Tonal Pitch Space

Tonal Pitch Space

Fred Lerdahl

2001

OXFORD
UNIVERSITY PRESS

Oxford New York
Athens Auckland Bangkok Bogotá Buenos Aires Calcutta
Cape Town Chennai Dar es Salaam Delhi Florence Hong Kong Istanbul
Karachi Kuala Lumpur Madrid Melbourne Mexico City Mumbai Nairobi
Paris São Paulo Shanghai Singapore Taipei Tokyo Toronto Warsaw

and associated companies in
Berlin Ibadan

Published by Oxford University Press, Inc.
198 Madison Avenue, New York, New York 10016

Library of Congress Cataloging-in-Publication Data
Lerdahl, Fred, 1943–
Tonal pitch space / Fred Lerdahl.
p. cm.
Includes bibliographical references and index.
ISBN 0-19-505834-8; ISBN 0-19-514229-2 (pbk.)
1. Music—Theory. 2. Tonality. 3. Musical pitch. 4. Musical analysis. I. Title.
MT6.L36 T66 2001
781.2'3—dc21 00-031371

9 8 7 6 5 4 3 2 1

Printed in the United States of America
on acid-free paper

Preface

A few years after Ray Jackendoff and I finished *A Generative Theory of Tonal Music* (Lerdahl and Jackendoff 1983; hereafter GTTM), fresh theoretical ideas began to intrude on my time for composing. The only way to unburden myself of them was to work them out and write them down. By the late 1980s I had published four articles that explored new territory: "Timbral Hierarchies (1987)," "Cognitive Constraints on Compositional Systems" (1988a), "Tonal Pitch Space" (1988b), and "Atonal Prolongational Structure (1989a)." All except the pitch-space article dealt with issues in contemporary music, reflecting my compositional interests. I soon sensed that in these separate articles a larger theory was taking shape and decided to weave them together into a book. It was unclear what the unifying thread should be. I tried and abandoned building the book around "Cognitive Constraints . . ." The relationship between implications of research in music cognition and the systematic needs of composers could not be pursued beyond a point of useful generalization, and certainly not at the level of rigor demanded of a treatise in music theory.

Only gradually did I grasp the many potentials latent in the pitch-space article. Its starting point was not the obvious spatial aspects of music, such as room acoustics or pitch height, but empirical evidence that listeners of varying degrees of training and of different cultures hear pitches (and pitch classes), chords, and regions as relatively close or distant from a given tonic and in an orderly way. The pitch-space article developed a quantitative model of these intuitions. Subsequently I initiated the model's application to the analysis of actual music, sketched some chromatic spaces, and used the model to quantify patterns of tension and relaxation (Lerdahl 1992, 1994a, 1996).

These separate efforts have come together in this volume, conceived around the central idea of pitch space. Earlier material is here revised, elaborated, and merged with new work into an integrated theory of music cognition and an associated system of analysis. As background, chapter 1 reviews the goals, idealizations, and rule system of the GTTM theory and surveys its analytic components, concentrating on the derivation of prolongational structure and surrounding issues. Chapter 2 presents the diatonic pitch-space model and relates it to previous and current research in music theory and psychology. The principle of the shortest path becomes a basis for deriving prolongational structure. Chapter 3 combines the pitch-space model with prolongational structure by tracing pitch-space paths at multiple prolongational levels. Different path representations are shown, and the narrative potential of this method of analysis is illustrated. Chapter 4 shows how an essential aspect of musical expression, that of tension and relaxation as pitch events unfold, can be modeled by computing pitch-space distances between events connected in the prolongational tree. Another fundamental aspect of musical expression, that of degrees of attraction between pitches and chords, is also quantified, leading to a fresh perspective on melodic and harmonic expectations. Chapter 5 takes up the issue of how listeners locate a tonic, as preparation for an approach to harmonic functionality based on prolongational position. The approach is applied to various musical grouping schemas. Chapter 6 generates chromatic tonal spaces by modifying variables in the diatonic distance formula. Subsequent delineation of preferential constraints on the form of tonal spaces leads to a metrical analogy, including a subtheory of metrical attractions. Chapter 7 applies the spaces developed in chapter 6 to chromatic tonal music from Wagner to Bartók. Chapter 8 considers some consequences of flat (or atonal) pitch space and advances an approach to atonal prolongational and functional structures based less on the cognitive construct of pitch space than on psychoacoustic principles.

My spatial explorations began not with pitch but with timbre. As this topic lies outside the scope of this study, I shall say a few words about it here. The article "Timbral Hierarchies" (1987) describes how I generated simple computer-music sounds, all on the same pitch and at the same dynamic but differentiated timbrally (by manipulating formants) so as to yield perceptually equidistant timbral intervals along specific timbral dimensions. The goal was to construct perceptually viable prolongational patterns of tension and relaxation out of timbre alone—in short, to begin to explore Schoenberg's (1911) vision of timbral organization. I found that ordering timbral intervals along a single axis was musically and cognitively impoverishing. With as few as nine equally spaced vowels arrayed on two axes of brightness, however, I was able to create intelligible timbral prolongational structures of up to twenty-five events, including passing and neighboring functions, transpositions and inversions, departures and returns, and partial and full repetitions. There could be no timbral octave; the sounds were arranged on each axis on an ordered scale of perceived tension. These timbral études of changing vowels on a single pitch were musically minimal, but they made the point that through computer synthesis it is possible to construct the beginnings of a timbral syntax. They also suggested the broader point that a space of elements must be arrayed in at least two dimensions for music of any cognitive complexity. The next step was to explore the spatial idea in the realm of pitch.

Although this volume's focus on pitch space has inevitably led to an emphasis on tonal rather than atonal music (tonal pitch space and tonality are in a sense synonymous), the last three chapters trace ways in which the space evolved toward atonal structures. In the process these chapters shape an implicit historical narrative and provide one basis for analyzing recent music. When I matured musically in the late 1960s, the reigning view was that Schenkerian theory explained tonal music and twelve-tone theory (with its set-theoretic offshoot) explained twentieth-century music. I have never been comfortable with this dichotomy and have endeavored to develop a framework for understanding music that incorporates both the relatively unchanging cognitive foundations of the musical mind and the historical continuities that underlie changes in musical style.

I attach special importance to the approach to tonal tension and attraction developed in chapter 4 because these conceptions have a great deal to do with musical expression, a subject that cries out for better understanding. At first glance it might seem odd to claim a relationship between music's great emotional power and numerical outputs of rules. However, emotional reactions to music depend on (unconscious) understanding. In a successful cognitive theory there can be no opposition between quantification and affective response. On the contrary, a musically sophisticated and psychologically relevant formal model can clarify general assertions about musical expression made from a literary or philosophical perspective and bring them to a more explanatory level of understanding.

GTTM sets forth a theory of rhythmic structure that requires no extension here (except tangentially, with respect to grouping schemas and metrical attractions). GTTM's pitch theory, however, is incomplete. As the preceding overview suggests, *Tonal Pitch Space* addresses this shortcoming, in ways that I could not have envisioned when writing GTTM. There is nothing unanticipated, however, in the underlying conceptual continuity with GTTM. As in the earlier book, I view music theory as a branch of cognitive science. I am concerned not just with creating intellectually or aesthetically pleasing pitch constructs but also with proposing ones that model the unconscious intuitions of experienced listeners of the musical idioms under consideration. Where possible, I relate my constructs to the empirical literature in music perception and cognition. I attempt to make my proposals precise enough to be testable. Unlike standard music-theoretic practices, which leave it to the analyst to apply the relevant theoretical constructs to actual music, my approach is equally concerned with specifying the principles by which listeners infer the proposed constructs. One of my ideals for a music theory is that it assign automatically a limited range of preferred hearings according to cognitively viable principles. (To be sure, I do not wish all music theories to have this goal. There are many purposes and functions for theories of music.)

The goal of computational explicitness notwithstanding, various aspects of this theory remain unfinished. This is inevitable for an undertaking of this scope. Ultimately, however, I am less interested in completeness than in fruitful ideas. If faced with two solutions to a theoretical problem, one of them formally complete but musically flawed or psychologically implausible, the other formally incomplete but musically satisfying and psychologically believable, I choose the latter, because it provides something valuable to build upon. Nor do I eschew applying, from time to time, the concepts and representations of the model in an informal, more traditionally analytic way. A theory grounded in cognition should be extensible to informal musical discourse.

South Hadley, Massachusetts F.L.
October, 2000

Acknowledgments

It is a pleasure to acknowledge some of the people who and institutions that helped me during the long gestation of this work. Pride of place goes to Ray Jackendoff, in whose company I learned how to do the kind of music theory that matters most to me. Without our prior work together, this volume would have been inconceivable.

Just as our collaboration was drawing to a close, I had the good fortune to participate—thanks to Karl Pribram and Diana Deutsch—in three Ossiach conferences (1980, 1983, 1985) organized by Juan Roederer. These meetings opened my eyes to the worlds of psychoacoustics and experimental music psychology. Around the same time, I spent a number of residencies and visits at IRCAM (1981, 1983, 1984, 1988, 1991). This was my introduction to the world of computer music. Jean-Baptiste Barriére, Tod Machover, Stephen McAdams, Yves Potard, and David Wessel supported and assisted me in undertaking a number of computer-music projects. For various technical and logistical reasons none of these projects was completed, but working on them proved a gold mine for subsequent theorizing.

My thoughts about pitch space germinated not only from my timbral studies but also from the theoretical work of Daniel Werts (1983) and especially the psychological research of Carol Krumhansl (1983, 1990). Articles by David Lewin (1982) and Richard Taruskin (1988)—though they would hardly have guessed it—led me to novel conceptions of harmonic functionality and nondiatonic tonal organization, respectively. Conversations with William Rothstein in the late 1980s sharpened my understanding of the relationship of my work to Schenkerian analysis. A probing remark in 1987 by Célestin Deliège concerning cognitive constraints ignited my attempt at an atonal prolongational theory. In 1991 Emmanuel Bigand helped crucially on the issue of tonal tension by suggesting that it might have something to do with pitch space. (I had previously tried to find the solution purely in terms of patterns of prolongational branchings.) In 1994 Caroline Palmer advised my pursuit of the quantification of harmonic tension to the point reached here. Steve Larson's (1994) work on tonal forces motivated my theory of tonal attractions.

At Columbia University, my doctoral students Kevin Mooney and Mine Dogantan provided historical background on nineteenth-century music theories. John Halle sustained my conviction in the pertinence of the theory for contemporary compositional practice. David Temperley both clarified the theory of attractions and pushed me toward an alternative approach to tonic-finding. Joshua Fineberg helped refine the treatment of atonal prolongations and its relation to tension.

It was through a series of lectures that I gave in 1990 at the Sibelius Academy in Helsinki that I began to see how I could organize my disparate ideas into a coherent framework. In 1990–1991 I benefited from a fellowship to begin this work from the National Endowment for the Humanities, with further support arranged by Dean Paul Boylan at the University of Michigan and Vice President Martin Meisel at Columbia University. During 1993–1994 I was a Fellow at the Center for Advanced Study in the Behavioral Sciences in Palo Alto, California, with support provided by the Andrew W. Mellon Foundation. Traces can be found in the following pages of valuable conversations with the other members of the CASBS Music Cognition Group: Jamshed Bharucha, Robert Gjerdingen, Carol Krumhansl, Leonard Meyer, Eugene Narmour, and Caroline Palmer. I am grateful to them all.

Portions of this book originated in material from invited lectures. The work on cognitive constraints was developed for a conference on that topic in 1987 in Geneva, Switzerland, organized by Etienne Darbellay. The theory of atonal prolongations was originally advanced in 1988 at an IRCAM conference organized by Stephen McAdams and resumed for a session, put together by Miguel Roig-Francoli, of the 1996 annual meeting of the Society for Music Theory. My journeys into pitch space were initiated at a 1990 music psychology conference at Ohio State University organized by Mari Riess Jones. Work on the analysis of chromatic music and on functionality was reported at the 1994 annual meeting of the Society for Music Theory at a special session, arranged by Justin London, devoted to the tenth anniversary of the publication of GTTM. The approach toward generating chromatic spaces was sketched in 1994 at an ESCOM conference in Liège, Belgium, organized by Irène Deliège. The analogy between tonal space and metrical grid was proposed in 1998 in the Poland lecture I was privileged to give at a second music psychology conference at Ohio State University, organized by David Huron.

Louise Litterick, David Temperley, and Carl Voss read the complete manuscript and made many suggestions about content and style that significantly improved the book. Further comments by Christopher Hasty, Jonathan Kramer, and an anonymous reader, as reviewers for Oxford University Press, were invaluable for the final revisions. Joan Bossert initially undertook this project at OUP, and

Bruce Phillips provided patient encouragement for it. Maribeth Payne, Maureen Buja, and Cynthia Garver skillfully oversaw the publication processs. Barbara Wild did the expert copyediting. A subvention from the Society for Music Theory helped defray costs of the complex musical figures, which were superbly realized on the computer by Don Giller.

Here and there in this volume I have reworked material from earlier publications (Lerdahl 1988a, 1988b, 1989a, 1989b, 1991, 1992, 1994a, 1994b, 1996, 1997b, 1999). I gratefully acknowledge permission from Academic Press, the American Psychological Association, *Analyse Musicale*, *Contemporary Music Review*, *Current Musicology*, *Journal of Music Theory*, *Music Perception*, and Overbird Press. Belmont Music Publishers granted permission to reproduce the first part of Schoenberg's *Klavierstuck*, Op. 33a.

This book is dedicated with love to my wife, Louise Litterick, and my children, Julie, Ruth, and Sophie.

Contents

Abbreviations

GTTM	*A Generative Theory of Tonal Music* (Lerdahl and Jackendoff (1983)
ic	interval class
pc	pitch class
PR	preference rule
TR	tranformational rule
WFR	well-formedness rule
α	attraction function
δ	distance function
Δ	composite distance function
boldface letter	tonal region or key (e.g., **C** = C major; **c** = C minor)

Tonal Pitch Space

1 *Theoretical Foundations*

OVERVIEW OF GTTM

Goals

This volume builds an original edifice of music theory on the foundations of Ray Jackendoff's and my *A Generative Theory of Tonal Music* (GTTM; 1983). It may therefore prove useful to summarize and slightly extend the earlier theory before embarking on the new one.

A listener familiar with a musical idiom organizes its sounds into coherent structures. GTTM attempts to characterize those musical structures that are hierarchical and to establish principles by which the listener arrives at them for a work in the Classical tonal idiom. These principles are stated as a musical grammar, or system of rules, that generates the structure that the listener associates with the signal. Figure 1.1 schematizes the form of the theory: the rules take as input the sound signal as organized psychoacoustically into a "musical surface" and attempt to give as output a structural description that models aspects of the heard structure.

GTTM proposes four types of hierarchical structure simultaneously associated with a musical surface. Grouping structure describes the listener's segmentation of the music into units such as motives, phrases, and sections. Metrical structure assigns a hierarchy of strong and weak beats. Time-span reduction, the primary link between rhythm and pitch, establishes the relative structural importance of events within the rhythmic units of a piece. Prolongational reduction develops a second hierarchy of events in terms of perceived patterns of tension and relaxation.

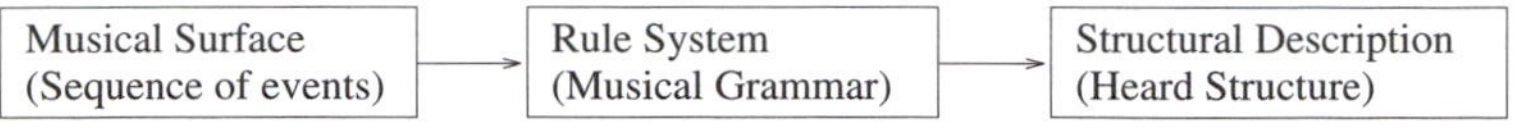

FIGURE 1.1 The form of generative music theory.

The four hierarchies integrate (leaving aside feedback effects) as in Figure 1.2. From the grouping and metrical structures the listener forms the time-span segmentation over which the dominating-subordinating relationships of time-span reduction take place; and from the time-span reduction the listener projects the tensing–relaxing hierarchy of prolongational reduction. In addition, both kinds of reduction depend for their operation on stability conditions among pitch configurations. The stability conditions represent features of the tonal system as a whole rather than event structures in a specific piece. GTTM mostly ignores the stability conditions. They form the centerpiece of this study, treated through the concept of pitch space.

GTTM treats music theory as the branch of theoretical psychology concerned with modeling the musical mind (Sloboda 1985). In the spirit of recent cognitive theory (Fodor 1983; Jackendoff 1987), the musical mind is seen as possessing characteristics of modularity, specialization, automaticity, speed, impenetrability to consciousness, and corresponding brain localization. This perspective does not deny cross-faculty influences or the effect of conscious processes on musical understanding in trained individuals. The strategy, rather, is to isolate the spontaneous musical cognitive capacity as an idealized object of study. The theory seeks to be sufficiently precise in its formulations that its concepts, rules, and predictions can in principle be tested by the methods of experimental psychology.

For practical reasons, GTTM concentrates on the idiom of Classical diatonic tonal music, but its thrust is to model musical understanding beyond the response to any particular idiom. Along the lines of Chomsky (1965), it attempts to distinguish between rules that are specific to a musical idiom and rules that apply universally. The term "universal" is meant not in a geographical or historical sense but in a psychological one. To assert that a rule is universal is to claim that it represents a natural propensity of the musical mind. But even a universal principle cannot apply if the input does not trigger it. A totally nonperiodic rhythmic sequence will not lead to the inference of a metrical grid, nor will drum music bring principles of pitch organization into play. So the inapplicability of a rule in a given

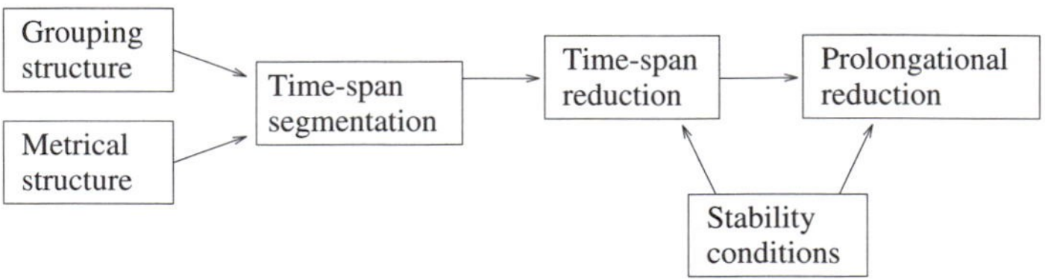

FIGURE 1.2 A flow chart of GTTM's components.

instance does not necessarily invalidate its status as a mental principle. What is required, rather, is that a putative universal apply in the same way whenever it is called into play. It must be evaluated in terms of its general psychological plausibility, its coherence and parsimony within the theory, and the empirical evidence for or against it.

While the issue of universality will not be emphasized in this volume, it is implicit in the chapters that extend the range of the theory beyond the diatonic idiom. Various details of the theory, such as the measure of distance between events, are adjusted to accommodate differing features of the input. More abstract principles remain unaltered. The general picture emerges of a theory whose details change with musical style but whose underlying constructs are constant, reflecting permanent features of musical understanding.

Idealizations

Any theory must simplify the phenomena it addresses in order to formulate suitable insights and generalizations. GTTM makes assumptions analogous to those found elsewhere in cognitive science. First, it takes as given the musical surface (the aural perception of pitches, timbres, durations, and dynamics), ignoring the complex process by which the surface is constructed from the acoustic signal. In the same spirit, the notated score is taken—minus bar lines but with the addition of harmonic roots and tonal orientations—to represent the surface. Second, GTTM assumes an "experienced listener." In reality no two listeners are exactly alike, nor are any two hearings by the same listener. Given familiarity with an idiom, however, the ways in which a piece is understood are highly constrained. A theory of musical understanding needs to characterize these common constraints as a framework for studying individual differences. Third, the theory provides structural descriptions not for how the music is heard as it unfolds in time but for the final state of a listener's understanding. It is doubtful whether a substantive theory of real-time listening processes can be developed without first considering the nature of the information these processes deliver. (Jackendoff [1991] outlines a promising approach to real-time processing based on GTTM's structures and rules.) Most music theories tacitly accept these three simplifying assumptions, and this work continues them.

A fourth limitation concerns the distinction between hierarchical and associational structures (Meyer 1973). By "hierarchy" is meant an organization of discrete elements such that one element is perceived to subsume or contain other elements. The elements do not overlap, subsumption is recursive, and at any given level the elements are adjacent. By "association" is meant the relative closeness or distance that is judged to exist between ideas. An idea is closely associated with another if it takes few psychologically viable operations to change one into the other. Motivic and timbral relations are usually regarded as associational. While GTTM's rule system depends in part on associations (in the form of "parallelisms") for the assignment of hierarchical structure, it does not have a component for representing associational structure. This is so for three reasons. First, it is attractive to concentrate on hierarchies, since it is known throughout psychology that learning and memory are enhanced if a subject is able to organize the input in a hierarchical manner (some classic citations are Miller, Galanter, and Pribram 1960; Simon 1962; and Neisser 1967). Studies in music psychology have shown that the absence of perceived hierarchy substantially reduces the listener's ability to learn and remember structure from musical surfaces (Deutsch 1982b; Krumhansl 1990). Second, the degree of association of ideas depends in part on how they are embedded within a hierarchy. If they receive similar hierarchical descriptions they are more likely to be judged as closely related. Third, and on a practical level, it is difficult to make a substantive theory of associations. Within music theory this remains relatively uncharted territory.

A fifth idealization in the GTTM theory is the construal of a musical surface as a single sequence of discrete events that assemble into hierarchically organized groupings. This view excludes polyphonic lines from independent representation. However, lines are never completely unrelated in tonal music. The idealization remains plausible to the extent that simultaneous lines are also part of a single ongoing flow. Within this framework, prolongational reduction connects horizontally related events at multiple structural levels in terms of repetition, departure, and return. This study expands the treatment of homophonic linear connections through the theory of melodic attractions, which provides one basis for understanding voice leading ("Melodic Tension" and "An Attractional Approach to Harmony" in chapter 4). Further discussion of polyphonic groupings is deferred to "Issues in Prolongational Theory" later in this chapter.

The rule system

Essential to GTTM's psychological orientation is its rule system. Each of its rhythmic and reductional hierarchies is generated by its own set of rules. Across each set there are three rule types. Well-formedness rules (WFRs) establish the strict hierarchical organization of each component. Transformational rules (TRs) permit modifications on musical surfaces so that certain hierarchically ill-formed phenomena, such as grouping overlaps, can be treated as well formed. Preference rules (PRs) establish which formally possible structures correspond to a given musical surface.

The PRs, which do the major work of analysis within the theory, pick out features in the music that influence the listener's intuitions. In the grouping component, for example, one PR marks a potential grouping boundary at a pause; another detects thematic parallelism between two groups that are potentially far apart at the surface, assigning them parallel grouping positions; and a third encodes the effect of large-scale harmonic structure on grouping decisions. As these instances suggest, some PRs are local in application, others are global, and some relate effects across components. Out of their interaction emerges the "preferred," or most coherent, analysis of the piece in question. A musical passage in which the various PRs reinforce one another strikes the listener as clear or prototypical. Where the rules conflict, the structure seems vague or ambiguous and more than one description may be assigned. The rule system is thus gradient rather than categorical; that is, the PRs mark not the correctness or incorrectness of an analysis but its relative viability within a framework of limited alternatives. Although this feature may seem unusual by comparison with standard linguistic grammars, it is normal in theories of vision (Marr 1982) and has broad application for cognitive systems (Jackendoff 1987). The connectionist approach in psychology (Rumelhart and McClelland 1986) treats cognition in terms of individual factors that converge in a gradient fashion on "goodness-of-fit" solutions. Optimality theory in phonology (Archangeli and Langendoen 1997) also has the flavor of a PR system. In short, GTTM's rule system possesses features in common with much recent theorizing in cognitive science.

Ideally, the PRs should be stated quantitatively so that when they interact a clear overall result is obtained. Thus a metrical preference for strong beats on stressed events might conflict with another rule that prefers in-phaseness with the associated grouping structure and the quantification would resolve the issue. But achieving quantification is not straightforward. The effect of a rule depends on its surrounding context, for instance, how much an event is stressed compared to its neighbors. Even a clear local result might be overridden by a global consideration: the contextually marked stress might act as a syncopation within a larger metrical regularity. GTTM avoids these difficulties by giving only general indications about a rule's typical strength. However, it motivates each rule psychologically, states it precisely, and applies it consistently. GTTM's aspiration, largely realized, is for the rules to be predictive enough to be adaptable to empirical testing.

This study continues to introduce PRs. But its most characteristic formal procedure turns out to be not PRs but a kind of WFR that is designed not to specify hierarchical structure but to spell out how to do something. These are well-formedness rather than preference rules because they are obligatory. Often they are algorithmic. This difference reflects not a change of attitude but a change in subject matter. Pitch-space theory proves to be fundamentally numerical; as a result, so are its spin-offs, the methods for calculating tonal tension and attraction.

Interestingly, the most difficult component to treat in quantitative terms remains grouping structure, seemingly the simplest of the organizations under consideration. The principles of musical grouping are largely adaptations of general Gestalt principles of auditory perception (Deutsch 1982a; Handel 1989; Bregman 1990). They are hard to quantify because the factors involved in determining grouping boundaries vary continuously over any given dimension and interact with one another in complex ways. In addition, more than other structural aspects, grouping is susceptible to the influence of performance nuances (Kramer 1988). This theoretical difficulty becomes concrete in performing a musical analysis. It is sometimes troublesome to determine the grouping structure of a piece, but once that is in place the rest mostly follows like clockwork.

A REPRESENTATIVE ANALYSIS

Rhythmic structure

To illustrate the GTTM theory, let us derive a hierarchical analysis of the Bach chorale "Christus, der ist mein Leben," concentrating on the prolongational component. The most relevant derivational factors for particular stages of structure will be referred to informally rather than by identifying PRs as such.

The grouping analysis, which appears in slur notation beneath the music of the chorale in Figure 1.3, is simple and unambiguous. There are no salient groupings beneath the phrase level, as there would be, for example, from motivic and textural differentiations in the Classical style. The chorale's phrase endings are marked by breaks and cadences. A rest plus attack-point distance establishes a larger grouping boundary in bar 4. Symmetry reinforces these grouping boundaries.

A metrical grid is inferred through a pattern-matching process between the accentual flux in the musical signal—in GTTM's terms, "phenomenal accents"—and a learned repertory of well-formed metrical structures. The listener makes the best fit between the phenomenal accents and the most suitable grid. Because beats do not have duration but are conceptual points in time, GTTM notates metrical structure by rows of dots, as in Figure 1.4. To the left of each row is the note value for the duration between beats at that level. The attack patterns and the steady harmonic rhythm establish the quarter-note level. At the half-note level there is a temporary ambiguity due to the initial repetition of the tonic chord. This level is settled by the first half of bar 2 with the long melodic note, the lack of harmonic change on the second beat, and the change in rhythmic activity in the inner voices. The long melodic note also cues the assigned grid for the whole-note level, supported by the preference for strong beats early in a group. Hypermetrical levels (those larger than the notated bar) are uncertain in this piece, due to the conflict between early strong beats, which would place hypermetrical beats on the downbeats of odd measures, and long notes, which would put them on the

FIGURE 1.3 Bach chorale "Christus, der ist mein Leben."

FIGURE 1.4 Metrical grid for the first phrase of the Bach.

downbeats of even measures. If we assume that the former principle prevails, a hypermetrical beat is placed on the downbeat of bar 1.

Extremely small or large metrical levels tend to be less salient than those that converge around seventy beats per minute. This is so presumably for biological reasons (a correlation with the human pulse rate), reinforced by the stylistic cues that give rise to metrical judgments. For any given piece the theory designates such a moderate metrical level, called the tactus, as most salient. In the chorale it is the quarter-note level, by virtue of the attacks, harmonic rhythm, and customary tempo.

One might generalize from GTTM's conception of the tactus. Along similar lines, the phrase level is almost always salient, while very small groups, unless isolated motivically, tend to be perceptually marginal and groups larger than the period can be uncertain. Thus the grouping analogue to the tactus is the phrase. Likewise, in pitch reduction it is hard for listeners to grasp relationships between events that pass by at a very fast tempo, and long-range pitch connections can be difficult to grasp. But reductional connections at a tactus tempo and within a phrase are relatively easy to grasp. Thus all the components manifest optimal hierarchical levels for processing within a middle range.

We turn now to the time-span component, which comprises two parts, a hierarchical segmentation into units and a hierarchy of events within those units. The segmentational part is rhythmic in character and derives from the grouping and metrical components, both of which apportion time spans, either from one grouping boundary to the next or from one beat to the next. The resulting grouping and metrical spans can be in or out of phase with one another. When they are out of phase, a single perceptually most salient segmentation must be determined, so that a single time-span reduction can be constructed over it. This is done as follows. At large levels, all groups are time-span segments. At small levels, there are spans from beat to beat in the metrical grid. At intermediate levels, adjustments must sometimes be made in the metrical spans so that they do not overlap grouping boundaries. Weak beats belong as afterbeats to the previous

FIGURE 1.5 Time-span segmentation for the first phrase of the Bach.

strong beats unless grouping boundaries intervene, in which case they belong as upbeats to the following strong beats.

Figure 1.5 shows the time-span segmentation within the first phrase of the chorale, in which the grouping and meter are out of phase by one beat. Note the augmented span *x* and the truncated span *y* caused by the grouping boundaries. As such bracketing derives automatically from the grouping and metrical analyses, it will be omitted in subsequent representations.

Time-span reduction

A musical reduction is a way to represent hierarchical relationships among pitch events in a piece. Events judged as relatively embellishing are "reduced out" recursively, leaving at each stage a residue of structurally more important material.

Heinrich Schenker's (1935/1979) well-known approach to reduction has both a metaphysical and an aesthetic basis, depends on an a priori construct (the *Ursatz*) that has a pervasive top-down influence on an analysis, is informal in its application, and emphasizes voice-leading features. GTTM's, in contrast, has a psychological aim, has no metaphysical givens, proceeds by rule, and emphasizes rhythmic and harmonic features. In both approaches, structural importance is a question not of surface salience but of syntactic stability.

GTTM restricts reduction to that of a strictly nested, constituent hierarchy, allowing the use of a tree notation. As in Figure 1.6, a right branch signifies subordination to a previous event, a left branch to a succeeding event. Event e_2 is subordinate to (or embellishes) e_1, e_3 is subordinate to e_4, and e_4 is subordinate to e_1. Hence there is an underlying stage in which e_2 and e_3 have been reduced out and e_4 is adjacent to e_1. (We return to the issue of strict branching later in this chapter, in "Issues in Prolongational Theory.")

Time-span reduction evaluates the importance of events within the framework of the time-span segmentation. The most stable event in a segment is its "head," and other events in the unit are elaborations of the head. Each head goes on to the next larger segment for comparison against another head, up to the level of the whole piece. Figure 1.7 illustrates the time-span reduction for the first phrase

FIGURE 1.6 Illustration of strict branching.

FIGURE 1.7 Time-span reduction for the first phrase of the chorale.

of the chorale, with the tree above and a corresponding musical notation beneath the music. The correspondence is indicated by the letter labeling of the nodes in the tree and in the levels in musical notation.

The choices for head in this passage are determined mainly by relative harmonic stability. In detailing this process, let us refer to events, for convenience and without further theoretical claim, by Roman-numeral designations, supplemented as needed by careted Arabic numerals for melodic scale degrees. At level e the embellishing eighths in bar 2 disappear. In the first half of bar 1, I is more stable than V^6; in the second half of bar 1, IV^6 is more stable than V^4_2/IV; in the first half of bar 2, the V on the downbeat is more prominent than its elaborated repetition. At intermediate level é (created by the augmented span designated *x* in Figure 1.5), the upbeat I, despite the greater stability of its melodic note, is subordinate to the following I because the latter is on a downbeat and, more important, because it affords stronger global prolongational connections. (Alternatively, in the corresponding musical notation at the bottom of Figure 1.7, the two opening Is are fused, as shown by the horizontal bracket at level e; the resultant I shows the lower F at level d.) At level d in bar 1, I is more stable than IV^6; in bar 2, I is more stable than V.

Further reduction depends on the notions of structural beginning and structural ending (or cadence), which articulate grouping structure at the phrase and larger levels. The essential motion of a phrase takes place between these two points. A structural beginning is the most stable event before the cadence in a phrase and usually takes place early in the phrase. A cadence is a harmonic/melodic formula at the end of a phrase and is marked for retention in the reduction at the levels for which it plays a role. The importance of a particular structural beginning or cadence depends on its position in the larger grouping structure. If it abuts a boundary of a larger group, it serves as a structural beginning or cadence for that group as well as for its own phrase. Figure 1.8 schematizes the hierarchical function of each beginning and cadence (marked [b] and [c] in the diagram) in the grouping structure of the chorale.

Figure 1.9 gives the time-span reduction for the entire chorale, using the musical notation only. Levels a–c in Figure 1.9 correspond to the phrasal structural beginnings and cadences of Figure 1.8; note how both members of the cadences are retained at the levels for which they function. Elaborations internal to phrases appear in levels d–e. (No attempt is made to remove the parallel fifths and octaves that lie just below the musical surface.)

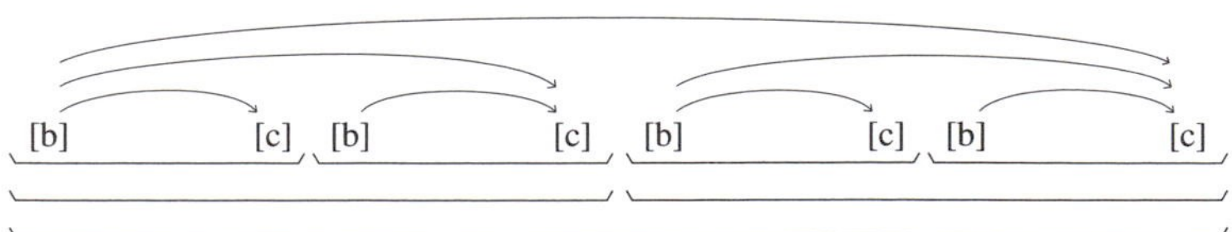

FIGURE 1.8 Nested structural beginnings and cadences (marked [b] and [c]) for the entire chorale.

FIGURE 1.9 Time-span reduction for the entire chorale.

The suppression of the tree notation in Figure 1.9 reflects a reevaluation of the role of time-span reduction. In GTTM this component has two functions, first as an independent representation of event importance and second as a stage in the derivation of the prolongational reduction. Here the emphasis is on the second function. GTTM's stipulation of two tree structures has the disadvantage of necessitating two analytic graphs for a piece, one for the rhythmic analyses and the time-span reduction, the other for the prolongational analysis. Bypassing the time-span tree permits all the components to be represented in a single graph. It also puts priority on the prolongational reduction, which is of greater musical and psychological interest. At the same time, it would be a mistake to eliminate the time-span component altogether. Because it evaluates events as heard in the rhythmic structure, this kind of reduction contains essential information for the prolongational analysis, which requires rhythmic as well as pitch values to establish its tensing and relaxing patterns. Indeed, a similar step would be needed for Schenkerian analysis if it were to aspire to the status of a predictive theory. There are, for example, any number of tonics in a piece; it is their differing rhythmic positions that determine which are structural and which are incidental.

Principles of prolongational reduction

As an initial simplification, prolongational events are usually indicated by the melody/bass skeleton. In effect, this step constitutes a transformational operation on surface events, the deletion of inner voices, in order to concentrate on the more salient soprano and bass. To the extent that deletion at underlying levels is performed, one can speak not only of horizontal reduction, in which subordinate events in a sequence are removed, but also of vertical reduction, in which pitches within individual events are removed.

Prolongational relationships are represented by branchings in a tree diagram and equivalently by slurs between note heads in musical notation. As shown in Figure 1.10, right branches stand for a tensing motion (or departure), left branches for a relaxing motion (or return). The degree of tension or relaxation between two events depends on the degree of continuity between them (this statement is refined in "The Harmonic Tension Model" in chapter 4). For both right and left branching there are three kinds of branching connection: strong prolongation, in which an event repeats; weak prolongation, in which an event repeats in altered form (by triadic inversion or by change in melodic note over the same harmony); and progression, in which an event connects to a contrasting event. Strong prolongation is indicated by a node with an open circle, weak prolongation with a filled-in circle, and progression with no circle. In the slur notation, also shown in Figure 1.10, slurs correspond strictly to tree branchings, with dashed slurs for strong prolongations, a combination of dashed and solid slurs for weak prolongations (depending on whether the bass or the soprano has moved), and solid slurs for progressions. For clarity, in this volume stems and flags are added to note heads of relatively superordinate events. The tree notation more clearly projects patterns of tension and relaxation, while the slur notation better conveys linear

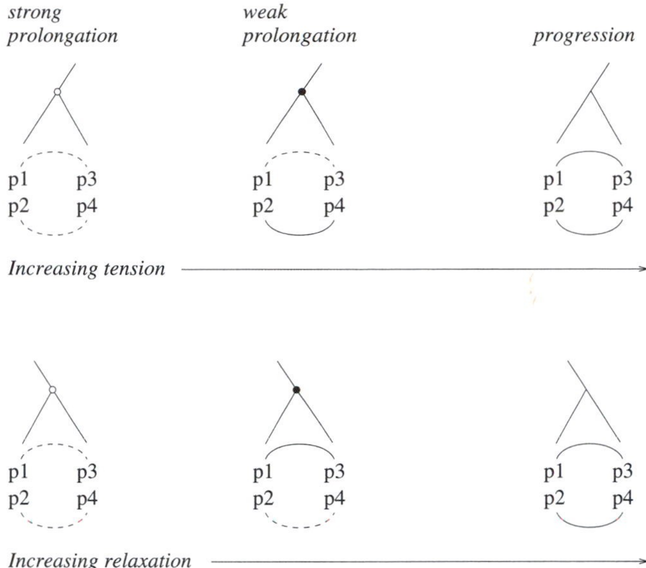

FIGURE 1.10 Repertory of prolongational branchings.

connections. Nevertheless, because the tree notation creates a visual obstacle between the music and its structural description, this study often dispenses with it in favor of notes and slurs.

The term "prolongation" resonates with shifting meanings over the centuries and belongs to no single tradition. In Schenkerian theory it usually means "composing out" (Schenker's own intention for the term is open to debate). GTTM's word for "composing out" is "elaboration": if one event composes out, or elaborates, another event, the former is subordinate to the latter. GTTM's use of "prolongation," however, often indicates a specific kind of elaboration, in which the elaborating event is either literally or functionally identical to the elaborated event. This meaning reflects ordinary English usage: the repeat of an event "prolongs" the event. However, when one is referring more generally to "prolongational reduction," GTTM's usage is closer to the Schenkerian one.

A prolongational analysis is constructed by stages from the events available in global to local levels of the corresponding time-span reduction. This top-down procedure, in contrast to the bottom-up construction of time-span reduction, is requisite because the prolongational function of an event can be judged only from its surrounding context. As the tree elaborates, it forms progressively smaller and more numerous prolongational regions (spans bounded by the immediately superordinate branches at that point in the prolongational analysis). Prolongational regions play a role comparable to time-span segments in that both carve up the musical surface into the nested spans over which reduction takes place.

It is illegal to attach an event outside its prolongational region, because that would violate the top-down construction of the prolongational tree. Take the

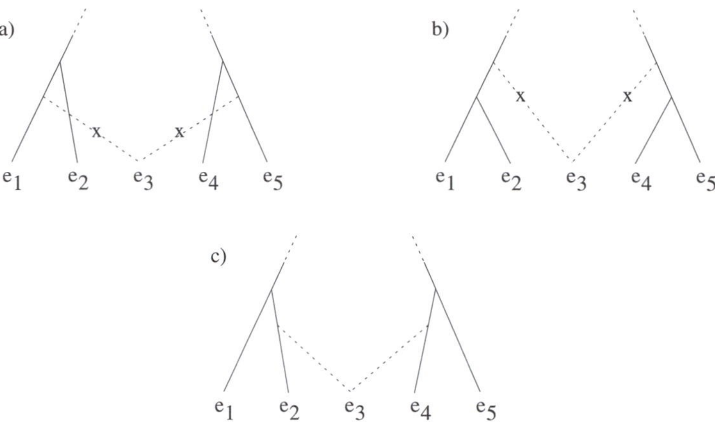

FIGURE 1.11 Well-formedness constraints on prolongational branchings.

string of five events e_1–e_5 in Figure 1.11, in which e_2 has already connected to e_1 and e_4 to e_5. E_3 therefore lies in the region e_2–e_4. It cannot cross branches to connect to e_1 or e_5, as indicated by the dashed branches in Figure 1.11 a; nor can it attach to e_1 or e_5 at a level higher than e_2 or e_4, as in Figure 1.11b, since these connections would lie outside the region e_2–e_4. Rather, it must branch to either e_2 or e_4, as in Figure 1.11c.

Only one or two events (or occasionally three) come up for assignment within any particular prolongational region at any given stage in a prolongational derivation. These events connect to the end points of the region in the most stable way and in a manner that achieves an optimal branching pattern. Later in this chapter, "Issues in Prolongational Theory" deals with optimal branching. In chapters 2 and 4 the factor of stability, which GTTM sketches as a set of verbally stated conditions, will be developed with precision in terms of pitch-space distance. Here I wish only to refine the relationship between a time-span reduction and its associated prolongational reduction. Suppose that the sequence under consideration is at time-span level L_n. Then, with one exception, the events to be assigned prolongational analysis at that stage are those at L_n. The exception is full repetition, yielding a right-branching strong prolongation, the most stable possible prolongational relationship. Because it is so stable, an event that forms it can be accessed not only at L_n but also at L_{n-1}. That is, the relative lack of rhythmic importance of the repeated event, reflected by its appearing at the next smaller time-span level, is compensated by its perfect stability of connection. But a repeated event at L_{n-2} cannot be so accessed, for in that case it is rhythmically too weak to be considered at that stage of derivation. This tight yet somewhat flexible relation between the two reductions is called the interaction principle. Figure 1.12 illustrates the principle schematically: time-span level a and possibly level b provide the events for prolongational level a, time-span level b and possibly level c provide the events for prolongational level b, and so on. The dashed arrows that angle from lower time-span levels signify that these connections are possible only

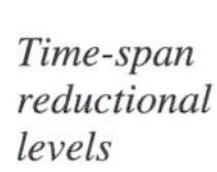

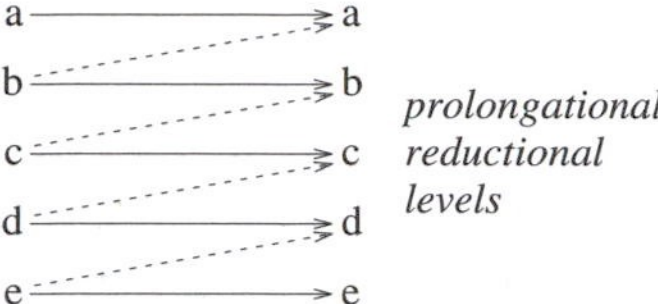

FIGURE 1.12 Schematic representation of the role of the interaction principle in deriving prolongational analysis from time-span reduction.

in the case of right strong prolongation. As a result of the interaction principle, the main difference between the time-span and prolongational reductions is in the way events connect, not in their levels of hierarchical importance.

It might be supposed that the exception for right strong prolongation would be mirrored by a similar treatment of left strong prolongation. In fact, the latter hardly ever occurs. Given the sequence $e_1 \rightarrow e_2$ at any prolongational level and given that e_1 and e_2 are identical, one typically hears e_2 as a repetition of e_1 rather than e_1 as an anticipation of e_2. Only a special circumstance, such as e_1 occurring on an upbeat just before e_2 on a downbeat, might override the tendency to hear repetitions retrospectively rather than prospectively. This tendency could be stated as a rule, but it is not necessary to do so. The rhythmic positions of e_1 and e_2 almost always ensure that e_1 is more important in the time-span reduction and hence that e_2 forms a right strong prolongation to it. Therefore, left strong prolongation does not enter as an exception into the interaction principle.

GTTM does not treat prolongational branchings by level, as it does for time-span reduction, in the sense of layered horizontal slices of events. Rather, prolongational events are related only through nodes of the tree (or, equivalently, through slurs). As Figure 1.12 implies, however, it is useful to establish strict prolongational levels. In addition to clarifying prolongational derivations, they facilitate the construction of prolongational pitch-space paths, the topic of chapter 3. The most effective method is simply to equate prolongational levels with derivational order. Consider the hypothetical Figure 1.13, in which the letters at the nodes signify prolongational levels derived from time-span levels. A simple letter labeling means that the derived prolongational level of the event in question cor-

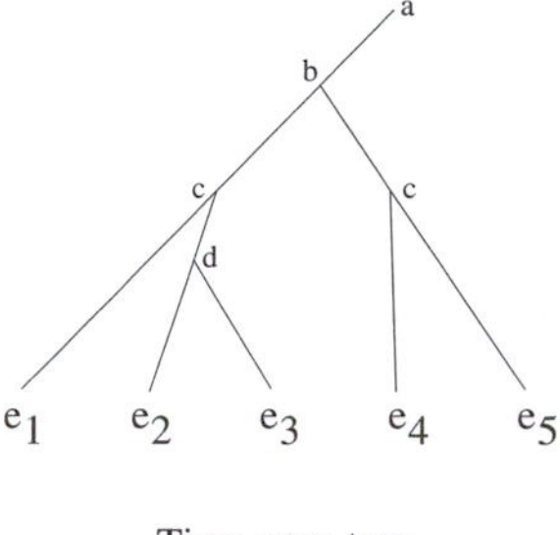

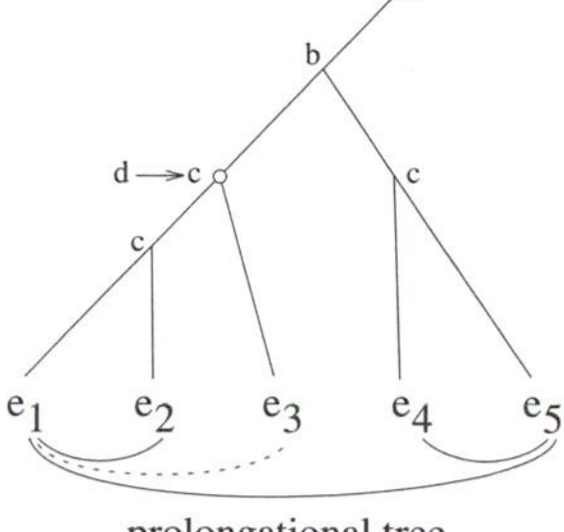

FIGURE 1.13 Abstract illustration of the derivation of prolongational analysis from time-span reductional levels.

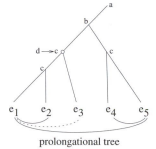

responds to its equivalent time-span level. An arrow between two labels means that the derived prolongational level to the right comes from the nonequivalent time-span level to the left. In this figure, all the events except e_3 derive from the equivalent time-span level. The indication "d→c" means that e_3, which repeats e_1, appears at time-span level d but is promoted by the interaction principle to prolongational level c.

Constructing a prolongational analysis

Enough has been said about prolongational derivation to undertake a prolongational analysis of the Bach chorale. Figure 1.14 builds by stages a prolongational reduction for the chorale's first phrase. The derivation follows the course laid out by the interaction principle. As shown by the node labels, the dominating event in the time-span reduction is the $I^{\hat{3}}$ on the downbeat of bar 1 (from level a in Figure 1.9), and the next available events are the V–I cadence in bar 2 (from level c in Figure 1.9). These events make the optimally stable prolongational connections in Figure 1.14a: the two $I^{\hat{3}}$s form a right strong prolongation, and the V is a relaxing left progression into the following I. The next available event (from level d in Figure 1.9) is the IV^6, which relaxes into the V as a dominant preparation in Figure 1.14b. As a balance to this closing double relaxing motion, Figure 1.14b adds at this stage (from level e in Figure 1.9) a tensing right progression for the V^6 from the opening I. Figure 1.14e completes the prolongational connections for the remaining events of the phrase (from level e in Figure 1.9 and the musical surface): V^4_2/IV resolves into IV^6, and local prolongations elaborate both the opening I and the cadential V.

We now derive the prolongational analysis for the entire chorale down to time-span level e in Figure 1.9. Time-span level a yields the prolongational tree in Figure 1.15a. This is a typical shape for a coherent prolongational structure: the $I^{\hat{3}}$ weakly prolongs into the final resolution (because $I^{\hat{3}}$ is less stable than $I^{\hat{1}}$); and within that frame the final cadential V attaches to the cadential $I^{\hat{3}}$ as a resolving

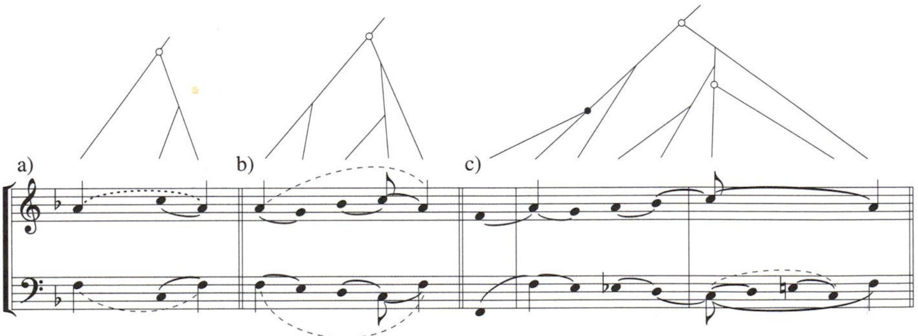

FIGURE 1.14 Prolongational analysis of the first phrase of the Bach chorale, represented in three stages.

progression. Time-span level b yields Figure 1.15b: $I^{\hat{3}}$ cadencing the second phrase strongly prolongs the opening $I^{\hat{3}}$, and the I/V (I of V) cadence at the end of the third phrase branches either from the I of bar 4 or to the final cadential V. However, both alternatives relegate the return to $I^{\hat{3}}$ at the beginning of the fourth phrase (shown in parentheses in Figure 1.15b) to a subordinate position between two Vs. It makes little sense to attach the returning $I^{\hat{3}}$ to either V, for that would make this tonic part of a dominant elaboration. The interaction principle comes to the rescue by going back to time-span level b, searching one level lower to time-span level c and finding this $I^{\hat{3}}$ there, and attaching it as a strong prolongation to the $I^{\hat{3}}$ in bar 4. The I/V in bar 6 then connects as a departure within this tonic prolongation. The result is Figure 1.15c, which replaces Figure 1.15b. This is a typical application of the interaction principle. Figure 1.15d adds the remaining events from time-span level c. In prolongational region bars 1–3, the $I^{\hat{3}}$ that cadences the first phrase branches as a right strong prolongation off the opening $I^{\hat{3}}$ (as in Figure 1.14a), and the I^6 on the downbeat of bar 3 weakly prolongs the

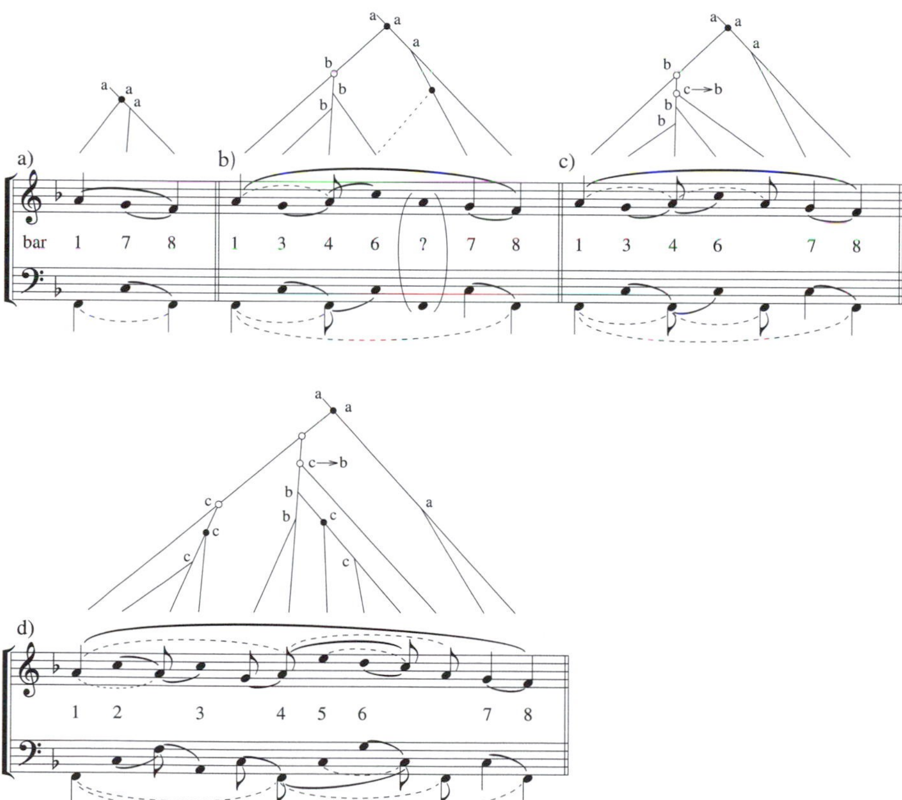

FIGURE 1.15 Derivation of levels a–d of the prolongational analysis of the entire chorale.

cadential $I^{\hat{3}}$ in bar 2. In prolongational region bars 4–6, the I/V on beat 2 of bar 5 and the cadential V/V in bar 6 attach to the cadential I/V, transposing at a smaller level the shape of Figure 1.15a.

The remaining unattached events fall within phrases. The first phrase has been discussed. In the second phrase, shown in Figure 1.16a, the I on beat 3 of bar 3 weakly prolongs the I^6 two beats earlier; the other events are passing. One might ask, though, whether the $I^{\hat{3}}$ on beat 3 could not instead be a strong right prolongation off the $I^{\hat{3}}$ that cadences the first phrase. The answer is no: the $I^{\hat{3}}$ on beat 3 of bar 3 appears two levels (level e) below the I^6 (level c), and the interaction principle cannot reach down more than one level to find a strong prolongation. At time-span level d this $I^{\hat{3}}$ has been displaced by the cadential V. In other words, this $I^{\hat{3}}$ is in too weak a rhythmic position to have such prolongational importance. Figure 1.16b makes the point in a different way by rewriting it as a I^6, a musically acceptable solution that demonstrates that this $I^{\hat{3}}$ is not structural to the phrase but a product of local voice leading. By contrast, it would be unthinkable to replace the cadential $I^{\hat{3}}$ in bar 4 with a I^6. This example illustrates the limits of the interaction principle. In the third phrase, time-span level d provides the vi/V

FIGURE 1.16 Derivation of intraphrasal prolongational connections (continuing from Figure 1.15)

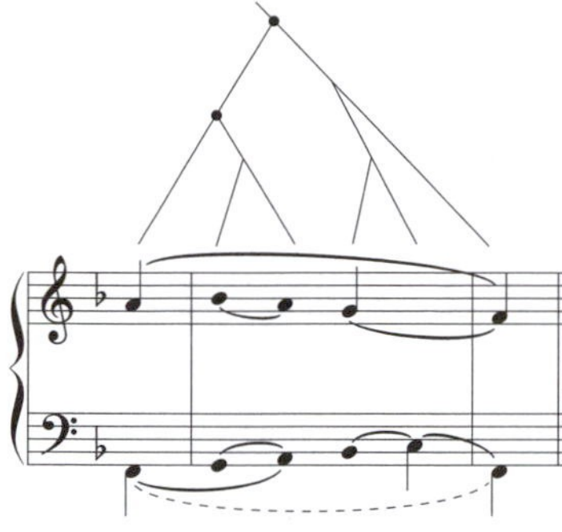

FIGURE 1.17 Prolongational analysis of the fourth phrase treated as a self-contained unit.

in bar 5, yielding the branching in Figure 1.16c. In the fourth phrase, shown in Figure 1.16d, the $I^{\hat{3}}$ prolongs into the I^6 followed by full closure.

The endings of the second and fourth phrases do not branch with their beginnings because they articulate not just their own phrases but larger groups as well. It is customary to assign prolongational connections only from a global perspective. Figure 1.17 illustrates how the fourth phrase would look if treated as a self-contained unit. Note how structurally similar it is, transposed, to the third phrase (Figure 1.16c). In addition, the fourth phrase resembles and completes the second phrase, melodically by descending to $\hat{1}$ instead of returning to $\hat{3}$, harmonically through the inclusion of a dominant preparation.

Figure 1.18 assembles the preceding analyses into what will be the standard reductional format in this book. Above the music is the prolongational tree, and immediately below are the metrical and grouping structures. Next comes the time-span reduction. At the bottom, corresponding to the tree, appears the prolongational reduction in slur notation, given in two stages for clarity.

Observations and comparisons

The analysis in Figure 1.18 suggests a few observations that are not directly represented in the hierarchical notations. First, the most embedded event in the entire reduction, hence the moment of greatest tension, is the ii/V in bar 5, which coincides with the melodic high point, the tonic F toward which the melody has been striving. The expressive force of this moment is due to this combination of stable melodic goal and unstable harmonic support.

Second, the chromatic D♭ in the last phrase recalls the E♭ in the opening phrase. These inflections, which are conspicuous in such a diatonic setting, hold parallel positions in their respective phrases. Both occur at identical metrical positions and belong to events that share similar branching positions. They are associations that cut across the hierarchical analysis.

Third, note how the prolongational groupings (branching clusters) cut across the grouping structure (the phrases), contributing to an ongoing flow over and above the formal articulations. Specifically, the cadence of the first phrase prolongs into the second phrase and the cadence of the second prolongs into the third.

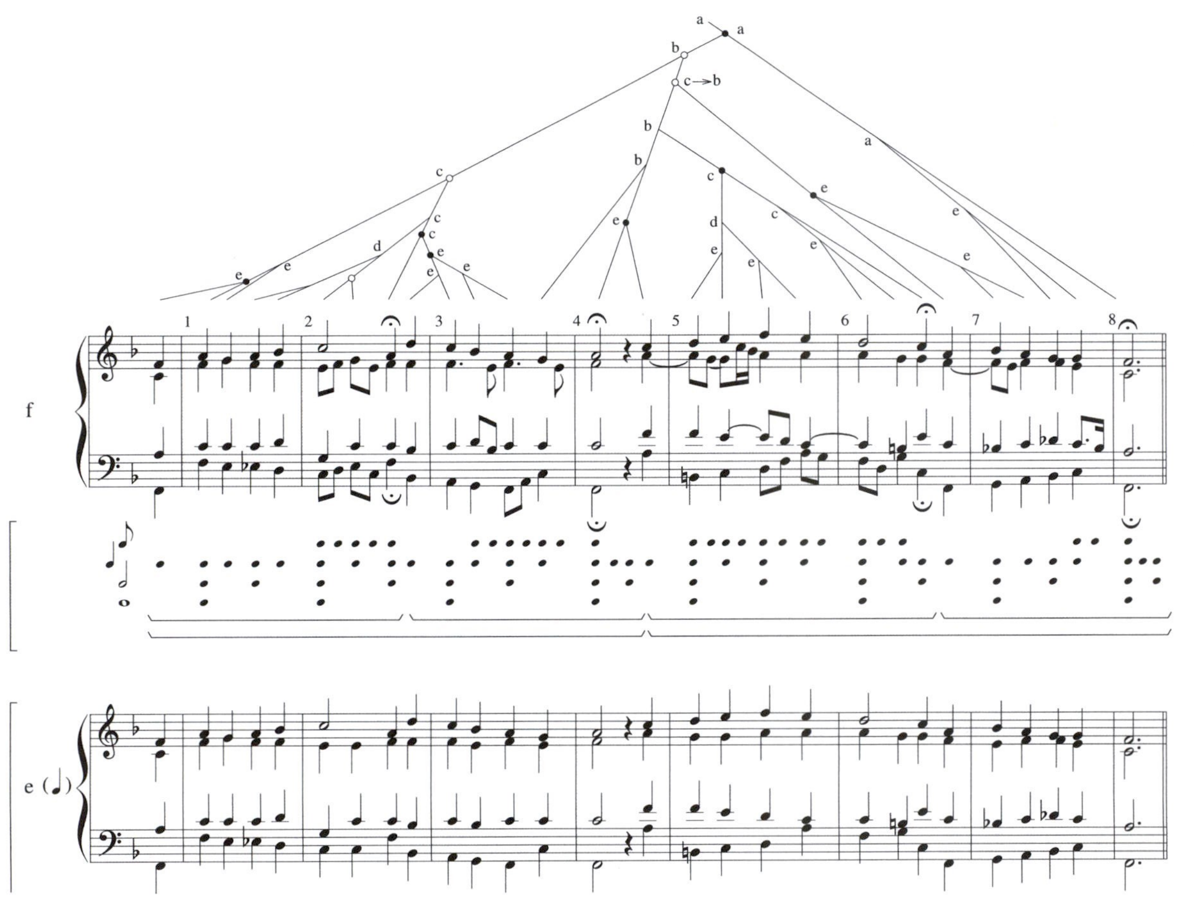
a
b
c→b
c
d
e
f
e (♩)
Meter and grouping
1
2
3
4
5
6
7
8

FIGURE 1.18 Complete hierarchical analysis of the Bach chorale.

Only at the end of the third phrase, as a breath before the final resolution, are the two kinds of grouping congruent in any larger sense. But immediately the fourth phrase starts with a repetition of the $I^{\hat{3}}$ that cadences the second phrase, crossing over the strong grouping boundary in bar 4. More generally, nineteenth-century analytic approaches (for example, Marx 1837–1847) tended to emphasize motivic, phrasal, and sectional parsings. Schenker, with his composed-out voice-leading structures, went to the opposite extreme. In my view, it is important to strike a balance between prolongational structure and phrasal form. (William Rothstein 1989 expresses a similar view from within the Schenkerian paradigm.) In GTTM this structural counterpoint is revealed through a comparison of its grouping and prolongational analyses.

It is instructive to compare the prolongational analysis in Figure 1.18 with the Schenkerian analyses of the chorale in Forte and Gilbert (1982), Neumeyer (1987), and Beach (1990). Allen Forte and Steven Gilbert treat $\hat{5}$ as the primary tone (the melodic Cs in bars 2,4, and 6), creating an *Urlinie* descent through the B♭-A-G in bar 7. As the C throughout lacks root-position tonic support, its choice must be based on salience rather than stability. To achieve the obligatory *Urlinie* descent through $\hat{4}$, Forte and Gilbert bypass the root-position tonic that begins the fourth phrase in favor of the harmonically unsupported B♭ on the downbeat of bar 7. According to this theory, the progression at the beginning of the fourth phrase is better interpreted as a prolonged melodic A over a bass arpeggiation, elaborated by a neighbor note in the soprano with a passing note in the bass (as in Figures 1.16e and 1.17). Figure 1.19 attempts to translate Forte and Gilbert's reading into GTTM's notation; evidently they count the I^6 as a prolongation of V.

David Neumeyer treats the high F in bar 5 as the head tone for an $\hat{8}$-line that descends to $\hat{5}$ by bar 6, after which he follows Forte and Gilbert's solution. Neumeyer seems to mix reductional features with intuitions of the organization of pitch space, in which the octave elaborates into the fifth and the fifth into the triad (see chapter 2). David Beach objects to Neumeyer's reading because of the high F's weak harmonic support and opts for a $\hat{3}$-line in an analysis similar to that of Figure 1.18.

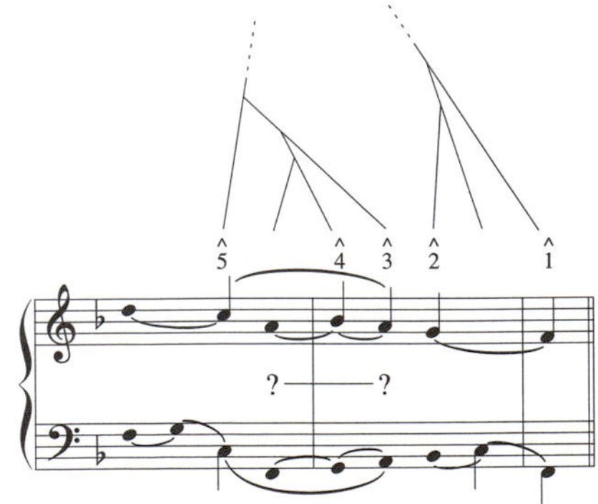

FIGURE 1.19 A translation into GTTM's prolongational notation of Forte and Gilbert's reading of the fourth phrase of the chorale.

It should be clear by now that the GTTM theory cannot generate the Forte-Gilbert or Neumeyer analyses. The theory is too wedded to rhythmic and harmonic factors, too little influenced by a priori schemas, and too governed by rule for such possibilities to arise. That it comes up with Beach's $\hat{3}$-line is a consequence not of a theoretical commitment to preordained structures but of what emerges as most stable in this particular analysis.

ISSUES IN PROLONGATIONAL THEORY

Prolongational good form

The tree in Figure 1.15a was described as having a typically coherent shape. Figure 1.20 repeats the tree as an abstraction: I→V-I, analyzed as a left weak prolongation that encloses a left progression. GTTM calls this structure the "basic form." Unlike the *Ursatz*, which it superficially resembles, the basic form is not an a priori generating structure but a description of a common reductional state, reflecting the trajectory from structural beginning to cadence. This basic form occurs as often as it does because it realizes a number of converging stability factors that are simple and frequently available at or near the musical surface: prolongation of the tonic, root-position harmonies, the standard cadence, and diatonic downward stepwise melodic motion that resolves on $\hat{1}$.

GTTM goes on to suggest a slightly more complex branching configuration called normative prolongational structure, depicted skeletally in Figure 1.21a. It consists of a tensing departure from the structural beginning followed by a relaxing motion into the cadence, all contained within a phrase or larger group. Subordinate material can precede the first superordinate branch, take place between the superordinate branches, or succeed the cadence. The cadence itself usually has two members (either V→I or V→deceptive resolution), but in the half-cadence the second member is absent. The left branch into the cadence acts as a dominant preparation. If a phrase lacks this element, the resolution feels incomplete. The branchings do not connect at the top as a prolongation in Figure 1.21a because this connection is not a requirement. While tonic prolongation is typical, it may not occur if a modulation is involved or if the larger context brings about more global connections (as in the fourth phrase of the Bach chorale). Yet normative structure can exist in such cases. The main intuition about normative structure is that a complete cadenced group tenses and relaxes internally, regardless of the attachment of its superordinate end points. GTTM claims that this pattern is an

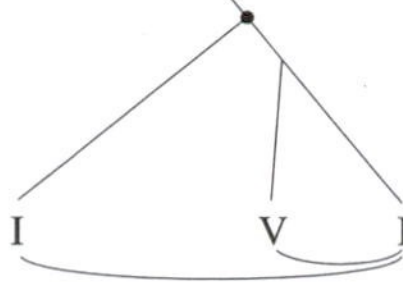

FIGURE 1.20 Prolongational basic form.

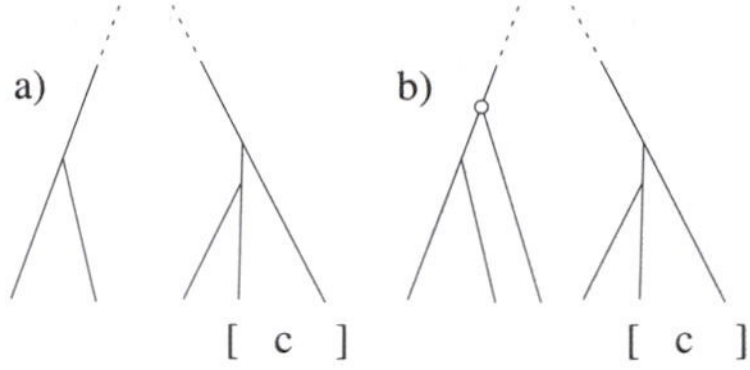

FIGURE 1.21 Normative prolongational structure: (a) its minimal tensing–relaxing pattern; (b) variant with return of the opening.

organizing principle for the listener and thus states it as a PR that influences branching formations.

Figure 1.21b shows a common variant of normative structure in which there is an internal prolongation of the structural beginning after the structural departure. This variant is common in phrases in the Classical period and, at a larger level, stands for the reprise in rounded-binary and sonata forms.

The idea that the listener prefers certain basic tensing-relaxing patterns is a powerful one, for it grounds prolongational structure in gestures that lie in physical action, which necessarily involves states of exertion and repose. Moreover, if these gestures are limited in number and if they combine at multiple structural levels, then prolongational patterns, while potentially infinite in variety, are usually quite repetitive. This combination helps explain why tonal music is varied yet learnable. In fact, I have only two other such patterns to propose. Together with normative structure, I call this three-pronged repertory prolongational good form.

The first of these other patterns, the balance constraint, says that if events at the next subordinate level are framed by a strong or weak prolongation, the listener seeks to connect them so that left and right branches are equally distributed. Assume at any prolongational level the sequence of events e_1–e_2–e_3–e_4 and assume further that e_4 repeats e_1 in a prolongation that encloses e_2 and e_3. How should e_2 and e_3 attach? Because e_1 and e_4 form a prolongation, they must be equally relaxed. And because e_2 and e_3 are subordinate within e_1–e_4, they must be tenser than e_1 and e_4. Suppose first that e_2 tenses off e_1, as in Figure 1.22a. Then the

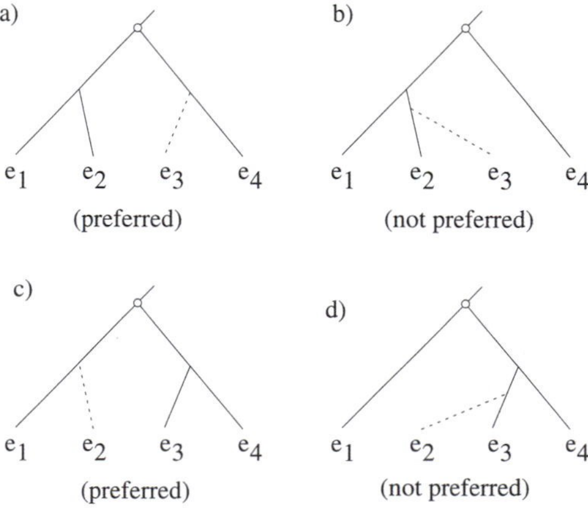

FIGURE 1.22 The balance constraint.

preferred branching for e_3, indicated by the dashed branch, is to e_4, for the resulting configuration balances a tensing departure with a relaxing return. The alternative in Figure 1.22b would implausibly exhibit a double tension followed by no relaxation within an overall equilibrium. Figure 1.22c–d shows the reverse situation in which e_3 connects first, with the same result.

The second pattern, the recursion constraint, says that if two events are left- or right-subordinate to another event, they should attach so that they are recursively rather than independently subordinate. Let us deal only with progressions. Assume at any prolongational level the sequence e_1–e_2–e_3, such that e_1 dominates e_2 and e_3. Suppose that e_3 tenses directly off e_1. Then the preferred branching for e_2, indicated by the dashed branch, is to e_3, as in Figure 1.23a, rather than directly to e_1, as in Figure 1.23b, for the latter would mean that e_2 and e_3 tense off e_1 in an unrelated way.

A third interpretation, in Figure 1.23c, is prohibited on grounds of well-formedness: if e_2 connects directly to e_1, e_3 cannot then attach directly to e_1 because the connection would lie outside e_3's prolongational region (as in Figure 1.11b); therefore, e_3 can only attach to e_2. Figures 1.23d–f reverse Figures 1.23a–c so that e_3 dominates, with the same result. The overall effect of this constraint is to promote linear connectedness in waves of tension and relaxation.

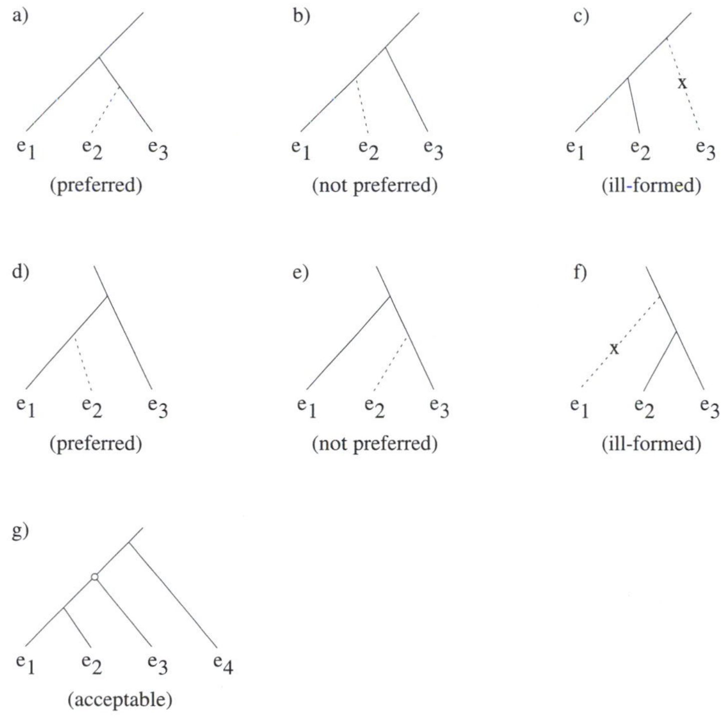

FIGURE 1.23 The recursion constraint.

There are limitations on the scope of the recursion constraint. First, it does not apply if one of the subordinate events precedes and the other succeeds the more structural event. Second, it applies within but not across the conceptual boundaries between nonharmonic tones, chords, and regions. Thus if a nonharmonic tone embellishes a chord, the nonharmonic tone's branch does not count with the chord's branch. Likewise, a chord's branch within a region does not count with a branch that connects to an event in another region. Elaborations of nonharmonic tones, chords, and regions take place on different planes (this notion will become clearer once the pitch-space model is introduced in chapter 2). Finally, although the constraint applies to prolongations (strong or weak) as well as to progressions, albeit more weakly because of the lack of change of tension, it does not apply to a combination of progressions and prolongations, for prolongations articulate the spans within and across which recursive progressions take place. Repeated left or right branches that alternate prolongations and progressions, as in Figure 1.23g, are acceptable.

The following formulation summarizes this discussion:

PROLONGATIONAL GOOD FORM

(1) *Normative prolongational structure* (adapted from GTTM) For cadenced groups, prefer to include:
- (a) a structural beginning and a cadence
- (b) optionally, a right-branching prolongation that is the most important direct elaboration of the structural beginning
- (c) a right-branching progression that, except for (b), is the most important direct elaboration of the structural beginning
- (d) a left-branching progression that is the most important direct elaboration of the first element of the cadence.

(2) *Balance constraint* At any level, for events e_2 and e_3 immediately subordinate within the strong or weak prolongation e_1–e_4, prefer the attachment of e_2 to e_1 and e_3 to e_4.

(3) *Recursion constraint* At any level, for events e_j and e_k subordinate to e_i, prefer, if e_j directly attaches to e_i, the direct attachment of e_k to e_j; and if e_k directly attaches to e_i, prefer the direct attachment of e_j to e_k; both subject to the conditions that
- (a) e_j and e_k are both to the left or to the right of e_i
- (b) e_i, e_j, and e_k form all progressions or all prolongations
- (c) e_i, e_j, and e_k are all either harmonic events within a region or events located in different regions.

Underlying levels of the Bach chorale will illustrate the three kinds of prolongational good form. Figure 1.24a gives time-span reductional level d for the first phrase (taken from Figure 1.9). The balance constraint induces a left departure rather than a predominant function for the IV^6. However, at level e, shown in Figure 1.24b, the V^6 takes over the departing function, so the IV^6 can now act as a genuine predominant. The branching in Figure 1.24b exemplifies the minimal

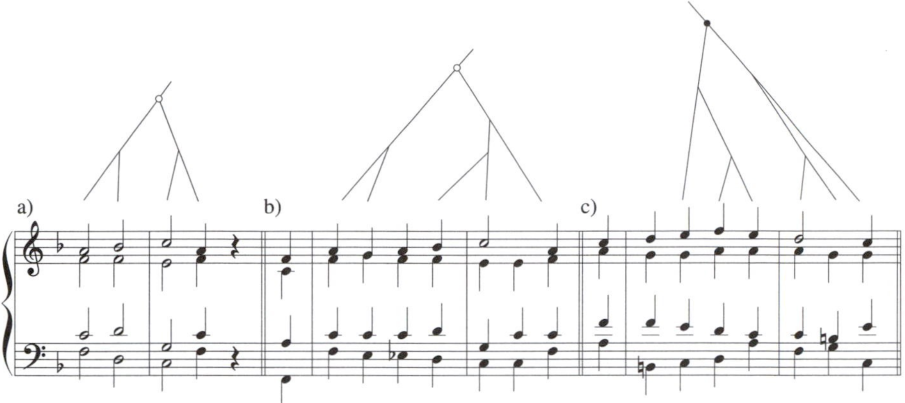

FIGURE 1.24 Illustrations of prolongational good form, taken from underlying levels in Figure 1.18: (a) the balance constraint; (b) normative prolongational structure; (c) the recursion constraint.

conditions for normative structure. Figure 1.24c, also taken from time-span level e, shows how the recursion constraint controls the branching in the third phrase. Both ii and vi elaborate their local tonic, I of C major, but not independently: vi attaches to I and ii to vi.

The prolongational analysis in Figure 1.18 violates prolongational good form only once, and that very weakly, in the nonrecursive right strong prolongations of the opening tonic at levels b and c. Recursive elaboration takes place a number of times in approaches to cadences, and normative structure occurs in the first and third phrases. Its omission in the second phrase is important to the continuity of the chorale, for otherwise that phrase—with its second cadence on the tonic and the succeeding pause—would seem too closed. The third phrase manifests not only normative structure but also the basic form, making it a rather complete unit in the subsidiary region. Normative structure is absent in the fourth phrase because there is no functional departure but instead a neighboring-passing motion at the downbeat of bar 7. As a result, the double relaxation at the end functions less for the phrase than for the chorale as a whole.

The optimal branching patterns of prolongational good form are preferential rather than mandatory because they interact with branching assignments based on stability. This interaction can be formulated as a two-stage process: (1) observing the interaction principle, assign prolongational branchings according to stability factors; and (2) correct the resulting branchings where needed so as to conform to prolongational good form.

On strict branching

It might be felt that the distinctions invoked for prolongational good form are artifacts of a tree notation that itself is a questionable way of representing a pitch

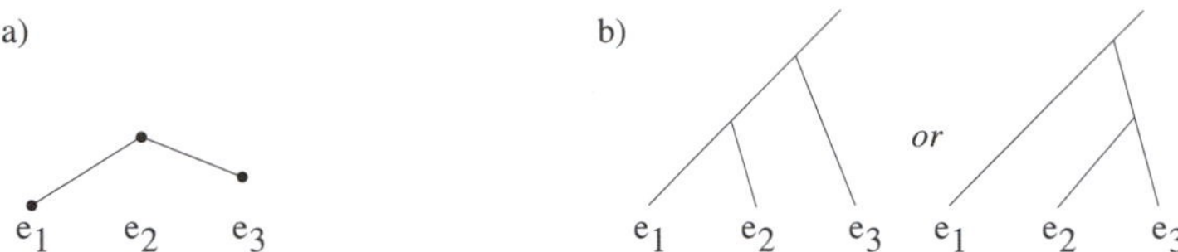

FIGURE 1.25 Representations of tension and relaxation: (a) by a curve on a graph; (b) by strict branching, with the subordinate branch to the right or to the left.

reduction. Specifically, it might be argued that elaborations should not have to attach to single superordinate events, as the tree (and slur) notation requires. Strict branching appears to be in conflict with the interpretation of prolongational structure as nested patterns of tension and relaxation. Given successive events e_1, e_2, and e_3 at any prolongational level and assuming that e_1 and e_3 are superordinate to e_2, $e_1 \rightarrow e_2$ increases tension and $e_2 \rightarrow e_3$ decreases tension. This tensing–relaxing pattern can be graphed as in Figure 1.25a, with events arrayed on the x-axis and relative tension on the y-axis. By the strict branching condition, however, e_2 must attach either to e_1 or to e_3, as in Figure 1.25b (disregarding nodal type or the recursion constraint). In this connection, Steve Larson (1997) makes a helpful distinction between affixes (prefixes or suffixes) and connectives. Strict branching is appropriate, he argues, for affixes such as escape tones or appoggiaturas but not for connectives such as passing and neighboring tones. As it is a matter of elementary counterpoint that there is stepwise motion to and from a passing or neighboring tone, why not say that passing or neighboring embellishment is simply subordinate between two relatively structural tones, without its having to be a constituent of the one or the other?

While this argument has merit, theoretical parsimony encourages retention of strict branching. Adding the option of "in-betweenness" to that of "belongingness" would complicate prolongational representation and derivation. This is so even for neighboring motion. The immediate stages of reduction for the opening melody of Mozart's G minor Symphony are given in Figure 1.26, with the neighboring E♭s acting as prefixes rather than just as connectives. This is so because the E♭s group with the following quarter-note Ds, in accordance with the overall rhythmic-motivic organization of the passage. In many cases, to be sure, it is not so clear whether a neighbor belongs to the preceding or succeeding tone. There

FIGURE 1.26 Three levels for the opening melody of Mozart's G minor Symphony, I.

is a sliding scale for neighboring belongingness. But the application of other relevant criteria tips the balance one way or the other (GTTM, section 8.2). Generally speaking, the embellishing neighbor attaches to whichever structural tone is more proximate, as summed across all the perceptually relevant dimensions. In the Mozart, the critical proximity dimension is that of shared membership within a rhythmic group.

Just as any nonconstituent subordination translates into a branching structure by invoking comparative proximity, so any graphic curve converts into a tree: an object at a trough between events at surrounding peaks attaches to one or the other peak by comparing their relative height or relative closeness. Such an approach is familiar in psychology; see, for example, Tverksy and Hutchinson (1986). Gilbert Youmans (1994) takes a similar approach specifically with respect to GTTM, in the context of a linguistic-literary analysis. Because the tree notation conveys more information than do nonconstituent hierarchies or graphic curves, there is reason to favor it as a means of representation.

An alternative is to loosen strict hierarchy in favor of a network model. A network is an organization in which the elements link at nodes without restriction to unique branching. Typically a network represents a web of interconnecting associations. GTTM does not assert that all musical relationships are hierarchical—far from it. However, to make headway toward a theory of associations, it is crucial to separate out those relations that can be described hierarchically. In the sketchy forms suggested by Robert Gjerdingen (1988) and Richard Cohn and Douglas Dempster (1992), an entirely network approach is weakly constrained and is unlikely to yield a useful system of analysis.

It is feasible, however, to represent connectives in network fashion within what is otherwise a strictly hierarchical framework. Figure 1.27a treats the connective e_2 this way by attaching it to both e_1 and e_3. This is a formal notation for saying that e_2 lies between the more structural e_1 and e_3. Better yet, the representation in Figure 1.27b lets us have it both ways: the solid branch signifies strict branching to the most proximate superordinate event, while the dashed branch adds the alternative attachment, creating a local network. In this volume I shall often finesse the issue in this manner. For example, the analysis of the first phrase of the chorale might add the two dashed branches in Figure 1.28. The V^4_2/IV on the third beat of bar 1 is the point of maximal tension in the phrase, the point of reversal between right and left branching patterns. The dashed branch from the V^6 to the V^4_2/IV conveys the tension motion, and the solid branch from the V^4_2/IV to the IV^6

a)

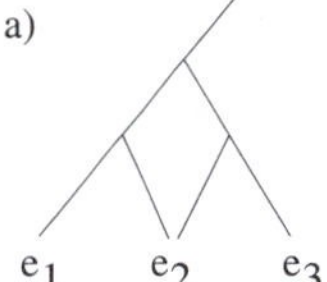

b)

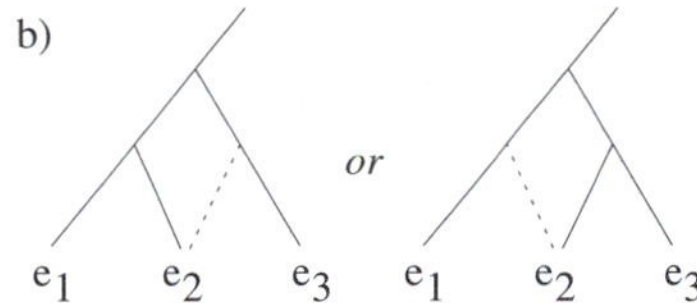

FIGURE 1.27 Alternative representations for Figure 1.25: (a) a network representation; (b) a combination strict branching and network notation.

FIGURE 1.28 Prolongational analysis of first phrase of "Christus, der ist mein Leben" using the optional notation of dashed branching when shifting from right to left branching.

expresses the subsequent relaxation. As the notation implies, the solid branch is primary, for the V_2^4/IV is closer to the IV^6 than to the previous V^6. The addition of the dashed branch, while strictly speaking superfluous, conveys the shift from tension to relaxation. Likewise and on a smaller scale, the double passing tones after the downbeat of bar 2 primarily elaborate the structural V. The dashed branch goes to the ensuing V^6, showing the small reversal from tension to relative relaxation within the weak prolongation of the V. ("The Principle of the Shortest Path" in chapter 2 and "Melodic Tension" in chapter 4 will ground this approach in terms of pitch-space distance and attraction.)

In summary, strict branching is defensible as a representation of relative closeness in subordinative attachment. But combined left/right networklike branchings, within an otherwise strictly hierarchical representation, offer a viable alternative for certain connectives, especially when using a combination of solid and dashed branches to signify relative connectivity.

Toward an enrichment of the grouping component

As mentioned in "Overview of GTTM," the grouping component collapses parsings within individual polyphonic lines into a single grouping structure for the passage as a whole. Although this idealization is useful, it simplifies the grouping structure of many musical passages. How might this and other aspects of the grouping component be enriched?

A first and fundamental step would be to incorporate Gestalt principles adapted from research on general auditory scene analysis (Bregman 1990). To make sense of the environment, the auditory system automatically organizes the incoming auditory signal into simultaneous, continuous streams—for instance, a speaking voice, a humming air vent, and a car honking outside the window. Two complementary aspects are at work. On the one hand, the ear fuses mutually varying sonic components into single sources or objects. The objects may vary acoustically over time, but they are nevertheless perceived as coherent entities so long as the variance is not disruptive. On the other hand, simultaneous sources with contrasting acoustic features acquire separate perceptual identities. These principles carry over to music (McAdams and Bregman 1979; Huron 2000). A complex pitch has many overtones but is perceived as one object even if, say, its vibrato or loudness changes. This holds true to a lesser extent for chords (especially consonant ones) and mixed orchestral timbres. The division of the musical flow into the elementary objects of analysis that GTTM calls pitch events—single pitches and chords—is thus an act of low-level grouping. Next, if two pitches are perceived as separate objects that are registrally proximate and timbrally similar, they tend to be heard as part of a single line. If they are registrally far apart or timbrally dissimilar, the ear is likely to assign them to simultaneous separate lines.

The local rules in GTTM's grouping component invoke the same criteria but in a vertical way. If two adjacent events are temporally or registrally proximate and otherwise acoustically similar, the ear tends to group them together. If they are not proximate and similar, one hears them as belonging to different groupings of events, such as different motives or phrases. GTTM thus treats auditory scenes from one angle. A more complete grouping component would incorporate the principles of similarity and proximity along a number of psychoacoustic and musical dimensions in order to parse the musical signal first into events and then into horizontal as well as vertical units of events. This program lies outside the scope of this volume.

It is possible, however, to outline how polyphonic groupings, assigned by application of GTTM's grouping rules independently to each stream, combine into a single overall grouping structure that becomes in phase with the metrical grid. To emphasize that the issue of polyphonic groupings pertains not just to contrapuntal music, let us consider the nominally homophonic opening phrase of the first movement of Mozart's Sonata, K. 333, in Figure 1.29. Respective groupings for the melody and accompaniment are placed above and below the music. Each subphrasal grouping of the melody begins with an anacrusis to the downbeat of each bar. This segmentation is determined by the comparatively long duration at the end of each of these groups and, at the next larger level, by motivic parallelisms and symmetry. Each corresponding group in the accompaniment begins after an eighth rest on the downbeat of each bar. Thus the two groupings, while equivalent in their time-span lengths and nesting structures, are out of phase both with each other and with the metrical structure.

Perceptually, this misalignment is a mere surface disturbance. How this is so is demonstrated in the time-span reduction in Figure 1.29. At level d the accompaniment lines up with the spans of the metrical grid, so that the eighth-note delays appear on downbeats. The dashed lines show how the melodic pitches on the upbeats and afterbeats at level d relocate at level c to their downbeats. At level b the basic melodic-harmonic motion of the phrase, $\hat{5}\rightarrow\hat{4}\rightarrow\hat{3}$ over I→ii→V^7→I emerges, and the grouping becomes not two out-of-phase patterns but a single

FIGURE 1.29 Polyphonic groupings and reductional analysis of Mozart's Sonata, K. 333, I, bars 1–4.

structure. The psychological claim is that the listener automatically performs this reduction and hence experiences the passage in terms of a fundamentally single grouping structure. The prolongational analysis at the bottom of Figure 1.29 illustrates the process in reverse: at level 1 the passage is homophonic, but at level 2 the respective slurs of the soprano and bass overlap temporally, showing the partial independence of the lines.

The general principle, then, is that locally out-of-phase polyphonic groupings converge into an overall homophonic grouping at an underlying reductional level. In tonal music, constraints on the treatment of nonharmonic tones and on harmonic formation ensure unification at an early reductional stage. The reductional process also relocates events so that out-of-phase surface groupings begin on metrical downbeats at underlying levels. The following chapters will assume these analytic steps.

Abstractions and transformations of surface events

Cohn and Dempster (1992) distinguish between "representational" and "inclusional" hierarchies. In the former, the leaves of the tree persist as leaves at underlying levels; in the latter, nonsurface structures are abstractions from the leaves. The reductional hierarchies in GTTM are representational. For example, a $I^{\hat{3}}$ chord at the musical surface persists in being a $I^{\hat{3}}$ chord at the underlying levels for which it continues to function. Underlying events in Schenkerian theory, in contrast, are in some sense abstractions, even though they are represented by musical notation.

It is easy to say that underlying events are somehow abstract. It is much more difficult to develop a formal theory that assigns specific abstract structure to underlying events, and in a way that corresponds to the listener's presumed internal representations. GTTM avoids this morass. It is concerned with derivation of prolongational structure rather than with underlying abstractions of already assigned prolongations. But the issue of the abstraction of underlying events remains an important one. Without making firm theoretical claims, I should like to outline an approach to the issue. The idea is that the specific content of an event degrades and generalizes in memory, depending on the framework in which it is experienced. Consequently, at any prolongational level, only what is needed in that context is retained through a transformational operation. Unlike GTTM's transformations, these operations do not turn ill-formed into well-formed hierarchies but modify the content or placement of events at underlying levels.

For instance, in the last bar of the Bach chorale "Ich bin's, ich sollte büssen" in Figure 1.30, the tenor leaps from F to B♭ in order to avoid the parallel fifths that would have resulted between soprano and tenor if the tenor had descended stepwise, in typical fashion, from F to E♭–D♭–C. The inner voice leading in the last bar is thus purely local in function (elegantly carried out, to be sure, by filling in the gap from the previous A♭–F leap). Beneath there is a more abstract under-

FIGURE 1.30 The final phrase of Bach's chorale "Ich bin's, ich sollte büssen," together with an abstract representation at an underlying level.

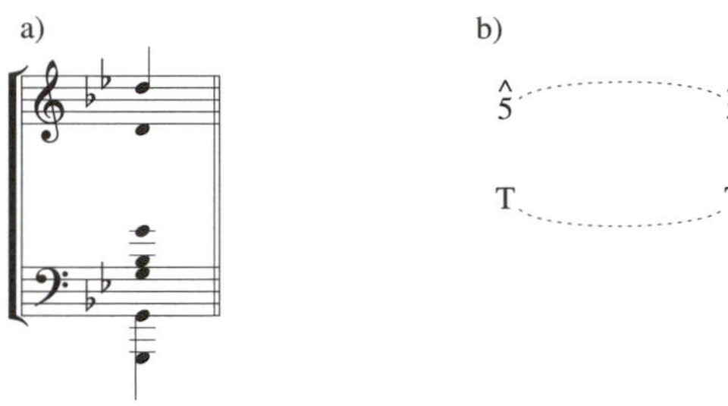

FIGURE 1.31 Mozart's G minor Symphony, I: (a) the opening surface "event" after normalization; (b) an abstract global representation of the opening event prolonging to its return at the beginning of the recapitulation.

lying representation in which such details play no role. At this level only the structural beginning and cadence of the phrase remain, and only the outer voices are retained, with scale degrees given in the soprano and root functions designated in the bass. The transformations in question are deletion and labeling of abstracted relations.

In another illustration, Figure 1.31a gives the verticalized surface content of the structural beginning of the opening phrase of Mozart's G minor Symphony. This verticalization is itself a temporal abstraction. The unusual spacing of the event is immaterial to the larger form of the movement. At the global level at which this event prolongs to the beginning of the recapitulation, it matters only that it is a root-position G minor triad with $\hat{5}$ on top. Or, more abstractly, perhaps it only matters that it is a tonic chord with $\hat{5}$ on top, as in Figure 1.31b (where "T" indicates harmonic function rather than a particular triadic realization). The representation of the G minor triad changes depending on the context in which it is viewed. Just as events in a sequence relate to one another hierarchically, so a single event has hierarchical depth.

Bach's C major Prelude from Book I of *The Well-Tempered Clavier* provides instances of transformation to an underlying event not present at the musical surface and of underlying registral transfer. Figure 1.32a gives the progression in bars 21–23. At an underlying level, however, this passage is best represented by the ii$^{6}_{5}$ in Figure 1.32b on the view that the E in bar 21 is a suspension that needs to resolve to D, even though at the surface this happens only obliquely in bar 23.

Registral transfer occurs at the most global level of the Prelude. As sketched in Figure 1.33, the opening I$^{\hat{3}}$ descends an octave, leading through the underlying ii$^{6}_{5}$ to V$^{\hat{2}}$ in the lower register. But the resolution to the final I$^{\hat{1}}$ takes place an octave higher, recovering the original register. At the next prolongational level, shown beneath, the second I$^{\hat{3}}$ and the ii$^{6}_{5}$ in the lower octave reduce out, leaving

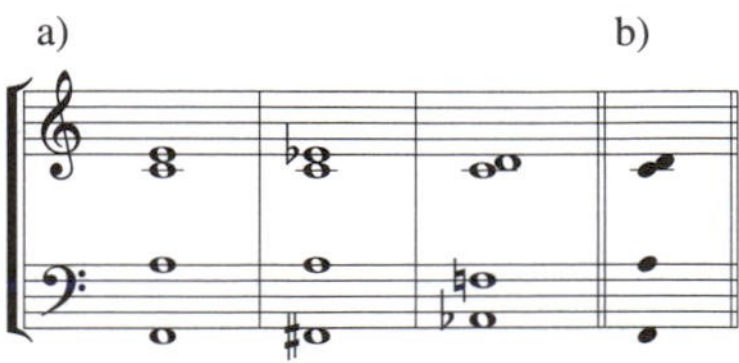

FIGURE 1.32 Bach's C major Prelude (WCT I): (a) the progression in bars 21–23; (b) the functional harmony that underlies bars 21–23.

FIGURE 1.33 Global levels of Bach's C major Prelude, showing the registral transformation of the cadential $V^{\hat{2}}$.

the $V^{\hat{2}}$ between the opening $I^{\hat{3}}$ and the closing $I^{\hat{1}}$. At this point and not before, and in order to achieve stepwise motion in the reduction, the $V^{\hat{2}}$ is raised to the upper octave. The arrow represents the transformational operation. (Compare GTTM, Example 10.11, as well as Schenker's [1932] well-known analysis.)

When to activate and how to specify the content of transformations such as those for Figure 1.30–33 is theoretically problematic. Registral transformation in Figure 1.33 may be fairly direct, but often it is not as clear as it is in Figure 1.32 whether an event is suppressed at the surface and, if so, what it should consist of at underlying levels. Abstracting event features at the level of the phrase as in Figure 1.30 may seem relatively straightforward, but what the nature of an event is at a global level such as in Figure 1.31 is far from obvious.

The first theme group and transition of the first movement of Beethoven's *Waldstein* Sonata motivates more speculative operations on surface events, including their temporal adjustment. The score in Figure 1.34 is transformed into a quasi-chorale texture in Figure 1.35. All the registers collapse into the central one, the voices simplify into four smoothly moving parts, each bar of music has the value of a quarter note within a larger $\frac{4}{4}$ hypermeter, the harmonic rhythm evens out into quarter-note motion, and the phrase structure becomes regular. This regularity is achieved by one expansion and three deletions: the end of the first phrase—bar 13 in Figure 1.34—is expanded to represent four bars; bar 21 is deleted; bars 23–28 are compressed to a four-bar grouping; and bars 29–30 are deleted after the downbeat of bar 29. The notes in parentheses stand for normative, unstated voice leading in place of the arpeggiated octaves in bars 12–13 in Figure 1.34. To clarify the correspondences, the bar numbers from Figure 1.34 are placed at the beginning of each notated bar in Figure 1.35. Surface features trigger the expansion and deletions: there is a fermata in bar 13; bar 21 is an "extra" measure that breaks up the regularity of the parallelism between bars 5–8 and 18–22; the six-bar unit in bars 23–28 is caused by direct repetition; and bar 29 elides with bar 31, eliminating the arpeggiating flourish between these points. As a result of these transformations, the brilliant improvisational surface of Figure

FIGURE 1.34 Beethoven's *Waldstein* Sonata, Op. 53, I, up to the beginning of the second theme group.

FIGURE 1.34 (Continued)

FIGURE 1.35 Normalized version of Figure 1.34.

1.34 becomes two neatly parallel phrases in Figure 1.35, each comprising four hypermeasures divided into subgroupings of 1+1+2 and ending in a half-cadence. Figure 1.35 also brings out the quasi-inversional relationship between the two phrases: in the first, the statement of the material sequences down a whole step, with the bass descending chromatically to the dominant of the parallel minor region; in the second, the statement sequences up a whole step, with the soprano ascending chromatically to the dominant of the parallel minor, E minor, for the new region, E major.

The changes wrought in Figure 1.35, which resemble the rhythmic reductions and normalizations carried out by present-day Schenkerians (as in Schachter 1980 and Rothstein 1989, 1990), multiply the problem of when and how to specify underlying transformations. Some might be satisfied just to conclude that Figure 1.35 illuminates the underlying schematic structure of Beethoven's surface. The theoretically more ambitious program of deriving Figure 1.35 by rule would require a method for recognizing standard schemas and ways of converting deviations from those schemas into their prototypes. Given this daunting task, the crutch of the constraining power of an encompassing *Ursatz* schema would seem too enticing to resist. I take the psychologically more plausible position that schematic prototypes arise out of a convergence of simple cognitive principles that are available at or near musical surfaces. Based on such principles, one might go on to invoke constraints of rhythmic good form, roughly parallel to prolongational good form. For example, a phrase is optimally four or eight bars long so that it can remain in a constant relationship to the hypermeter (GTTM, section 11.4). The transformation, say, of a nine-bar into an eight-bar phrase is a way of representing the relationship between the deviation and its prototype. While such an approach appears to be promising, I shall not undertake it with any thoroughness here but instead shall take it for granted where useful, so that the resulting structures can serve as a platform for other theoretical explorations.

2 *Diatonic Space*

THE CONCEPT OF PITCH SPACE

Tonal and event hierarchies

It is necessary first to distinguish between an event hierarchy and a tonal hierarchy (Bharucha 1984b). An event hierarchy, which is typically cast as a pitch reduction, represents hierarchical relationships inferred from a sequence of events. Event hierarchies have long been a concern of music theory, although it was not until Schenker that the pitch analysis of an entire piece took such a form. The prolongational structures discussed in chapter 1 form event hierarchies. A tonal hierarchy, in contrast, corresponds to GTTM's stability conditions and embodies the hierarchical relations that accrue to an entire tonal system beyond its instantiation in a particular piece. Such a hierarchy is atemporal in that it represents more or less permanent knowledge about the system rather than a response to a specific sequence of events. This knowledge arises from listening experience. Within bounds, exposure to a different musical idiom gives rise to a different tonal hierarchy. Tonal and event hierarchies are interdependent developmentally. Exposure to music is a prerequisite for internalizing a tonal hierarchy, yet a complex event hierarchy cannot be constructed without such a schema. They bootstrap each other into existence (Deutsch 1984).

This chapter develops a model of the tonal hierarchy, not only for its intrinsic importance but also in order to flesh out the stability conditions that the GTTM theory relies on to generate pitch reductions. Later chapters will explore other theoretical and analytical consequences of the model.

Previous approaches

In both music theory and music psychology there are traditions that express the tonal hierarchy by geometric models. These traditions correlate spatial distance with intuitive musical distance. For example, the region (or key) of G major is understood to be closer to C major than A♭ major is to C major. Within a C major context, the chord V is closer to I than is ii; the pitch D is closer to C than is D♭. Observe that "closer" does not necessarily mean more proximate in log frequency; in that sense, D♭ is closer to C than is D. Rather, D is closer in the sense that it lies within the C major scale while D♭ does not. The distance in question is not acoustic but cognitive. A spatial model is a way to represent this kind of internalized knowledge.

In music theory this approach originated in the Baroque period, when tempered scales came into use, as a device for teaching smooth modulation. Johann David Heinichen (1728) proposed the regional circle in Figure 2.1a, in which the major circle of fifths alternates with its relative minor counterpart. Such a representation depends on the group-theoretic feature that progression by perfect fifth passes through all the members of the chromatic collection before returning to the starting point. Adjacent moves on the circle stand for close modulations and nonadjacent moves for more distant modulations. However, Heinichen's circle did not reflect tonal practice—D minor and A minor are not closer to C major than are F major and G major—so alternative proposals were made by Johann Mattheson (1735) and others. All of them took advantage of the circle of fifths but similarly foundered in the handling of major–minor relationships, for which a single circle provides too impoverished a space. David Kellner (1737) made progress by suggesting the structure in Figure 2.1b, which links relative minor-major regions in a double circle of fifths. This satisfied relative minor relationships but continued to neglect parallel minor relationships. Later on, Gottfried Weber (1821–1824) (anticipated by Vial 1767; see the frontispiece of Lester 1992) invoked the chart in Figure 2.1c. The circle of fifths appears on the vertical axis, with relative and parallel major–minor relationships alternating on the horizontal axis. G major, F major, A minor, and C minor are all equidistant regions from C major, and so on by transposition throughout. Because distances along each axis are invariant, regardless of the horizontal or vertical starting point, a geometrical projection of this chart would take the form not of a three-dimensional sphere but of a four-dimensional toroidal structure.

Music theorists have also been concerned with another level of tonal proximity, chord relatedness within a region. Usually this concern has appeared in the guise of recommended fundamental-bass or root progressions (Rameau 1722; Sechter 1853; Piston 1941–1978), though in the Riemannian tradition it arises in the form of an optimal ordering of functional harmonic classes (T→S→D→T). David Lewin (1987), following Hugo Riemann (1902), briefly discusses harmonic progression in terms of a spatial format mentioned later.

The psychological tradition has focused more on pitches and pcs (pitch classes) than on regional or harmonic relationships. Pitches close in log frequency are perceived as near to one another, and so are pitches in a 2:1 frequency ratio. To

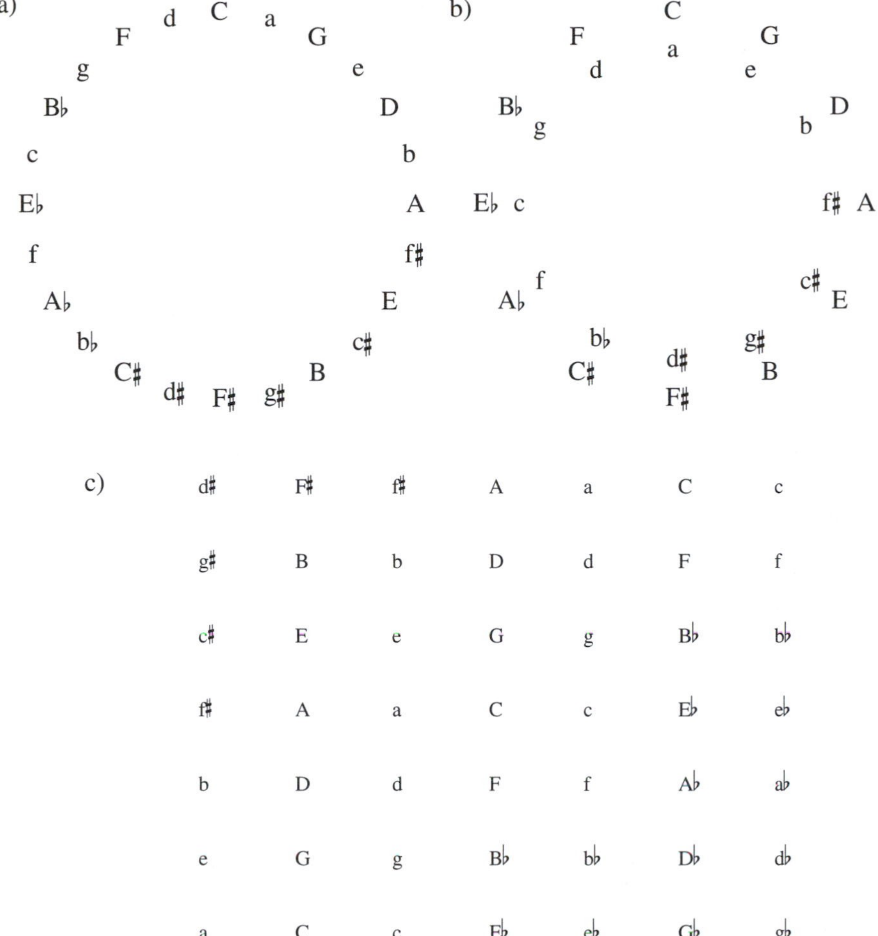

FIGURE 2.1 (a) Heinichen's regional circle; (b) Kellner's regional circle; (c) Weber's regional chart.

model these two kinds of proximity, M. W. Drobisch (1855) suggested that pitch height be represented on a helix, with octave recurrences placed proximally on the vertical axis of the turning helix. Roger Shepard (1982) extends this approach to include other closely related intervals such as the perfect fifth. Combining the semitone and fifth cycles, for instance, yields the double helix in Figure 2.2a, which Shepard calls the "melodic map."

Another pitch space, and one with a long history in music theory, is the lattice structure in Figure 2.2b, in which the horizontal axis is laid out in perfect fifths and the vertical axis in major thirds. It was first proposed by the mathematician L. Euler (1739) as a way of representing just intonation. If pitches are compressed into one octave, intervals can be figured by multiplying ratios along the lattice.

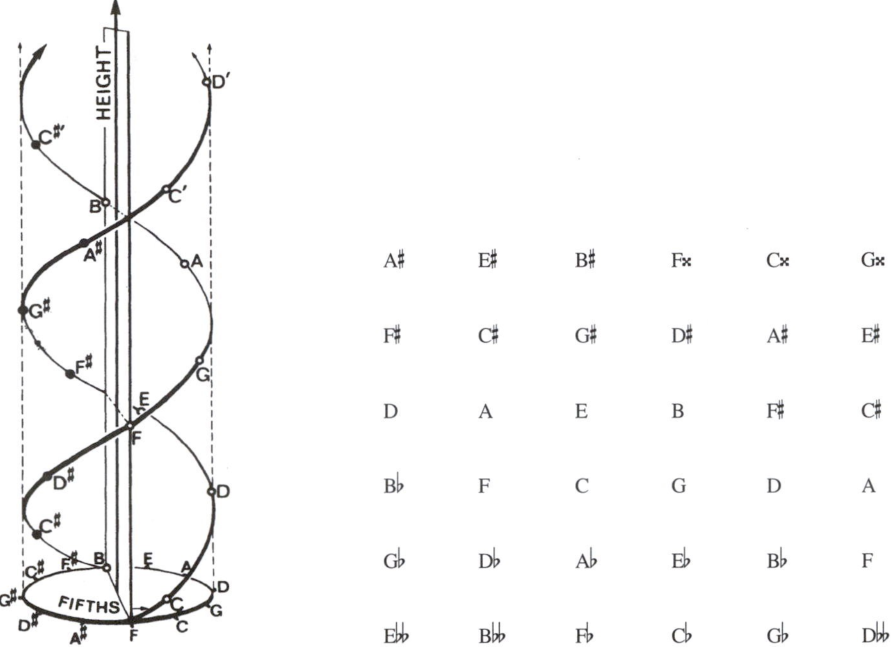

FIGURE 2.2 (a) Shepard's melodic map (Reproduced by permission of Academic Press); (b) Riemann's *Tonnetz*.

Thus the large major second C-D is traced in Figure 2.2b from C eastward to G and D, which equals 3:2 × 3:2 = 9:4, or 9:8, while the small major second C-D is traced from C northward to E and westward to A and D, which equals 5:4 × 2:3 × 2:3 = 20:36, or 40:36 = 10:9. Hermann von Helmholtz (1863/1885) and Arthur von Oettingen (1866) took up this representation, the latter employing it as well for harmonic description. Influenced by Oettingen, Riemann used this *Tonnetz* (table of relations) in various ways throughout his career (Mooney 1996). The structure has also been invoked by Renate Imig (1970) and Christopher Longuet-Higgins (1962), the latter again motivated by considerations of just intonation. Adjusted to equal temperament, it corresponds to Shepard's (1982) "harmonic map." By combining major-and minor-third cycles, Gerald Balzano (1980, 1982) arrives at an almost equivalent space, rotated so that the perfect fifth cycle rather than the minor-third cycle forms a diagonal. The equal-tempered *Tonnetz* has enjoyed a resurgence of interest in the neo-Riemannian work of Cohn (1997), Brian Hyer (1995), David Kopp (1995), and Lewin (1992), among others.

A problematic aspect of invoking the equal-tempered *Tonnetz* is that the historically prior and syntactically central diatonic collection arises only as a secondary feature. The chromatic collection is assumed as foundational for the Classical tonal system. From this foundation, equal-interval cycles are generated, creating symmetrical multidimensional models. Shepard's melodic map is made up of two strands of whole-tone scales, and his harmonic map employs thirds cycles (as do the corresponding models mentioned earlier in this section). But only the fifth cycle is basic to the diatonic system, which in many respects is asymmetrical. Other interval cycles do not assume musical significance until the rise of chromaticism in the nineteenth century.

Historical issues aside, and quite briefly (we shall revisit issues relating to the *Tonnetz*), the space in Figure 2.2b is inadequate on two grounds, not as a representation for just intonation but as a psychological model. First, its distances are empirically incorrect. In a C major context, one does not hear, for example, the pitch F as closer to the tonic than D or A♭ as closer than A. Second, although the original motivation of space had to do with intervals between pitches, Riemann applies it freely to chords and regions, thereby conflating levels of description.

This second point is germane to all the models mentioned here. The spaces in Figure 2.1 express relative proximity among tonal regions, and those in Figure 2.2 represent (or should represent) the relative proximity of pcs in a tonal context. Between these two categories lies the relative proximity of chords within a region. Even supposing the existence of an adequate model for a single level, how can the three levels relate in one overall model?

The experimental work of Carol Krumhansl and her associates (summarized in Krumhansl 1983, 1990) points toward a resolution of these issues. They investigate listeners' responses for the cognitive proximity of pcs, chords, and regions in relation to an induced tonic. For each level, multidimensional scaling yields a geometric solution that perspicuously represents the patterns implicit in the data. The pc level takes the form of the cone in Figure 2.3a, in which the most stable pcs appear at the bottom and the least stable at the top. The layering in Figure 2.3a bears out the familiar observation (for instance, in Meyer 1956) that in Classical tonality the tonic is most stable, then the other tonic triad members, then the remaining diatonic pcs, then the nondiatonic pcs. The chordal level, in relating pairs of chords within a diatonic context, appears as in Figure 2.3b. As one might expect, IV and V turn out to be closest to I. The regional level receives the toroidal mapping in Figure 2.3c. This result, which has been replicated in a number of ways over a variety of subjects, approximates the Weber space in Figure 2.1c.

Diana Deutsch and John Feroe (1981) propose a theory of encoding of pitch sequences that suggests a novel approach with respect to Krumhansl's results. In the tradition of psychological coding theory (Simon and Sumner 1968; Restle 1970), they hypothesize that listeners structure tonal sequences by means of hierarchically organized alphabets. The superordinate alphabet is the octave; then come triads and seventh chords, then the diatonic scale, and finally the chromatic scale, essentially as in Figure 2.3a. With empirical support from Deutsch (1980), they argue that the more parsimoniously a melody can be represented in terms of these alphabets, the easier it is for the listener to encode the sequence. Although Deutsch and Feroe's interest is in the processing of event hierarchies (they use a notational equivalent of GTTM's time-span trees, introduced in Lerdahl and Jackendoff [1977]), their theory has two implications for pitch-space theory. First, the alphabets themselves belong to the tonal hierarchy but take an algebraic rather

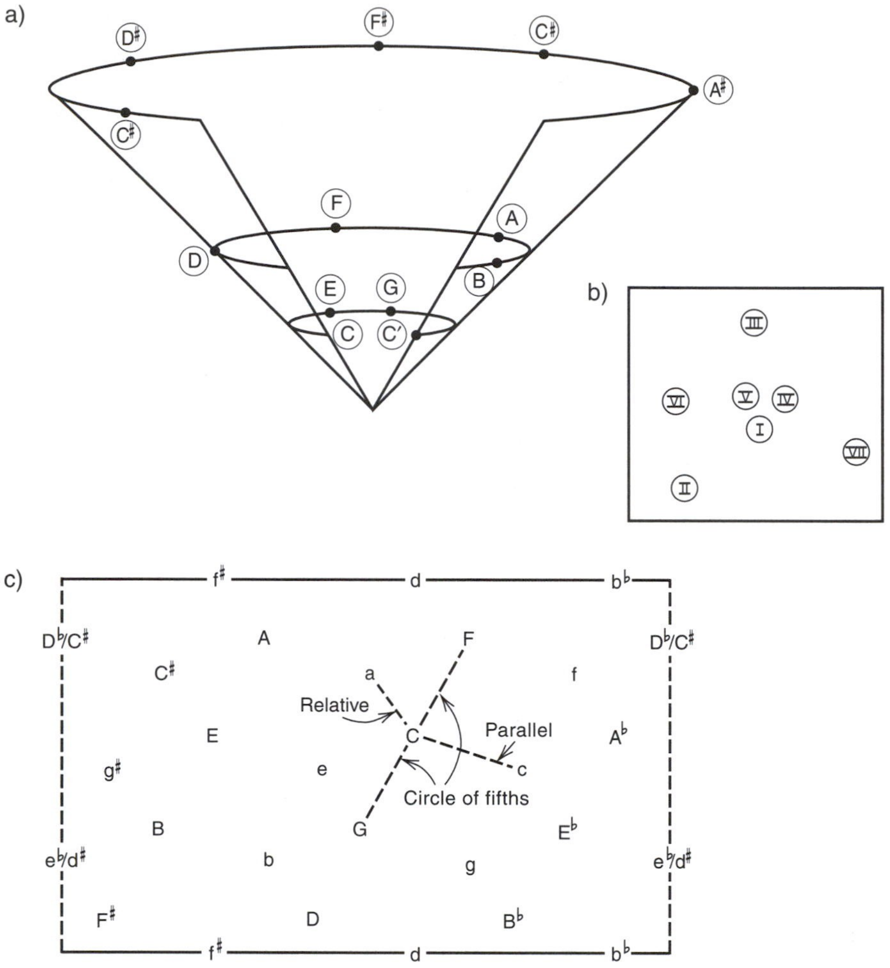

FIGURE 2.3 Krumhansl's spatial representations derived from empirical data: (a) pc proximity (Reproduced by permission of Academic Press); (b) chordal proximity; (c) regional proximity. Sections (b) and (c) copyright © by the American Psychological Association; adapted with permission.

than geometric form. Second, unlike the spaces mentioned earlier, the alphabets are organized like a musical reduction: the content of one level elaborates the content of its immediately superordinate level.

This survey motivates the following conclusions. First, GTTM's stability conditions correspond to the tonal hierarchy, which can be modeled by a multidimensional space in which spatial distance equals cognitive distance. We do not know how the brain calculates cognitive distance; it might be useful to cast the model in algebraic form. Second, an algebraic representation can be conceived as a stratified hierarchy in which the more stable elements at one level repeat at the next larger level. Such a formulation can give the tonal hierarchy an abstract structure similar to an event hierarchy. Third, an adequate theory of diatonic space must incorporate the three levels of pitch class, chord, and region into one model, which represents relative proximity for all elements at each level and shows how the levels interconnect. Fourth, the model should treat the chromatic collection not as the parent structure but as one level of a hierarchical organization in which the asymmetrical diatonic collection and the triad have at least comparable prominence. Interval cycles other than the fifth should not play a central role in the model. Fifth, the model should mirror empirical findings.

The next sections develop such a model. For convenience, I continue to call the model diatonic space, even though the diatonic collection is only part of the story and the model is fundamentally numerical rather than spatial in concept. The model usually treats the abstractions of pcs and ics (interval classes) rather than specific pitches and intervals, although at various points it will be useful to refer to the latter.

The basic space

Let us posit the "basic space" of Figure 2.4a, a rendering of Deutsch and Feroe's idea of hierarchically organized alphabets. It also reflects the empirical results displayed geometrically in Figure 2.3a. Level a is octave (or root) space, level b is fifth space, level c is triadic space, level d is diatonic space, and level e is chromatic space. In contrast to Deutsch and Feroe, a fifth space is included here, because the fifth is more stable than the third of a triad and because the fifth becomes the basis for shifting the space. The seventh-chord level is excluded because in Classical music seventh chords have little independent status, the interval of a seventh usually behaving as a local dissonance governed by voice-leading principles. If, however, a seventh is judged to be harmonic, it can be added at the triadic level.

Figure 2.4a is oriented toward a tonic chord in C major, notated in Roman-numeral fashions as I/**I**, or I/**C**. Chords are designated in nonbold type, regions

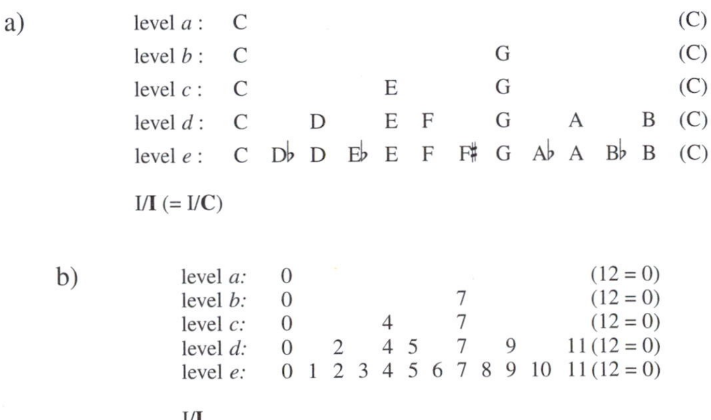

a)
level *a* : C (C)
level *b* : C G (C)
level *c* : C E G (C)
level *d* : C D E F G A B (C)
level *e* : C D♭ D E♭ E F F♯ G A♭ A B♭ B (C)
I/**I** (= I/**C**)
b)
level *a:* 0 (12 = 0)
level *b:* 0 7 (12 = 0)
level *c:* 0 4 7 (12 = 0)
level *d:* 0 2 4 5 7 9 11 (12 = 0)
level *e:* 0 1 2 3 4 5 6 7 8 9 10 11 (12 = 0)
I/**I**

FIGURE 2.4 The basic space: (a) using letter names; (b) in numerical format.

in boldface. The space shifts for other chords and regions, as explained later. A pc numerical representation proves useful for this purpose, achieved by translating Figure 2.4a into Figure 2.4b, where C = 0, C♯ (or D♭) = 1, D = 2, . . . B = 11. The numerical notation brings out the basic formal feature that level e provides a closed cycle of elements, with adjacent elements separated by the same interval. It would be possible to describe the space on the basis of ics rather than pcs and, in keeping with the untempered origin of the diatonic system, to derive the chromatic level by interval from the diatonic level. This program is not necessary for our purposes here.

The basic space itself is obvious—we are all aware of octaves, triads, and diatonic and chromatic scales—yet it has great explanatory power. First of all, it meets the listed requirements. The space is algebraic. Each level of the space elaborates into less stable pcs at the next smaller level; conversely, the more stable pcs at one level continue on to the next larger level. The structure is asymmetrical and represents the diatonic scale and the triad directly. As will be seen, the only cyclic operator is the fifth. Changes in the space yield a unified treatment of pc, chord, and regional proximity. The quantified distances tally with the empirical evidence.

The next sections quantify distances and transform the space for the pc, chordal, and regional levels. The basic space remains oriented to I/**C**; different orientations would yield equivalent results. Geometric projections for pc, chordal, and regional distances are developed from the calculations. It should be kept in mind, however, that the theory primarily resides in the algebraic model. After each level's technical presentation I discuss theoretical issues pertinent to that level.

THE PITCH-CLASS LEVEL

Pitch-class and pitch proximity

The distance of the other pcs from the tonic pc0 can be calculated both vertically and horizontally. Vertical distance gives the depth of embedding of a pc by counting the number of levels down in the basic space that a pc first appears. Figure 2.5a does this for each pc in Figure 2.4.

Distance along the horizontal dimension is usually measured in terms of specific pitches rather than of pcs. Let pitches p0, p1 . . . p11, p12 be contained within an octave. Horizontal distance relies on a generalized notion of step and skip. In traditional usage, a step takes place between adjacent members of the chromatic or diatonic collection and an arpeggiation occurs between adjacent members of a triad. It is conceptually unifying, however, to think of arpeggiation as stepwise motion in triadic space. One can also speak of a step in fifth space. This is the sense, for instance, in which the sequence p0→p4→p12 involves a skip (between p4 and p12), whereas the sequences p0→p7→p12 and p0→p4→p7→p12 do not. Likewise, a leap of an octave is a step in octave space, but a leap of two octaves is a skip. A step, in short, is adjacent motion, and a skip is nonadjacent motion, along any level of the space. Figure 2.5b counts steps in this fashion for levels c–e of Figure 2.4.

a)

Vertical distance from pc0:	0	4	3	4	2	3	4	1	4	3	4	3
Pitch class:	*0*	*1*	*2*	*3*	*4*	*5*	*6*	*7*	*8*	*9*	*10*	*11*

b)

Horizontal distance from pc0:													
	0				1			1					(0)
	0		1		2	3		3		2		1	(0)
	0	1	2	3	4	5	6	5	4	3	2	1	(0)
Pitch:	*0*	*1*	*2*	*3*	*4*	*5*	*6*	*7*	*8*	*9*	*10*	*11*	*(0)*

c)

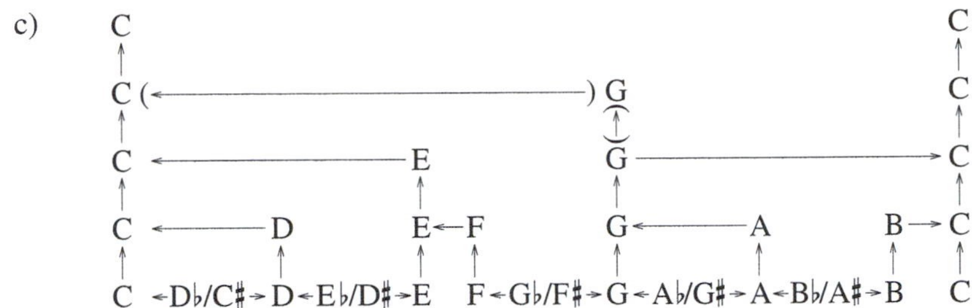

d)

Combined distance:	0	5 6	4	6 6	3	5	7 6	2	6 7	5	7 6	4
Pitch:	C	D♭/C♯	D	E♭/D♯	E	F	G♭/F♯	G	A♭/G♯	A	B♭/A♯	B

FIGURE 2.5 Pc and pitch proximity in the basic space: (a) vertical depth of pc embedding; (b) number of horizontal steps for each level; (c) stepwise horizontal and vertical pitch paths; (d) number of moves for each pitch in (c).

One can also add up the shortest number of steps at all levels of the space that a pitch takes to reach p0. For instance, p5 is two steps from p0: one step at the diatonic level from p5 to p4 and another step at the triadic level from p4 to p0. Distances at level e can depend on chromatic spelling: using letter names, D♭ is one step from C; but under the implications of usual spelling, C♯ is two steps from C (C♯→D, D→C). If the ultimate point of stability is conceived to be the C at the top of the structure, the vertical embedding and horizontal steps of Figures 2.5a and 2.5b combine into the pathlike representation of Figure 2.5c. The number of moves for each pitch in Figure 2.5c is tabulated in Figure 2.5d. Thus in Figure 2.5c there are five arrows from D♭, and six from C♯, to C at the top of the structure. The values in Figure 2.5d must be interpreted strictly in terms of I/I.

A related way to conceive pc distance is in terms of a geometric mapping of the basic space. The pcs of level e (the chromatic collection) form equidistant points on a circle, and the pc at level a (the root) forms a single point on an orthogonal plane. Lines traced around the circle at different levels generate the cone in Figure 2.6 (compare Figure 2.3a). Absolute distances between pcs at intermediate levels become smaller as the cone narrows, reflecting changes in adjacency; compare, for instance, the distances from pc0 to pc4 at the chromatic, diatonic, and triadic levels. In terms of Figure 2.5, the cone's y-axis maps vertical

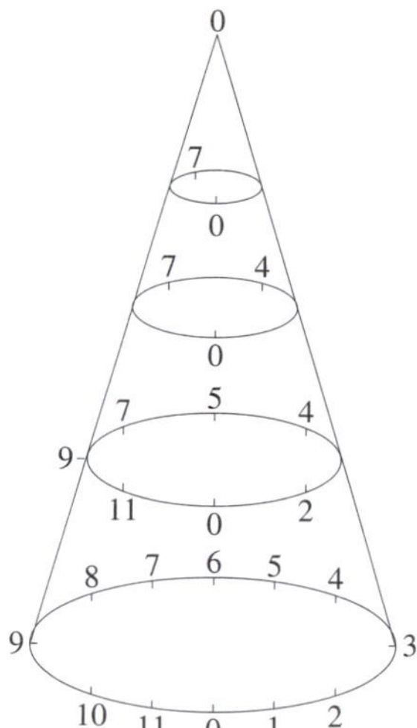

FIGURE 2.6 The pc cone.

depth of embedding (Figure 2.5a) and the x-axis represents step distances at any level (Figure 2.5b). Figure 2.4 is an unwrapped version of the cone.

Reflections on steps

Even though the steps at each of the fifth, triadic, and diatonic levels are unequal in log frequency, they are cognitively equal in the sense that they are steps within those levels. The counting in Figure 2.5b assumes this view. Such will also be the case when the step/skip distinction is extended to chords.

The differences in step sizes serves another cognitive function. The disposition of unequal steps at the diatonic level fulfills Balzano's (1980, 1982) psychologically relevant group-theoretic criteria of "uniqueness" and "coherence." Uniqueness demands that the ordered set of step sizes that begins from each pitch in the collection be different in each case. Counting up in semitones, the ordered set at the diatonic level from p0 is 2–2–1–2–2–2–1, from p2 it is 2–1–2–2–2–1–2, and so on in nonduplicating fashion. This feature arises only for collections with asymmetrical step configurations and permits unambiguous "position finding" (Browne 1981).

The coherence criterion preserves the intuitive correspondence between number of steps taken and distance traversed: a larger number of steps must correlate with a greater distance on the chromatic scale. For the diatonic scale, the only ambiguous interval in this respect is the tritone, which comprises three steps as an augmented fourth but four as a diminished fifth. An example of an incoherent collection is the harmonic minor scale, in which the stepwise augmented second between the sixth and seventh scale degrees is equal in distance to the minor thirds that elsewhere take two steps to traverse; hence, from this point of view, the common melodic preference for the upward raised sixth or downward lowered seventh. (Coherence can also be described in terms of maximal evenness

[Clough and Douthett 1991; Agmon 1996], as discussed in "Related Issues" in chapter 6.)

Balzano adds another criterion, "simplicity," which ensures orderly transposition of a collection. To describe simplicity in the framework used here, let us extend the step/skip distinction to transposition, such that a "transpositional step" moves a collection one step along an interval cycle and a transpositional skip is more than one transpositional step. A simple collection, then, is one that is capable of subtracting and adding a progressively larger number of new pcs, measured from the starting point, with each successive transpositional step. For the diatonic collection, one transpositional step on the fifth cycle subtracts one pc and adds another; a second transpositional step subtracts another and adds another; and so forth, until the cycle is completed. A restricted version of simplicity stipulates that a new pc must be chromatically adjacent to the pc it replaces. In moving from **C** to **G**, for instance, pc6 replaces and is adjacent to pc5. This significant property of the diatonic system enables stepwise modulation using diatonically altered stepwise melodic patterns. (A collection that is simple must also be unique.)

Some perspective can be gained by comparing two other familiar collections, the pentatonic and the octatonic, which, like the diatonic collection, have steps in two sizes. The pentatonic collection meets all three criteria: the step pattern 2–2–3–2–3 satisfies uniqueness; the steps and skips are coherent; and transposition by fifth meets the restricted version of simplicity. For example, in moving from C to G, pc11 replaces pc0 (although, unlike the diatonic case, there is the disadvantage that the replaced pc is at a superordinate level of the space). In contrast, the symmetrical octatonic collection satisfies only coherence. The nonunique step pattern 1–2–1–2–1–2–1–2 repeats four times per octave (Messiaen's [1944] "charm of impossibilities"); this in turn yields just two nonsimple transpositions that are equal in pc turnover (four) from the original collection.

The criteria of uniqueness and coherence apply as well to the triadic and fifth levels of diatonic space. The triadic level generates unique permutations of the three step sizes 4–3–5 (again counting in semitones); similarly, the fifth level has the unique step pattern 7–5. In both, the smallest interval is more than half the size of the largest, yielding coherence. Put another way, if the octave divided 6–6, uniqueness would not be satisfied; if it divided 4–8, coherence would not be satisfied. Likewise, if the fifth divided, say, 5–2, coherence would again not be satisfied. The picture emerges of hierarchically organized steps in which, at successive levels, steps form irregular patterns employing step sizes that are minimally different from one another.

The horizontal and vertical moves in Figure 2.5c illustrate two further and related features of the basic space. First, there is no subordinate pitch that is not adjacent to, hence a step from, a superordinate pitch. Second, steps between two pitches at superordinate levels mostly become skips at subordinate levels (the exceptions being between p7–p12 at the fifth and triadic levels, and between p4–p5 and p11–p12 at the diatonic and chromatic levels). It is easy to imagine a musical system in which these features are comparatively absent. For instance, as shown in Figure 2.7a, the triadic level could be omitted from diatonic space, reflecting the absence of harmony in many musical idioms. As a result, p4 would not be

a)

0											
0							7				
0		2		4	5		7		9		11
0	1	2	3	4	5	6	7	8	9	10	11

b)

0											
0							7				
0		2		4			7		9		
0	1	2	3	4	5	6	7	8	9	10	11

c)

0											
0							7				
0				4			7				
0		2		4			7		9		
0	1	2	3	4	5	6	7	8	9	10	11

FIGURE 2.7 Superordinate adjacency and subordinate elaboration in tonal space: (a) diatonic space without the triadic level; (b) pentatonic space without the triadic level; (c) pentatonic space with the triadic level added.

adjacent to a superordinate pitch. This may partly explain why predominantly melodic idioms often gravitate toward the pentatonic rather than the diatonic collection; for as Figure 2.7b reveals, pentatonic space meets both conditions. However, if a triadic level is included in pentatonic space, as in Figure 2.7c, the second condition is seriously violated: the step between p4 and p7 at the triadic level is not elaborated at the pentatonic level.

Linear completion

The two features just mentioned are significant for the treatment of dissonance. (The following qualitative account is elaborated by a quantitative treatment in "Melodic Tension" in Chapter 4.) Moving down in the space brings increasing dissonance, to be relieved by moving up again. More deeply embedded pitches are comprehended in terms of their adjacent superordinate context. The syntax of passing and neighboring tones depends on this circumstance. The anchoring of dissonances to their more consonant neighbors (Bharucha 1984a), in particular by subsequent stepwise resolution, encourages intelligible motion within the space.

This perspective sheds light on melodic closure, which can be thought of as dissonance resolution on a larger scale. Leonard Meyer (1973) and Eugene Narmour (1977, 1990) hypothesize that a diatonic step implies continuation in the same direction and, likewise, an arpeggiated line implies continuation along the arpeggiation. In a I/**I** (or I/**C**) context, C→D inplies E, C→E implies G, and so on. Relative melodic closure, hence relative absence of implication, happens when a more stable melodic point is reached. Thus C→D achieves partial closure on E, but not as much as E→D does upon reaching C. C4→E4→G4 finds closure on C5. In these terms, all of these implications consist of one-directional stepwise moves at any level of the basic space. Closure is attained to the extent that the last member of the sequence is superordinate within the space.

Schenker's (1935/1979) central voice-leading procedure, the *Zug* (linear progression), can be seen in the same way. Defined as an upward or downward diatonic stepwise progression bounded by pitches of the prolonged harmony, it operates at any level in an event hierarchy and unites line and harmony into one conception. The *Urlinie* is a special case of the *Zug* at the deepest structural level: over a prolongation of the tonic harmony, it outlines a downward diatonic span from a tonic chord tone to the tonic note. A *Zug* at any level traverses level d of the basic space with end points that belong to level c. (Changes in the harmonic orientation of the space of course alter the particular content of a *Zug*.) While Meyer focuses only on subsequent resolution, Schenker stipulates stepwise motion throughout the melodic span. This contrast in emphasis resembles at a larger scale the difference between an appoggiatura and a passing tone: the former can be approached by skip but must resolve by step, whereas the latter must be both approached and left by step. Schenker's (1910–1922) earlier insistence on the passing tone as the generative dissonance contains the seed of the *Zug*.

The following definition generalizes aspects of melodic closure and the *Zug:*

> LINEAR COMPLETION consists of one-directional stepwise motion at any level in the basic space, such that the boundary pitches of the line are superordinate in the space.

In the context of I/**C**, the progression p0→p1→p2 is complete at the diatonic level; p0→p2→p4 (forming a *Zug*) is complete at the triadic level; both p0→p4→p7 and p0→p2→p4→p5→p7 (the latter again forming a *Zug*) are complete at the fifth level; p0→p7→p12 is complete at the octave level; and so forth. The end points of a complete line can also belong to a level more than one stage above the level in question. The chromatic line p4→p5→p6→p7 is complete at the triadic level; the major or minor scale is complete at the octave level. Although most Classical melodies explore completion at the diatonic and triadic levels, some acquire distinctiveness by emphasizing other combinations of levels. Beethoven's Ninth Symphony begins with a navigation of fifth space, eventually filling it in with triadic and diatonic elaborations. The motivic material of the first movement of the *Eroica* Symphony often bypasses diatonic space in favor of a combination of triadic and chromatic spaces (Epstein 1979). The famous C♯ in bar 7 motivates a number of dramatic passages in its varied search for linear completion.

Completion occurs not only at the musical surface of a piece but also at underlying reductional levels. Incomplete lines reduce out quickly, leaving a residue of completion at deeper levels. A *Zug* collapses into a representation of the harmony embodied in its end points (Rothstein 1990). Linear completion is a fundamental voice-leading principle of tonal music.

THE CHORDAL LEVEL

Chord proximity within a region

We turn to the next conceptual level of diatonic space, the chord. From the perspective of the tonal hierarchy, a chord (triad) is a *Klang* abstracted away from specific register or spacing (Riemann 1893). Chords are represented at level c in the basic space (Figure 2.4), with level b giving the fifth in the chord and level a the root.

The model employs two familiar factors in calculating the proximity of any two chords within a tonal region, the diatonic circle of fifths and common tones. These factors originate in the top two levels of the basic space. The circle of fifths is central because root motion by fifths is basic to cadences and pervasive at all levels of tonal organization. There are psychoacoustic and group-theoretic grounds as well: the prominence of the third partial in most pitched sounds; the generation of the diatonic collection and of all the diatonic triads via the fifths cycle. The common-tone factor is warranted because the sharing of pcs—of octave space—is a strong link between two chords. Psychoacoustically, the second partial is especially strong. Pitches an octave apart match partials. Octave equivalence is the foundation for any group-theoretic approach to pitch.

The diatonic circle-of-fifths operation takes place at the triadic, fifth, and octave levels, leaving the content of the diatonic level intact:

> CHORDAL CIRCLE-OF-FIFTHS RULE Move the pcs at levels a–c of the basic space four steps to the right (mod 7) on level d or four steps to the left.

The rule is stated as four, rather than three, steps to the right or left in order to honor the custom of the circle of fifths rather than the circle of fourths. Its formulation with respect to level d rather than level e automatically incorporates the single diminished fifth between pc11 and pc5, since here are there two semitones at level d, 11 to 0 and 4 to 5.

Applying the chordal circle rule once, twice, and thrice to the right starting from I/**I** (Figure 2.4b) yields the structures in Figures 2.8a–c. (The significance of the underlined numbers will be discussed shortly; the triad in Figure 2.8a is labeled V/**I**, or more simply as V, and so on.) Repeated application yields a closed triadic cycle, (0 4 7), (2 7 11), (2 5 9), . . . (0 5 9), (0 4 7), shown in geometric format in Figure 2.9 with only the pc numbers for chordal roots indicated. The number of applications of the rule in any given instance measures the circle distance between two chords. In an extension of a distinction discussed in the previous section, a step occurs between adjacent chords in Figure 2.9 and a skip takes place between nonadjacent chords. For example, the progression I→V is a step, but I→ii is a skip.

These shifts in the space cause pcs to return, forming common-tone relationships with I. In Figure 2.8, V has one common tone with I, ii has no common tones, and vi has two common tones. Root motion by thirds maximizes common-tone relationships. But it is not enough merely to say that two chords share one

a)

							$\underline{7}$				
		$\underline{2}$					7				
		$\underline{2}$					7				$\underline{11}$
0		2		4	5		7		9		11
0	1	2	3	4	5	6	7	8	9	10	11

V/**I**

b)

		$\underline{2}$									
		$\underline{2}$							$\underline{9}$		
		$\underline{2}$			$\underline{5}$				$\underline{9}$		
0		2		4	5		7		9		11
0	1	2	3	4	5	6	7	8	9	10	11

ii/**I**

c)

									$\underline{9}$		
				$\underline{4}$					$\underline{9}$		
0				4					$\underline{9}$		
0		2		4	5		7		9		11
0	1	2	3	4	5	6	7	8	9	10	11

vi/**I**

FIGURE 2.8 Applications of the chord-circle rule to generate other chords within a region.

0(I)

5(IV) 7(V)

11(vii°) 2(ii)

4(iii) 9(vi)

FIGURE 2.9 The diatonic cycle of fifths, or chord circle.

or two pcs. The strength of pc duplication depends on hierarchical location, with the root of a chord being most important, the fifth less so, and the third least so. These weightings are articulated in the space by the number of times a pc appears in it. Conversely, the common-tone distance between two chords depends on the number of distinctive, or noncommon, pcs between the two. In order to include the differences in weight of the root, fifth, and third in the new chord, its distinctive pcs must be counted at all levels. As the underlined numbers in Figure 2.8 indicate, V has four distinctive pcs in the space in relation to I, ii has six distinctive pcs, and vi again has four distinctive pcs. This will be our measure of common-tone distance.

How do these two factors interact to measure the overall distance between two chords in a region? It might be thought sufficient just to associate a pair of numbers (j,k) with chord distance, where j = the shortest number of steps on the circle of fifths and k = the number of distinctive pcs. The distance from I to V would then be described as (1,4), to ii as (2,6), and to vi as (3,4). This notation reveals, for example, that even though ii is closer to I on the circle of fifths, vi shares more common tones with I, and that even though vi shares two common tones with I and V shares only one common tone, $k = 4$ for both because the root of V is a common tone and the root of vi is not. It is desirable, however, to take the further step of combining the two factors to produce one overall measure of distance. The simplest way to do this is additive:

CHORD DISTANCE RULE (first version) $\delta(x \rightarrow y) = j + k$, where $\delta(x \rightarrow y)$ = the distance between chord x and chord y; j = the number of applications of the chordal circle-of-fifths rule needed to shift x into y; and k = the number of distinctive pcs in the basic space of y compared to the those in the basic space of x.

This little algorithm fits intuition well. Figuring from I, $\delta(\text{I} \rightarrow \text{V}) = 1 + 4 = 5$, $\delta(\text{I} \rightarrow \text{ii}) = 2 + 6 = 8$, and $\delta(\text{I} \rightarrow \text{vi}) = 3 + 4 = 7$. If the chord-circle rule is similarly applied to the left, the same values result for IV, vii°, and iii, as shown in Figure 2.10. (Differentiation could be made by assigning negative numbers for leftward movement on the circle and taking the absolute value; for example,

a)

```
          5
0         5
0         5     9
0   2   4 5   7 9     11
0 1 2 3 4 5 6 7 8 9 10 11
```

δ(I→IV) = 1 + 4 = 5

b)

```
                      11
          5           11
    2     5           11
0   2   4 5   7   9   11
0 1 2 3 4 5 6 7 8 9 10 11
```

δ(I→vii°) = 2 + 6 = 8

c)

```
        4
        4             11
        4     7       11
0   2   4 5   7   9   11
0 1 2 3 4 5 6 7 8 9 10 11
```

δ(I→iii) = 3 + 4 = 7

FIGURE 2.10 Derivation of some chord distances within **I**.

Distance:	0	8	7	5	5	7	8
Chord:	I	ii	iii	IV	V	vi	vii°

FIGURE 2.11 Summary of chord distances within **I**.

a)

```
                  9
        4         9
0       4         9
0   2   4 5   7   9   11
0 1 2 3 4 5 6 7 8 9 10 11
```

δ(vi→vi) = 0 + 0 = 0

b)

```
          5
0         5
0         5       9
0   2   4 5   7   9   11
0 1 2 3 4 5 6 7 8 9 10 11
```

δ(vi→IV) = 3 + 4 = 7

FIGURE 2.12 Example of δ's transpositional invariance, with vi reset to 0.

0(I)

9(vi) 4(iii)

5(IV) 7(V)

2(ii) 11(vii°)

FIGURE 2.13 The common-tone circle (within a region).

δ(I→IV) = 1-11 + 4 =5. I have not found this refinement necessary.) All these results are symmetrical: δ(x→y) = δ(y→x).

Figure 2.11 summarizes δ for each triad within **I**. The results are what one might anticipate: V and IV are equally close to I; vi and iii are next; ii and vii° are more distant.

The results are invariant under transposition. Figures 2.12a–b illustrate by calculating δ(vi→IV), resetting the values for vi to 0. Just as with vi in comparison to I, j = 3, k = 4, and δ = 7. This procedure works in the general case. It also suggests a way to enrich the concept of a chordal step, for which we have so far had only a circle-of-fifths account (Figure 2.9). In Figure 2.11, root motion by thirds is next in proximity to motion by fifths (δ =7 as opposed to δ = 5). From this second kind of proximity a second triadic cycle can be generated, (0 4 7), (4 7 11), (2 7 11), . . . (0 4 9), (0 4 7). Projected geometrically, it yields the common-tone circle of Figure 2.13, in which stepwise motion again takes place between adjacent chords. Because of δ's transpositional invariance, these steps are conceptually equidistant from one another, overriding the major or minor quality of any particular third motion.

Figure 2.14 combines the two circles of Figures 2.9 and 2.13. The vertical axis represents the fifths circle and the horizontal axis the thirds circle. The chords on the horizontal axis are more widely spaced, reflecting the larger value for δ for chords a third apart than for chords a fifth apart. Diagonal moves are still larger and might be called chordal skips. The area enclosed by dashes represents the center of the space—the "chordal core"—shorn of most of its internal repetitions.

Because both axes in Figure 2.14 are circular, the chart can be converted into a toroidal structure with a unique location for each element. Figure 2.15 depicts this structure so that the vii° chords at each corner are the same. Imagine the left and right edges, as indicated by the dashed lines, as identical, and similarly with the top and bottom edges. Each chordal cycle forms a continuous "stripe" around the surface of the toroidal structure, with Figure 2.15a showing the vertical fifths cycle and Figure 2.15b the horizontal thirds cycle. (A torus is usually represented as a three-dimensional doughnut, with one axis around the doughnut tube and the other around the circumference. I employ the looser term "toroidal structure" because the geometry in question is more conveniently thought of as two orthogonal cylinders in four dimensions or as a four-dimensional sphere. Another way to picture the geometry is to think of latitudes and longitudes on Earth's three-dimensional sphere. Latitudes are parallel, but longitudes converge on the points of the north and south poles. In a toroidal structure, however, the longitudes must also be parallel.)

vii°	ii	IV	vi	I	iii	V
iii	V	vii°	ii	IV	vi	I
vi	I	iii	V	vii°	ii	IV
ii	IV	vi	I	iii	V	vii°
V	vii°	ii	IV	vi	I	iii
I	iii	V	vii°	ii	IV	vi
IV	VI	I	iii	V	vii°	ii

FIGURE 2.14 Chordal space, created by combining Figures 2.9 and 2.13. The dashes enclose the "chordal core."

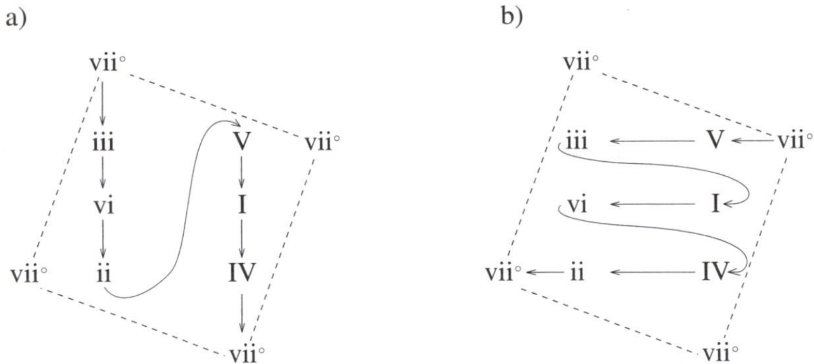

FIGURE 2.15 Toroidal representation of chordal space.

Motion along the toroidal structure takes place along its two-dimensional surface. Because of this, the toroidal and chart representations are interchangeable in principle. The toroidal version may be preferable at a conceptual level, but the chart is more practical.

Chordal space and harmonic progression

Beginning with Jean-Philippe Rameau (1722), music theorists have been concerned with principles of chord progression. Rameau (1737) restricted fundamental-bass progressions to those intervals present in the *corps sonore* (the triad formed by harmonic partials 1–6), which is to say to the intervals of a fifth and a third (Christensen 1993). He invented the *double emploi* largely in order to circumvent a progression such as IV→V; it now became IV→(ii)→V. Ink was likewise spilled by nineteenth-century fundamental-bass theorists over which root progressions are acceptable (Wason 1985). Like Rameau, Simon Sechter (1853) restricted progressions to root motion by fifths and thirds. Since root progressions by seconds happen in real music, Sechter, like Rameau, was obliged to interpose intermediate fundamentals or, conversely, to relate more than one chord to a single fundamental. Thus I→ii became I→(vi)→ii. These maneuvers led to bizarre harmonic glosses, especially in the hands of Sechter's pupil Anton Bruckner, who expanded the system so that any triad could be interpreted not only as $\hat{3}-\hat{5}-\hat{7}$ but also as even $\hat{5}-\hat{7}-\hat{9}$ over a missing root.

In terms of chordal space, Rameau and Sechter allowed only vertical or horizontal adjacent motion in the chordal space of Figure 2.14. If diagonal motion in chordal space counts as a skip, they permitted only stepwise chordal motion. From our perspective, they confounded the tonal and event hierarchies. Having intuited something like the chordal space of Figure 2.14, they went on to apply it to musical sequences. There is no reason, however, that chord progressions, any more than melodic progressions, should prohibit skips. Music relies on all kinds of disjunctions.

Half a century after Sechter, Schenker (1906), with his more hierarchical and linear approach, eliminated unwanted progressions by treating them as voice-leading elaborations of *Stufen* (abstracted scale steps). This was an improvement but not a solution. Voice-leading chords are still chords, each with its own location in pitch space.

Chordal space also bears on Riemann's (1893) function theory. For each of his three harmonic pillars, I, IV, and V, he conceived of harmonic substitutions a root-third away that retain the original function of tonic, subdominant, or dominant (Mickelsen 1977). A substitute a third below gives tonic function to vi, subdominant function to ii, and dominant function to iii. A substitute a third above gives tonic function to iii, subdominant function to vi, and dominant function to vii (in **C**, Riemann's vii is a B minor chord rather than a diminished triad—but we can overlook this systematic oddity). Thus iii and vi vary in function, depending on context. These relationships are implicit in the core of Figure 2.14. The central vertical axis yields the three harmonic pillars. On the horizontal axis, I is flanked by vi and iii, IV by ii and vi, and V by iii and vii°. This correspondence is due, on the one hand, to his harmonic pillars' being on the circle of fifths and, on the other, to the harmonic substitutes' sharing two common tones with their parent functions. (In chapter 5, "Function as Prolongational Position" treats the issue of functionality from another perspective.)

THE REGIONAL LEVEL

Chord proximity across regions

The next stage is evaluation of distances between chords in different regions. We begin with regional shifts—that is, with changes in diatonic collection. Contrasting terminology is widely used for chromatic moves at different levels of event hierarchies: "applied" or "secondary" dominant for momentary regional shifts, "tonicization" for intermediate shifts, and "modulation" for global shifts. For our purposes these distinctions are immaterial except as expressions of levels of regional motion.

Calculating regional distance depends on moving the diatonic level on the circle of fifths:

REGIONAL CIRCLE-OF-FIFTHS RULE Move the pcs at level d of the basic space seven steps to the right (mod 12) on level e or seven steps to the left.

This rule differs from the chordal circle rule in applying level e to level d instead of applying level d to levels a–c. For example, applying the rule once to the right changes the **C** diatonic collection in Figure 2.16a to the **G** diatonic collection in Figure 2.16b.

The number of applications of the regional circle rule is a partial measure of the distance between two regions. Repeated application of the rule produces the complete chromatic circle of fifths, shown in Figure 2.17 with only the roots given. As with Figure 2.9, regional stepwise motion can be thought of as adjacency on the chromatic circle.

a)

0		2		4	5		7		9		11
0	1	2	3	4	5	6	7	8	9	10	11

b)

0		2		4		6	7		9		11
0	1	2	3	4	5	6	7	8	9	10	11

FIGURE 2.16 An application of the region-circle rule to generate the G major collection from the C major collection.

It is important to see that circle-of-fifths operations apply at two conceptual levels, once for chords within a region and once for regions. The chordal circle rule generates triads on the diatonic cycle of fifths; the regional circle rule generates diatonic scales on the chromatic cycle of fifths. The distance from tonic C major to tonic C minor is 3 on the regional circle (that is, three counterclockwise steps in Figure 2.17) and then 0 on the chordal circle (Figure 2.9), whereas the distance from tonic C major to tonic A minor is 0 on the regional circle and then 3 (clockwise) on the chordal circle. The parallel and relative minor tonics are the same distance from I/I in equal but opposite ways.

The regional rule suggests enlarging the preliminary chord distance rule:

CHORD DISTANCE RULE (full version) $\delta(x \rightarrow y) = i + j + k$, where $\delta(x \rightarrow y)$ = the distance between chord x and chord y; i = the number of applications of the regional circle-of-fifths rule needed to shift the diatonic collection that supports x into the diatonic collection that supports y; j = the number of applications of the chordal circle-of-fifths rule needed to shift x into y; and k = the number of distinctive pcs in the basic space of y compared to those in the basic space of x.

Until now i has always equaled 0. The simplest way to calculate i is to count the number of changes in flats and sharps in the key signature. The value for i is computed first, then the value for j. The steps taken in applying j lead directly from the first to the second chord, no matter whether the new tonic is passed

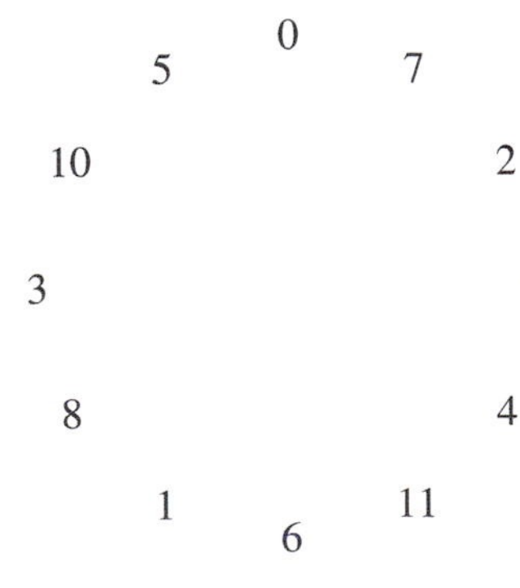

FIGURE 2.17 The chromatic circle of fifths, or the region circle.

through or not. Thus in δ(I/**I**→vi/♭**VI**), *i* = 4 (tonic C to tonic A♭), but *j* = 1 (chord root C to chord root F). The values for *k* typically include distinctive pcs at the diatonic level as well as higher levels. As before, the formula is transpositionally invariant.

There is a question as to how to treat the minor mode, which conventionally has three versions, the natural, harmonic, and melodic. I prefer to view this matter in terms of scale-degree voice-leading tendencies. The raised seventh degree appears as the leading tone when rising to the tonic and as a result is part of V and vii°. A raised sixth usually happens in voice-leading situations where a melodic augmented second with the raised seventh would otherwise arise. These are all context-dependent inflections within a diatonic, hence natural-minor, framework, so I shall regard the natural minor as basic. However, for V and vii° the raised seventh will be assumed. A consequence of this view of the minor mode is that variable *i* is the same for relative major/minor collections. Kellner's double circle (Figure 2.1b) implicitly relies on this assumption. However, *j* shifts as before, so the overall result is not equivalent. For example, *i* = 1 for both δ(I/**I**→I/**IV**) and δ(I/**I**→i/**ii**), but *j* = 1 for δ(I/**I**→I/**IV**) and *j* = 2 for δ(I/**I**→i/**ii**).

Figures 2.18–2.20 give various examples of interregional chordal distances. Figures 2.18a and 2.18b juxtapose the dominant chord heard as dominant (V/**I**, or "V of **I**") and as tonicized (I/**V**, or "I of **V**"). Because in the latter case *i* as well as *j* shifts once and because pc5 changes to pc6 in diatonic space, the overall distance of I/**V** from I/**I** is two units greater than that of V/**I**. Figures 2.18c and 2.18d similarly juxtapose an A major triad as V/**d** and as I/**A**, with the former three units smaller than the latter. Such distinctions are crucial to musical understanding—V/**ii** really feels closer to I/**I** than I/**VI** does—so it is important that the model be able to express these differences.

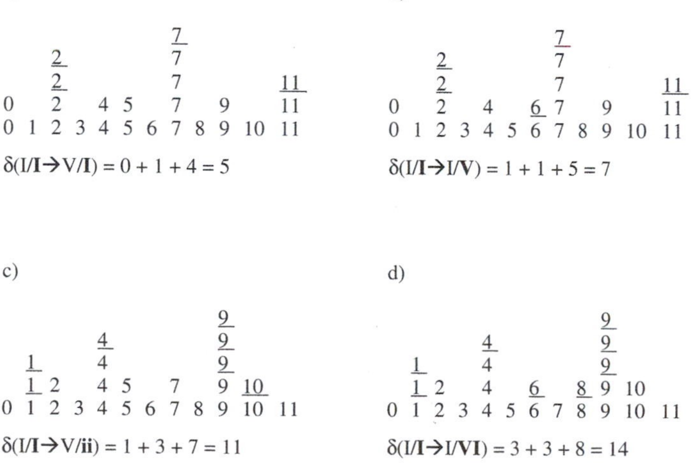

FIGURE 2.18 Examples of interregional chordal distances.

a)

		2									
		2							9		
		2			5				9		
0		2		4	5		7		9	10	
0	1	2	3	4	5	6	7	8	9	10	11

δ(I/**I**→i/**ii**) = 1 + 2 + 7 = 10

b)

				4							
				4							11
				4			7				11
0		2		4		6	7		9		11
0	1	2	3	4	5	6	7	8	9	10	11

δ(I/**I**→i/**iii**) = 1 + 3 + 5 = 9

c)

											11
						6					11
			3			6					11
0			3	4		6	7		9		11
0	1	2	3	4	5	6	7	8	9	10	11

δ(I/**I**→V/**iii**) = 1 + 2 + 8 = 11

d)

					5						
0					5						
0					5				9		
0		2		4	5		7		9	10	
0	1	2	3	4	5	6	7	8	9	10	11

δ(I/**I**→I/**IV**) = 1 + 1 + 5 = 7

e)

0											
0							7				
0				4			7			10	
0		2		4	5		7		9	10	
0	1	2	3	4	5	6	7	8	9	10	11

δ(I/**I**→V^7/**IV**) = 1 + 0 + 2 = 3

FIGURE 2.19 Further examples of interregional chordal distances.

Figures 2.19a and 2.19b compare i/**ii** and i/**iii**; the latter is slightly closer to I/**I**. Figure 2.19c adds V/**iii**, for which δ is larger than for i/**iii**. However, Figures 2.19d and 2.19e similarly compare I/**IV** and V/**IV**, to show that, in certain cases, the nontonic chord of a secondary region is closer to I/**I** than its local tonic is. The seventh has been included at the triadic level in Figure 2.19e to indicate how sevenths are treated when they have harmonic status. Exclusion of the seventh would decrease *k* by one, so that δ = 2. The low value for δ arises from the surface identity between the originating and goal chords; only the frame of reference changes.

Figures 2.20a and 2.20b juxtapose tonic chords in the relative and parallel minor regions. The values for *i* and *j* are reversed, and the value for *k* is identical despite the contrasting distribution of distinctive pcs; so the overall result is the same.

When a tone or chord from a nearby region appears in passing, the intuition is less of moving to the region than of borrowing from it. In a major-mode context, iv or vii^{o7} borrows from the parallel minor. Conversely, the raised leading tone in minor borrows from the parallel major. Movements in minor often end with a borrowed major tonic (the Picardy third). All these cases are instances of

a)

									9		
				4					9		
0				4					9		
0		2		4	5		7		9		11
0	1	2	3	4	5	6	7	8	9	10	11

δ(I/**I**→i/**vi**) = 0 + 3 + 4 = 7

b)

0											
0							7				
0			3				7				
0		2	3		5		7	8		10	
0	1	2	3	4	5	6	7	8	9	10	11

δ(I/**I**→i/**i**) = 3 + 0 + 4 = 7

FIGURE 2.20 Distances of the relative and parallel minor tonic chords.

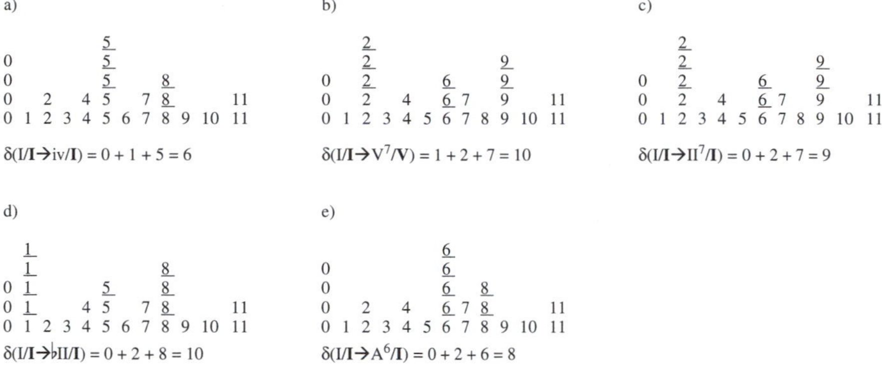

FIGURE 2.21 Distances from I/**I** of some borrowed chords.

"mixture." Applied dominants can be viewed similarly. For example, V^6_5/**V** easily substitutes for ii^6_5/**I** as a predominant in a cadential progression. It is cumbersome to specify a move to the **V** region for the V^6_5/**V**; rather, the fourth scale degree has been inflected upward, in a borrowing from the **V** region. (In Riemannian theory, the two receive contrasting functions, S for ii^6_5/**I** and D/D for V^6_5/**V**.)

The pitch-space model represents borrowing simply by staying within the home region and registering chromatically inflected pcs as needed. That is, i = 0, j behaves as before, and k includes all chromatic pcs. Figure 2.21 illustrates, starting with iv/**I** in Figure 2.21a. In Figures 2.21b–c, V^7/**V** is calculated first as a regional shift, then as a borrowing; note that the spatial configurations are identical but that i has a different value. Borrowings for ♭II/**I** (the Neapolitan) and an "Italian" augmented-sixth chord are shown in Figures 2.21d–e. For the latter, following tradition (perhaps dubiously), pc2 is assumed as the missing root; hence j = 2. Augmented sixths can be viewed as borrowing from **i** and **V** simultaneously.

Even though the model can express borrowing, it does not provide a mechanism for deciding whether a given case is best interpreted as a borrowing or a regional shift. This is a PR situation that involves context. "Function as Prolongational Position" in chapter 5 returns to this topic briefly.

Regional space

The chord distance rule works well for measurements to chords in nearby regions but yields rather obscure results for chords in distant regions. This is a fault not of the rule but of the task at hand. It is relatively easy to hear an E major chord as V/**vi** or as I/**III**, but how is one to hear the chord as III/♯**i** in the computation δ(I/**I**→III/♯**i**)? How is one to understand an A♭ minor chord in a I/**I** context? To grasp their spatial locations, distant chords must be placed in intermediate frameworks in which they are not so distant. In other words, to be intelligible they must be reached by modulatory stages. However, modulation is an expression not of chords but of regions. The model must move beyond the chordal level and address the region as a level in itself. Regions need to have specifiable distances from one another.

More than a pitch or a chord (or even a pc or a chord class), a region is an abstraction, an emergent property of the hierarchically related pcs and chord classes that belong to it. But the model requires any pitch object, even an abstract one, to be representable by a specific form of the basic space. Let us concretize a region directly in terms of its tonic—that is, by its scale (level d) and its tonic chordal configuration (levels a–c). The proximity of a secondary region can then be measured as the distance of its local tonic from the overall referential tonic. The reasonable assumption is that the distance of a local tonic is a reliable indicator of the distance of the region it represents.

Regional space can now be built in the same way as chordal space. First the local tonics are selected that have the smallest values for δ. These are I/**V**, I/**IV**, i/**vi**, and i/**i**, for all of which $\delta = 7$. This is the case even though the specific values of i, j, and k vary; see Figures 2.18b (I/**V** = 1 + 1 + 5), 2.19d (I/**IV** = 1 + 1 + 5), 2.20a (i/**vi** = 0 + 3 + 4), and 2.20b (i/**i** = 3 + 0 + 4). The fifth-related regions (I/**V** and I/**IV**) are placed on one axis and relative and parallel minor relationships (i/**vi** and i/**i**) on the other. Then δ is transposed to generate two cycles, vertically in fifths and horizontally in minor thirds for every parallel major-minor pair. Because δ is the same in all directions (in contrast to chordal space), the elements on this structure are equidistant. The result is Figure 2.22a, which is equivalent to the Weber space (Figure 2.1c). Figure 2.22b translates the note names of 2.22a into Roman numerals, with "i/♯**ii**" abbreviated as "♯**ii**," and so on.

Just as the chordal chart (Figure 2.14) can be viewed toroidally (Figure 2.15), so the regional chart in Figure 2.22 can be conceived as the toroidal structure in Figure 2.23, such that each element has a single location. As before, opposite parallel edges wrap around both vertically and horizontally. The elements on the upper and lower edges line up in this realization, but those on the left and right are just adjacent to their edges. In regional space, unlike chordal space, each axis exhibits not one stripe but parallel stripes: two on the fifths axis, for the major-mode and minor-mode cycles; three on the minor-thirds axis, expressing each minor-third cycle. The arrows in Figure 2.23a trace the major-mode fifths cycle, the arrows in Figure 2.23b the minor-mode fifths cycle. The 0–3–6–9 minor-thirds cycle appears directly on the central horizontal stripe in all the illustrations. Figure 2.23c draws the 1–4–7–10 cycle and Figure 2.23d the 2–5–8–11 cycle. It will prove more practical to refer to the chart representation in Figure 2.22.

With regional space in place, there is no obstacle to developing intelligible measurements between distantly related chords. The crucial point is the concept of the pivot. Distance calculations have not been problematic for chords in nearby regions because these regions share chords that can function as pivot chords from one region to another. As chromatic changes reach more distant regions, however, direct pivot chords disappear, requiring intermediate pivots that have not yet been taken into account.

Pivot chords can be thought of as points of tonic reorientation along a regional stepwise path. Regional access might at first be considered just in terms of vertical

a)

D♯	**F♯**	**f♯**	**A**	**a**	**C**	**c**
G♯	**B**	**b**	**D**	**d**	**F**	**f**
C♯	**E**	**e**	**G**	**g**	**B♭**	**b♭**
F♯	**A**	**a**	**C**	**c**	**E♭**	**e♭**
b	**D**	**d**	**F**	**f**	**A♭**	**a♭**
e	**G**	**g**	**B♭**	**b♭**	**D♭**	**d♭**
a	**C**	**c**	**E♭**	**e♭**	**G♭**	**g♭**

b)

♯ii	**♯IV**	**♯iv**	**VI**	**vi**	**I**	**i**
♯vi	**VII**	**vii**	**II**	**ii**	**IV**	**iv**
♯i	**III**	**iii**	**V**	**v**	**♭VII**	**♭vii**
♯iv	**VI**	**vi**	**I**	**i**	**♭III**	**♭iii**
vii	**II**	**ii**	**IV**	**iv**	**♭VI**	**♭vi**
iii	**V**	**v**	**♭VII**	**♭vii**	**♭II**	**♭ii**
vi	**I**	**i**	**♭III**	**♭iii**	**♭V**	**♭v**

FIGURE 2.22 Regional space, created by combining the fifths cycle and the parallel/relative major-minor cycle: (a) representation of regions by name of key; (b) representation as subregions oriented to C major.

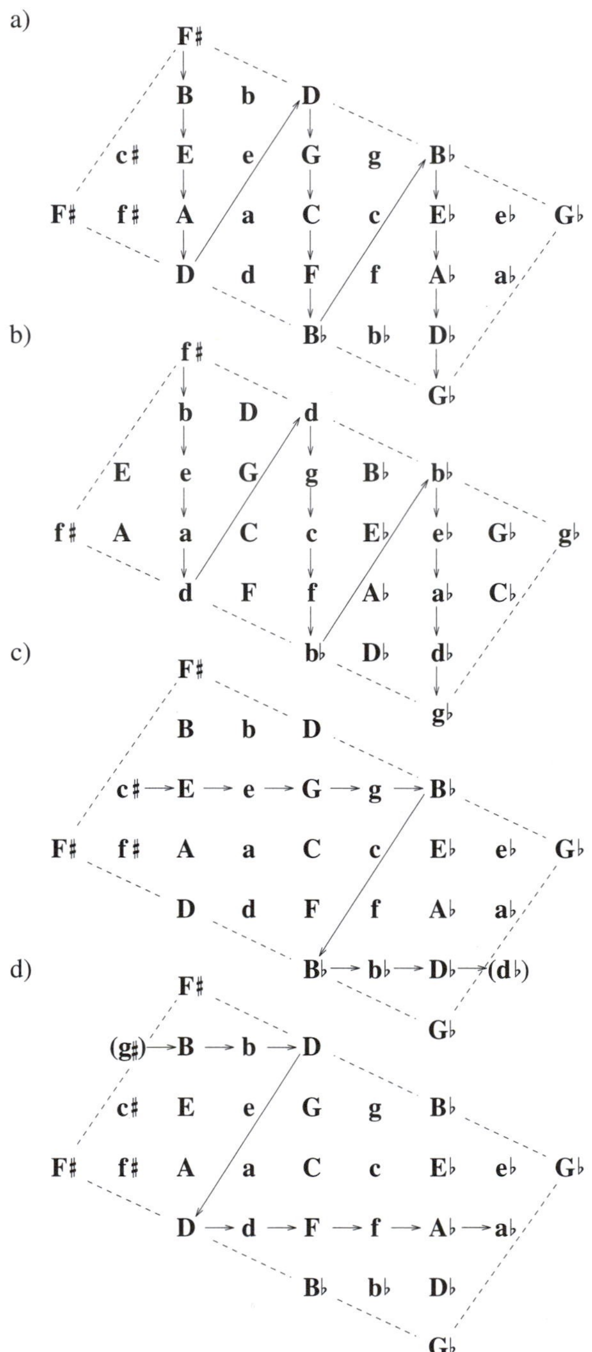

FIGURE 2.23 Toroidal representation of regional space.

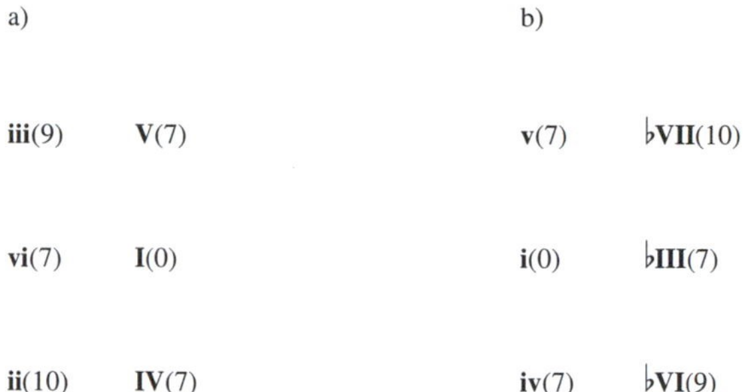

FIGURE 2.24 Representative pivot regions, together with their distance values from **I** and **i**, respectively.

or horizontal adjacency in Figure 2.22b. Thus **VI** is two steps to the west but three steps to the north of **I**. So far this makes sense, since it is indeed a shorter route to **VI** via **vi** than via **V** and **II**. However, this conception would make **ii** as well as **VI** and **II** two steps (rather than one step) away from **I**, an intuitively undesirable result. This problem might be rectified by including diagonal motion as stepwise; but then **v**, too, would be a step from **I**, even though intuitively **v** is accessed from **V** or **i** instead.

The difficulty can be resolved by isolating those local tonics that double as chords in the home region. As the fragment of regional space in Figure 2.24a shows, in relation to **I** these pivoting tonics include **ii**, **iii**, **IV**, **V**, and **vi**. The diagonal steps to **v** and **iv** are excluded, as is the seventh scale degree, which is not adjacent even diagonally in regional space. The value of δ is given in parentheses for each region. Figure 2.24b provides in reverse the pivoting tonics available from **i**. Again the values of δ are included, this time with **i** reset to 0.

Let us call six-regional units as in Figures 2.24a and 2.24b pivot regions and the centers of these regions pivot-region tonics. A move from one pivot region to another is accomplished either by sliding stepwise up and down the fifths axis in Figure 2.22 or by flipping sideways to linked parallel regions such as those in Figure 2.24. By way of illustration, Figure 2.25a shifts the home pivot region of Figure 2.24a northward one notch and Figure 2.25b shifts the home pivot region eastward to the nonoverlapping adjacent unit of Figure 2.24b. The squares indicate I as the home region, and the arrows and circles show the reorientations. A major-key pivot-region tonic is always located in the right central position, a minor-key pivot-region tonic in the left central position. Diagonal shifts are permitted if the new pivot-region tonic belongs in the first pivot region. Thus **iii** as pivot-region tonic can be accessed from **I** directly in Figure 2.25c, avoiding the intermediate step of V in Figure 2.25d.

In short, the usual vertical, horizontal, and diagonal moves remain available within a pivot region; but if a target region is not in the home pivot region, the pivot region is moved stepwise, in the ways indicated in Figure 2.25, until the region can be accessed. Symbolically,

REGIONAL DISTANCE RULE $\Delta(\mathbf{I}\rightarrow\mathbf{R}) = [\delta_1(\mathbf{P}_1\rightarrow\mathbf{P}_2)] + [\delta_2(\mathbf{P}_2\rightarrow\mathbf{P}_3)] \ldots + \delta_n(\mathbf{P}_n\rightarrow\mathbf{R})$, where $\Delta(\mathbf{I}\rightarrow\mathbf{R})$ = distance from the home pivot-region tonic **I** to the target region **R**; δ_1 = the pivot-region step from the first pivot-region tonic $\mathbf{P}_1$ to the second pivot-region tonic $\mathbf{P}_2$, and so on; and $\delta_n(\mathbf{P}_n\rightarrow\mathbf{R})$ = the distance from pivot-region tonic $\mathbf{P}_n$ to **R**, once **R** lies within the shifted pivot region. Steps within square brackets apply only if the condition for $\delta_n(\mathbf{P}_n\rightarrow\mathbf{R})$ is not met.

If desired, the chord designation for δ can be reset each time to **I** (or **i**). For example, $\Delta(\mathbf{I}\rightarrow\mathbf{v}) = \delta_1(\mathbf{I}\rightarrow\mathbf{V} = \mathbf{I}) + \delta_2(\mathbf{I}\rightarrow\mathbf{i}) = 7 + 7 = 14$. Another example: $\Delta(\mathbf{I}\rightarrow\mathbf{III}) = \delta_1(\mathbf{I}\rightarrow\mathbf{iii}=\mathbf{i}) + \delta_2(\mathbf{i}\rightarrow\mathbf{I}) = 9 + 7 = 16$. An example with one more step: $\Delta(\mathbf{I}\rightarrow\sharp\mathbf{i}) = \delta_1(\mathbf{I}\rightarrow\mathbf{iii}=\mathbf{i}) + \delta_2(\mathbf{i}\rightarrow\mathbf{I}) + \delta_3(\mathbf{I}\rightarrow\mathbf{vi}) = 9 + 7 + 7 = 23$; or, verbally, "move from **I** to **iii**, then to **iii**'s parallel major, **III**, then to **III**'s relative minor." By this point, however, it is easier to grasp the calculations if the regions are indicated not by Roman numeral but by letter name: $\Delta(\mathbf{I}\rightarrow\sharp\mathbf{i}) = \Delta(\mathbf{C}\rightarrow\mathbf{c}\sharp) = \delta_1(\mathbf{C}\rightarrow\mathbf{e}) + \delta_2(\mathbf{e}\rightarrow\mathbf{E}) + \delta_3(\mathbf{E}\rightarrow\mathbf{c}\sharp) = 9 + 7 + 7 = 23$. Figure 2.26a presents this path in spatial format. But if **c♯** is understood as **d♭**, the derivation might be $\Delta(\mathbf{C}\rightarrow\mathbf{d}\flat) = \delta_1(\mathbf{C}\rightarrow\mathbf{c}) + \delta_2(\mathbf{c}\rightarrow\mathbf{A}\flat) + \delta_3(\mathbf{A}\flat\rightarrow\mathbf{D}\flat) + \delta_4(\mathbf{D}\flat\rightarrow\mathbf{d}\flat) = 7 + 9 + 7 + 7 = 30$; this is shown spatially in Figure 2.26b. This is a longer route than the one in Figure 2.26a.

Figure 2.27a lists the smallest value for Δ for all the major and minor regions in relation to I. These values are most easily reached by moving the pivot regions

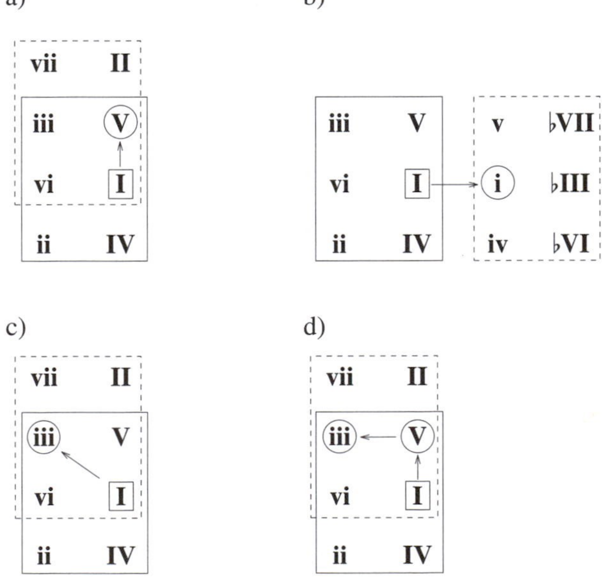

FIGURE 2.25 Examples of shifting pivot regions into adjacent pivot regions.

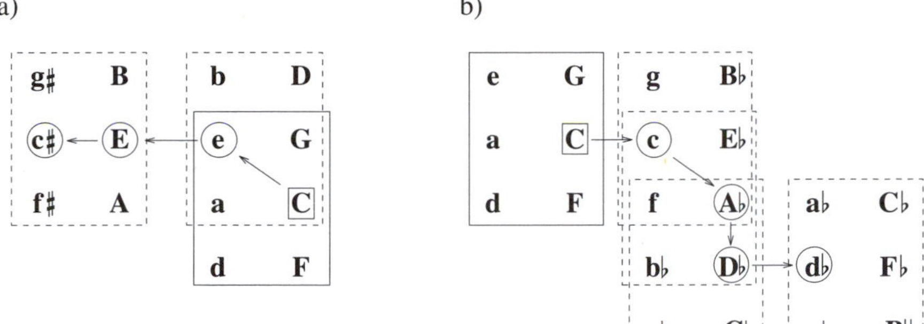

FIGURE 2.26 Examples of shifting pivot regions into nonadjacent pivot regions.

a)

Region:	**I**	**i**	**♭II**	**♯i**	**II**	**ii**	**♭III**	**♭iii**	**III**	**iii**	**IV**	**iv**
Δ:	0	7	23	23	14	10	14	21	16	9	7	14

Region:	**♯IV**	**♯iv**	**V**	**v**	**♭VI**	**♭vi**	**VI**	**vi**	**♭VII**	**♭vii**	**VII**	**vii**
Δ:	30	21	7	14	16	23	14	7	14	21	23	16

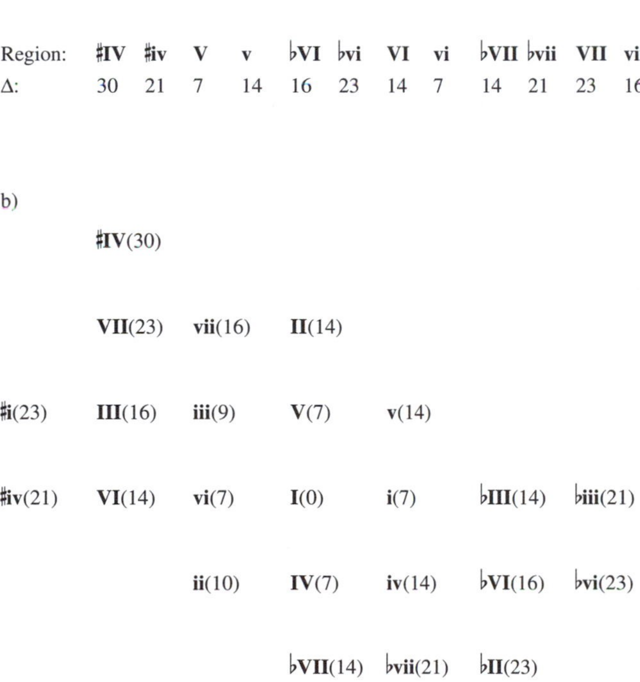

FIGURE 2.27 Summary of regional distances from **I**: (a) in table format; (b) as represented in regional space.

in Figure 2.24 through pivot-region shifts. Figure 2.27b places the values of Figure 2.27a on the regional chart.

The region distance rule is a special case—moving from I/**I** to I/**R**—of the general case in which distance is computed from any chord (tonic or not) in a given pivot region to any other chord (tonic or not) in any other pivot region. The special case has proven useful in acquiring an overall picture of regional distances. The general case is rarely needed in an analysis of a tonal piece, for usually a chromatic progression across regions can be interpreted as taking place within a pivot region. For the sake of completeness, however, the rule is as follows:

CHORD/REGION DISTANCE RULE $\Delta(C_1/\mathbf{R}_1 \rightarrow C_2/\mathbf{R}_2) = [\delta_1(C_1/\mathbf{R}_1 \rightarrow I/\mathbf{P}_1)] + [\delta_2(\mathbf{P}_1 \rightarrow \mathbf{P}_2)] + [\delta_3(\mathbf{P}_2 \rightarrow \mathbf{P}_3)] \ldots + \delta_n(I/\mathbf{P}_n \rightarrow C_2/\mathbf{R}_2)$, where $\delta_1(C_1/\mathbf{R}_1 \rightarrow I/\mathbf{P}_1) =$ the distance of C_1 in $\mathbf{R}_1$ to pivot-region tonic $\mathbf{P}_1$, which contains $C_1/\mathbf{R}_1$; $[\delta_2(\mathbf{P}_1 \rightarrow \mathbf{P}_2)] + [\delta_3(\mathbf{P}_2 \rightarrow \mathbf{P}_3)] \ldots =$ intermediate pivot-region shifts; and $\delta_n(I/P_n \rightarrow C_2/\mathbf{R}_2) =$ the distance from pivot-region tonic $\mathbf{P}_n$, which contains $C_2/\mathbf{R}_2$, to C_2 in $\mathbf{R}_2$. (δ_1 is given the optional brackets because it does not apply if the starting point is $I/\mathbf{P}_1$.)

δ_2 and δ_3 act as in the region distance rule cited earlier. δ_n by itself corresponds to the earlier treatment of δ in the chord distance rule: it computes from a pivot-region tonic to any chord within its pivot region.

By way of improbable example: $\Delta(\text{vi}/\mathbf{F} \rightarrow \text{V}/\mathbf{b}) = \delta_1(\text{vi}/\mathbf{F} \rightarrow \text{I}/\mathbf{C}) + \delta_2(\text{I}/\mathbf{C} \rightarrow \text{i}/\mathbf{e}) + \delta_3(\text{i}/\mathbf{e} \rightarrow \text{V}/\mathbf{b}) = (1 + 2 + 7) + 9 + (1 + 2 + 8) = 10 + 9 + 11 = 30$. Figure 2.28a provides the calculation for $\delta_1(\text{vi}/\mathbf{F} \rightarrow \text{I}/\mathbf{C})$ and Figure 2.28b for $\delta_3(\text{i}/\mathbf{e} \rightarrow \text{V}/\mathbf{b})$; $\delta_2(\text{I}/\mathbf{C} \rightarrow \text{i}/\mathbf{e})$ is taken from the table in Figure 2.27.

a)

		2									
		2							9		
		2			5				9		
0		2		4	5		7		9	10	
0	1	2	3	4	5	6	7	8	9	10	11

$\underline{0}$											
$\underline{0}$							$\underline{7}$				
$\underline{0}$				$\underline{4}$			$\underline{7}$				
0		2		4	5		7		9		$\underline{11}$
0	1	2	3	4	5	6	7	8	9	10	11

$\delta(\text{vi}/\mathbf{F} \rightarrow \text{I}/\mathbf{C}) = 1 + 2 + 7 = 10$

b)

				4							
				4							11
				4			7				11
0		2		4		6	7		9		11
0	1	2	3	4	5	6	7	8	9	10	11

						$\underline{6}$					
	$\underline{1}$					$\underline{6}$					
	$\underline{1}$					$\underline{6}$				$\underline{10}$	
	$\underline{1}$	2		4		6	7			$\underline{10}$	11
0	1	2	3	4	5	6	7	8	9	10	11

$\delta(\text{i}/\mathbf{e} \rightarrow \text{V}/\mathbf{b}) = 1 + 2 + 8 = 11$

FIGURE 2.28 Distance calculations for steps 1 and 3 of $\Delta(\text{vi}/\mathbf{F} \rightarrow \text{V}/\mathbf{b})$.

Remarks on Schoenberg space

The concept of musical space preoccupied Arnold Schoenberg throughout his career. He proposed regional spaces in both his treatises on tonal harmony (Schoenberg 1911/1978, 1954/1969), advancing first an equivalent of the Kellner space (Figure 2.1b), later an equivalent of the Weber space (Figures 2.1c and 2.22). It is uncertain how much he was aware of historical precedents. (David Bernstein [1991] offers evidence that Schoenberg was influenced by a chart in Erpf [1927] that resembles the Weber space.) Neither Weber nor Schoenberg generated his model from elements and operations, as I have with the chord distance rule. They presumably intuited the equidistance from I/**I** of I/**V**, I/**IV**, i/**vi**, and i/**i** and then constructed their charts by iteration of that module. Weber was explicit in this method of construction, thereby arriving at different orders of modulation. Schoenberg was more elliptical, although his "cross" (**C** in the middle flanked by **G** and **F** on the vertical axis and **a** and **c** on the horizontal axis) resembles the first stage of Weber's modular construction.

Schoenberg (1941/1975) also invoked musical space in his central essay on twelve-tone composition, largely to justify simultaneous and sequential presentations of the row. This feature of twelve-tone music contrasts with tonal syntax, which differentiates between principles of relatedness for melody and harmony, most obviously in the treatment of the interval of a second. A case can nonetheless be made that just as Schoenberg constructed his large-scale twelve-tone forms by analogy with tonal forms, so he built twelve-tone space by analogy with tonal space. Each pc in twelve-tone space has multiple positions, depending on set orientation instead of scale and chord orientation. The chordal level emerges from subsets of the row, roughly in the way that triads are subsets of scales (only "roughly" because twelve-tone space does not have the hierarchical organization of the basic space, so there is no analogue to the reductional relationship between triads and scales). The regional level affords the best correspondence: within the framework of hexachordal combinatoriality, two or more sets create a twelve-tone regional unit that transposes to nearby or distant regions, where distance can be measured by interval cycles of transposition (as with variable i in δ) and by segmental invariance across different set forms, creating common subsets (by analogy with variable k in δ). These regional units facilitate a sort of modulation within the twelve-tone universe (as discussed, for example, in Lewin 1968). Although moves within twelve-tone space are not as cognitively transparent as those within tonal space (Lerdahl 1988a), the analogies are interesting, and they help explain how Schoenberg was able to erect such an intellectually rich system.

Combined geometrical representations

Numerical distances have been derived within an integrated framework for all three levels of pitch space, and for each level a geometrical mapping has been proposed. It will prove useful, especially for developments in chapter 3, to assemble a geometrical version of the levels in combination.

III	V	vii°	iii	V	vii°
VI	**iii**	III	vi	**V**	iii
ii°	iv	VI	ii	IV	vi
III	V	vii°	iii	V	vii°
VI	**vi**	III	vi	**I**	iii
ii°	iv	VI	ii	IV	vi
III	V	vii°	iii	V	vii°
VI	**ii**	III	vi	**IV**	iii
ii°	iv	VI	ii	IV	vi

FIGURE 2.29 A two-dimensional representation of the combined chordal and regional toroidal structures.

The chordal and regional tori share fundamental features: both are constructed by closed cycles of fifths and thirds; steps are equidistant along these cycles. Hence the two structures can be combined into the chordal/regional space of Figure 2.29. A fragment of regional space is shown, and for each such region the chordal core is given, with appropriate major/minor adjustments in chord quality. Each regional designation doubles for "I" or "i" at the chordal level. The chordal pattern repeats in the regional pattern. For example, beginning at the upper left on the horizontal axis, III-V-vii° corresponds to **III-iii-V-v-♭VII-♭vii** (compare Figure 2.22b); each region doubles only because of parallel major-minor relationships. On the vertical axis III-VI-ii° corresponds to **iii-vi-ii**. Moreover, the proximity of chords across regions emerges in the representation. In **I**, for example, V is closest to **V**; conversely, in **V**, IV is closest to **I** (IV/**V** and I/**I** are both C major triads), and so on throughout the space, horizontally and diagonally as well as vertically. The representation exhibits self-similarity at two levels of pitch space.

This representation causes multiple spatial repetition of a given triad. For example, the C major chord appears as I/**I**, IV/**V**, V/**IV**, III/**vi**, and VI/**iii**. This redundancy is an artifact of the geometric mapping and is absent from the underlying algebraic representation. In the latter, the C major chord is always (0 4 7) at level c, (0 7) at level b, and (0) at level a. Its regional interpretation is determined by the content of level d (the scalar level), as well as by other factors discussed in "Finding the Tonic" in chapter 5.

How does the pc level integrate with chordal/regional space? Here the solution is less evident, for the basic space, while the generator of the regular chordal and regional spaces, has levels comprised of irregular intervals. Viewed geometrically, and as shown in Figure 2.6, the basic space is a cone, which in the usual representation is sliced and unwrapped. If each chord label in chordal space is replaced by its basic-space configuration, the result is the pc/chordal model in Figure 2.30. Given a large-enough page, and as suggested by the boldface **I** in the figure, the model could be extended to include the regional level as well.

```
            4
            4                    11
            4        7           11
0     2     4  5     7     9     11
0  1  2  3  4  5  6  7  8  9  10 11
```

(iii)

```
                     7
      2              7
      2              7           11
0     2     4  5     7     9     11
0  1  2  3  4  5  6  7  8  9  10 11
```

(V)

```
                                 11
               5                 11
      2        5                 11
0     2     4  5     7     9     11
0  1  2  3  4  5  6  7  8  9  10 11
```

(vii°)

```
                           9
            4              9
0           4              9
0     2     4  5     7     9     11
0  1  2  3  4  5  6  7  8  9  10 11
```

(vi)

```
0
0                    7
0           4        7
0     2     4  5     7     9     11
0  1  2  3  4  5  6  7  8  9  10 11
```

(I)

```
            4
            4                    11
            4        7           11
0     2     4  5     7     9     11
0  1  2  3  4  5  6  7  8  9  10 11
```

(iii)

```
      2
      2                    9
      2        5           9
0     2     4  5     7     9     11
0  1  2  3  4  5  6  7  8  9  10 11
```

(ii)

```
               5
0              5
0              5           9
0     2     4  5     7     9     11
0  1  2  3  4  5  6  7  8  9  10 11
```

(IV)

```
                           9
            4              9
0           4              9
0     2     4  5     7     9     11
0  1  2  3  4  5  6  7  8  9  10 11
```

(vi)

FIGURE 2.30 The core of pc/chordal space.

The directional orientation of a chordal and regional structure is immaterial as long as it has orthogonal fifths and thirds axes. A chordal or regional y-axis, for instance, could point in any direction. (Weber's chart in fact reverses east–west directions on the x-axis in comparison to the orientation of Schoenberg's and my models.) The combined chordal/regional space, however, must match orientations between fifths and thirds axes between the two levels, so that the interlevel patterns noted in connection with Figure 2.29 hold. A pc cone is orientationally unconstrained.

THE PRINCIPLE OF THE SHORTEST PATH

Nothing in the discussion so far selects the route between two chords. The rules for chord distance state that given chords C_1 and C_2 in regions $\mathbf{R}_1$ and $\mathbf{R}_2$, $\delta(C_1/\mathbf{R}_1 \rightarrow C_2/\mathbf{R}_2)$ can be calculated to a certain value. Thus the distance from I/**I** to a G major chord can be computed as δ(I/**I**→V/**I**). But the G chord has other locations in chordal/regional space. Its distance can be treated, for example, as δ(I/**I**→I/**V**) or δ(I/**I**→III/**iii**) or δ(I/**I**→IV/**II**). The G chord can also be reached through an intermediate point, such as δ(I/**I**→i/**i**) to δ(i/**i**→V/**i**). Unless there is countervailing evidence, however, a G chord that follows I/**I** will be heard as V/**I**. This is so because it is the simplest interpretation; it requires the least cognitive effort. Throughout this chapter, we have been implicitly observing a fundamental principle:

PRINCIPLE OF THE SHORTEST PATH The pitch-space distance between two events is preferably calculated to the smallest value.

This rule requires the most contextual, most efficient choice. It has some kinship to the Gestalt principle of *Prägnanz*, which Kurt Koffka (1935) states as: "Psychological organization will always be as 'good' as the prevailing conditions allow." In this case, "goodness" equals least distance in a learned schema of pc, chordal, and regional relationships. The shortest path more vividly suggests the principle of least action in physics, which grew out of classical conceptions of force and motion and which recently has played a central role in quantum electrodynamics (Feynman 1965; Mehra 1994). Generally, the change of a dynamic system from one state to another takes the smallest amount of time and/or distance possible in response to the forces that impinge on it. A thrown ball arcs in a parabola because that is the path of least action, given the force and direction of the throw and the force of gravity.

The principle of the shortest path is responsible for the chordal and regional mappings. It lies behind the chordal/regional method of reaching a locally nontonic chord directly from its pivot-region tonic rather than by first accessing the chord through its local tonic. It also operates at the pc level of diatonic space. In Figure 2.5, for instance, p4 (E) is counted directly as $\hat{3}$ in the tonic triad rather than merely as a member of the diatonic and chromatic collections. The evaluation of pitch stability in Figure 2.5d (which combines the values in Figure 2.5a and 2.5b) depends on this interpretation.

The principle provides the crucial link between pitch space and prolongational structure. GTTM's chief preference rule for time-span reduction (TSRPR 2) calls on somewhat imprecise stability conditions to select, within a given span, the most stable pitch event for continuation to the next larger level. Through the interaction principle, this rule strongly influences the associated prolongational reduction, which assigns the most stable connections for events within a given prolongational region (PRPR 3). The role of the stability conditions in determining a time-span and prolongational reduction can now be cast quantitatively in terms of pitch space:

TIME-SPAN STABILITY Of the possible choices for the head of a time-span T, prefer the event that yields the smallest value for δ (orΔ if necessary) in relation to the superordinate context for T.

PROLONGATIONAL CONNECTION Of the possible connections within a prolongational region R, prefer the attachment that yields the smallest value for δ (or Δ if necessary) in relation to the superordinate end points of R.

The preference for the smallest value means that the principle of the shortest path is in operation: the listener prefers the most stable choice, and the most stable choice is the one that is closest within the "superordinate context." This context differs somewhat between the two kinds of reduction. In time-span reduction, it is the local tonic implied by the events in T; in prolongational reduction, it comprises the events that frame R.

To see how the time-span rule works and to acquire a sense of its scope, let us return to the opening phrase of the Bach chorale analyzed in chapter 1. Level c of Figure 2.31 provides the quarter-note time-span level with the half-note time-span segmentation immediately below. For each half-note span, the rule calculates the distance of each quarter-note event from the local tonic and selects the one with the smallest value. The choice of local tonic depends strictly on the evidence within the time span in question. In the first half of bar 1, the F and C chords are measured in relation to I/**F**; in the second half of bar 1, the F$^{\flat 7}$ and the B♭ chords are measured in relation to I/**B♭**; in the first half of bar 2, the C chords are measured in relation to I/**C**; and in the second half of bar 2, the F chord stands alone. The distance values are given beneath the events in Figure 2.31 and derive from the chord distance rule (chords related by fifth yield δ =5). The augmented span that begins in bar 1 then selects between the two F chords, with the second chosen for global reasons discussed in "A Representative Analysis" in chapter 1. The winners at level c appear at level b. The procedure repeats at level b, which gives the half-note time-span level with the whole-note time-span segmentation. In bar 1 the F and the B♭ chords are measured in relation to I/**F**, and in bar 2 the C and F chords are measured in relation to I/**F**. The result is level a. (For simplicity, and without causing any real difference in this case, cadential retention of the V at level a is ignored.)

FIGURE 2.31 Application of the pitch-space version of the rule of time-span stability carried out for three levels of the Bach chorale "Christus, der ist mein Leben."

The treatment of time-span stability as pitch-space distance overlooks two aspects that properly belong to the stability conditions: the effect of the specific pitches of a triad that occur in the bass or soprano and the role of nonharmonic tones (which would be present in bar 2 of Figure 2.31 if the analysis began at the eighth-note level). These issues are deferred to "The Harmonic Tension Model" in chapter 4, which also incorporates the rule for prolongational connection into a pitch-space version of the interaction principle. Furthermore, the account here does not really explain how the local tonic for time-span T is determined. This important matter is treated in "Finding the Tonic" in chapter 5; again, the solution lies in the principle of the shortest path.

Despite these temporary gaps, it is possible to see how the shortest path replaces GTTM's stability conditions in building the phrase's prolongational structure. The derivation places the results in Figure 1.14 on firmer theoretical ground. In Figure 2.32, distances between adjacent chords are listed between the staves. Two relevant pitch-space calculations that may not be obvious are given in Figure 2.33. Following the interaction principle, the prolongational analysis begins with the events at time-span level a from Figure 2.31 and, because they are identical, attaches them as a strong prolongation at prolongational level a in Figure 2.32a. The IV^6 and the cadential V at time-span level b arise for consideration within the prolongational region between the opening I and the cadential I. The distance IV^6$\leftrightarrow$V is greater ($\delta = 8$) than the distances IV^6$\leftrightarrow$I and V$\leftrightarrow$I (in both cases, $\delta = 5$), so the principle of the shortest path favors connecting IV^6 and V not to each other but to I. By the balance constraint, the IV^6 attaches to the opening I and the V attaches to the cadential I, as in Figure 2.32b.

Next come the remaining events at time-span level c. At this stage there are four prolongational regions to be considered, shown beneath the music in Figure 2.32c. Regions R_1, R_3, and R_4 present no difficulty. In R_1 the anacrustic $I^{\hat{1}}$ weakly prolongs to the structural $I^{\hat{3}}$; in R_3 there is no further event to attach; in R_4 the elaborating V is closer to its immediately preceding downbeat ($\delta = 0$) than to the

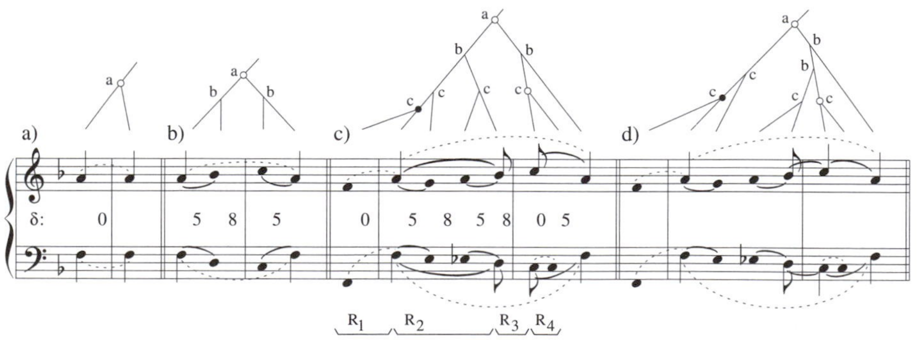

FIGURE 2.32 Application of the pitch-space version of the rule of prolongational connection in correspondence to Figure 2.31.

0											
0							7				
0				4			7				
0		2		4	5		7		9	10	
0	1	2	3	4	5	6	7	8	9	10	11

					$\underline{5}$						
0					$\underline{5}$						
0			$\underline{3}$		$\underline{5}$				$\underline{9}$		
0		2	$\underline{3}$		5		7		9	10	
0	1	2	3	4	5	6	7	8	9	10	11

$\delta(\text{V/}\mathbf{F}\rightarrow\text{V}^7\text{/}\mathbf{B}\flat) = 1 + 1 + 6 = 8$

										10	
					5					10	
		2			5					10	
0		2		4	5		7		9	10	
0	1	2	3	4	5	6	7	8	9	10	11

$\underline{0}$											
$\underline{0}$							$\underline{7}$				
$\underline{0}$				$\underline{4}$			$\underline{7}$				
0		2		4	5		7		9	10	
0	1	2	3	4	5	6	7	8	9	10	11

$\delta(\text{IV}\rightarrow\text{V}) = 0 + 2 + 6 = 8$

FIGURE 2.33 Distance calculations for two progressions in Figure 2.32.

ensuing I ($\delta = 5$). R_2 is more complicated. The distance $\text{V}^6/\mathbf{F}\leftrightarrow\text{V}^4_2/\mathbf{B}\flat$ ($\delta = 8$) is greater than the distances $\text{I}\leftrightarrow\text{V}^6$ ($\delta = 5$) and $\text{V}^4_2/\mathbf{B}\flat\leftrightarrow\text{I}^6/\mathbf{B}\flat$ (again $\delta = 5$); so V^6 attaches to I and $\text{V}^4_2/\mathbf{B}\flat$ attaches to $\text{I}^6/\mathbf{B}\flat$. But now prolongational good form is not fulfilled: there are two unrelated progressions off the $\text{I}^{\hat{3}}$, the V^6 and the IV^6, a violation of the recursion constraint; and there is no dominant-preparing left branch that leads into the cadential V, leaving normative structure unsatisfied. Both conditions are met if the IV^6 connects instead to the cadential V, as in Figure 2.32d. This is the preferred prolongational analysis of the phrase.

This short example, with its combined employment of the principle of the shortest path and prolongational good form, is representative of how the theory derives a prolongational analysis.

EMPIRICAL ISSUES

Issues of quantification

The reader might accept the pitch-space model in general but question some of its specifics. Let me consider four issues of this kind.

Issue 1. The values for δ in Figures 2.8 and 2.10, from which Figure 2.14 derives, do not always mirror musical behavior. First, at the chordal level, ii often functions in its first inversion as a dominant-preparation voice-leading variant of IV, not as a "real" ii, in which case $j = 1$, not 2. Second, partly to avoid the diminished fifth between the fourth and seventh scale degrees, iii is often approached by upward rather than downward fifth motion, in which case $j = 4$, not 3. This value would reflect the typically greater remoteness (in major) of the harmonic as opposed to the melodic third degree. Third, the characterization of vii° favors its role in a circle-of-fifths sequence rather than its common voice-leading dominant function, in which latter case $j = 1$, not 2 (since Rameau, vii° has been treated as a V^7 with a missing root). The revised values for these chords would then be $\delta(I \rightarrow ii) = 1 + 6 = 7$, $\delta(I \rightarrow iii) = 4 + 4 = 8$, and $\delta(I \rightarrow vii^{o}) = 1 + 6 = 7$. Alternative values for these chords might be selected for different contexts.

As a first response, chordal space need not directly reflect voice-leading factors. Voice-leading tendencies arise from features of the basic space (see "Melodic Tension" in chapter 4) and are instantiated in event hierarchies, to which chordal space is but one input.

A second response concerns formal parsimony and structural simplicity. Take just the case of iii, the cause of the greatest discrepancy between model and data. One can see the difficulty in Figure 2.3b and even more critically in Krumhansl's (1990) Table 7.7, which represents the results of the experiment that is most relevant to this question. It would appear that, in this instance, listeners are less attentive to the two common tones between I and iii (variable *k*) than to iii's distance from I on the circle of fifths (variable *j*). Another possibility is that the experimental question ("How well does chord x fit, in a musical sense, in the given context?") triggers not only responses of chordal stability but also the subject's stylistic sense of frequency of occurrence. Perhaps iii receives a weaker value not because it is so distant but because it does not occur very often. Whatever the reason for the discrepancy, treating iii outside of the shortest path would make for a less parsimonious theory. It would be a special case. Such treatment would also compromise transpositional invariance, so that the chordal chart would no longer be regular. From their studies of mental images, Shepard and Lynn Cooper (1982) contend that the mind abstracts away from the messiness of external input to construct and transform symmetrical, architecturally robust structures. Analogously, pitch space must be regular and standardized if it is to apply to a variety of instances in manifold contexts.

Similar questions could be raised at the regional level. Although the values in Figure 2.27 are mostly adequate, there a few exceptions. For instance, Δ(**I**→♭**II**) seems to be too large. Perhaps ♭**II** is just odd: the Neapolitan has a special history as a replacement for ii° in minor, allowing ♭II to insinuate itself as a pivot chord; and ♭**II** frequently appears in connection with the enharmonic treatment of the "German" augmented-sixth chord ($G^6 = V^7$/♭**II**), a chromatic shortcut that lies outside the purview of the model. However, a related difficulty—because ♭**VI** lies in ♭**II**'s path—is that Δ(**I**→**III**) and Δ(**I**→♭**VI**) seem slightly disproportionate in comparison to Δ(**I**→**II**) or Δ(**I**→♭**VII**).

The solution to this set of problems lies in style-dependent transformations of regional space, a topic deferred for treatment in chapters 3 and 6. Briefly, the idea is that the regular regional space of Figure 2.22 is the standard framework against which alternatives are optimized. When a style takes advantage of a particular alternative, the topology bends or folds to bring certain regions closer together. One can trace a coherent historical evolution in these changes.

Issue 2. There is a question concerning perceived asymmetry in relation to psychological prototypes. Prototypical entities are those judged to be most typical or central within a category (Rosch 1975; Rosch and Mervis 1975). In the color domain, for instance, red is perceived as more focal than pink. Nonsimple prototypes usually decompose into simpler default features (Jackendoff 1982). A prototypical chair has a flat surface, a back, and four legs of a certain height. The extent to which defaults are not filled is a mark of how deviant an instance is within its category. Experiments have established across many domains that the degree of perceived similarity between a prototype and other members of the category is asymmetrical: nonprototypical members are judged to be closer to the prototype than the latter is to the former. Pink is closer to red than red is to pink; a three-legged low-backed chair is closer to a standard chair than vice versa.

Krumhansl (1979, 1990) finds just this kind of asymmetry between stable and unstable tones. For example, in a I/**C** context, leading-tone B is judged as closer to prototypical tonic C than C is to B. In a V/**C** context, the reverse tendency holds: B, not C, is harmonic, so C is judged closer to B than the reverse; and so forth for other configurations of the basic space. Noting that asymmetries are not easily representable by geometric models of pitch, she argues that such models need to be supplemented by nongeometric components. I would stress instead that pitch space represents a steady-state schema. In an obvious psychophysical sense, the distances from B to C and from C to B are identical. "Melodic Tension" in chapter 4 offers a more satisfactory explanation for perceived asymmetries, based on a theory of attractions.

Issue 3. The spatial mappings are not quite Euclidean. For example, in the chordal toroidal structure, the nonrepeating core of which is given here as Figure 2.34, the measurements on the north–south axis are 5 and those on the east–west axis are 7. The southwest and northeast diagonals, however, are 8, even though by the Pythagorean theorem—assuming a flat plane—they should be 8.6 (the square root of $5^2 + 7^2$). Similar problems arise in the regional toroidal structure. In Figure 2.24a there is a small discrepancy in the diagonals: δ(**I**→**iii** = 9, but δ(**I**→**ii**) = 10. Their Euclidean distances should be 9.9 (the square root of $7^2 + 7^2$).

In response, the heart of the theory lies in the basic space and its algebraic transformations. Insofar as the geometrical projections are "real," the musical mind may modify discrepancies—again along the lines of Shepard and Cooper—to form regular structures, more or less as it adjusts between just intonation and equal-interval tuning.

Issue 4. It might be argued that the chord distance rule compares, so to speak, apples and oranges. Why should the steps on the circle of fifths (variables *i* and *j*) and the number of distinctive pcs (variable *k*) combine in a simple additive fashion? Why not another formula, perhaps one that includes coefficients?

There are two responses. First, the simple additive model correlates well with the experimental data. It also affords, as has been seen, attractive connections to the music/theoretic literature. A more complex model would be preferable only if it achieved better results.

Second, they are all apples anyway. We so closely associate pitches an octave apart and even categorize them as pcs, because of their psychoacoustic relatedness.

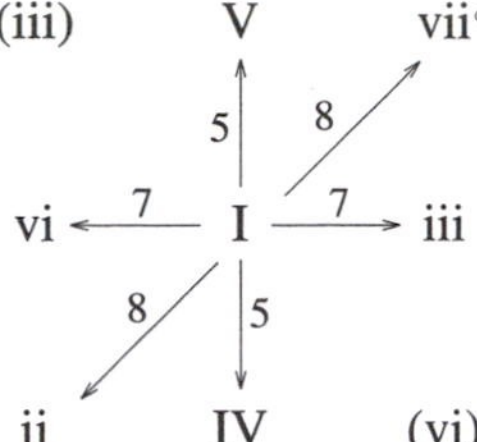

FIGURE 2.34 Distance values from I in the chordal core.

The fifth is the next most related interval. (Slight mistunings do not alter degrees of relatedness, for in normal musical contexts intervals are perceived categorically [Burns and Ward 1982].) However, moving by octaves does not change pc space. It is the factor of the fifth that reorients the space, as treated by *i* and *j*. When the space shifts, pcs do or do not return, as treated by *k*. If other related intervals, especially the major third, affected modifications of the space, other variables would have to be included; but this turns out to be unnecessary.

More generally, music theorists have gotten used to the idea, especially since the advent of twelve-tone and pc-set theory, that the octave is an interval different in kind from the other intervals. From a psychoacoustic viewpoint it differs only in degree. In employing the three variables together, the model takes a stance linked (but not restricted) to the psychacoustic perspective.

Evidence and explanation

An experiment typically tests a preexisting theory. Such is the case, for example, with Irène Deliège's (1987) validation (with emendations) of GTTM's local grouping preference rules. But the reverse also happens: experiments may demand an explanatory framework or suggest further theoretical ideas. This is the case with the model here, which initially was inspired by Krumhansl's empirical results. A theory has been needed to explain the observed regularities.

The model accommodates empirical evidence in a number of ways. To begin with, the structure of the basic space reflects psychoacoustically related stylistic features. A descent through levels a–e (Figure 2.4) brings increasing sensory dissonance between adjacent pcs at a given level. Level a offers the principal virtual pitch of the collections in levels b and c (Terhardt 1974). That is, when hearing a chord, the ear tries to match the pitches to the harmonic template of the natural overtone series. This pattern-matching process accounts for the perception of missing fundamentals and chordal roots. If a chord does not fit the template well, the ear weakly infers multiple roots of varying strength. If the chord fits the template, the ear infers a single root. The octave, fifth, and major triad match the template optimally and give an unambiguous root. The minor triad is somewhat conflicted in this regard, although the traditional root does correspond to the pc of the strongest virtual pitch. (Incidentally, virtual pitches—which were not yet postulated at the time—underlie intervallic roots in Hindemith's [1937/1942] theory of harmony, rather than the difference [or combination] tones upon which he relied to ground his intuitions.) For the major triad, level b provides the second most salient pitch, the fifth (assuming a standard timbre, with partial n at roughly $1/n$ amplitude of that of the fundamental); level c adds the major third, the third most salient pitch (Thompson and Parncutt 1997). For the minor triad, the weightings for the third and fifth are more ambiguous (Terhardt, Stoll, and Seewann 1982). The parallel treatment of the fifth and third of the minor triad is justified by parallel usage of major and minor triads in tonal music. These roles of basic-space levels are also reflected, broadly speaking, in historical practice: level b serves as the harmonic norm for resolution for much medieval and non-Western music, level c for Classical tonal music.

Between levels c and d appears a conceptual line that separates harmony and melody. This has a partly psychoacoustic basis. When a periodic sound wave reaches the inner ear, an area of the basilar membrane is stimulated, the peak of which, transmitted and resolved through the auditory pathways, causes the perception of a single pitch. If two periodic signals stimulate overlapping areas, the perturbation causes a sensation of "roughness." In most pitch ranges this sensation arises from intervals less than a minor third and is strongest at the interval of about a quarter-tone. This area of overlapping is called the critical band. Reinier Plomp and W. J. M. Levelt (1965) modernized Helmholtz's (1863/1885) beating theory of dissonance by demonstrating the role of the critical band in judgments of sensory consonance (also see Roederer 1973). Intervallic inversions (minor second to major seventh, and so on) retain their quality of dissonance or consonance in proportion to the strength of their partials inside or outside the critical band. In the basic space the intervals at levels a–c lie outside the critical band, in consequence of an aesthetic ideal of harmonic euphony that existed throughout much of Western music history. Indeed, the various triads (major, minor, diminished, and augmented) are the only trichords that meet this condition.

Level d, whose adjacent pitches fall inside the critical band, provides the melodic bedrock for many musical idioms, with level e offering inflectional possibilities. Relevant in this regard is the perceptual attention band, which is coextensive with the critical band. When a pitch sounds, listeners focus on other pitches within the attention band more than on those outside it, much as they notice objects near each other in the visual field more quickly than objects that are far apart (Scharf et al. 1987; Bharucha 1996). The attention band thus provides a kind of glue for sequential pitches. In pursuit of linear connectedness, melodies tend to proceed largely by intervals within this band. Large sequential intervals, by contrast, have a greater tendency to be heard in separate streams (Bregman 1990). (Scharf et al. hint at a common basis for the attention and critical bands, although the physical mechanisms that underlie it are not yet fully understood. Evidently the neural firing that gives rise to the critical band is an aspect of the attentive process.)

It may be superfluous to add that there is nothing obligatory about these correspondences between pitch space and psychoacoustics. Rather, the psychoacoustics provide a set of possibilities of which a musical system can take advantage. Western tonality has done so, but other systems might or might not pursue this route.

Lerdahl (1988b) reviews specifics of the experimental support of the pc, chordal, and regional distance values given by the model here. Briefly, the pc level is ratified by Krumhansl's original probe-tone study (1979; Figure 2.3a), by Krumhansl and Edward Kessler's (1982) key profiles, and by the correspondence between Figure 2.5c and Amos Tversky and J. W. Hutchinson's (1986) nearest-neighbor analysis of Krumhansl's data. The chordal level is confirmed by Krumhansl, Jamshed Bharucha, and Kessler's (1982) multidimensional scaling solution of the relatedness of chords within a key (Figure 2.3b) and by Krumhansl's (1990) analysis of her chord-probe experiments. The regional level is supported by Krumhansl and Kessler's (1982) derivation of regional space from the pc hierarchy (Figure 2.3c) and by Krumhansl's (1990) similar derivation of the same structure from the chordal hierarchy. There is some evidence for the notion of pivot regions in Krumhansl and Kessler's finding that listeners exercise greater effort in evaluating modulations to distant as opposed to close regions.

When used to calculate tension–relaxation patterns (see "The Harmonic Tension Model" in chapter 4), the pitch-space model receives strong empirical support (Bigand, Parncutt, and Lerdahl 1996; Krumhansl 1996). In spite of the intricacies of deriving tension values, listeners hear these patterns directly and forcibly.

Krumhansl's (1990) empirical analysis highlights the interrelatedness of the pc, chordal, and regional levels. Along with approximating the empirical findings for each level, this theory combines the three levels into one overall model. Distances at each level are determined by variables—octaves (pcs) and fifths—that are manifest at the top two levels of the space and that have not only a psychoacoustic but also a developmental basis. The octave and fifth are salient partials in the human voice and are in inevitable part of the organism's conditioning even before birth (Lecanuet 1996; Abrams and Gerhardt 1997).

As is usual in cognitive psychology, Krumhansl's results are statistical in nature because they average data from a population of responses. She undertakes further statistical analysis in search of patterns in the observed regularities and finds striking correlations between, on the one hand, the quantitative distribution of all the pcs in actual compositions ("tone durations") and, on the other, listeners' internalized pc and chordal hierarchies. She concludes that pc surface salience is crucial developmentally (Krumhansl 1990). After all, nursery tunes are strongly diatonic and emphasize the tonic and dominant pitches. While the argument is persuasive with respect to learning, it does not explain what mental computations listeners perform once they have internalized average tone durations in an idiom. In highly evolved styles such as Wagner's or Brahms's, tone profiles and tone durations are less likely to correlate. As GTTM demonstrates for event hierarchies, once a style is learned, listeners infer organization far beyond what is given by surface features. The same is true, in my view, for the tonal hierarchy. Listeners respond to structures more than to statistical norms.

Even though the model presented here succeeds empirically, it might not be the best one. The musical mind could reach similar distance values by other means. In this connection, Riemann's harmonic theory has recently been recast as a set of formal transformations (Lewin 1982, 1987, 1992; Hyer 1995; Kopp 1995; Mooney 1996; Cohn 1996, 1997, 1998; Douthett and Steinbach 1998). Krumhansl (1998) finds that an application of a combination of these transformations fits her earlier data somewhat better for nonmusicians than does the model here. Should this model be replaced by the neo-Riemannian one?

The relevant neo-Riemannian transformations are R (for "relative," equivalent to *Parallelklang* in German), L (for "leading tone" or *Leittonwechselklang*), P (for "parallel" major-minor), and D (for "dominant"). R moves the fifth of a major triad up a whole step or the root of a minor triad down a whole step, as in Cmaj→Amin or Cmin→E♭maj. (Riemann, in search of symmetry, considered the fifth of a minor triad to be its root, but this need not concern us here.) L moves the root of a major triad down a half step or the fifth of a minor triad up a half step, as in Cmaj→Emin or Cmin→A♭maj. P exchanges the third of a major or minor triad, as in Cmaj↔Cmin. In contrast to R, L, and P, which reverse chord quality, D keeps the same chord quality by shifting a triad up or down the cycle of fifths, as in Cmaj→Gmaj or Cmin→Fmin. Figures 2.35a–d display these four

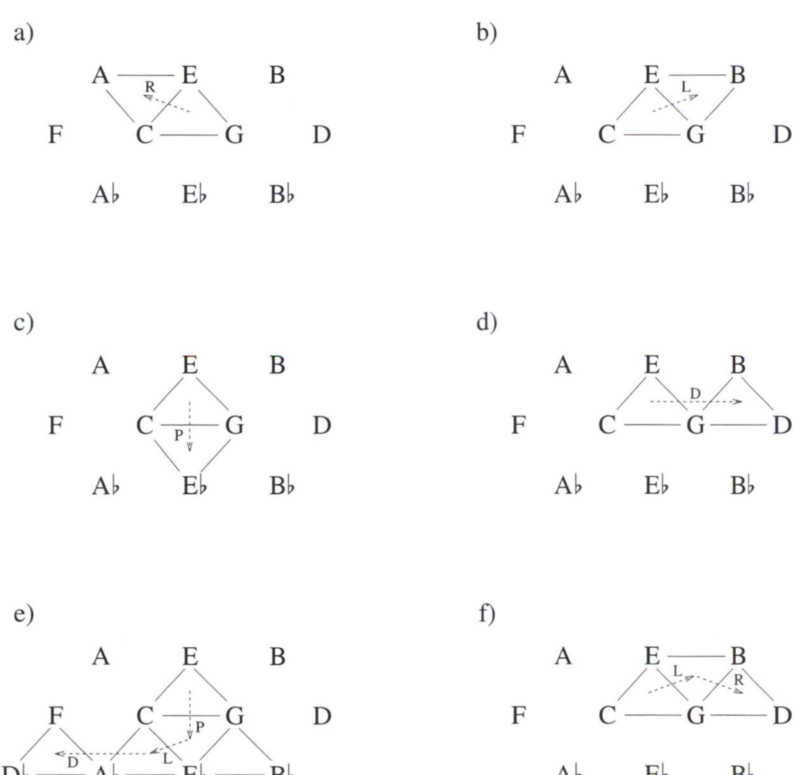

FIGURE 2.35 Illustrations of neo-Riemannian transformations.

transformations employing a slightly modified version of the *Tonnetz* (adapted from Riemann 1915). In the original just-intonation-inspired version in Figure 2.2b, the minor-third axis must be read off the northwest–southeast diagonal and there is an unwanted semitonal axis on the southwest–northeast diagonal. The modified version places the major- and minor-third axes on an equal footing, each at a sixty-degree angle from the horizontal fifths axis, in the process suppressing the semitonal axis. R, L, and P flip the triad-triangle over on its side by retaining two pcs (Figures 2.35 a–c, respectively), while D, which keeps only one pc, shifts the triangle horizontally (Figure 2.35d).

Krumhansl computes distances between triads by counting the minimal number of transformations it takes to move from one triad to another. For example, $\delta_{\text{neo-R}}$(Cmaj→D♭maj) = P + L + −D = Cmaj→Cmin→A♭maj→ D♭maj, as shown in Figure 2.35e. The order is important because these transformations are not commutative (for instance, applying L + P + −D to Cmaj would yield Amaj). Specifying the minimal number of transformations is essential because a chord can be reached in any number of ways; the minimal number is, in effect, the shortest path. Indeed, the path for $\delta_{\text{neo-R}}$(Cmaj→D♭maj) follows a trajectory similar to that computed by the current model here in Figure 2.27: δ(I/**C**→I/**D♭**) = I/**C**→i/**c**→I/**A♭**→I/**D♭** = 7 + 9 + 7 = 23. This correspondence is not unexpected, for Riemann's *Tonnetz* can be seen as a modification of regional space (Figure 2.22), by merging parallel major-minor regions on the y axis, rotating the whole regional structure ninety degrees clockwise, and then rotating the new x axis thirty degrees counterclockwise. At a fundamental level, however, the spaces are dissimilar: the letters in the *Tonnetz* denote pcs, while in Figure 2.22 they stand for regions.

Its correlations and related geometry notwithstanding, there are drawbacks with the neo-Riemannian approach as a cognitive pitch-space model. (Some of these points were mentioned in "The Concept of Pitch Space" earlier in this chapter.) First, even though the diatonic collection forms a compact region in the space (Longuet-Higgins 1962), its distances between pcs have no rationale outside the triads of which they are a part. In Figure 2.35a, for instance, G and A are not adjacent within the context I/**C**. In short, scalar distances are violated in the *Tonnetz*. It seems infelicitous for a theory of diatonic space to downplay the diatonic scale, which is almost as overlearned an alphabet as the triad and is constantly accessed on a par with and in relation to chord and region.

Second, even though the *Tonnetz* represents triads rather directly, it treats all pcs in a chord as equal, ignoring the concept of chordal root, which since Rameau has been fundamental to tonal theory. As a consequence, triadic progressions are viewed solely through the lens of efficient voice leading (minimal linear motion; see Cohn 1998). The progression I→vi, for example, is accomplished not by root motion but by the stepwise motion of the R transformation. While this treatment may be appropriate in certain contexts, in many it is not. (This point does not apply to recent work in the German Riemannian tradition, such as de la Motte [1988], in which chords are referred to by their traditional roots.)

Third, the *Tonnetz* treats triads without the framework of regions. The triadic motion Cmaj→D♭maj is not the same as I/**C**→I/**D♭**; the former effects a change in chord, not necessarily in region. To be in a region is an abstraction that involves location with respect to tonic and scale. Such a conception lies outside the neo-Riemannian framework.

Fourth, the D transformation is needed along with with R, L, and P to attain the best empirical fit in Krumhansl's analysis, yet in the neo-Riemannian system D is a greater transformation than R, L, and P, which keep two common tones rather than just one. Indeed, D is formally superfluous: as shown in Figure 2.35f, D = L + R. As in its neglect of the diatonic scale, the system underplays the cycle of fifths at the chordal level.

Fifth, neo-Riemanian theory has typically been applied to chromatic passages in late tonal compositions, but its application to standard diatonic passages is awkward. For example, granting the D transformation as an independent transformation, I→IV→V→I becomes −D + 2D + −D (where "−D" designates leftward movement in Figure 2.35). 2D could be replaced by another operation that accomplishes upward whole-tone motion in all voices, but the addition of more transformations would complicate the system (Riemann 1880 in fact takes such a step). In brief, the neo-Riemannian version is just as elaborate as the Roman-numeral description; yet, unlike the latter, it omits diatonic scale degrees and root motions. Furthermore, the argument that listeners switch between two systems—that Roman-numeral analysis describes diatonic listening while neo-Riemannian transformations apply to chromatic listening—is implausible as a psychological position. It is problematic in particular for late tonal music, which moves smoothly between diatonicism and chromaticism even within a single phrase. Any viable analytic system for this music must be capable of treating its chromatic and diatonic elements with comparable smoothness. Chapters 3 and 6 will show how diatonicism and chromaticism combine within one overall system.

Sixth, in connection with point 2, neo-Riemannian theory disregards the underlying psychoacoustics. This would be questionable for any music theory, but it is especially so for a theory in which the fundamental harmonic unit is the triad, because of its prominence with respect to both spectral and virtual pitches. As discussed, the psychoacoustic prominence of the members of the major triad, and to a lesser extent of the minor triad, falls in the ordering of root, then fifth, and then third. The neo-Riemannian implicit denial of an extraformalistic basis for music theory contrasts with the attitude of Riemann himself. He not only ascribed roots to triads but also consistently sought a scientific foundation for his harmonic theories, first in the psychoacoustics of Helmholtz (1863/1885)—his misadventure with the undertone series notwithstanding—and later in the research of early experimental psychologists such as Carl Stumpf (1890).

Standing back from these various points, what is really tested in Krumhansl's experiments? Listeners rate how well a pitch fits into a tonally induced context. However, the extrapolation from tone-probe profile to regional mapping is imperfect. One does not really know how to understand the pitch D♭ in a I/**C** context, for the information is undertermined. The D♭ might imply a voice-leading chromaticism, a triad of uncertain function, or possibly **I/D♭**. Under such contextually impoverished circumstances, it is not surprising that neo-Riemannian transformations perform well, for they maximize common-tone relationships. Krumhansl (1998) concludes that the empirical success of the neo-Riemannian transformations reduces to the principle of pitch proximity, which these transformations maximize. It is notable that neo-Riemannian transformations succeed best for nonmusicians. I suspect that this is so because nonmusicians are less likely than musicians to infer levels of pitch space not elicited directly in the experimental task. Further research presumably will show that given sufficient surface information, listeners infer all levels of the basic space. My conclusion, then, is that the psychoacoustic relevance and theoretical richness of the approach presented here outweigh the empirical stalemate, which up to this point is based on rough-grained data.

Richard Parncutt (1989, 1994) develops an explicitly psychoacoustic model of tonal harmony. He extends Terhardt's virtual-pitch model to develop plausible measures for chord relatedness. Parncutt's quest has been to establish a direct link between psychoacoustics and the cognition of harmony without a stage of mental representation. Pivotal factors in his approach parallel those in the pitch-space model, however. The relatedness of chords depends on a weighted virtual-pitch commonality approximated by the chord distance rule, which also relies on common tones (variable k) and fifth relatedness (variables i and j). This convergence accounts for the good correlations between his and my predictions (Bigand, Parncutt, and Lerdahl 1996).

Convergent evidence from different sources usually argues in favor of complementarity of approaches. One might contend, however, that the cognitive operations imputed by my music-theoretic model are nonexistent or at least secondary, since its predictions can be approximated on psychoacoustic grounds. Yet Parncutt himself steps well beyond psychoacoustics per se. My view is that psychoacoustics provide a necessary but insufficient foundation, a range of options for structuring potential and ease of learning, that the musical mind has at its disposal. One set of rich potentialities has been realized by diatonic tonality. Listeners familiar with this music develop cognitive representations and operations for processing it, including the basic space and its transformations and mappings.

How might these cognitive representations and operations be instantiated in the brain? Bharucha (1987, 1991, 1996) seeks to explain Krumhansl's data patterns by means of neural-net computational modeling, which, while differing in many respects from actual neurons and their synaptic connections, appears to come closer to brain behavior than does an abstract computational model such as the pitch-space theory presented here. He supplements his approach with close attention to the physiological and psychological evidence.

The model here can nevertheless be made to look more brainlike. Instead of numbering pcs by C = 0, C♯ = 1, . . . B = 11, let pitches be located from from left to right with C arbitrarily at the left. Figure 2.36a represents this by marking

a)

1 1 1 1 1 1 1 1 1 1 1 1
C C♯D D♯E F F♯G G♯A A♯B

b)

1 0 1 0 1 1 0 1 0 1 0 1
1 1 1 1 1 1 1 1 1 1 1 1

c)

1 0 1 0 1 0 1 1 0 1 0 1
1 1 1 1 1 1 1 1 1 1 1 1

d)

1 0 0 0 0 0 0 0 0 0 0 0
1 0 0 0 0 0 0 1 0 0 0 0
1 0 0 0 1 0 0 1 0 0 0 0
1 0 1 0 1 1 0 1 0 1 0 1
1 1 1 1 1 1 1 1 1 1 1 1

e)

0 0 0 0 0 0 0 1 0 0 0 0
0 0 1 0 0 0 0 1 0 0 0 0
0 0 1 0 0 0 0 1 0 0 0 1
1 0 1 0 1 1 0 1 0 1 0 1
1 1 1 1 1 1 1 1 1 1 1 1

f)

0 0 0 0 0 0 0 1 0 0 0 0
0 0 1 0 0 0 0 1 0 0 0 0
0 0 1 0 0 0 0 1 0 0 0 1
1 0 1 0 1 0 1 1 0 1 0 1
1 1 1 1 1 1 1 1 1 1 1 1

FIGURE 2.36 Quasi-neural representations of the basic space: (a) representing pitches neutrally by location; (b) the C major scale in binary numbers; (c) the G major scale; (d) I/**C**; (e) V/**C**; (f) I/**G**.

each pitch neutrally as "1"; a pitch's identity is determined solely by its location. Certain well-established features of cortical organization are germane at this point. First, there is a tonotopic arrangement (mapping to physical location along a given dimension—in this case, by frequency) of pitches not only on the basilar membrane but also in the auditory cortex (Weinberger 1999). Second, neurons constantly fire at a low level; one neuron transmits to another across a synaptic gap once a threshold is reached in firing activation. Third, neurons in specific cortical areas are organized in layers, such that firings at one level transmit to neurons at the next level (Churchland 1986). Bearing these features in mind, let the 1s in Figure 2.36a now signify a subthreshold level of constant firing. If a pitch sounds, its activation at the lowest level exceeds the threshhold and transmits to the next level, where again it is represented by 1. If the pitch does not sound, the lowest level does not transmit and it is represented at the second level by 0. Thus Figure 2.36b represents a C major scale, Figure 2.36c a G major scale (in both cases again following the convention that C is displayed to the left, C♯ to its immediate right, and so on). If a C major triad sounds along with the C major scale, three more neuronal levels come into play, with firings weighted so that the third level represents the triad C-E-G, the fourth level the fifth C-G, and the fifth level the root C. Figure 2.36d stands for I/**C**, Figure 2.36e V/**C**, and Figure 2.36f I/**G**. Any scale or chord in any region can be represented by a layered pattern of 1s and 0s. The number of 1s for each pc corresponds to its degree of neuronal activation.

This binary translation of the basic-space representation broadly resembles the architecture of Bharucha's neural nets. It will be necessary, in addition, to abstract input pitches into pcs (perhaps along lines suggested by Deutsch's [1969] netlike diagram). A further issue is how far the modeled spatial organization of chords and regions is realized in the physical arrangement of neurons in the auditory cortex, by analogy with spatially mapped feature detectors in the visual cortex

(Hubel and Wiesel 1962; Marr 1982). Marc Leman (1995) describes a self-organizing neural network for chords that approximates the toroidal configuration of Krumhansl and Kessler (1982). Although the neurobiological evidence is not yet available, it is possible that such an organization is realized in the brain as well—that there is a physical correlate to the multidimensional spatial mappings advanced in this chapter.

3 *Paths in Pitch Space*

PROLONGATIONAL PATHS

The concept of pitch-space paths

This chapter explores somewhat informally the analytic potential of the geometric representations developed in the last chapter. Figure 3.1 provides the score of Chopin's E major Prelude, Figure 3.2 its hierarchical description (we bypass discussion of the derivation). Figure 3.2 abbreviates the musical surface by representing the soprano-bass skeleton at the quarter-note time-span reductional level and by diminishing the note values from the quarter note to the sixteenth note, so that a full measure corresponds to a phrase, or four-bar hypermeasure, in Figure 3.1. This is a convenient if not fully explicit way to represent metrical and hypermetrical grids (the notation is adapted from Schachter 1980). The rest of the figure is laid out as in Figure 1.18. At a global level, the piece projects strong prolongations from the opening to the beginning of the second phrase and from there to the beginning of the third. Within each phrase there is a tensing-to-relaxing pattern, with the final relaxation resolving to full stability.

Consider how alike the first and third phrases begin yet how dissimilar their effects are. The first phrase is almost wholly diatonic, while the third modulates to a distant place, returning home at the last moment. A reductional graph (Schenkerian or otherwise) that displays chromatic versus diatonic voice-leading elaborations cannot begin to capture this difference. Rather, the third phrase is

FIGURE 3.1 Chopin's E major Prelude.

remarkable for its pitch-space journey. If events situate mentally in pitch space, then prolongational analysis should take place over that space.

This idea was implied in the reductional method outlined in "The Principle of the Shortest Path" in chapter 2, for pitch-space distances were calculated there at each prolongational level. But that method does not convey paths in a direct way. For an intuitively transparent charting of pitch-space journeys, I turn instead to the geometrical representations. The notion of tracing the unfolding of events in a musical space was implicit in the eighteenth-century models for correct modulation and in the subsequent theories of Weber, Riemann, and Schoenberg. Recently the idea has been explicit in Lubin (1974), Krumhansl and Kessler (1982), Carpenter (1983), and Werts (1983). However, none of these writers employs the range of spaces to be utilized here, nor do they combine pitch-space paths with prolongational analysis.

One formal point must be reviewed first. For pitch-space paths, labeled prolongational levels are indispensable, for each level has its own path. The prolongational levels in Figure 3.3a can be read as the horizontal slices in Figure 3.3b. Each sequence in Figure 3.3b takes a path in pitch space. A piece of any size has many prolongational levels and hence many paths. Lest this seem too abstract, think of the beginning of the first movement of Beethoven's *Waldstein* Sonata (Figure 1.34). At the surface, the opening harmonic progression is I–V^4_2/**V**–V^6; for the subphrase groups in bars 1–4 and 5–8, the music sequences down a step; at the level of theme groups, the piece modulates from **C** to **E** (bar 1 to bar 35). This unexceptional description has already suggested paths at three prolongational levels.

My task here is to provide a clear account of such intuitions. I imagine a model in which prolongational trees reach down to events in multidimensional space-time, uniting the tonal and event hierarchies in one representation. This is obviously not feasible on a two-dimensional page; and even if it were, the page would be so cluttered as to be unreadable. Piecemeal graphs must suffice.

Paths in regional space

Let us begin with the regional space of Figure 2.22a and plot paths for the second and third phrases of the Chopin E major Prelude, based on the prolongational levels in Figure 3.2. The first phrase is not discussed in the following analysis because it remains resolutely in the tonic region; Chopin is preparing by contrast the adventure to follow. Figure 3.4 treats the second phrase to the beginning of the third. Only the relevant portions of regional space are shown. The arrows mark paths from one region to another. Starting and ending regions are squared, and intermediate regions are circled. Figure 3.4a describes prolongational level a, a simple loop around the E major tonic, signifying the (non)motion from the structural beginning of the second phrase to that of the third. At level b, shown in Figure 3.4b, the path divides the octave into equal intervals (in this case, major thirds), a common nineteenth-century technique that Chopin pioneered. The remaining regions, all passed through fleetingly, are shown in Figure 3.4c.

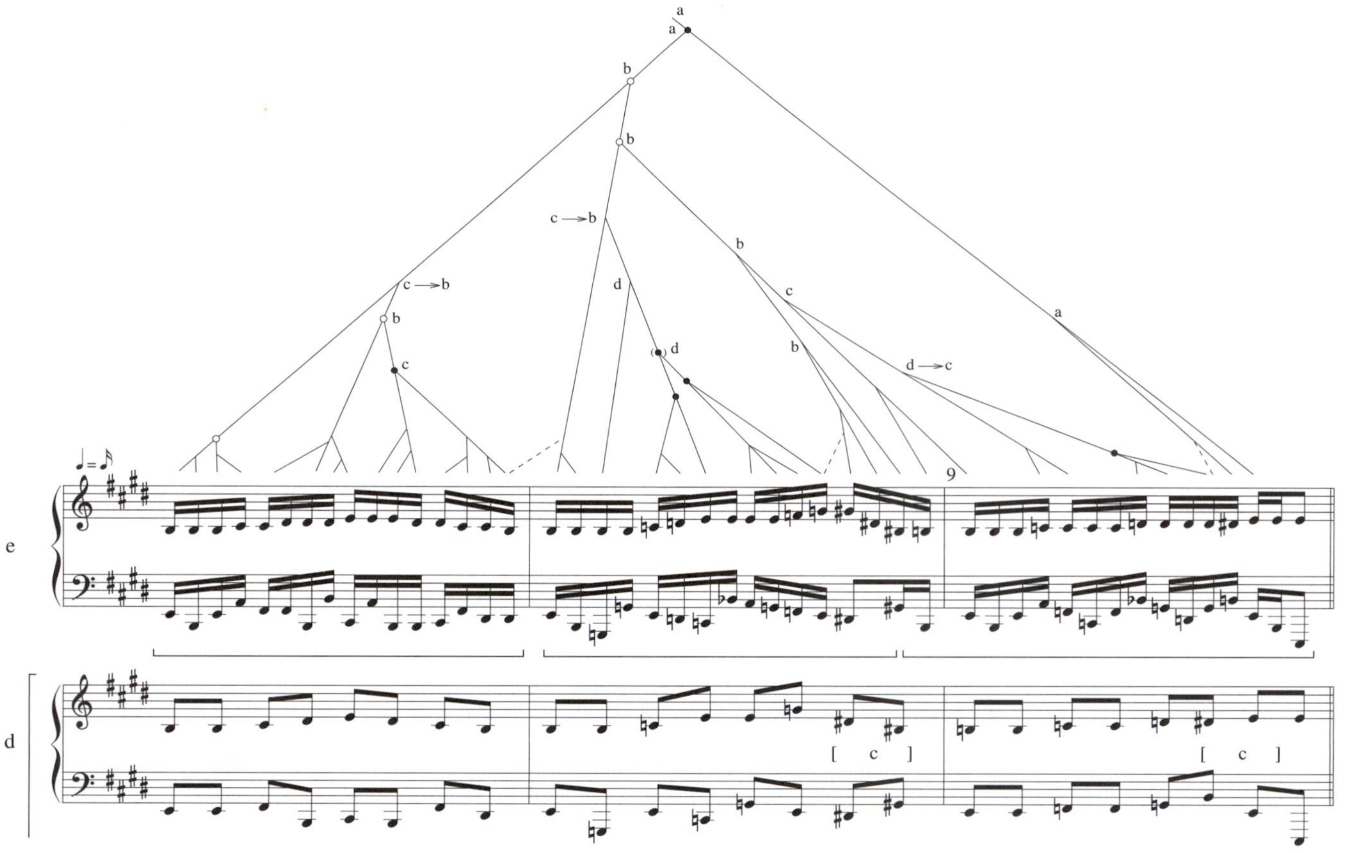

a
a
b
b
c → b
c → b
b
d
b
c
(•) d
c
b
a
d → c
9
e
d
[c]
[c]

FIGURE 3.2 Reductional analysis of the E major Prelude.

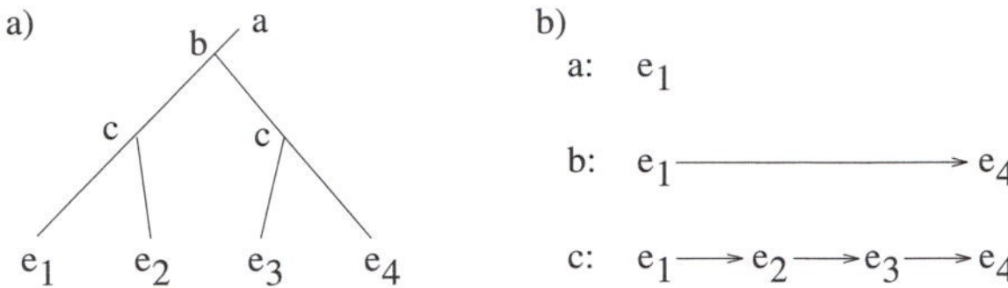

FIGURE 3.3 Trees and levels: (a) a hypothetical tree for four events designated by level; (b) the levels notated as horizontal slices.

In Figures 3.4b–c the journey in the unfolded toroidal structure begins and arrives on different **E**s. Instances of this kind happen especially when a path cannot be construed in diatonic terms. Such is the case here: bars 7–8 of the score are notated in **A♭** rather than **G♯** not only for readability but also as a consequence of repeated moves toward the flatted sixth degree. **C** is heard in terms of **E**, **A♭** in terms of **C**. The next major-third move would arrive at **F♭**, the enharmonic equivalent of **E**. The need to hear **F♭** as **E** demands that **A♭** be understood as **G♯**—which, in a global view, it is anyway. Chopin effects the change between the **A♭** arrival and the passing **g♯** chord. Is the second **E** the same as the first or is it conceptually a different **E**? If regional space is viewed toroidally with one location per region, there is one **E**. The geometry erases pure diatonicism on both its axes. But if the space is represented as an unfolded chart, as in the figure, the two **E**s can have different locations. A consequence of this representation is that there are contrary interpretations at different prolongational levels: the same **E** in Figure

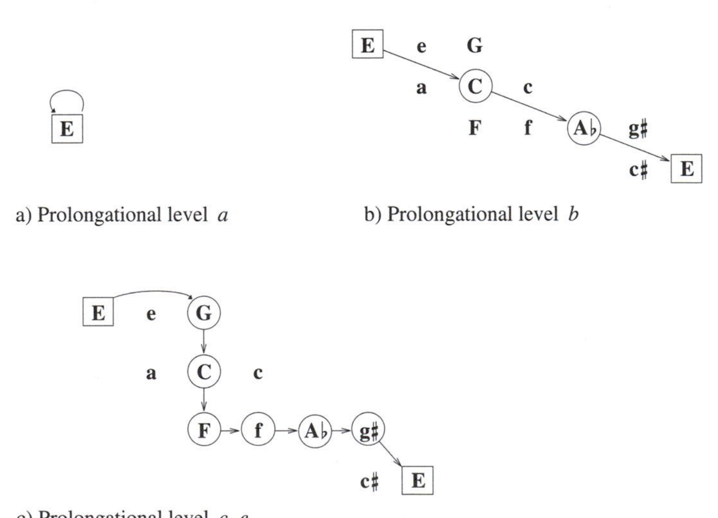

FIGURE 3.4 Paths in regional space for the second phrase of the Chopin E major Prelude.

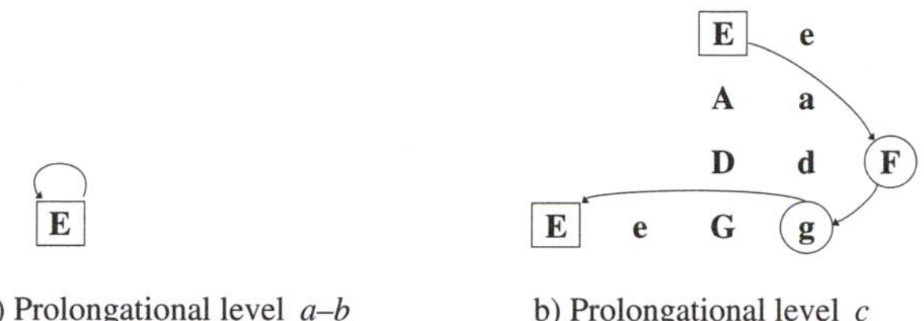

a) Prolongational level *a–b* b) Prolongational level *c*

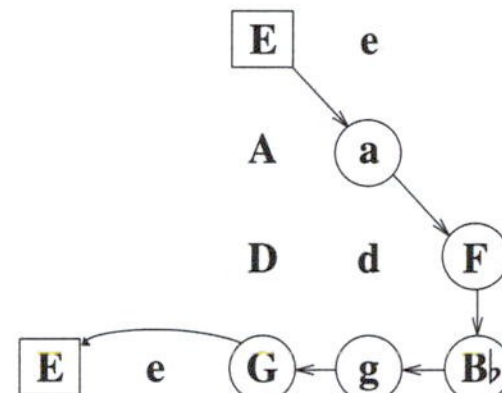

c) Prolongational level *d*

FIGURE 3.5 Paths in regional space for the third phrase of the E major Prelude.

3.4a but different ones (**E** and **E** = **F♭**) in Figure 3.4b. Such multiple locations are artifacts of the chart representation.

Figure 3.5 maps the paths for the third phrase at three stages of prolongational analysis. Observe in Figure 3.5c the motion from **G** to the final **E**. As in chapter 2, it is useful at this level of abstraction to invoke the distinction between step and skip. Until this point, the regional shifts have been stepwise: each arrow moves to a vertically, horizontally, or diagonally adjacent region. But here there is a decided regional skip, from **G** over **e** to **E**. This progression reverses the progression at the beginning of the second phrase, the start of the chromatic journey.

Figure 3.6 combines the levels of Figures 3.4 and 3.5 into one representation. The squared regions refer to Figures 3.4a and 3.5a, the solid arrows specify the paths for Figures 3.4b and 3.5b, and the dashed arrows include the subordinate regions traversed in Figures 3.4c and 3.5c.

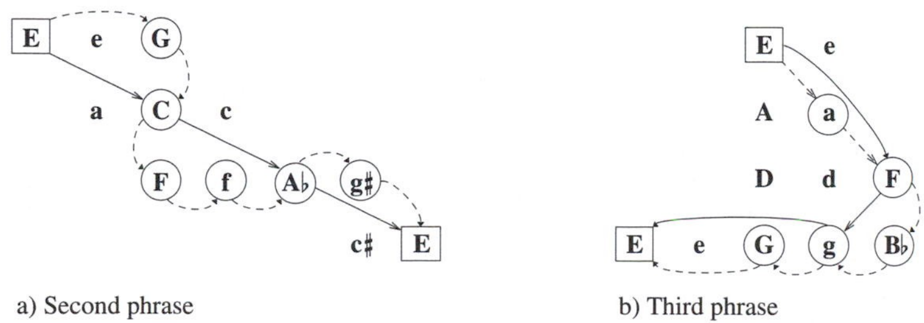

a) Second phrase b) Third phrase

FIGURE 3.6 Multileveled representation of regional paths.

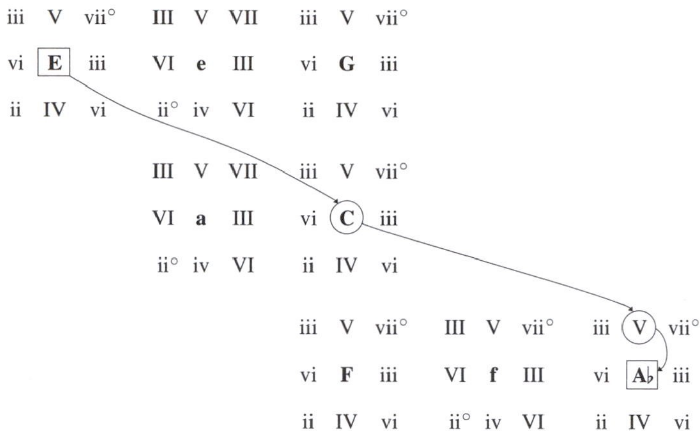

a) Prolongational levels *a–b*

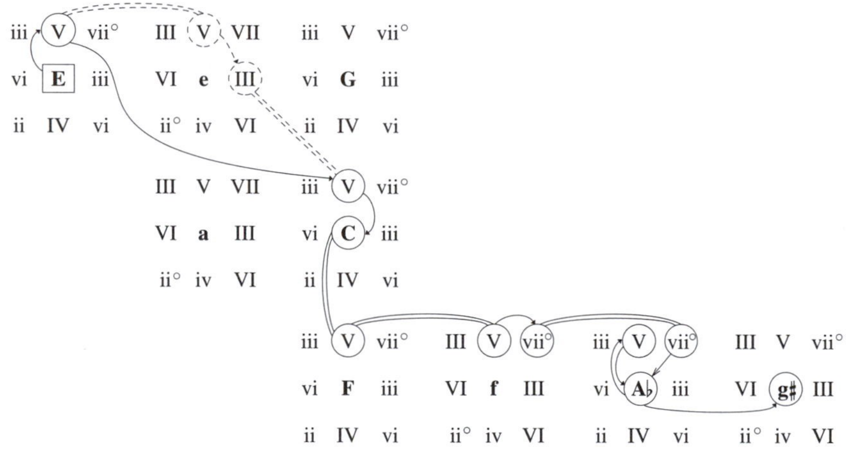

b) Prolongational levels *c–e*

FIGURE 3.7 Chordal/regional representation of paths in the second phrase of the E major Prelude.

Paths in chordal/regional space

Paths through regional space collapse the distinction between chord and region by representing, in effect, only the tonic chord of each region. In the second phrase, for instance, the G major triad (bar 5 in Figure 3.1) is hardly a region, but it is represented as **G** in Figure 3.4c because there is no V/**C** available in the representation. In contrast, **F** stands for a region (bar 6) that is traversed without any statement of its tonic chord. More generally, the leaves of a prolongational tree are pitch events, but the categories in regional space are regions, so the correspondence between the two can only be approximate.

To capture finer distinctions, we must invoke the chordal/regional space in Figure 2.29. Fragments of this representation are given for the second phrase of the Chopin in Figure 3.7, in which prolongational paths are traced. (For convenience, prolongational levels cluster into groups of two or three at a time.) Parallel lines symbolize "pivots," or single events at the musical surface that are reinterpreted as two identical events in different parts of the space.

Figure 3.7a corresponds to Figure 3.4b, with the addition of the cadential V in bar 8, so as to take account of all the events in prolongational level b in Figure 3.2. In Figure 3.7b, which corresponds to Figure 3.4c, the G triad is designated not as I/**G** but as V/**C**. (The dashed arrows and circles will be discussed shortly.) When I/**C** arrives (beat 3 of bar 6) after a $\hat{5}\rightarrow\hat{1}$ diatonic descent in the bass, B♭ has arrived in an inner voice, turning it into V^7/**F**. In this reading, these two functions are separated in the space, connected in the path by a pivot designation; I/**C** exists just beneath the surface. **F** and **f** (bars 6–7) appear as regions passed through without local tonic realizations. The voice crossings in bars 6–8 convert the V^7/**F** into an enharmonically pivoting vii^{o7} that climaxes on the cadential $^6_4$/**A♭** (downbeat of bar 8). This $^6_4$/**A♭**, preceded as it is by a dominant function, and in the spirit of much nineteenth-century (as opposed to eighteenth-century) usage, has tonic status in its immediate context. The motion through **g♯** brings the music back toward I/**E** to open the third phrase. (This interpretation follows Edward Aldwell and Carl Schachter [1979] in treating the A major triad on the downbeat of bar 7 as a passing consequence of multiple voice crossings. This triad is startling precisely because it does not fit within the pitch-space trajectory of the phrase as a whole.)

Figure 3.8a, which corresponds to Figure 3.5b, charts the path for the intermediate levels of the third phrase. Figure 3.8b accords with the local levels from Figure 3.5c.

Now consider the dashed arrows and circles in Figures 3.7b and 3.8b and recall the principle of the shortest path. Where the music necessitates a modulatory jump, one attempts to turn the regional skip into a series of steps. The dashed arrows and circles represent such medial points of interpretation. In Figure 3.7b, the G major chord is interpretable as III/**e** on the way from **E** to **C**. In Figure 3.8b, the A minor chord can be understood as i/**a** on the way from **e** to **F** and the G major chord as iii/**e** (mirroring Figure 3.7b) en route from **G** to **E**.

Paths in scale-degree space

Figures 3.7 and 3.8, while a distinct improvement on the regional paths of Figures 3.4 and 3.5, fail to show the piece revolving around different forms of the mediant. There are four possible mediant harmonies: g♯ minor and G major, directly available from **E** and **e**, respectively; and G♯ major and g minor, accessed from the intermediate locations of **g♯** and **G**, respectively. The piece exploits all four possibilities: the first chromatic event is a G chord (bar 5); the climax resolves to I/**G♯**(**A♭**), followed by a transitional g♯ chord (bar 8); and the stepwise regional pro-

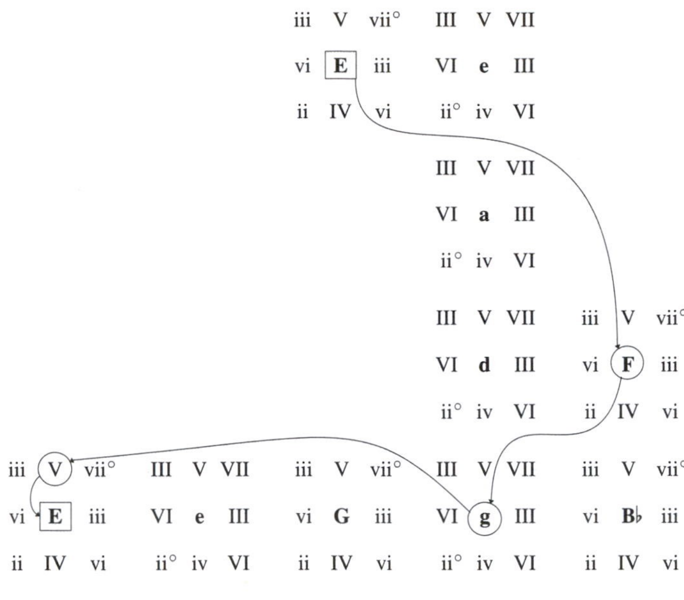

b) Prolongational level *c*

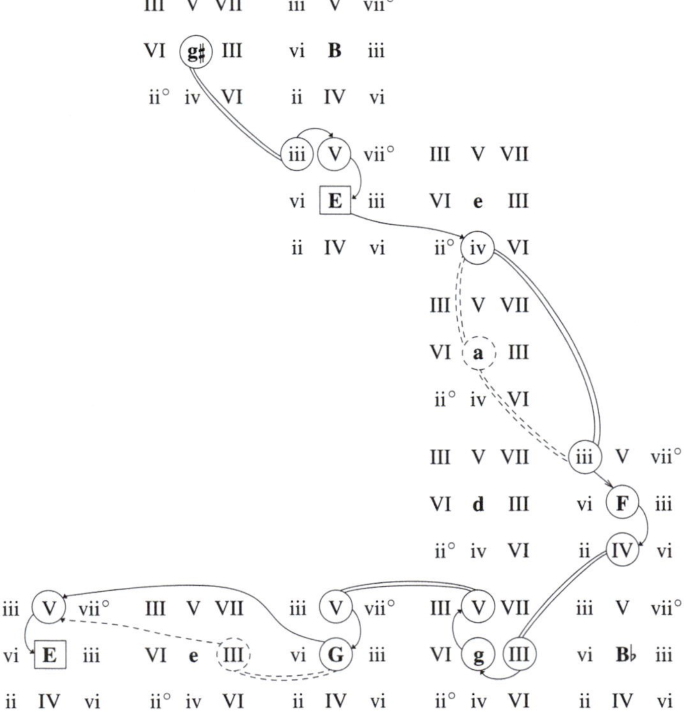

b) Prolongational level *d*

FIGURE 3.8 Chordal/regional representation of paths from the end of the second phrase through the third phrase of the E major Prelude.

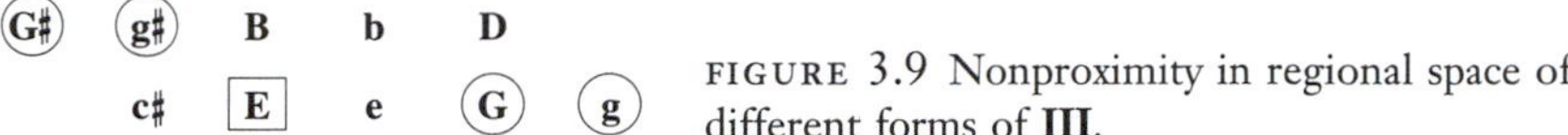

FIGURE 3.9 Nonproximity in regional space of different forms of **III**.

gression of the third phrase reaches **g-G** (bar 11) before the final resolution (this feature is discussed by Aldwell and Schachter). However, as can be seen in Figure 3.9, regional space splits the four mediant regions into two clusters, **G♯-g♯** and **G-g**. Should these clusters clump together to reflect the generalization that they are all forms of the abstraction we call the mediant? Is another axis needed to accomplish this?

There is a better solution. Figure 3.10 brings out a correspondence discussed in "The Regional Level" in chapter 2 between the chordal and regional spaces, a result of the generation of both spaces by fifths and thirds axes. Vertically and horizontally, parallel major/minor regions combine to form the same ordering as at the chordal level: iii moves vertically down to vi and ii, just as **III-iii** do to **VI-vi** and **II-ii**; iii moves horizontally to V and vii°, just as **III-iii** do to **V-v** and **♭VII-♭vii**; and so on. On the basis of this relation, the arrows in the figure signify an optional mapping of regional onto chordal space. All chromatic harmonies, including the various mediant structures, are diatonicized in the process. (This idea is implicit in Roman-numeral notation, which assigns a diatonic scale degree to harmonic roots, often including chromatically altered contexts such as ♭VI or ♯IV.) However, since a scale degree is an abstraction rather than a specific pitch configuration, Figure 3.11 depicts scale-degree space by Arabic numerals with carets rather than by Roman numerals, which retain specific chordal associations. Because the space is so repetitive, it will be useful to trace paths through adjacent steps on the chart representation. The dashed square encloses the part of the space that corresponds to the chordal core in Figure 3.10.

Figures 3.12–14 give scale-degree paths for the Prelude at levels that agree with levels in the prolongational analysis in Figure 3.2 and with the chordal/regional paths presented earlier. The first phrase in Figure 3.12a moves from I to V and loops around the V. In Figure 3.12b the phrase is drawn out twice by moves from V to VI, sidestepping I before settling on V.

Most of the musical interest of the second and third phrases is ironed out at the level of abstraction given in Figures 3.13 and 3.14. But that the scale-degree

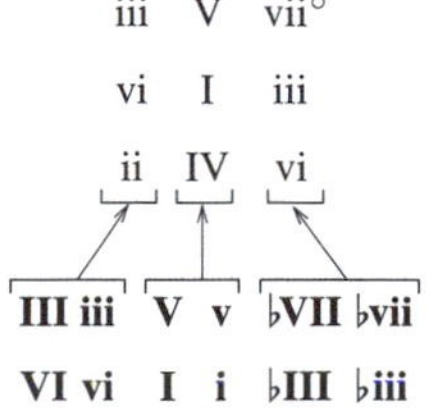

FIGURE 3.10 Correspondence between the chordal and regional spaces.

$\hat{3}$	$\hat{5}$	$\hat{7}$	$\hat{2}$	$\hat{4}$	$\hat{6}$	$\hat{1}$
$\hat{6}$	$\hat{1}$	$\hat{3}$	$\hat{5}$	$\hat{7}$	$\hat{2}$	$\hat{4}$
$\hat{2}$	$\hat{4}$	$\hat{6}$	$\hat{1}$	$\hat{3}$	$\hat{5}$	$\hat{7}$
$\hat{5}$	$\hat{7}$	$\hat{2}$	$\hat{4}$	$\hat{6}$	$\hat{1}$	$\hat{3}$
$\hat{1}$	$\hat{3}$	$\hat{5}$	$\hat{7}$	$\hat{2}$	$\hat{4}$	$\hat{6}$

FIGURE 3.11 Scale-degree space.

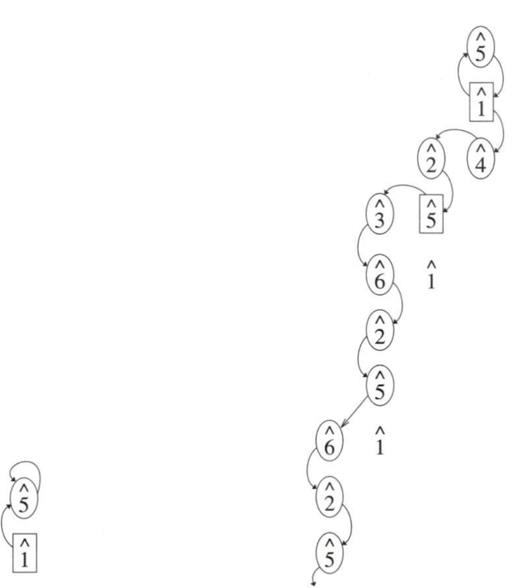

a) Prolongational levels *a–b* b) Prolongational levels *c–e*

FIGURE 3.12 Scale-degree representation of paths in the first phrase of the E major Prelude.

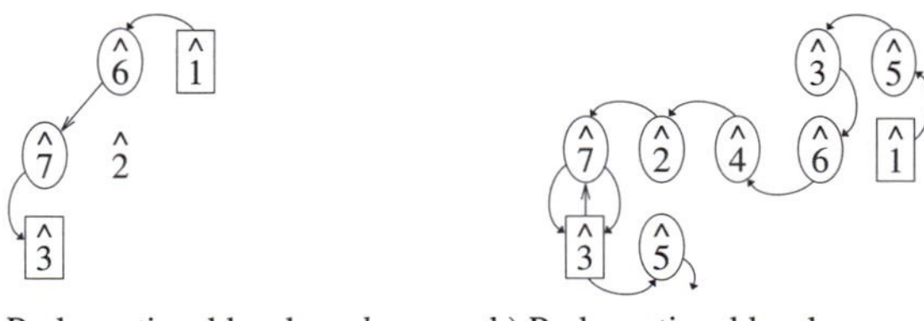

a) Prolongational levels *a–b* b) Prolongational levels *c–e*

FIGURE 3.13 Scale-degree representation of paths in the second phrase of the E major Prelude.

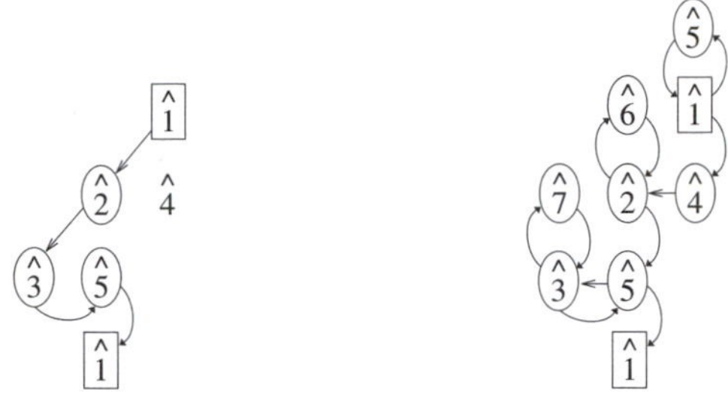

a) Prolongational level *c* b) Prolongational levels *d–e*

FIGURE 3.14 Scale-degree representation of paths in the third phrase of the E major Prelude.

representation has intuitive validity is suggested by Figure 3.15, which recomposes the second and third phrases (simplifying the figuration) with all but a few local chromaticisms taken out. (Purists can realize a full diatonic version by ignoring the remaining accidentals.) There is now one mediant harmony. Another telling detail in the unmodified version concerns the A major chord at the downbeat of bar 7, treated as an incidental consequence of the voice crossings in bars 6–7. There is also a sense in which this event shines through from the diatonic substratum that otherwise has been painted over at the chromatic surface. Figure 3.15 shows how smoothly the A major chord fits into the diatonic transform.

FIGURE 3.15 Diatonic realization of the second and third phrases of the E major Prelude.

Pc/chordal paths

By analogy with the treatment of chord sequences as paths in chordal/regional space, linear sequences of individual pitches can be modeled as paths in pc/chordal space. In this representation, each pitch is marked by its location in a particular configuration of the basic space, and successive basic spaces are arrayed according to their positions in chordal/regional space (as in Figure 2.30). A short melodic passage in a single region will illustrate. (At this level of detail, a longer modulatory passage would not fit on a page; the principle does not change.) Figure 3.16 represents paths in pc/chordal space for the melody of the first two bars of the E major Prelude (as in chapter 2, C is always set to 0). Again paths are traced through groupings of prolongational levels taken from Figure 3.2, first at a reduced level, then through the surface sequence. The topmost position of a given pc is the one designated in a particular configuration of the basic space, on the assumption that an event is understood in its most stable available position. Figure 3.16a shows B going to D♯ over the framing I–V progression. (Note that the I chord, being tonic, is shown in boldface, just as in the chordal/regional representation.) In Figure 3.16b, as in the scale-degree representations, the chordal core is spread out as a chart to bring out the stepwise motion from ii to V. The B and the C♯ change location in the space as they are harmonically reinterpreted. The D♯ on the second beat of bar 2 is treated as an anticipation, showing how diatonic nonchordal pcs are rendered at the scalar level (chromatic nonchordal pcs would be represented at the chromatic level).

Pc distances can be misleading in this representation, not only because it must squeeze into two dimensions but also because each configuration of the basic space faces northward. One could imagine a multidimensional realization in which pc cones revolve contextually, their tips pointing toward adjacent events in order to minimize distances.

For these two bars it would be much easier to write "$I^{\hat{5}} \rightarrow V^{\hat{7}}$" and then "$I^{\hat{5}} \rightarrow V^{\hat{5}} \rightarrow I^{\hat{5}} \rightarrow IV^{\hat{6}} \rightarrow ii^{\hat{6}} \rightarrow V^{\hat{7}}$," perhaps in conjunction with the prolongational slur notation. Are paths in pc/chordal space worth the price in notational complexity? The answer is yes, in precisely this sense: the model integrates lines into the overall spatial framework so that distances at all levels are characterized in a principled way. The model places a pc within the space of a chord, which has a location in a region, which has a position in relation to other regions. As a piece unfolds at various prolongational levels, each pc in a line has an exact address.

Yet it must be acknowledged that the structure of melodic lines can also transcend their harmonic instantiations. The E major Prelude is interesting in this regard. Figure 3.17 repeats from levels c–d in Figure 3.2 the prolongational slurs for the melody but places stems on the structural notes of the tonic triad, rather than on prolongationally superordinate pitches, in order to show how the pitches of the triad guide the melodic shape. The line of the first phrase rises diatonically from $\hat{5}$ to $\hat{8}$ and falls back; its linear thrust is present regardless of the particular chords. A similar process occurs in the second phrase with heightened intensity. The melody moves more quickly by step from $\hat{5}$ to $\hat{8}$ (= $\hat{1}$) over modulating

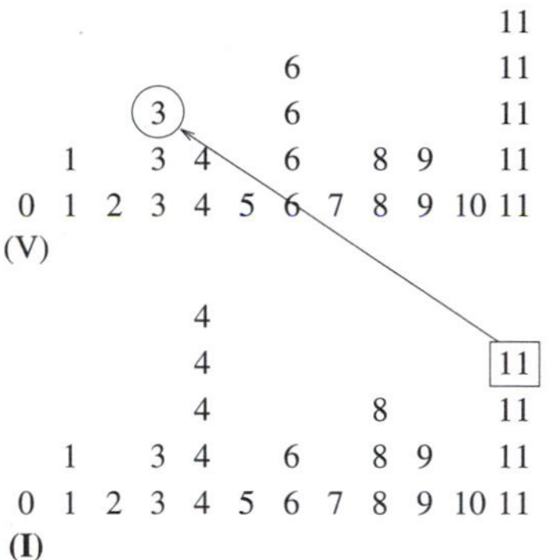

a) Prolongational levels *a–b*

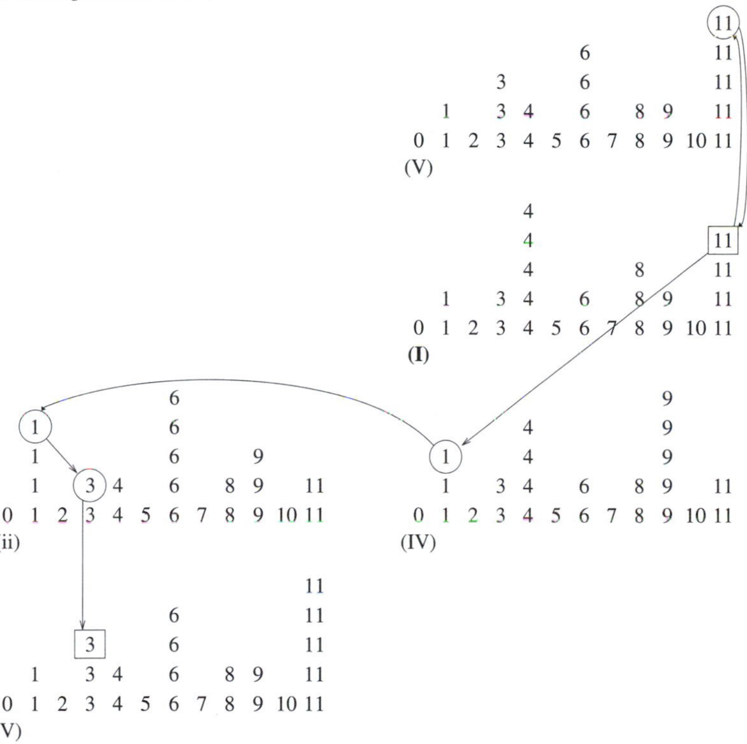

b) Prolongational levels *c–e*

FIGURE 3.16 Pc/chordal representation of paths in bars 1–2 of the E major Prelude.

harmonies and from there to $\hat{3}$ (Ab = G♯) over a climatic **A♭**$^{6}_{4}$. Linear completion is arrested because the harmony undercuts the goal tones, E and G♯. The third phrase retraces more slowly a stepwise ascent from $\hat{5}$, this time resolving on $\hat{8}$ with full tonic support. The power of the final arrival on $\hat{8}$ results not only from its rhythmic position at the end of a four-bar phrase but also from the frustrated

FIGURE 3.17 A combination of the prolongational structure of the melody of the E major Prelude, shown by the slurs, and the melody's salient arpeggiation of the tonic triad, represented by the stemmed notes.

trajectories of the first two phrases. The $\hat{8}$ of the first phrase and, even more, the $\hat{3}$ of the second are salient but not stable; the final $\hat{8}$ is both salient and stable.

The pitch-space theory does not derive the superior status of the stemmed notes in Figure 3.17 because it interprets melodic pitches within their harmonic contexts. It shows the high E in the first phrase to be a neighbor to D♯ and the high A♭ in the second phrase to be tonally unstable. The stemmed notes provide an alternative hierarchy not incorporated in the theory presented here, a framework for the melody that arises by reference to the global tonic and supported by contour salience.

The spatial models and paths discussed in this section can be summarized as follows. Regional paths trace modulational patterns but do not connect events within regions. Chordal/regional space rectifies this shortcoming and, tied to prolongational levels, provides a good account of chord progressions in pitch space. Scale-degree space illuminates the diatonic substratum that underlies much chromatic music. Pc/chordal paths model the extent to which we hear lines in the context of chord progressions.

REGIONAL PROLONGATIONS

The score of Chopin's E minor Prelude appears in Figure 3.18, its event analysis in Figure 3.19. As a shortcut, the latter begins, except for the registrally complex bars 15–18, at the two-bar level (level d) in the time-span derivation. Prolongational levels e–f give some linear shape to the chromatically descending harmonies, prolongational levels c–d reveal their stepwise diatonic underpinnings, and prolongational levels a–b display the skeleton of the antecedent–consequent period that constitutes the form of the piece. (This Prelude causes difficulties for Schenkerians in search of a properly descending $\hat{5}$-*Urlinie*. Forte and Gilbert [1982] propose an "interruption" at $\hat{4}$ rather than $\hat{2}$. Schachter [1995] treats the *Urlinie* descent as not interrupted and transfers it to the tenor voice across phrases. These alternatives are discussed in Justin London and R. Rodman [1998], whose preferred reading, which the analysis in Figure 3.19 somewhat resembles, forsakes a full *Urlinie* descent in favor of retaining features of the melodic surface at underlying levels. Their approach relates to the discussion of schematic tension in "Functions and Schemas" in chapter 5.)

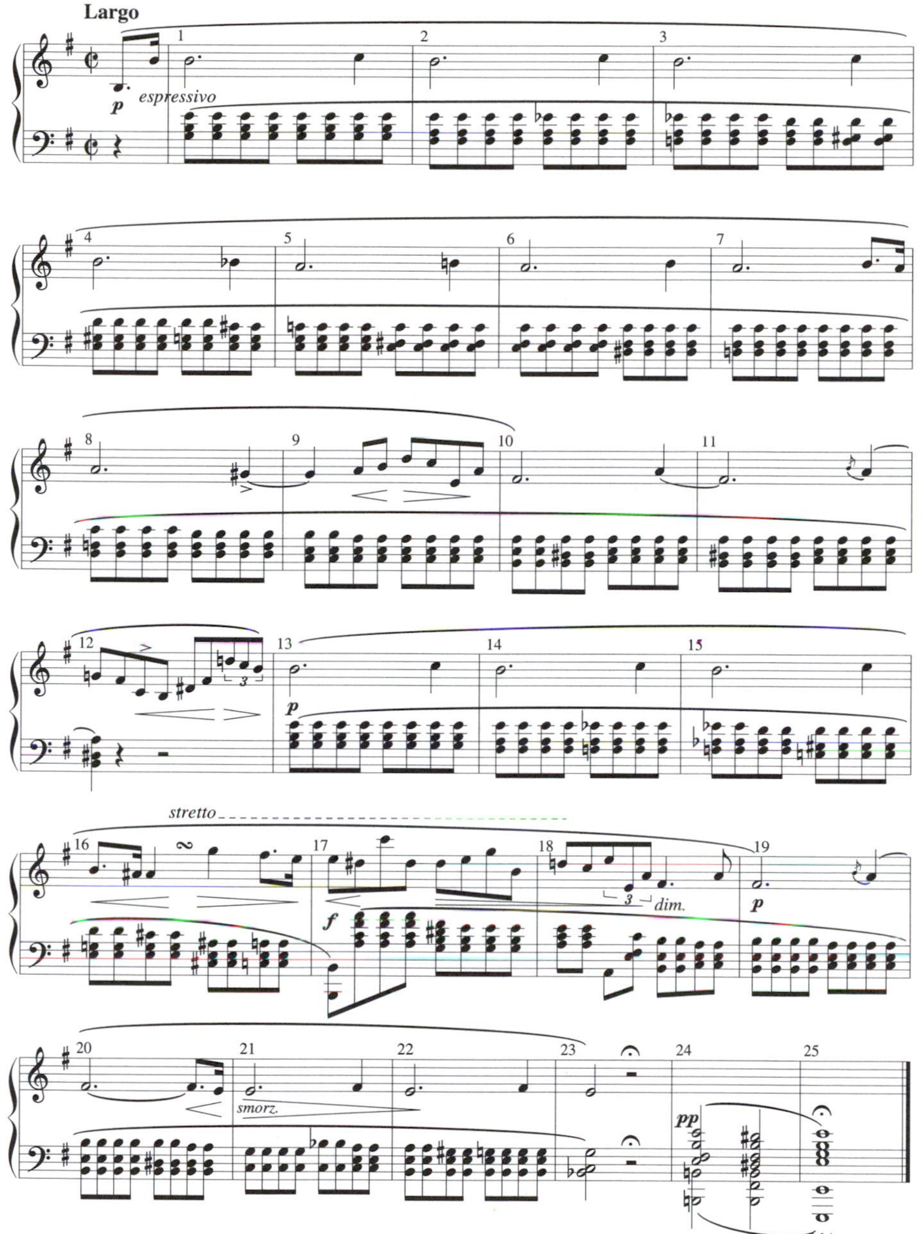

FIGURE 3.18 Chopin's E minor Prelude.

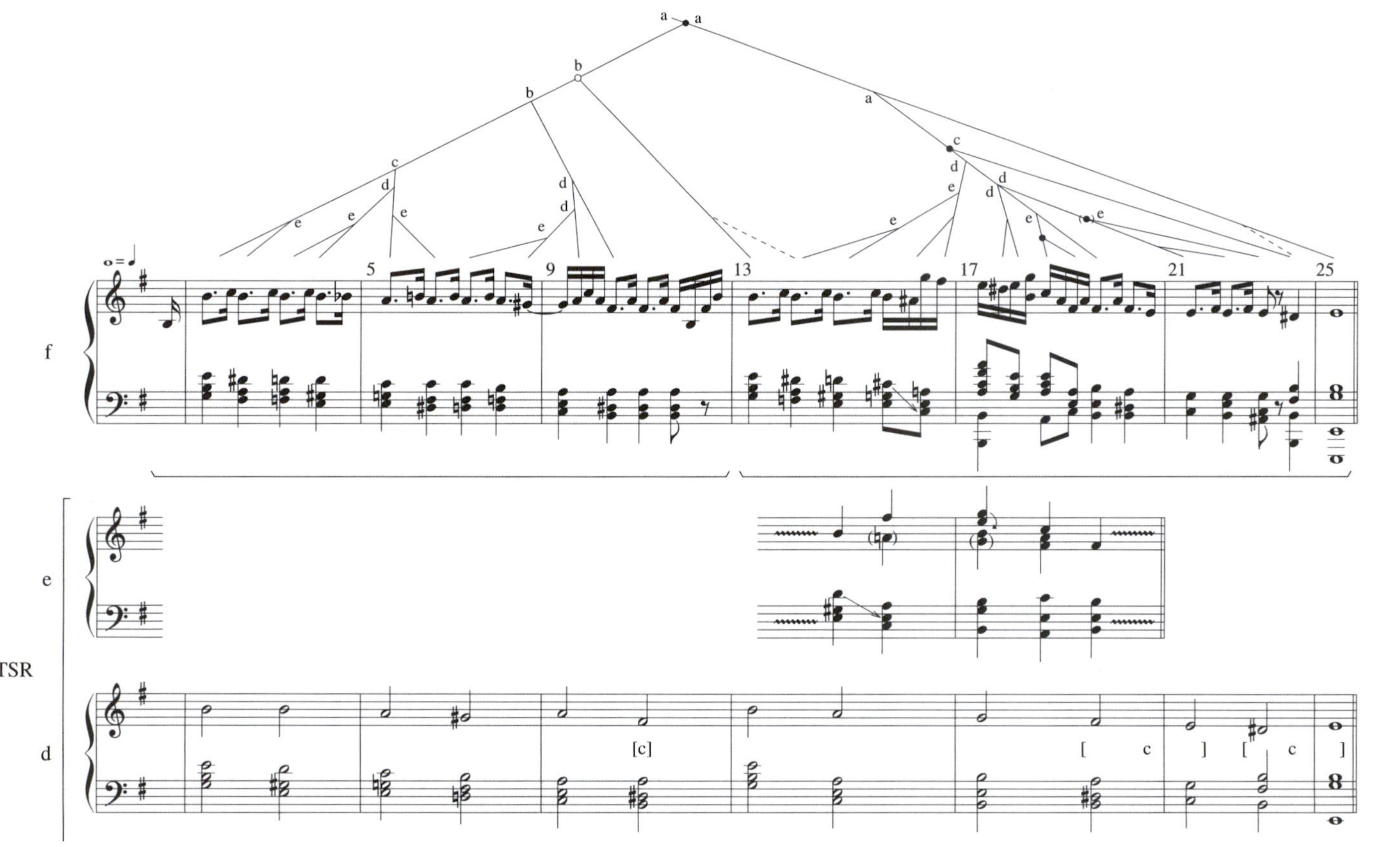

f
e
TSR
d
5
9
13
17
21
25
[c]
[c] [c]

FIGURE 3.19 Reductional analysis of the E minor Prelude.

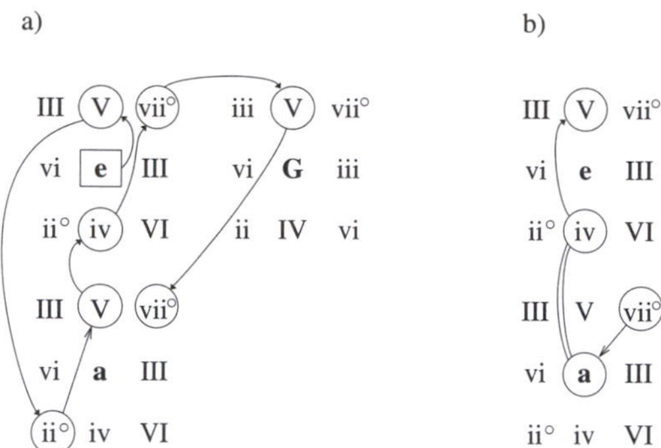

FIGURE 3.20 Pitch-space journey in the first phrase of the E minor Prelude: (a) bars 1–8; (b) bars 8–12.

Although the chords are products of voice leading, they are also objects that move through pitch space. Consider the first phrase (bars 1–12) from this perspective. Figure 3.20a gives the journey, tracing the event sequence at prolongational level f up to bar 8, just before the dominant preparation emerges. The music passes through the regions of **iv, i**, and **III** (bars 3–4, 5–6, and 7, respectively) without arriving on their tonics. Not to capture these regional references would be to miss an important part of the phrase's meaning. In these measures the melody freezes and the harmonies hover; much is implied, but nothing is fulfilled. Figure 3.20b resumes and completes the phrase (bars 8–12) at the moment when the harmony disambiguates and the melody opens up.

This passage provides an embryonic instance of a technique that is pervasive in later composers such as Wagner and Debussy. Analytic discussions of Wagner's harmony (for example, Bailey 1977; Lewin 1984; and McCreless 1982) habitually refer to key areas as of primary importance, regardless of the presence or absence of tonic resolution. Indeed, regions in chromatic music often acquire a vividness far beyond the individual events and linear connections that realize them. In a reduction of a Classical tonal passage, the remaining event at an underlying level is normally the tonic to which the subordinate events refer; thus the reduction reflects the frame of reference. But an event reduction can be misleading in cases where, at various structural levels, no tonic event is available to emerge as superordinate.

These considerations call for a level of analysis that assigns hierarchical structure directly to regions, beyond the level of the pitch event. A regional prolongational analysis can be constructed from the regions traversed in the chordal/ regional representation at successive prolongational levels. These sequences of regions become the units of reductional analysis. The derivation proceeds in the same way as event reduction, including time-span reduction and use of the interaction principle; that is, rhythmic factors must be taken into account, and connections are determined by the shortest regional path.

To add distinctions to the notation, let whole note heads refer to regions whose tonics are stated and black note heads to regions whose tonics are not stated. Note heads in parentheses indicate regions that are briefly borrowed from. Strong prolongations obtain between whole notes, leaving weak prolongations for connections that involve implied tonics. Slurs accord with branchings, with dashed slurs reserved for strong prolongations.

Figure 3.21 provides regional prolongational analyses for the two Chopin Preludes; their trees derive level by level from their event prolongational analyses (Figures 3.2 and 3.19). The leaves—that is, the objects at the ends of branches—in Figure 3.21a, which stand for regions, match those of Figure 3.2, which stand for events, reflecting that in this piece the chief regions have local tonic realization. The underlying chromaticism of the second and third phrases is emphasized by the chromatic disposition of regions in Figure 3.21a. The analysis of the E minor Prelude in Figure 3.21b, in contrast, diverges from its event prolongational structure in Figure 3.19, reflecting the absence of resolution on intermediate tonics. The regions are diatonically related, revealing that not far beneath the chromatic surface this Prelude's tonal structure is diatonic.

Because the sequences of regions in Figure 3.21 variously duplicate the regional paths of Figures 3.4–6 and the chordal/regional paths of Figures 3.7–8 and 3.20, one might argue that regional prolongational reduction is unnecessary. This kind of analysis, however, does not just list multileveled sequences of regions. It also gives them their own prolongational connections and displays their hierarchical relationships directly rather than through an indirect comparison of event paths at different levels of detail. Regional prolongations are satisfying in another way as well. The GTTM conception of the pitch event—any discretely sounding pitch or vertical combination of pitches—embraces only two of the three strata of pitch space, those of the pitch and of the chord. The notion of regional prolongational analysis includes the third stratum, the region, completing a correspondence between the levels of pitch space and the objects of reduction.

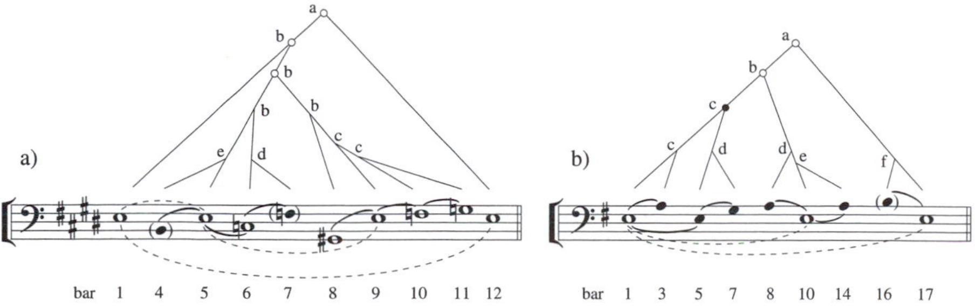

FIGURE 3.21 Regional prolongational analyses: (a) the E major Prelude; (b) the E minor Prelude.

PARALLEL MIXTURE

Collapsing regional space

In regional space adjacent regions are all equidistant. While this arrangement presumably causes no difficulties for the fifths axis, it might raise questions for the thirds axis. For eighteenth-century music, relative major–minor relations seem closer than parallel ones. Bach moves with ease from **I** to **vi** and from **i** to **III** but rarely from **I** to **i** or from **i** to **I** (discounting the Picardy third, which is a surface coloring rather than a regional change). From Bach to Wagner one can trace an evolution. Haydn in his minor-mode sonata movements typically retains the expository shift to the major mode for the second-theme group in the recapitulation, thereby ending the movement in major. Local parallel borrowings become increasingly common in Mozart and Beethoven. For Schubert, parallel major-minor mixture becomes a stylistic signature, as in his G major Quartet or C major Quintet. This tendency continues in Chopin and Berlioz. By mature Wagner, it is often pointless to attempt to decide whether a passage is in the major or in its parallel minor mode because of the constant shifts and borrowings between them. The practice of nineteenth-century chromaticism reaches the opposite pole in this respect from the practice of the eighteenth century.

How is the development to be treated theoretically? Imagine that regional space folds on the creases in Figure 3.22. Let horizontally adjacent pairs of regions be more closely related if they lie between the creases than if they do not. In Figure 3.22a, **f♯-A, a-C**, and **c-E♭** fall between the creases, reflecting eighteenth-century practice, and in Figure 3.22b, **A-a, C-c**, and **E♭-e♭** fall between the creases, reflecting much nineteenth-century practice. Alternatively, more closely related horizontal regions can be placed in closer proximity. Figure 3.23a does this for Figure 3.22b: parallel regions clump together, mirroring the extensive use of parallel mixture but nevertheless identifying parallel modes as separate structures. This space suits Schubertian practice. If mixture is complete, the space further collapses into Figure 3.23b, in which a given region designates not its major or minor version but a merged combination of the two. While the vertical axis continues to exhibit the circle of fifths, the horizontal axis directly expresses the minor-third cycle and the major-third cycle emerges on the northwest–southeast diagonal. Figure 3.23b thus resembles the Riemann space shown in Figure 2.2b, if the latter is taken as representing regions rather than pitches and if one of its axes is rotated. The collapsed regional space in Figure 3.23b corresponds to the frequent practice of Wagner and later composers who employ a highly chromatic tonal style.

The original regional space, in which adjacent regions are equidistant in all directions, is the tonal prototype that most listeners internalize; but it can squeeze or stretch along the lines of Figure 3.22 to accommodate stylistic variants. The variant that fully combines parallel modes has had particular historical force and is worth exploring in its own right. Figure 3.23a represents an intermediate stage in which the ordering of regions has not changed but in which horizontal equi-

a)

d♯	F♯	f♯	A	a	C	c
g♯	B	b	D	d	F	f
c♯	E	e	G	g	B♭	b♭
f♯	A	a	C	c	E♭	e♭
b	D	d	F	f	A♭	a♭
e	G	g	B♭	b♭	D♭	d♭
a	C	c	E♭	e♭	G♭	g♭

b)

d♯	F♯	f♯	A	a	C	c
g♯	B	b	D	d	F	f
c♯	E	e	G	g	B♭	b♭
f♯	A	a	C	c	E♭	e♭
b	D	d	F	f	A♭	a♭
e	G	g	B♭	b♭	D♭	d♭
a	C	c	E♭	e♭	G♭	g♭

FIGURE 3.22 Regional space with folds: (a) between relative major-minor regions; (b) between parallel major-minor regions.

distance is sacrificed. The end product of this tendency, Figure 3.23b, again achieves equidistance in all directions.

Untransformed regional space arises from the chord distance rule as a mapping from a referential tonic to other proximate tonics. How, then, do the structures in Figure 3.23 derive from the rule? One approach, suggested by a line of thinking in Werts (1983), is to expand the number of pcs at the diatonic level to include all the major and minor possibilities, thus creating a nondiatonic collection; on that basis to develop a basic space to which the chord distance rule applies; and from that to build a chordal/regional space that includes all the major-minor chordal possibilities. It might be hoped that interregional measurements would reflect the spatial distributions in Figure 3.23. Such an approach, however, seems not only impractical but also conceptually questionable. Just as the variants of the minor scale are inflections on the natural minor diatonic scale, so parallel mixture retains its diatonic origins in the abstraction of the scale degree. Figure 3.24a lists the scale degrees of the major mode, of the minor mode with variants on $\hat{7}$ and $\hat{2}$ ($\flat\hat{2}$ is common in chromatic music, often as an upper chromatic leading tone to the tonic), and finally of the "mixed mode," which combines the possibilities from the first two. Figure 3.24b illustrates the results for the mixed mode oriented to

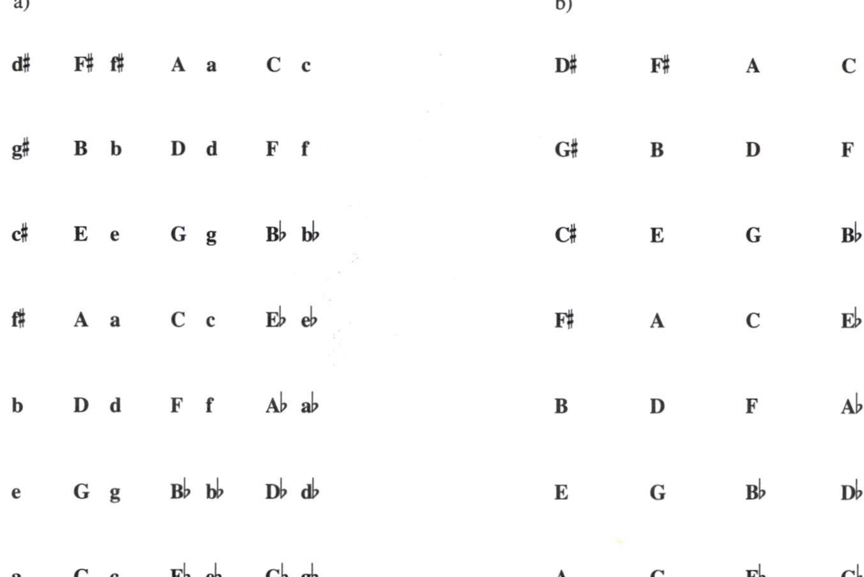

FIGURE 3.23 Spatial unification of parallel major-minor regions: (a) partial mixture of parallel regions; (b) complete mixture of parallel regions.

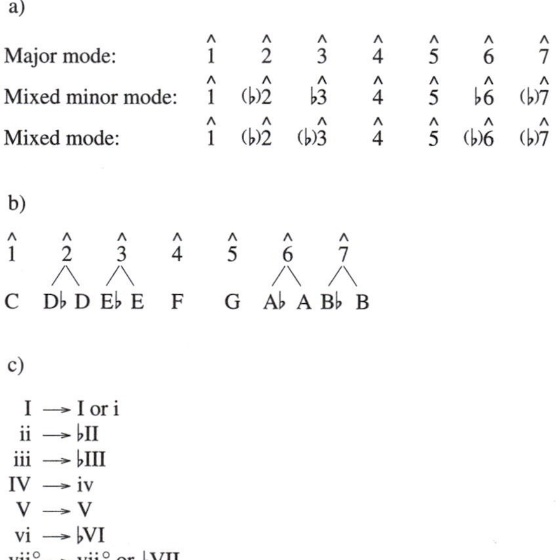

FIGURE 3.24 The mixed major-minor mode: (a) characteristic scale-degree inflections; (b) optional scale-degree inflections in **C**; (c) chordal mapping from the major to the mixed mode.

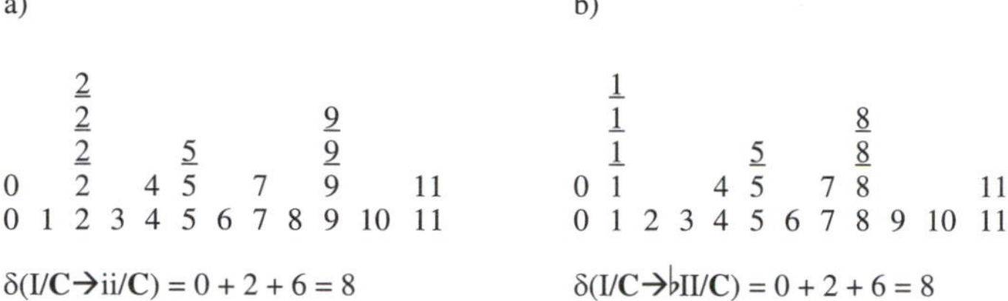

FIGURE 3.25 Equivalent distances for inflected chords.

C. Each branching from scale degree to pc represents an inflectional option. Figure 3.24c enumerates chords that typically occur on each scale degree, mapped for convenience from the major to the mixed mode. Through ♭$\hat{2}$, ♭$\hat{3}$, ♭$\hat{6}$, the mixed mode tends to convert minor triads in the major mode into major triads.

Once modal variants are viewed as optional realizations of abstract scale degrees, no change is required to derive chordal distances from a tonic. Figure 3.25 illustrates for ii and ♭II of **C**. Figure 3.25a is standard, but in Figure 3.25b the inflectional option of ♭$\hat{2}$ and ♭$\hat{6}$ is taken, with the result that these pcs at the diatonic level are not counted as noncommon in the *k* variable. Consequently, in the mixed mode ii and ♭II are equidistant from the tonic and by the same values (0 + 2 + 6). Such would be the case for any mixed-modal chord on any scale degree. This treatment is a generalization from the practice in chapter 2 for the minor mode, where V and vii° substitute for their natural-minor but uncharacteristic counterparts, v and ♭VII. Thus, as shown in Figure 3.26, the chordal/regional representations for major-mode **C**, minor-mode **c**, and mixed-mode **C** have the same geometry.

The argument does not yet justify the transformed regional spaces in Figure 3.23. Let us assume that distances on the fifths axis remain unchanged, since the way one region is treated carries over to its transposition a fifth higher or lower. The distance between relative major-minor tonics likewise remains unchanged, because the *i* and *k* variables in δ can continue in the major-mode option and the *j* variable must still equal 3. Therefore, as before, δ(I/**C**→i/**a**) = 0 + 3 + 4 = 7 (see Figure 2.20a). That leaves parallel regions for consideration. Here the *j* variable equals 0 no matter what; in the original calculation, δ(I/**C**→i/**c**) = 3 + 0 + 4 = 7 (see Figure 2.20b). If the mixed-modal inflectional options ♭$\hat{3}$, ♭$\hat{6}$, and ♭$\hat{7}$ are taken, the *i* and *k* variables also revert to 0, so δ(I/**C**→i/**c**) = 0 + 0 + 0 = 0. This is the situation modeled in Figure 3.23b. Figure 3.23a represents a non-

a)			b)			c)		
iii	V	vii°	III	V	vii°	♭III	V	vii°
vi	**C**	iii	VI	**c**	III	♭VI	**C**	♭III
ii	IV	vi	ii°	iv	VI	♭II	iv	♭VI

FIGURE 3.26 Modal representations of chordal/regional space: (a) the major mode; (b) the minor mode; (c) one possible realization of the mixed mode.

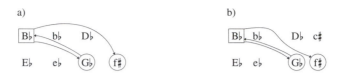

FIGURE 3.27 Modulation in bars 1–48 of Schubert's posthumous B♭ Sonata, I: (a) in standard regional space; (b) in partially mixed regional space.

derived transitional point between the untransformed and completely mixed states of regional space.

Two applications

Partially collapsed regional space might have little relevance at local levels yet play an important role in the larger organization of a piece. The first movement of Schubert's posthumous B♭ Sonata is a good example. The piece begins in **B♭**, goes to **G♭** (bar 20), and returns to a restatement of the opening theme in **B♭** (bar 36), after which it modulates to **f♯** (= **g♭**) (bar 48) to launch the second theme group. If modeled in untransformed regional space, the progression takes the path in Figure 3.27a, which leaps from **B♭** to **G♭** and back, and then jumps even further, from **B♭** to **g♭**. But the experience of this music is not of such regional discontinuity. There is little sense, for example, that **b♭** is silently traversed in order to reach **G♭**. The transformed space in Figure 3.27b allows these regional shifts to be modeled by diagonal steps between pairs of major-minor regions. At the same time, **G♭** and **f♯** retain their individual identity and ought not to be collapsed completely.

The rest of the exposition and development sustain the regional pattern of Figure 3.27b. Leaving aside the reductional analysis, Figure 3.28 displays the major regional moves up to the beginning of the recapitulation. **B♭** goes to **f♯**, as just discussed; the second theme then moves to its relative major, I/**A** (bar 58), which then prolongs as V/**d**. (Incidentally, because **f♯** is really **g♭**, **g♭**'s relative major is really **B𝄫**. Beyond its local behavior, this music depends not on diatonicism but on enharmonic equivalence. It is therefore not surprising that the **B♭** at the recapitulation in Figure 3.28 is in a different location than the **B♭** at the beginning.)

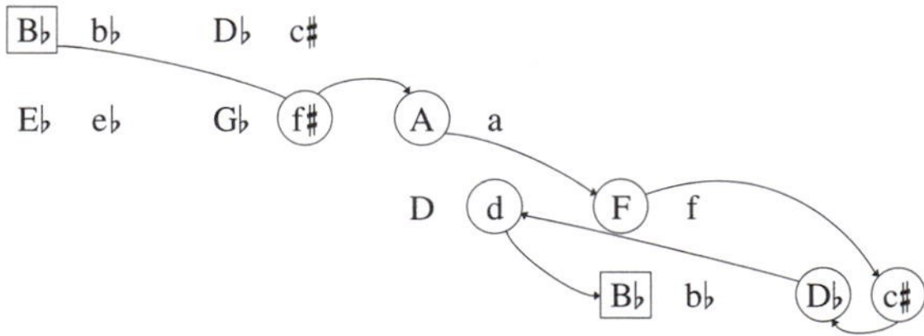

FIGURE 3.28 Global regional path for the exposition and development of the Schubert B♭ Sonata.

After a number of local regional digressions the exposition settles in **F** (bar 80). Thus the overall pattern for the exposition forms a pair of major-third regional motions, **B♭** to **f♯** and **A** to **F**. The development begins with a sudden shift from **F** to **c♯** (= **d♭**) (bar 117), in parallel to **B♭-f♯** in the exposition. The development takes a wild pitch-space journey, but its structural points are clear. Texturally it divides into two sections, demarcated by a strong arrival on **D♭** (bar 149). The second section arrives on **d** (bar 173) before returning to **B♭** for the recapitulation (bar 216). The frame for the development is again one of interlocking third-related regions, **F** to **c♯** (= **D♭**) and **d** to **B♭**. The graph reveals this pattern by its recurrent paths on the northwest–southeast diagonal. Such patterns have a greater impact in listening to this movement than do large-scale linear connections. (See Cohn [1999] for a related discussion of this movement within the neo-Riemannian framework.)

The opening phrases of the Transfiguration music (the *Liebestod*) from Wagner's *Tristan und Isolde* are best modeled not by partial but by complete mixture of parallel regions. To keep a self-contained frame, Figure 3.29 provides the passage in its Act II incarnation, where the music stays in **A♭**, rather than in its return at the end of Act III, where it modulates to **B**. Figure 3.30 reduces Figure 3.29 to one event per bar, notated in diminished durational values to bring out the regular hypermeter. It will be convenient to refer to the hyperbar numbers in Figure 3.30.

Figure 3.31a illustrates how convoluted the pitch-space journey would be if the first bar (and, by parallelism, succeeding bars) were modeled in untransformed chordal/regional space. More convincing is the path in mixed chordal/regional space shown in Figure 3.31b, with the prolongational structure given above. ♭III/**A♭** (= ♭VI/**E♭**) is now easily available, so there is no need to move fictitiously to **a♭** and **e♭**. In bars 2–3, this unit sequences up the minor-third cycle until **A♭** is again reached. Figure 3.32 picks up the path from this point until the end of the phrase. After the pattern-breaking move to **G♭** in bar 4, the music returns on a partial semitone cycle, **G♭** to **G** to **A♭** (with a momentary passage through **E♭** en route). The overall modulatory design of the entire passage emerges transparently in the regional representation in Figure 3.33.

The minor-third transpositional cycle pervades much of *Tristan*, but why does the semitone cycle appear in this passage? Here we must turn to Act III, most of which revolves around **f**, the home of the English horn lament. Near the end, as King Marke cries his last woe, the strings quietly interrupt three times, intoning the first bar of the Transfiguration, first in **F**, then **G♭**, then **G**. Isolde, who has swooned over Tristan's body, is rising from the despair of **f**, in a composing out of the chromatically rising *Sehnsucht* (yearning) motive (bars 2–3 of the Act I Prelude), to begin the Transfiguration in **A♭**. The semitonal regional ascent in this part of the Transfiguration recaptures this moment as she reaches for a high A♭ supported by an A♭ tonic harmony. The palpable feeling of climactic rise in the phrase leading up to this arrival (the equivalent of bars 15–21 in Figure 3.29) is a consequence not just of surface features (tremolo and crescendo) but of this underlying regional ascent. Having achieved high $\hat{8}$/**A♭**, in the region of love, she can enter **B**, the polar opposite of **f** and the region of spiritual ecstasy.

FIGURE 3.29 Opening phrases of the Transfiguration music from *Tristan* (version in Act II).

FIGURE 3.29 (Continued)

FIGURE 3.30 Time-span reduction of Figure 3.29.

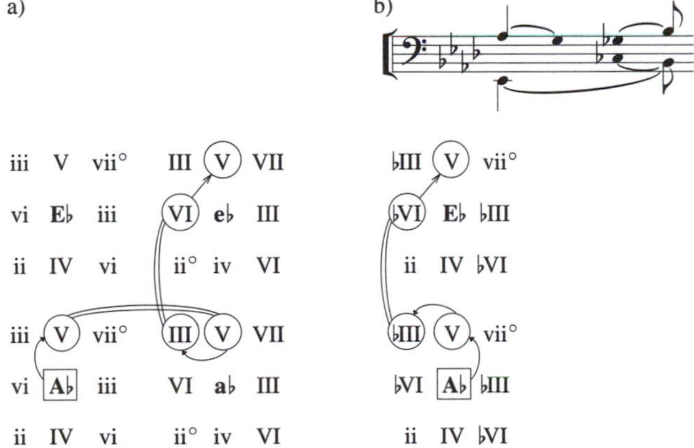

FIGURE 3.31 Chordal/regional representations for bar 1 of Figure 3.30: (a) in untransformed space; (b) in mixed space.

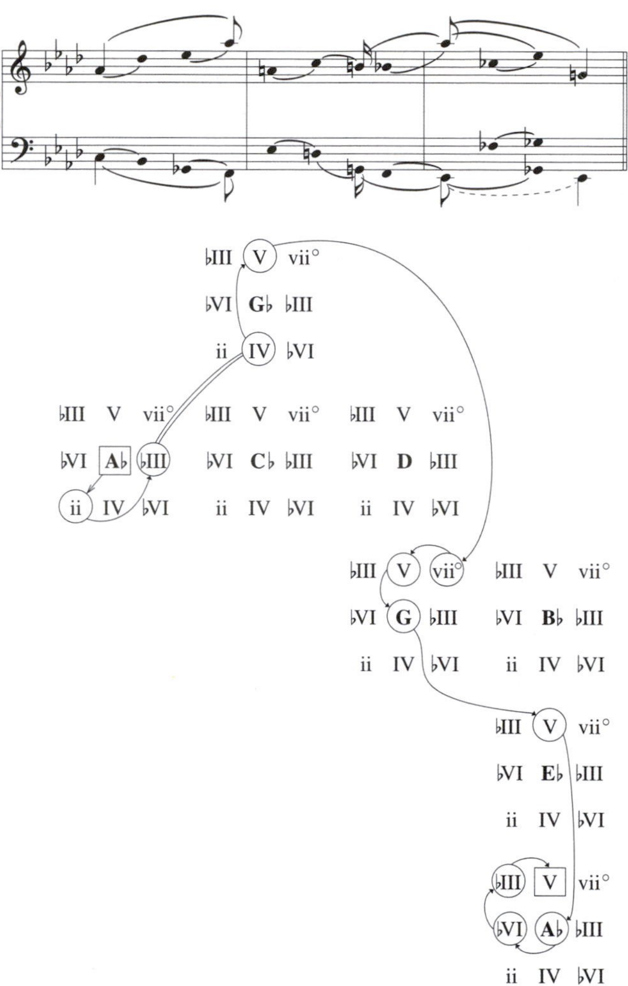

FIGURE 3.32 Chordal/regional representation for bars 3–6 of Figure 3.30.

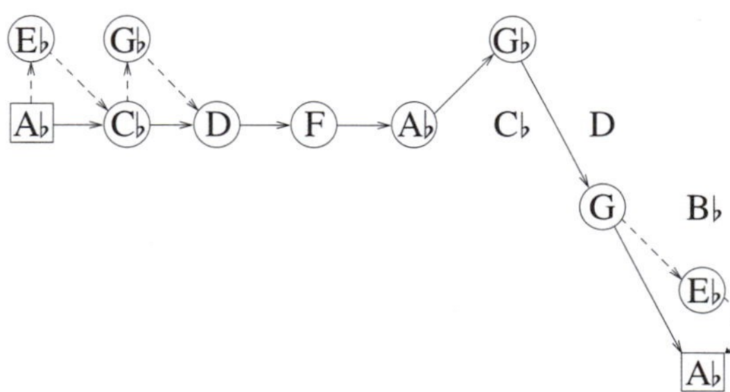

FIGURE 3.33 Regional path of the Transfiguration music (Figure 3.30) in collapsed regional space.

Figure 3.34 provides the reductional backdrop to the path analyses in Figures 3.31–33. A regional prolongational analysis is added at the bottom. As would be expected in music as intricately chromatic as this, there are viable analytic alternatives. One of these is shown in prolongational levels d–e by the dashed branch and parenthetical dashed slurs that connect the high A♭ and low F at the end of bar 4 to A♭ and E♭ on the downbeat of bar 6. Of particular interest, however, are the $^6_4$ chords that saturate the passage. Although they appear to resolve immediately to their dominants, they also behave as (local) tonics. As a result, the climactic arrival on the downbeat of bar 6 attaches by the interaction principle as a prolongation of the previous tonic chords, producing an oddly shaped tree. The alternative, to treat the A♭$^6_4$ arrival as a standard cadential embellishment, is offered by dashed branches and parenthetical slurs. When the passage returns at the end of Act III, the cadential V^7/**A♭** elides in favor of the modulation to I$^6_4$/**B**, strengthening by its absence the interpretation of the climactic A♭$^6_4$ as a tonic prolongation.

NARRATIVE PATHS

Parsifal's journey to redemption

Some of the remarks on the Transfiguration music have intimated that pitch-space paths can embody expressive meaning, at least in a dramatic context. This section explores this potential for Wagner's *Parsifal*, which builds in a more consistent way on the regional patterns in *Tristan*. *Parsifal* is about journeys, physical and spiritual, so it should not be surprising if trajectories in tonal space have symbolic significance, functioning as superleitmotives, so to speak, that govern small and large stretches of musical progression.

Let me reverse the east–west directions on the x axis of the untransformed regional chart—which, except here, follows Schoenberg's orientation—so as to reflect Weber's orientation. As remarked in "The Regional Level" in chapter 2, from a formal and psychological point of view the orientation is immaterial. The internal evidence of *Parsifal* speaks for the Weber space in its original distribution, arranged for diatonic contexts as in Figure 3.35a, with **A♭** at the midpoint of each edge of the chart and **D** in the middle. For chromatic contexts I employ its partially collapsed variant in Figure 3.35b; completely collapsed space is less apposite here because in *Parsifal* parallel regions symbolize expressive polarities. Chordal space takes the same orientation as regional space.

The ensuing discussion justifies the overall geography for chordal and regional spaces given in the narrative map of Figure 3.36: direct ascent, or motion upward by fifths, points toward heaven; direct descent, or motion downward by fifths, points toward the tangible world; motion by thirds to the right (=*das Recht*) points toward Christian truth (as conceived by Wagner); motion by thirds to the left (=*sinistra*) points toward Christian sin (as conceived by Wagner). These meanings are fluid: "heaven" might be replaced by "salvation," "the tangible world" by "earth," "truth" by "good," "sin" by "evil." Diagonal trajectories blend features of the directions they combine: a northeast trajectory reaches for redemption, while a southwest trajectory manifests sin in the world.

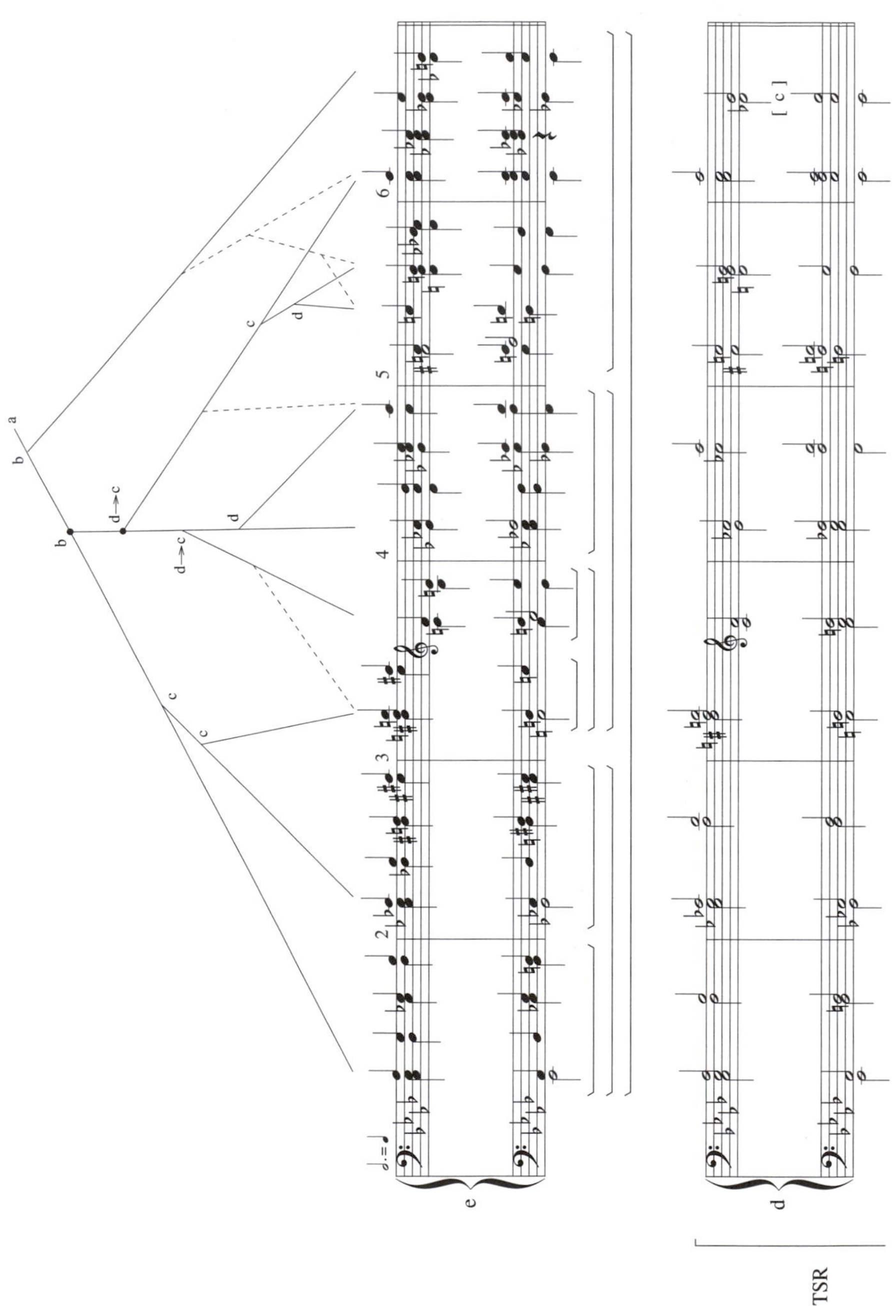

a
b
b
d→c
d→c
c
c
c
d
d
e
d
[c]
TSR

FIGURE 3.34 Reductional analysis of the Transfiguration music.

a)

D	b	B	g♯	A♭	f	F	d	D
G	e	E	c♯	D♭	b♭	B♭	g	G
C	a	A	f♯	F♯	e♭	E♭	c	C
F	d	D	b	B	g♯	A♭	f	F
B♭	g	G	e	E	c♯	D♭	b♭	B♭
E♭	c	C	a	A	f♯	F♯	e♭	E♭
A♭	f	F	d	D	b	B	g♯	A♭
D♭	b♭	B♭	g	G	e	E	c♯	D♭
G♭	e♭	E♭	c	C	a	A	f♯	G♭
B	g♯	A♭	f	F	d	D	b	B
E	c♯	D♭	b♭	B♭	g	G	e	E
A	f♯	F♯	eb	E♭	c	C	a	A
D	b	B	g♯	A♭	f	F	d	D

FIGURE 3.35 Regional space reoriented for *Parsifal*: (a) untransformed space; (b) partially collapsed space.

b)

D	b	B	g♯	Ab	f	F	d	D
G	e	E	c♯	D♭	b♭	B♭	g	G
C	a	A	f♯	F♯	e♭	E♭	c	C
F	d	D	b	B	g♯	A♭	f	F
B♭	g	G	e	E	c♯	D♭	b♭	B♭
E♭	c	C	a	A	f♯	F♯	e♭	E♭
A♭	f	F	d	D	b	B	g♯	Ab
D♭	b♭	B♭	g	G	e	E	c♯	D♭
G♭	e♭	E♭	c	C	a	A	f♯	F♯
B	g♯	A♭	f	F	d	D	b	B
E	c♯	D♭	b♭	B♭	g	G	e	E
A	f♯	F♯	e♭	E♭	c	C	a	A
D	b	B	g♯	A♭	f	F	d	D

FIGURE 3.35 (Continued)

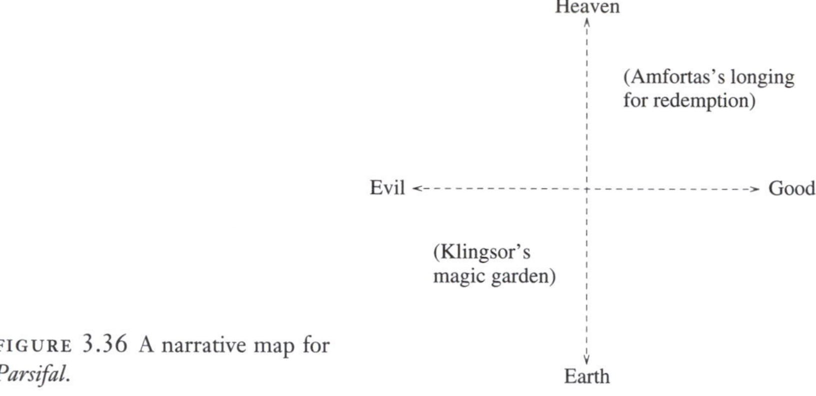

FIGURE 3.36 A narrative map for *Parsifal.*

Figure 3.37 provides the Communion (*Liebesmahl*) theme at the beginning of the Prelude to Act I. Beneath the music are its implied harmonies (realized in the repeat in bars 9–14), its grouping structure, and its prolongational analysis. The Wound and Spear motives form the central subgroups of the theme. Of the outer subgroups, the first expresses the Mystery of the ritual that surrounds the grail, and the last takes a turn toward Sorrow, particularly in the variation it takes in the parallel statement of the Communion theme in **c** (bars 20–25) and related passages. (These and all other names are mere labels that stand for complex semantic and emotive associations that vary in context.) Of particular interest is the tonal ambiguity at the end of bar 2. The line has risen on offbeats to span an A♭ octave, at which point linear completion is arrested by the reversal to a metrically and dynamically accented G, transforming $\hat{8}$/**A♭** into neighboring ♭$\hat{6}$/**c**. This moment foreshadows the larger drama: full ascent is blocked by the catastrophe of

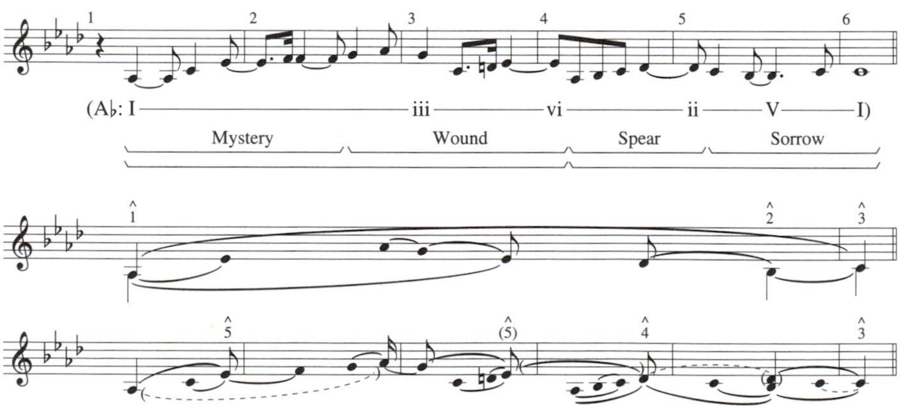

FIGURE 3.37 The grouping and prolongational analyses of the Communion theme (Prelude to Act I, bars 1–6).

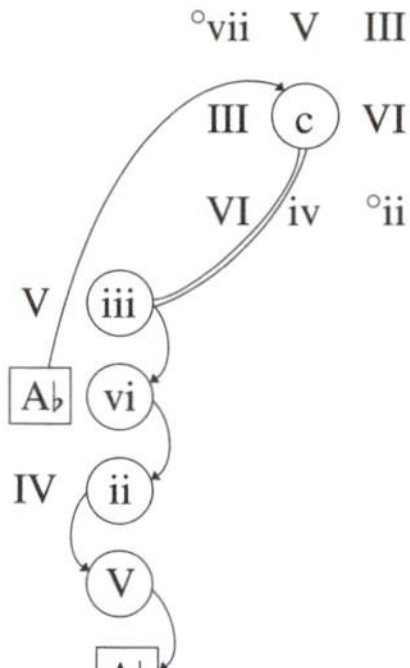

FIGURE 3.38 The chordal/regional path for the harmonized repeat of the Communion theme (bars 9–14).

Amfortas's wound (bar 3), which symbolizes the agony of his sexual fall and consequent spiritual impotence. Only by recapture of the spear (bar 4) can **A♭** be returned to legitimately. The line settles in partial closure, from above and below, on $\hat{3}$/**A♭** (bar 6), suggesting that resolution remains a real but unfulfilled hope.

Already in bars 3 and 4 there is a juxtaposition of D and D♭. These pcs are associated with the wound and the spear, respectively. But recovery of the sacred totem is not so near to home (that is, to **A♭**) as diatonic D♭. Redemption will require a perilous journey to the most remote regions from **A♭** in regional space, **d** and **D**.

Figure 3.38 traces the Communion theme's chordal/regional path from its subsequent harmonization (bars 9–14): I/**A♭** to i/**c**, the latter pivoting as iii/**A♭** and resolving down the cycle of fifths to I. **A♭** and **c** are located with respect to each other just as in Figure 3.35. The subsequent harmonic unfolding in **A♭** follows the shortest path within the chordal chart. In keeping with the narrative map, motion to the northeast symbolizes Amfortas's longing for redemption, and downward motion conveys grounding in the earthly domain of the knights of the grail. The path starts to the northeast because it is here that the wound thwarts the high A♭, causing the longing. The ensuing retreat downward soothes the pain by returning gradually to the home location of the grail, I/**A♭**.

Figure 3.39 gives the Communion theme's unharmonized parallel phrase (bars 20–25) and an indication of its subsequent harmonization (bars 28–33), with the slurs above the music providing the essentials of its prolongational analysis. The association with the wound is intensified by the transposition to **c**. The main departure within the phrase, the striking jump to **e**, follows from the transposed

FIGURE 3.39 The parallel phrase of the Communion theme (bars 20–25).

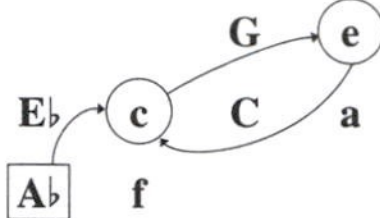

FIGURE 3.40 The combined regional path for the original and parallel phrases of the Communion theme.

leading tone. Later in Act I the same progression occurs as Gurnemanz tells of Amfortas's wounding; it also foreshadows the latter's anguished Act I aria, which begins in **e**.

Figure 3.40 plots paths at the regional level for the original and transposed phrases, employing untransformed regional space because of the mostly diatonic context. The major-third division of the octave from **A♭** to **c** to **e** extends the northeast trajectory of Figure 3.38 and falls back. There is no further ascent to **A♭** by this route. Beyond the yearning for redemption, this path symbolizes Amfortas's flight from the sinister Klingsor, whose motive moves in the opposite direction, again in a major-third division of the octave and in uniformly dark minor triads. Figure 3.41 shows this motive and its regional path, this time using partially collapsed space because of the chromatic context. Infected as he is by Klingsor, Amfortas's own motive similarly begins with an arpeggiation of an augmented triad.

After the statements of the Communion theme comes the rectitudinous Grail theme (the "Dresden Amen"), given in Figure 3.42 (bars 39–41). Unlike its shadowed predecessor, the Grail melody rises an untroubled octave. Its chordal path does not struggle upward but moves confidently to the right until its grounding downward to I/**A♭**.

The first fully westward trajectory takes place just after the appearance of the eastward-moving Grail theme, in the sequential presentation of the Faith motive (bars 45–51). As shown in Figure 3.43, the motive maps leftward from **A♭** to **C♭** (= **B**) to **D**, anticipating the primary modulational scheme of the entire drama. The implication is that faith must confront and vanquish sin in order to recover

FIGURE 3.41 Klingsor's motive and its regional path.

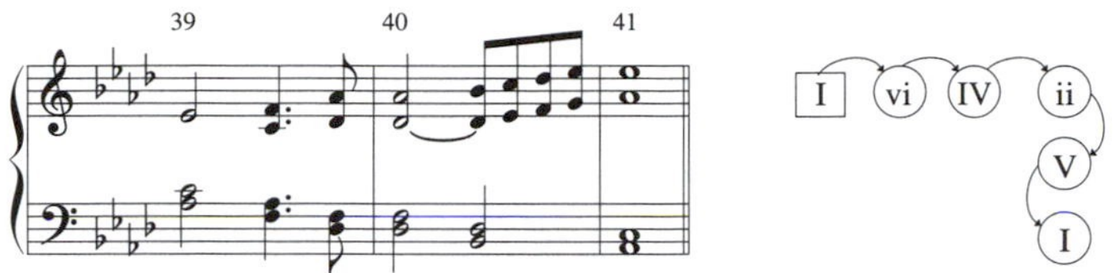

FIGURE 3.42 The Grail theme (bars 39–41) and its chordal path.

FIGURE 3.43 The presentation of the Faith motive (bars 45–55) and its chordal/regional path.

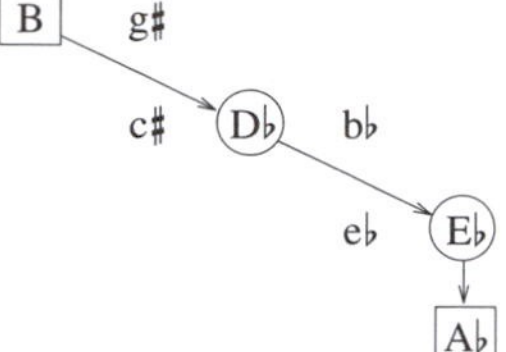

FIGURE 3.44 Regional path for the continuation of the Faith motive (bars 60–66).

the spear and hence the health of the society of the grail. The continuation of this phrase (bars 51–55), however, hints that the task will be arduous: after a northeast groping for redemption, the tonal path retreats toward its starting point and cadences with the Sorrow motive in **e♭**.

All of the directions mentioned in connection with the narrative map have been illustrated at the chordal or regional level except for direct northward ascent. I shall return to this point. A related issue concerns the absence on the map of a northwest–southeast diagonal. The musical reason is that this direction gives rise to the major-second transpositional cycle, which, in part because it lacks common tones between adjacent tonic triads, is less useful for chromatic tonality than the minor-third and major-third cycles. Nevertheless, Wagner occasionally has recourse to a southeast direction. As shown in Figure 3.44, in the continuation of the Faith motive (bars 60–66) the phrases sequence through **C♭**, **D♭**, and **E♭** before returning to **A♭**. This trajectory is consonant with the semantics of the narrative map ("earthly good"). In contrast, it is hard to imagine what a northwest trajectory might signify, and Wagner does not take this route.

In a characteristically Wagnerian dialectic, diatonicism in *Parsifal* stands for nature and faith, chromaticism for magic (good or bad) and sin. Granted the narrative map, motion to the right tends to be diatonic/chordal, as in the Grail motive, and motion to the left tends to be chromatic/regional, as in Klingsor's motive. More complex entities such as the Communion theme, which mixes grace and suffering, partake of both domains. Most music theory situates chromaticism in opposition to diatonicism, as if the former were an intrusion on the tonal system (see Proctor [1978] on this issue). An advantage of the spatial approach is its capacity to bring these oppositions into a unified representation.

The principle of the shortest path applied at successive prolongational levels is integral to the narrative under construction. Compare the opposite trajectories of Figure 3.40, which signifies a longing for redemption, and Figure 3.41, which represents the evil Klingsor. Both trajectories track a major-third cycle. Why then does **A♭** in Figure 3.40 reach **e** by a northeast path through intermediate **c** when **e** could be also accessed to the southwest, as happens between **b** and **g** in Figure 3.41? The answer is that **e** in Figure 3.40 is not directly accessible from **A♭**, for it is prolongationally nested within **c**; and the shortest distance from **c** to **e** is to the northeast. In Figure 3.41, in contrast, **g** is adjacent to **b** at the musical surface and thus connects in that theme's prolongational path. The opposite trajectories of the two passages are genuine from a theoretical standpoint, and their polar narrative interpretations follow.

The final section of the Prelude resumes the Communion theme in a beautiful expansion (bars 80–106) that plays a central role throughout *Parsifal.* As we glean from Amfortas's Act I monologue, the passage expresses his perception of the Communion ritual through the lens of his prior harrowing journey to Klingsor's magic garden, where he succumbed to Kundry's allure, lost the spear, and suffered the wound. He now blasphemously equates his unappeasable desire, externalized in his wound, with the Savior's wound on the Cross. The passage dramatizes both his spiritual longing and his spiritual affliction.

Figure 3.45 displays the expansion in relation to its model. The top line repeats from Figure 3.37 the opening statement of the Communion theme together with its progression of leitmotives. The expansion, shown only in the melody, reads from left to right down the two pages; parallel passages align vertically. The Mystery and Wound motives repeat twice in sequence, the last time with an extension of the Wound motive. Then the Spear and Sorrow motives repeat twice in sequence, the last time through an extension of the Sorrow motive in the form of the Sin-torment (*Sündenqual*) motive. Finally, the beginning of the Wound motive returns, again repeated twice, and the line sinks, an octave below its highest reach, into semicompletion.

The narrative behind this expansion is inseparable from its regional journey. The theme first reprises the opening move from **A♭** to **c** (bars 80–82). But the intrusion of a diminished-seventh chord foreshadows the upcoming modulations around the minor-third cycle and propels a repeat of the Wound motive that reroutes the phrase to V/**C♭** (bar 84). Amfortas is beginning to relive his journey to Klingsor's magic garden. The sequence takes the third phrase (a variant of bars 28–33) to **d**, the region furthest from the holy realm of **A♭** and hence a symbol of death. (In this connection, in Act I Kundry informs Parsifal of his mother's death through a cadence in **d**; Amfortas's Act I monologue cadences on V/**d** as he longs for extinction; in Act III the uncovering of Titurel's coffin and Amfortas's ensuing plea for death are in **d**.) After dwelling on the Wound over V/**d** (bars 91–93), Amfortas reaches with increasing urgency for a vision of the Spear, the agent not only of his wound but also of his redemption, as the modulations resume their course around the minor-third cycle from **d** to **f** (bars 95–98). The deceptive cadences bring no respite and he falls into despondency in the form of the Sin-torment expansion (bars 98–100), and finally into an exhausted contemplation of the Wound (bars 100–103), before emerging on a V/**A♭** that pleads for resolution.

Figure 3.46a brings out the underlying voice-leading patterns in this passage. Scale degrees are numbered and bracketed in relation to their local regions. The local melodic prolongations first extend $\hat{5}$ by transposition along the minor-third cycle and then, with the emergence of the Spear motive, seek linear completion through ($\hat{5}$)-$\hat{4}$-$\hat{3}$-$\hat{2}$-$\hat{1}$ as the cycle continues. These motions remain unresolved, including the framing one in **A♭**. Beneath the musical notation, the regions that are passed through are listed and connected in a regional prolongational analysis. Figure 3.46b specifies these same relationships as a westward path through partially collapsed regional space. This trajectory recalls the one in Figure 3.43. But unlike the earlier case, in which Faith turned from **D** back toward its starting point, here the path continues in the same direction beyond **d** all the way to **A♭** on the other side, signifying Amfortas's return to the halls of the grail after his disastrous experience in the magic garden. But is it the same **A♭**? If represented toroidally with one location per region, then yes, it is the same **A♭**. But when represented as an unfolded chart, the two **A♭**s can be viewed as conceptually different. No doubt Amfortas has returned home, but home is no longer the same; the Order is in decay. He began his journey in righteousness at the **A♭** at the right edge of the narrative map and ends up in sin at the **A♭** at its left edge. This trajectory is the perfect emblem for the broken leader who is now barely able to perform his role.

Granted these different **A♭**s and their significations, the narrative quest of *Parsifal* can be framed as follows: Which **A♭** will redeem Amfortas and the Order, and how is it to be reached? The narrative map points toward the northmost **A♭** as the place of salvation, and such will prove to be the case; but this **A♭** must be reached by a particular route. The prophecy in Act I hints the way:

FIGURE 3.45 The final section (bars 80–106) of the Act I Prelude as an expansion of the Communion theme.

Durch Mitleid wissend,	Through compassion enlightened,
der reine Tor;	the innocent fool;
harre sein,	wait for him,
den ich erkor.	whom I have chosen.

The home region for the Innocent Fool (*reine Tor*) theme is **d**, with a plagal cadence on I/**D**. This means that Parsifal, the innocent fool, must travel toward death and redeem Amfortas's sin by transforming **d** to **D**. The plagal motion further suggests moving northward in chordal space. The true path, we discover, is to proceed westward from **A♭** on the minor-third cycle to **d/D** and to ascend from there by fifths to **A♭**.

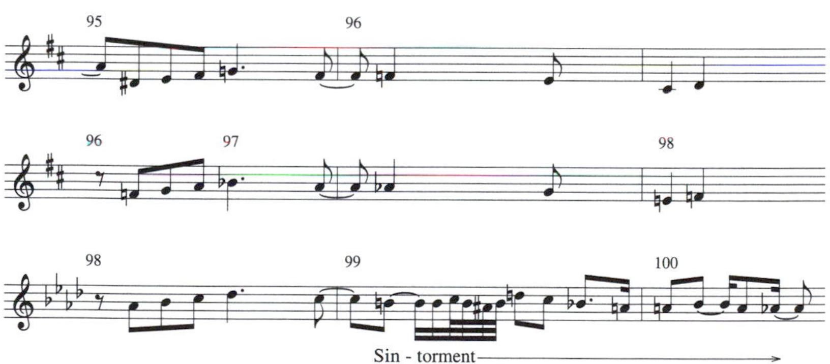

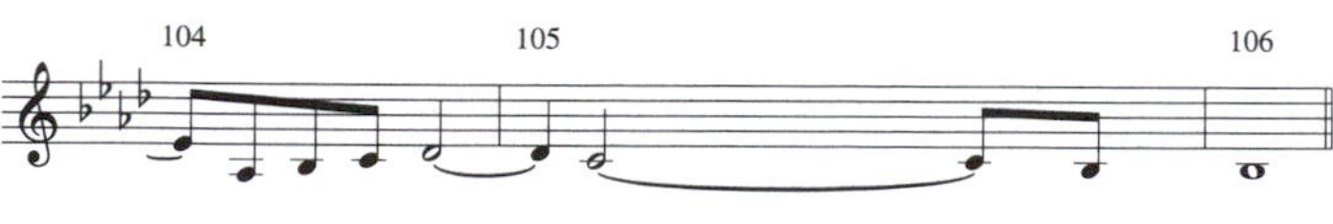

FIGURE 3.45 (Continued)

FIGURE 3.46 Prolongational analysis and regional path for the final section of the Act I Prelude.

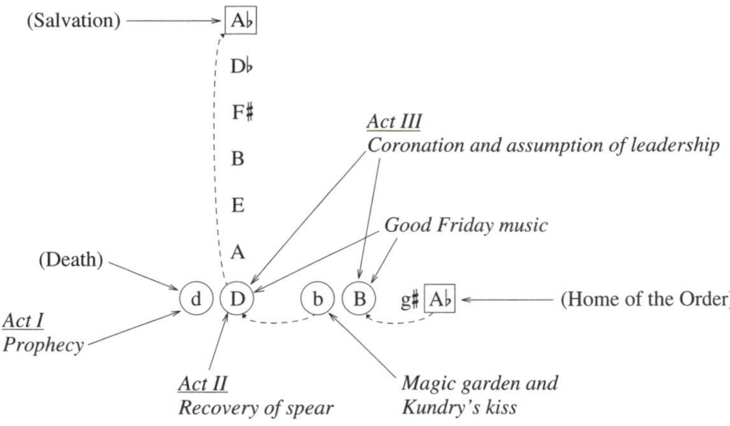

FIGURE 3.47 Stages in Parsifal's journey to redemption.

In the second scene of Act I, Parsifal uncomprehendingly witnesses Amfortas's agony. Yet Parsifal has understood enough to undertake, in Act II, the westward journey to Klingsor's realm, whose tonal region is **b**. The turning point in the drama, Kundry's kiss, occurs just after an evaded cadence in **b** in the middle of Act II. By the end of Act II, after a tonally ambiguous passage in **d** during which Kundry tries one last time to embrace him, Parsifal seizes the spear, in a transformation of Klingsor's motive, over a blazing **D** major triad. However, his trauma in the magic garden has been so great that he is unable to return with the spear directly to the realm of the grail, but loses his way, as depicted in the Prelude to Act III. When, in the first scene of Act III, he comes back to take over from Amfortas and restore vitality to the Order, Parsifal must symbolically trace once again the path to **b** and **d**, in order to complete the healing in a spirit of responsibility and compassion. This inner action is accomplished by transforming **b** and **d** into **B** and **D**. Gurnemanz blesses Parsifal, whose motive triumphs in a great climax in **B**. Assuming Amfortas's office, Parsifal in turn blesses Kundry, whose torment melts into the Good Friday music in **B** and **D** as the real magic of Spring replaces the false magic of Klingsor's garden (the head of the Good Friday theme is a variant of the Mystery motive). They go to the temple of the grail, where Parsifal announces his victory, with his motive now in **D**, a resumption of its statement in **B**, and a reply to Amfortas's lament in **d** earlier in the scene. The regions of **b** and **d** have been redeemed, and the ascent from **D** to **A♭** can take place. Figure 3.47 summarizes these remarks.

The motion from **D** to **A♭** happens twice, both times locally from **D♭** via the Neapolitan chord in the Innocent Fool theme (♭II/**D♭** = D major chord), as a sign that the prophecy has been fulfilled. The first time, as Parsifal calls, "*Enthüllet den Gral, öffnet den Schrein!*" (Reveal the Grail, open the shrine!), the progression moves down, not up, the cycle of fifths, as shown in Figure 3.48. The cause of the southward trajectory is both tonal and narrative. The close of the Act I Prelude, with its rising woodwind echoes of the Mystery motive over V/**A♭** (bars 106–

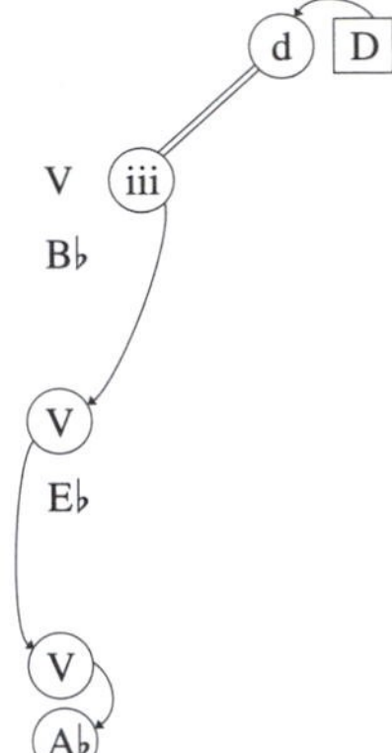

FIGURE 3.48 The first resolution from **D** to **A♭** (end of Act III).

113), has demanded resolution, a feat that Wagner accomplishes here, as Lewin (1984) discusses, by a transformation of these echoes so that they begin on D rather than on D♭ and close on I/**A♭**; compare Figures 3.49a–b. It was suggested in connection with Figure 3.37 that recovery of the spear would necessitate a journey to **d/D**. This mission having been accomplished, Parsifal can now reconcile **d/D** and **A♭** in the same phrase. The progression goes down rather than up because the descending-fifth chordal progression at the end of the Act I Prelude can be completed only by adding the final descending fifth. This trajectory grounds **d/D** in **A♭**.

Before the second motion from **D** to **A♭** there occurs the remarkable passage in Figure 3.50. The Grail motive (Figure 3.42) transforms into the harmonies of Klingsor's motive (Figure 3.41) through repeated flattening of the descending-thirds chord progression. The reason for this leitmotivic combination is that the

FIGURE 3.49 Comparison of (a) the completion of the end of the Act I Prelude and (b) the first resolution from **D** to **A♭** at the end of Act III. Only the soprano-bass skeletons are given. (After Lewin 1984.)

FIGURE 3.50 The Grail motive infiltrated by the harmonies of Klingsor's motive.

miracle of the grail failed because of Amfortas's sin and all power lay with Klingsor. By recapturing the spear, Parsifal has appropriated Klingsor's magic and refructified the ritual; and it is just during this passage that the grail begins to glow again.

In its usual form, Klingsor's motive has enough diatonic melodic pitches to be interpreted as modulatory at the regional level. Here, with no independent melody and given the association with the Grail theme, the reference functions chiefly at the chordal level. The progression can be modeled using a transformed version of chordal space along the lines of Figure 3.26c. Figure 3.51 shows the initiating **E♭** flanked by chromatically altered III and ♭vi, creating a cycle of major-third root-intervals. Plugging Figure 3.50 into this altered space results in the path in Figure 3.51b. In terms of altered scale steps, as indicated in parentheses, the G chord is ♭IV and the e♭ chord is not a minor tonic but 𝄫ii. At this point the music "modulates" back into diatonic chordal space in **D♭**. This interpretation enables the path for the passage to correspond to that of the Grail theme in its original version (compare Figure 3.42). In terms of the narrative map, Klingsor's motive has been rerouted from a southwest direction to a largely eastward one. Parsifal has metamorphosed evil into good. (Lewin dissects this passage in terms of Riemann functions; "Analyses of Triadic Chromatic Tonal Music" in chapter 7 returns to it from a hexatonic perspective.)

Now that Parsifal has taken over Klingsor's magic, it is time for the long-promised ascent from **D** to **A♭**. Again the Innocent Fool theme brings the music from **D♭** to **D**, at which point a long rising plagal sequence begins through the fusion of the Mystery and Grail motives shown in Figure 3.52. Its dramatic func-

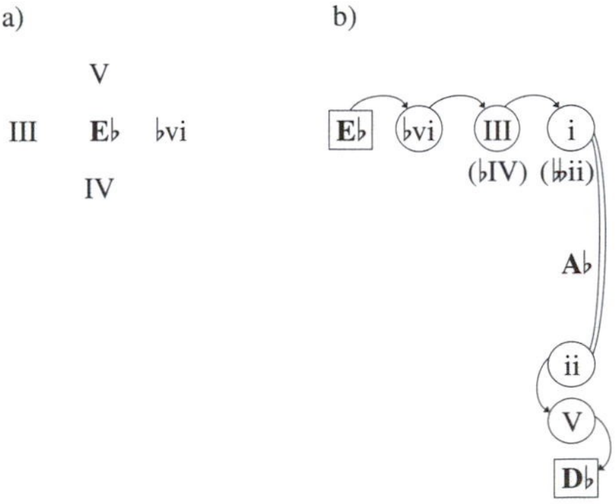

FIGURE 3.51 An adaptation of chordal space: (a) altered chords on the horizontal axis, creating a major-third cycle; (b) path for the passage in Figure 3.50.

FIGURE 3.52 The Mystery and Grail motives combined.

tion is to celebrate the regeneration of the mystery of the grail. More profoundly, its linear function is to provide a way, at last, for the initial octave rise in the Communion theme (Figure 3.37) not to be thwarted at its goal but to find full realization. Better yet, the combination passes a step beyond the octave, setting in motion the harmonic sequence that drives the music ever upward until the chorus reaches high A♭, the final vocal note in the drama. The simple but powerful harmonic sequence is graphed in Figure 3.53. Near its conclusion there is a single deviation, the striking interpolation of A minor within **D♭**, a last nod in the direction of Klingsor as Kundry sinks lifeless to the ground. Finally, with one more plagal step, **A♭** is attained and prolonged.

Figure 3.54 superimposes the narrative map on the principal tonal axes of *Parsifal*. Amfortas's path moves east to west from **A♭** to **A♭** (Prelude to Act I). Parsifal duplicates this path to the **d/D** center point, literally (Act II) and then symbolically (Act III), and from there, in the final action, he spans the **A♭** on the south–north axis. Perhaps it is not too fanciful to note that, taken together, this picture forms a cross with the wound in the middle.

Compositional use of the Weber space

Although this theory is concerned with how music is cognized rather than with how it is composed, there is no reason not to suppose that from time to time

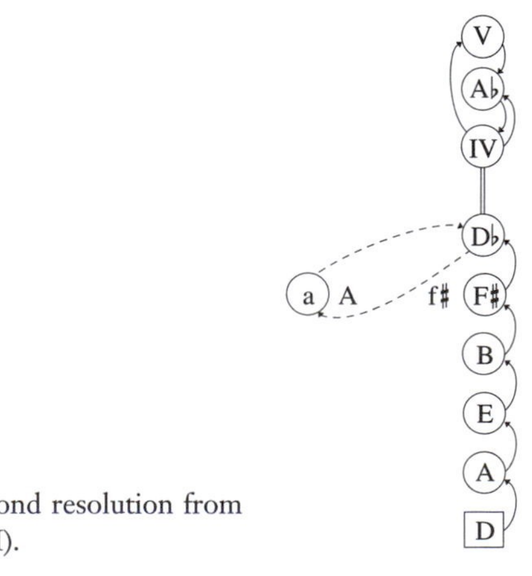

FIGURE 3.53 The second resolution from **D** to **A♭** (end of Act III).

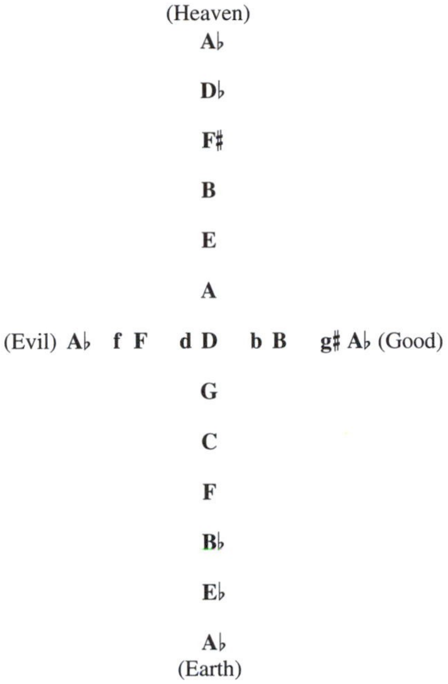

(Heaven)
A♭
D♭
F♯
B
E
A
(Evil) **A♭ f F d D b B g♯ A♭** (Good)
G
C
F
B♭
E♭
A♭
(Earth)

FIGURE 3.54 The narrative map superimposed on the main tonal paths of *Parsifal.*

composers have consciously taken advantage of concepts that the theory includes. Such would seem to be the case with *Parsifal* and the Weber space, for the correspondences between the two can hardly be accidental. I digress on this point for its own sake and not to shore up my tonal/narrative interpretation, which must stand on its own merits.

Beyond the internal evidence of tonal/narrative paths, there are clues that Wagner knew and used the space. Consider the verbal exchange that launches the Transformation interlude of Act I:

Parsifal: *Ich schreite kaum, doch wähn' ich mich schon weit.*
I scarcely move, yet I imagine myself already far.
Gurnemanz: *Du sieh'st mein Sohn, zum Raum wird hier die Zeit.*
You see, my son, here time becomes space.

During this exchange Gurnemanz and Parsifal begin their magic journey to the temple of the grail. As they sing, the music sequences diatonic phrases on the minor-third cycle, which accounts for why Parsifal feels that he is traveling far without effort. Gurnemanz's reply alludes not only to the miraculous physical change in time and space that they are undergoing but also to the temporal unfolding of the music in tonal space.

For his 1951 Bayreuth production of *Parsifal,* Wagner's grandson Wieland included in the Festival handbook a verbal diagram, "Parsifal's Cross: A Psychological Diagram," laid out in the shape of a cross (Spotts 1994; reprinted in the liner notes of the Boulez LP recording on Deutsche Gramaphon). The design approximates the narrative map: the Savior is at the top, Mother Earth at the bottom, Klingsor at the left, the Order (represented by Titurel) at the right. Wieland's placement of the kiss at the center of the cross is dramatically true but does not quite fit the tonal map, in which the wound and death lie at the center. While the subject matter of *Parsifal* may have been Wieland's only impetus for this diagram, one wonders if he found a suggestive sketch of this sort among his grandfather's papers.

It would be helpful to know whether Richard Wagner was familiar with Weber's *Versuch einer geordeneten Theorie der Tonsetzkunst* (1821–1824). Aside from his early self-instruction from the writings of J. B. Logier (Wagner 1992), which have no bearing on the Weber space, little is known of Wagner's technical studies. We do know, however, that Weber's *Versuch* ran through second and third editions (1824 and 1832) and became a standard reference work of the period (Hoffman 1980; Werts 1983); for instance, Weber's regional chart appears as a pedagogical device in Lobe (1851). We also know from his autobiography that Wagner was acquainted with Schumann in the 1840s in Dresden and from Schumann's diaries that Schumann thoroughly studied the *Versuch* (Wagner 1992; Schumann 1971).

There is internal evidence, albeit not as elaborate as that for *Parsifal*, that Schumann himself utilized the Weber chart as a tool for organizing regions in his song cycles. Arthur Komar (1971) observes that the regions in *Dichterliebe* follow a fairly regular pattern that involves fifths and thirds. He offers a convoluted explanation for the pattern and tries to slot it into a quasi-Schenkerian graph. Whatever the virtues of the Schenkerian method, they do not extend to the loose tonal organization of a song cycle. The regional path in Figure 3.55, which utilizes the fold representation from Figure 3.22a, is both less ambitious and more illuminating. The unit of analysis is the tonic of each song, and there is no attempt to organize the sequence into a prolongational hierarchy. Beginning in **f♯** (the first song, "Im wunderschönen Monat Mai," is ambiguous between prolonging V/**f♯** and I/**A**), the cycle moves back and forth within one fold of the space. The sequence gradually descends down the fifth axis until, at "Ich hab' im Traum geweinet," it crosses the seam to the adjacent fold and then continues to descend until **c♯** is reached. The cycle has come full circle and in a sense could begin again, with the I of the **D♭** coda pivoting as V/**f♯**. It is tempting to ascribe narrative significance to this pattern, but Heine's elusive poetry does not offer an easy interpretation. At the least, the stark "Ich hab' im Traum geweinet" signals a change in mood that conforms to the crossing from one fold to the next.

The poetry of *Frauenliebe und Leben*, in contrast, projects a clear if apparently conventional narrative attended by the relatively transparent regional scheme in Figure 3.56. The first five songs form a palindromic path, from **B♭** to **E♭** to **c** and back. **B♭** signifies the woman's emotional home in her feelings for her loved one. The movement from **B♭** to **E♭** to **c** passes through adoration to doubt, and the reversal through **E♭** back to **B♭** answers with engagement and wedding. With this action closed, the regional skip across the seam to the sixth song, **B♭** to **G**, depicts the change in her life brought about by marriage and

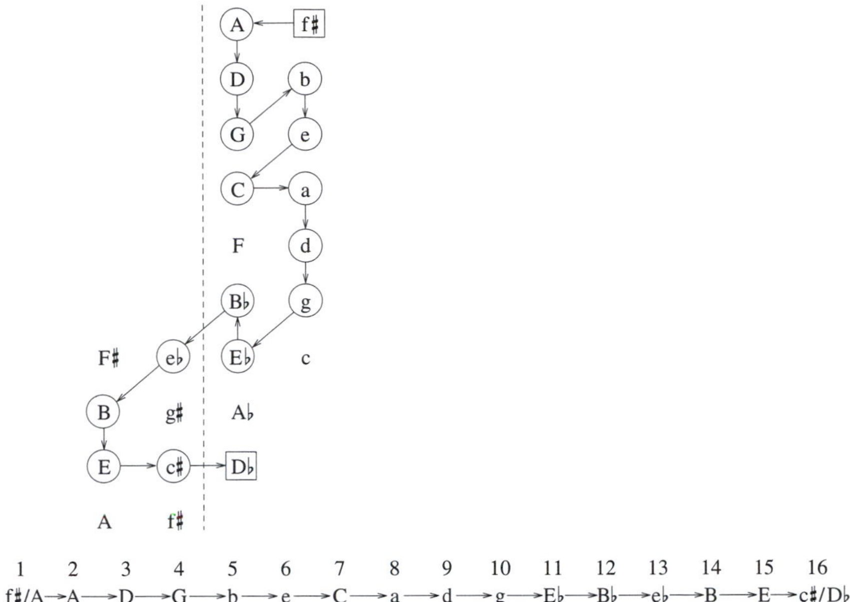

FIGURE 3.55 Regional journey in Schumann's *Dichterliebe*. The numbers refer to the songs in order.

pregnancy. Just as engagement led to wedding by a rising fifth from **E♭** to **B♭**, so pregnancy brings the joy of motherhood from **G** to **D**. These two songs (the sixth and seventh) portray the period of her marriage and exist in their own spatial fold. Then the husband dies and the seam is crossed again to **d** in the eighth song. The return home in the **B♭** coda expresses her consolation in lived recollection.

Schubert's song cycles do not reveal predominantly stepwise, comparably patterned regional paths. Figure 3.57 illustrates with the path for his one cycle with a strong narrative, *Die schöne Müllerin. Winterreise*, not shown, presents an even greater tangle. Evidently, Schumann did, but Schubert did not, exploit the Weber chart.

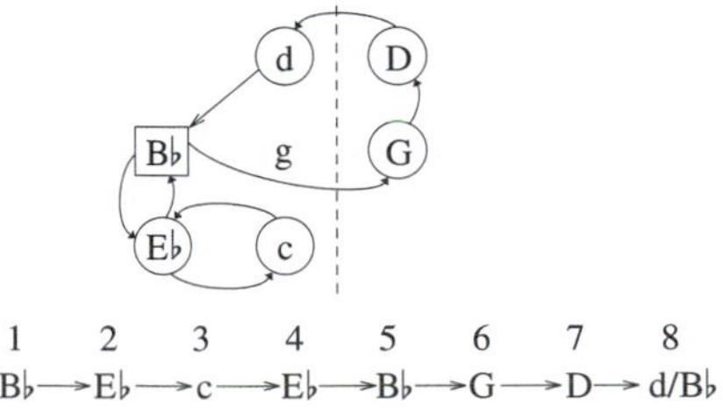

FIGURE 3.56 Regional journey in Schumann's *Frauenliebe und Leben*.

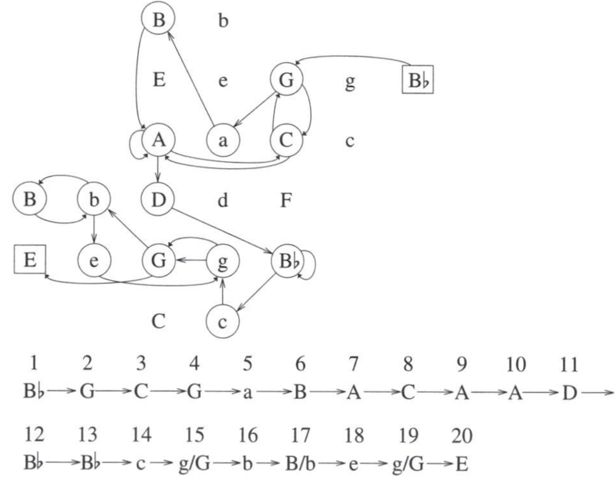

FIGURE 3.57 Regional journey in Schubert's *Die schöne Müllerin*.

A note on semantic paths

The narrative paths just discussed depend directly or indirectly on verbal discourse. Can tonal paths be narrative without words? There is a growing literature on purely musical narrativity that I shall not attempt to assess. An approach from linguistic theory, however, is worth a brief remark because it is so congenial to pitch-space paths.

Jackendoff (1982) advances a semantic theory based on the notion that there is a level of thought, which he calls conceptual structure, that underlies verbal and other cognitive behavior. He demonstrates that all kinds of verbal utterances depend tacitly on concepts of spatial location and motion. For instance, the syntax of temporal expressions parallels that of spatial expressions and relies on spatially conceived time. Spatial concepts appear to belong to conceptual structure itself, which divides the world into such basic categories as "thing," "location," "event," and "direction." Verbs and prepositions specify places or paths in relation to starting, intermediate, and terminating objects. Just as a ball can be at a certain location or move to, above, below, through, or around an object, so can an idea or feeling be or move in space.

Granted that conceptual structure operates on spatial location and motion and granted that music is a form of thought, it follows that music is implicated in space and motion. This is so not only for musical terminology, which cannot do without spatial terms such as "interval," "neighbor," "up" and "down," "step" and "skip," and so on, but also in the organization (chapter 2) and motion (chapter 3) of musical objects themselves. Pitches and chords have locations in pitch space. They can remain stationary, move to other pitches or chords that are close or far, or take a path above, below, through, or around other musical objects.

None of this imbues musical places and paths with semantic content in a strict linguistic sense. Besides, the connection between the semantics of a sentence and the narrative of a story is anything but simple—although stories, too, cannot do without places and paths. The point, rather, is that an utterance, a narrative, and a musical passage all share an abstraction, that of objects and paths moving in time through space. This commonality is one reason that music, when allied with words, can participate as an equal partner in the unfolding of a narrative.

4 *Tonal Tension and Attraction*

THE HARMONIC TENSION MODEL

Tension and pitch space

Fundamental to the experience of tonal music is the hearing of patterns of tension and relaxation as the events in a piece unfold. Although GTTM's prolongational component models aspects of this experience, its repertory of branchings (Figure 1.10) does not register an exact amount of tension or relaxation within or across its three categories of strong prolongation, weak prolongation, and progression. The key to rectifying this imprecision is conversion of the metaphor of instability/stability into that of tension/relaxation: the more unstable two events are with respect to each other, the further apart two events are in pitch space and the greater the tension that exists for one in relation to the other. The pitch-space rules quantify the degree of stability from one event to another, hence their tensional states. Furthermore, in a hierarchical view, tonic orientation establishes the point of stability against which the instability of other events is measured. If the first of two prolongationally connected events is closer to the governing tonic, the motion from the first to the second event increases tension by the distance between them. If the second is closer to the governing tonic, the motion from the first to the second decreases tension by the distance between them. These considerations hold at any reductional level.

Before we proceed, let it be noted that there are other kinds of musical tension than those accounted for by the methods described here. There is the surface tension of a crescendo, a rise in melodic contour, or a suddenly dense texture.

There is the tension that results from the deviation from or conflict between phrasal and harmonic schemas (see "Functions and Schemas" in chapter 5). There is metrical tension (see "A Metrical Analogy" in chapter 6). There is the psychological tension measurable by the extent to which preference rules are satisfied (Temperley and Sleator 1999). This chapter does not treat these kinds of tension.

Sequential and hierarchical tension

Listeners understand music both sequentially and hierarchically. They inevitably hear one event after another; they also organize the surface in terms of structural events and their elaborations. Let us assume, broadly speaking, that naive listeners stay close to the surface while experienced listeners tend to hierarchize it. Here I idealize the situation by modeling strict sequential and strict hierarchical hearings. In the sequential model, pitch-space distances are calculated from one event to the next. In the hierarchical model, distances are calculated down the prolongational tree, so that an event inherits tension values from prolongationally more important events.

Consider bars 1–9 of the first movement of Mozart's Sonata K. 282, shown in Figure 4.1. This passage constitutes the first theme group and transition into the beginning of the second theme group of this miniature sonata form. To simplify matters at the outset, Figure 4.2 provides bars 1–4 at the quarter-note level of the associated time-span reduction. This "surface," treated as a sequence of chords, will be assigned tension values, first sequentially and then hierarchically. Events are numbered and labeled with Roman numerals for reference. Event 11 is interpreted as an immediately underlying, predominant ii^7; the B♭ in the soprano is an appoggiatura that does not resolve until the change of harmony on the following beat. The rest of the labeling is straightforward.

Figure 4.3 provides the sequential calculations for the passage. The simple rule is as follows:

> SEQUENTIAL TENSION RULE (short version): $T_{seq}(\mathbf{y}) = \delta(x_{prec} \rightarrow \mathbf{y})$, where $\mathbf{y}$ = the target chord, x_{prec} = the chord that immediately precedes $\mathbf{y}$ in the sequence, $T_{seq}(\mathbf{y})$ = the tension associated with $\mathbf{y}$, and $\delta(x_{prec} \rightarrow \mathbf{y})$ = the distance from x_{prec} to $\mathbf{y}$ (using $\delta[x \rightarrow y] = i + j + k$).

Events in Figure 4.3 are always located by the shortest path. For example, event 7 is interpreted as V^4_2/**ii** because that is the closest place for that pc configuration in relation to event 6. The target event in each calculation is given in boldface. Event 1 is counted from a hypothetical event 0, and the progression from event to event follows in order. (A few progressions are omitted as redundant: $\delta[1 \rightarrow \mathbf{2}]$ and $\delta[5 \rightarrow \mathbf{6}] = 0$ because the chords directly repeat; $\delta[12 \rightarrow \mathbf{13}]$ is the same as $\delta[9 \rightarrow \mathbf{10}]$. The issue of chordal inversions will be taken up shortly.) It simplifies matters to represent incomplete triads and seventh chords as complete triads, although this step is not required in the pitch-space model. (A missing triad member could be subtracted or a seventh could be added at the chord level of the basic

FIGURE 4.1 Mozart's Sonata, K. 282, I, bars 1–9.

FIGURE 4.2 Quarter-note level of the time-span reduction, bars 1–4.

```
      3
      3             10
      3       7     10
0   2 3   5   7 8   10
0 1 2 3 4 5 6 7 8 9 10 11
```

δ(I/**I**→I) = 0 + 0 + 0 = 0
δ("0"→**1**)

```
                    10
          5         10
    2     5         10
0   2 3   5 7   8   10
0 1 2 3 4 5 6 7 8 9 10 11
```

δ(I→V) = 0 + 1 + 4 = 5
δ(2→**3**)

```
          (5)
0         (5)
0     3   (5)     9
0   2 3   5   7   9 10
0 1 2 3 4 5 6 7 8 9 10 11
```

δ(V→vii°/**V**) = 1 + 1 + 6 = 8
δ(3→**4**)

```
                    10
          5         10
    2     5         10
0   2 3   5   7   9 10
0 1 2 3 4 5 6 7 8 9 10 11
```

δ(vii°/**V**→I/**V**) = 0 + 1 + 4 = 5
δ(4→**5**)

```
0
0             7
0       4     7
0   2   4 5   7 8   10
0 1 2 3 4 5 6 7 8 9 10 11
```

δ(I/**V**→V/**ii**) = 1 + 2 + 8 = 11
δ(6→**7**)

```
          5
0         5
0         5     8
0   2   4 5   7 8   10
0 1 2 3 4 5 6 7 8 9 10 11
```

δ(V/**ii**→i/**ii**) = 0 + 1 + 4 = 5
δ(7→**8**)

```
                    10
          5         10
    2     5         10
0   2 3   5   7 8   10
0 1 2 3 4 5 6 7 8 9 10 11
```

δ(i/**ii**→V/**I**) = 1 + 1 + 5 = 7
δ(8→**9**)

```
      3
      3             10
      3       7     10
0   2 3   5   7 8   10
0 1 2 3 4 5 6 7 8 9 10 11
```

δ(V→I) = 0 + 1 + 4 = 5
δ(9→**10**)

```
          5
0         5
0         5     8
0   2 3   5   7 8   10
0 1 2 3 4 5 6 7 8 9 10 11
```

δ(I→ii) = 0 + 2 + 6 = 8
δ(10→**11**)

```
                    10
          5         10
    2     5         10
0   2 3   5   7 8   10
0 1 2 3 4 5 6 7 8 9 10 11
```

δ(ii→V) =0 + 1 + 4 = 5
δ(11→**12**)

```
      3
      3             10
      3       7     10
0   2 3   5   7 8   10
0 1 2 3 4 5 6 7 8 9 10 11
```

δ(V→I) =0 + 1 + 4 = 5
δ(12→**13**)

FIGURE 4.3 Sequential distance calculations for the progression in Figure 4.2.

space.) Listeners tend in any case to fill out an incomplete triad into a conceptual *Klang;* and the sevenths in seventh chords will be treated below in another fashion. Following tradition (Rameau 1722), the vii^{o6}/**V** (event 4) is represented as a dominant with a missing root; hence the pcs in parentheses. It may seem at first that this vii^{o6}/**V**, since it functions merely as an applied dominant, resolves not to I/**V** but to V/**I**. But remember that this reading is blindly sequential. As will be discussed momentarily, only under a somewhat larger hearing is event 5 interpreted as V/**I**. The same holds for the i/**ii** (event 8).

Figure 4.4 lists the results from Figure 4.2 in tabular form. For each T_{seq}(**y**) the designation (x_{prec}→**y**) is listed so as to clarify the calculation in question, and the Roman-numeral designation for **y** is given in brackets. The first three columns supply the resulting values in the chord distance rule. The right column sums the numbers in each row, yielding the distance value between the two events in question. These values convey not a tensing or relaxing in relation to a governing tonic but the tension of moving from one event to the next. In this view, there is no larger perspective on the increase in tension, say, from event 6 (I/**V**) to event 7 (V^4_2/**ii**). Rather, the comparatively great tension attached to the V^4_2/**ii** in the progression I/**V**→V^4_2/**ii** results from these events being temporally adjacent but somewhat far apart in chordal/regional space. The values as a whole give a clear shape to the phrase: the first subphrase (through the first half of bar 2) tenses at its

	pitch-space distance			total
	i	j	k	
T_{seq}(0→**1**) [I/**I**]	0	0	0	**0**
T_{seq}(1→**2**) [I]	0	0	0	**0**
T_{seq}(2→**3**) [V^6]	0	1	4	**5**
T_{seq}(3→**4**) [vii^{o6}/**V**]	1	1	6	**8**
T_{seq}(4→**5**) [I/**V**]	0	1	4	**5**
T_{seq}(5→**6**) [I/**V**]	0	0	0	**0**
T_{seq}(6→**7**) [V_2/**ii**]	1	2	8	**11**
T_{seq}(7→**8** [i/**ii**]	0	1	4	**5**
T_{seq}(8→**9**) [$V^4{}_2$]	1	1	5	**7**
T_{seq}(9→**10**) [I^6]	0	1	4	**5**
T_{seq}(10→**11**) [ii^7]	0	2	6	**8**
T_{seq}(11→**12**) [V^7]	0	1	4	**5**
T_{seq}(12→**13**) [I]	0	1	4	**5**

FIGURE 4.4 Sequential values of Figure 4.3 put into tabular form.

middle, and the second subphrase (the second half of bar 2 to the downbeat of bar 4) begins in a relatively high state of tension and then levels off.

Figure 4.5 adds to Figure 4.2 the prolongational analysis that is needed as input to the hierarchical tension model. In this approach, the distance of an event is measured from the superordinate event to which it attaches in the tree. Right branching keeps events in temporal sequence, but left branching does not. Figure 4.6 provides the breakdown on these distances. Certain progressions that occur a number of times are listed only once, with multiple references as indicated. In each instance, the numbered ordering for δ(x→y) comes from the branchings in Figure 4.5.

The results from Figure 4.6 are displayed in Figure 4.7 up to the column "local total." At this point another factor is added: the column "inherited value" lists the value that each target event receives from superordinate branchings. For instance, event 7 inherits 7 from event 8, event 8 inherits 5 from event 9, event 9 inherits 0 from event 10, and event 10 inherits 0 from event 1; so the inheritance of event 7 is 7 + 5 + 0 + 0 = 12. The inherited value is then added to the local total to arrive at the "global total" for each target event. Symbolically,

> HIERARCHICAL TENSION RULE (short version): $T_{loc}(\mathbf{y}) = \delta(x_{dom}\rightarrow\mathbf{y})$; and $T_{glob}(\mathbf{y}) = T_{loc}(\mathbf{y}) + T_{inh}(x_{dom})$, where **y** = the target chord, x_{dom} = the chord that directly dominates **y** in the prolongational tree; $T_{loc}(\mathbf{y})$ = the local tension associated with **y**; $\delta(x_{dom}\rightarrow\mathbf{y})$ = the distance from x_{dom} to **y** (= $i + j + k$); $T_{glob}(\mathbf{y})$ = the global tension associated with **y**; and $T_{inh}(x_{dom})$ = the sum of distance values inherited by **y** from chords that dominate x_{dom}.

Some specifics in Figures 4.6 and 4.7 require explanation. As in the sequential analysis, event 4 (vii^{o6}/**V**) locally orients event 5 as I/**V**. However, the larger voice

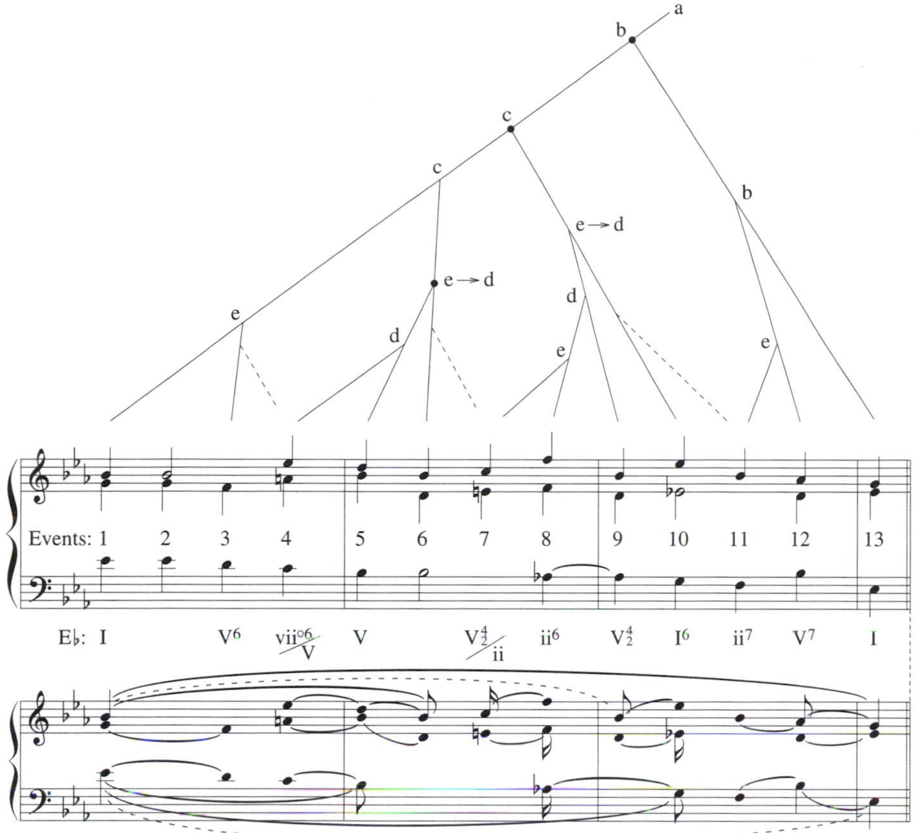

FIGURE 4.5 Prolongational reduction of Figure 4.2.

leading (the prolongation of the melodic B♭ from bar 1) causes event 5 to elaborate event 6, which branches higher than the local **V** region and thus functions as V/**I**. Hence I/**V** must convert into V/**I**, as shown in Figure 4.6c. The same considerations apply to event 8, which must convert from i/**ii** into ii/**I**. But in this case there is only a single ii to accomplish the transformation, so an evaluation on the single event δ(8→**8**) is required to Figure 4.6f. Figure 4.7 combines the two steps δ(9→**8**) and δ(8→**8**) in the inherited value for event 8. This step provisionally quantifies the pivot function. (In Figure 2.33 and in effect by graphing pivots with double lines throughout chapter 3, I have taken the slight shortcut, to avoid fussiness, of not counting the translation of an identical event from one region to another, as is done in Figure 4.6f.)

A complementary way to view pivots is to slice the prolongational analysis into levels of prolongational sequences. In Figure 4.8, prolongational level c does not deviate from the tonic region. The moves to **V** and **ii** emerge only at levels d and e, respectively. The act of listening integrates all three levels and

a)
```
      3
      3             10
      3       7     10
0   2 3   5   7 8   10
0 1 2 3 4 5 6 7 8 9 10 11
```
δ("I"→I) = 0 + 0 + 0 = 0
δ("I"→**1**)
δ(1→**2**)
δ(1→**10**)
δ(1→**13**)

b)
```
                    10
          5         10
    2     5         10
0   2 3   5 7   8   10
0 1 2 3 4 5 6 7 8 9 10 11
```
δ(I→V) = 0 + 1 + 4 = 5
δ(1→**3**)
δ(1→**6**)
δ(10→**9**)
δ(13→**12**)

c)
```
                    10
          5         10
    2     5         10
0   2 3   5   7   9 10
0 1 2 3 4 5 6 7 8 9 10 11
```
δ(V/**I**→I/**V**) = 1 + 0 + 1 = 2
δ(6→**5**)

d)
```
         (5)
0        (5)
0     3  (5)      9
0   2 3   5   7   9 10
0 1 2 3 4 5 6 7 8 9 10 11
```
δ(I/**V**→vii°/**V**) = 0 + 1 + 5 = 6
δ(5→**4**)

e)
```
          5
0         5
0         5     8
0   2 3   5   7 8   10
0 1 2 3 4 5 6 7 8 9 10 11
```
δ(V/**I**→ii/**I**) = 0 + 1 + 4 = 5
δ(9→**8**)
δ(12→**11**)

f)
```
          5
0         5
0         5     8
0   2   4 5   7 8   10
0 1 2 3 4 5 6 7 8 9 10 11
```
δ(ii/**I**→i/**ii**) = 1 + 0 + 1 = 2
δ(8→**8**)

g)
```
0
0             7
0       4     7
0   2   4 5   7 8   10
0 1 2 3 4 5 6 7 8 9 10 11
```
δ(i/**ii**→V/**ii**) = 0 + 1 + 4 = 5
δ(8→**7**)

FIGURE 4.6 Local hierarchical distance calculations for Figure 4.5.

	pitch-space distance *i*	*j*	*k*	*local total*	*inherited value*	***global total***
T_{glob}("I"→**1**) [I/**I**]	0	0	0	0	0	**0**
T_{glob}(1→**2**) [I]	0	0	0	0	0	**0**
T_{glob}(1→**3**) [V^6]	0	1	4	5	0	**5**
T_{glob}(5→**4**) [vii^{o6}/**V**]	0	1	5	6	7	**13**
T_{glob}(6→**5**) [I/**V**]	1	0	1	2	5	**7**
T_{glob}(1→**6**) [V/**I**]	0	1	4	5	0	**5**
T_{glob}(8→**7**) [V_2/**ii**]	0	1	4	5	12	**17**
T_{glob}(9→**8**) [ii/**I** = i/**ii**]	1	1	5	7	5	**12**
T_{glob}(10→**9**) [V_2]	0	1	4	5	0	**5**
T_{glob}(1→**10**) [I^6]	0	0	0	0	0	**0**
T_{glob}(12→**11**) [ii^7]	0	1	4	5	5	**10**
T_{glob}(13→**12**) [V^7]	0	1	4	5	0	**5**
T_{glob}(1→**13**) [I]	0	0	0	0	0	**0**

FIGURE 4.7 Table of the local hierarchical values from Figure 4.6, together with values inherited from the prolongational tree. The global total for each target event = local total plus inherited value.

FIGURE 4.8 Prolongational branchings c–e (from Figure 4.5) notated as three separate levels.

interprets these fleeting tonicizations as chromatic enrichments of the home region.

Figure 4.9 plots the values from Figures 4.4 and 4.7 graphically, with the sequence of events on the x axis and tension on the y axis. The filled-in nodes connected by dashed lines record the sequential values, and the open nodes connected by solid lines record the hierarchical values. The hierarchically derived curve captures the same tension peaks at events 4, 7, and 11 as the sequentially derived curve does. But because of the inherited values, the hierarchical peaks are magnified and a sense of gradual relaxation toward the tonic in events 7–10 is conveyed. In addition, the hierarchical valleys become more pronounced, particularly at the tonic returns at events 10 and 13. These are welcome refinements. At the same time, it is unsettling that the tension associated with events 10 and

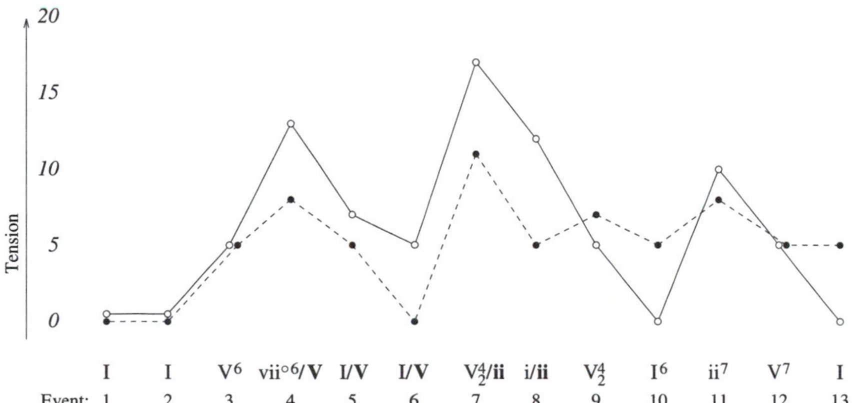

FIGURE 4.9 Graphic representation of the sequential and hierarchical tension values in Figures 4.4 and 4.7. The filled-in nodes connected by dashed lines record the sequential values, and the open nodes connected by solid lines record the hierarchical values.

13 should be the same in the hierarchical analysis. Event 10 feels tenser than event 13. True, the prolongational analysis shows how event 10 is less structural than event 13; and the difference in tension is partly due to rhythmic function (event 10 is in the middle of the phrase; event 13 resolves it). Even so, event 10 is tenser purely as a pitch structure, for it is in inversion and event 13 is not. Figures 4.4 and 4.5 cannot register this fact because their hierarchical tension values derive from a space that is built from pcs rather than pitches.

A related issue is the lack of treatment of dissonance. If it were the actual surface of K. 282 that were under scrutiny rather than a simplified version of it, the analysis would have to take sevenths, passing and neighboring tones, and suspensions into account.

These considerations suggest that the sequential and hierarchical models should be supplemented by an additional factor, "surface dissonance," which evaluates the psychoacoustic tension caused by surface features of an event. The sensory dissonance of an event is affected by which pitches are in the bass and which in the soprano, as well as by the presence or absence of sevenths and nonharmonic tones. Surface dissonance therefore subdivides into three variables: "scale degree," which tracks the melodic note over the triad that supports it ($\hat{1}$, $\hat{3}$ or $\hat{5}$ of the triad); "inversion," which counts whether a chord is in root position or inversion; and "nonharmonic tone," which evaluates all nonharmonic tones, including chordal sevenths. Melodic notes on $\hat{3}$ or $\hat{5}$ are tenser than melodic notes on $\hat{1}$, but they are less tense than chords in inversion, which receive a value of 2; so let us say that melodic notes on $\hat{3}$ or $\hat{5}$ add a tension value of 1. Chords in inversion receive an added value of 2 because the chordal level of the basic space is two levels down from the root. Diatonic nonharmonic tones receive a value of 3 and chromatic nonharmonic tones a value of 4, because they occur three and four levels down in the space, respectively. Sevenths receive an added value of 1, because if they were treated as harmonic their pitch-space values would be one tension unit greater than they would be otherwise (the *k* variable would add 1 at the chordal level). These numerical values are first approximations pending empirical feedback; nor do they incorporate contextual nuances that distinguish, say, the tension of one nonharmonic tone from that of another.

The question as to whether a seventh is harmonic or nonharmonic has a long history in music theory. The stance taken here is simply one of bookkeeping: rather than counting some sevenths as harmonic and others as nonharmonic, it is simpler, and it does not alter the results, to leave the chordal level of pitch space as purely triadic and evaluate the seventh elsewhere in the model.

As in the chord distance rule, the variables for sensory dissonance combine additively:

SURFACE TENSION RULE $T_{diss}(\mathbf{y})$ = scale degree (add 1) + inversion (add 2) + nonharmonic tone (add 1 for sevenths, 3 for diatonic nonharmonic tones, and 4 for chromatic nonharmonic tones), where $T_{diss}(\mathbf{y})$ = the surface tension associated with chord **y**; scale degree = chords with $\hat{3}$ or $\hat{5}$ in the melodic voice; inversion = chords with $\hat{3}$ or $\hat{5}$ in the bass; and nonharmonic tone = any pc in **y**'s span that does not belong to **y**.

Surface dissonance then combines with pitch-space distance to arrive at an overall tension value. For sequential tension,

SEQUENTIAL TENSION RULE (long version) $T_{seq}(\mathbf{y}) = T_{diss}(\mathbf{y}) + \delta(\mathbf{x}_{prec} \rightarrow \mathbf{y})$.

Figure 4.10 carries out this procedure, adding the variables for surface dissonance to the numbers from Figure 4.4.

The picture for hierarchical tension is somewhat more complicated. An event's surface dissonance belongs to the event itself rather than to the larger musical form. In the hierarchical model, therefore, surface dissonance contributes to the local total for an event but does not figure into its inherited value, which reflects the larger prolongational context. Thus the local tension for **y** equals the surface dissonance of **y** plus the pitch-space distance to **y** from its directly superordinate event in the prolongational tree (= [scale degree + inversion + nonharmonic tone] + [$i + j + k$]). The inherited value of **y** equals the sum of the pitch-space distances (excluding surface dissonance) of the superordinate events to which **y** directly and indirectly attaches; and the global tension of **y** equals the local tension for **y** plus **y**'s inherited value. Symbolically,

HIERARCHICAL TENSION RULE (long version) $T_{loc}(\mathbf{y}) = T_{diss}(\mathbf{y}) + \delta(\mathbf{x}_{dom} \rightarrow \mathbf{y})$; and $T_{glob}(\mathbf{y}) = T_{loc}(\mathbf{y}) + T_{inh}(\mathbf{x}_{dom})$.

	surface dissonance			*pitch-space distance*			***total***
	sc.-deg.	inv.	nh.t.	*i*	*j*	*k*	
T_{seq}(0→**1**) [I/**I**]	1	0	0	0	0	0	**1**
T_{seq}(1→**2**) [I]	1	0	0	0	0	0	**1**
T_{seq}(2→**3**) [V^6]	0	2	0	0	1	4	**7**
T_{seq}(3→**4**) [vii^{o6}/V]	1	2	0	1	1	6	**11**
T_{seq}(4→**5**) [I/**V**]	1	0	0	0	1	4	**6**
T_{seq}(5→**6**) [I/**V**]	0	0	0	0	0	0	**0**
T_{seq}(6→**7**) [V$_2$/**ii**]	0	2	1	1	2	8	**14**
T_{seq}(7→**8** [i/**ii**]	1	2	0	0	1	4	**8**
T_{seq}(8→**9**) [V$^4{}_2$]	0	2	1	1	1	5	**10**
T_{seq}(9→**10**) [I^6]	1	2	0	0	1	4	**8**
T_{seq}(10→**11**) [ii^7]	0	0	1 + 3	0	2	6	**12**
T_{seq}(11→**12**) [V^7]	1	0	1	0	1	4	**7**
T_{seq}(12→**13**) [I]	1	0	0	0	1	4	**6**

FIGURE 4.10 Long version of sequential tension: surface dissonance plus sequential pitch-space distance (the latter taken from Figure 4.4). "Sc.-deg." = scale degree; "inv." = inversion; "nh.t." = nonharmonic tone.

	surface dissonance			*pitch-space distance*			*local total*	*inherited value*	***global total***
	sc.-deg.	inv.	nh.t.	*i*	*j*	*k*			
T_{glob}("I"→**1**) [I/I]	1	0	0	0	0	0	1	0	**1**
T_{glob}(1→**2**) [I]	1	0	0	0	0	0	1	0	**1**
T_{glob}(1→**3**) [V^6]	0	2	0	0	1	4	7	0	**7**
T_{glob}(5→**4**) [vii^{o6}/V]	1	2	0	0	1	5	9	5 + 2	**16**
T_{glob}(6→**5**) [I/V]	1	0	0	1	0	1	3	5	**8**
T_{glob}(1→**6**) [V/**I**]	0	0	0	0	1	4	5	0	**5**
T_{glob}(8→**7**) [V_2/**ii**]	0	2	1	0	1	4	8	5 + 7	**20**
T_{glob}(9→**8**) [ii/**I** = i/**ii**]	1	2	0	1	1	5	10	5	**15**
T_{glob}(10→**9**) [V_2]	0	2	1	0	1	4	8	0	**8**
T_{glob}(1→**10**) [I^6]	1	2	0	0	0	0	3	0	**3**
T_{glob}(12→**11**) [ii^7]	0	0	1 + 3	0	1	4	9	5	**14**
T_{glob}(13→**12**) [V^7]	0	0	1	0	1	4	6	0	**6**
T_{glob}(1→**13**) [I]	1	0	0	0	0	0	1	0	**1**

FIGURE 4.11 Long version of hierarchical tension: surface dissonance plus hierarchical pitch-space distance (the latter taken from Figure 4.7).

Figure 4.11 expands Figure 4.7 for $T_{glob}(\mathbf{y})$, showing the same waves of tension and relaxation as before but amplifying them through the additional factors of surface dissonance. Now there is a difference between event 10 (T = 3) and event 13 (T = 1), and it is possible to treat nonharmonic tones.

Stepping back from motivating and stating rules, it should be noted that prolongational structure itself is derived so as to minimize the distance between events within a prolongational region (see "A Representative Analysis" in chapter 1 and "The Principle of the Shortest Path" in chapter 2). A preferred prolongational analysis thus also minimizes tension. To put it the other way around, a comparatively low tension profile is a measure of how "good" a prolongational analysis is—not "good" in an aesthetic sense (indeed, a piece with little tension is likely to be rather dull) but in the sense of the Gestalt principle of *Prägnanz*. Work in the preference-rule computer modeling of harmony and meter (Temperley and Sleator 1999) compares and rates the efficacy of analyses in related ways.

A hierarchical tension analysis

We are now in a position to deal with the actual music of K. 282 rather than a simplified version of it. Interestingly, it proves fruitless to do a sequential tension analysis of the musical surface. Take for instance beat 1 of bar 2, given in Figure 4.12. The appoggiatura E♭ is understood in terms of the following D, and the passing C is understood in terms of the following B♭. The eighth-note level shows this in time-span reductional format. Further, the B♭ on the the fourth sixteenth of beat 1 is heard not only as a delay at the eighth-note level but also as an anticipation of the B♭ on beat 2 at the quarter-note level. Thus the roles of the first, third, and fourth sixteenth notes of beat 1 cannot be represented in a purely sequential model, for their sense depends on notes that follow them. Such situations are characteristic of all but the most unornamented musical surfaces. To comprehend a piece, listeners must perform at least a minimal reduction of surface

FIGURE 4.12 Melodic surface of K. 282, I, bar 2, beats 1–2, together with its time-span reduction at the eighth-note and quarter-note levels.

embellishments. I shall therefore set aside the sequential model for now. It will resurface in a different guise in "An Attractional Approach to Harmony" later in this chapter.

Let us proceed with the hierarchical tension analysis of the surface of bars 1–9. To set the stage, Figure 4.13 sketches the larger context for this segment. After an initial prolongation of **I**, the analysis shows (as one would expect) a prolongation of **V** from the second-theme group to the end of the exposition. The opening I/**I** attaches to the global tonic at the end of the movement, and the I/**V** at the beginning of the second-theme group in bar 9 attaches to the global dominant that concludes the exposition.

The prolongational analysis is broken up for readability into the two graphs in Figures 4.14 and 4.15 (bars 1–4 and 4–9, respectively). Because of a grouping overlap, the I on the downbeat of bar 4 serves a double function, as the resolution of the first phrase in Figure 4.14 and as the beginning of the second phrase in Figure 4.15. Events down to the level of the sixteenth note are numbered for reference; hence the numbering does not correspond to that of the previous figures. The grace notes and trills in the right hand of bars 4–9 are left out, and the arpeggiations of the chords in the left hand are fused in the time-span reduction. As a means of locating the events in the prolongational graphs and in the tension table (shown in Figure 4.17), the events in the graphs are separated between each

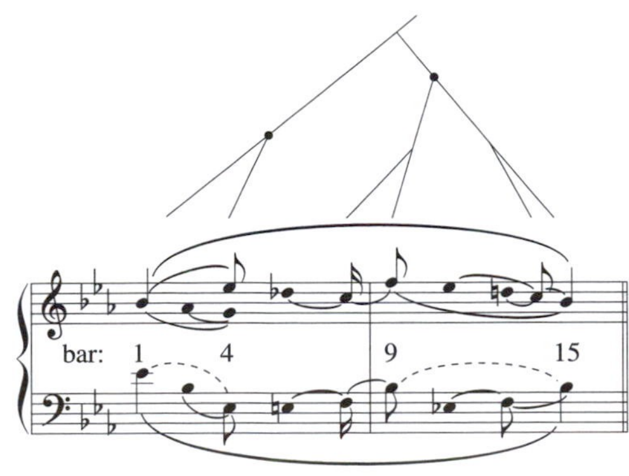

FIGURE 4.13 Global prolongational analysis of the exposition of K. 282, I.

FIGURE 4.14 Prolongational analysis of K. 282, I, bars 1–4.

FIGURE 4.15 Prolongational analysis of K. 282, I, bars 4–9.

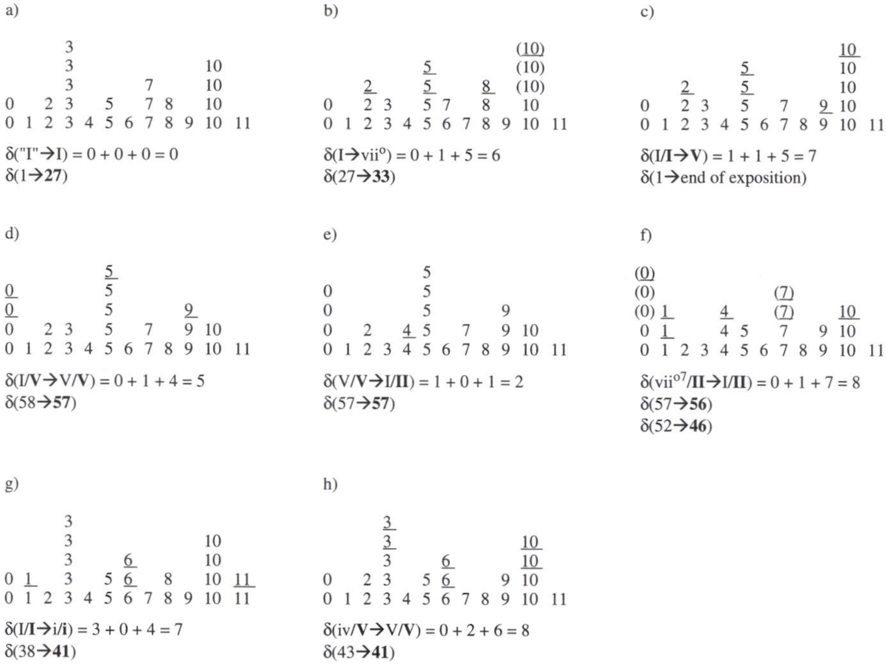

a)

```
      3
      3               10
      3     7         10
0   2 3   5   7 8     10
0 1 2 3 4 5 6 7 8 9 10 11
```

δ("I"→I) = 0 + 0 + 0 = 0
δ(1→**27**)

b)

```
                      (10)
          5           (10)
    2     5     8     (10)
0   2 3   5 7   8     10
0 1 2 3 4 5 6 7 8 9 10 11
```

δ(I→vii°) = 0 + 1 + 5 = 6
δ(27→**33**)

c)

```
                      10
          5           10
    2     5           10
0   2 3   5   7     9 10
0 1 2 3 4 5 6 7 8 9 10 11
```

δ(I/**I**→**V**) = 1 + 1 + 5 = 7
δ(1→**end of exposition**)

d)

```
          5
0         5
0         5       9
0   2 3   5   7   9 10
0 1 2 3 4 5 6 7 8 9 10 11
```

δ(I/**V**→V/**V**) = 0 + 1 + 4 = 5
δ(58→**57**)

e)

```
          5
0         5
0         5       9
0   2   4 5   7   9 10
0 1 2 3 4 5 6 7 8 9 10 11
```

δ(V/**V**→I/**II**) = 1 + 0 + 1 = 2
δ(57→**57**)

f)

```
(0)
(0)             (7)
(0) 1     4     (7)   10
0   1     4 5   7   9 10
0 1 2 3 4 5 6 7 8 9 10 11
```

δ(vii°7/**II**→I/**II**) = 0 + 1 + 7 = 8
δ(57→**56**)
δ(52→**46**)

g)

```
      3
      3               10
      3     6         10
0 1   3   5 6   8     10 11
0 1 2 3 4 5 6 7 8 9 10 11
```

δ(I/**I**→i/**i**) = 3 + 0 + 4 = 7
δ(38→**41**)

h)

```
      3
      3               10
      3     6         10
0   2 3   5 6     9   10
0 1 2 3 4 5 6 7 8 9 10 11
```

δ(iv/**V**→V/**V**) = 0 + 2 + 6 = 8
δ(43→**41**)

FIGURE 4.16 Some local hierarchical distance calculations for bars 4–9.

quarter-note beat by a vertical single line and between each measure by a vertical double line. In the table they are correspondingly separated between each quarter-note beat by a horizontal single line and between each measure by a horizontal double line.

Figure 4.16 provides the most critical calculations for local hierarchical distances in bars 4–9. These will be referred to later. Figure 4.17 displays the tension table for Figures 4.14 and 4.15 in a format like that in Figure 4.11. As before, each **y** appears in temporal sequence; harmonic changes are included in brackets. In the scale-degree column, in addition to the distinctions discussed earlier, 1 is added when the melody is in the upper octave and on $\hat{1}$ over the chord in question. This slight increase in tension is due not to a nontonic scale degree but to change from the normative tessitura. The inherited values proceed as before, by tracing each **y**'s $T_{inh}(x_{dom})$ through the table, in correspondence with the tree. This is done by counting the $i + j + k$ value for each event that directly or indirectly dominates **y**. For example, event 45 (the E♭ appoggiatura on beat 3 of bar 7) inherits 8 from event 46 (see Figure 4.16f), which inherits 0 from event 52, which inherits 7 (5 + 2) from event 57 (Figures 4.16d–e), which inherits 7 from the V at the close of of the exposition (Figure 4.16c), which inherits 0 from the global tonic. Thus event 45's total inheritance = 8 + 0 + 7 + 7 + 0 = 22. To this is added event 45's surface dissonance, which equals 4 because of the chromatic appoggiatura, yielding a global total of T(ev 45) = 26. All the other calculations are performed in comparable fashion.

A word is required about events 57 and 39 (event 39 for the current point equals event 41, from which it differs only in its melodic note). As with the pivots cited earlier, event 57 has a dual interpretation depending on its contextual scope. Very locally, it is tonicized as I/**II**; but at the level at which event 43 (V^7/**V**) anticipates and attaches to it, it assumes the global function of V/**V**. In terms of distance values, δ(I/**V**→I/**II**) = 1 + 1 + 5 = 7, whereas δ(I/**V**→V/**V**) = 0 + 1 + 4 = 5. The conversion from the latter to the former, or δ(V/**V**→I/**II**) = 1 + 0 + 1 = 2, takes place at prolongational level d. Figure 4.17 shows both calculations, with those from the global perspective in parentheses. Event 39 brings up another kind of dual interpretation, not one of prolongational level but one of prospective versus retrospective hearing. At first, event 39 sounds like a right-

	surface dissonance			*pitch-space distance*			*local total*	*inherited value*	***global total***
	sc.-deg.	inv.	nh.t.	*i*	*j*	*k*			
T_{glob}("I"-->**1**) [I/**I**]	1	0	0	0	0	0	1	0	**1**
T_{glob}(1-->**2**)	0	0	2	0	0	0	2	0	**2**

T_{glob}(1-->**3**) [I]	1	0	0	0	0	0	1	0	**1**

T_{glob}(1-->**4**) [V^6]	0	2	0	0	1	4	7	0	**7**
T_{glob}(4-->**5**)	0	2	0	0	0	0	2	5	**7**

T_{glob}(7-->**6**)	0	2	2	0	0	0	4	7 + 6	**17**
T_{glob}(9-->**7**) [vii^{o6}/**V**]	1	2	0	0	1	5	9	7	**16**
======									
T_{glob}(9-->**8**)	0	0	3	0	0	0	3	7	**10**
T_{glob}(12-->**9**) [I/**V**]	1	0	0	1	0	1	3	5	**8**
T_{glob}(11-->**10**)	0	0	3	0	0	0	3	5	**8**
T_{glob}(12-->**11**)	0	0	0	0	0	0	0	5	**5**

T_{glob}(1-->**12**) [V/**I**]	0	0	0	0	1	4	5	0	**5**

T_{glob}(15-->**13**)	0	2	3	0	0	0	5	17	**22**
T_{glob}(15-->**14**)	0	2	1	0	0	0	3	12 + 5	**20**
T_{glob}(16-->**15**) [V_2/**ii**]	0	2	1	0	1	4	8	5 + 7	**20**

T_{glob}(21-->**16**) [ii/**I** = i/**ii**]	1	2	0	1	1	5	10	5	**15**
T_{glob}(16-->**17**)	1	2	0	0	0	0	3	5 + 7	**15**
T_{glob}(17-->**18**)	0	0	3	0	0	0	3	12	**15**
=======									
T_{glob}(21-->**19**)	0	2	1 + 3	0	0	0	6	5	**11**
T_{glob}(21-->**20**)	0	2	1	0	0	0	3	5	**8**
T_{glob}(22-->**21**) [V_2]	0	2	1	0	1	4	8	0	**8**

T_{glob}(1-->**22**) [I^6]	1	2	0	0	0	0	3	0	**3**
T_{glob}(22-->**23**)	1	2	0	0	0	0	3	0	**3**
T_{glob}(23-->**24**)	1	2	0	0	0	0	3	0	**3**

T_{glob}(26-->**25**) [ii^7]	0	0	1 + 3	0	1	4	9	5	**14**

T_{glob}(27-->**26**) [V^7]	0	0	1	0	1	4	6	0	**6**
=======									
T_{glob}(1-->**27**) [I/**I**]	1	0	0	0	0	0	1	0	**1**

T_{glob}(27-->**28**)	1	0	0	0	0	0	1	0	**1**

T_{glob}(31-->**29**)	1	0	0	0	0	0	1	0	**1**

FIGURE 4.17 Hierarchical tension values, bars 1–9.

	surface dissonance			*pitch-space distance*			*local total*	*inherited value*	***global total***
	sc.-deg.	inv.	nh.t.	*i*	*j*	*k*			
T_{glob}(31-->**30**)	0	0	3	0	0	0	3	0	**3**
T_{glob}(27-->**31**)	1	0	0	0	0	0	1	0	**1**
=======									
T_{glob}(33-->**32**)	0	2	3	0	0	0	5	6	**11**

T_{glob}(27-->**33**) [vii^{o6}]	0	2	1	0	1	5	9	0	**9**

T_{glob}(36-->**34**)	1	2	0	0	0	0	3	6	**9**

T_{glob}(36-->**35**)	0	2	3	0	0	0	5	6	**11**
T_{glob}(33-->**36**)	1	2	0	0	0	0	3	6	**9**
=======									
T_{glob}(38-->**37**)	0	2	3	0	0	0	5	0	**5**

T_{glob}(27-->**38**) [I^6]	1	2	0	0	0	0	3	0	**3**

T_{glob}(41-->**39**) [iv^6/V]	1	2	0	0	0	0	3	12 + 8	**23**

T_{glob}(41-->**40**)	0	2	3	0	0	0	5	12 + 8	**25**
T_{glob}(43-->**41**)	1	2	0	0	2	6	11	12	**23**
=======									
T_{glob}(43-->**42**)	0	0	1 + 3	0	0	0	4	12	**16**
T_{glob}(57-->**43**) [V^7/V]	1	0	0	0	0	1	2	7 + 5	**14**

T_{glob}(43-->**44**)	1	0	0	0	0	0	1	12 + 1	**14**

T_{glob}(46-->**45**)	0	0	4	0	0	0	4	14 + 8	**26**
T_{glob}(52-->**46**) [vii^{o7}/**II**]	1	0	0	0	1	7	9	14	**23**

T_{glob}(46-->**47**)	1	0	0	0	0	0	1	14 + 8	**23**
=======									
T_{glob}(52-->**48**)	1	0	0	0	0	0	1	14	**15**
T_{glob}(50-->**49**)	0	2	0	0	1	4	7	14	**21**
T_{glob}(48-->**50**)	1	0	0	0	0	0	1	14	**15**
T_{glob}(52-->**51**)	1	2	0	0	1	4	8	14	**22**

T_{glob}(57-->**52**)	1	0	0	0	0	0	1	14	**15**
T_{glob}(54-->**53**)	1	2	0	0	1	7	11	14	**25**
T_{glob}(52-->**54**)	1	0	0	0	0	0	1	14	**15**
T_{glob}(56-->**55**)	1	2	0	0	0	0	3	14+8	**25**

T_{glob}(57-->**56**)	1	2	0	0	1	7	11	14	**25**

T_{glob}(58-->**57**) [V/V=I/**II**]	1	0	0	1(0)	1	5(4)	8(6)	7(5)	**15(11)**
=======									
T_{glob}("V"-->**58**) [I/**V**]	0	0	0	0	0	0	0	7	**7**

FIGURE 4.17 (Continued)

branching minor coloration of the tonic, in which case δ(I⁶/**I**→i⁶/**i**) = 7 (Figure 4.16g). But already by the downbeat of the next bar it retrospectively behaves as a left-branching minor subdominant heading toward the new region of **B♭**, in which case δ(iv⁶/**V**→V⁷/**V**) = 8 (Figure 4.16h). This left-branching interpretation is taken, in slight violation of the shortest path, because it enables normative prolongational structure to be satisfied for this phrase. Since the V⁷/**V** is embedded with respect to the global tonic, the iv⁶/**V** then inherits further values, making it one of the tenser moments in the entire excerpt.

Figure 4.18 completes this analysis by graphically plotting the values from Figure 4.17 over the music from Figures 4.14 and 4.15. Beneath the music the two large phrases are labeled A (bars 1–4) and B (bars 4–9); within A are subphrases

a_1 and a_2, and within B are subphrases b_1 and b_2. The archetypal tension pattern is to begin in relative relaxation, to tense in the middle, and to relax toward closure. This pattern occurs for subphrases a_1 and b_1, for phrases A and B, and for the entire section A + B, projecting them all as articulated units. Moreover, each of these units (except A) concludes, after the intervening tension, in a state of relaxation that is nonetheless greater in tension than at its onset. This composite upward trajectory helps propel the music forward from its beginning. If the end of the exposition or of the entire movement were under consideration, the balances in phrasal tension would tip the other way. The exceptions to the archetypal pattern are the structurally parallel subphrases a_2 and b_2, which both begin in tension and move toward relaxation with momentary crests before their cadences. The high tension that starts a_2 and b_2 prevents them from seeming like phrase beginnings and instead integrates them into their larger phrases. The crests magnify the subsequent sharp falls in tension that mark the phrase endings.

Reformulation of the interaction principle

The enriched tables for hierarchical tension employed in Figures 4.11 and 4.17 can be read as a gloss on the three branching categories for prolongational reduction. Because inheritance (T_{inh} in the hierarchical tension rule) is irrelevant to immediate branching, the column "inherited value" can be ignored for this purpose, and the relevant function becomes not T_{glob} but T_{loc}. The gloss is this: (1) if for any $T_{loc}(\mathbf{y})$ there is no change between x_{dom} and $\mathbf{y}$ in the columns for surface dissonance and if **y**'s pitch-space distance values are all 0, the result is a strong prolongation; (2) if there is a change in the column for scale degree or inversion and if **y**'s pitch-space distance values remain at 0, the result is a weak prolongation; and (3) if any of **y**'s pitch-space distance values are not 0, the result is a progression.

This perspective suggests a reformulation of GTTM's interaction principle, which, as will be recalled from "A Representative Analysis" in chapter 1, regulates the derivation of prolongational structure from the time-span analysis:

INTERACTION PRINCIPLE (revised from GTTM) To assign the prolongationally most important event e_k within prolongational region $(e_i\text{–}e_j)$,
(1) derive prolongational level ${}_{p}L_n$ from the most global available time-span level ${}_{ts}L_n$
(2) within $(e_i\text{–}e_j)$, choose from ${}_{ts}L_n$
 (a) the e_k that forms the smallest value between $T_{loc}(e_i \rightarrow \mathbf{e_k})$ and $T_{loc}(e_j \rightarrow \mathbf{e_k})$, and attach $\mathbf{e_k}$ to that e_i or e_j
 (b) except if there is a $T_{loc}(e_i \rightarrow \mathbf{e_k}) = 0$ at ${}_{ts}L_{n-1}$, in which case attach that e_k to e_j before returning to step (2a)
(3) repeat steps (2a–b) at ${}_{ts}L_{n-1}$ and ${}_{p}L_{n-1}$, and continue recursively until all events are assigned.

This version of the interaction principle incorporates the principle of the shortest path phrased in terms of the rule for hierarchical tension. Step (2b) enables a right-branching strong prolongation from an event at the next lower level to

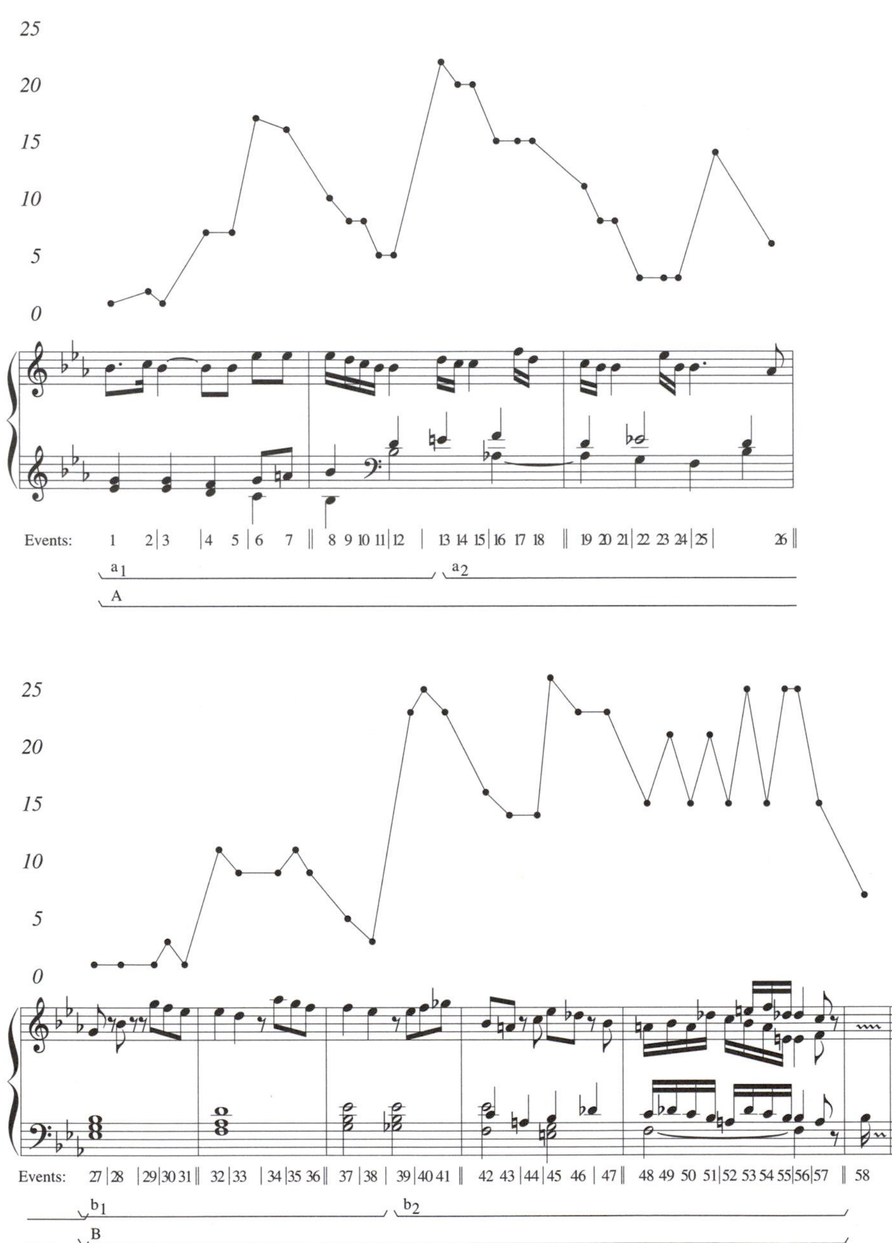

FIGURE 4.18 Graphic representation of the hierarchical tension values in Figure 4.17.

be assigned at the current level of derivation. The output of the interaction principle then interacts with the rule for prolongational good form (see "Issues in Prolongational Theory" in chapter 1) to determine the overall preferred branching structure.

MELODIC TENSION

Anchoring and asymmetry

The harmonic tension model evaluates tension at the levels of the chord and the region but does not address tension at the level of the individual pitch sequence—that is, at the level of melody—except through the distinction between harmonic and nonharmonic tones. I turn now to a central aspect of melodic tension and relaxation, the resolution of a dissonant pitch to a consonant neighbor. Invoking principles of proximity and asymmetry, Bharucha (1984a) provides a psychological account for this "anchoring principle." The Gestalt principle of proximity is familiar. According to the principle of asymmetry (see "Empirical Issues" in chapter 2), and assuming a I/**C** context, unstable B is judged as closer to stable C if B precedes C than if C precedes B. The basis of anchoring, then, is the psychological need for an unstable pitch to be assimilated to an immediately subsequent proximate and stable pitch, which is its cognitive reference point (Rosch 1975). Classical tonal syntax manifests these psychological factors in its treatment of basic voice-leading dissonances: the passing tone, the neighboring tone, the suspension, and the appoggiatura all resolve by step to the next pitch.

The basic space and its transformations by the chord distance rule do not reflect these perceptual asymmetries but take for granted that, for example, the distances from B to C and from C to B, or from I to V and from V to I, are the same. Here I shall offer another kind of solution to the asymmetry question after first developing and illustrating a quantification of the anchoring principle.

The melodic attraction rule

Figure 4.19 repeats the basic space, oriented to I/**C**. Because melody is the concern, upper C is included and each letter name stands for a pitch rather than a pc. The calculations work out better if the fifth level, necessary for harmonic and

Depth of Embedding	*The basic space with the fifth level omitted*												
0	C												C
1	C				E			G					C
2	C		D		E	F		G		A		B	C
3	C	C♯	D	D♯	E	F	F♯	G	A♭	A	B♭	B	C

FIGURE 4.19 The basic pitch space oriented to I/**C**, with levels of embedding indicated.

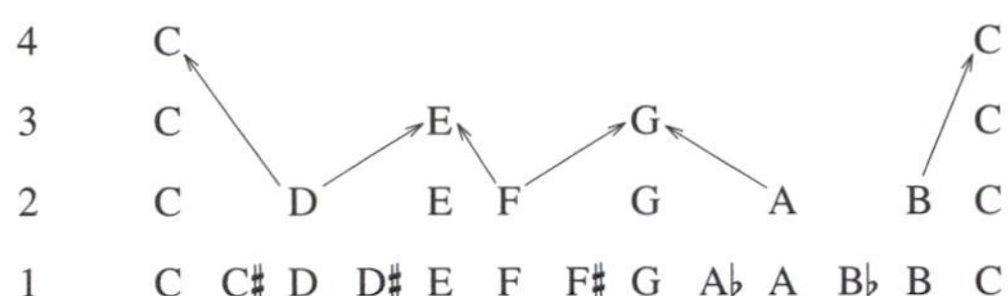

FIGURE 4.20 Neighboring attractions in a I/**C** context, with anchoring strength indicated by level.

regional modeling, is suppressed for melodic modeling; this places $\hat{3}$ and $\hat{5}$ at the same level. The depth of embedding of each level is given at the left. If each pitch is evaluated at its most stable embedding number, depth of embedding becomes a marker of how tense a pitch is in the context I/**C**. (With adjustments, this procedure corresponds to that used earlier in the values for the surface dissonance of nonharmonic tones.) Thus C has a melodic tension value of 0, C♯ of 3, D of 2, and so on. A rising C major scale has the tension sequence 0–2–1–2–1–2–2–0. If the chord changes, the basic space changes as well, leading to different embedding numbers for individual pitches.

A few definitions will facilitate the discussion. A neighbor to any pitch p_x at any level L_y is a pitch that is adjacent to p_x at L_y. For example, in a I/**C** context, C♯ and D are neighbors at the chromatic level, D and E are neighbors at the diatonic level, and E and C are neighbors at the chordal level. Assuming p_x is not present at L_{y+1}, an equal neighbor of p_x at L_y is a pitch that is adjacent but not present at L_{y+1}. A superordinate neighbor of p_x at L_y is both adjacent and present at L_{y+1}. A subordinate neighbor of p_x is not present at L_y but is both adjacent and present at L_{y-1}. In a I/**C** context, B is an equal neighbor to A, G is a superordinate neighbor to A, and A is a subordinate neighbor to G. A given pitch tends to anchor to or be relatively attracted to a superordinate neighbor. If p_x is more attracted to pitch p_y than p_y is to p_x, then p_y is an attractor for p_x.

The arrows in Figure 4.20 illustrate at the diatonic level the attractions to superordinate neighbors. These upward motions in the space, if they occur, assimilate the dissonances to the referential harmony and carry with them a reduction in tension (see "The Pitch-Class Level" in chapter 2). Figure 4.20 also reorders the numbering for embedding levels so that the least embedded level has the largest anchoring number. This second set of numbers represents the relative anchoring strength, or attractive power, of the pitches in a I/**C** context.

The more stable and the more proximate the attractor, the greater the tendency of the unstable pitch to anchor to it. These factors can be quantified. Relative stability, which is read off the vertical axis in Figure 4.20, is given by the ratio in anchoring strength between the two pitches. The attraction of D to E is 3/2 (anchoring strength 3 over anchoring strength 2), whereas the attraction of D to C is 4/2. Hence D is more attracted to C than to E. Melodic proximity is counted on the horizontal axis by the number of steps at the chromatic level between the two pitches in question. B is one semitone and D is two semitones from C. The greater the proximity, the greater the attraction; B is more attracted to C than is D. In other words, the attraction to the stable tone is inversely proportional to its distance. In the spirit of Newton's inverse-square law (the gravitational attraction between two masses is inversely proportional to the square of the distance between them), intuitions of anchoring appear to be modeled more accurately if the distance between the two pitches is squared. Thus the attraction by proximity of B to C equals $1/1^2$, whereas that of D to C equals $1/2^2$.

The following formula combines relative stability with distance:

MELODIC ATTRACTION $\alpha(p_1 \rightarrow p_2) = s_2/s_1 \times 1/n^2$, where p_1 and p_2 are pitches, with $p_1 \neq p_2$; $\alpha(p_1 \rightarrow p_2)$ = the attraction of p_1 to p_2; s_1 = the anchoring strength of p_1 and s_2 = the anchoring strength of p_2 in the current configuration of the basic space; and n = the number of semitone intervals between p_1 and p_2. (The stipulation $p_1 \neq p_2$ avoids denominator of 0.)

The inverse-square factor represents melodic attractions as behaving like a physical field. But the gravitational analogy as such need not be pressed. Quantificational details may require modification should future empirical evidence demonstrate the need. It is the explanatory factors embodied in the rule, stability and proximity, that really matter. Larson (1994, 1995) and Dirk Povel (1996) also propose these factors. The distinction of the attraction model here is that it quantifies these factors and integrates them into a larger theory of musical cognition.

The rule yields plausible results. Figure 4.21 carries out, in the context I/**C**, the attraction rule for each nontriadic diatonic pitch in relation to its triadic neighbors. At the right these attractions are generalized in terms of scale degrees. A dissonant pitch is most attracted to whichever superordinate neighbor has the higher value in the attraction rule. Thus, as shown by the numbers in the figure, B and D tend to anchor to C, F to E, and A to G. More specifically, B is strongly attracted to its single superordinate neighbor C, which is twice as stable and one semitone away. D is equidistant from C and E but is slightly more attracted to C because C is more stable than E. Conversely, F lies between two pitches, E and G, which are equally stable, but is more attracted to E because E is more proximate than G. A is weakly attracted to its single superordinate neighbor G, which is two semitones away.

$\alpha(B \rightarrow C) = 4/2 \times 1/1^2 = 4/2 = 2$ $[\hat{7} \rightarrow \hat{8}]$
$\alpha(D \rightarrow C) = 4/2 \times 1/2^2 = 4/8 = 0.5$ $[\hat{2} \rightarrow \hat{1}]$
$\alpha(D \rightarrow E) = 3/2 \times 1/2^2 = 3/8 = 0.375$ $[\hat{2} \rightarrow \hat{3}]$
$\alpha(F \rightarrow E) = 3/2 \times 1/1^2 = 3/2 = 1.5$ $[\hat{4} \rightarrow \hat{3}]$
$\alpha(F \rightarrow G) = 3/2 \times 1/2^2 = 3/8 = 0.375$ $[\hat{4} \rightarrow \hat{5}]$
$\alpha(A \rightarrow G) = 3/2 \times 1/2^2 = 3/8 = 0.375$ $[\hat{6} \rightarrow \hat{5}]$

FIGURE 4.21 Application of the attraction rule for nontriadic diatonic pitches in the context I/**C**. The attractors are superordinate neighbors.

FIGURE 4.22 Application of the attraction rule for nontriadic diatonic pitches in relation to their superordinate neighbors in the context i/c (assuming the natural-minor scale).

$\alpha(B\flat \rightarrow C) = {}^4/_2 \times {}^1/_{2^2} = {}^4/_8 = 0.5$	$[\hat{7} \rightarrow \hat{8}]$
$\alpha(D \rightarrow C) = {}^4/_2 \times {}^1/_{2^2} = {}^1/_2 = 0.5$	$[\hat{2} \rightarrow \hat{1}]$
$\alpha(D \rightarrow E\flat) = {}^3/_2 \times {}^1/_{1^2} = {}^3/_2 = 1.5$	$[\hat{2} \rightarrow \hat{3}]$
$\alpha(F \rightarrow E\flat) = {}^3/_2 \times {}^1/_{2^2} = {}^3/_8 = 0.375$	$[\hat{4} \rightarrow \hat{3}]$
$\alpha(F \rightarrow G) = {}^3/_2 \times {}^1/_{2^2} = {}^3/_8 = 0.375$	$[\hat{4} \rightarrow \hat{5}]$
$\alpha(A\flat \rightarrow G) = {}^3/_2 \times {}^1/_{1^2} = {}^3/_2 = 1.5$	$[\hat{6} \rightarrow \hat{5}]$

It is intuitively apparent that the greatest attraction is from $\hat{7}$ to $\hat{8}$, followed closely by $\hat{4}$ to $\hat{3}$; then come the weaker attractions of $\hat{6}$ to $\hat{5}$ and $\hat{2}$ to $\hat{1}$. The numbers in Figure 4.21 reflect this ordering.

As a complement to Figure 4.21, Figure 4.22 provides attractional calculations in the context i/**c**. $\hat{2}$ is pulled more strongly to $\hat{3}$ in the minor mode than in the major, as is $\hat{6}$ to $\hat{5}$, because of the resulting half-step distances. However, now $\hat{2}$ appears as less attracted to $\hat{1}$ than to $\hat{3}$, and $\hat{4}$ is equally attracted to $\hat{5}$ and $\hat{3}$. If to some ears these results seem counterintuitive, it may be because, as suggested by Schenker (1906) and Schoenberg (1911/1978), we construe the minor mode partly in imitation of the major mode. That is, the schema for major-mode attractions may interact with the attraction rule to modify the final judgment for minor-mode attractions. I shall disregard this presumed factor and keep to the results of the attraction rule. In one important respect, however, the minor mode is inflected both in imitation of the major mode and in a way supported by the rule: harmonic issues aside, $\hat{7}$ is typically raised in minor because the value $\alpha(B\flat \rightarrow C) = 0.5$ does not provide adequate centering on the tonic, especially in light of $\alpha(D \rightarrow E\flat) = 1.5$ and $\alpha(A\flat \rightarrow G) = 1.5$. The value for the raised leading tone, $\alpha(B \rightarrow C) = 2$, brings to the minor mode the needed attractional superiority of the tonic.

Now consider chromatic pitches that appear at the diatonic level of the space. If a new configuration of the space is invoked—for instance, when F♯ moves the space to a G major scale via the chord distance rule—everything proceeds as before under the new chordal/regional context. By contrast, if the chromatic pitch is interpreted as a diatonic inflection, as in the raised leading tone in minor, the space is altered at the inflection and the attraction rule proceeds accordingly. Two instances of diatonic inflection, D to D♯ and D to D♭, are given for the context I/**C** in Figure 4.23. D♯ is more attracted to E and less attracted to C than is the case with D in Figure 4.21, and D♭ is more attracted to C and less attracted to E than is D in Figure 4.21.

The melodic attraction rule works at the chromatic and triadic levels of the space as well. It applies at the chromatic level in a chromatic appoggiatura, for instance, or for a chromatic passing tone between diatonic neighbors. The rule predicts that the chromatic pitch is strongly attracted to resolve on a neighboring scale member, and very strongly so if the neighboring scale member is also an adjacent chord member. Thus, in the context I/**C**, $\alpha(C\sharp \rightarrow D)$ and $\alpha(D\sharp \rightarrow E)$ yield the large values given in Figure 4.24a. (If a chromaticism of this type were to resolve by an interval larger than semitone, it would not remain at the chromatic

a)

C C
C E G C
C D♯E F G A B C
C C♯D D♯E F F♯ G A♭A B♭B C

$\alpha(\text{D}\sharp \rightarrow \text{E}) = {}^{3}/_{2} \times {}^{1}/_{1^2} = {}^{3}/_{2} = 1.5$
$\alpha(\text{D}\sharp \rightarrow \text{C}) = {}^{4}/_{2} \times {}^{1}/_{3^2} = {}^{4}/_{18} = 0.22$

b)

C C
C E G C
C D♭ E F G A B C
C D♭ D D♯E F F♯ G A♭A B♭B C

$\alpha(\text{D}\flat \rightarrow \text{C}) = {}^{4}/_{2} \times {}^{1}/_{1^2} = 2$
$\alpha(\text{D}\flat \rightarrow \text{E}) = {}^{3}/_{2} \times {}^{1}/_{3^2} = {}^{3}/_{18} = 0.17$

FIGURE 4.23 Two chromatically inflected pitches in the context I/C, together with applications of the attraction rule.

level of the space but would be reinterpreted within some other diatonic/harmonic context.) At the triadic level, in contrast, the rule shows a negligible attraction of $\hat{3}$ and $\hat{5}$ to $\hat{1}$, as shown in Figure 4.24b. That is, $\hat{1}$ exerts little pull on $\hat{3}$ and $\hat{5}$ because the latter are already quite stable and are some distance away in semitones. (Remember that the attraction in question is melodic. Arpeggiation, being a harmonic phenomenon, lies outside the purview of the rule.) The scheme for numbering the levels of the basic space contributes to this difference in attractional force between the chromatic and triadic levels. The ratio for moving from the chromatic to the diatonic levels is $^2/_1$, while that for moving from the triadic to the root level is $^4/_3$, a smaller number. The more unstable a pitch, the more it needs to resolve.

The rule also applies to attractions to nonneighboring superordinate pitches, although their nonadjacency gives them relatively small values, as illustrated in Figure 4.24c. The attraction of A to C is close to twice as small as $\alpha(\text{A}\rightarrow\text{G})$ because of A's nonproximity to C, despite the latter's anchoring strength. The attraction of B to G is so tiny a value compared to $\alpha(\text{B}\rightarrow\text{C})$ that one scarcely thinks of B as being attracted to G at all. Still another example is $\alpha(\text{F}\rightarrow\text{C})$, again a minuscule value because of the large semitone distance. Indeed, the inverse-square factor renders inconsequential any attractions between pitches more than a major second apart. It is noteworthy that this interval before the critical drop in values corresponds to the width of the attention band (see "Empirical Issues" in chapter 2); one might also call it the attraction band.

a)

$\alpha(\text{C}\sharp \rightarrow \text{D}) = {}^{2}/_{1} \times {}^{1}/_{1^2} = 2$
$\alpha(\text{D}\sharp \rightarrow \text{E}) = {}^{3}/_{1} \times {}^{1}/_{1^2} = 3$

b)

$\alpha(\text{E} \rightarrow \text{C}) = {}^{4}/_{3} \times {}^{1}/_{4^2} = {}^{4}/_{48} = 0.08$
$\alpha(\text{G} \rightarrow \text{C}) = {}^{4}/_{3} \times {}^{1}/_{5^2} = {}^{4}/_{75} = 0.05$

c)

$\alpha(\text{A} \rightarrow \text{C}) = {}^{4}/_{2} \times {}^{1}/_{3^2} = {}^{4}/_{18} = 0.22$
$\alpha(\text{B} \rightarrow \text{G}) = {}^{3}/_{2} \times {}^{1}/_{4^2} = {}^{3}/_{32} = 0.09$
$\alpha(\text{F} \rightarrow \text{C}) = {}^{4}/_{2} \times {}^{1}/_{5^2} = {}^{4}/_{50} = 0.08$

FIGURE 4.24 Further applications of the attraction rule: (a) attraction of chromatic pitches to their diatonic neighbors; (b) attraction of triadic pitches to their tonic neighbor; (c) attraction of diatonic pitches to superordinate nonneighbors.

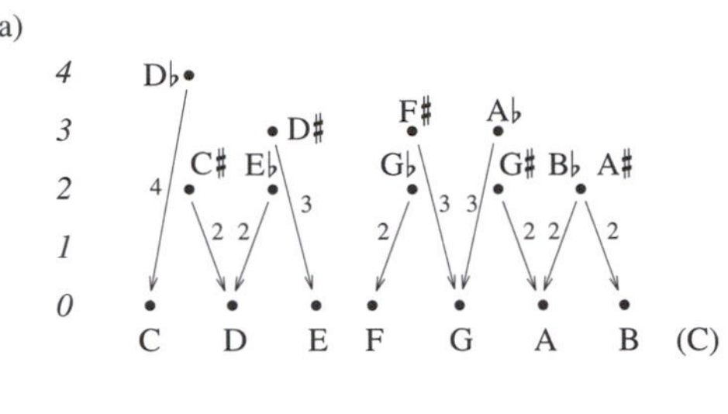

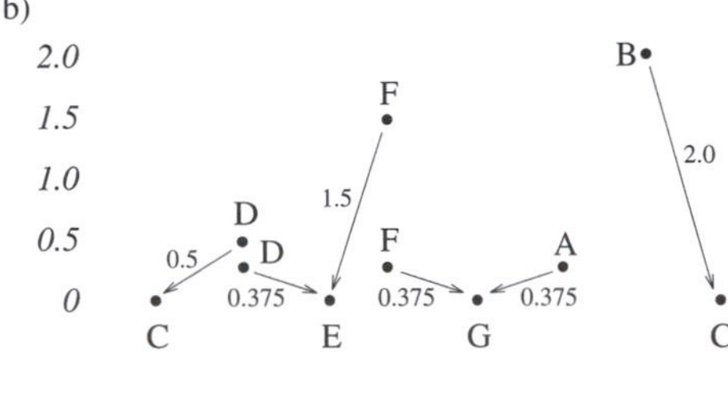

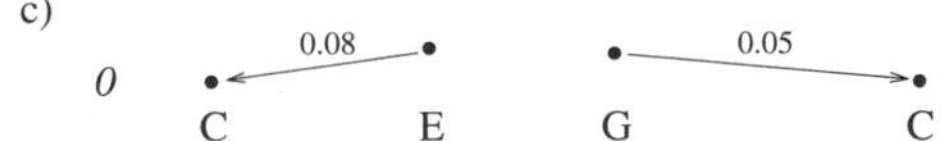

FIGURE 4.25 Graphic format for attractions to superordinate neighbors at all levels of the basic space in the context I/**C**: (a) chromatic to diatonic pitches; (b) diatonic to triadic pitches; (c) triadic pitches to the tonic pitch.

Figure 4.25 summarizes in graphic format the attractions to superordinate neighbors at all levels of the basic space for I/**C** (see Figures 4.21 and 4.24a–b). The graph breaks down into three parts for the chromatic, diatonic, and triadic levels. At each level the pitches are arrayed on the *x* axis and the attractional values on the *y* axis. The arrows indicate the goals and sizes of the attractions.

Historical precedents

Various strands in the history of music theory resonate with the melodic attraction rule. Briefly, Rameau's (1737) account of the attraction of nontonic pitches to the tonic resembles Newtonian descriptions of the gravitational pull of greater on lesser bodies (Christensen 1993). In a remarkable passage, J.-J. de Momigny (1806) proposes the inverse proportionality of proximity as the basis of pitch attractions, while rejecting gravity in the sense of downward pull (where "down" takes its conventional meaning in terms of musical register):

> To move regularly from a chord to another is to move each voice of the antecedent to the note of the consequent that attracts it, and this what musicians call "to resolve" . . . It follows from the need to resolve the notes of an antecedent chord by those of the consequent that there exists a true attraction or affinity between these notes . . . Like the attraction recognized in physics in relation to the inertia of bodies, this attraction acts in inverse relation to distance: a tone that is only half a step away from the one that

> has to follow it is much more powerfully attracted by it, than were it [separated] by a whole step . . . Since it is sometimes the lower tone that attracts the higher tone, and sometimes the higher that attracts the lower one, it follows that the attraction is not due to gravity but to proximity. (Translated in Dogantan 1997)

F.-J. Fétis (1844) asserts that the strong attractions of $\hat{7}$ to $\hat{8}$ and $\hat{4}$ to $\hat{3}$ lie at the heart of tonal behavior. Mathis Lussy (1874) refers to the attraction of the tonic as like that of planets to the sun and notes that proximate tones exert a greater attraction than distant ones (Dogantan 1997). Ernst Kurth (1920) views chromatic harmony as potential and kinetic energies surging toward stepwise resolution (Rothfarb 1988). Hindemith (1937/1942) gives special status in his theory of harmonic progression to the attractional force of semitone motion. Schenker (1921–1924) speaks of the "will of the tones," and his (1935/1979) *Urlinie* that begins on $\hat{5}$ or $\hat{3}$ follows anchoring tendencies. After establishment of the head tone on $\hat{5}$, $\hat{4}$ anchors on $\hat{3}$ and $\hat{2}$ on $\hat{1}$. The *Urlinie* that begins on $\hat{3}$ is contained within the $\hat{5}$ line. But the *Urlinie* that begins on $\hat{8}$ does not follow anchoring tendencies between $\hat{7}$ and $\hat{6}$, which partly accounts for its inferior status within that theoretical tradition. Victor Zuckerkandl (1956) ascribes scale-degree tendencies as in Figures 4.21–22 and asserts that "musical tones point to one another, attract and are attracted—hearing musical tones is hearing directional forces" Zuckerkandl, 35). Deryck Cooke (1959) attempts a lexicon of musical expression based on "what the notes are and what tensions exist between them" (Cooke, 40). He, too, arrives qualitatively at the attractional tendencies in Figures 4.21–22. Karol Berger (2000) discusses tonal tendencies in similar terms, ascribing to them intuitions of musical line and expression, and concludes that "a theory harmony is successful to the extent that it describes [one's] experience of the tonal tendencies of sounds correctly" (Berger, 33).

Attractional asymmetries

Up to this point we have considered only attractions to more stable pitches—that is, where $s_2 > s_1$. Not only does the Earth attract the moon, but also the moon attracts the Earth. Analogously, the attraction rule models the attraction of pitches to equally stable pitches, where $s_2 = s_1$, and to less stable pitches, where $s_2 < s_1$. Figure 4.26a performs this calculation at the diatonic level for equal neighbors, Figure 4.26b for subordinate neighbors.

Attractions where $s_2 > s_1$ are necessarily greater than where $s_2 \leqslant s_1$. This imbalance illuminates the issue of perceptual asymmetry. The distances between C and B and between B and C are the same, but the attractions on C and B are different. In the attraction rule the numerator and denominator for s_1 and s_2 invert when comparing α(p1→p2) and α(p2→p1), while $1/n^2$ remains the same. Therefore, the ratio between mutual attractions equals $s2/s1 \div s1/s2$. For B and C in a I/**C** context, $s_2/s_1 = 4/2$, so **B** is four times ($4/2 \div 2/4$) as attracted to C as C is to B: α(B→C) = 2 and α(C→B) = 0.5. When presented with the pairs B to C and C to B in a I/**C** context, the listener appears to merge this attractional

a)

$\alpha(A\rightarrow B) = {}^{2}/_{2} \times {}^{1}/_{2^2} = {}^{2}/_{8} = 0.25 \quad [\hat{6}\rightarrow\hat{7}]$

$\alpha(B\rightarrow A) = {}^{2}/_{2} \times {}^{1}/_{2^2} = {}^{2}/_{8} = 0.25 \quad [\hat{7}\rightarrow\hat{6}]$

$\alpha(E\rightarrow G) = {}^{3}/_{3} \times {}^{1}/_{3^2} = {}^{3}/_{27} = 0.11 \quad [\hat{3}\rightarrow\hat{5}]$

$\alpha(G\rightarrow E) = {}^{3}/_{3} \times {}^{1}/_{3^2} = {}^{3}/_{27} = 0.11 \quad [\hat{5}\rightarrow\hat{3}]$

b)

$\alpha(C\rightarrow B) = {}^{2}/_{4} \times {}^{1}/_{1^2} = {}^{2}/_{4} = 0.5 \quad [\hat{8}\rightarrow\hat{7}]$

$\alpha(C\rightarrow D) = {}^{2}/_{4} \times {}^{1}/_{2^2} = {}^{2}/_{16} = 0.125 \quad [\hat{1}\rightarrow 2]$

$\alpha(E\rightarrow D) = {}^{2}/_{3} \times {}^{1}/_{2^2} = {}^{2}/_{12} = 0.17 \quad [\hat{3}\rightarrow\hat{2}]$

$\alpha(E\rightarrow F) = {}^{2}/_{3} \times {}^{1}/_{1^2} = {}^{2}/_{3} = 0.67 \quad [\hat{3}\rightarrow\hat{4}]$

$\alpha(G\rightarrow F) = {}^{2}/_{3} \times {}^{1}/_{2^2} = {}^{2}/_{12} = 0.17 \quad [\hat{5}\rightarrow\hat{4}]$

$\alpha(G\rightarrow A) = {}^{2}/_{3} \times {}^{1}/_{2^2} = {}^{2}/_{12} = 0.17 \quad [\hat{5}\rightarrow\hat{6}]$

$\alpha(C\rightarrow E) = {}^{3}/_{4} \times {}^{1}/_{4^2} = {}^{3}/_{64} = 0.05 \quad [\hat{1}\rightarrow\hat{3}]$

$\alpha(C\rightarrow G) = {}^{3}/_{4} \times {}^{1}/_{5^2} = {}^{3}/_{100} = 0.03 \quad [\hat{1}\rightarrow\hat{5}]$

FIGURE 4.26 Applications, at the diatonic and triadic levels in the context I/**C**, of the attraction rule where $s_2 \leq s_1$: (a) attraction to equal neighbors; (b) attraction to subordinate neighbors.

differential with the perception of symmetrical distance between the two pitches. The result is an asymmetry in judging the similarity between subordinate and superordinate neighbors—not as great an asymmetry as the attractions claim on their own but one affected by them (compare Table 5.1 in Krumhansl 1990).

The ratio of asymmetry for the other pitches in a I/**C** context is as follows. D, like B, is four times $(4/2 \div 2/4)$ as attracted to C as C is to D ($\alpha[D\rightarrow C] = 0.5$ and $\alpha[C\rightarrow D] = 0.125$). Similarly, the subordinate diatonic neighbors to E and G are $9/4$ times $(3/2 \div 2/3)$ more attracted to them than the reverse. For equal diatonic neighbors the mutual attractions are identical $(2/2 \div 2/2)$. E and G are $16/9$ times $(4/3$

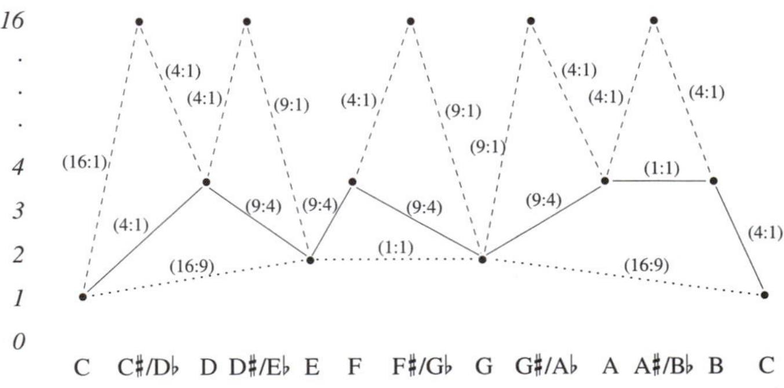

FIGURE 4.27 Ratios of asymmetrical attraction in the context I/**C**.

÷ ¾) as attracted to C as C is to E and G, and they are equally attracted to each other (⅓ ÷ ⅓). Finally, for chromatic pitches the ratio is 4 (²⁄₁ ÷ ½) for C♯↔D, E♭↔D, G♯↔A, B♭↔A, and A♯↔B; 9 (³⁄₁ ÷ ⅓) for D♯↔E and A♭↔G; and 16 (⁴⁄₁ ÷ ¼) for D♭↔C. Figure 4.27 graphs all these ratios, with C set at 1.0. This places E and G at 1.78 (1.0 × ¹⁶⁄₉), the other diatonic pitches at 4.0, and the chromatic pitches at 16. (Here, unlike in Figure 4.25, it is possible to represent all levels in a single two-dimensional graph, because the only variable is the ratio of asymmetry.) The arpeggiated ratios of the C major chord are connected by dotted lines, the diatonic ones by solid lines, and the chromatic ones by dashed lines. When embedding levels are combined with semitone distance, the steepness of a line reflects the degree of attractional asymmetry.

Ratios of asymmetry provide a means of interpreting what would otherwise be a troubling prediction of the attraction rule, namely, that attractions of stable to unstable pitches that are a half step away attain relatively high values compared to attractions of unstable to stable pitches that are a whole step or more away. For example, in a I/**C** context (not i/**c**!), α(D→C) and α(D→E♭) both equal 0.5, and α(E→F) = 0.67 whereas α(E→C) = 0.08. Intuitively, D is not equally attracted to C and E♭, nor is E more attracted to F than it is to C; rather, D is a nonharmonic tone that seeks not further tension toward chromatic E♭ but resolution most forcefully on C, and E is a stable harmonic tone with little attraction for nonharmonic F. The solution to this difficulty is that in each case the comparison should be not to other attractions but to the relative attraction exerted on the particular pitch in relation to the attractive force it exerts on other pitches. Relative attractions can be measured by ratios of asymmetry. As Figure 4.27 displays, the attraction of D to E♭ is ¼ of the attraction of E♭ to D, while the attraction of D to C is four times that of C to D; E's attraction to F is ⁴⁄₉ that of F to E, while E's attraction to C is ¹⁶⁄₉ that of C to E. It is as if D knew in advance the state of attraction that would arise if it moved to E♭ or C (or to any other pitch) and chose the route that would minimize further attractions on it; and similarly for E's potential to move to F or C.

This use of asymmetries does not constitute an alternative to the attraction rule. Rather, it is an interpretation that justifies the rule's predictions where they might otherwise seem questionable. The interpretation rests on the assumption that the cognitive system constantly seeks a lower attractional state.

Now consider the thorny issue of a pitch's attraction to itself. The melodic attraction rule skirts this issue by prohibiting $p_1 = p_2$ in order to avoid a denominator of 0. In other words, it avoids the highly undesirable result of approaching an infinite attraction through $\alpha(p_1 \rightarrow p_1) = \frac{s_1}{s_1} \times \frac{1}{0^2}$. While this result could be finessed in some ad hoc manner, it seems preferable to think about it in another way. Let us say that the tendency of a pitch not to move is a consequence not of self-attraction but of the shortest path. Even so, there is greater pressure for an unstable rather than a stable pitch to move; for example, in the context I/**C** and all else being equal, A♭ tends toward G, whereas G tends to remain stationary. This is again explained by ratios of asymmetry: A♭ is nine times as attracted to G as G is to A♭; G is only ¹⁶⁄₉ as attracted to C as C is to G. Therefore, A♭ has a much greater urge to move.

Attractional asymmetries shed light on intonational practices for instruments capable of continuous tuning. Even though intervals are symmetrically equidistant in a conceptual sense, in a musical context their tunings may not be. J. Fyk (1995) establishes that violinists tend to tune unstable pitches closer to their resolutions than is "correct." The effect is to enhance the need for resolution. Thus in the context I/**C**, B becomes closer in Hz to C in the motion B→C than would otherwise happen, increasing B's attraction to C by decreasing the distance. The motion from stable to unstable pitches, such as C→B, motivates no adjustment in tuning. Such intonational variances are unrelated to just intonation or any other intonational system. Fyk ascribes them to "tonality's gravitational pull"—in other words, to tonal attractions.

Attractions and expectations

The attraction rule predicts the attraction of any pitch p_x to any other pitch, whether superordinate, equal, or subordinate in the current configuration of the space. These predictions are "virtual" in that they do not determine what the next pitch in a melodic sequence will be. The next, or "realized," pitch might or might not be the pitch to which p_x is most attracted. However, the relative strengths of the attractions exerted on p_x strongly influence what pitch the listener expects to follow p_x. All else being equal, the pitch to which p_x is most attracted is the pitch that is most expected. This is my version of Meyer's (1956, 1973) and Narmour's (1977, 1990) implication/realization theory, which distinguishes between implied and realized pitches at successive points in a melody and hypothesizes which pitches are most implied. (Meyer [1956] uses the term "expectation," but he switches to "implication" in Meyer [1973]. I prefer "expectation" because it is explicitly psychological and does not evoke inapposite logical connotations.)

Should all the virtual attractions on p_x be combined in making a quantified prediction for its single most expected continuation? This step would seem unnecessary as well as complicated, for attractions more than a whole step away count for little. In a proposal related to this model, Bharucha (1996) restricts the problem to proximate attractors, treating them as opposite vectors; the hypothesized expectation is the difference between the two. In this model, for example, E and G are both attractors for F in opposite directions; the values are $\alpha(F \rightarrow E) = 1.5$ and $\alpha(F \rightarrow G) = 0.375$ (see Figure 4.21). The resultant expected continuation, then, would be F→E by the value $1.5 - 0.375 = 1.125$.

Although I, too, have taken this approach (Lerdahl 1996), the consequent profile dilutes the results of the attraction rule in a way that does not seem justified (although so far there is little empirical evidence to help decide the matter). It may turn out to be more accurate just to take attractional values as correlating directly with degrees of expected continuation. Thus, in a I/**C** context, the expectation F→E = 1.5, the expectation F→G = 0.375, and so on to other less likely continuations. This is the stance adopted here.

As Meyer and Narmour discuss, factors other than attraction also influence melodic expectations, such as style-specific patterns (melodic schemas) and good continuation (the tendency of a line to continue in the same direction and interval pattern). I shall dwell for a moment only on the latter, which Larson (1994) aptly calls melodic inertia. Imagine that you are in a spaceship in the midst of an asteroid belt. The ship's momentum propels it in a certain direction, but the gravitational forces of the asteroids constantly modify its trajectory. Larger and closer asteroids have a greater influence on the path of the ship than do smaller and more distant ones. So it is with pitches in an unfolding tonal melody. The more stable pitches are the larger asteroids, and the more proximate pitches are the closer asteroids. Continuing the analogy, melodic inertia and attraction form vectors that can reinforce or oppose each other. If the progression has been G→F, the expectation that E will follow is all the greater because of the strong attraction of F to E. But if the progression has been E→F, the strong attraction of F to E might be overridden by the inertial tendency of F to continue in the same direction to G.

A provisional way to quantify the interaction of melodic attraction and stepwise melodic inertia is to assign a constant of 1 to an inertial tendency and then add the greatest attractional value if their vectors are in the same direction but subtract the greatest attractional value if their vectors are in the opposite direction. If the resultant value is positive, the overall tendency is to continue in the same direction. If it is negative, the overall tendency is to return in the opposite direction. For example, in a I/**C** context, if G moves to F, the tendency to continue to E is reinforced by the fact that E is F's strongest attractor: tendency = inertia + attraction = 1 + 1.5 = 2.5. But if E moves to F, the tendency to continue to G is undermined by the contrary greatest attraction of F to E: tendency = inertia − attraction = 1 − 1.5 = − 0.5. Accordingly, the overall tendency, which in this case is much weaker than the first because of the opposing forces, is to return to E. This method does not take into account other factors that influence overall melodic tendency, such as motivic or elaborational pattern, but at least it captures the interaction of the inertial and attractional vectors in a stepwise context. (After melodic skips, stepwise reversal in direction is expected [Meyer 1973; Narmour 1990], and the interaction of melodic attraction and melodic direction would have to modified accordingly.)

The combined effect of attractions and inertia on expectations helps explain why diatonic linear completion is so important to tonal syntax (see "The Pitch-Class Level" in chapter 2). Inertia tends to keep a diatonic line moving by step in one direction, while the attractors at $\hat{5}$, $\hat{3}$, and $\hat{1}$ brake inertial motion. Termination of inertial motion on $\hat{7}$, $\hat{6}$, $\hat{4}$, or $\hat{2}$ leaves the line in a state of tension because it remains strongly attracted to, and hence tends toward, its superordinate neighbors $\hat{5}$, $\hat{3}$, or $\hat{1}$. Termination of a line on $\hat{5}$, $\hat{3}$, or especially $\hat{1}$ brings the line to a state of relative relaxation and nonexpectancy—in other words, to a state of relative closure—because at these points the attractions to subordinate neighbors are weak, leaving little compulsion to propel the line forward.

Regardless of the myriad virtual attractions exerted on p_x and the expected continuation from p_x, there is a realized pitch p_r that follows p_x. To keep track of what is computed, let the subscript "e" to the attraction rule signify the computation to the most expected pitch (equivalently, to the strongest virtual attraction)

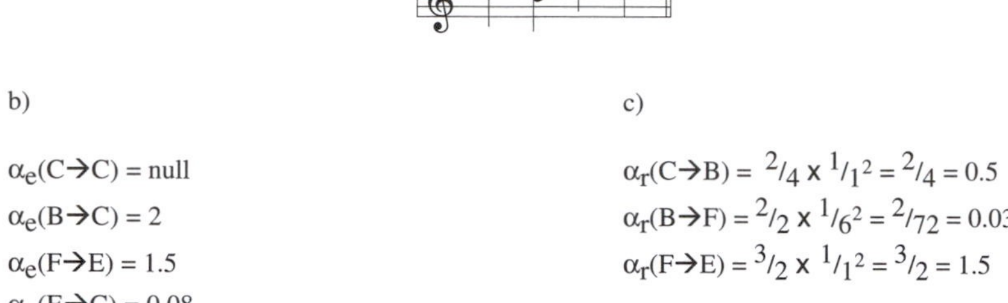

a)
b)
$\alpha_e(C \rightarrow C)$ = null
$\alpha_e(B \rightarrow C) = 2$
$\alpha_e(F \rightarrow E) = 1.5$
$\alpha_e(E \rightarrow C) = 0.08$
c)
$\alpha_r(C \rightarrow B) = {}^2/_4 \times {}^1/_{1^2} = {}^2/_4 = 0.5$
$\alpha_r(B \rightarrow F) = {}^2/_2 \times {}^1/_{6^2} = {}^2/_{72} = 0.03$
$\alpha_r(F \rightarrow E) = {}^3/_2 \times {}^1/_{1^2} = {}^3/_2 = 1.5$

FIGURE 4.28 The changing-note melodic pattern in (a), calculated in (b) for strongest virtual attractions and in (c) for realized attractions. The values in (b) are taken from Figures 4.21 and 4.24.

and the subscript "r" the computation to the realized pitch. The calculations for α_r can be performed not only for surface sequences but also for sequences at underlying levels.

As illustration, compare α_e and α_r for the melodic sequence C→B→F→E in Figure 4.28a. Meyer (1973) and Gjerdingen (1988) refer to this common Classical pattern as the changing-note archetype. The pattern is usually accompanied by paired phrase groupings with the progression I→V, V→I; but let us set aside the harmonic dimension for now. The α_e values are given in Figure 4.28b. There is no superordinate attractor for C because it is the tonic. B is strongly attracted to C, and F is almost equivalently attracted to E. This is the attractional source of the changing-note pattern: B and F are interchangeable because they have similar dynamic charges, so the resolution of one can replace that of the other. Finally, E is weakly attracted to C. The realized attractions are given in Figure 4.28c. Although C→B realizes a moderate attraction, B→F realizes an essentially empty attraction. B is of course impelled toward C. The difference between $\alpha_e(B \rightarrow C)$ and $\alpha_r(B \rightarrow F)$, $2 - 0.03 = 1.97$, measures B's unrealized, or denied, attractional potential. This potential discharges in the strong motion F→E, which is the one instance where $\alpha_e = \alpha_r$. This convergence provides partial closure for the sequence—partial because E is still drawn weakly to the attractor C.

With respect to attractional potentials, it can generally be hypothesized that $\alpha_e(p_1 \rightarrow p_2) - \alpha_r(p_1 \rightarrow p_3)$ = the power of implicative denial. For another example, suppose that a melody is on D with the expectation of resolving on C but that it goes to E instead. Then $\alpha_e(D \rightarrow C) - \alpha_r(D \rightarrow E) = 0.5 - 0.375 = 0.125$. But if D goes to F instead, the implicative denial is larger: $\alpha_e(D \rightarrow C) - \alpha_r(D \rightarrow F) = 0.5 - 0.11 = 0.39$. This proposal recasts Bharucha's opposing vectors in another guise.

This perspective on expectations illuminates a conundrum posed by Meyer (1961). Granted that listening to music is a form of communication, why do we enjoy a work that is so familiar that we remember in advance what will happen? Jackendoff (1991) answers by suggesting that the internal music processor is "informationally encapsulated," in the sense of Fodor (1983); that is, the unconscious processing of music continues blindly, no matter how well our conscious mind knows the music in question. To the internal processor, the musical input is always new. This theory elaborates Jackendoff's position. Whether or not an expected pitch is subsequently realized, the (unconscious) attractions on it are in operation by virtue of the structure of pitch space.

The difference between expected and realized attractions sheds light on Schenker's idealized voice leading beyond what I mentioned about linear completion. Schenker often replaces the vagaries of a musical surface with normalized linear progressions at underlying levels so that the lines realize the patterns of strongest virtual attraction (again, the "will of the tones"). The invocation of strongest attractions is, I think, a deeper justification for transforming underlying voice leading than arguments based just on systematic grounds internal to his theory.

AN ATTRACTIONAL APPROACH TO HARMONY

Voice-leading attractions

The concept of melodic attraction extends to harmonic progression, for the individual pitches in a chord seek stability just as do the pitches in a melody. In the terminology used here, the voices in a chord tend toward their attractors. The nonmelodic function of the bass, however, typically causes its strongest virtual and its realized melodic attractions to diverge. This being the case, I propose to compute only realized melodic attractions for all voices, always in the context of the pitch-space configuration of the second chord (see the next subsection for discussion of this point). Let us start with cases in which the bass progresses by root and the upper voices move as little as possible. This step both acknowledges standard bass motion and enables a convergence between expected and realized attractions in the upper voices. Where $\alpha_e = \alpha_r$, the subscript "e/r" is shown. Where a pitch repeats, the designation "null" is given, as in these cases the attraction rule does not apply. The overall realized voice-leading attraction of one chord to another is obtained by adding the attractions of the individual voices:

> VOICE-LEADING ATTRACTION $\alpha_{rvl}(C_1 \rightarrow C_2) = \alpha_{r1} + \ldots \alpha_{rn}$, where C_1 and C_2 are chords in which (at the very least) not all the pitches are identical; $\alpha_{rvl}(C_1 \rightarrow C_2)$ = the realized voice-leading attraction of C_1 to C_2; and $\alpha_{r1} + \ldots \alpha_{rn}$ = the sum of the realized melodic attractions for all the voices in C_1 to C_2.

Assume for now that all measurements are made in relation to I/**C** and consider the progression $V^7 \rightarrow I$ in Figure 4.29a. The voices are laid out as soprano, alto, tenor, and bass. The three upper voices resolve to their strongest attractors and the bass moves from G to C. The overall attractional strength, $\alpha_{rvl}(V^7 \rightarrow I)$, is therefore high. In the progression vi→I in Figure 4.29b, by contrast, the realized attractions in the outer voices are weak and the inner voices do not move at all. The result is a much smaller attractional total.

a)

$\alpha_{e/r}(F \rightarrow E) = 1.5$
$\alpha_{e/r}(D \rightarrow C) = 0.5$
$\alpha_{e/r}(B \rightarrow C) = 2$
$\alpha_{r}(G \rightarrow C) = 0.05$

$\alpha_{rvl}(V^7 \rightarrow I) = 4.05$

b)

$\alpha_{e/r}(A \rightarrow G) = 0.375$
$\alpha_{r}(E \rightarrow E) = \text{null}$
$\alpha_{r}(C \rightarrow C) = \text{null}$
$\alpha_{r}(A \rightarrow C) = 0.22$

$\alpha_{rvl}(vi \rightarrow I) = 0.595$

c)

$\alpha_{e/r}(F \rightarrow E) = 1.5$
$\alpha_{e/r}(D \rightarrow C) = 0.5$
$\alpha_{r}(B \rightarrow G) = 0.09$
$\alpha_{r}(G \rightarrow C) = 0.05$

$\alpha_{rvl}(V^7 \rightarrow I) = 2.14$

d)

$\alpha_{e/r}(E \rightarrow F) = 0.67$
$\alpha_{e/r}(C \rightarrow B) = 0.5$
$\alpha_{r}(G \rightarrow G) = \text{null}$
$\alpha_{r}(C \rightarrow G) = 0.03$

$\alpha_{rvl}(I \rightarrow V^7) = 1.2$

e)

$\alpha_{e/r}(B \rightarrow C) = 2$
$\alpha_{e/r}(F \rightarrow E) = 1.5$
$\alpha_{e/r}(D \rightarrow C) = 0.5$
$\alpha_{r}(G \rightarrow A) = 0.17$

$\alpha_{rvl}(V^7 \rightarrow vi) = 4.17$

FIGURE 4.29 Realized voice-leading attractions for (a) $V^7 \rightarrow I$; (b) vi→I; (c) $V^7 \rightarrow I$ with denial of the leading-tone resolution; (d) $I \rightarrow V^7$; and (e) $V^7 \rightarrow vi$. The values are taken from Figures 4.21, 4.24, and 4.26.

Figure 4.29c is identical to Figure 4.29a except that the tenor B resolves not to C but to G, filling out the C major triad. If the denial of B→C causes a lower value for this particular $\alpha_r(V^7 \rightarrow I)$ than seems fitting, it is because the listener tends to supply the resolution; that is, $\alpha_e(B \rightarrow C)$ mentally becomes $\alpha_{e/r}(B \rightarrow C)$, replacing, or at least accompanying, $\alpha_r(B \rightarrow G)$. The distinction between expected and realized attractions can blur for inner voices, which are perceptually masked compared to the soprano and bass.

Figure 4.29d reverses $V^7 \rightarrow I$ to $I \rightarrow V^7$, causing a substantial reduction in attractional value. This is the harmonic counterpart to melodic asymmetry. That is, even though $V^7 \rightarrow I$ and $I \rightarrow V^7$ are symmetrically equidistant in chordal space, V^7 is perceived as closer to I in the first progression because the attraction of V^7 to I is greater than that of I to V^7. Generally, the greater the attractions exerted on the voices of the first chord, the greater the reduction in attractional value when the order of the chords is reversed.

The $V^7 \rightarrow vi$ progression in Figure 4.29e yields a higher overall attractional value than does $V^7 \rightarrow I$ in Figure 4.29a because the bass G is more attracted to A than to C. While this comparison has a certain rightness with respect to the melodic lines, it violates the intuition that V^7 is more attracted to I than to vi. A harmonic component is lacking. Again the crucial factor is distance, this time not in semitonal distance but in chordal space, expressed by the chord distance rule as denominator. As with individual pitches, chordal attraction is inversely proportional to distance. This time, however, it does not seem advisable—purely in terms of the intuitive rightness of the output values—to square the distance. The voice-leading attraction rule appears as numerator. The resultant values are multiplied by a constant, a step that is not essential but helpful, as otherwise the values would be exceedingly small. The outcome combines the attraction and tension rules:

HARMONIC ATTRACTION $\alpha_{rh}(C_1 \rightarrow C_2) = K[\alpha_{rvl}(C_1 \rightarrow C_2)/\delta(C_1 \rightarrow C_2)]$, where $\alpha_{rh}(C_1 \rightarrow C_2)$ is the realized harmonic attraction of C_1 to C_2; constant $K = 10$; $\alpha_{rvl}(C_1 \rightarrow C_2)$ is as in the voice-leading attraction rule; and $\delta(C_1 \rightarrow C_2)$ is the distance from C_1 to C_2, with $C_1 \neq C_2$.

It will be recalled that the melodic attraction rule incorporates two factors, semitonal distance and the ratio of embedding between the two pitches. The harmonic attraction rule includes an equivalent factor of chordal distance but leaves vacant any factor of harmonic embedding (as distinct from melodic embedding). This difference is a consequence of dissimilarity between the spaces of pitches and chords. In the former (Figure 4.20), pitches take their places in a stratified hierarchy. In the latter (Figure 2.15), chords are symmetrically positioned on a toroidal structure, with none intrinsically superordinate to any other. Tonic orientation is not a matter of a multi-leveled chordal space; rather, it is a contextual abstraction from which other distances are directly or indirectly measured.

The current use of the chord distance rule here in effect reintroduces the short version of the sequential tension rule, T_{seq} (see "The Harmonic Tension Model" earlier in in this chapter), which proceeds from left to right employing only δ. Now, however, δ is in the denominator, for attractional and tensional values are inversely proportional.

Figure 4.30 fulfills the harmonic attraction rule for Figures 4.29a–b and d–e. The chord distance values are taken from "The Chordal Level" in chapter 2 except for $\delta(I \rightarrow V^7)$, for which the values are $0 + 1 + 5 = 6$. The resulting numbers are expressions of coexisting melodic and harmonic attractions. The attraction of V^7 to I is now larger than to vi, and the values for vi→I and I→V^7 are fittingly small. Indeed, the strong progression V^7→I is about ten times more attractional than the weak progression vi→I. The former is dynamic in its voice leading and moves to its harmonic neighbor; the latter is static in its voice leading and moves a greater distance in chordal space.

As presented, the harmonic attraction rule treats realized attractions. Yet it would be a shame to abandon the notion of virtual harmonic attractions. Let us say that virtual harmonic attractions exist between chords as measured not only

a) $\alpha_{rh}(V^7 \rightarrow I) = K[\alpha_{rvl}(V^7 \rightarrow I)/\delta(V^7 \rightarrow I)] = 10 \times {}^{4.05}/_{5} = 8.1$

b) $\alpha_{rh}(vi \rightarrow I) = K[\alpha_{rvl}(vi \rightarrow I)/\delta(vi \rightarrow I)] = 10 \times {}^{0.595}/_{7} = 0.85$

d) $\alpha_{rh}(I \rightarrow V^7) = K[\alpha_{rvl}(I \rightarrow V^7)\delta(I \rightarrow V^7)] = 10 \times {}^{0.825}/_{6} = 1.375$

e) $\alpha_{rh}(V^7 \rightarrow vi) = K[\alpha_{rvl}(V^7 \rightarrow vi)/ \delta(V^7 \rightarrow vi)] = 10 \times {}^{4.17}/_{7} = 5.96$

FIGURE 4.30 Realized harmonic attractions for cases (a), (b), (d), and (e) in Figure 4.29.

by attractions between voices but also by root motion, such that chordal-space distance between roots is inversely proportional to the virtual attractions between the roots. The chords that fill the C_1 slot in Figure 4.30 thus have multiple virtual attractions, just as do the pitches of a melody. Often the strongest attractor is not the chord that subsequently appears. The strongest attractor for V^7 is I, but the progression may turn out to be $V^7 \rightarrow vi$. The difference between the two values, $8.1 - 5.96 = 2.14$, expresses the unrealized potential of V^7 to resolve to I when it in fact moves to vi.

In this connection, it is a common observation (for instance, Bailey 1985) that in Wagner's music a deceptive cadential motion of some kind characteristically replaces the full cadence. Full cadences are underrepresented in this style. Why then do we not hear the deceptive progression as normative? Why does $V^{(7)}$ point to I (Hyer 1989)? The answer is that as long as the music invokes diatonic space, the space's attractional forces remain in effect. $V^{(7)}$ yearns for I despite its realization elsewhere.

Attractional context

The rules for melodic and harmonic attraction provide the mechanism for evaluating attractions between pitches or chords but do not specify the context in which pitches or chords are evaluated. This is a first approximation:

> ATTRACTIONAL CONTEXT (preliminary version) In measuring the attraction on event e_1 exerted by e_2, calculate the attraction in the context to which e_2 refers.

What is meant here by "context"? A simple version would stipulate only that there is a governing tonic to which each pitch relates. By this light, the melody in bars 1–4 of K. 282 ignores its harmonic instantiations and receives the realized attractional analysis in Figure 4.31, in which each melodic pitch is given a scale degree that represents its position in the I/E♭ configuration of the basic space. The realized attraction of each melodic pitch to the next is calculated sequentially

FIGURE 4.31 Realized attractional analysis for the melody of the first phrase of K. 282, calculated throughout in the context I/E♭.

in this unvarying context. The relative plausibility of this particular analysis comes from the fact that all the pitches in the melody belong to the **E♭** scale.

This analysis, however, fails to capture nuances of harmonic context. For instance, it does not identify the appoggiaturas on beats 1 and 3 of bars 2–3 and hence does not register their strong tendency to resolve. Nor does it register the effect of the applied dominants on beat 4 of bar 1 and on beat 3 of bar 2. More generally, pitches (whether harmonic or nonharmonic) exist in the context of chords and chords in the context of regions. It is necessary to articulate this hierarchy before returning to the issue of attractional context:

EVENT GOVERNANCE Assume any pitch p_x, chord C_x, and region $\mathbf{R}_x$. Then,
(1) p_x is governed by C_x if p_x takes place in the span over which C_x extends, from the onset of C_x to the onset of C_{x+1}; and
(2) C_x is immediately governed by $\mathbf{R}_x$ if C_x takes place in the span over which $\mathbf{R}_x$ extends, from the onset of $\mathbf{R}_x$ to the onset of $\mathbf{R}_{x+1}$; but
(3) if there is a pivot chord C_p, the span of $\mathbf{R}_x$ overlaps with that of $\mathbf{R}_{x+1}$, such that $\mathbf{R}_x$ ends and $\mathbf{R}_{x+1}$ begins with C_p.

In (2), the phrase "immediately governed by $\mathbf{R}_x$" means that there is no intervening region that governs C_x; for example, the vii^{o6} on beat 4 of bar 1 of K. 282 is immediately governed not by **E♭** but by local **B♭**. The provision in (3) for overlapping regions via pivot chords has a specific use that will be discussed in a moment.

The statement for event governance oversimplifies in two respects. First, as suggested by the relative plausibility of Figure 4.31, the interpretation of individual pitches does not completely depend on chordal governance (see the related discussion of pc/chordal and linear paths in "Prolongational Paths" in chapter 3). Second, among standard types of nonharmonic tones, condition (1) embraces passing tones, neighboring tones, suspensions, and appoggiaturas, but it does not cover anticipations. In K. 282, for example, the melodic D on the final sixteenth of bar 2 might best be interpreted as participating in the following V^4_2. This is an exception to the rule. But the statement suffices for most cases and will serve as a basis for a more adequate formulation of attractional context.

Let us proceed by means of examples from K. 282, assuming three melodic streams at the musical surface. A pitch's context can be represented by its scale degree and its Roman-numeral designation; such a description locates the pitch in a configuration of the basic space. However, a given pitch can have a number of such descriptions, depending on the perspective. For example, the appoggiatura D on beat 3 of bar 2 is $\hat{2}$ in relation to the root of its governing chord V^7/**f**; it is $\hat{6}$ in relation to its local tonic i/**f**; and, as in Figure 4.31, it is $\hat{7}$ in relation to the global tonic I/**E♭**. Of these possibilities, I propose a rather intricate treatment that is justified by the distinctions it affords. The idea is that a nonharmonic tone is heard in terms of the chord that governs it and a harmonic tone is heard in terms of the tonic of the region that immediately governs it. To clarify the counting, nonharmonic scale degrees will be bracketed. Thus, in Figure 4.32a, soprano D

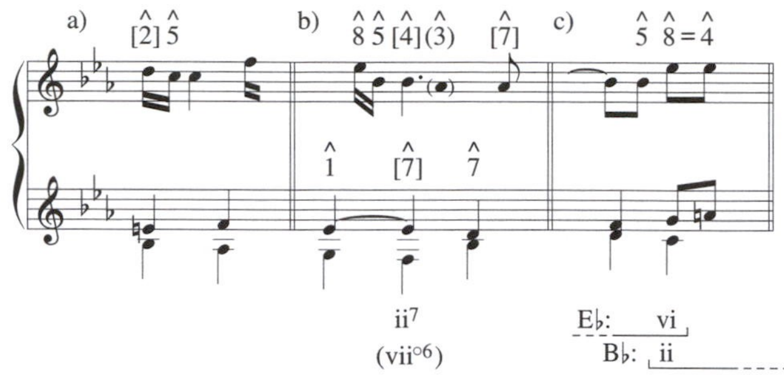

FIGURE 4.32 Scale-step designations from the first phrase of K. 282 using the principle of attractional governance: (a) from bar 2; (b) from bar 3; (c) from bar 1.

is designated as [$\hat{2}$] with respect to its governing chord V^7/**f**; and its resolution C, being harmonic, is $\hat{5}$ with respect to its local region **f**. Two more cases arise on beat 3 of the next bar, shown in Figure 4.32b. First, soprano B♭ functions as an appoggiatura to chord tone A♭, which does not arrive until the harmony changes. Because it is nonharmonic, B♭ is marked as [$\hat{4}$] in relation to the root, on the view that the underlying chord is the predominant ii^7. B♭'s implied resolution on $\hat{3}$ is given in parentheses; but when the resolution arrives, it is [$\hat{7}$]/V/**E♭**. Meanwhile alto E♭ becomes a suspended seventh that is marked as [$\hat{7}$] in relation to its root. Its resolution on D, which is harmonic, is $\hat{7}$ in relation to the governing tonic. (If soprano B♭ and alto E♭ are replaced by the resolutions they delay, the chord on beat 3 becomes vii^{o6}, in parallel with its equivalent place in the first subphrase, the vii^{o6} on beat 4 of bar 1. This alternative interpretation leads to issues of functionality to be addressed in the next chapter in "Function as Prolongational Position.")

At points of regional change in a realized attractional analysis, condition (3) of event governance comes into play. Assume, by a kind of regional inertia, that where there is more than one pivoting possibility, listeners reorient tonicity later rather than sooner. By this criterion, as shown in Figure 4.32c, the pivot between **E♭** and **B♭** in bar 1 occurs on beat 4 as vi/**E♭** = ii/**B♭**, turning soprano E♭ from $\hat{8}$/**E♭** into $\hat{4}$/**B♭** and alto G from $\hat{3}$/**E♭** into $\hat{6}$/**B♭**. At the next reductional level, however, the alto G on beat 4 reduces out, backing the pivot up to the $B\flat^6$ chord on beat 3. The location of a pivot thus varies according to the level of reduction. (Because "The Harmonic Tension Model" earlier in this chapter approaches this passage more globally, it treats the G as nonharmonic rather than as part of a C minor triad. This interpretation would change the attractional analysis slightly.)

This discussion motivates a detailed restatement of the context rule:

ATTRACTIONAL CONTEXT (final version) Assume pitches p_1 and p_2, chords C_1 and C_2, and regions $\mathbf{R}_1$ and $\mathbf{R}_2$, such that

(1) $p_1 \neq p_2$, but possibly $C_1 = C_2$ and $\mathbf{R}_1 = \mathbf{R}_2$

(2) p_1 is governed by C_1 and C_1 is governed by $\mathbf{R}_1$; p_2 is governed by C_2 and C_2 is governed by $\mathbf{R}_2$;

(3) if a realized attraction is computed and if
  (a) p_1 and p_2 are in the same stream and
  (b) $p_2/C_2/\mathbf{R}_2$ directly succeeds $p_1/C_1/\mathbf{R}_1$ at any given prolongational level,
then $\alpha(p_1/C_1/\mathbf{R}_1 \rightarrow p_2/C_2/\mathbf{R}_2)$, such that
(4) if p_1 is nonharmonic, it is evaluated within the basic-space configuration of $C_1/\mathbf{R}_1$
(5) if p_1 is harmonic, it is evaluated within the the basic-space configuration of $I/\mathbf{R}_2$.

Condition (1) disallows evaluation of identical pitches, as in the original melodic attraction rule; but $C_1 = C_2$ can occur if pitches move within the repeated chord, and $\mathbf{R}_1 = \mathbf{R}_2$ is the norm except in regional change. Condition 2 invokes event governance. Condition 3 is not needed unless realized attractions are computed; but if they are, 3a appeals to the integrity of polyphonic lines, and 3b generalizes to all prolongational levels. Condition 4 stipulates that a nonharmonic tone is evaluated within the chord that governs it. Condition 5 states that a harmonic tone is evaluated in the context of the tonic configuration of the goal region, no matter whether $\mathbf{R}_1 = \mathbf{R}_2$, $\mathbf{R}_1 \neq \mathbf{R}_2$ and C_1 is a pivot or $\mathbf{R}_1 \neq \mathbf{R}_2$ and there is no pivot.

Two attractional analyses

Figure 4.33 carries out at three levels a realized attractional analysis of the first phrase of K. 282—specifically at the surface and levels e–d in the time-span and prolongational reductions in Figure 4.14. At each level, scale-degree designations are given only for pitches for which the next level no longer supplies the immediate attractional context, either because at the latter level one of the pitches is reduced out or because the larger context causes a reinterpretation. The governing regions, bracketed below, include pivot overlaps in order to evaluate the attraction to and from each pivoting event. When evidence for the subsidiary region reduces out, as is the case of **f** at level a, the bracket disappears. If the analysis were to continue one more level, evidence for **B♭** would reduce out as well. Following the rule for attractional context, the scale-degree numbers in Figure 4.33 oscillate between counting from the root of the chord (for nonharmonic tones, including chordal sevenths) and counting from the tonic of the immediately governing region (for harmonic tones). In place of calculating each realized attraction, Figure 4.34 lists melodic attractional values between most of the scale degrees within fixed major and minor contexts. Many of these values are taken from Figures 4.21, 4.22, 4.24, and 4.26; the rest can be deduced from the melodic attraction rule. Because contexts change, it would be excessive to attempt a complete listing. Most of the cases in Figure 4.33 can be traced to the numbers in Figure 4.34.

Three details in bar 3 in Figure 4.33 require comment. First, on beat 3 at level c the attraction of B♭ to the chord-tone A♭ is shown through the parenthetically inserted A♭. But the B♭ remains at level b, causing an evaluation there from $[\hat{4}]$/ii/**E♭** to $[\hat{7}]$/V/**E♭**. Second, level b implies the polyphonic nature of the melody in bars 2–3. At level a, C→F and B♭→E♭ fuse, creating parallel streams, each yielding attractional values in its own right. Third, at level b the bass in bar 3 imitates the soprano in bars 2–3, continuing the parallel tenths with the structural soprano while articulating the cadence. If, however, at level a, the bass F on beat 3 is counted as part of the stream G→F→E♭, the result increases the realized attraction. This would be an alternative, coexisting interpretation (although a less pre-

FIGURE 4.33 Realized attractional analysis at three reductional levels of the three voices of the first phrase of K. 282, calculated using the final version of the rule of attractional context.

a) stepwise motion

major	*minor*
$\alpha(\hat{1}\rightarrow\hat{2}) = 0.125$	$\alpha(\hat{1}\rightarrow\hat{2}) = 0.125$
$\alpha(\hat{2}\rightarrow\hat{1}) = 0.5$	$\alpha(\hat{2}\rightarrow\hat{1}) = 0.5$
$\alpha(\hat{2}\rightarrow\hat{3}) = 0.375$	$\alpha(\hat{2}\rightarrow\flat\hat{3}) = 1.5$
$\alpha(\hat{3}\rightarrow\hat{2}) = 0.17$	$\alpha(\flat\hat{3}\rightarrow\hat{2}) = 0.67$
$\alpha(\hat{3}\rightarrow\hat{4}) = 0.67$	$\alpha(\flat\hat{3}\rightarrow\hat{4}) = 0.17$
$\alpha(\hat{4}\rightarrow\hat{3}) = 1.5$	$\alpha(\hat{4}\rightarrow\flat\hat{3}) = 0.375$
$\alpha(\hat{4}\rightarrow\hat{5}) = 0.375$	$\alpha(\hat{4}\rightarrow\hat{5}) = 0.375$
$\alpha(\hat{5}\rightarrow\hat{4}) = 0.17$	$\alpha(\hat{5}\rightarrow\hat{4}) = 0.17$
$\alpha(\hat{5}\rightarrow\hat{6}) = 0.17$	$\alpha(\hat{5}\rightarrow\flat\hat{6}) = 0.67$
$\alpha(\hat{6}\rightarrow\hat{5}) = 0.375$	$\alpha(\flat\hat{6}\rightarrow\hat{5}) = 1.5$
$\alpha(\hat{6}\rightarrow\hat{7}) = 0.25$	$\alpha(\flat\hat{6}\rightarrow\flat\hat{7}) = 0.25$
$\alpha(\hat{7}\rightarrow\hat{6}) = 0.25$	$\alpha(\flat\hat{7}\rightarrow\flat\hat{6}) = 0.25$
$\alpha(\hat{7}\rightarrow\hat{8}) = 2.0$	$\alpha(\flat\hat{7}\rightarrow\hat{8}) = 0.5$
$\alpha(\hat{8}\rightarrow\hat{7}) = 0.5$	$\alpha(\hat{8}\rightarrow\flat\hat{7}) = 0.125$

b) triadic arpeggiations

major	*minor*
$\alpha(\hat{1}\rightarrow\hat{3}) = 0.05$	$\alpha(\hat{1}\rightarrow\flat\hat{3}) = 0.08$
$\alpha(\hat{3}\rightarrow\hat{1}) = 0.08$	$\alpha(\flat\hat{3}\rightarrow\hat{1}) = 0.15$
$\alpha(\hat{3}\rightarrow\hat{5}) = 0.11$	$\alpha(\flat\hat{3}\rightarrow\hat{5}) = 0.06$
$\alpha(\hat{5}\rightarrow\hat{3}) = 0.11$	$\alpha(\hat{5}\rightarrow\flat\hat{3}) = 0.06$
$\alpha(\hat{5}\rightarrow\hat{8}) = 0.05$	$\alpha(\hat{5}\rightarrow\hat{8}) = 0.05$
$\alpha(\hat{8}\rightarrow\hat{5}) = 0.03$	$\alpha(\hat{8}\rightarrow\hat{5}) = 0.03$

c) some nontriadic skips

major	*minor*
$\alpha(\hat{1}\rightarrow\hat{4}) = 0.02$	$\alpha(\hat{1}\rightarrow\hat{4}) = 0.02$
$\alpha(\hat{4}\rightarrow\hat{1}) = 0.08$	$\alpha(\hat{4}\rightarrow\hat{1}) = 0.08$
$\alpha(\hat{8}\rightarrow\hat{6}) = 0.055$	$\alpha(\hat{8}\rightarrow\flat\hat{6}) = 0.03$
$\alpha(\hat{6}\rightarrow\hat{8}) = 0.22$	$\alpha(\flat\hat{6}\rightarrow\hat{8}) = 0.125$
$\alpha(\hat{2}\rightarrow\hat{4}) = 0.11$	$\alpha(\hat{2}\rightarrow\hat{4}) = 0.11$
$\alpha(\hat{2}\rightarrow\hat{6}) = 0.04$	$\alpha(\hat{2}\rightarrow\flat\hat{6}) = 0.03$
$\alpha(\hat{2}\rightarrow\hat{7}) = 0.11$	$\alpha(\hat{2}\rightarrow\hat{7}) = 0.11$
$\alpha(\hat{3}\rightarrow\hat{6}) = 0.03$	$\alpha(\flat\hat{3}\rightarrow\flat\hat{6}) = 0.03$
$\alpha(\hat{6}\rightarrow\hat{3}) = 0.06$	$\alpha(\flat\hat{6}\rightarrow\flat\hat{3}) = 0.06$

FIGURE 4.34 List of voice-leading attractions within major and minor contexts.

ferred one within the theory as a whole) to the standard $\hat{5}\rightarrow\hat{1}$ bass motion at the cadence.

The differences between the realized melodic attractions in Figures 4.31 and 4.33 are small except at the appoggiaturas. In each case, the attraction exerted on the appoggiatura is greater in Figure 4.33.

Figure 4.35 tabulates the results of level b in Figure 4.33 and sums the realized voice-leading attractions for each chord. The harmonic attraction rule, α_{rh}, takes these values to form the realized harmonic attractional analysis for the phrase. Events are numbered for reference as in Figure 4.2. The first progression, or *Prog*(1→2), a repeat of the opening I/E♭, has null realized attractional value because nothing moves. The attractional forces remain weak until the first peak

Prog(1→2)
$\alpha(B\flat \rightarrow B\flat) = \text{null}$
$\alpha(G \rightarrow G) = \text{null}$
$\alpha(E\flat \rightarrow E\flat) = \text{null}$
$\alpha_{rvl}(\mathrm{I}/\mathbf{E}\flat \rightarrow \mathrm{I}/\mathbf{E}\flat) = \text{null}$
$\alpha_{rh}(\mathrm{I}/\mathbf{E}\flat \rightarrow \mathrm{I}/\mathbf{E}\flat) = \text{null}$

Prog(2→3)
$\alpha(B\flat \rightarrow B\flat) = \text{null}$
$\alpha(G \rightarrow F) = 0.17$
$\alpha(E\flat \rightarrow D) = 0.5$
$\alpha_{rvl}(\mathrm{I}/\mathbf{E}\flat \rightarrow \mathrm{V}^6/\mathbf{E}\flat) = 0.67$
$\alpha_{rh}(\mathrm{I}/\mathbf{E}\flat \rightarrow \mathrm{V}^6/\mathbf{E}\flat) = 10 \times {}^{0.67}/_5 = 1.34$

Prog(3→4)
$\alpha(B\flat \rightarrow E\flat) = 0.02$
$\alpha(F \rightarrow A) = 0.04$
$\alpha(D \rightarrow C) = 0.17$
$\alpha_{rvl}(\mathrm{I}^6/\mathbf{B}\flat \rightarrow \mathrm{vii}^{o6}/\mathbf{B}\flat) = 0.23$
$\alpha_{rh}(\mathrm{I}^6/\mathbf{B}\flat \rightarrow \mathrm{vii}^{o6}/\mathbf{B}\flat) = 10 \times {}^{0.23}/_5 = 0.46$

Prog(4→5)
$\alpha(E\flat \rightarrow D) = 1.5$
$\alpha(F \rightarrow A) = 2.0$
$\alpha(D \rightarrow C) = 0.5$
$\alpha_{rvl}(\mathrm{vii}^{o6}/\mathbf{B}\flat \rightarrow \mathrm{I}/\mathbf{B}\flat) = 3.0$
$\alpha_{rh}(\mathrm{vii}^{o6}/\mathbf{B}\flat \rightarrow \mathrm{I}/\mathbf{B}\flat) = 10 \times {}^{3.0}/_5 = 6.0$

Prog(5→6)
$\alpha(D \rightarrow B\flat) = 0.08$
$\alpha(B\flat \rightarrow D) = 0.05$
$\alpha(B\flat \rightarrow B\flat) = \text{null}$
$\alpha_{rvl}(\mathrm{I}/\mathbf{B}\flat \rightarrow \mathrm{I}/\mathbf{B}\flat) = 0.13$
$\alpha_{rh}(\mathrm{I}/\mathbf{B}\flat \rightarrow \mathrm{I}/\mathbf{B}\flat) = \text{null}$

Prog(6→7)
$\alpha(B\flat \rightarrow C) = 0.375$
$\alpha(D \rightarrow E) = 0.25$
$\alpha(B\flat \rightarrow B\flat) = \text{null}$
$\alpha_{rvl}(\mathrm{IV}/\mathbf{f} \rightarrow \mathrm{V}^4{}_2/\mathbf{f}) = 0.625$
$\alpha_{rh}(\mathrm{IV}/\mathbf{f} \rightarrow \mathrm{V}^4{}_2/\mathbf{f}) = 10 \times {}^{0.625}/_8 = 0.78$

Prog(7→8)
$\alpha(C \rightarrow F) = 0.05$
$\alpha(E \rightarrow F) = 2.0$
$\alpha(B\flat \rightarrow A\flat) = 0.375$
$\alpha_{rvl}(\mathrm{V}^4{}_2/\mathbf{f} \rightarrow \mathrm{i}^6/\mathbf{f}) = 2.425$
$\alpha_{rh}(\mathrm{V}^4{}_2/\mathbf{f} \rightarrow \mathrm{i}^6/\mathbf{f}) = 10 \times {}^{2.425}/_5 = 4.85$

Prog(8→9)
$\alpha(F \rightarrow B\flat) = 0.03$
$\alpha(F \rightarrow D) = 0.11$
$\alpha(Ab \rightarrow A\flat) = \text{null}$
$\alpha_{rvl}(\mathrm{ii}^6/\mathbf{E}\flat \rightarrow \mathrm{V}^4{}_2/\mathbf{E}\flat) = 0.14$
$\alpha_{rh}(\mathrm{ii}^6/\mathbf{E}\flat \rightarrow \mathrm{V}^4{}_2/\mathbf{E}\flat) = 10 \times {}^{0.14}/_5 = 0.28$

Prog(9→10)
$\alpha(B\flat \rightarrow E\flat) = 0.05$
$\alpha(D \rightarrow E\flat) = 2.0$
$\alpha(A\flat \rightarrow G) = 1.5$
$\alpha_{rvl}(\mathrm{V}^4{}_2/\mathbf{E}\flat \rightarrow \mathrm{I}^6/\mathbf{E}\flat) = 3.55$
$\alpha_{rh}(\mathrm{V}^4{}_2/\mathbf{E}\flat \rightarrow \mathrm{I}^6/\mathbf{E}\flat) = 10 \times {}^{3.55}/_5 = 7.1$

Prog(10→11)
$\alpha(E\flat \rightarrow B\flat) = 0.04$
$\alpha(E\flat \rightarrow E\flat) = \text{null}$
$\alpha(G \rightarrow F) = 0.17$
$\alpha_{rvl}(\mathrm{I}^6/\mathbf{E}\flat \rightarrow \mathrm{ii}^7/\mathbf{E}\flat) = 0.21$
$\alpha_{rh}(\mathrm{I}^6/\mathbf{E}\flat \rightarrow \mathrm{ii}^7/\mathbf{E}\flat) = 10 \times {}^{0.21}/_8 = 0.26$

Prog(11→12)
$\alpha(B\flat \rightarrow A\flat) = 0.25$
$\alpha(E\flat \rightarrow D) = 1.5$
$\alpha(F \rightarrow B\flat) = 0.03$
$\alpha_{rvl}(\mathrm{ii}^7/\mathbf{E}\flat \rightarrow \mathrm{V}^7/\mathbf{E}\flat) = 1.78$
$\alpha_{rh}(\mathrm{ii}^7/\mathbf{E}\flat \rightarrow \mathrm{V}^7/\mathbf{E}\flat) = 10 \times {}^{1.78}/_5 = 3.56$

Prog(12→13)
$\alpha(A\flat \rightarrow G) = 1.5$
$\alpha(D \rightarrow E\flat) = 2.0$
$\alpha(B\flat \rightarrow E\flat) = 0.05$
$\alpha_{rvl}(\mathrm{V}^7/\mathbf{E}\flat \rightarrow \mathrm{I}/\mathbf{E}\flat) = 3.55$
$\alpha_{rh}(\mathrm{V}^7/\mathbf{E}\flat \rightarrow \mathrm{I}/\mathbf{E}\flat) = 10 \times {}^{3.55}/_5 = 7.1$

FIGURE 4.35 Realized harmonic attractional analysis for the first phrase of K. 282 at the quarter-note reductional level.

across the bar line in the semicadential progression vii^{o6}/**B♭**→I/**B♭**. The value for I/**B♭**→I/**B♭** is again null because there is no harmonic change. Then, alternating with deep valleys, the peaks occur at V^4_2/**f**→i^6/**f** and V^4_2/**E♭**→I^6/**E♭**, until the attractional rise to the cadence on the downbeat of bar 4, ii^7/→V^7/**E♭**→I/**E♭**.

Figure 4.36 graphs the α_{rh} values in Figure 4.35 in order to bring out the contrast between these attractional peaks and valleys. The plotting shows the attraction of Ev_x to Ev_{x+1} as located at Ev_{x+1}, but in actuality an attractional value expresses a relation between the two events. The irregular alternation in attractions creates a powerful rhythmic effect in counterpoint with the meter. There is a great attraction leading into the downbeat of bar 2; in the second half of bar 2 and the first half of bar 3 the strong attractions are displaced to the offbeats; this displacement is rectified by the strong attraction into the downbeat of bar 4. ("A Metrical Analogy" in chapter 6 will further develop the relationship between tonal attraction and meter.)

We turn now to the beginning of *Tristan und Isolde*, whose subject matter is attraction, physical and metaphysical. To embody this world view in tones, Wagner embraces chromatic voice leading, maximizing the potential for melodic attractions. The opening *Sehnsucht* leitmotive encapsulates the entire drama: motion toward tension followed by relaxation that does not resolve. Figure 4.37 exhibits these measures according to two interpretations, leading to somewhat different attractional results. The format is the same as in Figure 4.33 except that all the attractional values are included at level b so as to convey more directly the kinetic energy of the passage. Figure 4.38 displays the calculations for Figure 4.37 in a layout imitating that of the musical notation.

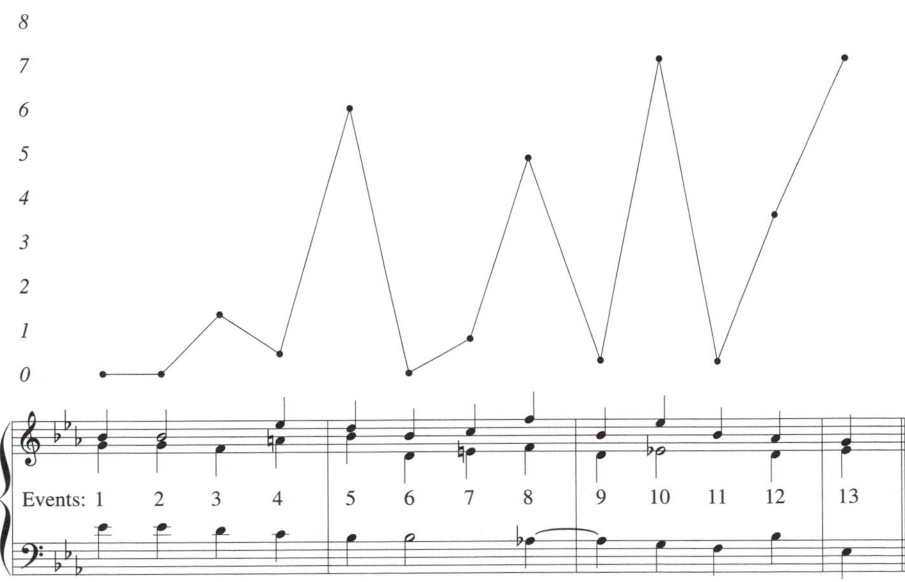

FIGURE 4.36 Graphic representation of the a_{rh} values in Figure 4.35.

FIGURE 4.37 Two interpretations of the voice-leading attractions for the Prelude to Act I of *Tristan und Isolde*, bars 1–3.

The reduction at level a in Figure 4.37 brings out the differences in interpretation. In (a), bar 1 implies i/**a**, and in bar 2 the G♯ is an appoggiatura to A, resulting in an augmented (French) sixth chord. In (b), bar 1 implies VI/**a** (or iv/**a**), and in bar 2 the G♯ is harmonic and A is passing, so that the Tristan chord functions as a real chord. Interpretation (a) for bar 1 can combine with interpretation (b) for bar 2, and vice versa. Even in Wagner's lifetime these various possibilities began to have advocates in the growing literature on this passage. Because it more easily fits Roman-numeral analysis, interpretation (a) became standard, although recently (b) has received persuasive support in Mitchell (1967). For comparative discussion, see Robert Wason (1985) and Jean-Jacques Nattiez (1990); Richard Taruskin (1997) includes a discussion of the passage in terms of tension and resolution. In my view, to insist on one correct reading would do violence to a passage in which ambiguity is an essential feature. However, Benjamin Boretz's (1972) and Forte's (1988) elevation of the Tristan chord as hierarchically superior to its resolution on V^7 misleads musically as well as dramatically, for it confuses the salience and associative strength of the Tristan chord with its syntactic role.

There are two major differences in voice-leading attraction between interpretations (a) and (b). In (a), alto F in bar 1 drives toward E, whereas in (b) it progresses less forcefully but over a longer trajectory to D♯ in bar 2. And in (a), soprano G♯ in bar 2 is more attracted to A than it is in (b), in which G♯'s energy

a)

		$\alpha(G\sharp \rightarrow A)$ $= {}^{2}/_{1} \times {}^{1}/_{1^2}$ $= 2.0$	$\alpha(A \rightarrow A\sharp)$ $= {}^{1}/_{2} \times {}^{1}/_{1^2}$ $= 0.5$	$\alpha(A\sharp \rightarrow B)$ $= {}^{3}/_{1} \times {}^{1}/_{1^2}$ $= 3.0$
$\alpha(A \rightarrow F)$ $= {}^{2}/_{4} \times {}^{1}/_{8^2}$ $= 0.01$	$\alpha(F \rightarrow E)$ $= {}^{3}/_{2} \times {}^{1}/_{1^2}$ $= 1.5$	$\alpha(E \rightarrow D\sharp)$ $= {}^{2}/_{3} \times {}^{1}/_{1^2}$ $= 0.67$	$\alpha(D\sharp \rightarrow D)$ $= {}^{2}/_{1} \times {}^{1}/_{1^2}$ $= 2.0$	
			$\alpha(B \rightarrow G\sharp)$ $= {}^{2}/_{2} \times {}^{1}/_{3^2}$ $= 0.11$	
			$\alpha(F \rightarrow E)$ $= {}^{3}/_{2} \times {}^{1}/_{1^2}$ $= 1.5$	

b)

		$\alpha(G\sharp \rightarrow A)$ $= {}^{2}/_{3} \times {}^{1}/_{1^2}$ $= 0.67$	$\alpha(A \rightarrow A\sharp)$ $= {}^{1}/_{2} \times {}^{1}/_{1^2}$ $= 0.5$	$\alpha(A\sharp \rightarrow B)$ $= {}^{3}/_{1} \times {}^{1}/_{1^2}$ $= 3.0$
$\alpha(A \rightarrow F)$ $= {}^{4}/_{3} \times {}^{1}/_{8^2}$ $= 0.02$	$\alpha(F \rightarrow E)$ $= {}^{2}/_{4} \times {}^{1}/_{1^2}$ $= 0.5$	$\alpha(E \rightarrow D\sharp)$ $= {}^{2}/_{3} \times {}^{1}/_{1^2}$ $= 0.67$	$\alpha(D\sharp \rightarrow D)$ $= {}^{2}/_{1} \times {}^{1}/_{1^2}$ $= 2.0$	
			$\alpha(B \rightarrow G\sharp)$ $= {}^{2}/_{2} \times {}^{1}/_{3^2}$ $= 0.11$	
			$\alpha(F \rightarrow E)$ $= {}^{3}/_{2} \quad {}^{1}/_{1^2}$ $= 1.5$	

FIGURE 4.38 Quasi-spatial layout of the computations for the interpretations in Figure 4.37.

is partly directed toward B in bar 3. In both readings, however, the progression into the half-cadential V^7 realizes strong attractions in three of the four voices. This factor causes high values in the realized harmonic attractional analysis in Figure 4.39. Here just the harmonic progression in bars 2–3 is computed, as represented by level a in Figure 4.37, since the presence of only one voice in bar 1 would unbalance the comparison. It is not obvious what root to assign to bar 2. The traditional if not entirely satisfactory solution for the augmented sixth is to call it an altered ii; this is done in interpretation (a) in Figure 4.39. But what is the root of the Tristan chord in interpretation (b)? The choice here is an altered vii, in which case there is no apparent functional change in the progression into

a)

$\alpha(A \rightarrow B) = 0.125$
$\alpha(D\sharp \rightarrow D) = 2.0$
$\alpha(B \rightarrow G\sharp) = 0.11$
$\alpha(F \rightarrow E) = 1.5$
$\alpha_{rvl}(ii^{\sharp 6}4_3/\mathbf{a} \rightarrow V^7/\mathbf{a}) = 3.735$
$\alpha_{rh}(ii^{\sharp 6}4_3/\mathbf{a} \rightarrow V^7/\mathbf{a}) = 10 \times {}^{3.735}/_5 = 7.47$

b)

$\alpha(G\sharp \rightarrow B) = 0.11$
$\alpha(D\sharp \rightarrow D) = 2.0$
$\alpha(B \rightarrow G\sharp) = 0.11$
$\alpha(F \rightarrow E) = 1.5$
$\alpha_{rvl}(vii^{\sharp 6}4_{\sharp 2}/\mathbf{a} \rightarrow V^7/\mathbf{a}) = 3.72$
$\alpha_{rh}(vii^{\sharp 6}4_{\sharp 2}/\mathbf{a} \rightarrow V^7/\mathbf{a}) = 10 \times {}^{3.72}/_7 = 5.31$

FIGURE 4.39 Realized harmonic attractional analysis for interpretations (a) and (b) at level a of Figure 4.37.

V. While this seems acceptable if the Tristan chord acts as a magnified appoggiatura, it penalizes the resulting harmonic attractional value in comparison to that of interpretation (a) because vii is further from V than ii is. In any case, the attractional values in both readings are very high.

The *Sehnsucht* motive does not end with the silence that follows it, for the V^7 is not at rest. As discussed in connection with Figure 4.30, the expectation of $V^7 \rightarrow$i(I) remains strong whether or not it is realized. That the resolution on i(I) is denied, here and in the sequences of the phrase and especially in bar 17, where there is a deceptive resolution to VI, propels the drama ever forward, eventually toward the climax of the love music in Act II, where V^7 is prolonged at great length and I is again thwarted (this time in **B**), and ultimately to the continuation and completion of the love music in the closing Transfiguration of Act III, where the progression $V^7 \rightarrow$(IV)$\rightarrow$I finally takes place. The regions change in these various attempts, but the real point is the force of the attractions, which remain unrealized until the concluding resolution.

TENSION, ATTRACTION, AND EXPRESSION

The relationship between tension and attraction

How does attraction as measured by the harmonic attraction rule (α_{rh}) relate to tension as measured by the harmonic distance rule (δ)? The harmonic attraction rule partly answers this question by incorporating voice-leading attraction with harmonic distance, so that harmonic attraction decreases with distance. But there are gaps in this answer. First, α_{rh} does not treat melodic elaborations that move faster than the harmonic rhythm. This is why α_{rh} is not applied to levels smaller than the quarter-note level in Figure 4.33 and the measure level in Figure 4.37. At smaller levels there is no harmonic change, so δ cannot apply there. Consequently, the attractional values for the smaller levels are calculated by α_r rather than by α_{rh}, and the output numbers between the two computations are incommensurate. In Figure 4.33, for example, the numbers that accompany the arrows at level c are not on the same scale as those at levels a–b. One could imagine an adjustment of some kind, but I shall not attempt this here.

A second, related issue is the divergent temporal scopes of the tension and attraction rules. Tension as measured by δ operates over longer stretches than does attraction as measured by α_r or α_{rh}, although the effects of all three rules attenuate over time. Over large spans we generalize events into abstractions that suppress the effect of specific voicings (see "Issues in Prolongational Theory" in chapter 1). This is why the attractional analysis of K. 282 (Figure 4.33) terminates at the half-note level; my intuition is that attractions measured at larger levels would be merely hypothetical. Intermediate and global prolongations depend not on attractions but on memory of structural features.

A third issue has to do with temporal direction of measurement. Sequential tension measurements take place from left to right, but hierarchical tension measurements occur in either direction. Attractional measurements take place either in some virtual dimension or, in the case of realized attractions, from left to right. In this respect, a realized attractional analysis is like a sequential tension analysis.

These qualifications notwithstanding, it is instructive to compare the harmonic tensional and attractional curves for bars 1–4 of K. 282 as represented at the quarter-note level of reduction. Figure 4.40 takes from Figure 4.9 the sequential and hierarchical tension curves (dashed and solid lines, respectively) and superimposes upon them, without regard to scale, the realized harmonic attractional curve (dotted line) from Figure 4.36. The tension peaks at events 4, 7, and 11 are

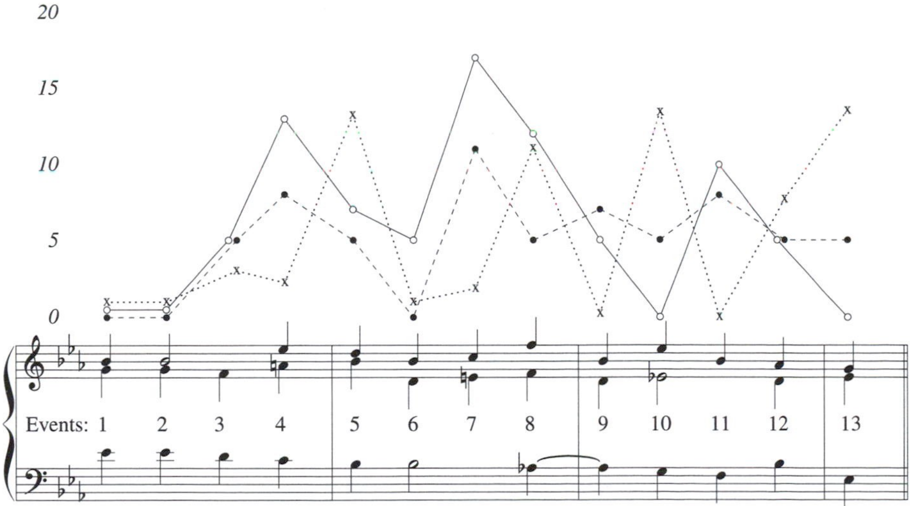

FIGURE 4.40 Comparison of the sequential and hierarchical tension analyses (dashed and solid lines, respectively) with the realized harmonic attractional analysis (dotted line) of bars 1–4 of K. 282. The sequential and hierarchical curves are taken from Figure 4.9 and the attractional curve is taken from Figure 4.36.

low in attraction; conversely, the attraction peaks at events 5, 10, and 13 are low in tension. Where there is a significant increase in tension, there is little attraction, and where there is a significant decrease in tension, there is great attraction. This stands to reason, for strong attractors are points of stability.

The closing bars of Richard Strauss's *Tod und Verklärung*, shown in simplified and abbreviated form in Figure 4.41a, cast a complementary light on the interaction of tension and attraction. In a manner reminiscent of the end of Isolde's Transfiguration, the preceding climax has resolved a dominant pedal with maximal attractional force, V^7→I/**C**. The progressions in Figure 4.41a, supporting the final repetitions of the *Verklärung* motive, then conclude the work peacefully. The first statement, I→♭VI/**C**, echoes **c**, the region of the hero's struggle with death. This is answered by the same progression within **C**, vi→I, and finally by I→I. The prolongational analysis beneath shows two neighboring motions; these are intensified by melodic appoggiaturas. Figure 4.41b provides a breakdown for δ(I→♭VI/**C**) = 10. (If the A♭ chord were treated not as a borrowing but as VI/**c**, δ would be somewhat larger—13 instead of 10—and consequently the α_{rh} value would be smaller.) δ(I→vi/**C**) = 7 (see Figure 2.11), and of course δ(I→I/**C**) = 0. The overall pattern for δ, displayed at the bottom of Figure 4.41a, is one of oscillation into considerable tension, then into less tension, and finally into no tension (except for the melodic appoggiaturas, which are left out of the calculation). Figure 4.41c computes α_{rh} within the attractional context I/**C** for each progression in the prolongational analysis. Because of ratios of asymmetry, I→♭VI/**C** brings a modest attraction and ♭VI→I/**C** responds with a substantial one. As with the Mozart, there is strong attraction into low tension. Next, I→VI/**C** smooths out I→♭VI/**C** by moving only one voice by a whole step, producing a very weak attraction; the return attraction is only slightly greater. The hero's soul is reaching quiescence. With α_{rh}(I→I/**C**) = 0, human striving ceases and the soul resides in perfect stasis.

Connections with other theories

Patterns such as those in Figures 4.40 and 4.41 have more than structural significance. A recurring idea in the history of musical thought is that tonal tension and attraction are central to musical expression. It is not easy to turn this conviction into a genuine theory of musical expression. Yet it is clear that such a theory must be grounded in a precise treatment of pitches and rhythms if its statements are to aspire to more than generalities.

A number of recent music theories have sought to relate tonal tension and attraction to expression, and in ways that relate to this chapter. Cooke's (1959) literal approach assigns specific emotional qualities to the dynamics of each melodic interval. Joseph Swain (1997) makes a case for patterns of tension and resolution as the chief source of musical expression. Perhaps the most influential theory of musical emotion has been that of Meyer (1956), in which the denial of expectation is hypothesized to cause affect. This means in our terms that in cases where $\alpha_e = \alpha_r$, the listener's response is one of satisfaction or completion with little affective arousal; in cases where $\alpha_e \neq \alpha_r$, the listener's response is one of surprise, frustration, or incompletion with accompanying strong affect. It may

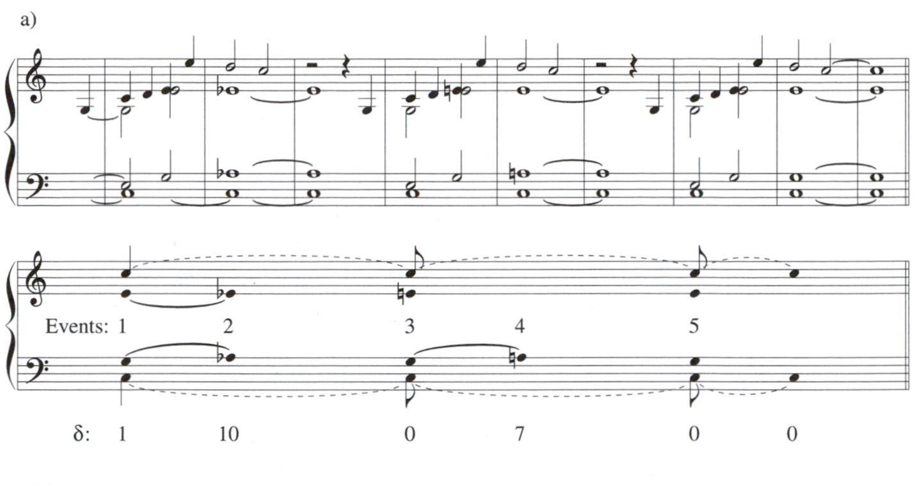

b)

$$\begin{array}{cccccccccccc}
 & & & & & & & & \underline{8} & & & \\
 & & & \underline{3} & & & & & \underline{8} & & & \\
0 & & & \underline{3} & & & & & \underline{8} & & & \\
0 & & 2 & \underline{3} & & 5 & & 7 & \underline{8} & & 10 & \\
0 & 1 & 2 & 3 & 4 & 5 & 6 & 7 & 8 & 9 & 10 & 11
\end{array}$$

$\delta(\text{I}/\mathbf{C} \rightarrow \flat\text{VI}/\mathbf{C}) = 0 + 3 + 7 = 10$

c)

Prog(1→2)

$\alpha(\text{C} \rightarrow \text{C}) = \text{null}$

$\alpha_r(\text{E} \rightarrow \text{E}\flat) = 0.33$

$\alpha_r(\text{G} \rightarrow \text{A}\flat) = 0.33$

$\alpha(\text{C} \rightarrow \text{C}) = \text{null}$

$\alpha_{rvl}(\text{I}/\mathbf{C} \rightarrow \flat\text{VI}/\mathbf{C}) = 0.66$

$\alpha_{rh}(\text{I}/\mathbf{C} \rightarrow \flat\text{VI}/\mathbf{C}) = 10 \times {}^{0.66}/_{10} = 0.66$

Prog(2→3)

$\alpha(\text{C} \rightarrow \text{C}) = \text{null}$

$\alpha_{e/r}(\text{E}\flat \rightarrow \text{E}) = 3$

$\alpha_{e/r}(\text{A}\flat \rightarrow \text{G}) = 3$

$\alpha(\text{C} \rightarrow \text{C}) = \text{null}$

$\alpha_{rvl}(\flat\text{VI}/\mathbf{C} \rightarrow \text{I}/\mathbf{C}) = 6$

$\alpha_{rh}(\flat\text{VI}/\mathbf{C} \rightarrow \text{I}/\mathbf{C}) = 10 \times {}^{6}/_{10} = 6$

Prog(3→4)

$\alpha(\text{C} \rightarrow \text{C}) = \text{null}$

$\alpha(\text{E} \rightarrow \text{E}) = \text{null}$

$\alpha_r(\text{G} \rightarrow \text{A}) = 0.17$

$\alpha(\text{C} \rightarrow \text{C}) = \text{null}$

$\alpha_{rvl}(\text{I}/\mathbf{C} \rightarrow \text{vi}/\mathbf{C}) = 0.17$

$\alpha_{rh}(\text{I}/\mathbf{C} \rightarrow \text{vi}/\mathbf{C}) = 10 \times {}^{0.17}/_{7} = 0.24$

Prog(4→5)

$\alpha(\text{C} \rightarrow \text{C}) = \text{null}$

$\alpha(\text{E} \rightarrow \text{E}) = \text{null}$

$\alpha_{e/r}(\text{A} \rightarrow \text{G}) = 0.375$

$\alpha(\text{C} \rightarrow \text{C}) = \text{null}$

$\alpha_{rvl}(\text{vi}/\mathbf{C} \rightarrow \text{I}/\mathbf{C}) = 0.375$

$\alpha_{rh}(\text{vi}/\mathbf{C} \rightarrow \text{I}/\mathbf{C}) = 10 \times {}^{0.375}/_{7} = 0.54$

FIGURE 4.41 The ending of Strauss's *Tod und Verklärung:* (a) the progression and its prolongational analysis; (b) computation for $\delta(\text{I}/\mathbf{C} \rightarrow \flat\text{VI}/\mathbf{C})$; (c) computations of α_{rh} for the progressions as numbered in the prolongational analysis in (a).

seem puritanical, however, to give denial all the credit for affective response. I would argue that it is not just the blockage of expected realization that counts but the entire interaction between the attractional field and the unfolding of events. The field pulls events in certain directions, whether they go there or not, and at every point the events cause the field itself to evolve. Out of this swirl of force and motion arises affect.

Meyer's work takes a formalistic turn in Narmour's (1990) implication–realization model. Narmour makes a hard distinction between innate and learned structures, and he asserts his basic principles of melodic implication to be innate. Perhaps for this reason, his model assumes a pitch space no more complex than the chromatic scale. While this may suffice for dealing with melodic inertia, it provides little structure for the melodic attraction rule, which demands a hierarchy of pitches as well as semitone distance. All the subtle distinctions in attractions between pitches depend on the pitch space given in Figure 4.19.

Suppose, nevertheless, that pitch space is flat. Narmour's assertion of the innateness of his melodic archetypes is clarified if its Gestalt basis is taken strictly. Using Gestalt psychoacoustic cues, humans try to carve the auditory input into streams. In flat pitch space, small intervals assure through proximity the coherence of a melodic stream. A leap creates the potential for a second stream to form, so the coherence of the original stream is best promoted by gradually redirecting the stream toward its initial channel in the least disruptive way. More precisely, to maintain a single stream, if the first interval is small, another comparable interval in the same direction is optimal (Narmour's "process"); if the first interval is large, a small interval in the reverse direction is optimal (Narmour's "reversal"). Alternating leaps between two registers, however, realize the potential for two coherent streams. In short, at this level of description, melodic implications appear to arise from the need to form coherent auditory streams. Gjerdingen (1994) offers evidence through computer modeling for this way of conceptualizing primitive melodic formation. This view also accords with Glenn Schellenberg's (1997) simplified and empirically promising treatment of Narmour's basic principles of melodic organization.

What, then, of the pitch space in Figure 4.19? As this space is a cultural construct, one might argue that the attraction rule applies just to diatonic tonal music, leaving only small and large intervals going up or down for a universal theory of melodic expectation. But the picture is not as simple as that. First of all, a rigid distinction between innateness and learning is difficult to maintain in face of the brain's capacity, even prenatally, to form neuronal connections in response to stimuli (Lecanuet 1996). Second, the structure of the basic space is not merely cultural but reflects both the human impulse to hierarchize and the ear's perception of differences in consonance and dissonance (see "Empirical Issues" in chapter 2). The basic space is thus a specific instantiation of general principles of organization. Third, Bharucha (1984a) explains anchoring in terms of psychological principles—proximity, stability, cognitive reference points—that have broad validity. One would therefore expect cultures to have a propensity to develop kinds of music that encourage conditions in which some version of the melodic attraction rule can operate (although, like all expectations, this one can be denied in a particular instance). In this view, the relationship between musical nature and nurture is not fixed but is interactive along favored developmental lines. If this reasoning is correct, hierarchical pitch space and the attraction rule should be part of a general theory of melodic expectation.

Bharucha (1996), resuming earlier threads in his own work and connecting his approach to the Meyer/Narmour tradition, develops the anchoring principle as a tonal force vector within a connectionist framework, in a formalism that the attraction rule resembles. Common factors include the inverse proportionality of semitonal distance and a weighting by ratio of the anchor and its unstable neighbor. Bharucha states the ratio in terms of attentional selectivity rather than levels of pitch space: a dissonant pitch is relatively salient (particularly if it falls on a strong beat) and draws attention to itself and to nearby stable tones, whose units are relatively active in the neural network; the focus of attention drives the appetite for resolution on those active units. The similarity between the two formalisms, coupled with the correspondence between the attention band and attractions of any significance as calculated by α, makes it evident that the two models are reaching toward the same goal from complementary perspectives. Moreover, that Bharucha refers to his formalism as the "yearning vector" indicates that he, too, senses the expressive dimension in tonal attraction. (See "Empirical Issues" in chapter 2 and "Melodic Tension" earlier in this chapter for related discussion.)

Starting from Bharucha's (1984a) anchoring principle and my pitch-space model, Larson (1994, 1995) treats tonal melody and prolongation as subject to the metaphorical forces of inertia, magnetism, and gravity. He argues that these forces are a source of expressive meaning in music and uses them as the basis of a model that correlates predictions of melodic expectations with empirical data (taken from Lake 1987). As mentioned, Larson's inertia corresponds to Meyer's good continuation and Narmour's process. The melodic attraction rule developed here quantifies and generalizes Larson's magnetic force. By gravity he means the tendency for melodic lines to descend by step (as a Schenkerian, Larson is especially committed to this notion). However, gravity appears to be dispensable: in the major scale, except for the leading tone, the strongest virtual attractions of nonchordal diatonic pitches are by stepwise descent anyway. If there is any downward tendency beyond what is accounted for by attractions, it may reside in the fact that the most relaxed register for vocal production lies in a rather low range (though not at the bottom). That is, the cause may be more physical than cognitive. Besides, what is "down" to us may be "up" or "away" in another culture. The use of spatial metaphors is universal in talking about music, but spatial orientations are not. There is reason, then, to drop gravity as a musical force.

What does Larson's and my employment of physical concepts mean? It would not be difficult to deconstruct if taken literally, so the facile answer is that space, paths, tension, attraction, and inertia are mere metaphors and no more. According to George Lakoff and Mark Johnson (1980; also Johnson 1987), however, human thought naturally takes the form of embodied metaphorical schemas such as "container," "location," "path," "tension," and "attraction." Pitch-space theory fits comfortably within this framework: a pitch is contained in a chord and a chord in a region; an event has a location; listening to music involves taking paths through pitch space; tension and attraction arise from the interaction of events unfolding through the structure of the space.

In a classic study, F. Heider and M. Simmel (1944; discussed in Pinker 1997) made a cartoon in which three dots moved so that they did not blindly follow physical laws, like balls on a billiard table, but seemed to interact with one another—trying, helping, hindering, chasing—in ways that violated intuitive physics. The dots' motions could be interpreted only as if they acted on their own energy and volition. It was as if they sped up or turned on their own, possessed of internal energy and in service of recognizable goals. Subjects who were shown the film effortlessly attributed animate agency to the dots. Antonio Damasio (1999, p. 70) discusses how, from similar experiments, perceivers make specific attributions of emotion to these abstract movements, depending on whether they seem to lurch with anger, jump with joy, or cringe with fear.

Such is the case with music. Here the dots are events, which behave like interacting agents that move and swerve in time and space, attracting and repelling, tensing and coming to rest. These motions are inherently expressive. The remarkable expressive power of music is a manifestation of the internalized knowledge of objects, forces, and motion, refracted in the medium of pitches and rhythms.

5 *Prolongational Functions*

FINDING THE TONIC

General principles

The theory of prolongations in pitch space, augmented by the treatment of tonal tension, suggests a novel approach to the refractory issue of tonal function. The approach relies fundamentally on tonal context. Because a piece's overall tonal context is its tonic, it is necessary first to develop a method for finding the tonic.

Up to this point the theory has assumed frames of reference. The rules in chapter 2 calculate pitch-space distances between any two events but do not orient a sequence of events to its tonic. Yet the formulation of the stability conditions in terms of pitch space ("The Principle of the Shortest Path" in chapter 2) depends on locating the tonic at any time-span or prolongational level: the tonic is the point of stability from which the distance of other events is directly or indirectly measured. Similarly, the calculations of tension ("The Harmonic Tension Model" in chapter 4) presume a tonic point of total relaxation at which T = 0 and from which the hierarchical tension of other events is measured. Thus the question of how the tonic is established would be central to the theory as a whole even if it were not needed to support a subtheory of functionality.

The question of tonic-finding has been treated in a number of ways in the psychological and theoretical literature (for example, Longuet-Higgins and Steedman 1971; Butler 1989; Krumhansl 1990; and Temperley 1996). Finding the tonic is a complex phenomenon and surely cannot be reduced to a single principle. Without pretending to completeness, I approach the issue through the principle of the shortest path. In this view, events are interpreted not only in the closest possible relation to one another but also in the closest proximity to a provisional tonic.

It follows that when a single note or chord sounds in isolation, the listener assumes that it is the tonic, for the shortest distance is from an event to itself. In terms of the algebraic pitch-space representation, the listener aligns the basic space to fit the pitch or chord in question, so that the pitch or chord is in the most stable position at the top of the basic space.

The picture becomes more complicated once a second pitch or chord sounds. Consider a few melodic cases. All else being equal, p0 followed by p2 is best interpreted as $\hat{1}\rightarrow\hat{2}$ in **C**, for only in this case is one of the pitches located at the top of the basic space, as illustrated by the pitches inside the solid lines in Figure 5.1a. (A pitch is counted at its most stable position, or highest level, in the basic space.) The alternative, $\hat{7}\rightarrow\hat{8}$ in **d**, is not available because in the minor mode $\hat{7}$ is raised when leading into $\hat{8}$. Somewhat less preferred possibilities are $\hat{4}\rightarrow\hat{5}$ in **G** and $\hat{5}\rightarrow\hat{6}$ in **F**, each of which places one of the pitches at the fifth level of the space, as shown in Figures 5.1b–c. Not at all preferred, and indeed quite bizarre, would be the construal of p0→p2 in Figure 5.1d as $\sharp\hat{4}\rightarrow\flat\hat{6}$ in **F♯**, because that would place p0 and p2 down in the space as chromatic alterations at the diatonic level. To take another example, p0 followed by p4 has two plausible interpretations, as $\hat{1}\rightarrow\hat{3}$ in **C** and as $\hat{3}\rightarrow\hat{5}$ in **a**, as shown in Figures 5.1e–f, with the former slightly preferred because there one of the pitches is at the top level. In Figure 5.1g, p0 followed by p5 yields $\hat{5}\rightarrow\hat{1}$ in **F**, for the two events are in the two top levels of the space. The alternative in Figure 5.1h, $\hat{1}\rightarrow\hat{4}$ in **C**, reaches down to the diatonic level for the second pitch.

The shapes of the boxed-in pitches in Figure 5.1 suggest that if the box is not a rectangle, the solution is not preferred. Rectangles can be drawn only for pitches that are adjacent at some level of the space, hence related by step in the sense of Figures 2.5b–c.

These melodic fragments indicate that the choice with the least overall embedding (that is, with the tallest rectangle) in the basic space guides the provisional assignment of tonic orientation. This criterion coincides with the shortest path if the basic space is seen as an unwrapped cone whose entrance is at its tip, with distances from the tip measured by depth of embedding (as in Figure 2.5a). The criterion includes the familiar claim that the stated or implied diatonic collection is a factor in finding the tonic; for if a (partial) collection fits at the diatonic level, it appears at a shorter distance from the tip than if (part of) it is available only at the chromatic level. Thus the diatonic factor is not an independent principle but a consequence of the shortest path as it applies to the basic space. The rare-interval criterion (Browne 1981; Brown and Butler 1981) is also not a truly independent principle but enters the picture as an efficient indicator of the diatonic level. Because a tritone or a minor second is comparatively rare in the diatonic collection, the presence of one of these intervals implies more about what the entire collection might be than would, say, a fifth or a major second. The elements of the presumed collection are given the least embedded interpretation in the space.

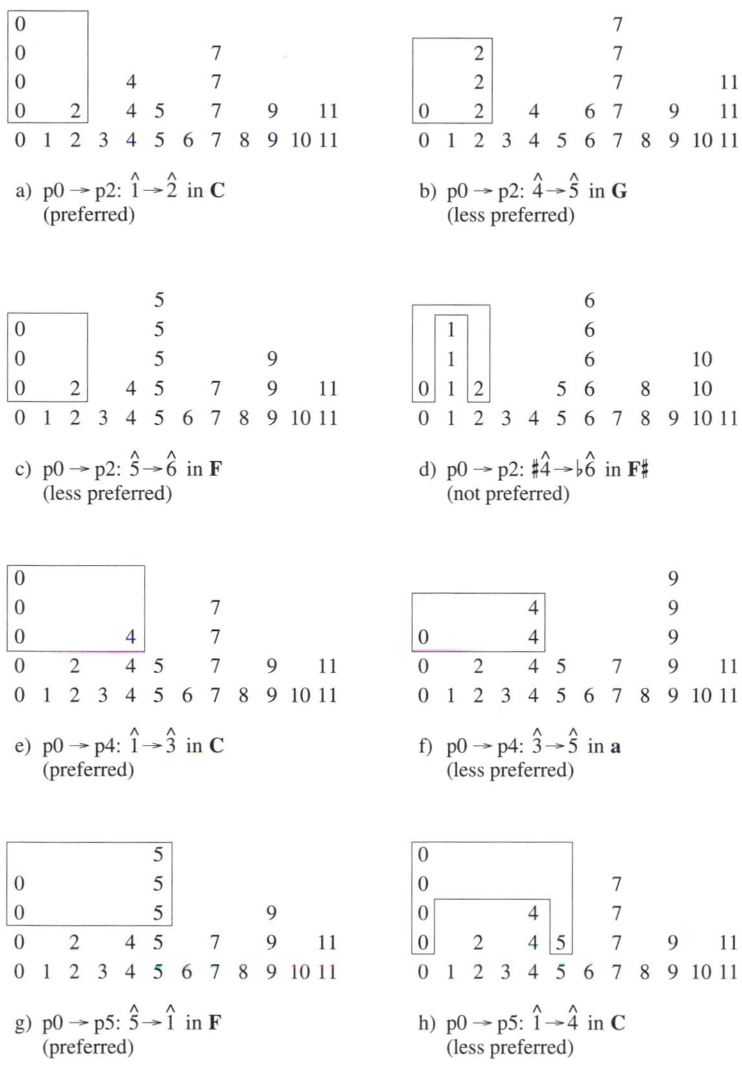

FIGURE 5.1 Tonic orientation for sequences of two pitches.

A progression of two chords must be treated somewhat differently than that of two pitches because, unlike the basic pc space, chordal space is not in itself organized hierarchically. In an intraregional chordal toroidal structure, the seven chords are evenly spaced. Each chord has a set of fixed minimal distances to the others, and none is intrinsically superordinate. In the pretonal modal system, the tonic can be the root of any of six chords on the structure (except for the diminished triad). Cadences and their relative importance in the grouping structure—features that emerge in a time-span reduction—determine local or global tonicity in a modal as well as in a tonal piece. But in the Classical tonal system, given a particular diatonic collection, there are only two modes, the major and the minor, and hence only two candidates for tonic. The chordal/regional spatial representation, with its alternation of major and minor configurations, reflects this duality of Classical tonality. The chordal toroidal structure, despite its uniformity, allows only two tonic orientations. This stylistic restriction simplifies the tonic-finding problem.

The shortest path continues to operate at the chordal level, both between two chords and with respect to their putative tonic. Optimally, one of the chords should itself be a tonic. Let us work through a few progressions, leaving aside questions of harmonic inversion, voice leading, style-specific cues, metrical and phrasal position, and normative temporal orderings. The progression C→d (a C major chord followed by a d minor chord), given in Figure 5.2a in the arrow/path notation, is best interpreted as **I**→ii in **C**, because that makes one of the events tonic. The reverse possibility of **d** is disqualified because, again, in the Classical tonal system $\hat{7}$ would be raised to C♯. A less preferred alternative to Figure 5.2a is the interpretation of C→d as V→vi in **F**, as in Figure 5.2b, with the tonic unstated. Another interpretation, I/**C**→i/**d** in Figure 5.2c, while it would permit both chords to be tonics, fails because the shortest path between C and d is not taken. For another case, the progression C→a offers two strong possibilities, I→vi in **C** and III→i in **a**, shown in Figures 5.2d–e. **C** is preferred because in the alternative $\hat{7}$ is uncharacteristically lowered. The progression C→F is ambiguous between I→IV in **C** in Figure 5.2f and V→I in **F** in Figure 5.2g. More information is needed to tip the balance between them, for instance if one of the two chords functions as tonic at the next larger reductional level. The progression F→G in Figure 5.2h, however, functions unambiguously as IV→V in **C**, even though neither states the tonic directly, for only the C diatonic collection, and therefore **C**, contains both chords. Similarly, a G^7 chord, which in the Riemannian tradition partakes of subdominant as well as dominant function (Harrison 1994), points by itself to the tonic as V^7/**C**. Finally, a good test case is the progression a→e. If understood as vi→iii in **C**, as in Figure 5.2i, the two chords are away from an unstated tonic. The interpretation i→v in **a** is unsatisfactory because of the lowered leading tone. That leaves iv→i in **e**, given in Figure 5.2j, as the preferred analysis.

The graphing in Figure 5.2 relies on the multiple locations of a given triad in chordal/regional space. As discussed in "The Regional Level" in chapter 2, this representational redundancy is a visual convenience and does not arise in the underlying algebraic model, in which distances are measured strictly by the chord distance rule.

In the reductional method described in "A Representative Analysis" in chapter 1, only two (or at most three) events come up for comparison within a given time span or prolongational region, so there is never a point in the analysis where tonic-finding depends on evaluating many events at once. Thus there is no need for an external criterion to limit the computation, such as invoking tone durations (as in Krumhansl 1990) or a temporal decay function (as in Temperley 1996). The hierarchy of spans and regions performs this task within the theory. Instead, the chief problem, which occurs already at the musical surface, is the determination

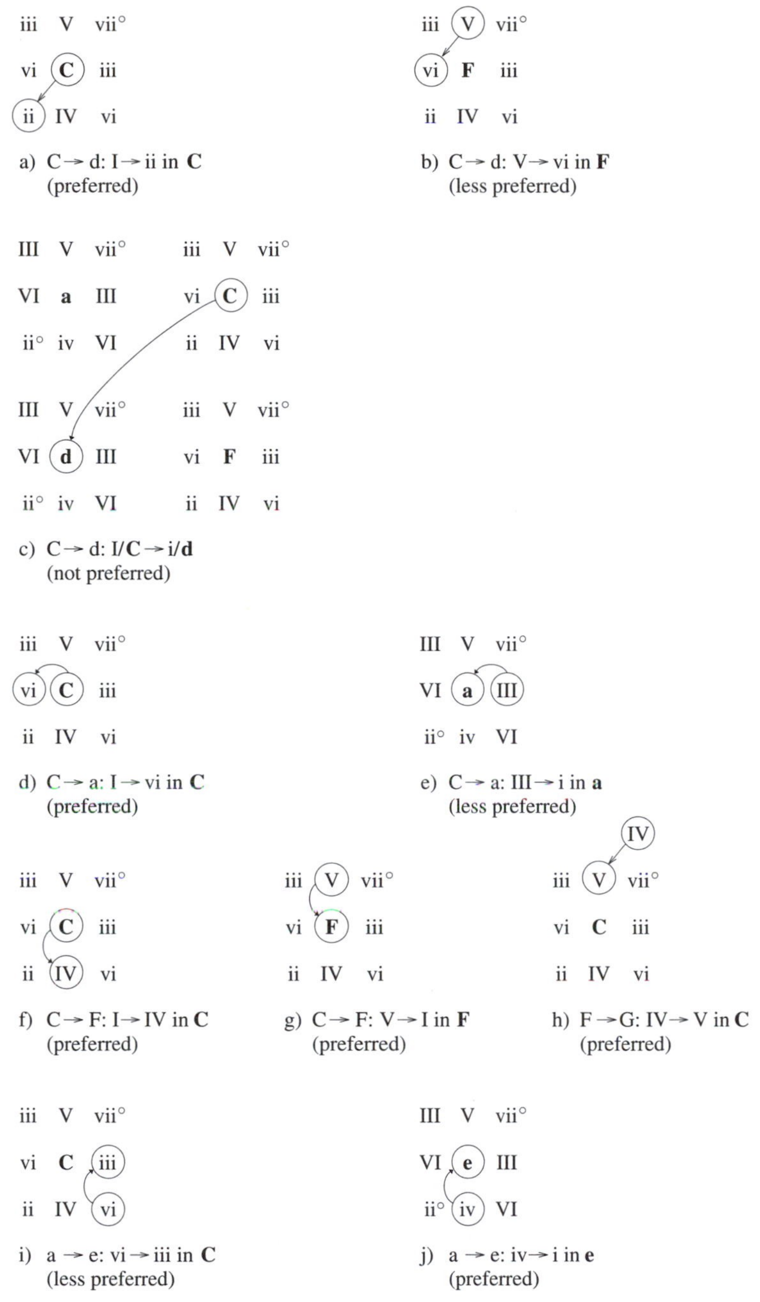

FIGURE 5.2 Tonic orientation for sequences of two chords in the same region.

of which tones are harmonic and which are nonharmonic. This seemingly trivial but in fact quite intricate complication lies outside our concerns here; let us proceed on the assumption that the theory makes the right distinctions.

The discussion so far has assumed that the pitches or chords in question belong in the same region. What if they do not? Suppose, for instance, that the chord progression C→E takes place at a reductional level in some time span or prolongational region of a piece. It would be implausible, say, to assign the C chord as V/**F** and the E chord as VI/**g♯**, as depicted in Figure 5.3a. The principle of the shortest path continues to apply. Assuming that the C chord and the E chord are in different regions, these regions should be as close as possible to each other, and one of the chords should optimally be a tonic. If the C chord is interpreted as I/**C**, the E chord suggests V/**a** or I/**E**, with the former preferred because I/**C**→V/**a** is a shorter distance than I/**C**→I/**E**. These possibilities are illustrated in Figures 5.3b–c. If, however, the E chord is assigned the location I/**E**, the C chord suggests VI/**e**, shown in Figure 5.3d.

Which choice is better, Figure 5.3b or Figure 5.3d? Each expresses one event as a tonic, to which the other event relates by the shortest path. In the chord distance rule, δ(I/**C**→V/**a**)= 0 + 4 + 6 = 10 and δ(VI/**e**→I/**E**) = 3 + 3 + 7 = 13; this slightly favors Figure 5.3b. But this advantage is overridden by a more powerful factor. Just one of the events will make the best connection in the prolongational reduction, which is to say that just one of the events will be closer to the tonic orientation of the next larger level. Thus if **C** is referential at the next level, the preferred interpretation is I/**C**→V/**a** (Figure 5.3b); if **E** is referential at the next level, the preferred interpretation is VI/**e**→I/**E** (Figure 5.3d). Ultimately, selection by reductional importance hangs on a supposition about the global tonic of the piece. Usually an expert listener will not be surprised at this level, although there are well-known cases, such as Chopin's Second Ballade, which begins in **F** and ends in **a**, or the last movement of Mahler's Fourth Symphony, which begins in **G** and ends in **E**, where a reductional decision is undermined by reference to two framing tonics. Such exceptional cases do not weaken the usual effectiveness of reductional importance in influencing tonic orientation.

The following preference rule summarizes this discussion:

TONIC-FINDING RULE To establish tonic orientation in any time span or prolongational region at any level,

(1) if single pitches are under consideration, prefer the interpretation that places the pitches at the highest locations in the current basic-space configuration

(2) if chords are under consideration, prefer the interpretation that connects the chords by the shortest chordal/regional paths, both

(a) with respect to one another and

(b) with respect to the putative tonic at that level (without violating characteristic diatonic inflections in minor)

(3) if two events within a region are equally close to a tonic under different interpretations, or if the events do not fit in the same region, prefer the

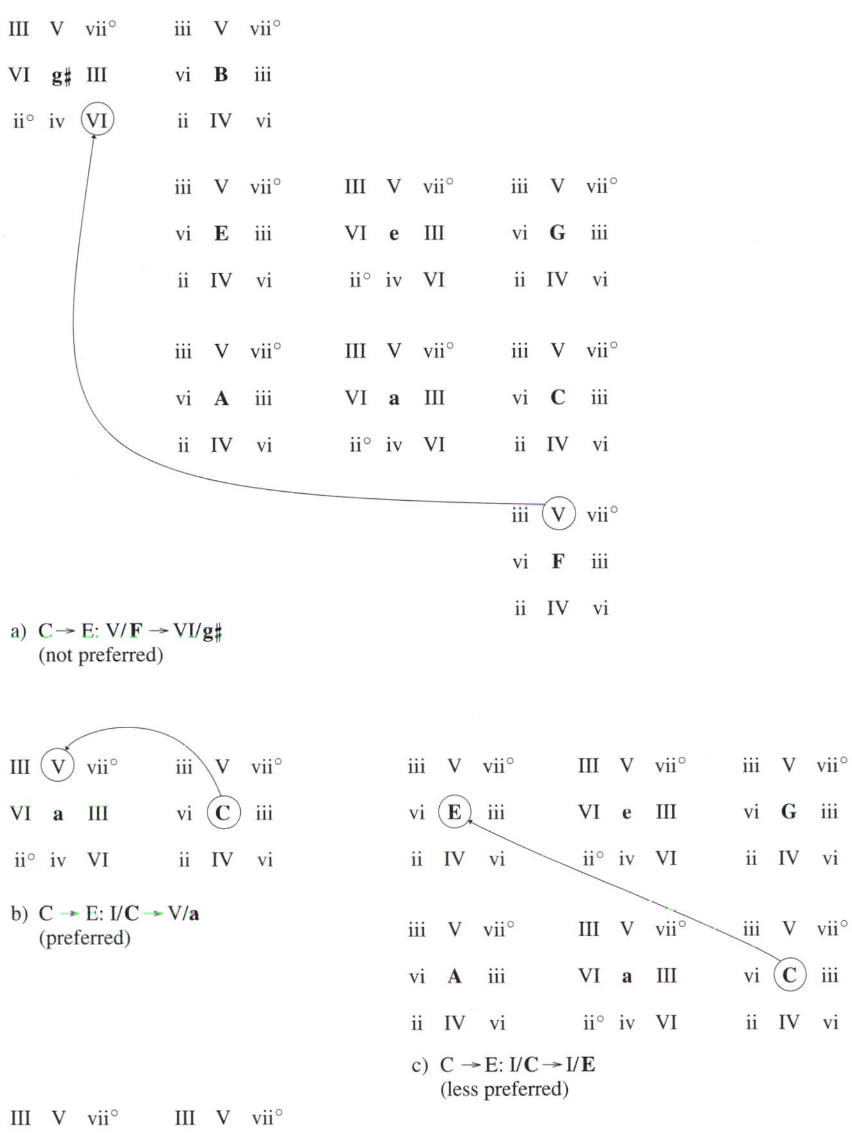

III V vii° III V vii°
VI **E** III VI **e** III
ii° iv VI ii° iv VI

d) C → E: VI/**e** → I/**E**
(preferred)

FIGURE 5.3 Tonic orientation for sequences of two chords in different regions.

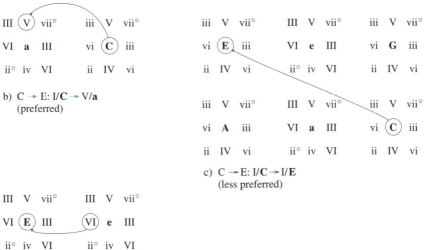

interpretation that forms the shortest path to the governing tonic at the next larger reductional level.

The statement that tonic orientation is computed at any time-span or prolongational level assumes that listeners constantly adjust tonic orientation at multiple stages, in search of the most stable or coherent overall structural representation. This plausible but intricate picture could be simplified somewhat if the theory were able to treat time-span reduction not as an independent derivational stage but merely as that part of the prolongational derivation that evaluates rhythmic information. I shall not pursue this possibility here.

The tonic-finding rule could be augmented by factors that do not involve the shortest path. The following analyses will refer to only one of these, the role of harmonic inversion: all else being equal, a chord in root position functions more strongly as a tonic than does a chord in inversion. For example, in the progression C→F^6, **C** is more likely heard as tonic, but in the progression C^6→F, **F** is more likely heard as tonic.

Condition (1) of the tonic-finding rule relates to Krumhansl's (1990) key-finding algorithm, which computes the best fit between tone durations (the total duration of each pc in a passage) and probe-tone profiles (the judged stability of each of the twelve pcs in relation to an induced tonic) for each of the twenty-four major and minor keys. The basic pc space approximates a given probe-tone profile in the form of an unwrapped cone, so condition (1) is a version of Krumhansl's best fit. However, the input in my approach is not tone durations, which are rough approximations of pitch importance, but segmented reductional sequences.

Before continuing, a digression: conditions (1) and (2) of the rule impact on an issue only partly related to tonic-finding, the harmonic interpretation of an unaccompanied melody. Like finding the tonic, chordal assignment is a question of spatial location. Take the melodic sequence C→E→D→F. It is optimally parsed into C→E and D→F so that each pair can rise from the diatonic to the triadic level; thus condition (1) can take on a parsing role. Now consider each pair of pitches. As discussed, C→E is best interpreted as $\hat{1}$→$\hat{3}$ in I/**C**, although it can also function as $\hat{3}$→$\hat{5}$ in i/**a**. D→F by itself is preferably interpreted as $\hat{1}$→$\hat{3}$ in i/**d**, but it can also function as the root and third of ii/**C**, vi/**F**, or iv/**a**. It can also act as $\hat{3}$→$\hat{5}$ in I/**B♭** or as the fifth and seventh of V^7/**C**. The full four-note sequence eliminates **d** because of the C and **B♭** because of the E, leaving **C, F**, and **a** as candidates for tonic region. Condition (1) favors **C** over **a**, since there is a C but not an A in the sequence, and condition (2b) favors **C** over **F**, since there is presumably a C chord but certainly not an F chord in the sequence. On these grounds, then, the implied chord progression is I→ii of **C**. But by condition (2a), I→V is a shorter distance than I→ii; so the final preferred harmonic interpretation of the sequence is I→V^7 of **C**.

Although I believe this approach has promise, I shall not pursue it further. There are too many issues to solve that fall outside our topic here, such as assigning implied polyphonic lines from a single melodic sequence, developing secure criteria for separating nonharmonic from harmonic tones, taking into account implied voice leading, and interfacing implied harmony with rhythmic structure. (See Temperley [1996] for substantial proposals on these issues.)

Three tonic-finding analyses

Passages in the literature will demonstrate the application of the shortest path in establishing tonic orientation. Figure 5.4 repeats from Figure 2.31 the time-span reduction, beginning at the quarter-note level, of the first phrase of the Bach chorale, "Christus, der ist mein Leben." In the discussion of Figure 2.31 it was stated without explanation that local tonicity is determined within each time span. Here is how the procedure works, mainly using condition (2) of the tonic-finding rule. In spans c_1 and c'_1, the shortest path arises if the progression is either I→V^6 in **F** or IV→I^6 in **C**; the former is preferred because the F chord is in root position and the C chord is in inversion. In span c_2, the shortest path obtains if the progression is V$^4_2$→I^6 in **B♭**. In spans c_3 and c_4, the default interpretations are I/**C** and I/**F**. At the next level, in span b_1 the alternatives are I→IV^6 in **F** and V→I^6 in **B♭**; the former is preferred because then the tonic is in root position. In span b_2, either I→IV in **C** or V→I in **F** is viable; the latter is preferred because, by condition (3), it permits the shortest path at level a_1, where **F** prevails as tonic.

These time-span reductional locations carry over in top–down fashion (by the interaction principle) into prolongational paths, as shown in Figure 5.5: at level a, I/**F** progresses to itself; at level b, the intermediate events act within **F**; at level

FIGURE 5.4 Time-span reduction of the first phrase of the Bach chorale "Christus, der ist mein Leben" (repeated from Figure 2.31).

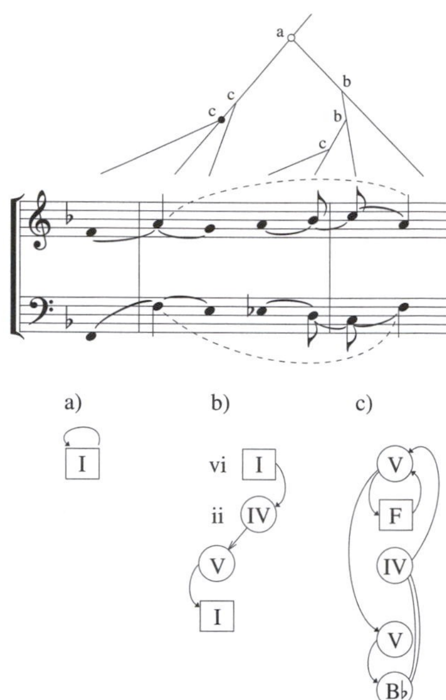

FIGURE 5.5 Prolongational paths for the levels in Figure 5.4 (the prolongation reduction is repeated from Figure 2.32d).

c, **B♭** is passed through, with I^6/**B♭** pivoting as IV/**F**. The move to **B♭** is necessary because the chord that begins span c_2 is located there and not in **F**. But there is no need to move to **C** for span c_3 (as there was in the bottom–up time-span analysis), for a more proximate C chord is available in **F**. The shortest path constrains the interpretation of the C chord within its prolongational context.

How does this intricate combination of bottom–up and top–down derivation reflect the listener's spontaneous ability to find the tonic? As argued in Jackendoff (1991), time-span and prolongational computations (along with grouping and metrical computations) are performed simultaneously in the course of listening. The time-span part of this process can be thought of as an ongoing evaluation of rhythmic importance while in search of the shortest prolongational path. Assignments are constantly assessed, revised, and provisionally settled upon at phrase boundaries. As the next phrase begins, usually just the final results for the previous phrase are retained, avoiding memory overload. A retrospective revision of tonic orientation at such a point is jolting, for it means changing what was already fixed.

We continue in a somewhat less detailed manner with two complex cases of tonic-finding. First consider bars 1–13 of the first movement of Beethoven's *Waldstein* Sonata (see Figure 1.34), as represented in Figure 5.6 in its "normalized" version (repeated from Figure 1.35). Let us proceed through Figure 5.6 from left to right, using its bar numberings instead of those of the sonata. The first inclination is to locate the first event as I/**C**, since the shortest path is from an event to itself (condition [2b] of the tonic-finding rule). The plot immediately thickens with V^4_2/**G**→I^6/**G** on beats 2–3 of bar 1. If bar 1 is heard as taking a regional shift,

FIGURE 5.6 Normalized version of Beethoven's *Waldstein* Sonata, Op. 53, I, bars 1–13 (repeated from Figure 1.35)

that is, as I/**C**→V^4_2/**G**→I^6/**G**, the resulting path, shown in Figure 5.7a, violates condition (2a). **C** nevertheless remains a candidate for global tonic because the G chord, unlike the C chord, is not in root position and therefore is intrinsically less stable. Condition (2a) instead suggests the interpretation IV→V^4_2→I^6 in **G**, as graphed in Figure 5.7b. The provisional prolongational structures that result from these two interpretations appear above each path; in each case, the tonic is head and other events are elaborations.

On the view that parallel passages are heard in parallel fashion, bar 2, which sequences the music of bar 1 down a whole step, ought to receive path and prolongational analyses analogous to bar 1. Figure 5.8a carries out this precept with respect to Figure 5.7a and Figure 5.8b with respect to Figure 5.7b. Both prolongational analyses take the further step of subordinating the head of the second sequential unit to that of the first. However, the path for Figure 5.8a lacks com-

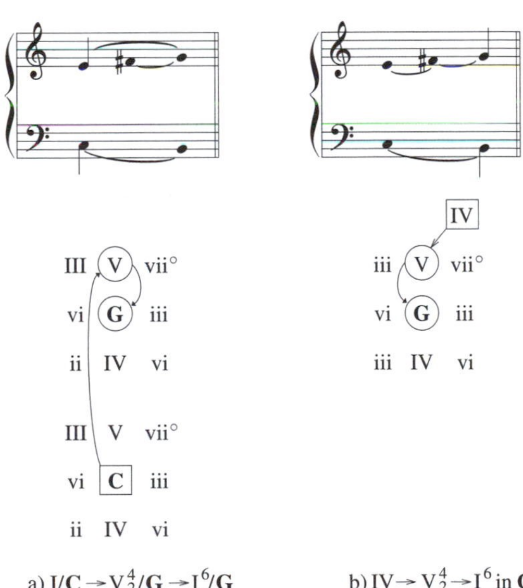

FIGURE 5.7 Competing paths for bar 1 of Figure 5.6. The resulting prolongational analysis is given above each pitch-space path.

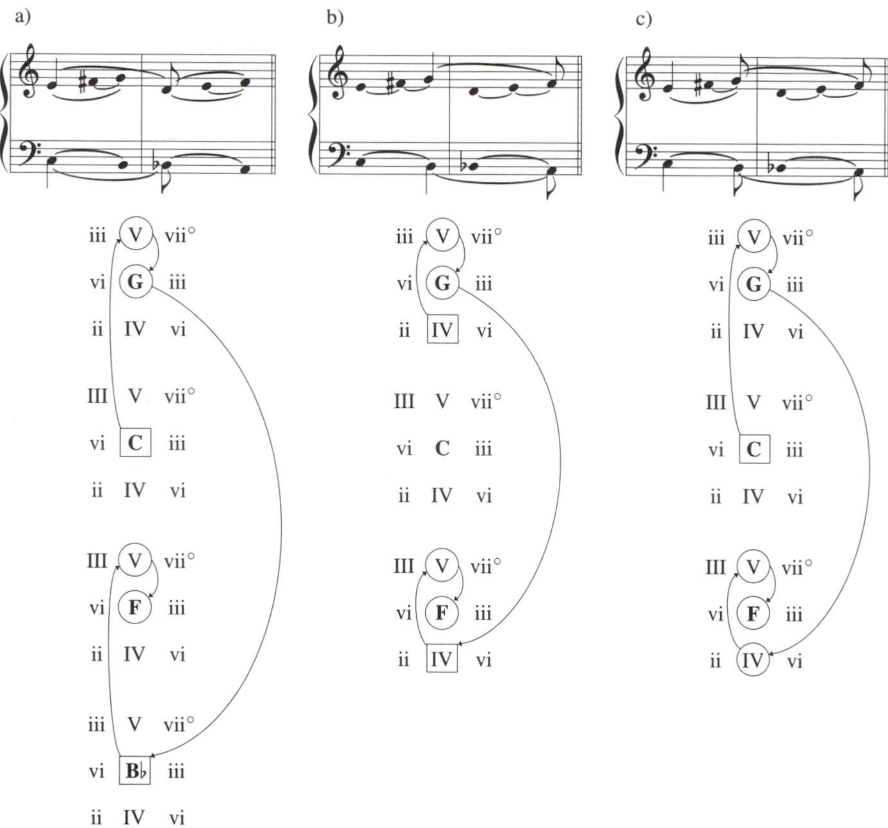

FIGURE 5.8 Competing paths for bars 1–2 of Figure 5.6.

pactness: each sequential unit moves to an adjacent region, and the two units traverse different sets of regions. And the path for Figure 5.8b lacks connectedness: although the path for each sequential unit is within a region, the two regions are no longer even adjacent. A more integrated solution is to discard parallelism and analyze the passage as a combination of Figures 5.7a–b in Figure 5.8c. Now the opening event is a stable I/**C**, and the parallel **B♭** chord is interpreted not as I/**B♭** but as IV/**F**, thereby bringing this foreign element closer to **C**.

The arrival of the V^7 on the downbeat of bar 3 dispels what remains of previous uncertainties about tonic orientation. In the time-span analysis, the V^7 is tagged as a half-cadence for the entire phrase. The ideal matching structural beginning for the half-cadence is the opening C chord interpreted as I/**C**, since this reading provides the shortest path at that level to the V^7 (condition [3]). This assignment causes the F^6 in bar 2 to pivot from its immediate function as I^6/**F** to a larger one as IV^6/**C**, which attaches prolongationally not to the previous V^6 but as a predominant to the V^7 in bar 3. The prolongational sketch in Figure 5.9 shows the larger connection between the opening I and the cadential V^7. The superordinate

FIGURE 5.9 Prolongational analysis for Figure 5.6.

stemmed notes in the bass trace a descending diatonic motion from I to V, filled in by chromatic passing notes. The extension of the V^7 into **c**, as an echoing gesture toward the flat side, does not obscure the basic trajectory of the phrase.

For completeness, Figure 5.10 slots Figure 5.9 into the usual format for a prolongational derivation. Figure 5.11 shows the pitch-space journey of the passage in correspondence with the two sets of prolongational levels at the bottom of Figure 5.10. The path in Figure 5.11a is very compact, for at these levels the tonicizations in **G**, **F**, and **c** have been eliminated, leaving a residue of I, V, and IV in **C**. The path in Figure 5.11b follows the one in Figure 5.8c up to beat 3 of bar 2, at which point I/**F** pivots as IV/**C**. The A♭ in the bass sets up the arrival on V/**c**, which then pivots as V/**C** in preparation for the next phrase group.

Observe that the journey in Figure 5.11b moves to adjacent regions in the northward, southward, and then eastward directions before returning to **C** for the second phrase group. If the *Waldstein* is to continue its highly charged regional exploration by modulating to adjacent regions and without covering previous ground, it must go westward. The second phrase group and transition do this. Prolongational derivation aside, Figure 5.12 displays the pitch-space journey for bars 14–35 of the score (Figure 1.34). The opening unit sequences not down but up a whole step, carrying the passage through a brief tonicization of **a** and pivoting to **e**, where, in parallel with the earlier V/**c** pivot to V/**C**, V/**e** pivots to V/**E** leading into the second theme group. (For related discussion of the beginning of the *Waldstein*, see Schoenberg [1954/1969] and Berry [1976].)

Consider now the opening of the Prelude to Act I of *Tristan und Isolde*. Bars 1–24 are provided in Figure 5.13. Figure 5.14 condenses the first section (bars 1–17) into a time-span reduction of four hypermeasures, omitting the cello anacruses as well as the thematic echoes in bars 12–15. No matter whether the G♯ in the first Tristan chord is interpreted as harmonic or as an appoggiatura, the three sequenced Tristan chords quickly reduce out, leaving a residue of half-cadential dominant sevenths until the deceptive cadence at bar 17. Each resolving dominant seventh in turn points to a tonic without resolving to it. The E^7 can be V^7/**A** or V^7/**a**, the G^7 can be V^7/**C** or V^7/**c**, and the B^7 can be V^7/**E** or V^7/**e**. The spatially most compact solution is V^7/**a**, V^7/**C**, and V^7/**e** (condition [2a] of the tonic-finding rule). Thus arises the progression V^7/**a**→V^7/**C**→V^7/**e**→V^7/**a**→VI/**a**, shown in prolongational notation in Figure 5.15a above the associated pitch-space path. By the balance constraint, the first E^7 connects to the G^7 and the B^7 connects to the second E^7. The shortest path reinforces this parsing: V^7/

FIGURE 5.10 Complete reductional analysis for Figure 5.6.

a→V⁷/**C** and V⁷/**e**→V⁷/**a** cover smaller distances than V⁷/**C**→V⁷/**e**. The second V⁷/**a** is structurally more important than its deceptive resolution, once again on the basis of the shortest path: V is closer to its tonic than is VI. (Hence there is no need for a special rule to stipulate right branching within deceptive cadences.) At the next larger reductional level the two E^7 chords form a strong prolongation, revealing that the governing tonic for the passage must be **a**. In spatial terms, the shortest path among the dominant sevenths is from V⁷/**a** to itself. Figure

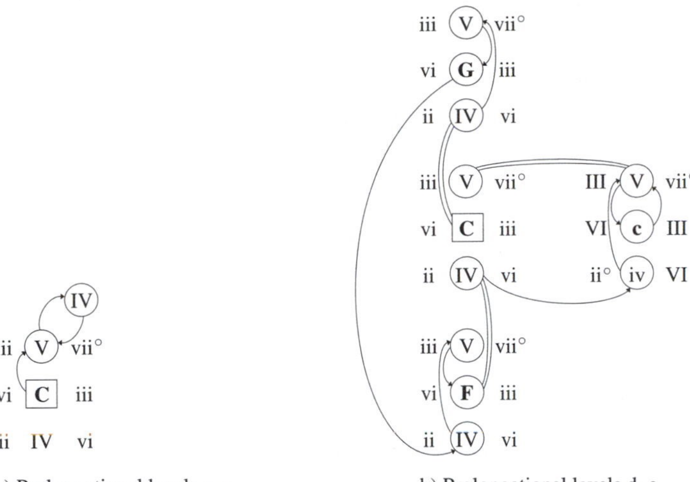

FIGURE 5.11 Pitch-space paths in correlation with the levels in Figure 5.10.

5.15b records this prolongational connection, with the path looping to V^7 before moving to VI.

The second section (bars 17–24) is presented in Figure 5.16 at the same time-span level as the first section in Figure 5.14. As the derivation of tonic orientations for this passage is intricate, it is helpful to refer to its grouping structure, shown at the bottom of Figure 5.16 as two parallel phrases, each in Bar form, $A_1A'_1B_1$ and $A_2A'_2B_2$. The VI/**a** that concludes the first section overlaps as an anacrusis to the second, for which it assumes a more local prolongational role.

The diatonic collections in the first phrase suggest three regions: **G, C**, and **d**. Only **C** can serve as pivot-region tonic (see "The Regional Level" in chapter 2), which means that if **C** is the governing tonic of the phrase, I/**G** and i/**d** have the potential to be reinterpreted as V and ii of **C**, yielding shortest paths. Hence the

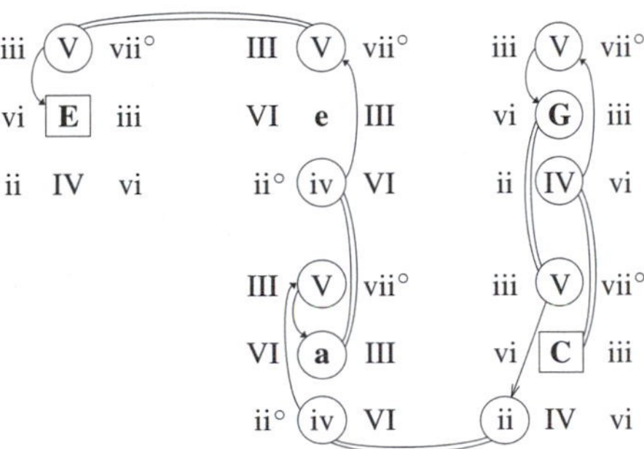

FIGURE 5.12 Pitch-space journey for bars 14–35 of the *Waldstein*.

FIGURE 5.13 Wagner, Prelude to Act I of *Tristan and Isolde*, bars 1–24.

FIGURE 5.14 Time-span reduction of bars 1–17 of the Prelude to *Tristan*.

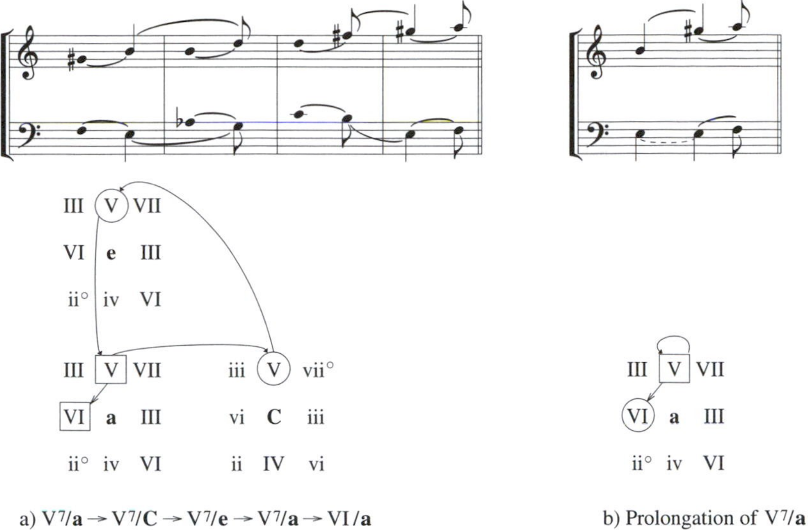

FIGURE 5.15 Prolongational structure and pitch-space path for bars 1–17.

larger picture inclines toward a **C** orientation. The details support this interpretation. Because the F♯s in A_1 and A'_1 follow from an F chord and lead to a G chord, they are understood less as representing **G** than as expressing an applied dominant to the G chord within the framework IV→V→I⁶ of **C** (condition [3]). And even though $\mathbf{B_1}$ ends locally in **d, d** cannot govern the phrase because the preceding C chord does not belong in **d**; rather, the d chord belongs in **C** (condition [2b]). Thus **G** and to a lesser extent **d** are fleeting regions that support V and ii in **C**. Figure 5.17a represents these results prolongationally and with an accompanying pitch-space path.

The second phrase also implies three regions, one for each subphrase of the Bar. A_2 continues in **d** from the first phrase, half-cadencing on V/**d** (the interpretation I/**A** would violate the shortest path). By sequential parallelism with A_2, A'_2

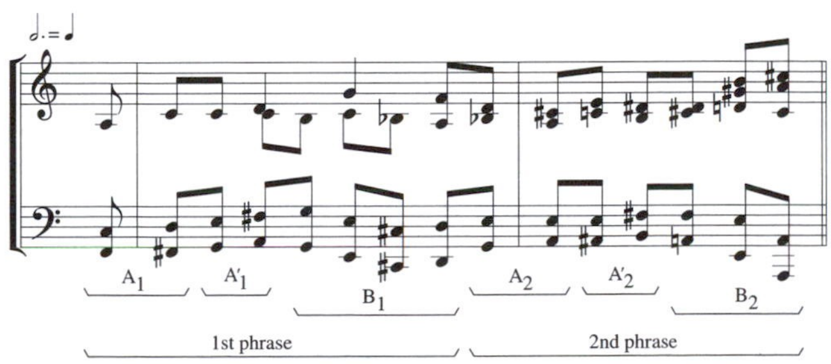

FIGURE 5.16 Time-span reduction of bars 17–24 of the Prelude to *Tristan*. The groupings are labeled according to Bar form.

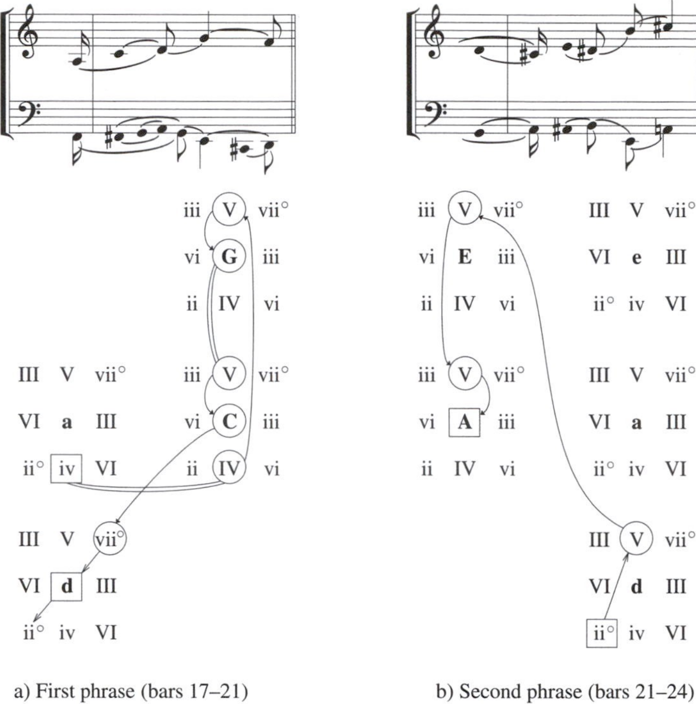

FIGURE 5.17 Prolongational structure and pitch-space path for the second section (bars 17–24).

moves to V/**E** (the alternative interpretation, V/**e**, is more remote from the continuation). B_2 closes with a V-I cadence in **A**. Coming at the end of the section, this full cadence has a time-span reductional importance that subsumes V/**E** as an embellishment of V/**A**, to which it connects by the shortest path (condition [3]). Figure 5.17b shows these relationships.

Figure 5.18 takes the superordinate stemmed events from Figure 5.17 and connects them at a higher prolongational and path level. This graph brings out that the first phrase centers on **C** and the second phrase drives toward **A**. That intermediate **d** bridges the two phrases is a contributing factor (along with the instrumentation and legato phrasing) to the obscuring of boundaries that is so important to the aesthetic effect of this music.

Figure 5.19 places Figures 5.17 and 5.18 in the context of a prolongational analysis of the entire passage (bars 1–24). To bring out the larger hypermeter, the graph incoporates, at the time-span level in question, the anacruses in the first section that were omitted in Figure 5.14; these remain reductionally ornamental because they are not harmonized. The graph also includes bars 12–15, which were deleted in Figure 5.14, in order to show that the hypermeter is periodic with or without the deletion. The grouping structure for both sections is labeled according

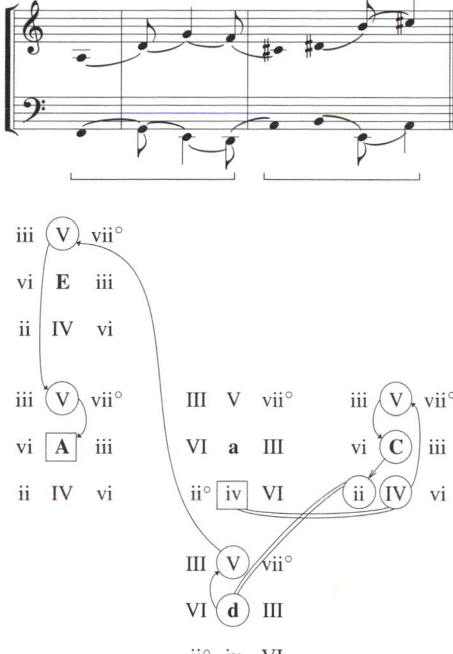

FIGURE 5.18 Prolongational structure and pitch-space path for the second section (bars 17–24) at a larger level than in Figure 5.17.

to Bar form; note that the second section doubles the harmonic rhythm and thus halves the length of the Bars (the last Bar is also metrically compressed, so that the arrival on I/**A** is destabilized rhythmically). The reduction would not be possible without reference at all levels to tonic orientation.

How do I^6/**C** and I/**A**, the dominating events in the two Bar phrases in the second section (bars 17–24), connect to the larger prolongational structure? Taking the shortest path, Figure 5.19 attaches the I^6/**C** to the VI/**a** that closes the first section (bar 17) and the I/**A** to the E^7 that governs the first section. At this level, the E^7 functions not as V^7/**a** but as V^7/**A**. At the most global level, the E^7 dominates the I/**A** because the latter is too embedded in the overall grouping structure to function for the entire Prelude; it is blocked by the interaction principle. Indeed, the Prelude as a whole prolongs V^7/**a**(**A**), for the reprise after the climax returns directly to this dominant seventh and not at all to I/**a**(**A**).

William J. Mitchell's (1967) Schenkerian analysis, by contrast, requires the **A** concert ending of the Prelude and elevates its first note, an unharmonized, anacrustic eighth-note A, to a structural role as an implied i/**a** directly prolonged to an alleged I/**A** in bar 44, over which he chooses a high C♯ as *Kopfton*. This interpretation confuses chord and region; the C♯ lacks tonic support, for it is harmonized by an A chord that acts locally as VI/**c♯**. Indeed, even if this C♯ were supported by I/**A**, the interaction principle would prevent its acting at a global level because of its nested position in the overall grouping structure. More generally, because he does not have recourse to pitch-space theory, Mitchell's methodology

a
b
c
d
d
d
e
e
e
e
f
f
f
f
f
2
6
10
18
22
A
A'
B
A
A'
B
A
A'
B
Bar
Bar
Bar
Bar
[c]
g
f
TSR

FIGURE 5.19 Prolongational analysis of bars 1–24 of the *Tristan* Prelude.

FIGURE 5.20 Regional prolongational analysis of bars 1–24 of the *Tristan* Prelude.

requires locating a global tonic to prolong, no matter how forced the result. He also analyzes bars 1–17 as prolonging a quasi-dominant E minor arpeggiation in the bass. But as the path in Figure 5.15a suggests, it is not the roots of the progression V^7/**a**→V^7/**C**→V^7/**e**→V^7/**a** that govern this section but rather the tonics to which these dominants refer. A regional prolongational analysis (see "Regional Prolongations" in chapter 3) of bars 1–24 will clarify the point. Figure 5.20 reveals that the regional progression in bars 1–17 is **a**→**C**→**e**→**a**, arpeggiating an A minor triad, and that the regions in bars 17–24 express the slightly elaborated motion **a**→**C**→**d**→**E**→**A**. The passage is normative at this level of abstraction. Wagner has replaced a standard chordal progression with an equivalent regional progression. This is why, despite its intense surface chromaticism, the beginning of the Prelude is tonally so grounded.

FUNCTION AS PROLONGATIONAL POSITION

On Riemannian functionality

With tonic-finding in place, we turn to the issue of tonal function, a focus of Riemannian theory. As noted in "The Chordal Level" in chapter 2, the core of the chordal chart, repeated as Figure 5.21, expresses the basic Riemann functions (with the exception of vii° in place of vii). The three harmonic pillars are in the central column, with T (tonic) in the center, D (dominant) above, and S (subdominant) below. The left column shows the relative or R versions—*Parallel* in German—of these pillars (submediant in the major mode), the right column their *Leittonwechsel* or L versions (mediant in the major mode). Thus there are three forms of T in the center row, of D in the top row, and of S in the bottom row. This arrangement is intuitively plausible to the extent that some of the R and L versions commonly substitute for pillars: vii° for V in cadences, vi for I in deceptive cadences, ii for IV in dominant preparations. Along the lines of Riemann (1893), the arrangement could be augmented by chromatic substitutions, as in the major-

	Parallel-klänge	*Pillars*	*Leitton-wechsel-klänge*
D:	iii	V	vii°
T:	vi	I	iii
S:	ii	IV	vi

FIGURE 5.21 Chordal space with basic Riemann functions.

minor mixed chordal space of Figure 3.26c. There is no reason, however, to follow Riemann in his functionally inversional treatment of the minor mode.

Although Riemann can be less than consistent on such matters, his functional designations represent not chords but abstract harmonic functions. For instance, S stands not for a IV chord but for "subdominant function," of which IV might or might not be the instantiation. But what does he mean by "function"? Apparently, it expresses a chord's meaning in relation to the three harmonic pillars (Kopp 1995). An E minor chord in **C** means either a tonic L or a dominant R, in the sense that it can be understood as a version of either T or D, respectively. The function theory alone does not say which interpretation to choose. The logic of chord progressions is dealt with elsewhere in Riemann's theory, through relationships of chord-root intervals and the table of relations (see Figures 2.2b and 2.35). The functional sequence T–S–D–T, which analysts such as Yizhak Sadai (1986) have identified as normative for tonal music, is an observation that employs the categories of the theory rather than a product of the theory, which is surprisingly unconstrained in its functional assignments (Mooney 1996).

The emphasis in neo-Riemannian theory (discussed in "Empirical Issues" in chapter 2) shifts from functional meaning to functional progression through the transformation of one *Klang* into another. *Klang* transformations can be traced as chordal paths, along the lines of Figure 2.35 (see, for example, Lewin 1992). Differences in spaces aside, this way of conceiving functionality resembles chapter 3's assignment of pitch-space paths, with the added step of labeling functions. However, the Riemann tradition has little conception of paths at different structural levels.

Despite broad similarities with neo-Riemannian paths and the arrangement in Figure 5.21, my approach to functionality falls outside the Riemannian conception. I propose that tonal function equals prolongational position. In other words, functionality is an epiphenomenon of prolongational structure. This formulation applies, with qualifications, to pitches as well as to chords, and it is not restricted to a Hegelian dialectical threesome. In this view, neither the location of a chord in pitch space nor the path traversed between two chords expresses functionality, except in the indirect sense that location and path help determine prolongational structure. Nor does the algebraic transformation of one chord into another, regardless of its intrinsic interest, express a musical function. In biology, functionality concerns the role of organisms in context. Just so with events in music.

The function rule

The following statement will guide the discussion:

> FUNCTION RULE Given the repertory of functions T (tonic), D (dominant), S (subdominant), Dep (departure), Ret (return), N (neighboring), and P (passing), assign them by prolongational position from global to local levels, such that
>
> (1) T belongs to any pitch or chord that is a (local) tonic as established by the tonic-finding rule

(2) D belongs to any chord
  (a) that is part of a labeled cadence, such that
    (i) for a full cadence, it left-branches into T, or
    (ii) for a half- or deceptive cadence, it left-branches to an underlying implied T, or
  (b) that is an applied (secondary) dominant
(3) S belongs to any chord that left-branches to D
(4) Dep belongs to any chord that is assigned a right-branching progression
(5) Ret belongs to a noncadential chord that is assigned a left-branching progression to a chord that itself is a right prolongation
(6) N belongs to any pitch or chord that is
  (a) directly subordinate within a strong prolongation or
  (b) a diatonic or chromatic step away from one of its directly superordinate events but not from the other ("incomplete N")
(7) P belongs to any pitch or chord that is
  (a) directly subordinate within a weak prolongation or
  (b) a left branch off Dep
(8) all functions transmit intact through strong or weak prolongations
(9) parallel passages preferably receive parallel functions.

First, some preliminary remarks on this rule. The top–down assignment of functions follows from the way prolongational structure is derived. Numerical subscripts can be added if there is further right or left branching; for example, $T \rightarrow Dep_1 \rightarrow Dep_2$, or $S_2 \rightarrow S_1 \rightarrow D \rightarrow T$. Conditions (2a[ii]) and (7b) may seem puzzling and will be discussed shortly. An applied dominant counts as D in condition (2b) because it imitates a cadence, with the resolving chord acting as a very local tonic. Usually the applied dominant reduces out at the next level, and the T to which it resolves assumes another function. The discussion of condition (5), a noncadential alternative to D, is deferred to the next subsection. Condition (8) enables functions to filter down through all levels of prolongational structure. Condition (9), as in GTTM's components, invokes the ubiquitous factor of parallel treatment of parallel passages.

Figure 5.22a illustrates T, D, and S with a list of their typical diatonic instantiations (conditions [1], [2a(i)], and [3]). V (or sometimes vii°) provides, by virtue of its formulaic cadential role, the entry to I, D→T. S can be anything other than I or V; of diatonic options, that includes ii, iii, IV, vi, and vii°. Because they share two pcs with V, however, iii and vii° yield voice-leading attractions (α_{rh}) for S→D that are weak in comparison to the strong attraction of V→I (see "An Attractional Approach to Harmony" in chapter 4). But IV and ii (and to a lesser extent vi), whose scale degrees $\hat{4}$ and $\hat{6}$ are adjacent to the root of V, offer strong attractions for S→D. As a result, the forceful options for realizing S→D→T in a common-practice context are few. These include chromatic alternatives for S, usually inflecting $\hat{4}$ or $\hat{6}$ or, in the case of augmented-sixth chords, both.

As Figure 5.22b suggests, anything but I qualifies as a departure (condition [4]; the list could be enlarged with chromatic chords). V functions in this context not

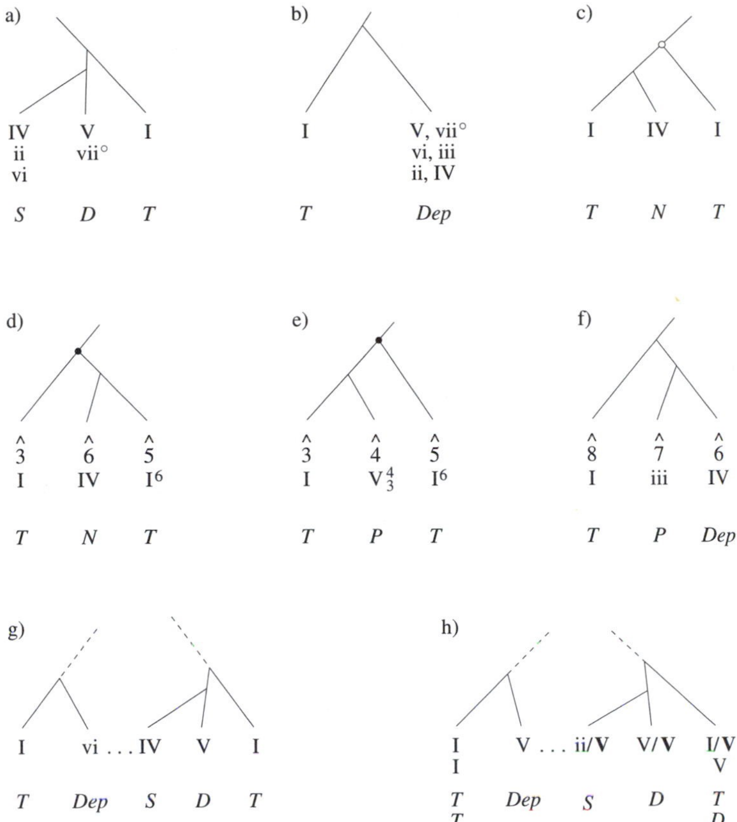

FIGURE 5.22 Schematic illustrations of some harmonic functions.

as D but as Dep. Similarly, in the "Amen" progression I→IV→I in Figure 5.22c, IV acts not as S but as N (condition [6a]). Functions depend not on root identity but on prolongational role. Figure 5.22d shows an incomplete N under a weak prolongation (one possible realization for condition [6b]). Figure 5.22e gives a standard P under a weak prolongation (condition [7a]). Figure 5.22f shows P acting instead as a left branch to Dep (condition [7b]) for a progression, $\mathrm{I}^{\hat{8}}$→$\mathrm{iii}^{\hat{7}}$→$\mathrm{IV}^{\hat{6}}$ studied in harmony treatises from Rameau to Sechter and Riemann (iii was not supposed to move by root-step to IV, so they had to devise explanations for this progression). That is, the basic motion is I→IV, elaborated by a passing $\hat{7}$ over III.

Figures 5.22g–h combine Figures 5.22a–b to show two functional realizations of normative prolongational structure. In Figure 5.22g, T→Dep . . . S→D→T is assigned to the progression I→vi . . . IV→V→I. The dots stand for whatever lies between Dep and S. In Figure 5.22h, the same normative structure takes the form of a tonicization, I→V . . . ii/**V**→V/**V**→I/**V**. At a larger level, shown directly beneath, evidence for **V** is absent, so I/**V** becomes V/**I**. This change corresponds to a different spatial location for the event and represents a hierarchically differentiated functional interpretation, D instead of T.

Why is the underlying I→V in Figure 5.22h not T→Dep instead? Because D belongs to a half-cadence, implying a left branch to a **T** that would be present if it were a full cadence (condition [2a(ii)]). Figure 5.23a represents this relationship (which could be stated as a transformational rule): the branch for the V is rerouted so that it connects to the superordinate I that the cadential I would have attached to if it had been present. This interpretation takes seriously the "half" in "half-cadence." Figure 5.23b shows a related operation for the deceptive cadence: V behaves as in the half-cadential D, and vi, which is less stable than V, becomes Dep. (Note that there is no tonic substitute in this scheme, in contrast to Riemannian theory, where the vi would be interpreted as a tonic *Parallelklang*.) In this way, a cadence, no matter which kind it is, branches and functions for the phrasal span specified by the time-span-reductional cadential labeling. The one constant function among these cadential types is D.

Behind Figures 5.22h and 5.23 lie two technical problems that require solutions. First, under what conditions is an event located in another region, rather than borrowed or inflected within the home region? This choice has been left open since its introduction in "The Regional Level" in chapter 2. Here the choice affects function. As a partial constraint on the interpretation, let us say that as the functional analysis proceeds down the tree, a single foreign event at a given level need not signify location within another region, but that two adjacent chords that belong in the foreign region do signify such location. For example, if a $D^{7}_{\sharp 3}$ is surrounded by other events that are entirely in **C**, it can be treated as an inflected ii/**C**; but if it is preceded or succeeded by another event that must belong in **G**, it is treated as V/**G**.

Second, at what level of functional derivation is an event (or two events) labeled a cadence? In the bottom–up time-span reduction, the procedure is clear: if V→I, V→null, or V→vi (or some other deceptive motion) occurs at the end of a group that has a structural beginning [b], then it is a cadence [c] (see "A Representative Analysis" in chapter 1). Prolongational reduction inherits the hierarchy thus created. Let us say that a functional analysis, as it derives from the prolongational reduction, accesses time-span cadential labeling. If an event arises that is labeled [c] at a given level in the time-span analysis, in the functional analysis it is assigned

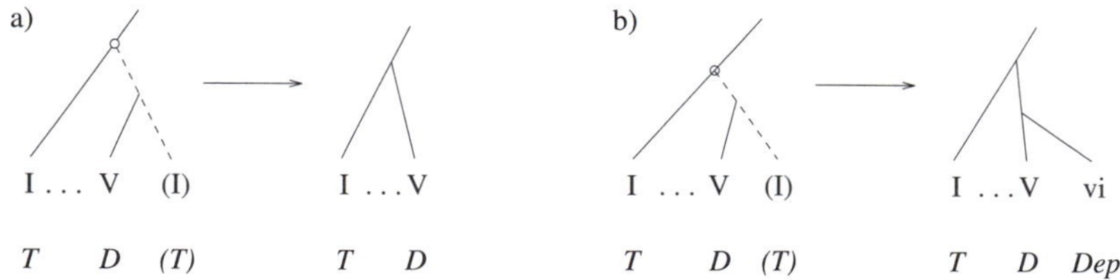

FIGURE 5.23 Functional cadential transformations: (a) the half-cadence; (b) the deceptive cadence.

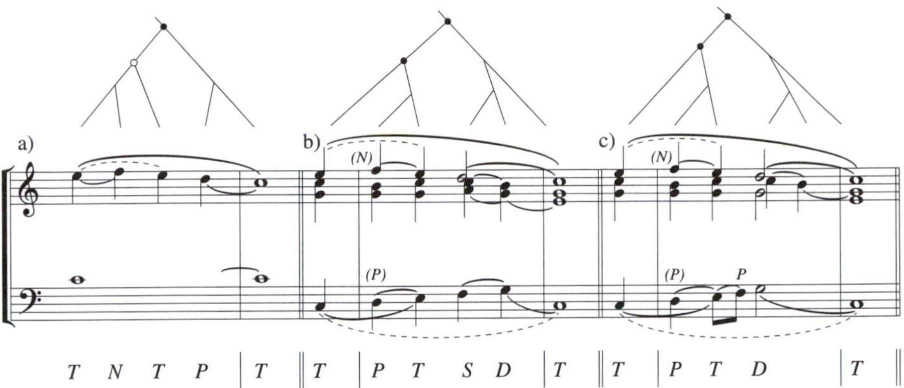

FIGURE 5.24 Nonharmonic functions: (a) *N* and *P* tones; (b) harmonic realization of (a), with subordinate labeling of *N* and *P* tones; (c) replacement of the ii^6_5 in (b) by a suspended V.

D (for a half-cadence), D→T (for a full cadence), or D→Dep (for a deceptive cadence).

Unlike T, D, S, and Dep, N and P can be harmonic or nonharmonic. In Figure 5.24a, nonharmonic N and P elaborate T. Figure 5.24b elaborates Figure 5.24a with chords to show that a chordal function such as P on the first downbeat can decompose into its voice-leading counterparts, in this case N in the soprano and P in the bass, both notated in parentheses to indicate their subordinate status. Strictly speaking, this step would require different prolongational analyses for each line at that level. Figure 5.24c varies Figure 5.24b so that the ii^6_5 on the third beat is suppressed, leaving only the alto suspension. The similarity between the two helped motivate Rameau's theory of supposition, which enabled him to treat all 2–3 (or 7–6) suspensions in the same way (Christensen 1993; Lester 1992). In this present approach, differentiation is made in chordal function, while their similarity is reflected in equivalent trees. The suspension in Figure 5.24c fills the role of S in Figure 5.24b.

Some functional analyses

We are now in a position to assign prolongational functions to actual pieces, beginning with the Bach chorale "Christus, der ist mein Leben" in Figure 5.25, which repeats, in two stages for clarity, the prolongational reduction from Figure 1.18. Beneath the phrase groupings are the functions displayed by prolongational level. The applications of the function rule can be traced down the tree. At the global levels in Figure 5.25a, the structural beginnings and cadences are represented, so the functions in operation are just T and D. The only point of reinterpretation comes at the end of the third phrase, whose arrival is D in relation

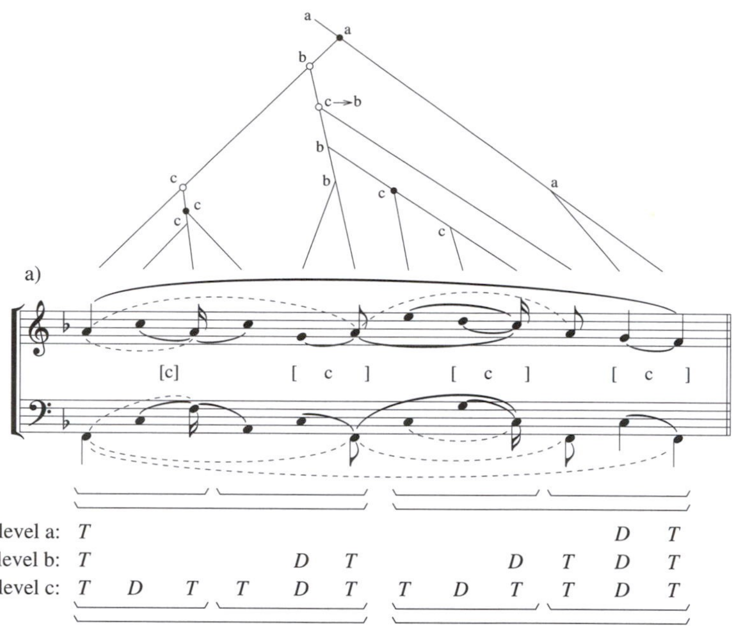

FIGURE 5.25 Function assignments for the Bach chorale "Christus, der ist mein Leben": (a) levels a–c; (b) levels d–e. The prolongational analysis is taken from Figure 1.18.

to **F** at level b but becomes T at level c, for at this reductional stage **C** is tonicized with its structural beginning and cadence.

The analysis continues in Figure 5.25b down to the quarter-note level, with one other point of reinterpretation in the first phrase at the IV, which is S at level d but a local T at level e because of the preceding applied dominant. Consequently, the phrase's normative progression T→Dep→ . . . S→D→T takes place across two levels. (See Keiler 1977 for a different kind of functional analysis of this phrase.) The second phrase begins with an incomplete N and prolongs T by means of P before proceeding to the cadence without S. After a connecting T extension, the third phrase moves via an incomplete N to a tonicized T, I^{3}/**C**, which elaborates by T→P→Dep (functionally comparable to Figure 5.22f) before settling into a S→D→T cadence (the high soprano F can be treated separately as N). The fourth phrase, like the second, extends T by P but, unlike the second, achieves functional closure by S→D→T.

Details aside, the main point about this formalized functional analysis is how smoothly it demonstrates usual intuitions about functionality. There is no need to invoke (neo)Riemannian transformations. The tree generates the functions.

Figure 5.26 gives a functional analysis of the normalized version of bars 1–13 of the *Waldstein* Sonata (see Figures 5.6 and 5.9). Level c elaborates T→D from level b into a normative half-cadential phrase, T→Dep→S→D. Levels d–e then supply the local tonicizing functions in **G** and **F** for bars 1–2 and add N and P extensions for bar 3, borrowed from **c**. In a very local view, the opening C major

FIGURE 5.25 (Continued)

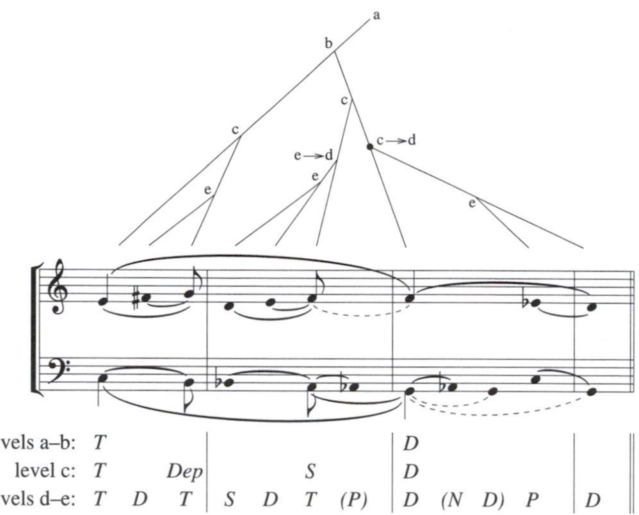

FIGURE 5.26 Function assignments for the normalized version of Beethoven's *Waldstein* Sonata, I, bars 1–13.

triad might have been S in **G** (taking the path in Figure 5.7b), but because of the global-to-local derivation of functionality, it has already inherited T in **C**.

Notions of functionality can influence prolongational interpretations rather than the other way around. Such may have been the case in Schenker's (1935/1979) well-known analysis of Schumann's song "Aus meinen Tränen sprießen" from *Dichterliebe*. The first phrase of the song is given in Figure 5.27. The issue concerns the reading of the A major triad in bar 2. Schenker's foreground graph places the bass A in parentheses, indicating that its role is to make the passing soprano C♯ consonant, and slurs the IV in the same bar around the putatively passing I$^{\hat{3}}$ to V in bar 3. He reinforces this interpretation by writing I–IV–V–I beneath bars 1–3. Evidently, in spite of his antipathy to Riemannian theory, he felt the need to realize the T–S–D–T schema.

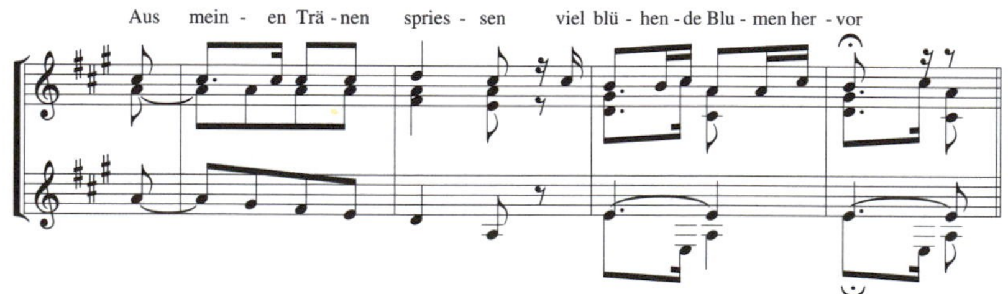

FIGURE 5.27 The first phrase of Schumann's song "Aus meinen Tränen sprießen" (from *Dichterliebe*).

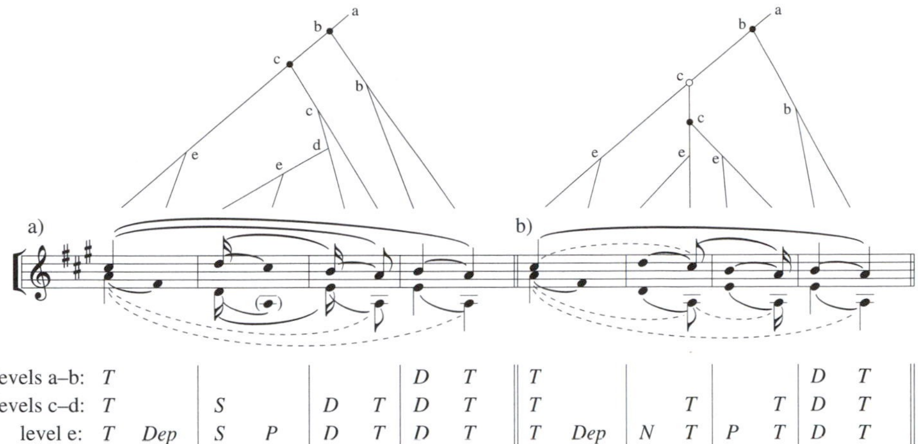

FIGURE 5.28 Function assignments for Figure 5.27: (a) adaptation of Schenker's analysis; (b) an alternative analysis.

To make a proper comparison, Figure 5.28a puts Schenker's analysis into the notation of my theory and assigns functions according to the function rule. The progression T→S→D→T emerges at levels c–d, and the C♯ in bar 2 receives P at level e. In a sense, this result validates the idea of function as prolongational position: to find a predominant, Schenker needs this prolongational analysis. However, the theory proposed here would arrive instead at the analysis in Figure 5.28b, in which the $\mathrm{IV}^{\hat{4}}$ in bar 2 is N between two $\mathrm{I}^{\hat{3}}$s. This result obtains because $\mathrm{I}^{\hat{3}}$ is more stable than $\mathrm{IV}^{\hat{4}}$ in the time-span analysis of bar 2, reinforced by a preference for maximizing strong prolongations so as to keep tension at a minimum. And because the phrasal cadence takes place in bar 4 rather than in bar 3, the noncadential $\mathrm{V}^{\hat{2}}$ in bar 3 becomes P between $\mathrm{I}^{\hat{3}}$ and $\mathrm{I}^{\hat{1}}$. This analysis reveals a less complete structure than Schenker's, because now there is no S-function and normative prolongational structure is not achieved. But then Schumann's setting of Heine's lyric is nonclosural and equivocal in other ways, notably in the disjunction in bar 4 (repeated at the end of the song) between the vocal half-cadence and its hesitant completion in the piano. A degree of structural incompleteness accurately reflects the poetics of the song. (For related discussion, see Dubiel 1990; Forte 1959; and Kerman 1980.)

Figure 5.29 revisits the two main interpretations of the opening of the *Tristan* Prelude. In the top line in Figure 5.29a, the G♯ is an appoggiatura to A and the chord is an augmented sixth; in Figure 5.29b the G♯ is a chord tone and the A is passing, so the operative sonority is the Tristan chord itself. From a traditional perspective, the augmented-sixth version is S (or possibly D/D), while the Tristan-chord version is problematic in both root and function. In the approach here, however, the two harmonic progressions are functionally identical, S→D, the V^7 receiving D because it is a half-cadence, in each case led into by a predominant

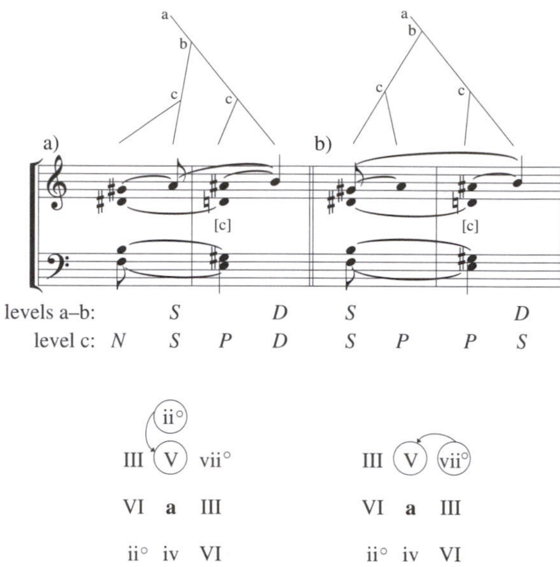

FIGURE 5.29 Function assignments for the beginning of the *Tristan* Prelude: (a) the augmented-sixth interpretation; (b) the Tristan-chord interpretation.

S. The function rule does not refer to the content of S, only to its branching status. The differences concern only the nonharmonic tones. The contrast between the two (aside from their somewhat divergent tensional values in Figures 4.37–39) arises instead from their spatial locations and paths, shown beneath the functional analyses. (As in "An Attractional Approach to Harmony" in chapter 4, the Tristan chord is treated as an altered vii° so as to give it a location in chordal/regional space.) Other historical disagreements within the augmented-sixth interpretation (such as whether the Tristan chord is an alteration of ii^{o7} or of V^7/**V**) would similarly be represented as a matter not of function but of location and path.

A difficulty for augmented-sixth advocates has been how to treat the third appearance of the Tristan chord in bar 10 (see Figure 5.13). If only for this reason, I adopt the Tristan-chord version in considering how the Bar as a whole functions harmonically (bars 1–17). The prolongational analysis in Figure 5.30, which duplicates that of Figure 5.15, yields D→D for the prolonged V^7/**a** at levels a–b, followed by Dep at the deceptive cadence in bar 17. At level c the analysis presents normative prolongational structure in an unusual realization in which V rather than I is prolonged. The V^7/**V** in bar 11, being a single event outside **a** at that level, acts as S. Level d shows the local sequencing of S→D in the contexts of **a, C**, and **e**.

Figure 5.31 continues the exploration of functionality in a more deeply chromatic setting, the somewhat reduced Act II version of the Transfiguration (first presented in Figure 3.30). It will be convenient to refer to the hyperbar number-

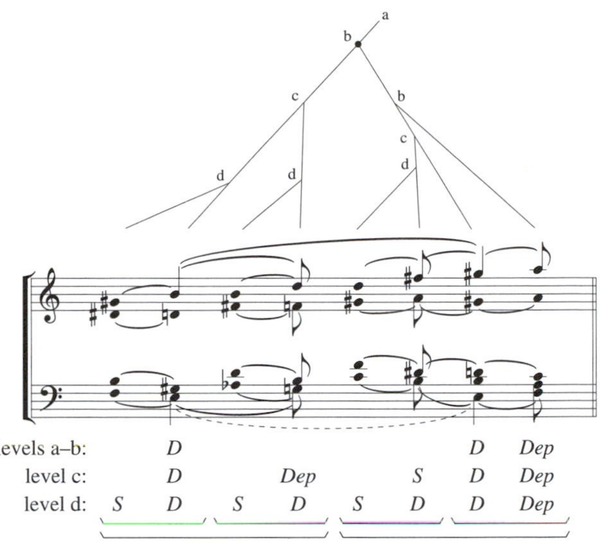

FIGURE 5.30 Functional analysis of bars 1–17 of the *Tristan* Prelude.

ings in Figure 5.31. The prolongational analysis repeats that of Figure 3.34 (without parenthetical alternate readings; in particular, the initial I^6_4 is treated as a tonic that prolongs up two octaves to the high A♭ on the downbeat of bar 6). Levels a–b of the function analysis show T→D, but in bars 1–4 at level c the sequence up the minor-third cycle introduces a new functional element. A♭$^6_4$→C♭$^6_4$→D$^6_4$ yields the right-branching T→Dep1→Dep2; then, by the shortest path, F$^6_3$ left-branches to A♭$^6_3$. If the A♭$^6_3$ is T, it may seem that the F$^6_3$ should be D. It is not, because the F$^6_3$ is noncadential—it simply lies on the minor-third cycle—and because the I is a right prolongation of an earlier I. The sense here is of return toward relative stability, and the branching specifies the Ret-function (condition [5] of the function rule). Ret is rarer in diatonic music, in which cadences usually accompany returns, than in chromatic music, in which the expanded harmonic vocabulary permits a variety of noncadential articulations.

Continuing at level c, the G major chord in bar 5 as yet has no context to be located in a region other than **A♭**, and so is P within a T-prolongation (albeit with noncontiguous voice leading). Only at level d does it acquire the adjacent context to be interpreted as a local I/**G**. At level e the phrase groupings achieve functional normality. In bar 1 the V^7 is Dep from the I^6_4 and the C♭ triad is S to the half-cadential V/**E♭**, yielding T→Dep→S→D. After repeating sequentially in bar 2, this functional progression elides in bar 3 but resumes in a new guise in bar 4, creating a functional rhyme between the first and second two-bar groups. This is a good example of how dissimilar surfaces can express matching functions. Finally, the I^6_4 on the downbeat of bar 6 is surrounded by Ret and Dep before semiclosure on the V^7. The Dep acts as an interpolation within I^6_4→V^7, recalling the sequence to **C♭** in bar 2 and similar modulations earlier in the scene.

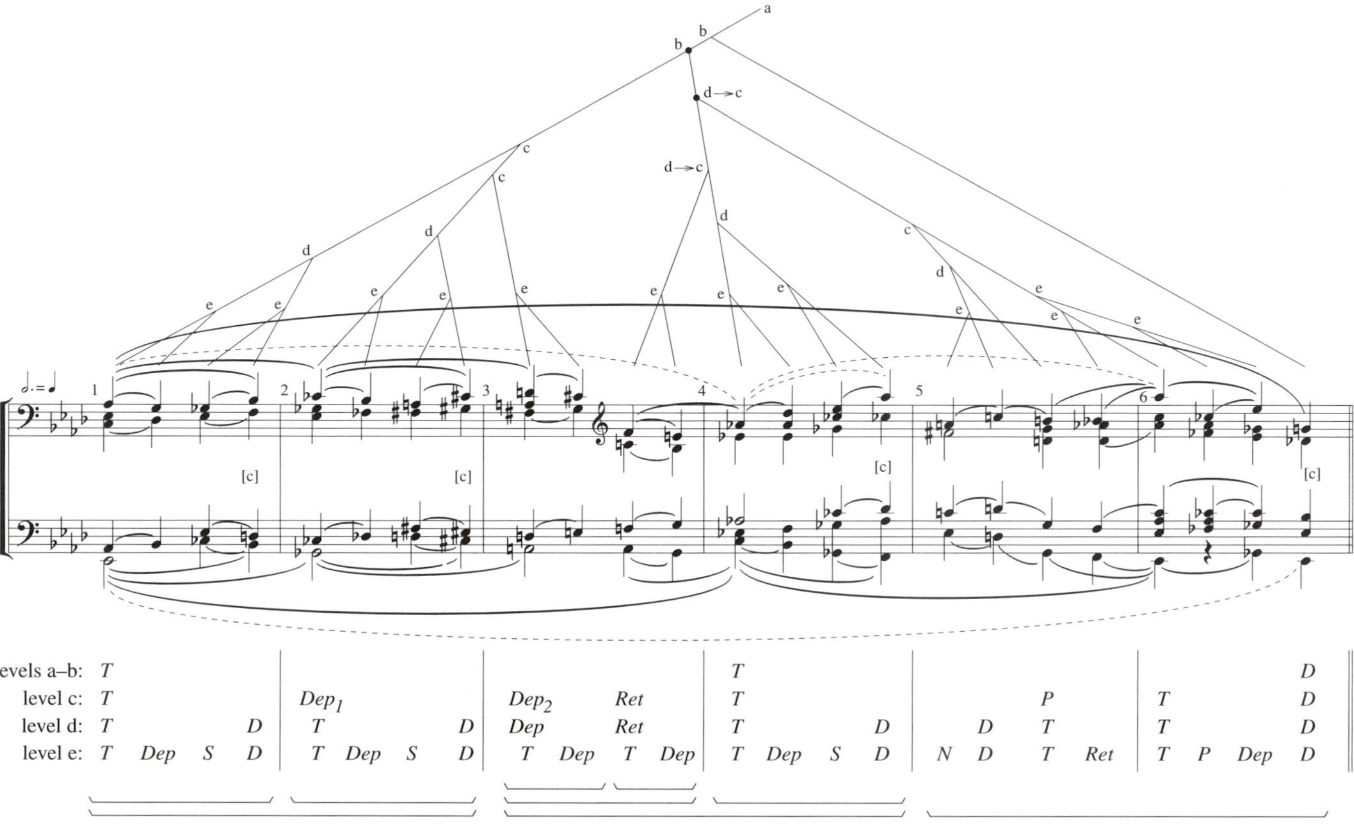

FIGURE 5.31 Functional analysis of the first section of the Transfiguration music from *Tristan* (Act II version).

Issues concerning functionality

To conclude this section, I briefly take up three issues concerning function: the status of the cadential $^6_4$, the role of functionality in long-range hearing, and the relationship between function and tension.

Issue 1. The distinction between chordal identity and chordal function sheds light on a peculiarity of current music-theory pedagogy, the cadential "V$^6_4$" chord. Because the $^6_4$ embellishes D in a context such as Figure 5.32a, some writers (for example, Beach 1967 and Aldwell and Schachter 1979) seek to make its role explicit by calling it a V$^6_4$ rather than the traditional I$^6_4$. However, this notation confounds the description with the rarer but indubitable V$^6_4$, which usually functions as P, as in Figure 5.32b. More important, the revision confuses root with function. As Riemann understood, Roman-numeral analysis is not equipped to represent harmonic function. It simply says which scale step the root of a chord is on in relation to the tonic and what the intervals are up from the bass. This is what the designation I$^6_4$ does. However, because the cadential $^6_4$ in its typical eighteenth-century usage is a nonharmonic embellishment, there the "I" in "I$^6_4$" may be misleading, and the locution "cadential $^6_4$" is preferable. In no way is the formation in Figure 5.32a a "V$^6_4$." The distinction between structure and function is elementary in the biological sciences, as witness the difference between anatomy and physiology. By the same token, a I$^6_4$ is a vertical structure, and its function varies with context. It can embellish D as P or N, and in nineteenth-century usage it can function as T.

Issue 2. Nicholas Cook (1987, 1994) claims that prolongational theories of any stripe assume an unrealistic ability on the part of average listeners to hear global closure. He adduces evidence that listeners discriminate poorly whether a piece begins and ends in the same key (for more encouraging evidence, see Marvin and Brinkman [1999]) and uses this evidence to argue against the efficacy of prolongational theories. However, closure and global prolongation are not a single issue. Closure is a composite phenomenon that involves melodic, harmonic, regional, rhythmic, gestural, and formal resolution. How much these factors converge at the end of a piece is a variable to which beginning and ending in the same key is but one contributor. Probably a more important contributor is the functional closure provided by S→D→T.

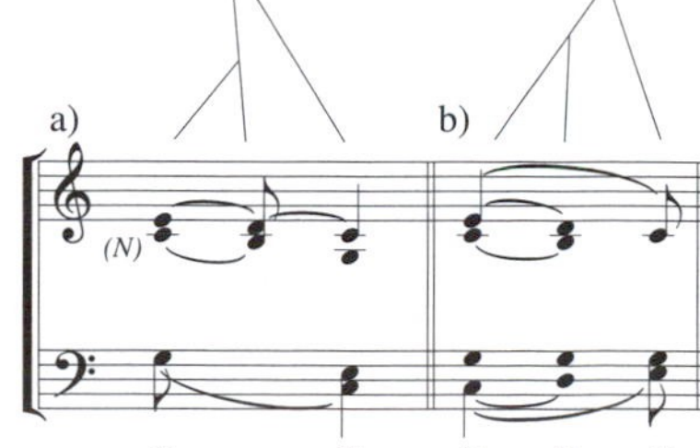

FIGURE 5.32 Functions for the $^6_4$ chord: (a) embellishing a dominant function; (b) passing function.

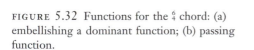

FIGURE 5.33 Beginning and ending of "Die zwei blauen Augen" of Mahler's *Lieder eines fahrenden Gesellen.*

Assume that most listeners hear global regional (non)returns as poorly as Cook claims (certainly they hear them less well than expert musicians like to admit). Take, for instance, "Die zwei blauen Augen" from Mahler's *Lieder eines fahrenden Gesellen*, which, as illustrated in Figure 5.33, begins on i/**e** and ends, with the same motive and instrumentation, on a framing i/**f**, as a symbol of the lovelorn protagonist who wanders away but cannot escape his grief. Unless they are attentive, listeners will probably suppose that the opening tonic has been prolonged rather than that a regional journey via **C** and **F** has taken place. Do they hear a different global structure than listeners who do notice the regional journey? Yes in terms of pitch-space paths—but no in terms of function. Both kinds of listener (accurately) perceive the beginning as tonic and the ending as tonic. Figure 5.34a shows the global regional journey for the attentive listener, Figure 5.34b the resulting

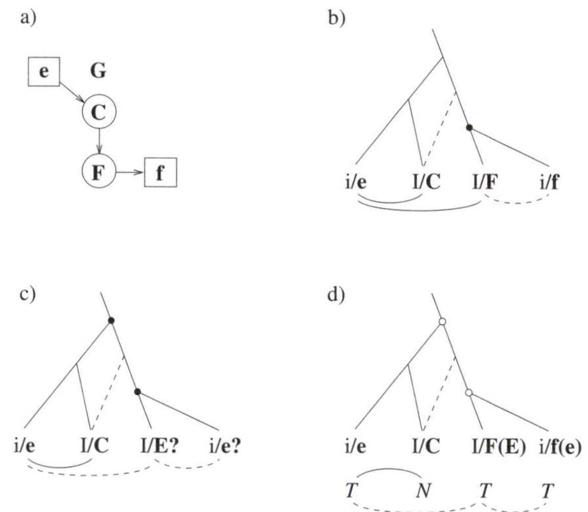

FIGURE 5.34 Global structure in the final song of Mahler's *Lieder eines fahrenden Gesellen*: (a) its regional journey; (b) the resulting prolongational structure; (c) representation of the inattentive listener's sense global tonic prolongation; (d) the song's global structure in terms of functional prolongations.

global prolongational tree. Figure 5.34c characterizes the less attentive listener's sense of global tonic prolongation. But Figure 5.34d suggests how, for all listeners, T prolongs no matter whether the opening region does or not.

Thus we arrive at the notion of the prolongation not of pitch events but of functions. Formally, this step means decoupling T from the overall prolongational tree and relying on less global applications of the tonic-finding rule, in this case at the level of the major sections of the song. From these T-assignments the other functions follow as usual. Equivalent T-functions, rather than regional strong prolongations, then connect as T-prolongations, where T-equivalency is defined by co-occurrence at the same time-span reductional level. In Figure 5.34d, i/**e** and i/**F** are equivalent at a reductional level just below that of the song as a whole, so their T-functions qualify as a T-prolongation. The codettalike i/**f** then receives T directly from i/**F**.

Although this theoretical move sounds abstract, it is a straightforward response to the fact that listeners pay more attention to local and intermediate levels of prolongational structure than to global ones yet also experience large-scale closure. To them (if not necessarily to performers, who must fit their eyes, voices, fingers, and lips to what they see and what they intend to sing and play), T-equivalencies are less abstract than global prolongations. However, because this theory is an idealized final-state theory rather than a processing theory (see "Overview of GTTM" in chapter 1), I shall not pursue this idea further. It suffices to indicate that the problem of hearing global prolongations does not jeopardize prolongational theory in any fundamental way. Rather, the theory, in conjunction with the current approach to functions, points to a nontrivial solution to the problem.

Issue 3. It may not be immediately obvious that the seven proposed functions improve on Riemann's three. (However, his three quickly become nine—see Figure 5.21—and many more once chromatic transformations enter the picture.) In particular, why not dispense with S and D as Riemannian remnants and stay within a fivefold repertory of T, Dep, Ret, N, and P? After all, the basic insight of this approach is that prolongational structure itself provides the basis for intuitions about function. In prolongational trees there are just three node types together with right and left branchings, representing nested patterns of tension and relaxation. The fivefold repertory covers the basic branching possibilities.

Despite this argument, I prefer to retain S and D, for they serve the important purpose of distinguishing cadential closure from noncadential Ret. The choice rests on how fine-grained one wishes a functional theory to be.

More radically, "The Harmonic Tension Model" in chapter 4 has shown how branching patterns in conjunction with pitch-space theory lead to quantitative values of hierarchical tension. Would it not be more "psychological" to eliminate functional categories altogether and rely simply on tension curves? To explore this possibility, Figure 5.35 lists the tension values for the progressions in Figures 5.22a, c, f, and h, using the short version of T_{glob}. (The long version is not needed because nonharmonic tones and specific melody/bass notes are not at issue here.) In an abbreviated notation, each distance δ appears next to the appropriate branch and the values are totaled beneath. In Figure 5.35d, the global branch between I/**I**

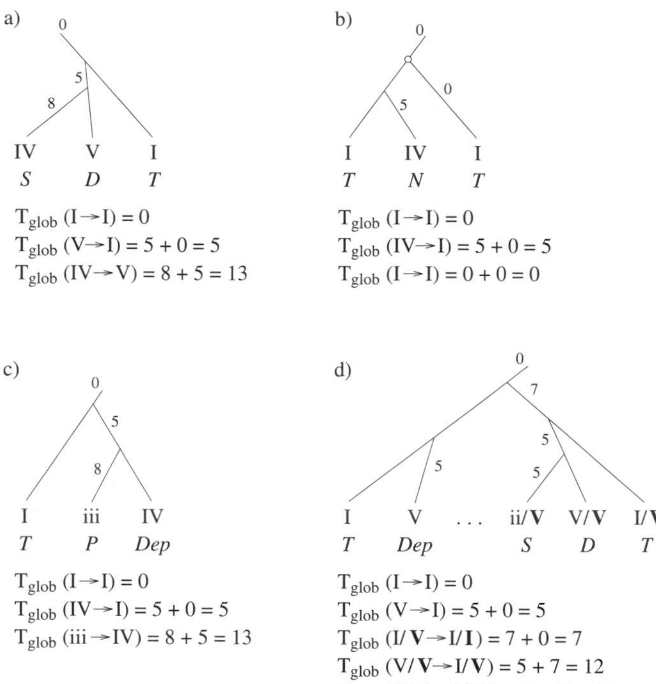

FIGURE 5.35 Tension calculations, using the short version of the hierarchical tension rule $[(T_{glob}(\mathbf{y}) = T_{loc}(\mathbf{y}) + T_{inh}(x_{dom})]$, for the progressions in Figures 5.22a, c, f, and h.

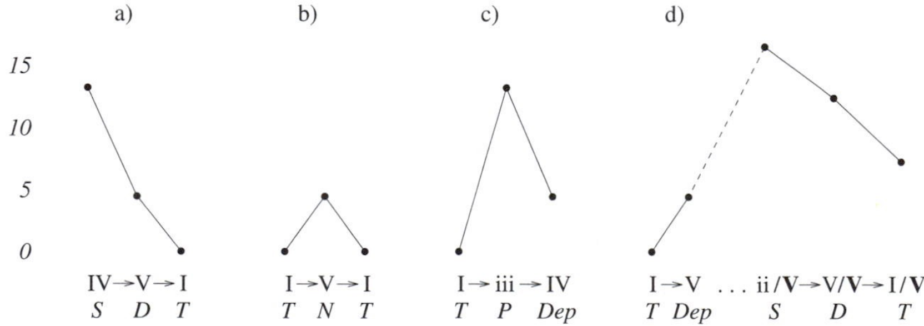

FIGURE 5.36 Tension graphs for Figure 5.35.

and I/V is connected to give a definite tension value for I/V. (At the more global level where I/V is interpreted as V/I, the tension value would decrease to T_{glob} (V/I→I/I) = 5 + 0 = 5.)

Figure 5.36 graphs the values for Figure 5.35. As is to be expected from the branching definitions of the various functions, S's initial state of tension relaxes via D into T (Figure 5.36a). N is tenser than its surrounding prolongation, which is at the same tension level on both sides (Figure 5.36b). Dep reflects an increase in tension, within which the further tension of P might occur (Figure 5.36c). Dep and S→D→T typically combine to form a normative tension curve for a phrase or section (Figure 5.36d).

Yet curves such as these are mere approximations of functionality, for they do not incorporate enough distinctions. They do not locate events in regions or identify classes of progressions at successive levels of analysis. The sevenfold functional repertory is useful because it strikes a balance between the specificity of event identities and the generality of tension curves, in order to unearth regular patterns in the unfolding of events.

FUNCTIONS AND SCHEMAS

The sentence

Even though tension curves do not replace functional analysis, they offer a gateway to exploring how local groupings function within phrases. We begin at the phrase level itself with normative prolongational structure, which expresses a stable beginning followed by tension and a closing cadential relaxation. Figures 5.37a–c summarize three representations for this overriding phrasal schema: as a branching abstraction (from Figure 1.21), as a simple tension curve (of which Figure 5.36d

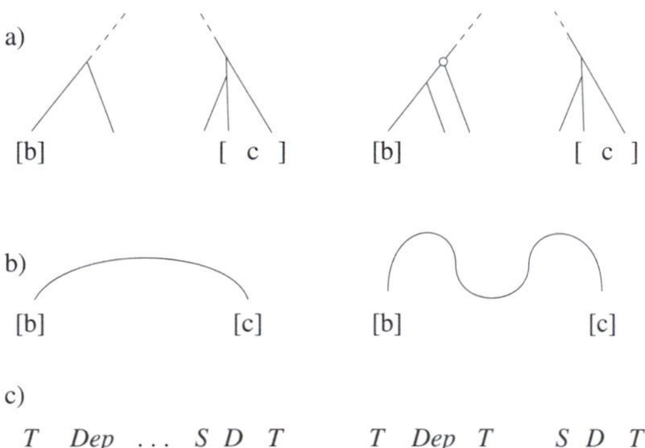

FIGURE 5.37 Three representations for normative prolongational structure: (a) as a branching structure; (b) as a tension curve; (c) as a functional analysis. Also given for each representation is the standard variant in which the structural beginning returns within the phrase.

is one realization), and as an expression of functions (as in Figures 5.22g–h). For each case, the standard variant is also given in which the structural beginning returns in the middle, creating a double tensing–relaxing pattern. This internal return lends added stability to the phrase as a whole.

These two related tension patterns represent the usual prolongational and functional contexts within which subphrasal groups behave. Consider the most pervasive Classical subphrasal schema, the sentence (*Satz*), whose groupings comprise a statement and counterstatement of equal length, followed by a continuation and cadence equal in length to the statement/counterstatement (Schoenberg 1967; Caplin 1998). The statement introduces a motive, and the counterstatement varies it in parallel fashion. The continuation, the least constrained part of the schema, develops the motive and leads into the cadence.

Figure 5.38 slots the appropriate normative prolongations and functions into two versions of the sentence. The numbers associated with the subphrasal groups indicate their usual time-span proportions, 1 + 1 + 2, which might take place within a notated four-, eight-, or sixteen-bar phrase. T→Dep expresses the rise in tension and S→D→(T) the relaxation demanded by normative prolongational structure. In Figure 5.38a, the statement is realized by T and the counterstatement by Dep; in Figure 5.38b, the statement is realized by T→Dep and the counterstatement by Ret→T. The continuation begins optionally in Figure 5.38a with T; it is unspecified in Figure 5.38b. In both cases, the final T is in parentheses because the cadence might be not full but half or deceptive.

Figure 5.38 effects a link between prolongational and functional structures on the one hand and subphrasal grouping structure on the other. In actual pieces this linking is not rigid. Schemas, musical or otherwise, are flexible constructs. Their identities as categories depend not on necessary and sufficient conditions but on degrees of confluence of multiple factors in PR fashion. Some factors are central, others peripheral. If the critical factors converge, the instance is prototypical of the schema. The boundaries of a schema are fuzzy (Rosch 1975; Jackendoff 1982; Gjerdingen 1988; see the related discussion of prototypes in "Empirical Issues" in chapter 2).

The abstractions of Figure 5.38 thus describe two closely related sentential prototypes. The opening phrase of Beethoven's Sonata Op. 2, no. 1, in Figure 5.39a exemplifies Figure 5.38a by showing the branchings and functions that fulfill the prototype. The opening phrase of his Sonata Op. 2, no. 3, in Figure 5.39b does likewise for Figure 5.38b (the varied repeat of the continuation is not shown). Many sentences, however, only partly fulfill their prototypes. For instance, the motivic-grouping arrangement of a sentence can occur without normative structure, as at the beginning of Beethoven's Sonata Op. 2, no. 2, in Figure 5.39c, in which ii in the counterstatement serves as Dep, leaving the phrase without S and effectively without a continuation as well. (Or, following the recursion constraint, if the ii is S, then there is no Dep.) As a result, this phrase is less complete than those in Figures 5.39a–b.

Another subtle divergence from functional prototypicality takes place in the opening of the *Waldstein* Sonata, again shown in normalized form in Figure 5.40.

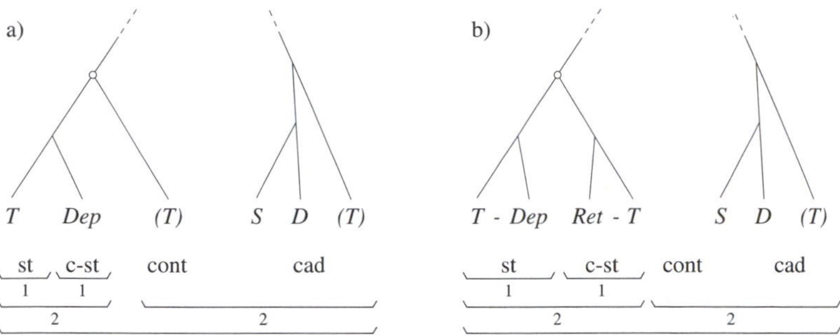

FIGURE 5.38 Two normative versions of the phrasal sentence ("st" = statement; "c-st" = counterstatement; "cont" = continuation; "cad" = cadence).

Dep is taken care of in the statement by the move to V^6 (= I^6/**G**), but S emerges as IV^6 (= I^6/**F**) not in the continuation but already in the counterstatement. Consequently, the half-cadential D arrives already at the beginning of the motivic continuation, within which it must subsequently extend so as to complete the needed time-span proportions. The premature locations of S and D lend this passage some of its expressive urgency.

Wagnerian Bar form, when at a phrasal rather than sectional level, has the same grouping structure and motivic treatment as the sentence. But the prolongational and functional features of the Bar are often rather different from the Classical sentence. The beginning of the *Tristan* Prelude deviates from sentential prototypicality in that, as discussed in connection with Figure 5.30, Dep takes off not from T but from a global D. The second Bar in bars 17–21, shown in Figure 5.41a, forms the odd functional progression Ret_2→Ret_1→T→Dep. The third Bar in bars 21–24 in Figure 5.41b lacks functional autonomy because it begins with Dep_2 from the closing Dep_1 of the previous Bar sentence. In short, these two Bars satisfy the grouping and motivic aspects of the sentence schema but do not meet its prolongational and functional criteria. The effect is to merge the two Bars into a continuous arc. However, Figure 5.41c reveals that these two Bars combine at the next larger level into a modulating realization of the standard sentential functional progression, T→Dep→S→D→T. The two phrases together form a functionally complete unit.

Galant gambits

Gjerdingen (1996) approaches the early Classical galant style in terms of voice-leading schemas familiar to cultivated listeners of the time. He places his treatment, which is based in part on Riepel (1755), against subsequent Romantic "essentialist" approaches, in which category he includes Riemann's function theory because it abstracts all harmony into three classes. In a related vein, Gjerdingen (1988) expresses reservations about hierarchical analytic approaches (Schenker's

FIGURE 5.39 Instances of the sentence, taken from the beginnings of (a) Beethoven's Sonata, Op. 2, no. 1, (b) Beethoven's Sonata, Op. 2, no. 3, and (c) Beethoven's Sonata, Op. 2, no. 2.

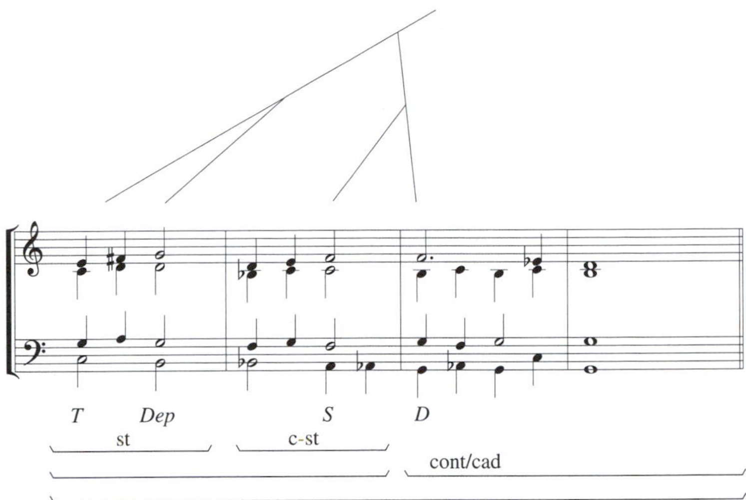

FIGURE 5.40 Nonprototypicality of the sentence that begins Beethoven's *Waldstein* Sonata.

Ursatz may be the most essentialist of music-theoretic constructs) and offers in their stead network connections to represent schematic behavior.

Gjerdingen's stance on functions and hierarchies notwithstanding, his proposals about schemas suggest a further enrichment of my theory—which, while not relying on any sort of essentialism, embraces both non-Schenkerian hierarchies and non-Riemannian functions. Figure 5.42 provides structural descriptions for the schemas that he invokes for the galant style. These descriptions represent prototypes; many variants are possible. The occasional parentheses indicate strong options within a schema. Figure 5.42a shows the $\hat{1}\rightarrow\hat{7}\rightarrow\hat{4}\rightarrow\hat{3}$ schema studied theoretically and historically in Gjerdingen (1988); it is a variant of Meyer's (1973) changing-note schema ($\hat{1}\rightarrow\hat{7}\rightarrow\hat{2}\rightarrow\hat{1}$ or $\hat{3}\rightarrow\hat{2}\rightarrow\hat{4}\rightarrow\hat{3}$). Its most distinctive feature is the soprano line, which more often than not occurs in this unadorned form only at an underlying reductional level. The bass and harmony can take a number of related forms, one of which is given in Figure 5.42a. As the minimal metrical grid indicates, the structural event that begins each paired group usually falls on a relatively strong beat. The prolongational structure begins in stability and extends it, yielding a functional progression, T→Dep→Ret→T (T→T at the next level), that is central to this schema, as are the paired groups associated with it.

Figure 5.42b shows the cadential schema of the galant style. The bass line, $\hat{4}\rightarrow\hat{5}\rightarrow\hat{1}$, supports either $\hat{4}\rightarrow\hat{3}\rightarrow\hat{2}\rightarrow\hat{1}$ or $\hat{2}\rightarrow\hat{1}\rightarrow\hat{7}\rightarrow\hat{1}$ or both simultaneously. The prolongational structure expresses relaxation. The functional progression S→P→D→T becomes S→D→T once the cadential $^6_4$ reduces out. Typically the $^6_4$ and the tonic arrival occur on relatively strong beats, and usually the subgroup that contains this schema includes preceding material.

FIGURE 5.41 Functionality in bars 17–24 of the *Tristan* Prelude: (a) nonfulfillment of normative structure in bars 17–21; (b) nonfulfillment of normative structure in bars 21–24; (c) functional normativeness for the two phrases combined.

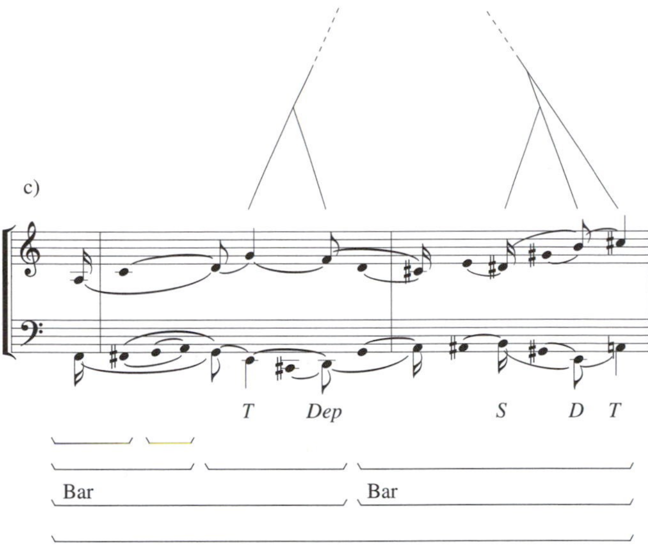

FIGURE 5.41 (Continued)

Figures 5.42c–d present two forms of the Romanesca. (This and related terms referred to here are historical associations employed by Gjerdingen.) Here the paramount feature is the diatonic descent of the bass from the tonic; the soprano is variable. In Figure 5.42c, the bass prolongs the tonic, replicating the prolongational and functional structure of Figure 5.42a within a single subgroup. In Figure 5.42d, the bass moves instead to the dominant, creating a slightly different tree.

Figure 5.42e shows the Prinner Riposte, in which the melody and bass move in parallel tenths, $\hat{6}\rightarrow\hat{5}\rightarrow\hat{4}\rightarrow\hat{3}$ against $\hat{4}\rightarrow\hat{3}\rightarrow\hat{2}\rightarrow\hat{1}$. Figure 5.42f elaborates the bass in Figure 5.42e with V→I, merging the ending of this schema with the harmonic aspects of Figure 5.42b.

Finally, Figure 5.42g presents the Fonte, whose basic feature is a sequence in paired groups from supertonic to tonic, supported by a circle-of-fifths progression. The realization of individual voices is fluid. In Figure 5.42g the soprano $\hat{5}\rightarrow\hat{4}\rightarrow\hat{3}$ accompanies either a root-motion bass, $\hat{6}\rightarrow\hat{2}\rightarrow\hat{5}\rightarrow\hat{1}$, or a line that emphasizes leading-tone motion, $\sharp\hat{1}\rightarrow\hat{2}\rightarrow\hat{7}\rightarrow\hat{1}$.

As Gjerdingen (1996) discusses and as Figure 5.43a displays, the first phrase of Mozart's K. 282 exploits three of these galant schemas: in bars 1–2 the modified Romanesca that leads into V, as in Figure 5.42d; in bars 2–3 the Fonte, with all three voices as shown in Figure 5.42g, but with the soprano and bass inverted; and, overlaying the Fonte, in bars 2–4 the Prinner with cadence, as in Figure 5.42f. Figure 5.43a isolates the branchings from the global prolongational analysis (Figure 4.14) so that they correspond explicitly to the schematic patterns in Figures 5.42d, f, and g. At the bottom of Figure 5.43a appear the critical scale steps

a) Variant of the changing-note schema

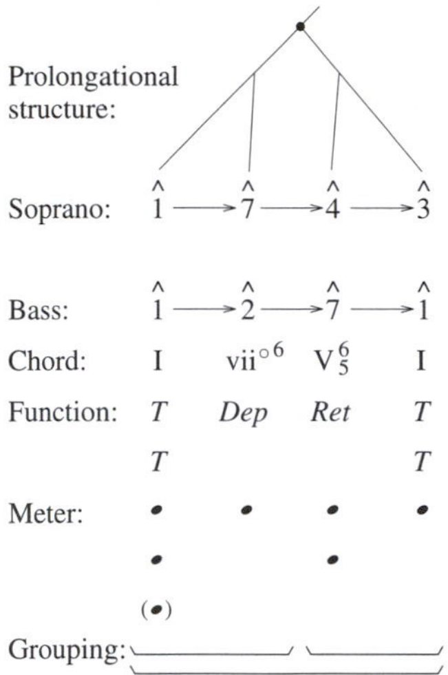

b) cadential schema

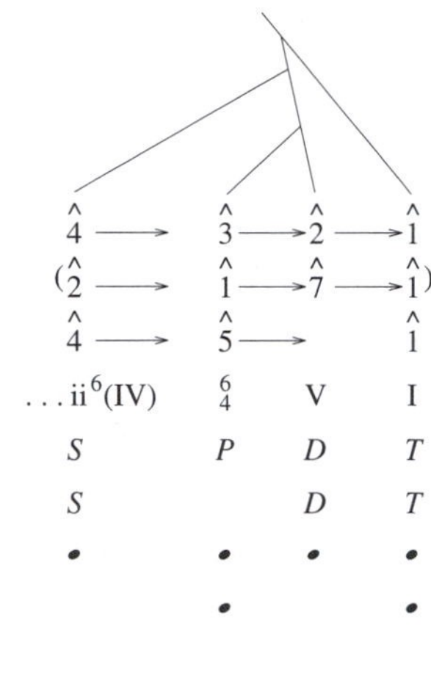

c) Romanesca

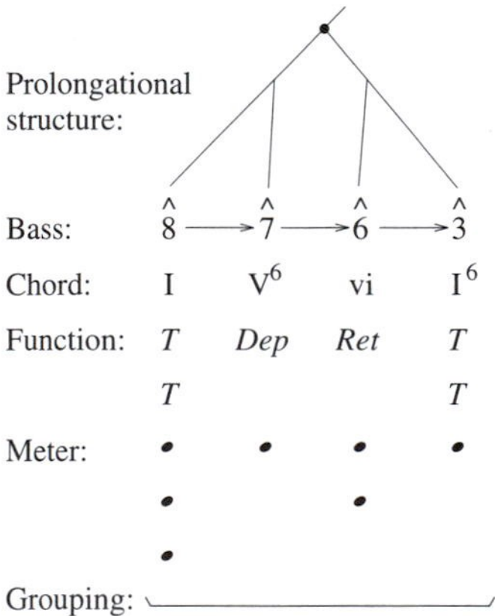

d) modified Romanesca

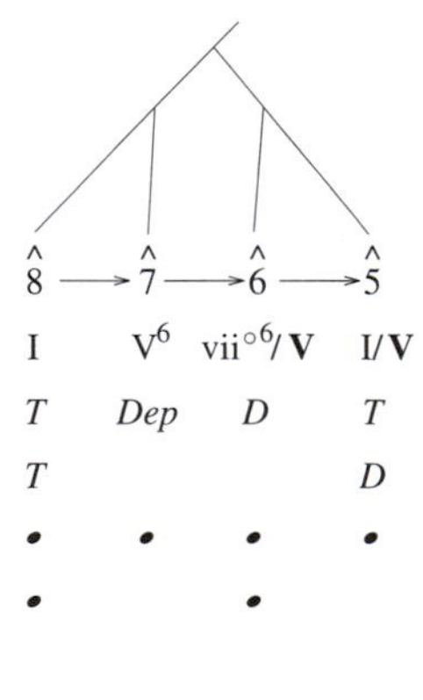

FIGURE 5.42 Some galant schemas.

e) Prinner Riposte

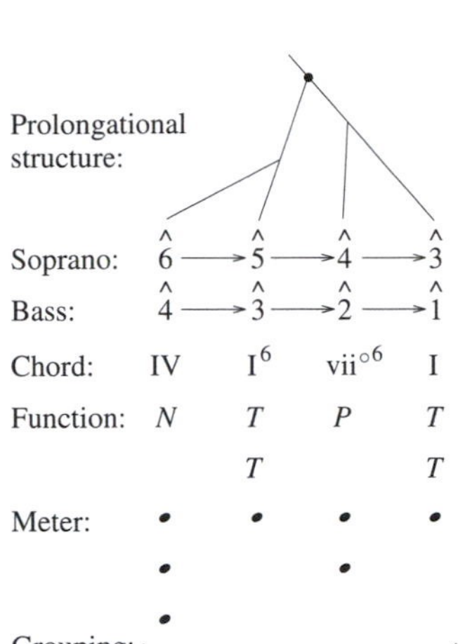

f) Prinner with cadence

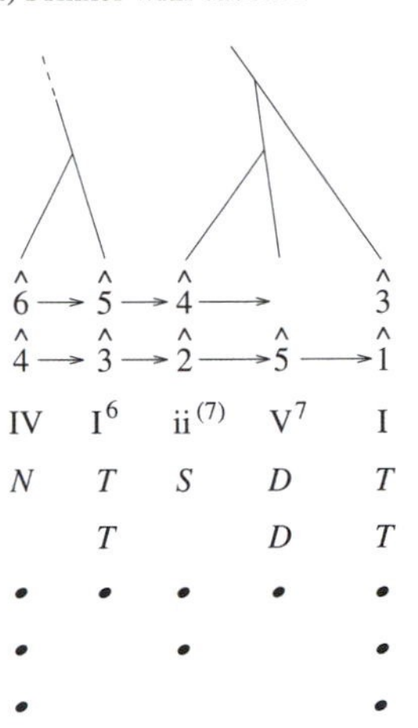

g) Fonte

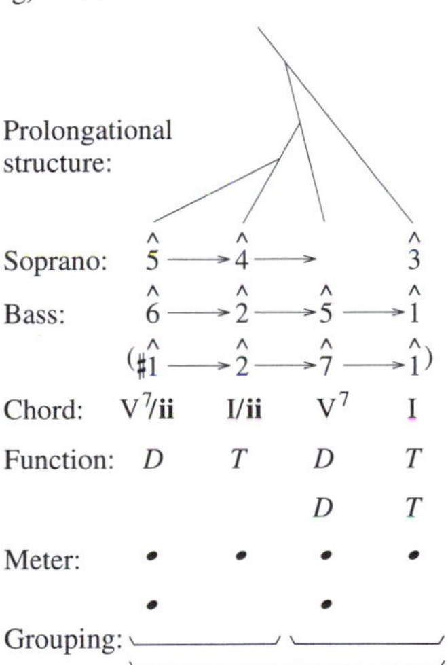

FIGURE 5.42 (Continued)

for the Romanesca and the Prinner with cadence, along with the relevant functional symbols for these two schemas and the Fonte. Note that the Fonte converts the N that normally begins the Prinner into a local D. Also, according to condition (5) of the function rule, the V^4_2 on the downbeat of bar 3 should receive Ret because the return to the ensuing I^6 is not cadential; by condition (9), however, it receives D in parallel with the preceding applied D→T. This assignment accords with the standard Fonte.

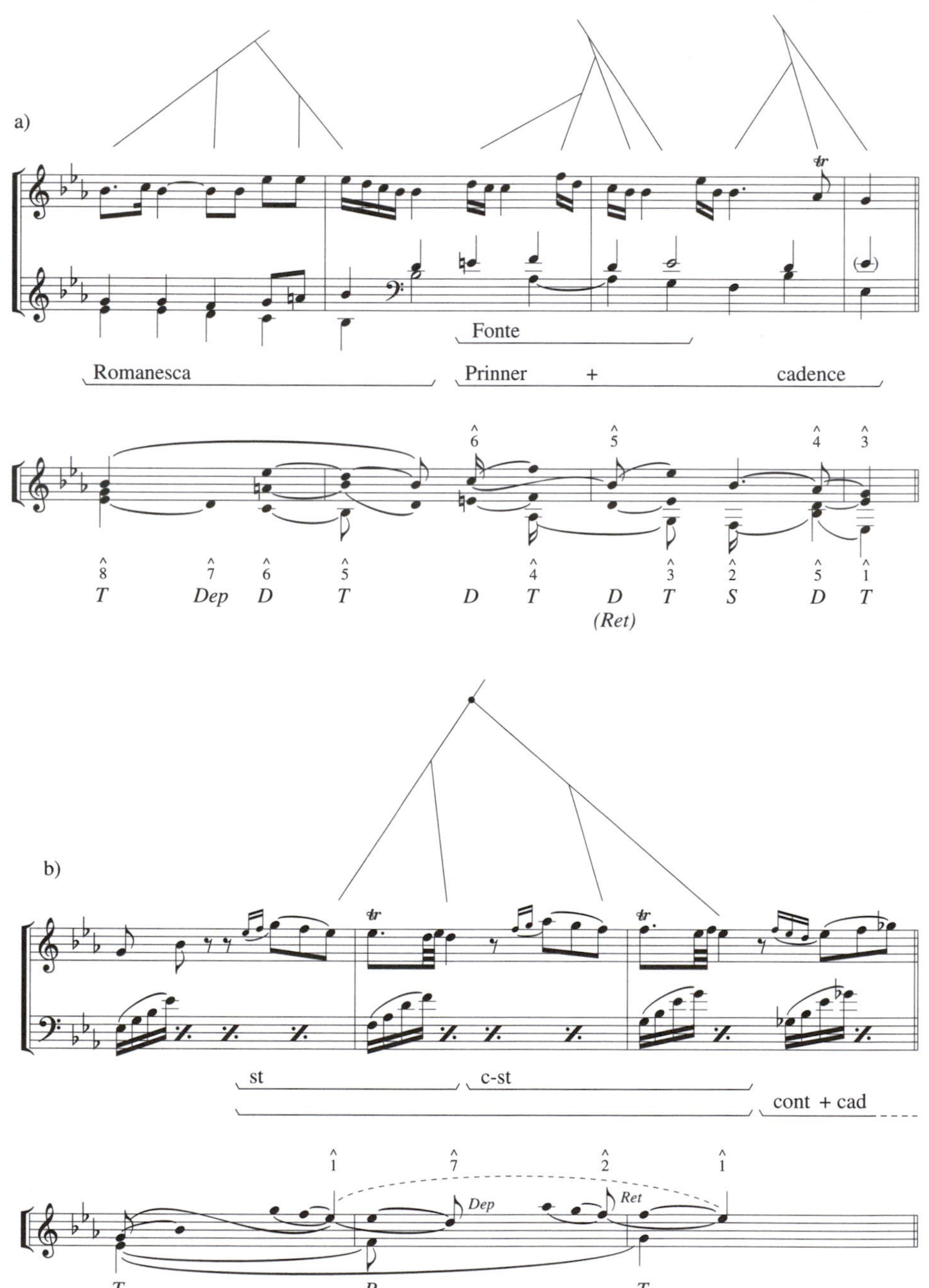

FIGURE 5.43 Galant schemas in Mozart's K. 282, I: (a) bars 1–4; (b) bars 4–6.

$$\text{Normative phrase} \longrightarrow \begin{bmatrix} \text{changing note} \\ \\ \text{Romanesca} \end{bmatrix} + \begin{bmatrix} \text{Prinner} \\ \\ \text{Fonte} \end{bmatrix} + \text{cadence}$$

FIGURE 5.44 Quasi-syntactic layout for the ordering of galant schemas.

Figure 5.43b continues the schematic analysis for the second phrase of K. 282 (compare Figure 4.15). This phrase is a sentence, with the statement and counterstatement filled by the changing-note schema, not in the version given in Figure 5.42a but in Meyer's $\hat{1}\rightarrow\hat{7}\rightarrow\hat{2}\rightarrow\hat{1}$ version. As a result, a simple T→P→T in the bass accompanies the requisite T→Dep→Ret→T in the soprano. The continuation and cadence, while meeting the conditions for the sentence, do not incorporate any of the galant schemas in Figure 5.42. One could go on with this movement in the same vein: the second theme group (bars 9–15) comprises a sentence with internal repetitions, with the continuation and cadence completed by the cadential schema; the brief development (bars 16–21) starts with an altered Fonte (as Gjerdingen remarks); and so forth.

As may be inferred from the Mozart, the repertory of galant schemas do not appear at arbitrary locations. Their prolongational and functional properties ordain their beginning, middle, and ending niches within an overarching normative prolongational structure. This ordering lends these schematic units a quasi-syntactic status. How this happens could be described in terms of tension and relaxation, but function symbols are more revealing. The various versions of the changing-note and Romanesca schemas occur at the beginnings of phrases, for they establish and extend T. The changing-note schema's paired subgroupings make it ideal for fulfilling the statement–counterstatement slots of a sentence. The Prinner Riposte and the Fonte generally take middle positions within phrases. In the Prinner Riposte, the opening N followed by an unstable T makes it unsuitable as a beginning, while P→T at its end does not mark closure. The Fonte's beginning is unstable, and its sequential construction implies continuation rather than closure. Thus the boundaries of the Prinner Riposte and the Fonte are open-ended. This very feature also makes the Fonte suitable to launch a development, which is a middle on a larger scale. Finally, both the cadential schema and Prinner plus cadence end a phrase with S→D→T.

Figure 5.44 summarizes these remarks in a format that loosely resembles that of syntactic rewriting rules. The brackets denote options within a position. These locations are not obligatory, however, and sometimes Classical composers play with alternative orderings. For example, the rondos of Mozart's Sonata, K. 281, and Schubert's posthumous B♭ Sonata begin with Fontes; Beethoven's Sonatas Op. 31, no. 3, and Op. 111 ostensibly begin with cadences. Such cases are exceptions.

In summary, galant schemas are more than surface patterns. They possess grouping, metrical, and tensing–relaxing prolongational structures. These prolongational structures translate into functional sequences that take the form of normative schematic orderings. Listeners attuned to the style usually know where they are in a piece, so to speak, because recognition of a schema also entails awareness of its temporal context.

Schematic tension

Not only subphrasal groupings but also groupings at the level of the phrase and higher assume schematic forms with normative orderings. The combinatorial possibilities increase with schematic size. Normative functional orderings within large schemas such as sonata or rondo tend to reduce this combinatorial explosion by channeling expectations of musical form as a piece unfolds in time. When these expectations are upset or when simultaneously projected schemas come into conflict, a schematic tension results that is different from but complementary to the patterns of tonal tension discussed in chapter 4. Like tonal tension, schematic tension demands resolution.

Let us explore this topic through Mendelssohn's *Gondollied* (Venetian Boat Song), Op. 30, no. 6, in Figure 5.45 (also analyzed in Rothstein 1989). My approach can be viewed as a sketch toward a theoretical grounding for William Caplin's (1998) neo-*Formenlehre* treatment of Classical form.

Like many instances of the nineteenth-century character piano piece, the *Gondollied* has a schematic frame, an introduction that establishes T and a coda that confirms S→D→T. The heart of the piece, our locus of inquiry, is a modification of the double-period schema, which itself is an expansion of the antecedent–consequent period. A prototypical antecedent–consequent period decomposes into the familiar structural features represented in Figure 5.46a: paired phrases of equal length, each beginning on a relatively strong beat (optionally with an anacrusis); the first phrase normatively progressing from T→Dep to S→D; the second phrase returning motivically and tonally to the start of the first phrase and answering the half-cadential $V^{\hat{2}}$ with a full cadence, $V^{\hat{2}}\rightarrow I^{\hat{1}}$. The full cadence expresses D→T in the home region or in a related region. The standard double period, whose global prolongational structure is sketched in Figure 5.46b at a level comparable to that in Figure 5.46a, extends this schema with a contrasting developmental phrase that arrives on a half-cadence and a fourth phrase that replicates in the home region the reprisal and closural features of the second phrase. The four phrases are conventionally designated as AA'BA'. The "8" beneath each phrase indicates both that the phrase lengths are equal and that for this piece their normative length is eight bars.

Using methods developed by Schachter (1980) and Rothstein (1989), Figure 5.47 rewrites the melody and basic harmony of the Mendelssohn to show how it approaches double-period prototypicality. The music is given in smaller note values to project the hypermeter. The first and second phrases (bars 7–14 and 15–22 in Figure 5.45) require no change. The third phrase (bars 23–30) eliminates an extension (bars 31–32) that derives from the introduction (bars 5–6). A passage that is interpolated in terms of the double-period schema (bars 33–36) is removed between the third and fourth phrases. Finally, the fourth phrase (bars 37–43) recovers its full length from the metrical deletion caused by an overlap with the coda (bars 43–44). This is the underlying phrasal form of the *Gondollied*.

(Continued)

FIGURE 5.45 Mendelssohn's second "Venetian Boat Song," Op. 30, no. 6 (from *Songs without Words*).

FIGURE 5.45 (Continued)

Figure 5.47 also reveals that the underlying phrasal form does not meet the functional requirements of the antecedent–consequent period or the double period. The first two phrases merely prolong I up to their cadences. The resulting functional progressions are T→D and T→D-T, without the internal tension and relaxation of Dep and S required of normative prolongational structure. Although the developmental third phrase includes Dep and S, the fourth phrase repeats the incompleteness of the second. It would have been easy to recompose these phrases to include Dep and S. A master of inventiveness at reprises, Mendelssohn found

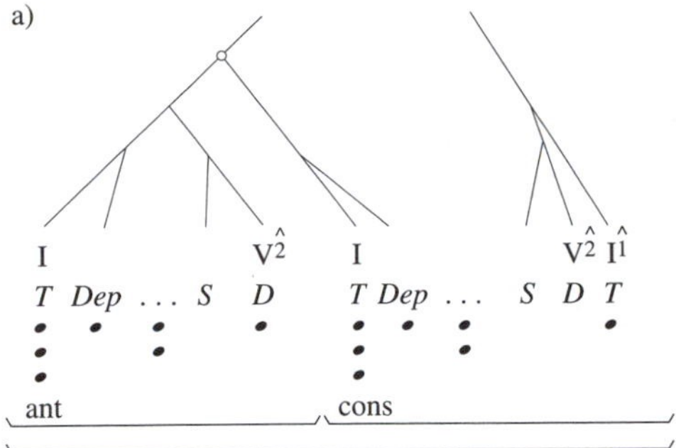

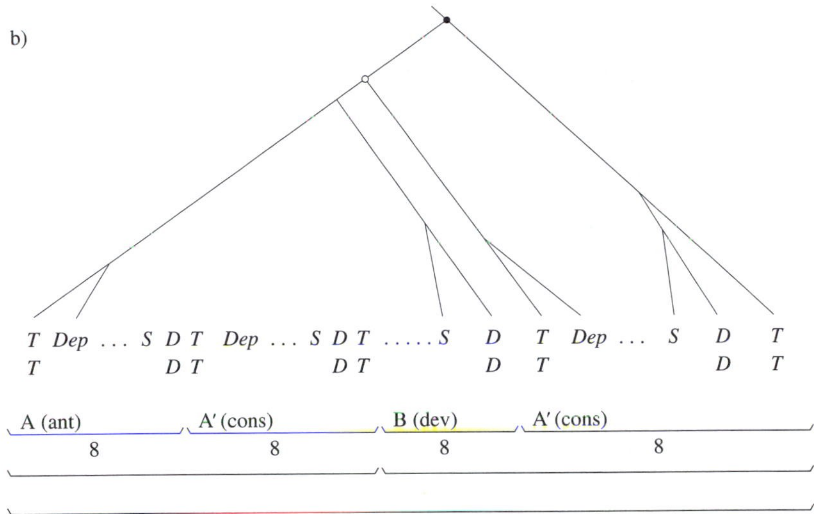

FIGURE 5.46 Schemas for (a) the antecedent–consequent period, and (b) the double period.

the more interesting solution in Figure 5.48. The function of the interpolated passage (bars 33–36) is to supply the missing global S. As at the beginning of the recapitulation of the first movement of the Italian Symphony, the melodic reprise then slips in over a tonic $\frac{6}{4}$, which proceeds to resolve in the middle of the phrase (bars 37–39). This premature harmonic closure leaves the rest of the phrase to spin out in functional superfluity, as if nothing unusual had happened (bars 39–43).

Two schemas are out of phase, between the functions demanded by normative prolongational structure and the necessity for a global cadence at the end of the double period. Figure 5.49 records this divergence in terms of the surface phrasal form of the piece, its global prolongational tree, and its basic functions. Harmonic S→D→T occurs over the interpolation and into the beginning of the reprising

FIGURE 5.47 Underlying double period for the Mendelssohn, written in smaller note values to bring out the hypermeter, and with harmonic functions given.

FIGURE 5.48 The interpolated phrase and its role in creating an S-function at the reprise.

A', without an accompanying melodic resolution. The global harmonic and melodic cadence at the end of A' in turn lacks a preceding S. The role of the coda, aside from its framing function, is to bring functional and cadential motion back into phase, by twice stating S→D→T in cadential gestures. The trills (bars 46 and 50) associate this action with the earlier interpolated passage (bars 33–36) that is misplaced in a functional-schematic sense. The reprise has been in a state of schematic tension, and the coda provides its retrospective resolution.

Although the analysis of the *Gondollied* has been presented in abbreviated form, it could be demonstrated to derive at every stage from the theory behind it—except in one important respect. The theory has not specified how to generate

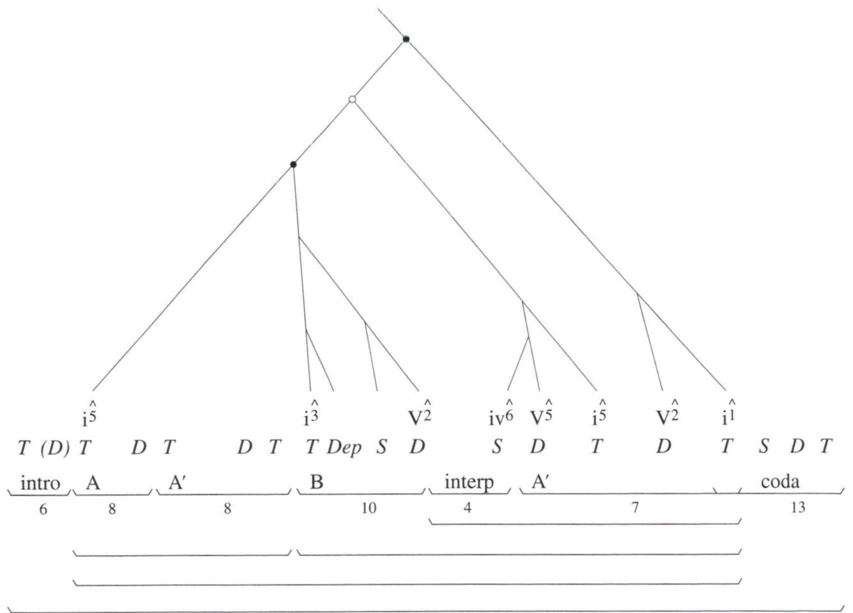

FIGURE 5.49 Surface phrase structure, global prolongational tree, and basic functions for the Mendelssohn.

underlying phrasal forms such as that in Figure 5.47. This entails three steps: (1) specifying a repertory of schemas, including their prototypical states; (2) providing a recognition mechanism for identifying a given schema as it appears in a musical surface, including whatever irregularities or anomalies a particular instance possesses in relation to its category; and (3) changing the surfaces of nonprototypical instances into their prototypes by transformational rules that delete or expand or otherwise modify the surfaces. Step (1) has already been sketched along the lines of Figure 5.38 for the sentence, Figure 5.42 for subphrasal galant schemas, and Figure 5.46 for the antecedent–consequent period. Step (3) has been illustrated informally for the *Gondollied* by the deletions of the introduction, transition after the third phrase and following subdominant passage, and coda and by the extension of the consequent phrase beyond its overlapped ending, so that the four phrases of the double period are shorn of extraneous elements and line up in normative lengths. Step (2), however, presents a formidable task that will not be undertaken here.

The ideas about schemas have nonetheless come far enough to suggest that we have been dealing with an emergent level of analysis. In prolongational and pitch-space structure the unit of analysis is the pitch event, that is, a pitch or chord. Here the unit is a level of grouping—subphrasal in galant schemas, the phrase in the sentence, multiple phrases in period construction—that possesses certain rhythmic, prolongational, and functional features. Schematic units take preferred orderings by virtue of their tension patterns. Experienced listeners often attend to the expectations, realizations, and alterations of these units as much as they do to the unfolding of the pitch events that compose them.

6 *Chromatic Tonal Spaces*

PITCH SPACE IN EVOLUTION

Nineteenth-century music frequently turns to chordal and regional motion by thirds as an alternative to motion by fifths. From a geometric perspective, this means taking nonvertical paths on the chordal and regional toroidal structures. Parallel major-minor mixture, which compresses horizontal motion, is one aspect of this process. Nonvertical motion in a straight line also creates interval cycles that divide the octave into equal parts. These divisions lead to new scales, the octatonic (comprising alternating half and whole steps) from the minor-third division and the hexatonic (comprising alternating half steps and minor thirds) from the major-third division.

This historical evolution can be modeled by spatial transformations. Figures 3.26c and 3.51 have illustrated how diatonic chordal space can be represented as chromatically inflected—in the first case through major-minor mixture, in the second through equal division of the octave. Figure 6.1 combines these features. In Figure 6.1a, **I/i** means that inflections close to the major mode lie to the left and those close to the minor mode lie to the right; the reverse holds for **i/I** in Figure 6.1b. Chords on the minor- and major-third cycles appear in each row in Figures 6.1a and 6.1b, respectively. The central rows exhaust the possibilities of triads related to the tonic by thirds: in Figure 6.1a, vi and then VI to the left, ♭III and then ♭iii to the right; in Figure 6.1b, ♭VI and then ♭vi to the left, iii and then III to the right. The upper and lower rows show corresponding relationships to the dominant and subdominant chords.

a)

III/iii	V/v	♭VII/♭vii
VI/vi	**I/i**	♭III/♭iii
II/ii	IV/iv	♭VI/♭vi

b)

♭iii/♭III	V/v	vii/VII
♭vi/♭VI	**i/I**	iii/III
♭ii/♭II	iv/IV	vi/VI

FIGURE 6.1 Chromatic alterations on the horizontal axis of chordal space to yield (a) cycles of minor thirds and (b) cycles of major thirds.

With its progressions of diatonically unrelated chords, chromatic tonal music often blurs the distinction between chord and region. Figure 6.1 reflects this trend through its pairing of parallel major and minor chords along interval cycles, so that it resembles partially collapsed regional space. Figure 6.2 summarizes from "Parallel Mixture" in chapter 3 the transformation, through progressive major/minor mixture, from diatonic through partially collapsed to fully mixed regional space. (In Figure 6.2c, each letter stands for a completely mixed region.) In all three representations, but most visibly in Figure 6.2c, the fifth cycle lies on the vertical axis, the minor-third cycle on the horizontal axis, and the major-third cycle on the northwest–southeast diagonal. The major-second cycle on the southwest–northeast diagonal is a stylistic option less frequently taken, in part because adjacent tonic triads on this diagonal do not share any common tones. Chapter 3 gives examples of all these trajectories, often at underlying reductional levels.

Whether regarded as progression at the chordal level, as in Figure 6.1, or as motion from tonic to tonic at the regional level, as in Figure 6.2, paths in these various directions produce familiar scalar collections. A three-step path of major (or minor) triads on the fifths cycle, such as F→C→G, yields the diatonic collection, as shown in Figure 6.3a using only the regional representation. A four-step path on the horizontal axis, such as A→C→E♭→G♭, yields the octatonic collection, as in Figure 6.3b. A three-step path on the northwest–southwest angle, such as E→C→A♭, yields the hexatonic collection, as in Figure 6.3c. The octatonic and

a)

E	**e**	**G**	**g**	**B♭**	**b♭**
A	**a**	**C**	**c**	**E♭**	**e♭**
D	**d**	**F**	**f**	**A♭**	**a♭**

b)

E e	**G g**	**B♭ b♭**
A a	**C c**	**E♭ e♭**
D d	**F f**	**A♭ a♭**

c)

E	**G**	**B♭**
A	**C**	**E♭**
D	**F**	**A♭**

FIGURE 6.2 Progressive compression of regional space along the horizontal axis: (a) a portion of diatonic regional space; (b) the same regions partially collapsed through major/minor mixture; (c) the same regions completely collapsed through major/minor mixture.

a) diatonic

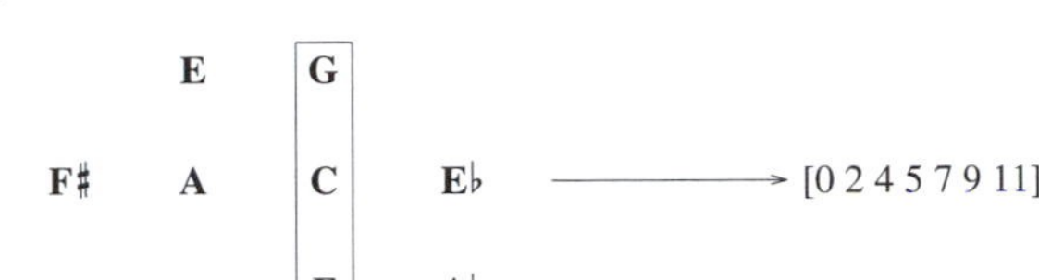

b) octatonic

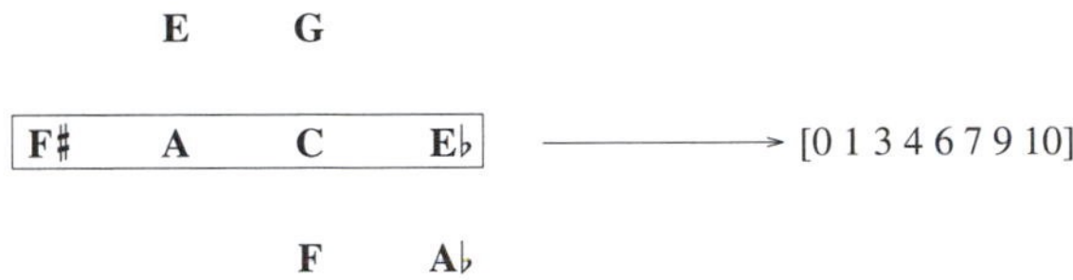

c) hexatonic

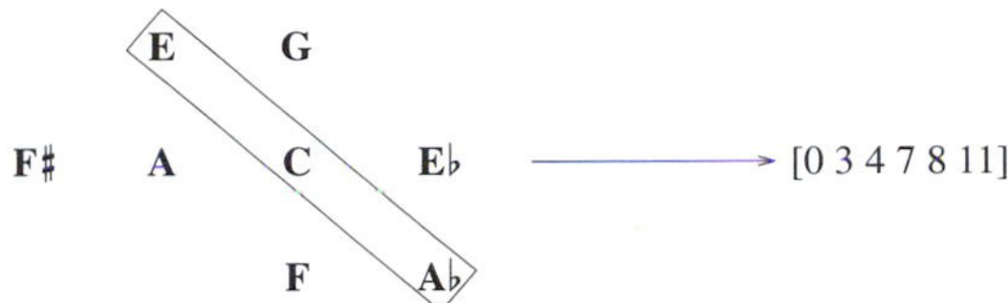

FIGURE 6.3 Derivation of diatonic, octatonic, and hexatonic collections from interval cycles of tonic chords in collapsed regional space.

hexatonic collections can equally well be read off the horizontal axes in Figures 6.1a and 6.1b, respectively.

The whole-tone scale has sources other than the alteration or compression of diatonic chordal/regional space. Generating it from root motion on the southwest–northeast diagonal of regional space is unconvincing if only because the whole-tone collection does not include major or minor triads. It is better to think of this collection as originating either from stepwise passing motion between triadic roots on the major-third cycle or, more important, from either of the two quasi-tonal chords that it does include, the augmented triad and the so-called French augmented-sixth chord. The first possibility is a result less of pitch space than of prolongational levels. The second possibility is explored later in this chapter.

Figures 6.1–3 suggest that the minor- and major-third divisions of the octave, together with the related octatonic and hexatonic collections, are not arbitrary stylistic developments but consequences of major-minor mixture and motion by thirds. Once music enters a truly octatonic or hexatonic realm, however, conventional scale steps no longer pertain and Roman-numeral analysis becomes unsuitable. For example, unless there is an overriding diatonic context, it is misleading to represent the chord progression C→E♭→F♯(G♭) as I→♭III→♯IV(♭V) in **C**—or, equally, as I/**I**→♭III/**I**→♭III/♭**III**. On its own, C→E♭→F♯ implies an octatonic context. Its spatial framework should therefore be not altered-diatonic but octatonic. New pitch spaces are required. Constructing these spaces and evaluating distances between them will be an intricate procedure whose analytic payoff will be demonstrated in chapter 7.

CONSTRUCTING CHROMATIC SPACES

Triadic/octatonic space

The first step in developing octatonic space is substituting an octatonic for a diatonic collection at the scalar level of the basic space, as shown in Figure 6.4, leaving the other levels unchanged. Unless other tunings are under consideration, which is not the case here, the chromatic level stays the same. The octatonic scale at level d begins with a half rather than a whole step because the alternative would not provide pcs 4 and 7 for representing the C major triad at level c. The assumption of the triad as the referential chordal sonority is appropriate for some but certainly not all octatonic music. Later on we consider some other chord types within the octatonic collection.

The second step is changing the cyclic intervallic operator at the chordal levels. In diatonic space, the operator is the chordal circle-of-fifths rule, one of whose justifications is that it exhausts the positions that a triad can take within the diatonic set. But even a single chordal fifth-step would bring the chord outside a given octatonic collection. For instance, the triadic move C→G would yield pc2 and pc11, which do not belong to the octatonic collection in Figure 6.4. The intervallic operator that generates the triads within a given octatonic collection is not the fifth but the minor third. Transposing repeatedly by ic3 up the octatonic scale in Figure 6.4 yields paired triadic circles, one major and the other minor: C→E♭→F♯→A→(C) and c→e♭→f♯→a→(c). For some octatonic passages the invocation of only one of these independent circles suffices, but it is more satisfactory to link them into one structure. This is accomplished by a third step, an operation that converts parallel major and minor triads into each other. This operation applied to the octatonic collection in Figure 6.4 produces four triadic pairs, C↔c, E♭↔e♭, F♯↔f♯, and A↔a.

This statement formalizes steps 2 and 3:

> OCTATONIC INTRAREGIONAL CHORD-CYCLE RULE To move from one triad to another within an octatonic collection,
> (1) move the pcs at levels a–c of the triadic/octatonic basic space two steps to the right (mod 8) on level d, or two steps to the left; and/or
> (2) move the single pc that is at level c but not at level b an ic1 to the only such option available at level d.

Condition (1) is adapted from the diatonic chordal circle-of-fifths rule. Applying it once to the right on Figure 6.4 yields the configuration in Figure 6.5a. Con-

level *a:*	0
level *b:*	0 7
level *c:*	0 4 7
level *d:*	0 1 3 4 6 7 9 10
level *e:*	0 1 2 3 4 5 6 7 8 9 10 11

FIGURE 6.4 Triadic/octatonic basic space.

dition (2) has no counterpart in diatonic space, which generates both major and minor triads on the fifths cycle. Applying this condition once to Figure 6.4 yields Figure 6.5b.

There are other ways of generating all the triads in an octatonic collection. One could simply shift each pc in a triad one step to the right along the octatonic collection, producing the chord sequence C–f♯–E♭-a–F♯–c–A–e♭–C. This would be analogous to moving I–ii–iii–IV–V–vi–vii°–I up the diatonic scale. Or one could invoke the R and P transformations of neo-Riemannian theory in alternation, R to move a triad by minor-third root motion, P to change chord quality. Condition (2) in the preceding rule accomplishes the same thing as the P transformation, but there is a subtle difference between condition (1) and the R transformation. Condition (1) moves triads by root motion, with the root weighted the most, next the fifth, the third the least, in line with the relative psychoacoustic salience of the members of the triad. The R transformation, by contrast, treats all triadic members equally and moves them by efficient voice leading rather than by root motion. The rule as stated better reflects the perspective of my theory. (See "Empirical Issues" in chapter 2 for related discussion.)

As in the diatonic case, a regional rule is needed for moving one octatonic collection to another—that is, for octatonic modulation. Because this scale repeats half and whole steps each t3, there are only three octatonic collections: [0 1 3 4 6 7 9 10] or oct0, for which t0 = t3 = t6 = t9; [1 2 4 5 7 8 10 11] or oct1, for which t1 = t4 = t7 = t10; and [2 3 5 6 8 9 11 0] or oct2, for which t2 = t5 = t8 = t11. Each octatonic set is named by reference to its first pc rather than by the nomenclature employed by Pieter van den Toorn (1983). Any of these scales could be listed as beginning with a whole step, which van den Toorn calls the melodic scale (because [0 2 3 5] is a subset of the diatonic as well as the octatonic scale), instead of a half step, which he calls the harmonic scale (because it permits a root-position triad to be built off its starting point). The regional circle-of-fifths

a)

```
      3
      3                10
      3        7       10
0 1   3 4   6  7    9  10
0 1 2 3 4 5 6  7  8 9  10 11
```

C→Eb

b)

```
0
0                 7
0     3           7
0 1   3 4   6     7    9 10
0 1 2 3 4 5 6     7  8 9 10 11
```

C→c

FIGURE 6.5 Triadic moves in octatonic space by conditions (1) and (2), respectively, of the octatonic chord-cycle rule, starting from the configuration in Figure 6.4.

rule could be taken over intact for the octatonic case, for t7 yields oct1 and t5 (= −t7) yields oct2. Equally possible are t1, t4, or t10 for oct1 and t2 (= −t10), t8 (= −t4), and t11 (= −t1) for oct2. The rule includes all these options:

> OCTATONIC REGION-CYCLE RULE Move the pcs at level d of the octatonic basic space one/four/seven/ten steps to the right (mod 12) on level e or the same to the left.

The octatonic chord-cycle and region-cycle rules serve as input to the octatonic chord distance rule, which takes the same variables as the diatonic case:

> OCTATONIC CHORD DISTANCE RULE $\delta_{oct}(x \rightarrow y) = i + j + k$, where $\delta_{oct}(x \rightarrow y)$ = the distance between chord x and chord *y; i* = the number of applications of the octatonic region-cycle rule needed to shift the octatonic collection that supports x into the octatonic collection that supports y; *j* = the number of applications of condition (1) of the octatonic intraregional chord-cycle rule needed to shift x into y; and *k* = the number of distinctive pcs in the basic space of y compared to basic space of x.

Condition (2) of the intraregional chord-cycle rule is ignored in variable *j* because it does not move the chordal root. The change in chord quality effected by condition (2) is instead registered by variable *k*.

Let us disregard octatonic modulation for the moment, keeping $i = 0$. Figure 6.6 provides calculations for δ_{oct} from a C major triad to all other triads in oct0.

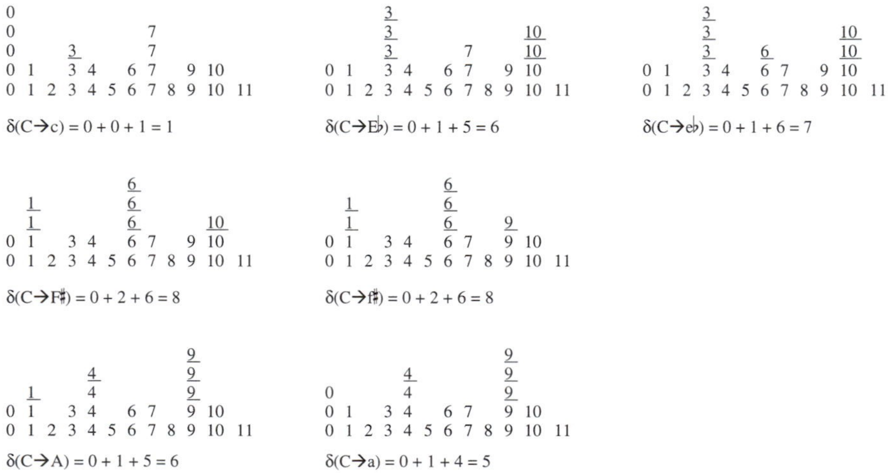

```
0
0                    7
0        3           7
0  1     3  4     6  7     9  10
0  1  2  3  4  5  6  7  8  9  10 11
```

$\delta(C \rightarrow c) = 0 + 0 + 1 = 1$

```
         3
         3                    10
         3           7        10
0  1     3  4     6  7     9  10
0  1  2  3  4  5  6  7  8  9  10 11
```

$\delta(C \rightarrow E\flat) = 0 + 1 + 5 = 6$

```
         3
         3                    10
         3        6           10
0  1     3  4     6  7     9  10
0  1  2  3  4  5  6  7  8  9  10 11
```

$\delta(C \rightarrow e\flat) = 0 + 1 + 6 = 7$

```
                  6
   1              6
   1              6           10
0  1     3  4     6  7     9  10
0  1  2  3  4  5  6  7  8  9  10 11
```

$\delta(C \rightarrow F\sharp) = 0 + 2 + 6 = 8$

```
                  6
   1              6
   1              6        9
0  1     3  4     6  7     9  10
0  1  2  3  4  5  6  7  8  9  10 11
```

$\delta(C \rightarrow f\sharp) = 0 + 2 + 6 = 8$

```
                           9
            4              9
   1        4              9
0  1     3  4     6  7     9  10
0  1  2  3  4  5  6  7  8  9  10 11
```

$\delta(C \rightarrow A) = 0 + 1 + 5 = 6$

```
                           9
            4              9
0           4              9
0  1     3  4     6  7     9  10
0  1  2  3  4  5  6  7  8  9  10 11
```

$\delta(C \rightarrow a) = 0 + 1 + 4 = 5$

FIGURE 6.6 Applications of the octatonic chord distance rule from a C major triad to all other triads contained in oct0.

Chord:	C	c	E♭	e♭	F♯	f♯	A	a
Distance:	0	1	6	7	8	8	6	5

FIGURE 6.7 Summary of chord distances from Figure 6.6.

The distinctive pcs in the new configuration are underlined. The values for *j* are counted by the shortest path. For example, for δ_{oct}(C→A), *j* = 1 to the left rather than 3 to the right. Figure 6.7 tabulates the distance values for Figure 6.6. As one would expect, δ_{oct}(C→c) is the smallest distance, followed by δ_{oct}(C→a) and then symmetrically by δ_{oct}(C→E♭) and δ_{oct}(C→A). Still further away are δ_{oct}(C→e♭) and finally δ_{oct}(C→F♯) and δ_{oct}(C→f♯).

These distances achieve a regular geometric pattern if the triads are arrayed spatially by shortest distances. For all parallel major/minor triads, $\delta = 1$, and for all minor-third-related triads of opposite quality, $\delta = 5$. Repeating these distances yields the irregular circular arrangement in Figure 6.8—to be precise, an octagon with alternating short and long sides. Counting from C, all the distances given in Figure 6.7 are measured around the circumference except for those to F♯ and f♯, which are reached by a direct line across the octagon rather than around its circumference. That is, δ_{oct}(C→F♯) = 8 is a shorter distance than Δ_{oct}(C→c→E♭→e♭ →F♯) = 1 + 5 + 1 + 5 = 12.

Any triad within a given octatonic collection can act as tonic. In this respect, octatonic music is more like modal diatonic music, in which any scale degree except that associated with the diminished triad can function as tonic, than Classical tonal music, which reduces tonic location within a diatonic collection to two options, the major and minor modes. But tonicity is more ambiguous for octatonic than for modal diatonic music because of the octatonic scale's intervallic repetitiveness, which makes position-finding within it quadruply redundant. As a result, judgments of octatonic tonicity depend more heavily on surface perceptual salience than they do for diatonic tonicity. For example, in a phrase that contains only pitches from oct0, if C begins and ends the phrase or if it is longer and louder than the other triads in the phrase, it is likely to be judged as most prominent and hence as (local) tonic. It is therefore pointless to specify in advance one of the triads in Figure 6.8 as tonic within oct0. It is sufficient in the abstract to employ an octatonic chordal/regional representation such as Figure 6.9a, in which **oct0** is given in boldface (indicating regional status), surrounded by the circular representation from Figure 6.8. However, if C is most prominent within an oct0

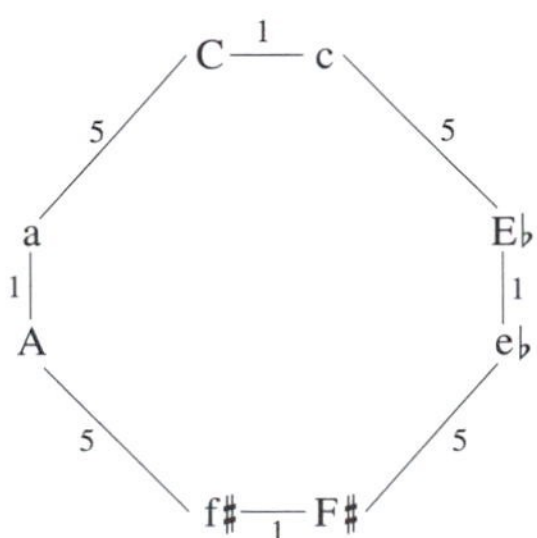

FIGURE 6.8 Spatial representation of triadic distances within oct0. The numbers indicate adjacent values for δ_{oct}.

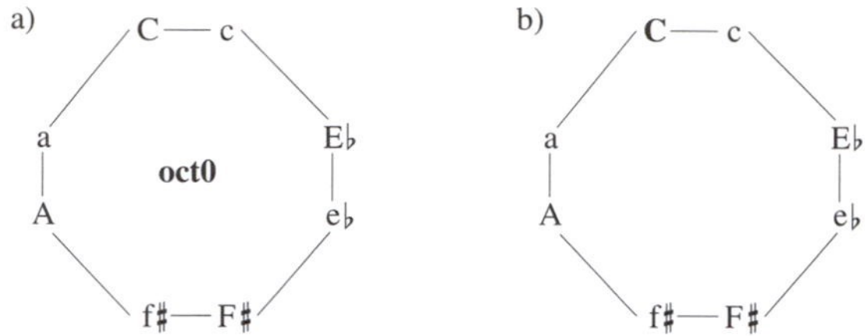

FIGURE 6.9 Alternative representations of octatonic chordal/regional space, notated for one region only.

passage, it might be preferable to adopt the representation in Figure 6.9b, in which **C** is in boldface, indicating its tonic status; this could be notated as $\mathbf{C}^{oct}$. This representation is analogous to the chordal/regional representation for a single region of diatonic space.

Modulation in octatonic as in diatonic music entails a change in scalar collection. Because tonicity within an octatonic collection is so ambiguous, I shall not attempt to build regional space by computing distances across collections from tonic to tonic, as was done for diatonic space, but shall simply calculate distances from collection to collection. This means disregarding the top three levels of the basic space and setting j = 0. Following the octatonic region-cycle rule, Figure 6.10a illustrates that motion from any of the three octatonic collections to any

a)

0	1		3	4		6	7		9	10		→		1	$\underline{2}$		4	$\underline{5}$		7	$\underline{8}$		10	$\underline{11}$
0	1	2	3	4	5	6	7	8	9	10	11		0	1	2	3	4	5	6	7	8	9	10	11

$\delta(\mathbf{oct0} \rightarrow \mathbf{oct1}) = 1 + 0 + 4 = 5$

	1	2		4	5		7	8		10	11	→	$\underline{0}$		2	$\underline{3}$		5	$\underline{6}$		8	$\underline{9}$		11
0	1	2	3	4	5	6	7	8	9	10	11		0	1	2	3	4	5	6	7	8	9	10	11

$\delta(\mathbf{oct1} \rightarrow \mathbf{oct2}) = 1 + 0 + 4 = 5$

0		2	3		5	6		8	9		11	→	0	$\underline{1}$		3	$\underline{4}$		6	$\underline{7}$		9	$\underline{10}$	
0	1	2	3	4	5	6	7	8	9	10	11		0	1	2	3	4	5	6	7	8	9	10	11

$\delta(\mathbf{oct2} \rightarrow \mathbf{oct0}) = 1 + 0 + 4 = 5$

b)

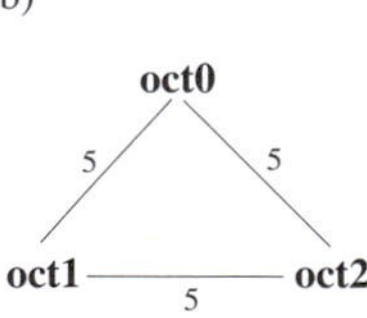

FIGURE 6.10 Octatonic regional distances: (a) calculations of δ_{oct}; (b) geometric mapping based on (a).

other always yields $k = 4$. There is no regional cyclic progression away from a given point, as is the case for diatonic space, in which each regional cycle-of-fifths step changes one pc in the diatonic collection, two steps change two pcs, and so forth. Rather, there is just one step from any octatonic collection to any other, so that $i = 1$ in each case. The three distances all sum to 5. Figure 6.10b maps this outcome as an equilateral triangle. This is the geometry of octatonic regional space.

Figure 6.11a combines the regional triangle with the circular representation in Figure 6.9a to form an overall picture of triadic/octatonic chordal/regional space.

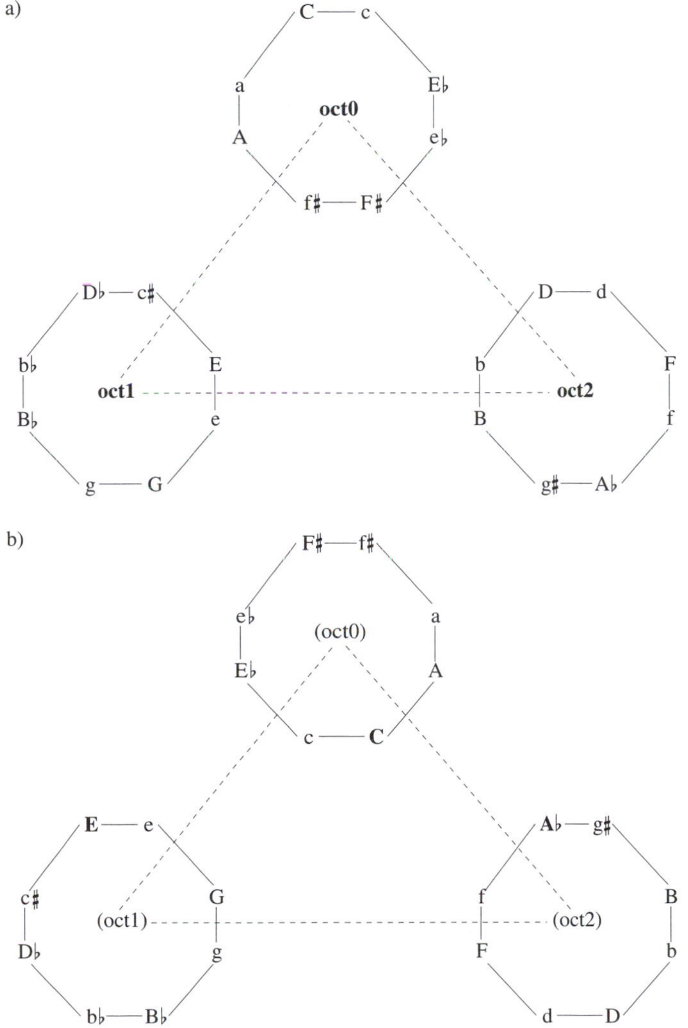

FIGURE 6.11 Triadic/octatonic chordal/regional space in its entirety, with two chordal orientations.

The solid lines connect adjacent chords within a region, the dashed lines the regions themselves. Chords within **oct1** and **oct2** are oriented so that they appear one and two semitones, respectively, above the chords in the equivalent orientation for **oct0**. These circular arrangements might be imagined, however, as revolving like wheels according to context, so that the shortest path is always taken. Suppose that a piece exploits the regional major-third cycle **C–E–A♭** as a complement to the intraregional chordal minor-third cycles. Then it might be useful to draw chordal/regional space as in Figure 6.11b, in which **C, E**, and **A♭** are local tonics in close mutual proximity. Compared to Figure 6.11a, the chord circles in **oct0** and **oct2** are rotated 180 degrees and the chord circle in **oct1** is rotated 90 degrees counterclockwise.

There is a slight wrinkle when computing δ_{oct} across regions. In diatonic space the cycle of fifths acts at the chordal as well as regional level, allowing variable *j* to access any chord in any region after variable *i* has done its work. But in octatonic space *j* generates a limited number of triads before cycling back to the starting point. To reach triads outside a region, variable *i* must be applied first, but this application erases the initial root-pc from which *j* is calculated. That the initial and goal root-pcs cannot both be present in the octatonic rule has the effect of erasing subtle distinctions in chord distances across regions; yet the change in chord root must still be taken into account. Therefore,

COROLLARY TO THE OCTATONIC CHORD DISTANCE RULE When calculating distances between chords across octatonic regions, let *j* always equal 1.

In effect, this stipulation eliminates the possibility of two chord steps for chords a tritone apart using the intrarregional chord-cycle rule.

Figure 6.12 carries out this approach for distances between C in **oct0** and all triads in **oct1**. All of these δ values are somewhat greater than intraregional chordal distances (compare Figure 6.7). The greatest distances are C→D♭, C→B♭, and C→b♭. Common pcs lead to lower values for C→e, C→G, and C→g and to a lesser extent for C→c♯ and C→E. Given the symmetries of octatonic space, it can be inferred that equivalent distances obtain for the other interregional triadic distances.

Triadic/hexatonic space

Triadic/hexatonic space is the formal twin of triadic/octatonic space. Figure 6.13 gives the basic triadic/hexatonic space, with only the scale level changed from that of diatonic or triadic/octatonic space. Because the scale alternates a minor second and a minor third, transposing it by ic4 yields the same collection, and shifting the chordal levels by the same amount generates all the triads within the collection. The following formulation differs from its octatonic counterpart only in the scalar level to which it refers:

```
1
1                 8
1         5       8
  1 2   4 5   7 8   10 11
0 1 2 3 4 5 6 7 8 9 10 11
```

δ(C→D♭) = 1 + 1 + 10 = 12

```
1
1                 8
1       4         8
  1 2   4 5   7 8   10 11
0 1 2 3 4 5 6 7 8 9 10 11
```

δ(C→c♯) =1 + 1 + 9 = 11

```
        4
        4               11
        4         8     11
  1 2   4 5   7 8   10 11
0 1 2 3 4 5 6 7 8 9 10 11
```

δ(C→E) = 1 + 1 + 9 = 11

```
        4
        4               11
        4     7         11
  1 2   4 5   7 8   10 11
0 1 2 3 4 5 6 7 8 9 10 11
```

δ(C→e) = 1 + 1 + 8 = 10

```
              7
    2         7
    2         7         11
  1 2   4 5   7 8   10 11
0 1 2 3 4 5 6 7 8 9 10 11
```

δ(C→G) = 1 + 1 + 8 = 10

```
              7
    2         7
    2         7     10
  1 2   4 5   7 8   10 11
0 1 2 3 4 5 6 7 8 9 10 11
```

δ(C→g) = 1 + 1 + 8 = 10

```
                    10
          5         10
    2     5         10
  1 2   4 5   7 8   10 11
0 1 2 3 4 5 6 7 8 9 10 11
```

δ(C→B♭) = 1 + 1 + 10 = 12

```
                    10
          5         10
  1       5         10
  1 2   4 5   7 8   10 11
0 1 2 3 4 5 6 7 8 9 10 11
```

δ(C→b♭) = 1 + 1 + 10 = 12

FIGURE 6.12 Calculations for δ_{oct} from a C major triad in **oct0** to all triads in **oct1**.

HEXATONIC INTRAREGIONAL CHORD-CYCLE RULE To move from one triad to another within a hexatonic collection,

(1) move the pcs at levels a–c of the hexatonic basic space two steps to the right (mod 6) on level d or two steps to the left; or
(2) move the single pc that is at level c but not at level b an ic1 to the only such option available at level d.

Condition (1) renders the chord circles C→E→A♭→(C) and c→e→g♯→(c), and condition (2) generates the pairs C↔c, E↔e, and A♭↔g♯. As in the octatonic case, all the triads in a hexatonic collection could be reached by other means, such as alternating the L and P neo-Riemannian transformations, but doing so would violate the spirit of this theory.

As a consequence of its repetition every major third, there are four hexatonic collections: [0 3 4 7 8 11] or hex0, for which t0 = t4 = t8; [1 4 5 8 9 0] or hex1, for which t1 = t5 = t9; [2 5 6 9 10 1] or hex2, for which t2 = t6 = t10; and [3 6 7 10 11 2] or hex3, for which t3 = t7 = t11. The scales are listed beginning with a minor third rather than in normal form—[0 1 4 5 8 9], and so on—because this is necessary if hex0 is to begin with a C major chord, in correspondence with the octatonic case. Moving from one hexatonic collection to another again par-

```
level a:  0
level b:  0             7
level c:  0       4     7
level d:  0     3 4     7 8        11
level e:  0 1 2 3 4 5 6 7 8 9 10 11
```

FIGURE 6.13 Triadic/hexatonic basic space.

allels the octatonic rule, except that the equivalent transpositional intervals must be changed:

HEXATONIC REGION-CYCLE RULE Move the pcs at level d of the hexatonic basic space one/five/nine steps to the right (mod 12) on level e or the same to the left.

There is a similar substitution for computing distances between triads in hexatonic space:

HEXATONIC CHORD DISTANCE RULE $\delta_{hex}(x \rightarrow y) = i + j + k$, where $\delta_{hex}(x \rightarrow y)$ = the distance between chord x and chord y; i = the number of applications of the hexatonic region-cycle rule needed to shift the hexatonic collection that supports x into the hexatonic collection that supports y; j = the number of applications of condition (1) of the hexatonic chord-cycle rule needed to shift x into y; and k = the number of distinctive pcs in the basic space of y compared to basic space of x.

COROLLARY: When calculating distances between chords across hexatonic regions, let j always equal 1.

Keeping $i = 0$, Figure 6.14 provides calculations for δ_{hex} from a C major triad to all other triads contained in hex0. The value for j is again assessed by the shortest path. Figure 6.15 tabulates the distance values for Figure 6.14. Again, δ(C→c) = 1. In parallel with δ_{oct}(C→a) = 5, δ_{hex}(C→e) = 5. Similarly, just as δ_{oct}(C→E♭) and δ_{oct}(C→A) = 6, so δ_{hex}(C→E) and δ_{hex}(C→A♭) = 6; again, δ_{oct}(C→e♭) = 7 and δ_{hex}(C→g♯ = 7. Figure 6.16 provides a geometrical mapping of hexatonic chordal space, based on shortest distances, yielding a hexagon with

```
0
0             7
0     3       7
0     3 4     7 8          11
0 1 2 3 4 5 6 7 8 9 10 11
```

δ(C→c) = 0 + 0 + 1 = 1

```
        4
        4                  11
        4     7            11
0     3 4     7 8          11
0 1 2 3 4 5 6 7 8 9 10 11
```

δ(C→e) = 0 + 1 + 4 = 5

```
        4
        4                  11
        4       8          11
0     3 4     7 8          11
0 1 2 3 4 5 6 7 8 9 10 11
```

δ(C→E) = 0 + 1 + 5 = 6

```
                8
      3         8
      3         8          11
0     3 4     7 8          11
0 1 2 3 4 5 6 7 8 9 10 11
```

δ(C→g♯) = 0 + 1 + 6 = 7

```
                8
      3         8
0     3         8
0     3 4     7 8          11
0 1 2 3 4 5 6 7 8 9 10 11
```

δ(C→A♭) = 0 + 1 + 5 = 6

FIGURE 6.14 Applications of the hexatonic chord distance algorithm from a C major triad to all other triads contained in hex0.

Chord:	C	c	e	E	g♯	A♭
Distance:	0	1	5	6	7	6

FIGURE 6.15 Summary of chord distances from Figure 6.14.

alternating short and long sides. All distances are measured around the circumference.

Employing the hexatonic region-cycle rule, Figure 6.17a calculates on the scalar level the distances of the other regions from **hex0**. Adjacent region-steps δ(**hex0**→**hex1**) and δ(**hex0**→**hex3**) = 4, but nonadjacent region-step δ(**hex0**→**hex2**) = 8. Symbolically, Δ(**hex0**→**hex2**) = δ(**hex0**→**hex1**) + δ(**hex1**→**hex2**) = 4 + 4 = 8; an alternate and equal route proceeds through **hex3** instead of **hex1**. Similarly, but not shown, δ(**hex1**→**hex2**) and δ(**hex2**→**hex3**) = 4, but δ(**hex1**→**hex3**) = 8. Thus hexatonic regional distances follow a city-block route. Figure 6.17b maps these distances as a square. Note, incidentally, that **hex0** and **hex2** are complementary hexachords, as are **hex1** and **hex3**. (In twelve-tone theory, the hexatonic collection is an all-combinatorial hexachord, labeled source-set E in Martino 1961.) Figure 6.18 combines Figures 6.16 and 6.17b to form triadic/hexatonic chordal/regional space. As in its octatonic equivalent, the orientations of the chords on the circles are arbitrary.

A comparison of Figures 6.11a and 6.18 reveals how reciprocal the octatonic/triadic and hexatonic/triadic chordal/regional spaces are. To simplify, count parallel major/minor triads as identical; that is, ignore the short sides of the chordal polygons. Then octatonic chordal space comprises a square and hexatonic chordal space an equilateral triangle; conversely, octatonic regional space comprises a triangle and hexatonic regional space a square. These complementary relations derive from the structures of the scales in question. The octatonic collection repeats every ic3, dividing the twelve chromatic pcs into four parts, and the hexatonic collection repeats every ic4, dividing the twelve chromatic pcs into three parts.

With the help of the corollary to the hexatonic chord distance rule, Figure 6.19a computes the distances between C in **hex0** and all triads in **hex1**. As in the octatonic case, all these values are greater than are those internal to **hex0**, with δ_{hex}(C→f), δ_{hex}(C→F), and δ_{hex}(C→a) the closest because they share the most common tones. Calculations for **hex3** would give matching values. Figure 6.19b performs δ_{hex} from C in **oct0** to a triad in **hex2**. The two-step move for variable *i* to reach **hex2** is matched by that for variable *j*. As this instance suggests, all triads in **hex2** build from the complementary hexachord, so they introduce the same number of noncommon tones at the upper levels of the hexatonic basic space. As

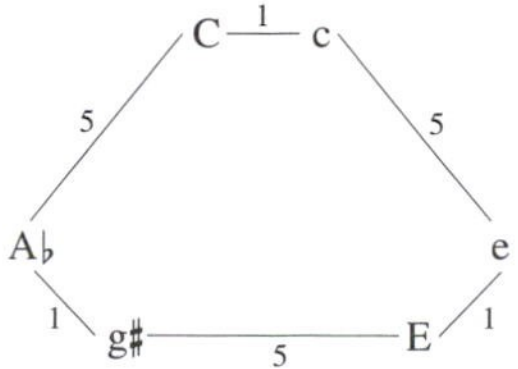

FIGURE 6.16 Spatial representation of triadic distances within hex0. The numbers indicate adjacent values for δ_{hex}.

a)

0 3 4 7 8 11 ⟶ 0 $\underline{1}$ 4 $\underline{5}$ 8 $\underline{9}$
0 1 2 3 4 5 6 7 8 9 10 11 0 1 2 3 4 5 6 7 8 9 10 11

δ(**hex0** ⟶ **hex1**) = 1 + 0 + 3 = 4

0 3 4 7 8 11 ⟶ $\underline{1\ 2}$ $\underline{5\ 6}$ $\underline{9\ 10}$
0 1 2 3 4 5 6 7 8 9 10 11 0 1 2 3 4 5 6 7 8 9 10 11

δ(**hex0** ⟶ **hex2**) = 2 + 0 + 6 = 8

0 3 4 7 8 11 ⟶ $\underline{2}$ 3 $\underline{6}$ 7 $\underline{10}$ 11
0 1 2 3 4 5 6 7 8 9 10 11 0 1 2 3 4 5 6 7 8 9 10 11

δ(**hex0** ⟶ **hex3**) = 1 + 0 + 3 = 4

b)

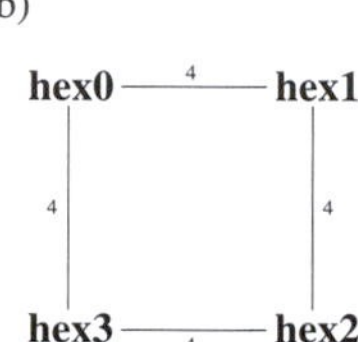

FIGURE 6.17 Hexatonic regional distances from **hex0**: (a) calculations of δ_{hex}; (b) a geometric mapping based on (a).

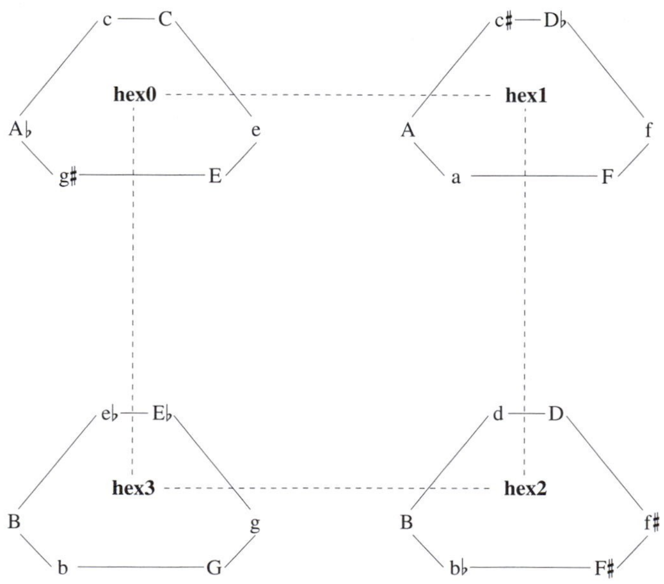

FIGURE 6.18 Triadic/hexatonic chordal/regional space.

a)

```
  1
  1              8
  1     4        8
0 1     4 5      8 9
0 1 2 3 4 5 6 7 8 9 10 11
```

δ(C→c♯) = 1 + 1 + 8 = 10

```
  1
  1              8
  1       5      8
0 1     4 5      8 9
0 1 2 3 4 5 6 7 8 9 10 11
```

δ(C→D♭) = 1 + 1 + 9 = 11

```
          5
0         5
0         5      8
0 1     4 5      8 9
0 1 2 3 4 5 6 7 8 9 10 11
```

δ(C→f) = 1 + 1 + 7 = 9

```
          5
0         5
0         5        9
0 1     4 5      8 9
0 1 2 3 4 5 6 7 8 9 10 11
```

δ(C→F) = 1 + 1 + 7 = 9

```
                   9
        4          9
0       4          9
0 1     4 5      8 9
0 1 2 3 4 5 6 7 8 9 10 11
```

δ(C→a) = 1 + 1 + 7 = 9

```
                   9
        4          9
  1     4          9
0 1     4 5      8 9
0 1 2 3 4 5 6 7 8 9 10 11
```

δ(C→A) = 1 + 1 + 8 = 10

b)

```
    2
    2              9
    2     5        9
  1 2     5 6      9 10
0 1 2 3 4 5 6 7 8 9 10 11
```

δ(C→d) = 2 + 2 + 12 = 16

FIGURE 6.19 Calculations for δ_{hex} from a C major triad in **hex0**: (a) to all triads in **hex1**; (b) to one triad in **hex2**.

a result, any triad in **hex2** reached from any triad in **hex0** has the identical large distance value. The same would hold between triads in **hex1** and **hex3**.

On the generality of the chord distance rule

Unlike the case for the diatonic pitch-space model, there is as yet little empirical data relevant to the octatonic and hexatonic models. (For partial evidence that supports the hierarchy of the octatonic basic space, see Krumhansl and Schmuckler 1986, also discussed in Krumhansl 1990.) Because of the structural ambiguity intrinsic to these spaces, it is unlikely that such evidence will be as robust as that for diatonic space. Moreover, since relatively little triadic/octatonic and triadic/hexatonic music has been written, listeners have not had comparable exposure to the music that these spaces represent. Consequently, should it be argued that only pc commonality, measured negatively by variable *k*, matters in constructing these spaces and that variables *i* and *j* can be thrown out, there is little external evidence to decide the matter. For octatonic space in Figure 6.6, except for the parallel major-minor move δ_{oct}(C→c), this argument would entail lowering δ_{oct}(C→E♭), δ_{oct}(C→e♭), δ_{oct}(C→A), and δ_{oct}(C→a) by 1 and δ_{oct}(C→F♯) and δ_{oct}(C→f♯) by 2. As a result, F♯ and f♯ would join e♭ as equally distant from C. The regional values in Figure 6.10a would reduce by 1. For hexatonic space in Figure 6.14, except for δ_{hex}(C→c), the same step would mean lowering all the chord distance values by 1. The regional values in Figure 6.17a would also reduce by 1 for δ(**hex0**→**hex1**) and δ(**hex0**→**hex3**), but for δ(**hex0**→**hex2**) the value would reduce by 2.

Granted the paucity of external evidence, are there internal grounds for deciding the issue? One might argue that counting only noncommon pcs in octatonic and hexatonic basic spaces is simpler and therefore preferable. However, the overall theory has greater force if the cycle rules and the distance rules for the diatonic, octatonic, and hexatonic spaces are all the same except for their intervallic operators and the scales over which they operate. This is the approach taken here, for it extends the generality of the theory in a nontrivial way. Further internal support for retaining variables *i* and *j* comes from the spatial irregularities that would result from removing them. Octatonic chordal space and hexatonic regional space would become less symmetrical.

Indirect support for these octatonic and hexatonic models comes from other music theories. Arthur Berger (1963) and van den Toorn (1983) anticipate the stratified hierarchy of octatonic basic space. Ernö Lendvai (1971), in proposing his axis system for Bartók's music, sets forth the octagonal arrangement in Figure 6.8, asserting that the system completes nineteenth-century tendencies toward relative and parallel major-minor relationships. Although he mixes chords and regions and does not mention the octatonic collection, his diagrams also suggest the triangular structure of octatonic regional space. Cohn (1996) illustrates his neo-Riemannian "hyperhexatonic" system with a spatial arrangement essentially identical to the hexachordal chordal/regional space of Figure 6.18.

As noted earlier, the octatonic and hexatonic chord-cycle rules could be stated in terms of neo-Riemannian transformations. Why then bother with the octatonic and hexatonic basic spaces and with their associated chord distance rules? First, these basic spaces instantiate cognitively valid hierarchies: the octatonic and hexatonic scales are built out of the chromatic scale, the triad is superordinate to either scale, and the triad itself has an internal hierarchy. Second, these rules create not only chordal but also regional spaces. Third, as already mentioned, the spaces and rules generalize from diatonic space. With minor adjustments, Schoenberg's chart of regions, Lendvai's axis system, and Cohn's hexatonic system all derive from the same formula. Because the chord distance rule retains its essential form, any phrase or passage that moves between the diatonic and chromatic tonal realms can be treated within a single system without sacrificing the genuine differences between them.

Nontriadic octatonic spaces

Just as level d of the basic space can be filled by collections other than the diatonic scale, so levels a–c can be completed by chords other than the triad. This subsection models three chordal substitutions over the octatonic scale. Figure 6.20a dis-

a)

0											
0							7				
0				4			7			10	
0	1		3	4		6	7		9	10	
0	1	2	3	4	5	6	7	8	9	10	11

b)

0											
0						6					
0			3			6				10	
0	1		3	4		6	7		9	10	
0	1	2	3	4	5	6	7	8	9	10	11

c)

0											
0						6					
0				4		6				10	
0	1		3	4		6	7		9	10	
0	1	2	3	4	5	6	7	8	9	10	11

FIGURE 6.20 Nontriadic octatonic basic spaces: (a) dom7/oct space; (b) Tristan/oct space; (c) F6/oct space.

plays dominant-seventh/octatonic or dom7/oct space, which is characteristic of some Debussy and Stravinsky. Its intervallic inversion at the chordal level, the half-diminished-seventh or Tristan chord, is the basis for the Tristan/oct space in Figure 6.20b. Wagner is interested in this chord less for its octatonic scalar properties than for its capacity to move around the minor-third cycle while retaining two common pcs at any transposition on the cycle. The harmonic constant in Scriabin's stylistic development, as pointed out by Taruskin (1988), is the French-sixth chord, which in his octatonic phase is embedded in the F6/oct space of Figure 6.20c. All three chord-types originate in earlier tonal practice and transpose around the minor-third cycle within an octatonic collection.

The terms "dominant seventh," "Tristan chord," and "French sixth" are merely descriptive in this context and do not imply functional behavior. I prefer not to refer to them in their normal forms—[0 2 5 8] for the dominant-seventh and Tristan chords, [0 2 6 8] for the French-sixth chord—because these orderings conceal their characteristic spacings.

Figure 6.21a computes the distances from the C^7 chord in Figure 6.20a to the other three-dominant-seventh chords in **oct0**. Variable *j* follows the intraregional octatonic chord-cycle rule. Figure 6.21b goes through the same routine from the Tristan chord in Figure 6.20b to the other three Tristan chords on the minor-third cycle. The validity of the top two levels of Tristan/oct basic space, in terms of root perception (Terhardt 1974), is undermined by the diminished fifth. The choice here is to be consistent with the treatment in Figure 6.21a and elsewhere concerning seventh chords. Figure 6.21c repeats the same procedure from the

a)

```
      3
      3                  10
   1  3         7        10
0  1  3  4    6  7    9  10
0  1  2  3  4  5  6  7  8  9  10  11
```

$\delta(C^7 \rightarrow E\flat^7) = 0 + 1 + 5 = 6$

```
                  6
   1              6
   1        4     6          10
0  1     3  4     6  7    9  10
0  1  2  3  4  5  6  7  8  9  10  11
```

$\delta(C^7 \rightarrow F\sharp^7) = 0 + 2 + 5 = 7$

```
                           9
            4              9
   1        4        7     9
0  1     3  4     6  7     9  10
0  1  2  3  4  5  6  7  8  9  10  11
```

$\delta(C^7 \rightarrow A^7) = 0 + 1 + 5 = 6$

b)

```
      3
      3                 9
   1  3        6        9
0  1  3  4     6  7     9  10
0  1  2  3  4  5  6  7  8  9  10  11
```

$\delta(C^{Tr} \rightarrow E\flat^{Tr}) = 0 + 1 + 5 = 6$

```
                  6
0                 6
0           4     6        9
0  1     3  4     6  7     9  10
0  1  2  3  4  5  6  7  8  9  10  11
```

$\delta(C^{Tr} \rightarrow F\sharp^{Tr}) = 0 + 2 + 3 = 5$

```
                           9
         3                 9
0        3           7     9
0  1     3  4     6  7     9  10
0  1  2  3  4  5  6  7  8  9  10  11
```

$\delta(C^{Tr} \rightarrow A^{Tr}) = 0 + 1 + 5 = 6$

c)

```
      3
      3                 9
   1  3           7     9
0  1  3  4     6  7     9  10
0  1  2  3  4  5  6  7  8  9  10  11
```

$\delta(C^{F6} \rightarrow E\flat^{F6}) = 0 + 1 + 7 = 8$

```
                  6
0                 6
0           4     6          10
0  1     3  4     6  7    9  10
0  1  2  3  4  5  6  7  8  9  10  11
```

$\delta(C^{F6} \rightarrow F\sharp^{F6}) = 0 + 2 + 1 = 3$

```
                           9
         3                 9
   1     3           7     9
0  1     3  4     6  7     9  10
0  1  2  3  4  5  6  7  8  9  10  11
```

$\delta(C^{F6} \rightarrow A^{F6}) = 0 + 1 + 7 = 8$

FIGURE 6.21 Applications of δ_{oct}: (a) from a C dominant-seventh chord to other dominant-seventh chords in **oct0**; (b) from a C Tristan chord to other Tristan chords in **oct0**; (c) from an F6 chord built on C to other F6 chords in **oct0**.

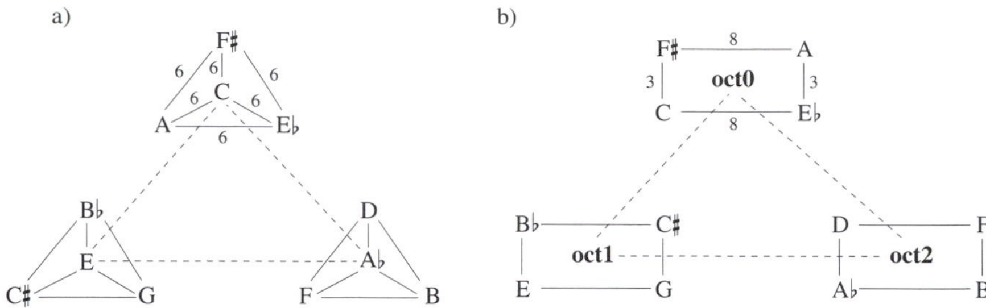

FIGURE 6.22 Geometric approximation of the distance values in Figure 6.21: (a) dom7/oct or Tristan/oct chordal/regional space; (b) F6/oct chordal/regional space.

French-sixth chord in Figure 6.20c to the other three such chords contained in **oct0**. The two tritones in the French sixth further weaken the top two levels of the basic space. In practice, root and bass become indistinguishable. Chords such as this, while still representable in the basic space, point to a breakdown in intuitions of the multileveled hierarchy of the space.

The distance values in Figures 6.21a–b are almost but not quite equal. Let us round off these values to 6, so that all four chords in dom7/oct space and all four chords in Tristan/oct space appear equidistant from one another. The result for either space is the set of chordal equilateral tetrahedrons in Figure 6.22a, arrayed as before on a regional triangle. In Figure 6.21c, however, French-sixth chords related by a tritone repeat the same pcs, whereas those a minor third apart form the complementary tetrachord within the octatonic collection. The difference in *k* values makes tritone-related chords significantly more proximate. Figure 6.22b is a rough attempt to draw these distances. Ideally, the chordal space should curve so that diagonal distances (between C and A, F♯ and E♭, and so on) are the same as the long edges of the rectangles. The representation of pitch or chordal tonicity is left open in Figure 6.22 because again this is a matter of contextual salience.

Whole-tone and mystic spaces

A further step in exploring chromatic tonal spaces is keeping the nontriadic chordal level intact and substituting another nondiatonic collection at the scalar level. Figure 6.23 takes this step from the F6/oct space of Figure 6.20c. Levels a–c are retained, but scalar level d is replaced in Figure 6.23a by the whole-tone scale,

a)

level *a:*	0											
level *b:*	0						6					
level *c:*	0				4		6				10	
level *d:*	0		2		4		6		8		10	
level *e:*	0	1	2	3	4	5	6	7	8	9	10	11

b)

level *a:*	0											
level *b:*	0						6					
level *c:*	0				4		6				10	
level *d:*	0	(1)		3	4		6		8		10	
level *e:*	0	1	2	3	4	5	6	7	8	9	10	11

FIGURE 6.23 Nontriadic octatonic basic spaces: (a) F6/wt space; (b) F6/mystic space.

creating F6/wt space, and in Figure 6.23b by Scriabin's so-called mystic scale, creating F6/mystic space.

There are parentheses around pc1 at level d in Figure 6.23b because the mystic collection is ordinarily thought of as having not seven but six pcs—[3 4 6 8 10 0] in this transposition. But often Scriabin inverts the collection—in this case, [1 0 10 8 6 4]—and combines it with itself to form the seven-pc set. The interval structure of the latter corresponds to both the rising melodic minor scale and the so-called acoustic scale (the major scale with raised fourth and flattened seventh, in imitation of the seventh and eleventh partials). Which name is used is likely to depend on chordal and tonic orientations. In Scriabin's usage, the seven-pc version can profitably be viewed as a hybrid of the octatonic and whole-tone scales—octatonic for the segment [10 0 1 3 4 6], whole-tone for the segment [4 6 8 10 0]. Evidently Scriabin conceived the octatonic and mystic collections as combining into a nine-pc mysterium scale—counting up stepwise, [7 9 10 0 1 3 4 6 8] in this transposition (Perle 1984).

The total intervallic repetitiousness of the whole-tone scale makes it instantly identifiable. Let us pass over statements of its chord-cycle, region-cycle, and δ_{wt} rules. The intraregional *j*-operator—the interval that generates all the French sixths within a whole-tone collection—is the major second. Figure 6.24a computes the distances from the configuration of Figure 6.23a to French-sixth chords built on the quasi roots D, E, and F♯ within the same whole-tone collection (distances built on B♭ and A♭ correspond to those on D and E, respectively). A tritone transposition duplicates the pcs of the first chord, creating a low *k* value that makes tritone-related French-sixth chords most closely related. The *i*-operator, equal to any odd-numbered chromatic steps, changes the scalar level into the other whole-tone scale, its complementary hexachord. Accordingly, any French-sixth chord built on **wt1** is equally distant from any chord in **wt0**; Figure 6.24b provides one instance. Chords aside, the distance between **wt0** and **wt1** is $\delta(\mathbf{wt0} \rightarrow \mathbf{wt1}) = 1 + 0 + 6 = 7$.

a)

		2									
		2						8			
0		2				6		8			
0		2		4		6		8		10	
0	1	2	3	4	5	6	7	8	9	10	11

$\delta(C^{F6} \rightarrow D^{F6}) = 0 + 1 + 5 = 6$

				4							
				4						10	
		2		4				8		10	
0		2		4		6		8		10	
0	1	2	3	4	5	6	7	8	9	10	11

$\delta(C^{F6} \rightarrow E^{F6}) = 0 + 2 + 5 = 7$

						6					
0						6					
0				4		6				10	
0		2		4		6		8		10	
0	1	2	3	4	5	6	7	8	9	10	11

$\delta(C^{F6} \rightarrow F\sharp^{F6}) = 0 + 3 + 1 = 4$

b)

	1										
	1						7				
	1				5		7				11
	1		3		5		7		9		11
0	1	2	3	4	5	6	7	8	9	10	11

$\delta(C^{F6} \rightarrow C\sharp^{F6}) = 1 + 1 + 13 = 15$

FIGURE 6.24 Calculations for δ_{wt} from a C French-sixth chord in **wt0**: (a) to other French-sixth chords in **wt0**; (b) to one French-sixth chord in **wt1**.

a)

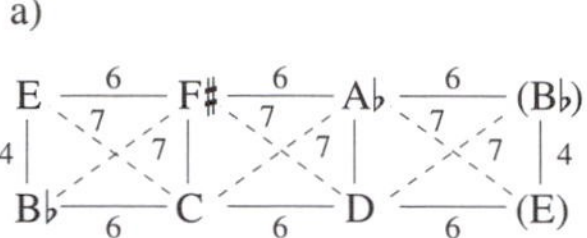

b)

E —— F♯ —— A♭ F —— G —— A
wt0 - - - - - 7 - - - - - wt1
B♭ —— C —— D B —— C♯ —— E♭

FIGURE 6.25 Spatial mappings of F6/wt space: (a) chordal distances within **wt0**; (b) chordal/regional space.

The intraregional distances in Figure 6.24a map into the structure in Figure 6.25a. As the chords in parentheses show, tritone-related pairs swap rows, so that, for example, the E at the upper left is the same as the E at the lower right. The geometric equivalent is a Möbius strip. Figure 6.25b combines the representation in Figure 6.25a with its single regional transposition, yielding F6/wt chordal/regional space.

RELATED ISSUES

Constraints on basic spaces

One could continue to build more basic spaces with other scalar or chordal substitutions, but the returns have already diminished. F6/mystic space applies to a handful of pieces by Scriabin, and F6/wt space is too uniform to be of much use at all. Besides, in both spaces the psychoacoustic ambiguity of the French-sixth root and fifth marginalizes levels a–b and therefore the validity of variable *j*. These spaces exist at tonality's edge.

What are the formal and psychological limitations on basic spaces? These can be developed as a combination of WFRs and PRs. The latter specify not absolute criteria for inclusion but a range of optimality along certain lines.

We begin with well-formedness conditions. First, as stated in "The Concept of Pitch Space" in chapter 2, a well-formed basic space is hierarchically organized. It consists of pcs arrayed in levels: each higher levels has fewer pcs than its immediately lower level, and a pc at a higher level is also a pc at lower levels. Figure 6.26a is ill-formed because level b is not a simplification of level c, and Figure 6.26b is ill-formed because pc7 is present at level c but not level d, nonsensically building the major triad over a whole-tone scale.

a)

0											
0							7				
0							7				
0		2		4			7		9		
0	1	2	3	4	5	6	7	8	9	10	11

b)

0											
0							7				
0				4			7				
0		2		4		6		8		10	
0	1	2	3	4	5	6	7	8	9	10	11

c)

0													
0							7						
0				4			7						
0		2		4		6	7		9		11		1
0	1	2	3	4	5	6	7	8	9	10	11	0	1

FIGURE 6.26 Three ill-formed basic spaces.

Second, each level of a well-formed basic space must duplicate at the octave. Level d of Figure 6.26c, in which p11 continues not to p0 but to p1, is ill-formed. It would make a jumble out of levels a–c. Indeed, the few musical systems around the world that employ scales that do not repeat at the octave also tend not to engage a harmonic dimension.

Third, the lowest level of a well-formed basic space must consist of pcs separated by equal adjacent ics. Throughout I am assuming a twelve-fold division of the octave, but others (Balzano 1980; Cohn 1997) have explored possibilities of other divisions. A special advantage of the twelvefold division is that it both permits attractive group-theoretic properties such as those that belong to the diatonic collection (see "The Pitch-Class Level" in chapter 2 and later in this chapter) and gives rise to intervals categorically perceived as approximating just intonation (Lerdahl 1988a). The latter feature enables a correlation between height of level in a basic space and the degree of sensory consonance of intervals between adjacent elements within a level. Such a correlation is crucial to the inference of levels of the basic space and can be counted as a preferred feature.

Next come two preferential constraints on the form of the reductional format. First, the number of pcs at a given level should approach half those at the next higher level. The F6/mystic space in Figure 6.23b, with its six-or seven-pc scale level, is preferable to the nine-pc F6/mysterium space in Figure 6.27a. The seven-pc version in Figure 6.23b is in turn preferable to the six-pc version, because in the former the reduction from twelve to seven pcs between levels e and d ($7/12 = 0.58$) and from seven to four between levels d and c ($4/7 = 0.57$) deviates less from half than does the reduction in the latter from six to four between levels d and c ($4/6 = 0.67$).

Second, the pcs at any level should be as uniformly distributed as possible, achieving maximal evenness (Clough and Douthett 1991). The mysterium space in Figure 6.27a, with its cluster of half steps between pc6 and pc10, falls short in this respect. Worse is the chromatic hexachordal space in Figure 6.27b, even though it meets the halving constraint.

Exact halving when combined with maximal evenness is itself undesirable, for it leads to total symmetry, impoverishing ic content and neutralizing position-finding. The aug-triad/wt space in Figure 6.27c illustrates. The equal-interval whole-tone scale has half the number of pcs of the chromatic scale, the equal-interval augmented triad half those of the whole-tone scale. The result is a space of undifferentiated steps at the scalar and chordal levels. Only somewhat more differentiated is F6/oct space (Figure 6.20c). For a basic space to afford unambig-

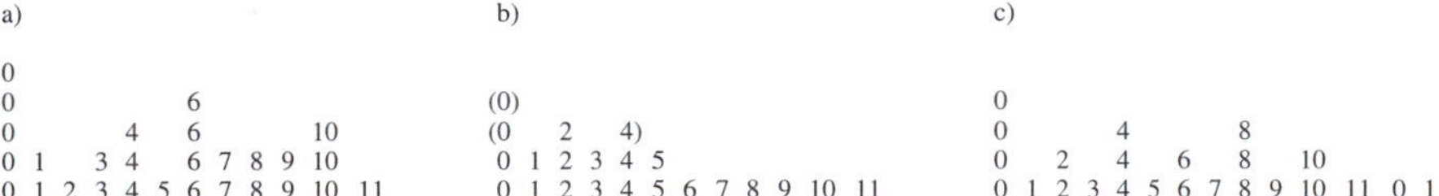

FIGURE 6.27 Some unpreferred basic spaces: (a) F6/mysterium space; (b) chromatic-hexachord space; (c) aug-triad/wt space.

uous position-finding, it must express uniqueness, in which each pc at a given level has an unduplicated set of intervallic relationships to the other pcs at that level. This occurs only when the intervallic distribution of a level is asymmetrical. Asymmetricality arises if the number of pcs at a given level is not a divisor of the number of pcs at the immediately lower level. The halving principle, then, must be modified to "almost half." This is the case anyway if the immediately lower level has an odd number of pcs; but if it has an even number of pcs, the immediately higher level should have half its pcs plus or minus one. For example, in triadic/diatonic space twelve pcs reduce not to six but to seven pcs between levels e and d and seven reduce to three between levels d and c.

The combination of halving from level to level and even distribution within a level ensures two related features mentioned in "The Pitch-Class Level" in chapter 2: a pc at any level below level a is adjacent to a pc that is also a pc at the next larger level; and, as much as possible, a step at any level above level e becomes a skip over a single pc at the next lower level. These features encourage the intelligibility of neighboring and passing functions, respectively.

The principles of halving, maximal evenness, and uniqueness combine to restrict step sizes at the scalar level. Almost-halving at the chromatic level leaves seven or five pcs at the scalar level. Maximal evenness distributes the pcs so that only two step sizes are present, a whole and a half step for the seven-note alternative (the diatonic scale) and a whole step and a minor third for the five-note alternative (the pentatonic scale). As counterexamples, the six-note mystic scale, [0 1 3 5 7 9], which has three step sizes, is not maximally even, nor is the harmonic minor scale, [0 2 3 5 7 8 11]. However, if the less preferred option of exact halving is taken, there are six pcs at the scalar level, and maximal evenness yields a whole-tone scale, which has only one step size. This scale, however, is not unique. That leaves a preference for precisely two step sizes at the scalar level.

Maximal evenness can be expressed in terms of coherence (again see "The Pitch-Class Level" in chapter 2), for the resulting distribution does not allow a single step at any part of a level to equal or exceed in chromatic distance two steps elsewhere in the level (Agmon 1996). A restricted version of coherence, in line with maximal evenness, stipulates that a larger step cannot be more than twice as large as a smaller one. In this version, the 1–2–1–2–1–2–1–2 pattern (counting up in semitones) of the octatonic scale is coherent (and maximally even), but the 1–3–1–3–1–3 pattern of the hexatonic scale is not.

Coherence applies more weakly to nonadjacent intervals, where the degree of evenness is perceptually less immediate. Consider all the possible combinations of five whole and two half steps; it does not matter which interval begins the sequence, for this only leads to modal variants. If the half steps are adjacent, as in the 1–1–2–2–2–2 semitonal intervallic pattern in Figure 6.28a, incoherence clearly appears between p0 and p2. If the pattern is 1–2–1–2–2–2–2 as in Figure 6.28b (this is the seven-pc version of the mystic scale or the ascending form of the melodic minor scale), incoherence appears more subtly in the three steps between p0 and p4, for elsewhere there are two steps between pitches four semitones apart. The most coherent pattern is that of the diatonic scale, 1–2–2–1–2–2–2, as in

a)

0 1 2 4 6 8 10
0 1 2 3 4 5 6 7 8 9 10 11

b)

0 1 3 4 6 8 10
0 1 2 3 4 5 6 7 8 9 10 11

c)

0 1 3 5 6 8 10
0 1 2 3 4 5 6 7 8 9 10 11

FIGURE 6.28 Scalar distributions that use two half and five whole steps.

Figure 6.28c, in which the half steps are distributed as evenly as possible (only the devilish tritone is suspect, there being three steps in one direction and four in the other). Similarly, the pentatonic intervallic pattern 2–2–3–2–3 is both maximally even and coherent, while the other possibility, 2–2–2–3–3, is neither.

Another preferential criterion is that there be precisely two intervallic generators at the scalar level. In an adaptation of Cohn's (1988) representation of transpositional combination, let the two generators be A and B and let the expression $A*B^x$ signify that ic A is transposed by ic B x times until the starting point is reached again without intervening pc duplication. When A= 0, the scale could be considered as generated by the single ic B; however, it slightly simplifies the discussion to refer to A = 0 as an ic and hence to regard all these cases as generated by two ics. Thus $0*1^{12}$ generates the chromatic scale by transposing ic identity (A = 0) by a semitone (B = 1) twelve times. The fifth cycle does the same: $0*7^{12}$ (or $0*5^{12}$) = the full chromatic collection. Smaller quasi exponents on the same ic pair generate the pentatonic and diatonic scales: $0*7^4$ = the pentatonic scale, $0*7^6$ = the diatonic scale. (All other fragments of the fifth cycle violate maximal evenness and coherence.) The remaining possibilities if A = 0 are $0*2^6$ = the whole-tone scale, $0*3^4$ = the diminished-seventh chord, $0*4^3$ = the augmented triad, and $0*6^2$ = the tritone dyad.

If A = 1, the possibilities for B are as follows. If B = 2, then $1*2^6$, or [0 1] transposed six times by ic2, yields the chromatic scale: [(0 1) (2 3) (4 5) (6 7) (8 9) (10 11) (0 1)]. The last dyad is repeated to show the return of the starting unit. Similarly, $1*3^4$ = the octatonic scale: [(0 1) (3 4) (6 7) (9 10) (0 1)]; and $1*4^3$ = the hexatonic scale: [(0 1) (4 5) (8 9) (0 1)]. $1*6^2$ generates a subset of the octatonic collection that is a familiar chord in twentieth-century music: [(0 1) (6 7) (0 1)]. B = 1 and B = 5 are not preferred because they yield pc duplication before cyclic completion: $1*1^{12}$ = [(0 1) (1 2) . . .], and $1*5^{12}$ = [(0 1) (5 6) (10 11) (3 4) (8 9) (1 2) . . .].

A $\geqslant$ 2 does not add to the list of preferred scales. For example, $2*3^4$ = oct2: [(0 2) (3 5) (6 8) (9 11) (0 2)]; $2*4^3$ = the whole-tone scale: [(0 2) (4 6) (8 10) (0 2)]. $2*5^{12}$ is not preferred because pcs duplicate: [(0 2) (5 7) (10 0) . . .]. However, $2*6^2$ yields a second familiar atonal chord: [(0 2) (6 8) (0 2)], the French-sixth subset of the whole-tone and octatonic collections.

Two of the pc sets thus generated, the French sixth and [0 1 6 7], have been referred to as chords rather than scales. This is partly because they are subsets of other pc sets generated by $A*B^x$. Given the hierarchical structure of basic spaces, it is natural to locate the French sixth and [0 1 6 7] at the chordal level above the scalar collections that contain them. Another reason for not preferring them as scales is that their larger adjacencies, a major third for the French sixth and a perfect fourth for [0 1 6 7], feel more like skips than steps. Intuitions about scales include a preference for small steps. Because of the inverse-square property of the melodic attraction rule (see "Melodic Tension" in chapter 4), attractions between pitches more than a major second apart are minuscule. The sense of stepwise motion between adjacent pitches depends in part on their mutual attraction. Yet another reason for not preferring [0 1 6 7] as a scale is that it violates the restrictive version of coherence; its larger adjacencies are more than twice the size of its smaller ones.

If the criterion of restricting stepwise motion to within a major second is observed strictly, not only are the French sixth and [0 1 6 7] eliminated as scales, but so are the diminished triad, the augmented triad, and the tritone dyad. So far, so good. But this criterion throws out the pentatonic and hexatonic scales as well. There is some plausibility here regarding the hexatonic scale, for it does not meet some of the other preferential constraints. But this result is unwelcome for the pentatonic scale. This example highlights the preferential status of all these criteria. The pentatonic scale is prototypically scalar in all respects except for its stepwise minor thirds; its violation of the criterion for small steps is overridden by all the other criteria.

Broadly speaking, scales and chords that are generated by two ics are quite symmetrical. If A = 0, a scale is self-symmetrical. For example, the white-note diatonic and pentatonic collections are self-symmetrical around D. The symmetry of these structures presumably makes them easier to learn and remember; hence, in part, their referentiality compared to that of the many more numerous asymmetrical pc sets.

The following statement summarizes this discussion:

CONSTRAINTS ON BASIC SPACE

Well-formedness conditions A basic space must

(1) consist of a closed group of pcs, with a single modulus operative at all levels (here the modulus is the octave)
(2) be hierarchically organized such that
    (a) at the lowest level, intervals between adjacent pcs are equal (here it is the twelve semitones)
    (b) every pc above the lowest level is also a pc at all lower levels
    (c) a pc that is relatively stable at level L is also a pc at L + 1
    (d) L + 1 has fewer pcs than L

Preferential conditions A basic space preferably

(1) correlates height of level in the space with the degree of sensory consonance of adjacent intervals within a level
(2) has almost half the pcs at L + 1 as at L
(3) expresses maximal evenness in its distribution of pcs at a given level (alternatively, has coherent steps at a given level)
(4) expresses a unique distribution of directed intervals
(5) has two step sizes at the scale level

(6) has two intervallic generators at the scale level, such that the starting point is reached again without intervening pc duplication
(7) has steps no larger than ic2 between adjacent pcs at the scale level.

Figure 6.29 displays how the scales and chords that have been discussed satisfy these preferences. (The harmonic minor scale is not included because it normally functions as an inflection on the diatonic scale; the mysterium scale is not included because it violates well-formedness condition [1] and hence is categorized as a nonscalar pc set.) The classification for sensory consonance relates scales to the chromatic level and chords to the relevant scale level. The reference for the major or minor triad is to the diatonic scale, the augmented triad to the whole-tone and hexatonic scales, the French-sixth chord to the whole-tone and octatonic scales, and [0 1 6 7] to the octatonic scale. The measure of consonance is a gross approximation of sensory roughness: if less than half the number of the most dissonant adjacent interval at the lower level appears at the higher level, the scale or chord counts as sensorily more consonant than the content of its immediately lower level. The classification for maximal evenness also relies on a comparison between levels. Scales are compared to the chromatic collection, but chords are judged in relation to their pertinent maximally even scales. The major or minor triad is referred to the diatonic scale, the augmented triad to the whole-tone and hexatonic scales, the diminished-seventh chord to the octatonic scale, the French sixth to the octatonic and whole-tone scales, and [0 1 6 7] to the octatonic scale. (If the major or minor triad were referred to the octatonic or hexatonic scales, it would be assigned "no," for the diminished-seventh chord is maximally even for the octatonic and the augmented triad for the hexatonic scale.) The rest of the table is straightforward.

How should these positive and negative answers combine in an overall typicality rating? The simple additive tally in Figure 6.30—the more yeses, the greater centrality of the scale or chord within its category—yields plausible results. The diatonic scale is the prototypical scale, followed by the pentatonic. The octatonic and seven-note mystic scales are next, then the whole-tone scale. The most deviant scale is the hexatonic. Similarly, the prototypical chord is the major or minor triad

	sensory consonance	*almost half*	*unique-ness*	*maximal evenness*	*two step sizes*	*two generators*	*small steps*
Scales							
Diatonic	yes	yes	yes	yes	yes	yes	yes
pentatonic	yes	yes	yes	yes	yes	yes	no
octatonic	yes	no	no	yes	yes	yes	yes
hexatonic	yes	no	no	no	yes	yes	no
whole-tone	yes	no	no	yes	no	yes	yes
mystic (7-note)	yes	yes	yes	no	yes	no	yes
Chords							
triad (maj/min)	yes	yes	yes	yes	no	no	no
dom7 (Tristan)	yes	yes	yes	yes	no	no	no
aug	yes	no	no	yes	no	yes	no
dim7	yes	no	no	yes	no	yes	no
F6	yes	no	no	no	yes	yes	no
[0 1 6 7]	no	no	no	no	yes	yes	no

FIGURE 6.29 Table of scales and constraints.

	Number of yeses	*Scales*	*Chords*
prototypical	7	diatonic	
	6	pentatonic	
	5	octatonic, mystic	
	4	whole-tone	maj/min triad, dom7/Tristan
	3	hexatonic	aug triad, dim7, F6
atypical	2		[0 1 6 7]

FIGURE 6.30 Typicality rating of the scales and chords in Figure 6.29.

(and its extension, the dominant-seventh or Tristan chord), followed by the augmented triad, the diminished-seventh and the French-sixth chords, and finally [0 1 6 7]. One could list any number of other pc sets as hypothetical scales or chords, but because they would meet virtually none of these preferences they would be poor candidates for levels of basic spaces.

Three patterns in Figure 6.29 deserve special comment. First, two of the three unique scales, the diatonic and pentatonic, do not express complete transpositional cycles, which would inevitably lead to duplication of directed intervals within a scale, but represent contiguous segments of $0{*}7^{12}$. They close their cycles by deviating one ic from ic5: ic6 for the diatonic, ic4 for the pentatonic. Similarly, the only unique chords in the list are the major/minor triad and its extension into seventh chords. Note that in all cases uniqueness and the almost-half criterion go together. This is because 7 and 5 are not divisors of 12, nor are 3 and 4 of 7; as a result, the larger number partitions unequally, creating unique directed intervals. Second, the criterion of two intervallic generators is powerful in the sense that it yields a complete list of the most regular scale types: diatonic, pentatonic, octatonic, hexatonic, and whole-tone. This list appropriately excludes the seven-note mystic scale. But the included hexatonic scale, while regular, is atypical in other respects. This circumstance explains why, despite its formal similarities to the octatonic scale (see the previous section), it is often disregarded in discussions of scales. Third, all the chords fail the small-step criterion. If they did not, their adjacent pcs would be too attracted to one another to coexist as stable verticalities. On the contrary, adjacent pcs in chords are preferably no smaller than a minor third, so as to avoid roughness. In preferred basic tonal spaces, the scalar level encourages attractions and the chordal level avoids roughness. (For a somewhat different comparison of scales, see Clough, Engebretsen, and Kochavi 1999.)

Tonal attractions in chromatic spaces

Tonal attractions behave in chromatic spaces just as they do in diatonic space, adjusting for differences in the spaces themselves. To illustrate, Figure 6.31a repeats (from Figure 4.20) triadic/diatonic basic space with the fifth level omitted and with anchoring strengths included. Beneath are the calculations of the melodic attraction rule for diatonic-scale pitches to their superordinate and equal neigh-

a)

Anchoring strength												
4	0											
3	0				4			7				
2	0		2		4	5		7		9		11
1	0	1	2	3	4	5	6	7	8	9	10	11

$\alpha_{tr/dia}(p11 \rightarrow p0) = {}^4/_2 \times {}^1/_{1^2} = {}^4/_2 = 2$

$\alpha_{tr/dia}(p5 \rightarrow p4) = {}^3/_2 \times {}^1/_{1^2} = {}^3/_2 = 1.5$

$\alpha_{tr/dia}(p2 \rightarrow p0) = {}^4/_2 \times {}^1/_{2^2} = {}^4/_8 = 0.5$

$\alpha_{tr/dia}(p2 \rightarrow p4) = {}^3/_2 \times {}^1/_{2^2} = {}^3/_8 = 0.375$

$\alpha_{tr/dia}(p5 \rightarrow p7) = {}^3/_2 \times {}^1/_{2^2} = {}^3/_8 = 0.375$

$\alpha_{tr/dia}(p9 \rightarrow p7) = {}^3/_2 \times {}^1/_{2^2} = {}^3/_8 = 0.375$

$\alpha_{tr/dia}(p9 \leftrightarrow p11) = {}^2/_2 \times {}^1/_{2^2} = {}^2/_8 = 0.25$

b)

0											
0							7				
0		2		4			7		9		
0	1	2	3	4	5	6	7	8	9	10	11

$\alpha_{5th/pent}(p2 \rightarrow p0) = {}^4/_2 \times {}^1/_{2^2} = {}^4/_8 = 0.5$

$\alpha_{5th/pent}(p9 \rightarrow p7) = {}^3/_2 \times {}^1/_{2^2} = {}^3/_8 = 0.375$

$\alpha_{5th/pent}(p2 \leftrightarrow p4) = {}^2/_2 \times {}^1/_{2^2} = {}^2/_8 = 0.25$

$\alpha_{5th/pent}(p9 \rightarrow p0) = {}^4/_2 \times {}^1/_{3^2} = {}^4/_{18} = 0.22$

$\alpha_{5th/pent}(p4 \rightarrow p7) = {}^3/_2 \times {}^1/_{3^2} = {}^3/_{18} = 0.17$

c)

Anchoring strength												
4	0											
3	0				4			7				
2	0	1		3	4		6	7		9	10	
1	0	1	2	3	4	5	6	7	8	9	10	11

$\alpha_{tr/oct}(p1 \rightarrow p0) = {}^4/_2 \times {}^1/_{1^2} = {}^4/_2 = 2$

$\alpha_{tr/oct}(p3 \rightarrow p4) = {}^3/_2 \times {}^1/_{1^2} = {}^3/_2 = 1.5$

$\alpha_{tr/oct}(p6 \rightarrow p7) = {}^3/_2 \times {}^1/_{1^2} = {}^3/_2 = 1.5$

$\alpha_{tr/oct}(p9 \leftrightarrow p10) = {}^2/_2 \times {}^1/_{1^2} = {}^2/_8 = 1$

$\alpha_{tr/oct}(p10 \rightarrow p0) = {}^4/_2 \times {}^1/_{2^2} = {}^4/_8 = 0.5$

$\alpha_{tr/oct}(p6 \rightarrow p4) = {}^3/_2 \times {}^1/_{2^2} = {}^3/_8 = 0.375$

$\alpha_{tr/oct}(p9 \rightarrow p7) = {}^3/_2 \times {}^1/_{2^2} = {}^3/_8 = 0.375$

$\alpha_{tr/oct}(p3 \leftrightarrow p1) = {}^2/_2 \times {}^1/_{2^2} = {}^2/_8 = 0.25$

d)

0											
0				4			7				
0			3	4			7	8			11
0	1	2	3	4	5	6	7	8	9	10	11

$\alpha_{tr/hex}(p11 \rightarrow p0) = {}^4/_2 \times {}^1/_{1^2} = {}^4/_2 = 2$

$\alpha_{tr/hex}(p3 \rightarrow p4) = {}^3/_2 \times {}^1/_{1^2} = {}^3/_2 = 1.5$

$\alpha_{tr/hex}(p8 \rightarrow p7) = {}^3/_2 \times {}^1/_{1^2} = {}^3/_2 = 1.5$

$\alpha_{tr/hex}(p3 \rightarrow p0) = {}^4/_2 \times {}^1/_{3^2} = {}^4/_{18} = 0.22$

$\alpha_{tr/hex}(p4 \leftrightarrow p7) = {}^3/_3 \times {}^1/_{3^2} = {}^2/_{18} = 0.11$

$\alpha_{tr/hex}(p8 \leftrightarrow p11) = {}^3/_3 \times {}^1/_{3^2} = {}^2/_{18} = 0.11$

(Continued)

FIGURE 6.31 Seven basic spaces with anchoring strengths and applications of the melodic attraction rule for scale pitches to their superordinate and equal neighbors.

bors (repeated from Figures 4.21 and 4.26a). The values are arranged in order of descending attraction. Figures 6.31b–g do likewise for fifth/pentatonic space, triadic/oct space, triadic/hex space, Tristan/oct space, F6/oct space, and F6/wt space. (If the octatonic scale were represented beginning with a major rather than a minor second, the strongest attraction would be $\alpha(p11 \rightarrow p0)$.)

Figure 6.32 puts all these values in a table in order to bring out attractional similarities and differences among spaces. Triadic/diatonic space displays a rather smooth distribution of attractional values, from $\alpha(p11 \rightarrow p0) = 2$ down to $\alpha(p9 \leftrightarrow p11) = 0.25$. Triadic/octatonic space is similar in this regard, for the scalar level again comprises half and whole steps. Triadic/hexatonic space, by contrast, shows a big gap in the middle of its attractional distribution, caused by its alternation of large and small scale steps. Thus, despite the formal affinities between

e)

Anchoring strength												
4	0											
3	0			3			6				10	
2	0	1		3	4		6	7		9	10	
1	0	1	2	3	4	5	6	7	8	9	10	11

$\alpha_{Tris/oct}(p1 \rightarrow p0) = {}^4/_2 \times {}^1/_{1^2} = {}^4/_2 = 2$

$\alpha_{Tris/oct}p4 \rightarrow p3) = {}^3/_2 \times {}^1/_{1^2} = {}^3/_2 = 1.5$

$\alpha_{Tris/oct}(p7 \rightarrow p6) = {}^3/_2 \times {}^1/_{1^2} = {}^3/_2 = 1.5$

$\alpha_{Tris/oct}(p9 \rightarrow p10) = {}^3/_2 \times {}^1/_{1^2} = {}^4/_{12} = 1.5$

$\alpha_{Tris/oct}(p1 \leftarrow\!\!\rightarrow p3) = {}^3/_2 \times {}^1/_{2^2} = {}^3/_8 = 0.375$

$\alpha_{Tris/oct}(p4 \leftarrow\!\!\rightarrow p6) = {}^3/_2 \times {}^1/_{2^2} = {}^3/_8 = 0.375$

$\alpha_{Tris/oct}(p10 \rightarrow p0) = {}^4/_3 \times {}^1/_{2^2} = {}^4/_{12} = 0.33$

$\alpha_{Tris/oct}(p7 \rightarrow p9) = {}^3/_3 \times {}^1/_{2^2} = {}^4/_{12} = 0.25$

f)

Anchoring strength												
4	0											
3	0				4		6				10	
2	0	1		3	4		6	7		9	10	
1	0	1	2	3	4	5	6	7	8	9	10	11

$\alpha_{F6/oct}(p1 \rightarrow p0) = {}^4/_2 \times {}^1/_{1^2} = {}^4/_2 = 2$

$\alpha_{F6/oct}(p3 \rightarrow p4) = {}^3/_2 \times {}^1/_{1^2} = {}^3/_2 = 1.5$

$\alpha_{F6/oct}(p7 \rightarrow p6) = {}^3/_2 \times {}^1/_{1^2} = {}^3/_2 = 1.5$

$\alpha_{F6/oct}(p9 \rightarrow p10) = {}^3/_2 \times {}^1/_{1^2} = {}^4/_{12} = 1.5$

$\alpha_{F6/oct}(p10 \rightarrow p0) = {}^4/_3 \times {}^1/_{2^2} = {}^4/_{12} = 0.33$

$\alpha_{F6/oct}(p1 \leftarrow\!\!\rightarrow p3) = {}^2/_2 \times {}^1/_{2^2} = {}^4/_{12} = 0.25$

$\alpha_{F6/oct}(p4 \rightarrow p6) = {}^3/_3 \times {}^1/_{2^2} = {}^4/_{12} = 0.25$

$\alpha_{F6/oct}(p7 \rightarrow p9) = {}^2/_2 \times {}^1/_{2^2} = {}^4/_{12} = 0.25$

g)

Anchoring strength												
4	0											
3	0				4		6				10	
2	0		2		4		6		8		10	
1	0	1	2	3	4	5	6	7	8	9	10	11

$\alpha_{F6/wt}(p2 \rightarrow p0) = {}^4/_2 \times {}^1/_{2^2} = {}^4/_8 = 0.5$

$\alpha_{F6/wt}(p2 \rightarrow p4) = {}^3/_2 \times {}^1/_{2^2} = {}^3/_8 = 0.375$

$\alpha_{F6/wt}(p8 \rightarrow p6) = {}^3/_2 \times {}^1/_{2^2} = {}^3/_8 = 0.375$

$\alpha_{F6/wt}(p8 \rightarrow p10) = {}^3/_2 \times {}^1/_{2^2} = {}^3/_8 = 0.375$

$\alpha_{F6/wt}(p10 \rightarrow p0) = {}^4/_3 \times {}^1/_{2^2} = {}^4/_{12} = 0.33$

$\alpha_{F6/wt}(p6 \rightarrow p4) = {}^3/_3 \times {}^1/_{2^2} = {}^3/_{12} = 0.25$

FIGURE 6.31 (Continued)

triadic/octatonic and triadic/hexatonic spaces, from an attractional perspective they are rather dissimilar. Triadic/hexatonic attractions more resemble those of F6/octatonic space, which also shows a gap between strong and weak stepwise attractions, this time caused by large and small adjacencies at the chordal level. Tristan/octatonic space shares its strongest attractions with F6/octatonic space, but its weaker attractions spread out more like triadic/octatonic space. The greatest contrast is between triadic/diatonic and triadic/octatonic spaces on the one hand and F6/wt space on the other. Because its scale steps are all major seconds, the attractions in F6/wt space are both weak and similar to one another; hence its bland quality. Fifth/pentatonic space, despite the formal closeness between the diatonic and pentatonic scales, is close to F6/wt space in its lack of strong attractions, again because it includes no minor seconds. Yet the distribution of attractions within fifth/pentatonic space is quite even. Fifth/pentatonic attractions are a weak version of triadic/diatonic attractions.

value	*tr/dia*	*5th/pent*	*tr/oct*	*tr/hex*	*Tris/oct*	*F6/oct*	*F6/wt*
2.0	11→0		1→0	11→0	1→0	1→0	
1.5	5→4		3→4 6→7	3→4 8→7	4→3 7→6 9→10	3→4 7→6 9→10	
1.0			9<-->10				
0.5	2→0	2→0	10→0				2→0
0.375	2→4 5→7 9→7	9→7	6→4 9→7		1<-->3 4<-->6		2→4 8→6 8→10
0.33					10→0	10→0	10→0
0.25	9<-->11	2<-->4	3<-->1		7<-->9	1<-->3 4<-->6 7<-->9	6<-->4
0.22		9<-->0		3→0			
0.17		4→7					
0.11				4<-->7 8<-->11			

FIGURE 6.32 Table of attraction values for the seven basic spaces in Figure 6.31.

Nondiatonic stepwise attractions bear on Cohn's (1997) neo-Riemannian treatment of the triad that employs the P, R, and L transformations (see "Empirical Issues" in chapter 2 and "Constructing Chromatic Spaces" earlier in this chapter). As he demonstrates, the triad is unique among trichords in its parsimonious voice leading, by which is meant that [0 3 7] alone transforms into (inversions of) itself by keeping two pcs stationary and moving the third pc a minor second (P or L) or major second (R). Combinations of these transformations yield not only the octatonic and hexatonic triadic cycles but also many other chromatic progressions. Implicit in this approach is the privileging of minor and major seconds in a system that otherwise ignores all basic-space levels except the chromatic and triadic. From our perspective, the source of this privileging is the high attractional values yielded by these intervals.

Nondiatonic harmonic attractions also adapt easily from the diatonic model. As dictated by the harmonic attraction rule, voice-leading attractions from one chord to another are summed, divided by the harmonic distance value δ for the space in question, and multiplied by a constant (again K = 10, as in "An Attractional Approach to Harmony" in chapter 4). Figure 6.33 gives two examples of realized nondiatonic harmonic attractions, one for a triadic progression in hexatonic space, the other for a Tristan-chord progression in octatonic space. The α values are taken from Figures 6.31d–e, the δ values from Figures 6.14 and 6.21b. (Because the lower voices in Figure 6.33b do not move, this example might be thought of as voice leading within a chord rather than as a harmonic progression; if so, the analysis would terminate with the α_{rvl} value.) The semitonal voice leading in both progressions leads to high attraction values, as is customary in highly chromatic tonal music.

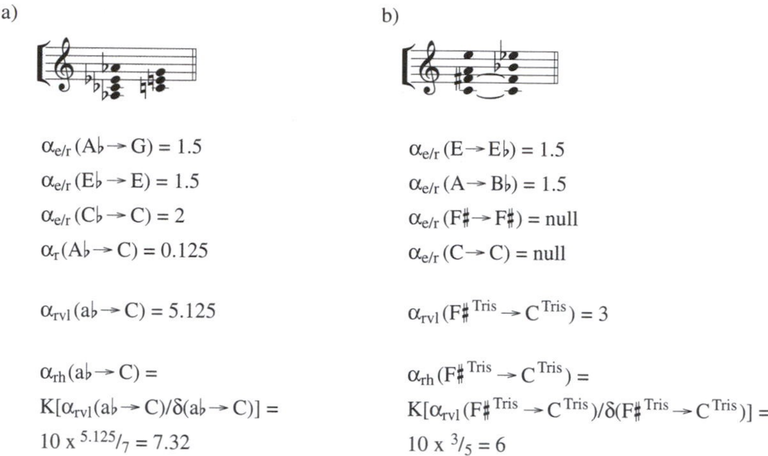

FIGURE 6.33 Realized harmonic attractions for two nondiatonic progressions: (a) a♭→C in triadic/hexatonic space; (b) F♯/Tristan→C/Tristan in Tristan/octatonic space.

Finding the preferred space

Granted the variety of spaces presented in this chapter, how does the listener infer the relevant space from the musical surface? The problem is comparable to establishing a metrical structure. In both cases, the task is done by pattern matching with respect to a limited repertory of possibilities. The best match is the one with the fewest violations between the surface and the repertory of available structures.

The following examples illustrate briefly how this process works. Along lines presented in GTTM, Figure 6.34 gives a simple rhythm accompanied by two possible metrical grids. To bring out the parallelism with space finding, the grid is inverted from its customary representation in GTTM. This makes it look like the stress grids employed in generative phonology (Liberman and Prince 1977; Hayes 1989; Halle and Lerdahl 1994). The two metrical rules triggered by this passage are to prefer a metrical structure in which strong beats align with the inception of relatively long events (that is, of relatively long interonset intervals) and to prefer parallel grids for parallel groups. The grid in Figure 6.34a meets

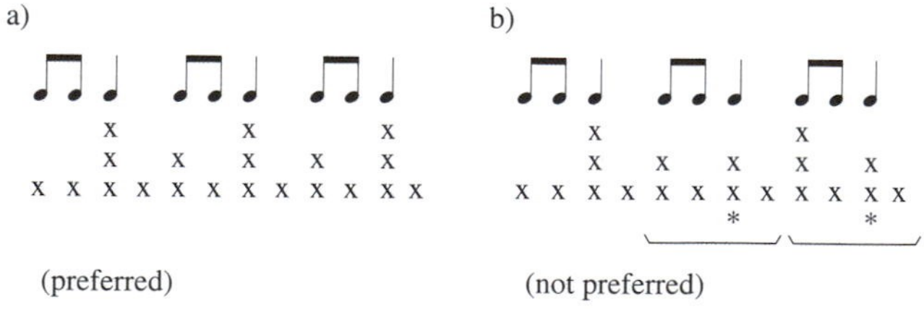

FIGURE 6.34 Pattern matching for establishing the preferred metrical grid.

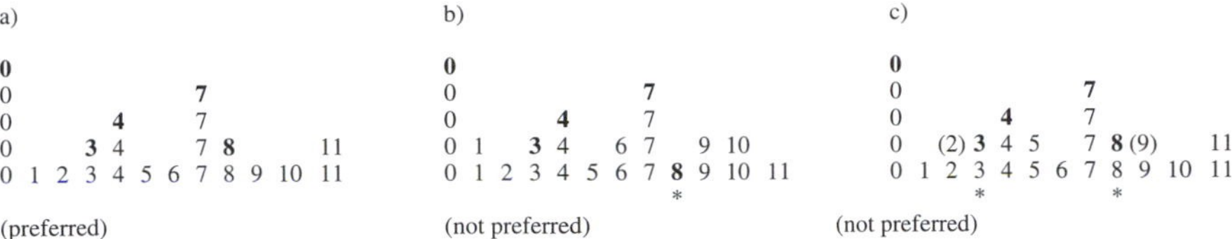

FIGURE 6.35 Pattern matching for establishing the preferred basic space, given the melodic sequence C→D♯→E→G→A♭.

both demands. The grid in Figure 6.34b fails to do so in four places: at the asterisks, the longer quarter notes fall on weaker beats; at the brackets, the repeated motive is not matched by parallel metrical structures. Other possibilities, such as a triple meter at the eighth-note level, would cause still more violations. The best match is Figure 6.34a, and it is the inferred structure.

Just as a style has a repertory of acceptable meters, so it has a repertory of acceptable spaces. Assume that the repertory includes exactly the scales and chords in Figure 6.29. The task is to find from that repertory the space that best matches the pitches given in the musical surface. For example, suppose that the melodic sequence C→D♯→E→G→A♭ appears in a way that projects the context of a C major triad. What is the preferred scalar level? The hexatonic possibility in Figure 6.35a places all the pitches in question at their highest possible locations, as indicated by the pitches in boldface. In other words, the hexatonic interpretation results in no violations. The octatonic possibility in Figure 6.35b succeeds until the A♭, which lies outside the putative octatonic collection. Consequently A♭ must be accessed at the chromatic level and is marked by an asterisk, indicating a single violation. Figure 6.35c interprets the pitches in terms of an inflected C major diatonic scale with $\sharp\hat{2}$ and $\flat\hat{6}$; this contortion would be plausible only if the surrounding context were diatonic. These two inflections count as two violations, so this configuration is still less preferred. Other possibilities would cause other violations. The hexatonic space wins.

GTTM treats the assignment of metrical structure as if one grid sufficed for an entire piece. While this holds for many Classical pieces, it is more accurate to say that the preferred metrical grid is generated and updated in the course of listening. There is metrical inertia once a grid is inferred; but if the pattern of phenomenal accents changes substantially, a different metrical grid may come into play. These considerations pertain to basic spaces as well. In the Classical idiom, triadic/diatonic space is the only basic space available. The listener seeks the best match—the preferred chordal/regional interpretation—between the surface and the possible configurations of the space. But in an idiom capable of projecting more than one tonal space, there is a prior step. The listener must generate an optimal fit between the surface and the repertory of available spaces. Again parallel to the metrical case, once a space is selected, subsequent events tend to be heard in terms of it, even in the face of increasing violations. But if a better match can be obtained by switching spaces, one does so in order to obtain a more stable interpretation. (David Temperley's [1997] harmony-finding rule deals with a comparable situation by assigning a penalty for a change of chordal root; the penalty is overridden only if a new root offers sufficiently fewer violations.)

Finding the preferred space can be viewed as taking the shortest path if, in the geometrical mapping, access to a basic space is taken through the tip of the pc cone. The pc at the tip is most stable, hence the point of entry to a space. In an optimal fit, pcs at the musical surface appear as close as possible to the tip. Thus in all cases in Figure 6.35, pcs 0, 4, and 7 are high up, reflecting the C major chordal context. Pc8 appears at the scale level in Figure 6.35a, but it is down at the chromatic level in Figure 6.35b and is inflected from the chromatic level in Figure 6.35c. Hence Figure 6.35a represents the shortest uninflected distance from the tip to all the presented pcs. In space-finding as well as in chord- and tonic-finding, computations take the shortest path.

Measuring interspatial distances

Beginning with Liszt and Wagner, space-switching, which I shall refer to as "hypermodulation," becomes idiomatic. A mechanism is needed for assigning distance values from one kind of space to another. The method presented earlier in this chapter—redefining the chord- and region-cycle rules using intervals that exhaust the transpositional possibilities and plugging the new versions into the original chord distance rule—is not feasible here. Within a space, the same scale or chord moves to another position. Across spaces, the scale- or chord-type changes.

One way to measure interspatial distances is to tally mismatchings of the structural features listed in Figure 6.29. A small number means that two structures are closely related, a large number that they are distantly related. The results, displayed in Figure 6.36, are credible, although one might quibble with this or that

a)

	dia	*pent*	*oct*	*hex*	*wt*	*mys*
dia	0					
pent	1	0				
oct	2	3	0			
hex	4	3	2	0		
wt	3	3	1	3	0	
mys	2	3	4	4	5	0

b)

	triad	*dom7*	*aug*	*dim7*	*F6*	*[0167]*
triad	0					
dom7	0	0				
aug	3	3	0			
dim7	3	3	0	0		
F6	5	5	2	2	0	
[0167]	6	3	3	1	0	0

FIGURE 6.36 Triangular matrix of nonmatching of features in Figures 6.29 between (a) pairs of scales and (b) pairs of chords.

particular weighting. The exercise suggests how abstract and various some of our intuitions about scalar and chordal relations are. The next step is to add scalar and chordal distances from Figures 6.36a and 6.36b, respectively, to determine overall interspatial distance, or δ_{is}. For example, δ_{is}(aug/hex→aug/wt) = hex-to-wt mismatch + aug-to-aug mismatch = 3 + 0 = 3; δ_{is}(tr/oct→[0167]/oct) = 0 + 6 = 6; δ_{is}(tr/dia→F6/oct) = 2 + 5 = 7. Yet even if the numbers turn out to correlate with listeners' judgments, the approach seems unsatisfactory, for it relates general properties rather than specific spatial configurations, and its factors have little to do with the distance rules employed for determining distances within regions.

The alternative approach adopted here is to consider spatial proximity as a form of similarity. The issue then resembles that of similarity between atonal pc sets, except that the latter do not have stratified structures in the sense of a basic space. Individual levels of contrasting basic spaces can nevertheless be compared. Atonal theory's standard similarity measures express degrees of total pc and ic commonality between sets (Forte 1973). In this pitch-space theory, pc commonality is represented negatively by variable *k* in δ: the more distinctive pcs between two scales or chords, the less similar and hence the more distant they are. There is no parallel to ic commonality, however. Variables *i* and *j* count the number of transpositional steps as determined by the region- and chord-cycle rules. These factors do not alter, much less compare, ic content. What then is the interspatial analogue to variables *i* and *j?*

Ic commonality in atonal theory usually relies on a comparison of one set's ic vector—its total number of instances for each ic—to that of another set. For example, a major or minor triad has no instances of ic1 or ic2, one each of ic3, ic4, and ic5, and none of ic6; so its interval vector is [001110]. Similarly, the ic vector of the dominant-seventh chord—or, equally, its inversion, the Tristan chord—is [012111]. The number of differences between the two sets of numbers—in this case, 0 + 1 + 1 + 0 + 0 + 1 = 3—can be taken as a measure of their similarity (with adjustments for comparisons between pc sets of differing cardinality; see Morris 1980). Such tabulations are probably more relevant for chords, which occur in different spacings and inversions, than for scales, for which the total ic content is perceptually less salient than the content of stepwise intervals. For instance, the ic vectors of the diatonic and octatonic scales are highly contrasting—[254361] for the diatonic, [448444] for the octatonic—in reflection of their respective asymmetrical and symmetrical constructions. But in another sense the two scales are alike in that they both comprise half and whole steps, a similarity that allows composers such as Stravinsky to move smoothly between the two.

Ic vectors may in any case be at too fine-grained a level of description to account for judgments of ic commonality. It is less crucial that the dominant-seventh chord has one more ic3 than the triad than that it has two ics, ic2 and ic6, that the triad lacks. Similarly, it matters less that the whole-tone scale has one more major second than the diatonic scale than that it does not have any minor seconds. The presence or absence of an ic is perceptually more important than its number of instances.

a)

	dia	*pent*	*oct*	*hex*	*wt*	*mys*
m2	yes	no	yes	yes	no	yes
M2	yes	yes	yes	no	yes	yes
m3	no	yes	no	yes	no	no

b)

	dia	*pent*	*oct*	*hex*	*wt*	*mys*
dia	0					
pent	2	0				
oct	0	2	0			
hex	2	2	2	0		
wt	1	1	1	3	0	
mys	0	2	0	2	1	0

c)

	dia	*pent*	*oct*	*hex*	*wt*	*mys*
dia	0					
pent	3	0				
oct	1	3	0			
hex	3	3	3	0		
wt	2	2	2	4	0	
mys	1	3	1	3	2	0

FIGURE 6.37 Comparison of step intervals in the scales from Figure 6.29: (a) presence or absence of step intervals for each scale; (b) matrix of pairwise differences in (a); (c) for nonidentical scales, addition of 1 to each of the values in (b).

Taking these observations together, I propose to measure intervallic commonality simply by comparing the presence or absence of ics for chords and of adjacent intervals for scales. Figure 6.37 carries out this procedure for the scales in Figure 6.29, Figure 6.38 for the chords in Figure 6.29. To achieve some standardization in the range of values between scales and chords, Figure 6.37c adds a constant of 1 to the scalar values in Figure 6.37b. Another reason for adding this constant is to prevent a value of 0 between nonidentical scales: even though steps in the diatonic, octatonic, and seven-note mystic scales may all be minor and major seconds, the scales in fact differ. In this accounting, the diatonic and octatonic scales, for example, resemble each other, and both are dissimilar to the hexatonic scale, which has minor thirds instead of major seconds. The triad resembles the dominant-seventh chord and augmented triad but is quite unlike the F6 and [0 1 6 7] chords. Dominant sevenths and F6 chords are rather similar. These results tie in with the similarities and differences in attractions between scalar neighbors displayed in Figure 6.32. Scales that possess the same step intervals project similar stepwise attractional patterns, with all the expressive power that degrees of attraction bring. Attractions between the nonstepwise intervals tabulated in ic vectors, by contrast, have little force.

Although this method is different in kind from counting transpositional steps, it acts somewhat like variables i and j in δ, in the very general sense that it measures a degree of change in a spatial configuration at both the scalar and

a)

	triad	*dom7*	*aug*	*dim7*	*F6*	*[0167]*
ic1	no	no	no	no	no	yes
ic2	no	yes	no	no	yes	no
ic3	yes	yes	no	yes	no	no
ic4	yes	yes	yes	no	yes	no
ic5	yes	yes	no	no	no	yes
ic6	no	yes	no	yes	yes	yes

b)

	triad	*dom7*	*aug*	*dim7*	*F6*	*[0167]*
triad	0					
dom7	2	0				
aug	2	4	0			
dim7	3	3	3	0		
F6	4	2	2	3	0	
[0167]	4	4	4	3	4	0

FIGURE 6.38 Comparison of chords from Figure 6.29: (a) presence or absence of ics for each chord; (b) matrix of pairwise differences in (a).

chordal levels. Variable *k*, representing pc noncommonality, remains as before. The following formula for interspatial distance thus bears some resemblance to that for intraspatial distances:

INTERSPATIAL DISTANCE RULE (first version) $\delta_{is}(x^{chord}/x^{scale} \rightarrow y^{chord}/y^{scale}) = (sc + 1) + ch + k$, where $\delta_{is}(x^{chord}/x^{scale} \rightarrow y^{chord}/y^{scale})$ = the distance between x^{chord}/x^{scale} and y^{chord}/y^{scale}; *sc* = the number of differences in the presence or absence of adjacent intervals between x^{scale} and y^{scale}; *ch* = the number of differences in the presence or absence of ics between x^{chord} and y^{chord}; and *k* = the number of distinctive pcs in the basic space of y^{chord}/y^{scale} compared to the basic space of x^{chord}/x^{scale}. (The motivation for adding 1 to *sc* was explained earlier.)

Figure 6.39 illustrates δ_{is} for a few cases within the framework $C^{chord}/\mathbf{C}^{scale}$ (that is, some chord-type with root C and some scale-type root C as tonic). The *sc* + 1 and *ch* values are taken from Figures 6.37c and 6.38b, respectively. In the first two cases the chord does not change, so *ch* = 0. In Figure 6.39a, *sc* + 1 = 1, and *k* = 4, as indicated by the underlined pcs in the space. In Figure 6.39b, *sc* + 1 = 3 and *k* = 2. Hence $\delta_{is}(C^{tr}/\mathbf{C}^{dia} \rightarrow C^{tr}/\mathbf{C}^{oct})$ and $\delta_{is}(C^{tr}/\mathbf{C}^{dia} \rightarrow C^{tr}/\mathbf{C}^{hex})$ both equal 5. In Figure 6.39c, the small move $C^{tr}/\mathbf{C}^{dia} \rightarrow C^{5th}/\mathbf{C}^{pent}$ brings the low value of 3. If the distance measurement were reversed, however, there would be more distinctive pcs because triadic/diatonic space has more members and levels than fifth/pentatonic space; the relation is not symmetrical. The other cases treat distances to chords outside of triadic/diatonic space. In Figures 6.39d–e, the combinations of *sc* and *k* values lead both $\delta_{is}(C^{tr}/\mathbf{C}^{dia} \rightarrow C^{F6}/\mathbf{C}^{oct})$ and $\delta_{is}(C^{tr}/\mathbf{C}^{dia} \rightarrow C^{F6}/\mathbf{C}^{wt})$ to equal 12. This relatively high value for chords and regions that do not move out of the orbit C/**C** results from the combination of substantial chordal and scalar changes.

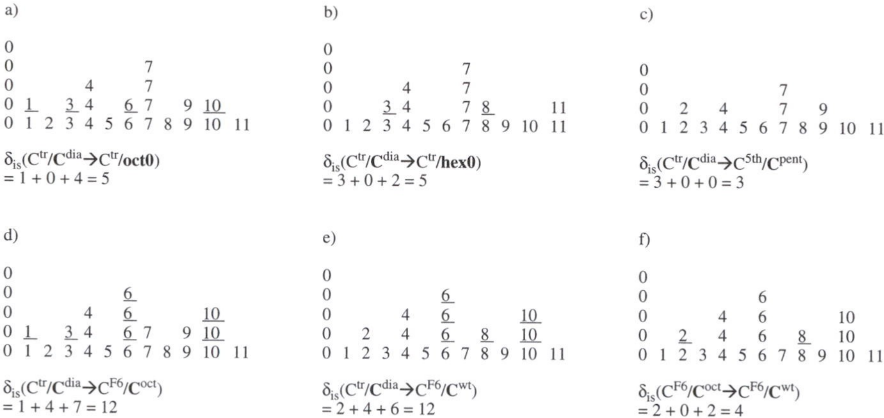

FIGURE 6.39 Applications of the first version of the interspatial distance algorithm within the framework C^{chord}/C^{scale}.

In Figure 6.39f, the retention of the same chord plus a relatively small change in scale results in a low distance value.

What happens if the measurement is to a chord with a different root or to another scale with a different tonic? In these cases, variables i and j must be reinstated; until now they have equaled 0. The full rule becomes:

INTERSPATIAL DISTANCE RULE (final version) $\delta_{is}(x^{chord}/x^{scale} \rightarrow y^{chord}/y^{scale}) = (sc + 1) + ch) + (i + j) + k$, where δ_{is}, sc, ch, and k are as before; i = the number of applications of the y^{scale} region-cycle rule to move the tonic orientation of x^{scale} to the tonic orientation of y^{scale}; and j = the number of applications of either the y^{chord} intraregional chord-cycle rule or the corollary to the y^{chord} chord distance rule (as the case may be) to move the root of x^{chord} to the root of y^{chord}.

Figure 6.40a–b illustrates the full version of δ_{is} without changing chord-type, so that $ch = 0$. In Figure 6.40a, $sc + 1 = 1$ (from Figure 6.37c); $i = 0$; and, by the octatonic intraregional chord-cycle rule, $j = 1$ in the transpositional step for

a)

3
3 10
3 7 10
0 1 3 4 6 7 9 10
0 1 2 3 4 5 6 7 8 9 10 11

$\delta_{is}(C^{tr}/C^{dia} \rightarrow Eb^{tr}/oct0)$
$= (1 + 0) + (0 + 1) + 9 = 11$

b)

7
2 7
2 7 11
1 2 4 5 7 8 10 11
0 1 2 3 4 5 6 7 8 9 10 11

$\delta_{is}(C^{tr}/C^{dia} \rightarrow G^{tr}/oct1)$
$= (1 + 0) + (1 + 1) + 7 = 10$

c)

3
3 9
1 3 7 9
1 3 5 7 9 11
0 1 2 3 4 5 6 7 8 9 10 11

$\delta_{is}(C^{tr}/C^{dia} \rightarrow E\flat^{F6}/wt1)$
$= (2 + 4) + (1 + 1) + 8 = 16$

FIGURE 6.40 Applications of the final version of the interspatial distance algorithm.

$C^{tr} \rightarrow E\flat^{tr}$. In Figure 6.40b, again $sc + 1 = 1$, $i = 1$ for **oct0→oct1**, and $j = 1$ by the corollary to the octatonic chord distance rule. In Figure 6.40c, $sc + 1 = 2$ and $ch = 4$ (from Figure 6.38b); $i = 1$ for **wt0→wt1**; and $j = 1$ by the corollary to the whole-tone chord distance rule (which, though not stated earlier, is parallel to the octatonic and hexatonic cases). This combination, in conjunction with k, leads to a high overall value, or a large distance between C^{tr}/**C**^{dia} and $E\flat^{F6}$/**wt1**.

These instances demonstrate the conceptual necessity of including not only variables sc and ch but variables i and j as well. The former variables measure the change in scale- and chord-type; the latter count transpositions of a scale-tonic or of a chord-root. Yet even with these distinctions, the proposed mechanism for measuring interspatial distances remains tentative. There is little empirical evidence to guide theory (Bruner [1984] is an exception). Moreover, outside of specific musical contexts, intuitions about interspatial distances are bewildering. Compare δ_{is}(C^{tr}/**C**^{dia}→G^{tr}/**oct1**) = 10 and δ_{dia}(I/**C**→I/**G**) = 7 (Figures 6.40b and 2.18b, respectively). G^{tr}/**oct1** is surely further from C^{tr}/**C**^{dia} than G^{tr}/**G**^{dia} is, but do these numbers accurately represent the right amount of difference? Is δ_{is}(C^{tr}/**C**^{dia}→$E\flat^{F6}$/**wt1**) = 16 (Figure 6.40c) really the same as δ_{dia}(I/**C**→I/**E**) = 16 (Figure 2.27), even though the latter is hardly the greatest distance possible in triadic/diatonic space? Maybe yes, in the sense that the structure of diatonic tonality generates more regions, hence greater possible distances, than do the structures of chromatic tonality. Debussy cannot modulate as far away from a tonic as Schubert can.

In the absence of empirical or reliable intuitive criteria, we are thrown back on purely theoretical criteria. I have opted for a relatively simple solution that incorporates what I believe to be the most relevant factors and presents them in a manner consistent with the diatonic theory, which itself rests on firm intuitive and empirical grounds.

A METRICAL ANALOGY

Formal parallelisms

I suggested earlier that finding a preferred space and finding a preferred metrical grid involve similar pattern-matching processes. Now I wish to pursue further the analogy between space and grid, as an extended digression that draws on themes developed in this and earlier chapters. After discussing formal parallelisms, I develop an approach to metrical attractions that may have some bearing on Christopher Hasty's (1997) concerns about the nonprocessive character of metrical grids.

The well-formedness conditions for basic spaces (see "Related Issues" earlier in this chapter) all have metrical counterparts. Just as pcs are abstractions of pitches by virtue of octave equivalence (condition 1), so beats form beat classes because of temporal periodicities. The equal intervals between adjacent pcs at the lowest level (condition 2a) are paralleled by equal intervals at the tactus and commonly at nearby metrical levels as well; this is GTTM's MWFR 4. However, in contrast to the formulation for basic spaces, the tactus is rarely the lowest metrical level. The parallel would be more complete if basic spaces were permitted a possibly irregular microtonal "inflectional level" below the chromatic level; this is a stylistic option beyond the purview of this volume. (Some idioms, such as Balkan dance music, alternate two and three subtactus beats at the tactus level. In these cases MWFR 4 does not apply. Temperley and Daniel Sleator [1999] suggest that even in quasi-regular contexts this metrical condition should be preferential rather than well formed, so as to accommodate tempo fluctuations. But from a well-formedness perspective, tempo fluctuations are mentally quantized, so that at a cognitive level quasi-regular spacing is indeed equal. In this respect, tempo fluctuations are like intonational variations in performance; cognitive adjustments are made for both in service of the operative mental representation.)

The relation between pcs at lower and higher levels (condition 2b) corresponds to the requirement that a beat at a higher level also be a beat at lower levels; this is GTTM's MWFR 2. The relative stability of pcs at higher pitch-space levels (condition 2c) is analogous to stronger beats at higher metrical levels. The reductional format of a basic space (condition 2d) is reflected in the stipulation that strong beats be two or three beats apart; this is GTTM's MWFR 3. Finally, unlike pitch-reductional trees, spaces and grids do not represent constituent hierarchies; that is, their elements do not belong to one or the other adjacent superordinate element but are just subordinate within their contexts. A consequence of all these parallelisms is that the representations for a basic space and a metrical grid, abstracting away from pc numbers on the one hand and from dots (or x's) on the other, have a similar appearance—especially when, as in Figure 6.34, the metrical grid is oriented with its fastest level at the bottom and its slowest one at the top.

Most of the preferential conditions for basic spaces have metrical analogues, too. The most robust ones follow from the metrical well-formedness requirement that strong beats be two or three beats apart. Thus the preference for almost half the pcs at level L + 1 compared to those at L (preferential condition 2) has a metrical correlate in triple relations between metrical levels and in combinations of duple and triple relations between levels. In the case of straight duple relations between levels, the "almost" must be dropped. Maximal evenness (condition 3) is fulfilled by duple or triple relations between levels or by a combination of them. The scalar preference for steps no larger than a major second (condition 7) roughly corresponds to the preference that strong beats at metrical level L + 1 be no more than three beats apart at L (according to MWFR 3, this is a well-formedness requirement). One tends, for example, to hear a $\frac{5}{8}$ bar as divided into 2 + 3 or 3 + 2 rather than as a single span with one strong beat and four weak ones.

The scalar preference for unique directed intervals (condition 4) is where space and grid part company, at least in Western tonal music, which favors equally spaced beats at all levels. Perhaps this is the case because if a grid is simple in the horizontal dimension, it organizes more easily into many levels in the vertical dimension. Vertical metrical depth, which is a stylistic characteristic of Classical tonal music, supports multileveled harmonic rhythms. Such symmetry is less fruitful if carried out in a pitch space. Figure 6.41 gives two pairs of symmetrical, isomorphic spaces and grids. The grid in Figure 6.41a represents a standard $\frac{3}{4}$ meter; its spatial counterpart is the aug/wt space in Figure 6.41b. Similarly, the

a)

x												(x)
x				x				x				(x)
x		x		x		x		x		x		(x)
x	x	x	x	x	x	x	x	x	x	x	x	(x)

b)

0												(0)
0				4				8				(0)
0		2		4		6		8		11		(0)
0	1	2	3	4	5	6	7	8	9	10	11	(0)

c)

x												(x)
x						x						(x)
x			x			x			x			(x)
x	x	x	x	x	x	x	x	x	x	x	x	(x)

d)

0												(0)
0						6						(0)
0			3			6			9			(0)
0	1	2	3	4	5	6	7	8	9	10	11	(0)

FIGURE 6.41 Isomorphic spaces and grids with completely symmetrical structures: (a) $\frac{3}{4}$ metrical grid; (b) aug/wt basic space; (c) $\frac{12}{8}$ grid; (d) tritone and diminished-seventh chord space.

grid in Figure 6.41c represents a $\frac{12}{8}$ meter; its spatial counterpart is a diminished-seventh chord bisected by a tritone, shown in Figure 6.41d. Even in Liszt or Scriabin it would be rare to find a combination of augmented triads and whole-tone scales, or a combination of tritones and diminished-seventh chords, without some additional complication. Western tonal music tends toward symmetrical grids but asymmetrical spaces.

The absence of harmony and counterpoint in many non-Western idioms, by contrast, leaves the horizontal aspects of their meters and rhythms free to develop in complex ways. Such is the case with North Indian and sub-Saharan African drum musics. African music, in particular, favors horizontally asymmetrical rhythmic constructions such as those in Figure 6.42. As pointed out by Jeff Pressing (1983) and Jay Rahn (1983), the second metrical level from the bottom in Figure 6.42a corresponds to the diatonic scale in Figure 6.42b. The equivalent level in Figure 6.42c corresponds to the pentatonic scale in Figure 6.42d. The durational realizations above the grids bring out these patterns, which can begin elsewhere in a cycle, creating quasi-modal variants. The two levels above the scale levels are less certain, however. The presented upper levels are to some extent implied by the durational patterns, and they yield well-formed grids. Alternatives for Figure 6.42a are the assignment of a regular meter with strong beats three eighths apart, creating a $\frac{12}{8}$ grid, or four eighths apart, creating a $\frac{3}{2}$ grid. According to D. Locke (1982), the $\frac{12}{8}$ interpretation, shown in Figure 6.42e, is the preferred one among practitioners of the idiom. Unlike Figure 6.42a, which changes bar lengths in order to align attack points with relatively strong beats, Figure 6.42e sets up a syncopated relationship between the irregular rhythms and the regular grid. Either way, the top levels in both Figure 6.42a and 6.42e give the cyclic strongest beat.

The grid representations in Figures 6.42a and 6.42c place the diatonic and pentatonic beat levels in a full hierarchical context. The criteria of almost-halving, maximal evenness, and uniqueness are met by these grids. The two-step criterion—condition (5) of the preferential conditions on basic spaces—is also met except at the third level of Figure 6.42a. The alternative interpretation in Figure

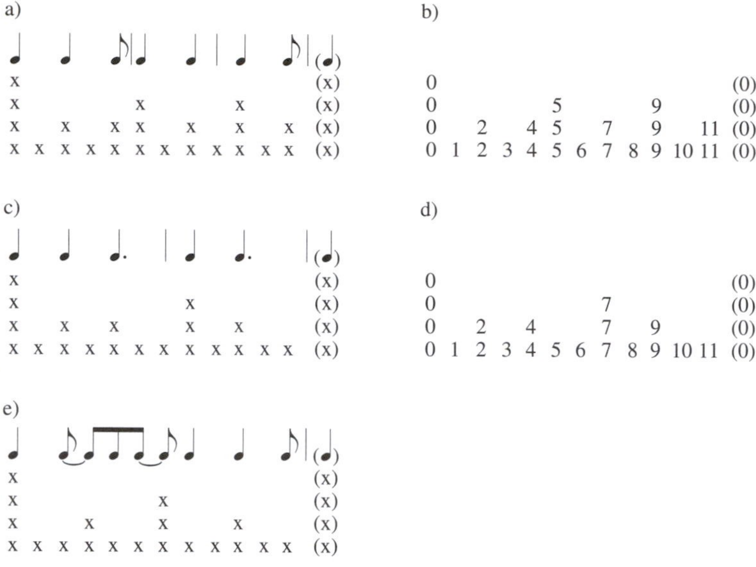

FIGURE 6.42 Isomorphism between preferred scales and characteristic West African rhythmic cycles: (a) is the metrical equivalent to the diatonic space in (b); (c) is the metrical equivalent to the pentatonic space in (d); (e) is the $\frac{12}{8}$ syncopated interpretation for the rhythmic pattern in (a).

6.42e retains uniqueness and two-stepness not as a metrical but as a rhythmic construct. As Balzano (1982) has argued for the diatonic and pentatonic scales, the prevalence of these rhythmic patterns presumably has arisen from their inherent potential for cognitive structuring. The appearance of identical pitch and rhythmic structures in unrelated cultures provides potent evidence for the psychological generality of the preferential constraints that lie behind them.

Metrical attractions

The formal similarities between space and grid suggest the development of a model of metrical attractions. Metrical attractions, however, are harder to conceptualize than tonal attractions. One reason is that intuitions about tonal attraction interfere with intuitions about a beat's metrical attraction. A second reason lies in the novelty of the idea of metrical attractions. In developing the theory of tonal pitch space, I have been guided by empirical data as well as by three centuries of pitch-space models in the music-theoretic literature. In developing a model of tonal attractions, I have drawn on a tradition in music theory even if as yet there is little empirical evidence. For a theory of metrical attractions, there is neither. I proceed entirely by analogy and intuition, in the hope that my ideas will lead to something revealing about musical behavior.

The basic intuition behind the notion of metrical attractions is that weak beats tend toward successive strong beats more than strong beats do toward successive

																		Anchoring strength
L(2):	x																(x)	3
L(1):	x								x								(x)	2
L(0):	x				x				x				x				(x)	1
L(-1):	x		x		x		x		x		x		x		x		(x)	0.5
L(-2):	x	x	x	x	x	x	x	x	x	x	x	x	x	x	x	x	(x)	0.33

FIGURE 6.43 A $\frac{4}{4}$ metrical grid with anchoring strengths.

weak beats. (Perhaps this is a motivation for Riemann's [1903] insistence on the upbeat-to-downbeat character of all phrase groupings.) A rhythmic figure stopping on the fourth beat of $\frac{4}{4}$, say, feels incomplete because there is a felt need to continue into the following downbeat. If the figure ends on the downbeat, however, there is less need to continue to the following weak beat, for the downbeat is relatively stable. As with tonal attractions, these metrical tendencies can also be stated in terms of expectations or implications (Narmour 1977, 1990).

The melodic attraction rule adapts to metrical attractions as follows. First, pitches exist in states of virtual attraction that are or are not realized, but meter exists in time. A pitch can be attracted to the left or the right in the basic space, but beats seem to be attracted only to the right (however, see later in this section). Let us provisionally restrict any beat attraction to the next adjacent beat at a given metrical level. Second, let us set the anchoring strength of the tactus metrical level, designated L(0), at 1, as shown in Figure 6.43. This step is needed because, unlike the case of the chromatic scale for tonal music, there is no a priori smallest metrical level; the smallest level can always subdivide. A referential value is needed, and it seems reasonable to give it to the tactus. By analogy with the anchoring strengths for the basic space in Figure 4.20, let the anchoring strengths of the next larger levels be L(1) = 2 and L(2) = 3; similarly, L(−1) = ½ and L(−2) = ⅓. The attraction of one metrical beat to the next is then proportional to the ratio of their anchoring strengths.

As long as beats at a given level are equidistant, it is not necessary to add the factor of distance between beats. The shape of the grid itself takes the distances into account and provides the requisite variations in attractional values. Hence,

METRICAL ATTRACTION RULE (short version) $\alpha(b_x \rightarrow b_{x+1}) = {}^{S_{x+1}}/_{S_x}$, where $\alpha(b_x \rightarrow b_{x+1})$ = the attraction of b_x to b_{x+1}; b_x and b_{x+1} are adjacent beats at the same metrical level; and s_x = the anchoring strength of b_x and s_{x+1} = the anchoring strength of b_{x+1} in the metrical grid.

If a given level has irregularly spaced beats, however, normally a combination of two and three, a distance variable needs to be included, again with attraction and distance in an inversely proportional relation. Unlike the case of tonal attractions, there does not seem to be any advantage here in squaring the distance:

METRICAL ATTRACTION RULE (full version) $\alpha(b_x \rightarrow b_{x+1}) = {}^{s_{x+1}}/_{s_x} \times {}^1/_r$, where $\alpha(b_x \rightarrow b_{x+1})$ = the attraction of b_x to b_{x+1}; b_x and b_{x+1} are adjacent beats at the same metrical level; s_x = the anchoring strength of b_x and s_{x+1} = the anchoring strength of b_{x+1} in the metrical grid; and r = the ratio of a beat's span to its normal span.

If a beat is three subbeats apart instead of the referential two, $r = 3/2$. Because of inverse proportionality, the effect is to weaken the attraction to the next stronger beat by $2/3$. If a beat is two subbeats apart in the context of three, $r = 2/3$ and the attraction to the next stronger beat increases by $3/2$. As these examples suggest, in the short version $r = 1$ tacitly, so that the second part of the equation equals 1 and can be ignored. The full version closely resembles the form of the melodic attraction rule. Quantificational modifications maybe required depending on future empirical results, but it is the explanatory factors that really matter. As with tonal attractions, these factors are stability (strength of beat in the metrical case) and proximity (time-span proximity in the metrical case).

Figure 6.44 applies the short version of the rule to some basic meters. Although standard note values are included for reference, it should be kept in mind that it is the attractions between beats, rather than between events, that is at issue. So long as a beat is inferred, it can be filled even by silence, as, for example, in the first movement of Beethoven's *Eroica* Symphony, bars 100–102, 124–131, 280, and so forth. A tie of an event into a strong beat can have a similar effect, as in the syncopated anticipation at the reprise in the "Ode to Joy" theme in the Finale of Beethoven's Ninth Symphony. In such cases, one might speak of an event as having an associated virtual metrical attraction to the following strong beat.

Beats in Figure 6.44 are given numerical subscripts corresponding to their tactus metrical positions. Since an attraction a beat apart at the same level equals 1, an attractional value more than 1 counts as relatively strong and a value less than 1 counts as relatively weak. The graphic plotting shows the attraction of b_x to b_{x+1} as located at b_{x+1}, but in actuality an attractional value expresses a relation between two beats. The changing directions and heights of the line convey the changing states of attraction. Figure 6.44a begins with $\frac{2}{4}$ and its elementary alternation between two attractional states. In the $\frac{3}{4}$ meter in Figure 6.44b, the rule says that b_1 is weakly attracted to b_2, b_2 neutrally to b_3, and b_3 strongly to b_1.

The picture becomes a little more complicated once a third metrical level is introduced. In the $\frac{4}{4}$ meter in Figure 6.44c, one should imagine a moderate tempo, so that the tactus remains at the quarter-note level. The first set of calculations, graphed by the solid line, shows oscillating but slightly asymmetrical attractions because of the differing attractional pulls of b_1 and b_3 in relation to b_2 and b_4. The second set of calculations, graphed by the dashed line to indicate that it is not the tactus level, shows a weaker, symmetrical oscillation between b_1 and b_3. Although the pattern of x's is the same for b_1 and b_3 in Figure 6.44c as it is for b_1 and b_2 in Figure 6.44a, in Figure 6.44c the attractional differences are less extreme, for the beats in question do not include the tactus. As a result, the ratio in question is not 2:1 but a smaller 3:2. But if Figure 6.44a is elaborated by an

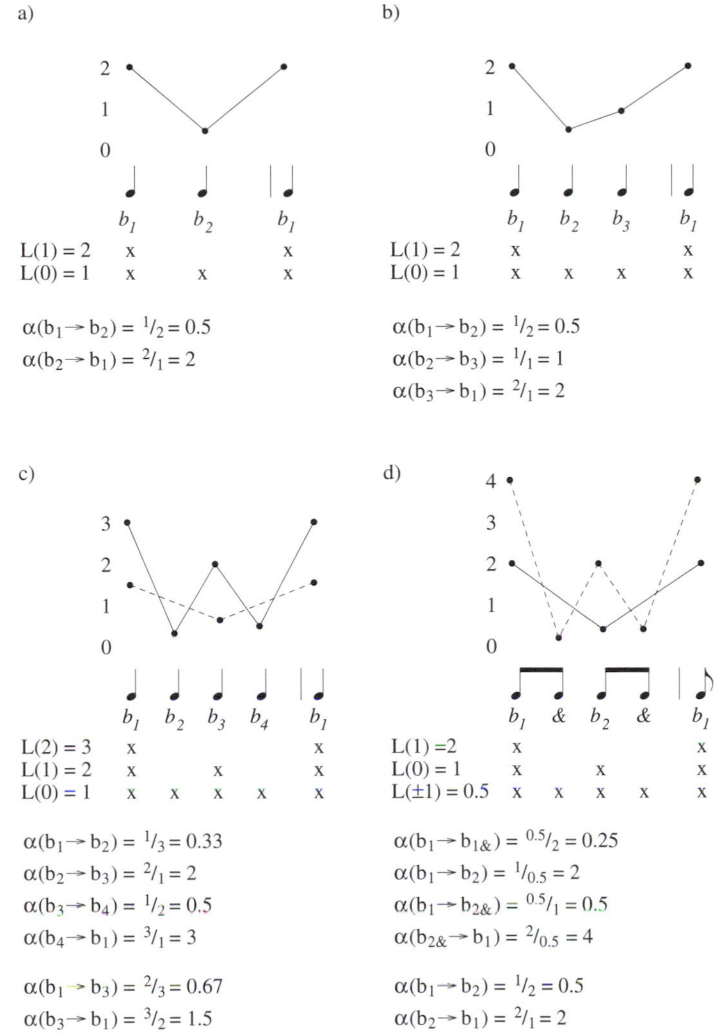

FIGURE 6.44 Some applications of the short version of the metrical attraction rule.

eighth-note level, as in Figure 6.44d, the tactus becomes the middle rather than the bottom level, and the ratio between b_1 and b_2 stays at 2:1.

Figure 6.45 applies the complete metrical attraction rule to a $\frac{5}{8}$ (2 + 3) meter (for notational convenience, the beats are numbered at the eighth-note level). For all beat lengths except one, there is no deviation from the normal span, so r = 1. However, for the second tactus beat (that is, b_3), r = 3/2. Therefore, the attraction of b_3 to following b_1 decreases by 2/3. The relevant comparison here is to b_2 and b_1 at the quarter-note level of $\frac{2}{4}$ in Figure 6.44d. There, $\alpha(b_2 \rightarrow b_1) = 2$; here $\alpha(b_3 \rightarrow b_1) = 1.33$. The temporal expansion causes a weaker attraction.

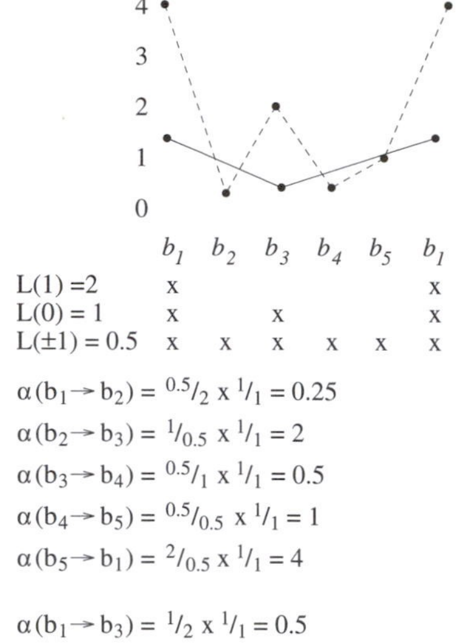

$\alpha(b_1 \rightarrow b_3) = {}^{1}/_{2} \times {}^{1}/_{1} = 0.5$

$\alpha(b_3 \rightarrow b_1) = {}^{2}/_{1} \times {}^{1}/_{3/2} = 1.33$

FIGURE 6.45 Application of the complete metrical attraction rule to a $\frac{5}{8}$ (2 + 3) meter.

The distance factor in the metrical attraction rule has bearing on swing rhythms in jazz, in which eighth notes on the beat are played somewhat longer than eighth notes on the "and" of beats. John Ito (1998) finds that variations in swing timing are surprisingly large. Hence it would not help to try to add extra microlevels of beats in the analysis. The effect of swing, rather, is to increase the attraction of the weak eighth to the following stronger beat. For instance, if the weak eighth occurs not at a "straight" halfway point across the quarter-note span but two-thirds of the way across, its attraction to the following stronger beat increases by three halves. Similarly, in a marchlike pattern of dotted eighths and sixteenths in the Baroque or Classical style, it seems fussy to add both subtactus eighth- and sixteenth-note levels (unless there is a texture of running eighth or sixteenth notes in other voices). Rather, the sixteenths feel like greatly delayed weak eighth notes, and the effect is one of propulsive attraction to the following strong beat.

Interaction of tonal and metrical attractions

Let us now apply the tonal and metrical attraction rules to the opening phrase of the third movement of Mozart's Piano Concerto no. 19, K. 459, given in Figure 6.46 together with its grouping and metrical analyses. The grouping and motivic structure forms a simple sentence. The meter is a straightforward $\frac{2}{4}$, with running eighth notes and the tactus at the quarter-note level. This is the pattern of Figure 6.44d. Although one might wish to posit a two-bar metrical level for a passage at this quick a tempo, the PR evidence for it is conflicting and effectively cancels this larger level out. (Depending on tempo, the tactus could instead be put at the half-note level. This alternative would make for small variations in the attractional values below.)

FIGURE 6.46 Mozart's Piano Concerto no. 19, K. 459, III, bars 1–4, together with its grouping and metrical analyses.

Roger Graybill (1994) treats this phrase in terms of its prolongational and gestural motions. He equates prolongational motion with Schenkerian reduction and defines gestural motion as motion to and from focal points within groups. He characterizes focal points in terms of both surface salience and metrical strength, more or less as in Cooper and Meyer (1960). Tonal and metrical attractional values go some way toward elucidating what he discusses qualitatively.

Figure 6.47 performs a realized voice-leading attractional analysis for the phrase at the quarter-note level of reduction (the inclusion of the repeated eighth notes would not add anything). To simplify, the filler inner voice is ignored. Figure 4.34 can be consulted for specific values of the melodic attraction rule. The values at the upbeat to bar 4 are calculated locally in relation to C major because of the applied dominant there. The soprano and bass attractions for each sonority sum to yield a single sequence of composite realized attractions. The curve above graphs these summed values. Although the attractional values themselves are

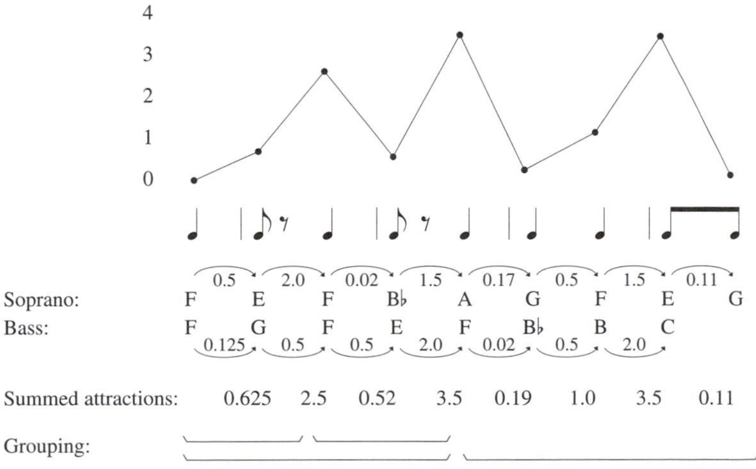

FIGURE 6.47 Tonal attractional analysis of the Mozart phrase.

placed between pitches to suggest their relational meaning, they are plotted on the curve at their points of arrival because, as in Figures 6.44–45, this placement better conveys the attractional ebb and flow. (The initial point on the curve, set to 0, is a convenient fiction.) For our purposes it is unnecessary to extend the analysis to harmonic as well as voice-leading attractions or to underlying prolongational levels.

The pattern in bars 1–2 of Figure 6.47 is one of weak tonal attractions into downbeats and strong attractions across grouping boundaries. The tonal and rhythmic structures are at odds. This pattern reverses with the cadential arrival at bar 4.

Figure 6.48 accomplishes a comparable task for the phrase's metrical attractions, again at the quarter-note level. There is a simple alternation between strong and weak attractions, just as in Figure 6.44a. Calculations at the eighth-note level, if carried out, would correspond to Figure 6.44d and would reflect the greater attractions from upbeat to downbeat caused by the eighth notes.

This regular alternation of strong and weak metrical attractions may indeed be too simple, for it does not take into account the effect of grouping boundaries on attractions. On one hypothesis, a grouping boundary between two beats inhibits the attraction of one to the next; hence the attraction of beat 1 to beat 2 in bars 1–2 would be less than in bar 3, where there is no interfering grouping boundary. Alternatively, it might be hypothesized that a grouping boundary after a weak beat sends its attraction not forward to the next beat but back to the previous strong beat. The Mozart passage provides no instance of this, but one can imagine a $\frac{3}{4}$ meter with a grouping boundary after the second beat, so that the second beat is attracted retroactively to the previous first beat. I incline toward the first over the second hypothesis because I am uncertain about the validity of time-reversing metrical attractions. However, it would be a challenging task to quantify the suppressing effect of grouping boundaries. Either of these possibilities would lend a suppleness to the theory of metrical attractions that at present it does not have and might elucidate aspects of expressive timing in performance.

How do tonal and metrical attractional values interact? When high pitch and high metrical attractions are in phase, there is an increase at attractional points of

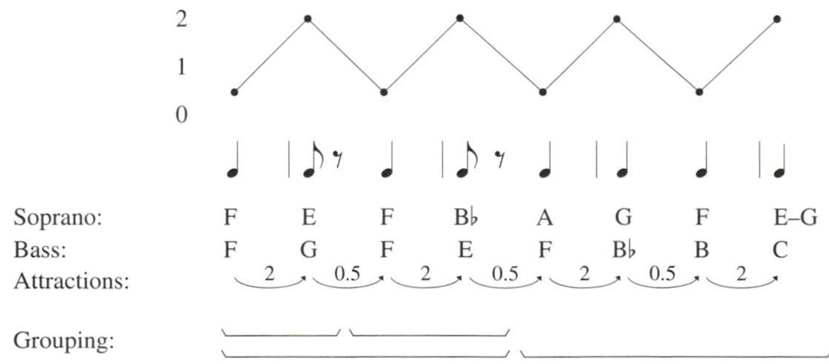

FIGURE 6.48 Metrical attractional analysis of the Mozart phrase.

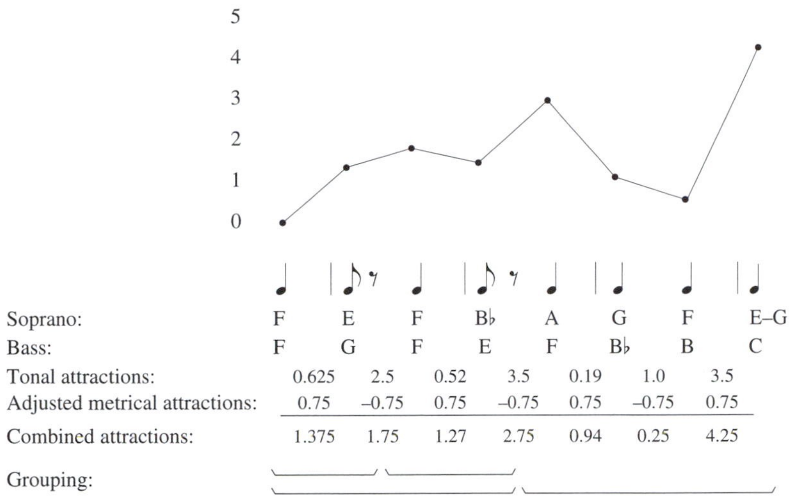

FIGURE 6.49 Combined tonal and metrical attractions.

arrival. This illuminates the pedagogical adage for chorale-writing, "strong progressions into strong beats." Conversely, when high tonal and metrical attractions are out of phase, the effect is to smooth out the competing attractions. The two kinds of attraction thus combine in an additive fashion. But even though the forms of the rules are almost the same, this does not mean that the numbers they produce are comparable. These values have meaning only within their own domains. A scaling coefficient is needed for normalizing the output values of the two kinds of attraction. To effect a provisional solution, Figure 6.49 subtracts 1.25 from each metrical attraction in Figure 6.48, so that the metrical values become 0.75 and −0.75, oscillating around 0. These metrical values add or subtract (as the case may be) from the melodic values in equal amount. The composite attractional curve begins evenly, moving to a high attractional value into the upbeat to bar 3, then dipping and finally cadencing into a still higher attractional value.

Graybill observes that the quarter-note level is metrically ambiguous. In terms of GTTM's metrical preference rules, there is a conflict between placing a downbeat on the event with the longest distance to the following attack point, which gives Mozart's barring, and placing it in phase with the grouping, which gives Graybill's alternative barring in Figure 6.50. Graybill's purpose in doing this is, in our terms, to align the points of tonal and metrical attraction so as to create a strikingly different gestural effect than in the original. The contrast is indeed instructive. Each metrical attraction in Figure 6.49 is reversed by the shifted metrical grid, resulting in the composite attractional curve in Figure 6.51. Each group now begins in a low state of attraction, producing a jagged overall trajectory. Attractions to the downbeats of bar 2 and especially bar 3 are emphasized, and the cadential arrival is underplayed. The shape of this curve is much less smooth than that in Figure 6.49.

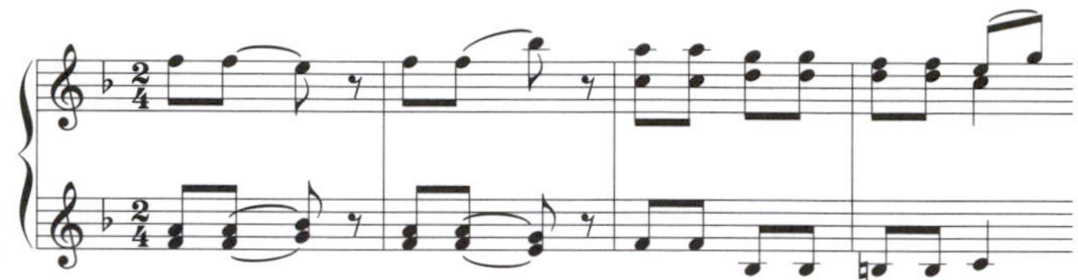

FIGURE 6.50 Rebarring of the Mozart phrase in order to align the points of tonal and metrical attraction.

How do tonal and metrical attractions influence musical performance? On a gravitational analogy, one might suppose that a high attraction would cause a shortening in the microtiming of events. But expressive timing often goes against prevailing tendencies, precisely in order to draw attention to them. In any case, it is unlikely that microtiming would change much in the Mozart phrase, which needs to move at regular pace. The differences in barring between the original and Graybill's alternative (Figures 6.46 and 6.50) are more easily brought out instead by dynamic contrasts, specifically by stressing the downbeats in each case. This suggests one kind of reason for preferring the original barring: the extra stresses fall on events that require attractional resolution, and making them more prominent increases expressivity.

In this connection, Caroline Palmer (1996) finds that in a performance of Mozart's K. 282 relatively strong microdynamics correlate with Narmour's (1996) predictions of low closure. In other words, events in states of high attraction tend to be played louder. Her study also finds that moments of tension, calculated as in Figure 4.17, tend to be played more slowly than moments of relative relaxation.

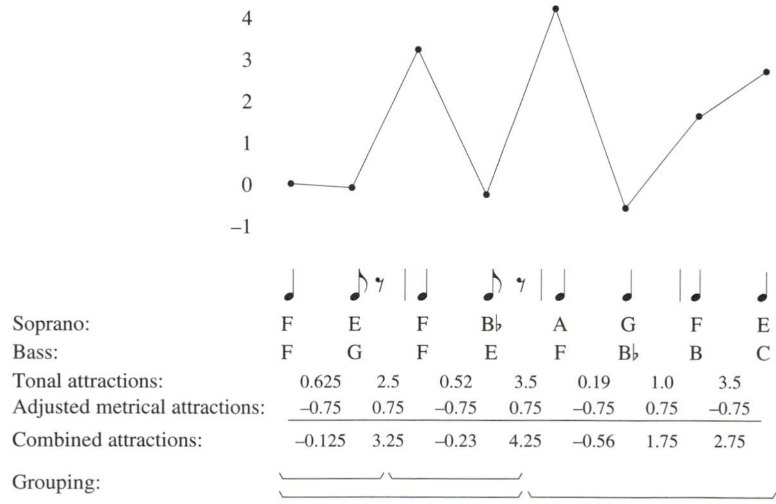

Soprano:	F		E		F		B♭		A		G		F		E
Bass:	F		G		F		E		F		B♭		B		C
Tonal attractions:		0.625		2.5		0.52		3.5		0.19		1.0		3.5	
Adjusted metrical attractions:		–0.75		0.75		–0.75		0.75		–0.75		0.75		–0.75	
Combined attractions:		–0.125		3.25		–0.23		4.25		–0.56		1.75		2.75	
Grouping:															

FIGURE 6.51 Combined tonal and metrical attractions for the rebarred version.

Both of these tendencies magnify points of intensity, making them more salient, and they appear to make a difference between an expressive performance and an inexpressive one. It will be interesting to see how well these factors correlate for a variety of performers, pieces, and musical styles.

In closing this section, it should be noted that the search for pitch-rhythm analogies is a recurring theme of twentieth-century music. Henry Cowell (1930) and Karlheinz Stockhausen (1957) observe that beats and pitches both arise from periodic vibrations, the one giving way to the other at around 20–25 Hz. They advocate durations and tempi in ratios equivalent to those of justly tuned intervals. Perceptually, however, there is a huge qualitative difference between pitch intervals and durational or tempo proportions. The analogy is merely conceptual. Similar problems attend the attempts of midcentury serialists (such as Babbitt 1962 and Boulez 1966) to map pitch or interval numbers onto rhythmic relationships. Their approach to musical time lacks a notion of the metrical grid and its interaction with grouping structure, as well as the relevant notion of pitch space, and their resulting mappings are cognitively opaque (see Lerdahl 1988a for related discussion).

Although I hope that the ideas sketched here will prove useful to composers, my immediate objective is a cognitive rather than a compositional one. This pitch-meter analogy arises from constructs, the basic space and the metrical grid, that are independently motivated and that have empirical support. That they look so much alike is a consequence of deep cognitive properties, expressed theoretically in such terms as reductional formats, maximal evenness, halving, and uniqueness. That these constructs permit a common approach to attractional intuitions brings them out of the realm of formalism and into the world of music as experienced.

7 *Prolongations in Chromatic Spaces*

ANALYSES OF TRIADIC CHROMATIC TONAL MUSIC

Some passages in Wagner

We are now in a position to apply chromatic spaces to actual music. Concepts and procedures from earlier chapters—prolongations, paths, tension curves, attractions, functions—transfer to these chromatic contexts.

Figure 7.1a repeats from Figure 3.50 the passage from *Parsifal* in which Klingsor's motive modifies the diatonic Grail motive. Figure 3.51 considers this progression as a chromatic transformation of diatonic space. From another perspective, however, the descending major-thirds progression takes place in triadic/hexatonic space. Following Lewin (1984, 1987), Cohn (1996) treats the passage with neo-Riemannian techniques. In this framework, the progression's chordal/regional path is the one in Figure 7.1b: E♭→b→G→e♭ in **hex3** space, then a hypermodulation to diatonic space, with the e♭ triad pivoting as diatonic ii/**D♭**. The **D♭** region is situated arbitrarily in relation to **hex3**. Distances values from chord to chord accompany the arrows. The values within **hex3** are taken transposed from Figure 6.15; the values within **D♭** are the usual diatonic ones. The shape of the path reflects the sense of the progression: full symmetry within **hex3**, followed by clear directionality in **D♭**.

The reinterpretation of the e♭ triad from hexatonic to diatonic space also involves a distance measurement by the interspatial distance rule. In Figure 7.2 the *ch*, *i*, and *j* variables = 0 because the chord is the same; *sc* + 1 = 3 (from Figure 6.37c); and *k* = 4 because of the changes at the scale level. The resulting distance

a)

b)

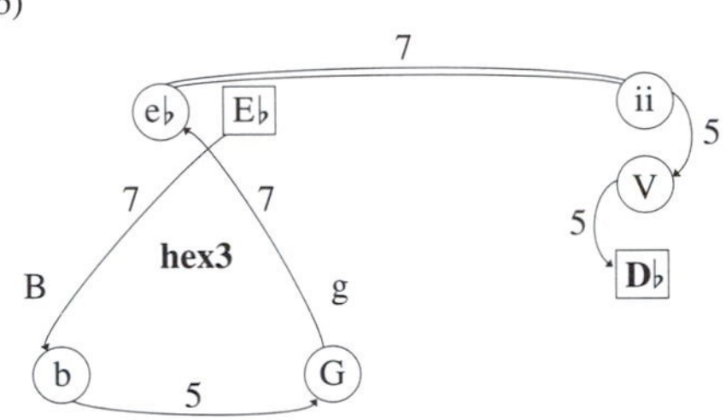

FIGURE 7.1 Triadic/hex space: (a) the combined Grail/Klingsor motive from Act III of *Parsifal* (repeated from Figure 3.50); (b) its chordal/regional path with distance values included.

of 7 represents the pivot shift. That the value assigned to this pivot is so high is a reflection of the cognitive effort to achieve reorientation from one space to the other.

Figure 7.3 provides a prolongational, functional, and tensional analysis of the Grail motive, first in its original diatonic version (transposed to **E♭** for comparison), then in the combined Grail/Klingsor version given in Figure 7.1. The progression in Figure 7.3a shows a standard realization of normative prolongational structure with accompanying functions. The progression in Figure 7.3b modulates from **E♭** to **D♭** as a result of the hexatonic transformation. In this limited context, **E♭** and **D♭** are assumed to be hierarchically equal; hence the top node does not express right or left branching. The tree shows a weak prolongation from the opening to the e♭ triad in bar 2 (weak because of the shift from major to minor). Consequently, the G triad functions not just as a second departure, as does its A♭ equivalent in Figure 7.3a, but as a return. The e♭ triad receives two branches for its double spatial location, e♭/**hex3** and ii/**D♭**. Each location has its own function, T for e♭/**hex3** and S for ii/**D♭**. Except for the complications in bar 2 of Figure 7.3b, the overall prolongational and functional assignments for Figures 7.3a and 7.3b are identical. In particular, Figure 7.3b keeps T at both ends of its trajectory. This functional correspondence

			3								
			3							10	
			3			6				10	
		2	3			6	7			10	11
0	1	2	3	4	5	6	7	8	9	10	11

			3								
			3							10	
			3			6				10	
0	1		3		5	6		8		10	
0	1	2	3	4	5	6	7	8	9	10	11

$$\delta_{is}(e\flat^{tr}/\mathbf{hex3}\rightarrow ii/\mathbf{D\flat}) = (3+0)+(0+0)+4=7$$

FIGURE 7.2 Distance computation for the pivoting e♭ triad from Figure 7.1.

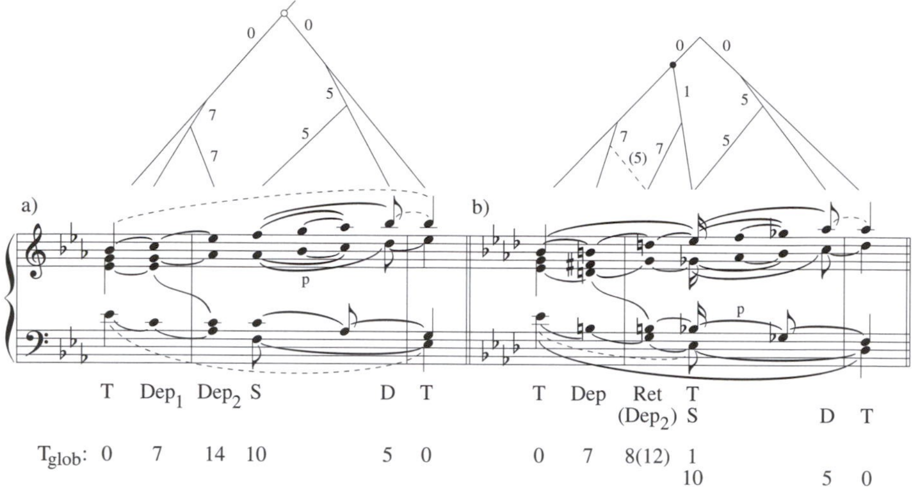

FIGURE 7.3 Prolongational, functional, and tensional analysis of two versions of the Grail motive: (a) diatonic version, transposed to **E♭**; (b) the combined Grail/Klingsor version.

in spite of divergent pitch-space paths contributes to the uncanniness of the chromatically transformed version.

The numbers next to the branches in Figure 7.3 represent δ values. For Figure 7.3a, these values are from δ_{dia}; for Figure 7.3b, they are from δ_{hex} and then from δ_{dia}, just as in Figure 7.1b. Beneath, these values are summed down the branches, using the short version of T_{glob}, to yield tension values for the two progressions. (There is no need to employ the long version of T_{glob}, since the features of surface dissonance are the same in both progressions.)

Figures 7.4a–b graph the tension values for Figures 7.3a–b, respectively. At first Figure 7.4b parallels Figure 7.4a: the tension of E♭→b in hexatonic space equals that of E♭→c in diatonic space. At this point the curves diverge. Figure 7.4a displays a direct tensing–relaxing pattern. In Figure 7.4b, the prolongational return in Figure 7.3b brings about a tensional plateau into the G chord and low tension at the e♭ minor triad. The spatial reinterpretation of the latter event then gives

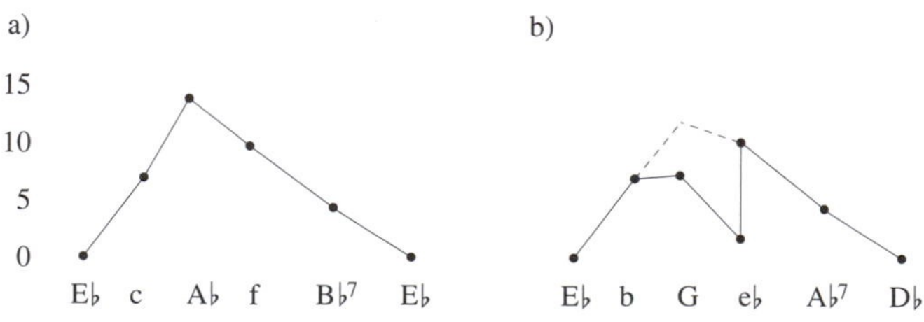

FIGURE 7.4 Graph of tension values for Figure 7.3a–b.

rise to the tensional climax of the phrase. But if a strong sense of transformation from the diatonic model is retained, one might hear the tensional curve shown by the dashed line, in parallel to Figure 7.4a; this curve comes from the values in parentheses in Figure 7.3b. The closing relaxation in both versions is the same.

An attractional analysis of these passages would show higher values in the chromatic version because of its many implied and realized semitonal motions. (See Figure 6.33a for an attractional analysis of a hexatonic thirds-related progression.) The expectations induced by these strong attractions compensate for the absence of the schematic expectations elicited by the diatonic version.

A passage in Act II of *Parsifal*, shown in Figure 7.5a (also discussed in Cohn 1996), has a complex spatial path. The music mixes the Grail motive with an aborted beginning of the Klingsor progression. Parsifal is recovering from Kundry's knowledge-bestowing kiss and in a hallucination struggles between Klingsor's pull and a vision of ritual of the Grail, which he did not comprehend at the end

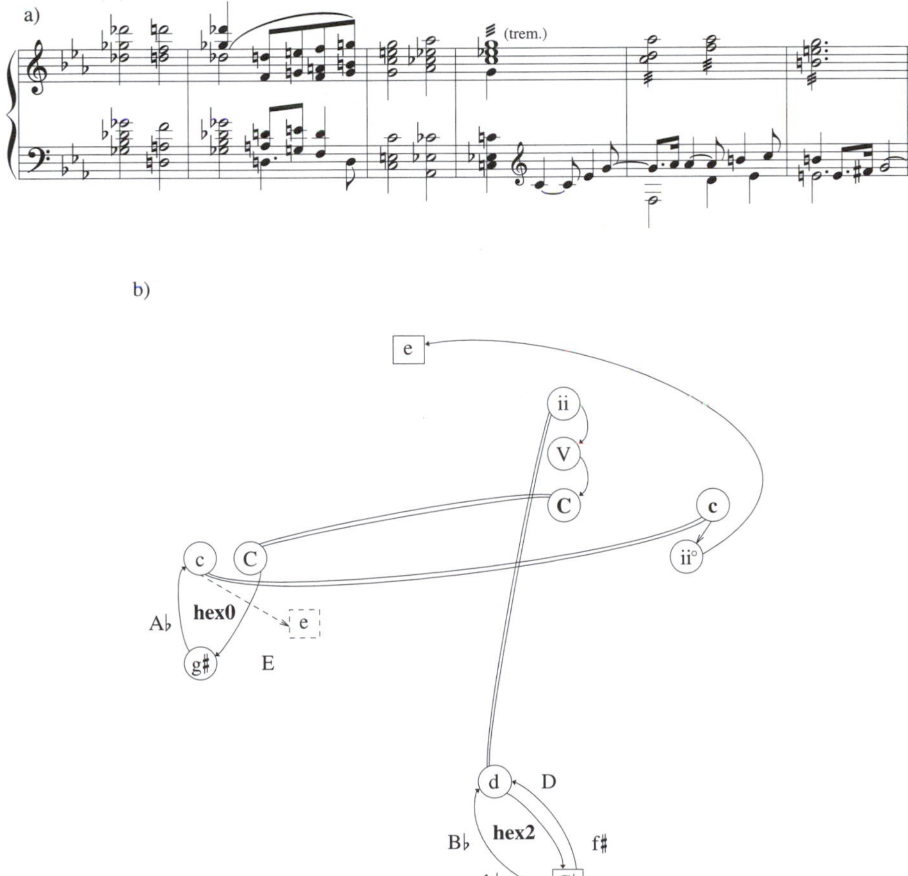

FIGURE 7.5 Pitch-space path for a passage from Act II of *Parsifal*.

of Act I. The pitch-space path, given in Figure 7.5b, represents a modulation within triadic/hexatonic space separated by linking moves into diatonic space, in keeping with the narrative and symbolic dimensions of the drama. The path begins in **hex2**, converts the d triad into ii/**C**, resolves to I/**C**, which then pivots as a C triad in **hex0**, and turns to c/**hex0** = i/**c** as the music evokes the minor-mode statement Communion theme, which also has a hexatonic component as it moves to **e**. The dashed path from c/**hex** to e/**hex** portrays the latter aspect, which would emerge at an immediately underlying prolongational level once the diatonic elements that express **c** reduce out.

There are many examples in Wagner in which surface diatonic features disappear into a triadic/octatonic substratum as a result of sequencing by minor thirds. Figure 3.46 illustrates how the last section of the Act I Prelude of *Parsifal* traverses the regional cycle **A♭→B→d→f→(b♭)→A♭**. A prolongational analysis of this passage would show an underlying progression of local tonic triads for the first three stages of this sequence. Closer to the surface is the same sequence at prolongational level c of the beginning of the Transfiguration in *Tristan*, given in Figure 3.34 (bars 1–4). Figure 7.6 traces this progression as a full clockwise path in **oct2** space. This representation complements the perspective of Figure 3.33, which shows the same underlying progression as a path in horizontally collapsed diatonic regional space.

At various points in *Tristan* the musical surface erupts with cycles of Tristan chords. Figure 7.7a gives an example, the *Sehnen* (longing) motive, which first occurs in Act II just before Tristan and Isolde settle down on the flowery bank. The three Tristan chords repeat those from the beginning of the Act I Prelude in rotated order (compare bars 2, 6, and 10 of Figure 5.13) and resolve, like the first phrase of the Prelude, to V^7/**a(A)**. Insofar as the Tristan chord acts as an altered vii^{o7} (see the discussion in connection with Figures 4.37 and 4.39b), this passage can be seen as an expanded appoggiatura. The plausibility of this view relies on the fact that, as illustrated in Figure 7.7b, the Tristan chords built on the same minor-third cycle resolve, each by a single semitone, to the same diminished-seventh chord (a feature exploited elsewhere in *Tristan*). Here, however, this reading shortchanges the effect of the Tristan chords, which do not resolve at all until the V^7/**a**(**A**). Another interpretation, taken in Figure 7.7c, is to treat the Tristan chords in Tristan/octatonic space, modulating to diatonic space at the E^7 chord. To facilitate the graphing, the tetrahedron structure of a region of Tristan/octatonic space (see Figure 6.22a) is simplified to a square. Each letter

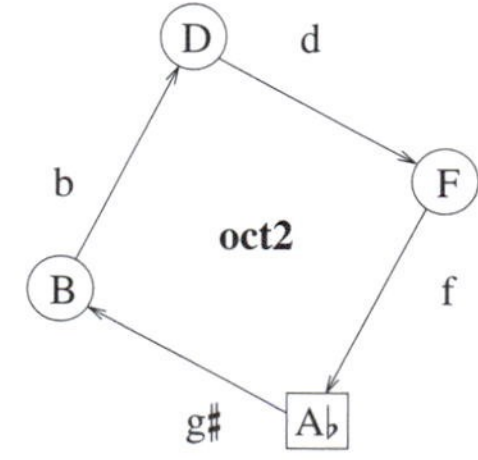

FIGURE 7.6 Triadic/octatonic path for an underlying prolongational level at the beginning of the Transfiguration music from *Tristan*.

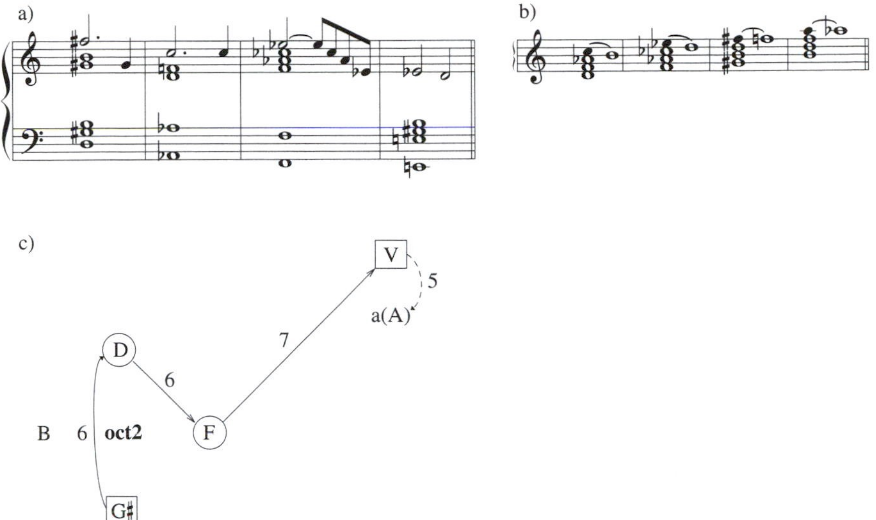

FIGURE 7.7 Analysis of the *Sehnen* motive from Act II of *Tristan*: (a) the motive; (b) voice-leading relationship of minor-third transpositions of the Tristan chord to a diminished-seventh chord; (c) pitch-space path of the motive in Tristan/**oct2** space into diatonic space.

stands for the root (assumed to be the lowest pitch of the chord built up in thirds) of a Tristan chord, and the four roots represent the four Tristan chords within the region. The path moves through A♭→D→F in **oct2** space to V^7/**a**(**A**) in diatonic space. (Because the root of the Tristan chord is ambiguous, the path might instead follow the bass motion, in which case the route would be D→A♭→F in **oct2**.) The δ values, taken from Figure 6.22a for the Tristan chords, accompany the arrows. The dashed arrow for δ(V→i/**a**[**A**]) indicates that even though this resolution does not arrive, the tension of V^7/**a**(**A**) is measured in relation to this goal.

Figure 7.8 computes the move from Tristan/octatonic to dom7/diatonic space. From the tables in Figures 6.37c and 6.38b, *sc* + 1 = 1 and *ch* = 0 (the Tristan chord, though not listed in Figure 6.38b, has the same ic structure as the dominant

					5						
					5						11
			3		5			8			11
0		2	3		5	6		8	9		11
0	1	2	3	4	5	6	7	8	9	10	11

				4							
				4							11
		2		4				8			11
0		2		4	5			8	9		11
0	1	2	3	4	5	6	7	8	9	10	11

$$\delta_{is}(F^{Tris}/\mathbf{oct2} \rightarrow V^7/\mathbf{A}) = (1 + 0) + (0 + 2) + 5 = 8$$

FIGURE 7.8 Distance computation for modulating from Tristan/octatonic to diatonic space in Figure 7.7.

seventh, its inversion). The tonic orientation of **oct2** is taken to be pc9, so $i = 0$. The postulated root of the Tristan chord is two steps away on the cycle of fifths from the root of the dominant seventh, so $j = 2$. The two chords share common pcs except, notably, for the root of the dominant seventh, bringing $k = 5$.

The distances from chord to chord in Figure 7.7 are quite uniform. This, along with the root-ambiguity of the Tristan chord and the symmetry (hence weak hierarchy) of the octatonic collection, makes uncertain the assignment of prolongational structure to the *Sehnen* motive. Perhaps the best solution, one that respects the recursion constraint as well as the 2 + 2 motivic structure of the phrase, is that in Figure 7.9. This reading gives an extended S-function to all the Tristan chords. The resulting tension values, presented at the bottom and again using the short version of T_{glob}, describe the phrase as beginning in great tension and subsiding to a state of low but unresolved tension. This gradual relaxing is reinforced by the surface features of descending tessitura and diminuendo.

If the tension at the beginning of this sequence seems excessive, it is because the spatial and prolongational uncertainties offset the usual effect of the nested left progressions. The weak harmonic motion and prolongational structure are compensated by voice-leading attractions. The realized attractions are undermined by linear octave displacements until the move into the V^7; but if the displacements are removed, at each point two voices remain stationary while two move by semitone. Figure 7.10a illustrates with idealized voice leading. The dashed slurs represent common tones between chords, the solid arrows half-step virtual attractions. These relationships could be computed as full harmonic attractions (see Figure 6.33b for such an accounting, transposed, of the first to the second chord). The root-ambiguities, however, make a summed voice-leading attractional analysis more germane (that is, without factoring in the inverse proportionality of δ). The numbers with the arrows in Figure 7.10a specify the voice-leading values, and Figures 7.10b–c break down how they are determined. Figure 7.10b omits the top level of the attractional basic space for the Tristan chords, in recognition of their perceptual fragility; the top level is reinstated, however, for the unambiguously rooted dominant seventh. Figure 7.10c applies the melodic attraction rule to these spaces. As will be recalled from "An Attractional Approach to Harmony" in chap-

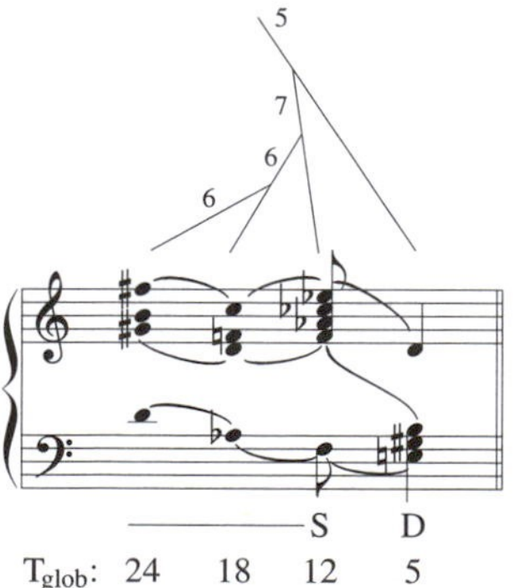

FIGURE 7.9 Prolongational, functional, and tensional analysis of the *Sehnen* motive.

a)

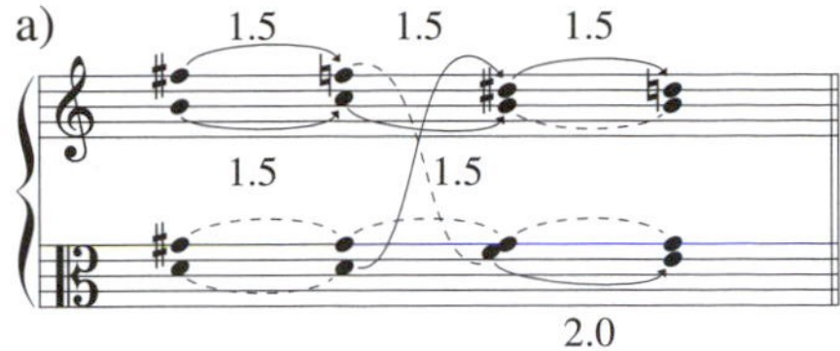

b)

Event 1

		2				6		8			11
0		2	3		5	6		8	9		11
0	1	2	3	4	5	6	7	8	9	10	11

Event 2

0		2			5			8			
0		2	3		5	6		8	9		11
0	1	2	3	4	5	6	7	8	9	10	11

Event 3

			3		5			8			11
0		2	3		5	6		8	9		11
0	1	2	3	4	5	6	7	8	9	10	11

Event 4

				4							
		2		4				8			11
0		2		4	5			8	9		11
0	1	2	3	4	5	6	7	8	9	10	11

c)

Prog(1→2)

$\alpha_{e/r}(F\sharp \rightarrow F) = {}^{3}/_{2} \times {}^{1}/_{1^2} = 1.5$

$\alpha_{e/r}(B \rightarrow C) = {}^{3}/_{2} \times {}^{1}/_{1^2} = 1.5$

$\alpha(G\sharp \rightarrow G\sharp) = \text{null}$

$\alpha(D \rightarrow D) = \text{null}$

$\alpha_{rvl}(1 \rightarrow 2) = 3.0$

Prog(2→3)

$\alpha_{e/r}(D \rightarrow D\sharp) = {}^{3}/_{2} \times {}^{1}/_{1^2} = 1.5$

$\alpha_{e/r}(C \rightarrow B) = {}^{3}/_{2} \times {}^{1}/_{1^2} = 1.5$

$\alpha(G\sharp \rightarrow G\sharp) = \text{null}$

$\alpha(F \rightarrow F) = \text{null}$

$\alpha_{rvl}(2 \rightarrow 3) = 3.0$

Prog(3→4)

$\alpha_{e/r}(D\sharp \rightarrow D) = {}^{3}/_{2} \times {}^{1}/_{1^2} = 1.5$

$\alpha(B \rightarrow B) = \text{null}$

$\alpha(G\sharp \rightarrow G\sharp) = \text{null}$

$\alpha_{e/r}(C \rightarrow B) = {}^{4}/_{2} \times {}^{1}/_{1^2} = 2$

$\alpha_{rvl}(3 \rightarrow 4) = 3.5$

FIGURE 7.10 Attractional analysis of the *Sehnen* motive: (a) idealized voice leading, with individual attractional values; (b) configurations of the basic space for the four chords of the motive; (c) expected/realized voice-leading attractions based on (b), summed to form the total realized voice-leading attractions for the progression.

ter 4, each attraction is computed in the framework of the goal event. For each progression the individual voice-leading values are summed at the bottom. The summed attractions are the same except for a slight increase progressing into the V^7, a consequence of the added root level for that chord in Figure 7.10b.

The values of summed attractions—3.0 and a little more—are only moderately large because the common tones between chords counterbalance the effect of the double semitonal motions. At the same time, the lack of significant attractional change projects stasis: the events motivate attractions, but each attraction leads to another commensurate one, protracting the longing.

A Debussy analysis

Behind much of Debussy's Prelude "La terrasse des audiences du clair de lune" (Book II, no. 7), three crucial passages of which are given in Figure 7.11, lies dom7/octatonic space, the chordal inversion of Tristan/octatonic space. Debussy

FIGURE 7.11 Passages from Debussy's Prelude "La terrasse des audiences du clair de lune" (Book II, no. 7): (a) bars 1–4; (b) bars 13–17; (c) bars 28–34.

c)

FIGURE 7.11 (Continued)

indeed pays homage to the inversional harmonic and motivic symmetries from the beginning of the *Tristan* Prelude in bars 13–14 of "La terrasse," shown in Figure 7.11b. Characteristically, Debussy's sonorous Tristan chord obliquely receives its strongest psychoacoustic (virtual pitch) root, C♯ in bar 16, so that it assumes D-function instead of the S-function of Wagner's linear Tristan chord.

The beginning of "La terrasse" in Figure 7.11a announces dom7/octatonic space by the diminished-seventh chord implicit within it. By way of explanation, the notes in the treble clef in Figure 7.12a invert Figure 7.7b: each dominant seventh whose root lies on the minor-third cycle C♯–E–G–B♭ is a semitone away from the opening diminished-seventh chord B–D–E♯–G♯. (Alternatively, the cycle [1 4 7 10] gives the roots of the possible dominants with flattened ninths on the cycle [2 5 8 11].) Unlike the Tristan chords in Figure 7.7b, the dominant sevenths have strong harmonic roots and unambiguous functionality and imply the tonics in the bass clef pointed to by the arrows. These tonics express the third minor-third cycle, F♯–A–C–E♭. Figure 7.12b models this closed tonal subsystem spatially. The δ values for the two minor-third cycles come from Figures 6.7 and 6.22a; those for the dominant-tonic relationships are from Figure 2.11. The subsystem thus combines two spaces, octatonic for "horizontal" and diatonic for "vertical" distances. Ultimately, diatonic dominates octatonic space in this piece, which globally prolongs V^7/**F♯** until the functional arrival of I/**F♯** in bar 34.

After the opening diminished-seventh chord come the four related dominant sevenths: E^7 in bar 1, G^7 in bars 1–2, and C♯^{7} and B♭^{7} in bar 3. The single pitch in bars 1–4 not in **oct1** (leaving aside the chromatic thirty-second notes in the high treble) is the neighboring F♯ in bar 1. This F♯, together with the salience of

a)

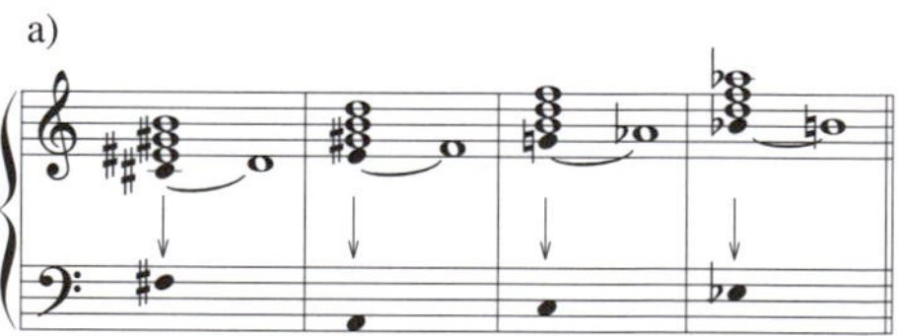

b)

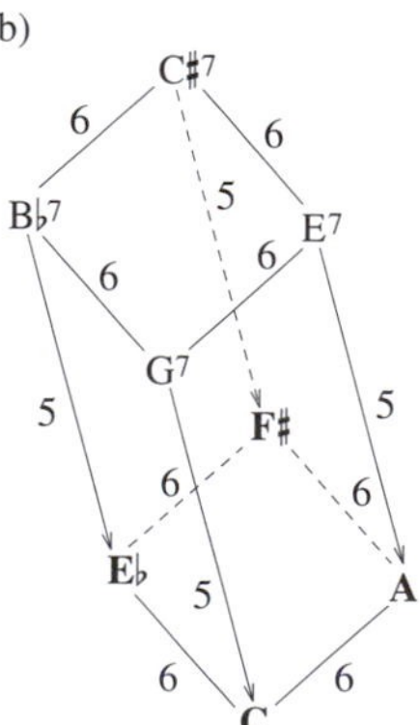

FIGURE 7.12 Tonal subsystem for dom7/octatonic space: (a) minor-third transpositions of the dominant-seventh chord on a diminished-seventh base, with implied $V^7 \rightarrow I$ resolutions; (b) spatial model of the relationships in (a).

a)

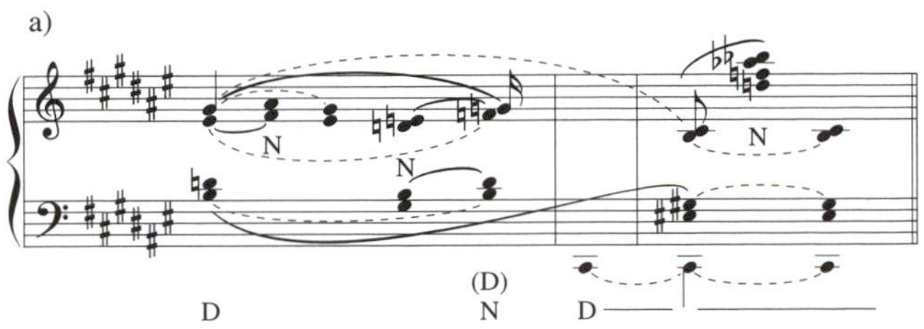

b)

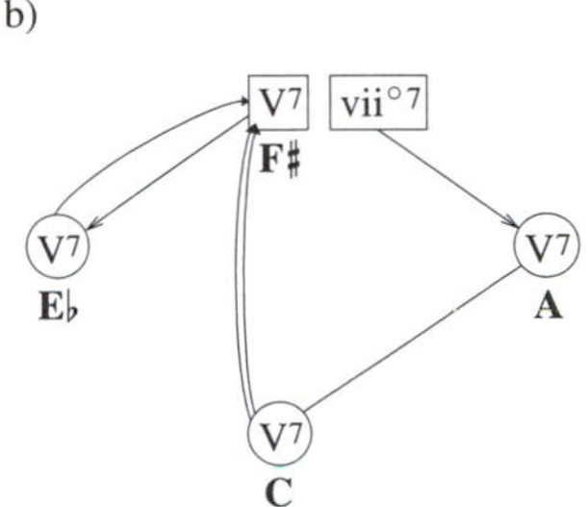

FIGURE 7.13 Prolongational, functional, and path analysis of bars 1–3 of "La terrasse."

the C♯⁷ chord and the diatonic melodic continuation in **F♯** in bars 3–4 (the parallel dominant sevenths in bars 3–4 are textural), already hints that the home region will be **F♯**. Of the tonic regions implied by these four dominant sevenths, all except **A** are traversed in the piece: **E♭** in bars 7 and 25–27; **C** in bars 27–30; and **F♯** in bars 1–6, 13–18, and 34–45.

Figure 7.13a provides a prolongational and functional analysis of bars 1–3. The diminished seventh retroactively acquires D-function once the low C♯ enters in bar 2. Neighboring motion takes place at every level, even in the descending thirty-second-note run not shown in the graph. These include a melodic N in bar 1, a harmonic N between the two D-functions of the opening vii°⁷ and the V⁷ in bars 2–3, and a "leaping" N within the V⁷ in bar 3. As the layout in Figure 7.12b is inconvenient for representing paths, the corresponding path analysis in Figure 7.13b resumes the familiar chordal/regional arrangement while maintaining the octatonic regional square. The pivoting double line between V⁷/**C** and V⁷/**F♯**, signifying a kind of equivalence, will be discussed shortly.

Figure 7.14a sketches the global prolongational and functional structure of "La terrasse." The quasi bar lines indicate the three main sections, bars 1–12, 13–31, and 32–45. Level a shows the global framework V⁷→I functioning as D→T. The initial dominant and resolving tonic diffuse over the musical surface (bars 1–3 and 34–39, respectively), but at this global level they are just V and I. The brackets at the end of the branches that lead to V and I signify their internal reduction and fusion at this level. Level b articulates the beginnings of the second and third sections with vii°♯⁷/**F♯** in place of a straight dominant. The vii°♯⁷ that commences the second section moves to V⁷(bar 16), which strongly prolongs the opening V⁷ by octave displacement. The vii°♯⁷ in the third section, by contrast, cadences into I

a)

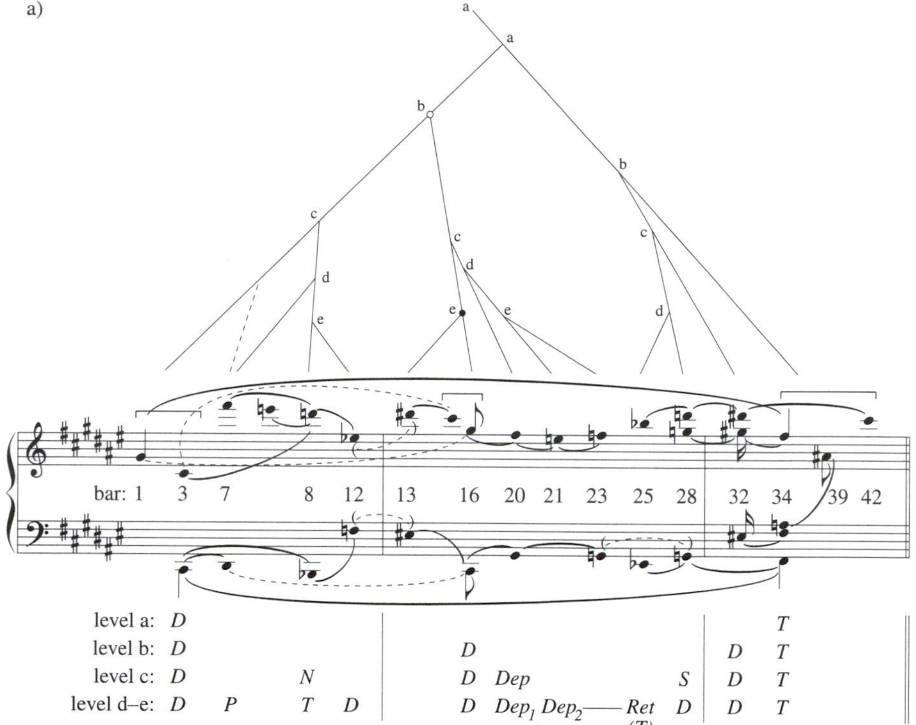

b)

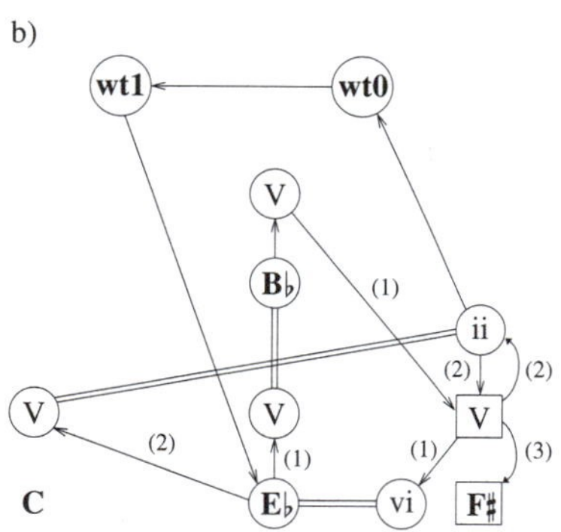

FIGURE 7.14 Prolongational, functional, and path analysis of global levels of "La terrasse."

(bar 34), as a kind of formal consequent; compare Figures 7.11b–c. To realize this interpretation, the time-span reduction, which is omitted, must assign the initial V^7 (bars 1–3) as a structural beginning and the resolving $vii^{\circ\sharp7}\rightarrow I$ as a cadential unit. Level c adds the **B♭** section in bars 8–12 as a neighbor between the first and second structural V^7s and starts to elaborate the middle section with a departure,

ii^7/**F♯** in bar 20, and an S-function, the G^7 in bars 28–31 (at this level acting as ♭II^{+6}/**F♯**). Normative prolongational structure is thereby attained. At level d comes the passing d♯ triad in bar 7. The middle developmental section departs further, now by hypermodulation to whole-tone space (bars 21–24), and returns after a caesura to the E♭ triad in bars 25–28 (which functions locally as I/**E♭** = T). At this level the G^7 in bars 28–31 functions as dominant of **C**. Level e adds a few more details. Not analyzed in the graph is the coda, with its triadic reference in bars 39–40 to the octatonic dominant-seventh cycle in bars 1–3 and its delicate allusions, by means of the Gs and Cs in bars 40–44, to the climactic V^7/**C** in bars 28–31.

Figure 7.14b traces the path for the bottom level of Figure 7.14a. For readability, the octatonic regional square of Figure 7.13b is unfolded, so that it corresponds to a portion of collapsed regional diatonic space (see Figures 3.23b and 6.3b). As in previous figures, the location of the whole-tone regions is arbitrary with respect to the rest of the space. One could calculate the interspatial δ values precisely, but this would take us into reductional minutiae beyond what is shown in Figure 7.14a. The numbers in parentheses next to the arrows specify orders of departure from locations for which there is more than one departure. In this interpretation, V^7/**C** (bar 28) pivots as an altered ii/**F♯**.

The tritone-related dominant sevenths in "La terrasse" raise larger issues of functionality. Recall from Figure 7.13b the double arrow that connects V^7/**C** and V^7/**F♯**. The G^7 in bar 2 (Figure 7.11a) sounds like V^7/**C** and realizes this potential in bars 28–31 (Figure 7.11c); but in this context and with the low C♯, the G^7 in bar 2 acts locally as an altered dominant, $V^7_{\flat 5}$/**F♯**. The low C♯ aside, the G^7 is an augmented-sixth chord with G and F (= E♯) as double leading tones to F♯. Similarly, the downbeat of bar 16 (Figure 7.11b), which grows harmonically and motivically out of bar 1, is—purely as a sonority—a French-sixth hybrid between C♯^{7} and G^7 (this is echoed in bars 34–35, the parallel place in the third section). From these instances, one might conclude that the G^7 in bars 28–31 has D-function not only locally in relation to **C** but also globally to **F♯**, particularly since in bar 31 the chord sequences baldly move around the octatonic cycle (one and a half times clockwise around the top square in Figure 7.12b), carrying implied D-function along with it. In addition, the low bass G in bars 28 and 30 connects to low F♯ in bar 34 without intervening pitches in that register (see the relevant slur in Figure 7.14a). According to the prolongational analysis, however, the ensuing $vii^{o\sharp 7}$ relegates this G^7 to a global S-function.

This case is hardly unique. The D-function of the ♭II^{+6} chord goes back at least to Schubert (Litterick 1996) and becomes common in chromatic tonal music; it is also standard in jazz, where it is referred to as a tritone substitution. At other times it functions as S, for instance in Scriabin's Prelude, Op. 48, no. 4 (Baker 1986). In bar 44 of Brahms's Intermezzo, Op. 76, no. 4, ♭II^{+6} functions as D; in bars 67–68 of his Intermezzo, Op. 117, no. 2, it functions as S. Both progressions are globally closural and are otherwise similar, including even their **B♭** tonality, except in one respect—the presence of an ensuing V^7 in Op. 117, no. 2, causing the ♭II^{+6} to be a second left branch. This circumstance is parallel to that of the climactic G^7 in "La terrasse." As with any event, the function of an augmented sixth is not preordained but depends on prolongational context.

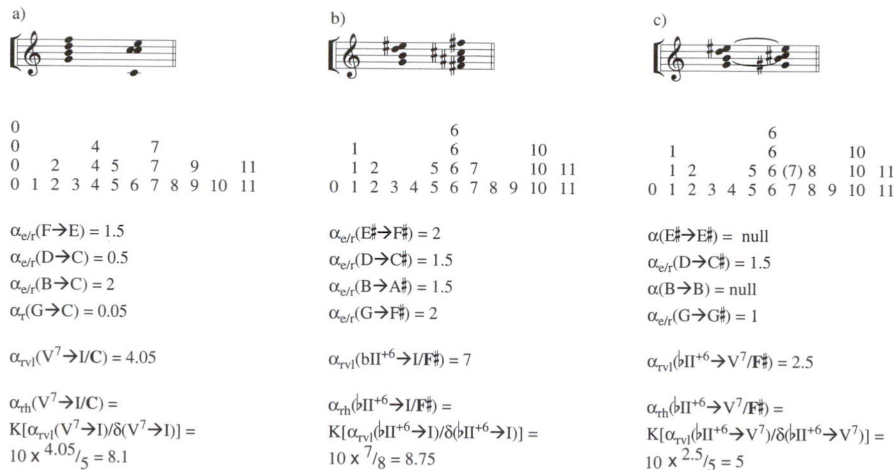

FIGURE 7.15 Three applications of the harmonic attraction rule.

The ability of $\flat II^{+6}$ to function as S is readily understandable: it is just an altered ii. But not all chords are successful D-substitutes. Why is $\flat II^{+6}$? The answer lies in the strong tonic attractions exerted upon it. Figure 7.15a (from Figures 4.29a and 4.30) applies the harmonic attraction rule to $V^7 \rightarrow I/\mathbf{C}$. Figure 7.15b does likewise for $\flat II^{+6} \rightarrow I/\mathbf{F\sharp}$. The goal contexts, I/**C** for Figure 7.15a and I/**F♯** for Figure 7.15b, are given in the basic spaces beneath the notated progressions (in Figure 7.15b the scalar level is chromatically inflected because of the altered ii). Beneath the basic spaces appear the strongest virtual attractions on the pitches, then the sum of those values, and finally the sum divided by the δ value (and multiplied by 10, as in "An Attractional Approach to Harmony" in chapter 4). Compared to Figure 7.15a, the greater attractions on the individual voices in Figure 7.15b are balanced by the greater distance between the chords. The values for both progressions are very high, indeed close. This is why $\flat II^{+6}$ substitutes so readily for V^7. By contrast, the attraction of $\flat II^{+6} \rightarrow V^7/\mathbf{F\sharp}$, given in Figure 7.15c, is only a little more than half that of the other two progressions, as a consequence of the two shared pcs between $\flat II^{+6}$ and V^7. A few details: for the attraction of G to G♯, the two pitches share the same scale degree, hence are at the same level of embedding; therefore, $\alpha_{e/r}(G \rightarrow G\sharp) = 2/2 \times 1/1^2 = 1$. If the realized bass motion were G→C♯, the calculation would be $\alpha_r(G \rightarrow C\sharp) = 3/2 \times 1/6^2 = 0.04$, and the value for $\alpha_{rh}(\flat II^{+6} \rightarrow V^7/\mathbf{F\sharp})$ would be 3.1. Either way, the relatively small value for $\alpha_{rh}(\flat II^{+6} \rightarrow V^7/\mathbf{F\sharp})$ leaves $\flat II^{+6}$ as S-function in somewhat equivocal position, for its stronger impulse is to function as D and to resolve directly to I. The G^7 in bars 28–31 of "La terrasse" operates within this web of tonal forces.

A note on neoclassic Stravinsky

Stravinsky's chordal norm during his neoclassic phase is the triad. Hence the structures utilized for Debussy's "La terrasse" apply to Stravinsky's many neoclassic passages in which the diatonic and octatonic collections intermix (Berger 1963; van den Toorn 1983). The pitch-space framework treats such shifting scalar collections not just as isolated structures but also as one level within a five-level basic space in which the other four levels do not change. The first movement of the *Symphony of Psalms*, for example, with its punctuating E minor triads, moves back and forth between $\mathrm{e}^{tr}/\mathbf{E}^{oct1}$ space and $\mathrm{e}^{tr}/\mathbf{E}^{phry}$ space. Figure 7.16a represents the two spaces and computes the distance from the former to the latter. All the levels of the basic spaces are the same except for the scalar levels. In spite of the hypermodulation, their distance from one another is very small, permitting easy transition between the two.

In addition to applying δ or α from event to event, the interpenetration of octatonic and diatonic structures can be approached through the dom7/octatonic subsystem pictured in Figure 7.12b. Figure 7.16b gives the beginning of the first movement and the ending of the third movement of the *Symphony of Psalms* (the latter passage also begins the third movement). The first-movement passage is in **oct1** and includes dominant sevenths of **E♭** and **C(c)**, the secondary and principal regions of both the second and third movements. As the arrows suggest, these strands culminate in the third movement in two streams that independently realize **E♭** and **C** just before the final resolution in notated bar 5 on a C chord. The δ values next to the arrows are taken directly from Figure 7.12b. In this case, the values represent not prolongational tension values but associative tensional connections across the span of the entire work. To effect a unitary prolongational structure for the **E♭/C** passage, however, it would be necessary to merge the two regions into a single region at an underlying level. **E♭** and **C** would merge into **c**, with the bass E at the end of bar 4 acting as an anticipation of the closing C major harmony. The measurement for the final cadential progression would thus become $\delta(\mathrm{i}/\mathbf{c}\rightarrow\mathrm{I}/\mathbf{C}) = 7$.

More generally, the mechanisms are in place to determine at all levels of a Stravinskian neoclassic work its various δ and α values, its geometric projections and paths, and its prolongational, tensional, and functional analyses. Adjustments would involve not global theoretical issues but stylistic details, in particular the separation of nonharmonic from harmonic tones, an area that is more ambiguous in this style than in Beethoven or Debussy. (The pitch-space theory is not designed, however, to deal with the remarkable registral spacings and doublings of Stravinsky's chords.)

PSYCHOACOUSTIC FACTORS IN PROLONGATIONAL ANALYSIS

Motivating the factors

Before moving on to more dissonant chromatic prolongations, we must consider the role that psychoacoustic features play in determining prolongational structure. The first of these is psychoacoustic salience. GTTM's time-span reductional PRs can be divided into two categories, those that compare relative pitch stability of the events within a given span or region and those that compare the relative

FIGURE 7.16 Stravinsky's *Symphony of Psalms:* (a) a distance measurement for the first movement; (b) the beginning of the first movement and the ending of the third movement, with realized harmonic implications from one to the other.

salience of events. Most aspects of the stability rules are reformulated in this study by distances in pitch space. In the salience category are GTTM's rules that select events in a registral extreme or strong metrical position; the latter, while not psychoacoustic per se, has the effect of salience by being a locus of attention (Jones and Boltz 1989). Even the practice of representing an event just by its bass and soprano depends on the relative salience of these voices because of the psychoacoustic masking of inner parts. Other salience factors not listed in GTTM include events that are comparatively long or loud or that are otherwise perceptually prominent in their immediate context.

Stability far outweighs salience in making reductional choices in diatonic tonal contexts. But with the rise of chromaticism, tonal stability begins to lose force, whether through ambiguity in projecting tonic orientation or through the use of the symmetrical scales explored in chapter 6. Salience fills the partial vacuum. For example, it influences certain choices in the reduction of "La terrasse" in Figure 7.14a. In bars 1–3, the C♯⁷ chord is selected because its bass note is at a registral extreme and because the low C♯ bass note in bar 2 and the C♯⁷ chord in bar 3 fall on downbeats. In bars 12–13, the Tristan chord wins over the more stable C♯⁷ chord because it is longer and on a downbeat.

For a more far-reaching example, consider contrasting significances ascribed in the literature to the opening C♯ of Debussy's *Prélude à l'après-midi d'un faune*. Felix Salzer (1952), relying exclusively on criteria of stability and on the view that the piece prolongs an E major tonic triad from beginning to end, treats the C♯ as a local upper neighbor to the immediately following B in bar 1, marked with "x" in Figure 7.17. At the other extreme, Matthew Brown (1993) relies implicitly on the greater salience of the C♯ compared to the B, by virtue of the C♯'s greater duration, pitch height, metrical position, and position at a grouping boundary. He treats

FIGURE 7.17 Debussy's *Prélude à l'après-midi d'un faune*, bars 1–13, with designations for three possible prolongational resolutions of the opening C♯.

the C♯ as prolonged over the Bs in the first phrase and through the next phrase, where the melody is harmonized beginning on a D major triad in bars 11–12, until the C♯ resolves to B over an E major triad in bar 13, marked with "z" in Figure 7.17. I prefer an intermediate interpretation: the arrival on an arpeggiation of an E major triad in bar 3, ending on a B of some duration, resolves the opening C♯ both melodically and harmonically at "y." The second phrase repeats this C♯–B motion with overt harmonization. In this view, the B at "x" is too fleeting and the implied harmony is too unstable for the C♯ to resolve as suggested by Salzer; yet the stability of the tonic in bar 3 is enough to override Brown's hearing of the opening C♯ as governing bars 1–13 in their entirety. This interpretation balances stability and salience. But the point is less to argue which of these interpretations is correct than to observe that they all lie on a single conceptual continuum, with stability criteria at one end and salience criteria at the other. It is doubtful that such a continuum would be useful for Beethoven. Its relevance for Debussy demonstrates that with the weakening of tonality brought about by chromaticism, salience has infiltrated the tonal system as an organizing principle. (Also see Figure 3.17 in this regard.)

Psychoacoustic salience is not the only principle of perceptual organization that influences reductional choices. In nontriadic chromatic tonal music it is not always obvious which pitches in a melodic line are harmonic and which are nonharmonic. For example, in the opening bars of Scriabin's Prelude, Op. 67, no. 1, in Figure 7.18, all the pitches belong to **oct0** except the A♭s on the downbeats of bars 1–3. Are the A♭s therefore nonharmonic? Are all the other melodic pitches harmonic? The principles of streaming and anchoring (see "Issues in Prolongational Theory" in chapter 1 and "Melodic Tension" in chapter 4) combine to provide answers for these questions. If two temporally adjacent sequential pitches are at least a minor third apart, they potentially coexist as members of different melodic streams or as members of an arpeggiated chord. But if the two pitches are a minor or major second apart, they fall within the same stream. In line with the anchoring principle, the first pitch is more ornamental and can be reduced out.

This reasoning applies to Figure 7.18 as follows. The A♭ in bars 1–2 is a fourth away from its successor E♭, so the two pitches belong to different chordal voices, the anchoring principle does not apply, and the A♭ is structural rather than or-

FIGURE 7.18 Scriabin's Prelude, op. 67, no. 1, bars 1–4, with reduction of the melodic line by the anchoring principle.

namental. The A♭ in bar 3, however, is less than a minor third away from ensuing F♯ and G, so it could be reduced out. In this case, however, the salience of the A♭ because of its metrical position, together with the parallelism that results from identical verticalities on the downbeats of bars 1–2 and 3, tips the PR balance in favor of retaining this A♭ as structural as well. Now consider the other melodic pitches in bar 1. The E♭ and E fall within a minor third, so E♭ resolves to E, as indicated by the arrow; likewise with G to G♭. In bar 3, the same considerations make F♯ resolve to G and B♭ resolve to A. In bar 4, D♭ resolves to C and A resolves to G. Above the music is the simplified melody shorn of all these ornamental tones.

The anchoring principle in its standard tonal application relies not just on subsequent proximity but also on the relative consonance of the second pitch. It may be asked whether an extension of the principle to melodic sequences in nontriadic contexts, where it is assumed (for our purposes here) that both pitches are equal with respect to consonance and dissonance, is justified. A brief answer is that because anchoring is pervasive in triadic music, listeners transfer it by habit to superficially similar contexts in nontriadic music; yet because there is little resolution of dissonance in the latter context, the effect is comparatively weak. A compatible but more probing answer is that anchoring depends on attractions, and the melodic attraction rule has two parts: s_2/s_1, which represents levels of stability (or relative consonance), and $1/n^2$, which represents proximity. In a nontriadic context where both pitches are at the same level, the effect of s_2/s_1 is neutralized: $s_2/s_1 = 1/1 = 1$. But $1/n^2$ nonetheless remains operative. If two pitches are a semitone apart, $1/n^2 = 1/1^2 = 1$, which expresses a moderate attraction; if they are two semitones apart, $1/n^2 = 1/2^2 = 0.25$, which is a rather weak attraction; if they are three semitones apart, $1/n^2 = 1/3^2 = 0.11$, which is a minuscule attraction. Thus even without the role of s_2/s_1, melodic attractions are felt, but the effect of the inverse-square factor renders inconsequential any attractions between pitches a minor third or more apart. Attractions within a half or whole step are strong enough to justify the practice of anchoring in contexts in which the distinction between harmonic and nonharmonic tones is obscure. (This conclusion fits with evidence concerning the perceptual attention band; see related discussion in "Empirical Issues," in chapter 2 and "Melodic Tension" and "Tension, Attraction, and Expression" in chapter 4.)

In addition to the horizontal factors of streaming and anchoring, vertical psychoacoustic factors play a role in prolongational structure. First, a short historical excursus. Closure in the late Middle Ages and early Renaissance is accomplished by the double-leading-tone (so-called Burgundian) cadence, as in Figure 7.19a. It is not necessary to compute every detail to see that from an attractional point of view this cadence achieves for fourteenth-century music what the V-I cadence

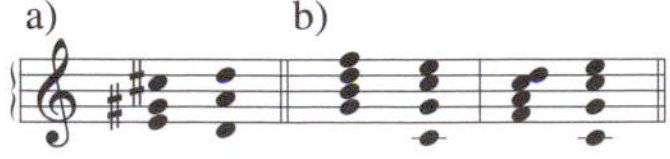

FIGURE 7.19 Basic cadences: (a) the double-leading-tone (Burgundian) cadence; (b) Rameau's authentic and plagal cadences.

does for eighteenth-century music. The upper voices resolve by leading tones, and the structural tenor also resolves by step, $\hat{2}\rightarrow\hat{1}$, the structural equivalent in that idiom to bass motion by fifth in the Classical period. The result is a very high α_{rvl} value and a low δ value (because stepwise motion in the tenor gives $j = 1$ in that idiom), yielding the strongest α_{rh} value available in the idiom. Vertically, the progression is from an inverted minor triad to an open-fifth sonority, $\substack{\sharp 6\\ \sharp 3}\rightarrow\substack{8\\ 5}$. In terms of both roughness and virtual pitches, syntactic resolution is reinforced by an increase in sensory consonance.

This correlation between musical and sensory consonance largely disappears in later centuries with the replacement of the double-leading-tone cadence by the V→I cadence. Nevertheless, Rameau (1722, 1737), in pursuit of a theory of harmony based first on simple ratios and then on the overtone series, and lacking a theory of pitch space, sought to increase the resolution of tonal tension by a corresponding increase in sensory consonance. Of his three essential chords, only the tonic was allowed to remain a pure triad; the dominant required a seventh, the subdominant an added sixth. His archetypal authentic and plagal cadences, shown in Figure 7.19b, thus involved not only syntactic but also sensory resolution. To maintain tension, he also included sevenths, even if they were not present in the musical surface, in midphrasal descending-fifth progressions until the arrival of the cadence (Lester 1992; Christensen 1993). From our perspective, however, incorporating a dissonant interval in pretonic chords (but not in the tonic itself) is an option but hardly an obligation within the Classical idiom. A remarkable feature of the triadic/diatonic system is that once local dissonances are stripped from the surface, all that remains, in a sense, are triads; yet intuitions of tension and relaxation remain powerful. It is the locations and paths of the triads in pitch space that induce these intuitions.

The role of sensory dissonance in shaping harmonic progression begins to reemerge in chromatic tonal music. *Tristan*, with its Tristan and dominant-seventh chords that seek triadic resolution, is emblematic. Yet the triad remains the governing sonority in Wagner. In Debussy, triads begin to share with other chord types the role of referential sonority, and progression by chord type becomes an increasingly important structural element. Ignoring complicating details, the chord-types in "La terrasse" move from seventh chords (bars 1–6), to triads (bars 7–11), to seventh chords (bars 12–20), to whole-tone chords (bars 21–24), to triads (bars 24–27), to seventh chords (bars 28–38), and to triads (bars 39–45). This parsing cuts across grouping boundaries as a way of enhancing continuity and is particularly striking over the caesura at the end of bar 24. As a result, however, it would be problematic to generate a prolongational analysis by chord-type, since prolongational analysis depends on time-span analysis, which obeys grouping boundaries. Even so, progression by chord-type broadly fits the prolongational tension pattern in Figure 7.14a. Whole-tone chords are generally more dissonant than dominant-seventh chords, which are more dissonant than triads. In the prolongational analysis, seventh chords dominate throughout most of the piece except for the tensing departure into the whole-tone passage in bars 21–24 and the final relaxation into triads and open fifths in bars 39–45. If the high-level events in Figure 7.14a are taken to represent their chord-types segments, the sensory dis-

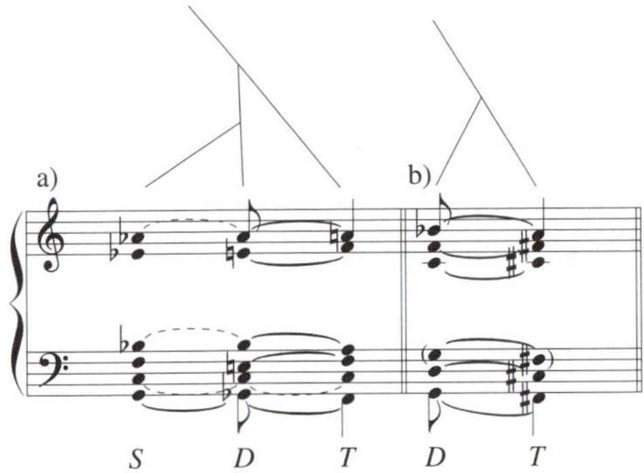

FIGURE 7.20 Progressions by chord type with prolongational and functional analyses: (a) Schoenberg's Chamber Symphony, Op. 9; (b) Schoenberg's Second String Quartet, Op. 10.

sonance of the chord-types as they unfold correlates with the tensing–relaxing structure of the prolongational tree. (This correlation ignores the triadic passages in bars 7–11 and 24–27, which instead are prolongationally subordinate because of their remote locations in pitch space.)

In Schoenberg's First Chamber Symphony, Op. 9, progression by chord-type becomes genuinely syntactic. Much of the work is controlled by its beginning progression in Figure 7.20a. To the ear, the chord-type progression fourth→whole-tone→triad is left-branching, hence S→D→T in function (local T in this case; the global tonic is not **F** but **E**). That this is so is a result not of tonal convention or salience or any other factor except sensory dissonance: the fourth chord is dissonant, the whole-tone chord is less so, and the triad is consonant.

The progression in Figure 7.20a employs strong semitonal attractions similar to those in Figures 7.15b and 7.19a. Schoenberg's Second String Quartet, Op. 10, takes a further step in Figure 7.20b. If semitonal voice leading to the tonic triad is kept in all voices, the resultant verticality is a fourth chord. The chord-type progression in Op. 10 contracts, skipping the whole-tone chord, to fourth→triad, functioning as D→T. Variants of this progression appear throughout the first and last movements of the Second Quartet, especially in their codas. As with Figure 7.20a, the progression implicitly depends on the perceptually based principles of anchoring by proximity and resolution of sensory dissonance. In this respect Schoenberg of this period is not far from Machaut.

The basic-space framework does not easily accommodate the progression in Figure 7.20a. Figure 7.21a includes all the pcs in Figure 7.20a at the scalar level, adds the pcs of the fourth chord at the chordal level, and adds a superordinate level in which the root is equated with the bass. The scalar level violates virtually all of the preferential constraints on basic spaces (see "Related Issues" in chapter 6). An alternative is considering the progression as hypermodulatory, in which case the fourth chord is supported by the diatonic collection in Figure 7.21b (pc2 is inferred from the horn call that follows the excerpted progression). But the pc content of the chord barely differs from that of the scale, seriously violating the halving constraint. Figure 7.21c continues the hypermodulatory interpretation of Figure 7.21b by assigning the whole-tone chord in Figure 7.20a to a whole-tone

a)

root level:								7				
chord level:	0			3		5		7	8		10	
scale level:	0			3	4	5	6	7	8	9	10	
chromatic level:	0	1	2	3	4	5	6	7	8	9	10	11

b)

root level:								7				
chord level:	0			3		5		7	8		10	
scale level:	0		2	3		5		7	8		10	
chromatic level:	0	1	2	3	4	5	6	7	8	9	10	11

c)

						6					
0				4		6		8		10	
0		2		4		6		8		10	
0	1	2	3	4	5	6	7	8	9	10	11

d)

							7				
0		2			5		7			10	
0	1	2			5	6	7		9	10	
0	1	2	3	4	5	6	7	8	9	10	11

e)

						6					
	1					6					
	1					6			9		
0	1	2			5	6	7		9	10	
0	1	2	3	4	5	6	7	8	9	10	11

FIGURE 7.21 Attempts at basic-space representations: (a) the fourth chord in Figure 7.20a; (b) the fourth chord in Figure 7.20a under a second interpretation; (c) the whole-tone chord in Figure 7.20a; (d) the fourth chord in Figure 7.20b; (e) the resolution to the triad in Figure 7.20b.

space. Again there is insufficient differentiation between the scalar and chordal levels. One must conclude that basic-space configurations are peripheral to the progression in Figure 7.20a. The role of pitch space is largely replaced by that of sensory consonance/dissonance.

The progression in Figure 7.20b fares somewhat better in terms of well-formedness in the basic-space representations of Figures 7.21d–e. A related space will be explored later in this chapter.

Three perceptual preference rules

The following reductional PRs summarize the preceding discussion and complement the PR for time-span stability (see "The Principle of the Shortest Path" in chapter 2):

SALIENCE CONDITIONS Of the possible choices for the head of a time-span T, choose an event that is
(1) attacked within the region
(2) in a relatively strong metrical position
(3) relatively loud
(4) relatively prominent timbrally
(5) in an outer-voice (high or low) registral position
(6) relatively dense (simultaneous attacks)
(7) relatively long in duration
(8) next to a (relatively large) grouping boundary
(9) relatively important motivically
(10) parallel to a choice made elsewhere in the analysis.

ANCHORING/REDUCTION RULE In a melodic sequence, if temporally adjacent pitches in a stream are less than a minor third apart and are comparably dissonant, choose the second pitch.

SENSORY CONSONANCE RULE In a harmonic sequence, choose the chord that is more consonant according to
(1) roughness
(2) clarity of harmonic root.

The list of salience factors augments the few salience rules given in GTTM and is taken from Lerdahl (1989a), where it was intended for atonal contexts. It is stated here in the context of chromatic tonal music in order to emphasize that salience always plays a reductional role, regardless of idiom. The strength of an individual factor depends not only on its immediate context with respect to that dimension—for example, how much louder an event is than the immediately preceding and ensuing events—but also on how it interacts with the other salience factors within and across events. To model this picture quantitatively would not be easy. Factors (9) and (10) go beyond salience per se to include associational factors that are still more difficult to measure.

The anchoring/reduction rule follows directly from the previous subsection. The two parts of the sensory consonance rule reflect critical-band theory and virtual-pitch theory and could be quantified along the lines of W. Hutchinson and L. Knopoff (1978) and E. Terhardt, G. Stoll, and M. Seewann (1982), respectively. The sensory consonance rule has in fact made a prior surreptitious appearance, in the factors of sensory dissonance in the long version of the hierarchical tension rule ("The Harmonic Tension Model" in chapter 4). There it was quantified in terms of syntactic features of tonal music—position of melodic note, chordal inversion, and nonharmonic tone—while here the measure is psychoacoustic.

The interaction of the three rules is complex. Anchoring might be overridden if the first of the two pitches is highly salient or relatively consonant. Furthermore, salience and sensory consonance are often in conflict. Any of these rules might be outweighed by the rule for time-span stability and the associated rule of prolongational connection, which both invoke some version of δ (see "The Principle of the Shortest Path" in chapter 2). Time-span stability in turn relates to the sensory consonance rule, in that stability normally arises out of a pitch space that correlates basic-space level with sensory consonance. Sensory consonance plays a reductional role, however, even if there is no multileveled space.

ANALYSES OF NONTRIADIC CHROMATIC TONAL MUSIC

A Scriabin analysis

We turn now at some length to Scriabin's Prelude, Op. 67, no. 1, whose beginning was treated by anchoring in Figure 7.18. Scriabin's late music, of which this short piece is an exemplar, takes place within nontriadic chromatic tonal spaces that project relationships analogous to those of traditional tonal practice.

Figure 7.22 gives the score of the Prelude. To which space (or spaces) does the music belong? Consider first the scale level. As illustrated in Figure 7.23a, the

FIGURE 7.22 Scriabin's Prelude, Op. 67, no. 1.

first verticality evokes the whole-tone collection, but the E♭ immediately contradicts that assumption and suggests the six-note mystic collection [3 4 6 8 10 0]. The pitches in the second part of bar 1—indeed, all of the pitches in the bar except the opening A♭—instead imply **oct0**; this impression is strengthened by the continuation in bars 3–4.

Figure 7.23b displays a close relationship among these three scales. A single chromatic adjacent move transforms a whole-tone scale into a six-note mystic

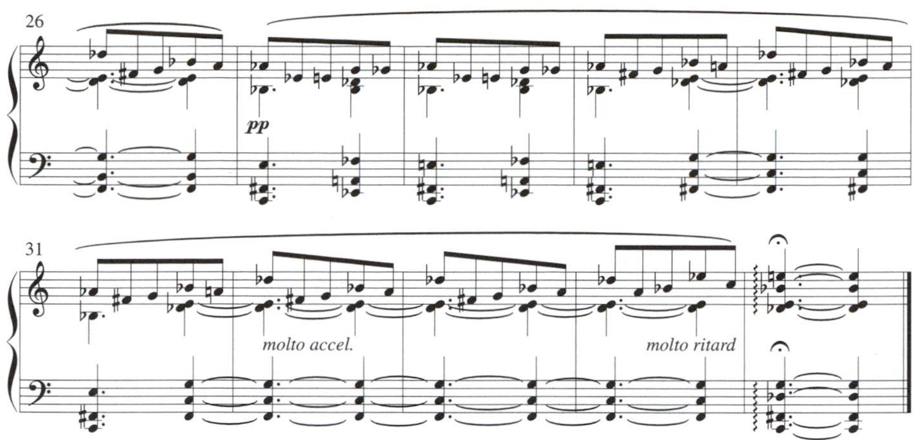

FIGURE 7.22 (Continued)

scale; alternatively, a single pc (in this case, pc2) in the whole-tone scale splits into its two chromatic neighbors to yield the seven-note mystic collection (including both pcs 1 and 3). The tritone-related pc (in this case, pc8) splits in the same way to form the octatonic scale. The mystic scale is thus an intermediary between the whole-tone and octatonic scales (Reise 1983; Taruskin 1988; Callender 1998). The chromatic stepwise motion at the surface of the piece strengthens by attraction the use of these transformations. For example, the A♭ on the downbeat of bars 1–3 is displaced melodically by G later in each of these bars and less directly by A in bar 3.

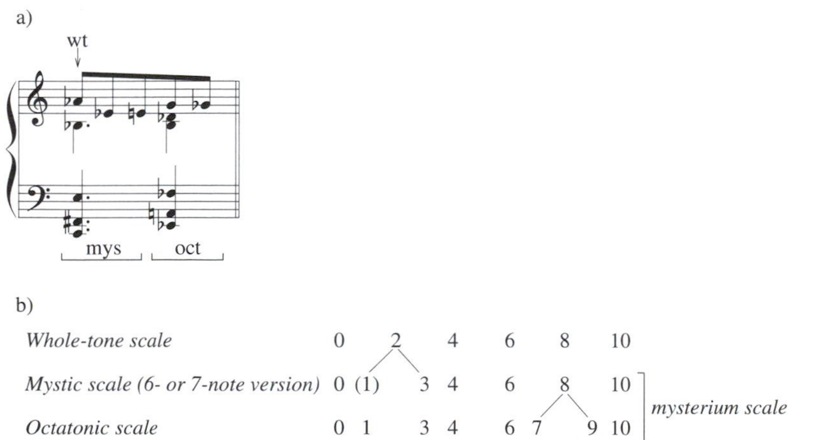

FIGURE 7.23 Finding the appropriate scale level for Op. 67, no. 1: (a) possibilities from bar 1; (b) relationships between the scales through substitution by chromatic neighbor.

Another way to view the mystic and octatonic scales, also included in Figure 7.23b, is to combine them as subsets of the mysterium scale (Pople 1983; Perle 1984). Thus all of the pcs in bar 1 become members of one collection. The rationale for this reading lies especially in the climactic chords in bars 15–16 and 19–20, which are rearranged transpositions of the combined two chords of bar 1 that support melodic lines transposed from bars 1 and 4. This approach allows the Prelude to be treated without scalar hypermodulation.

Figure 7.24a presents the transpositions of the mysterium scale as they appear in the Prelude, arrayed as ascending scales. The flagged pitch at the end of each scale turns that scale from an octatonic into a mysterium scale. The opening collection continues throughout the A section until the beginning of the B section in bars 13–14, where the pitches of the home transpositional level overlap with pitches of a new transpositional level that subsequently emerges in bars 15–16. This pattern repeats in bars 17–20. Unlike the octatonic scale, when transposed around the minor-third cycle the mysterium scale changes membership by subtracting one pc and adding another pc, analogously to diatonic scales transposed by fifths. Scriabin takes advantage of this feature in bars 19–27 by sequencing

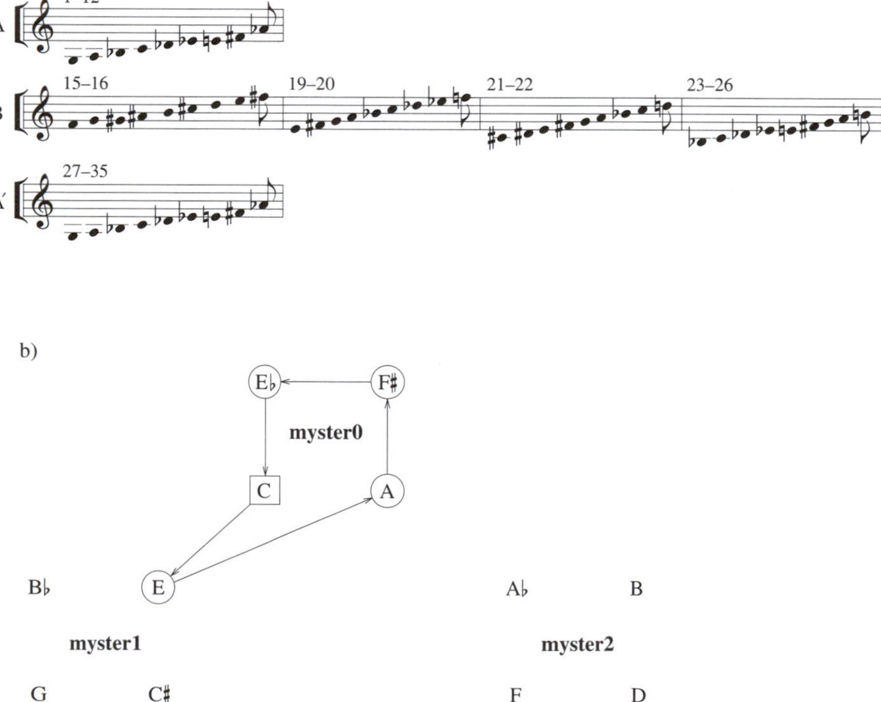

FIGURE 7.24 Transpositions of the mysterium scale in Op. 67, no. 1: (a) as scalar lists displayed by bar numbers; (b) as a path in mysterium regional space.

down by minor thirds. The effect is of a gradual return to the home region for the nonmodulating A' section.

Thus there are two modulatory levels at the mysterium-scale level, a smaller one that modifies a given octatonic collection and a larger one that moves the octatonic collection itself. Micromodulation transposes the mysterium collection by minor thirds or tritones, macromodulation by any other interval. In the Prelude there is one scalar macromodulation, to the climax in bars 15–16. The repeat a semitone lower in bars 19–20 returns to the general region of the A section but not to its specific region, which is then reached by micromodulatory sequencing. Rather than compute these distances, which involve only slight modifications of octatonic space, Figure 7.24b takes the shortcut of depicting mysterium regional space as a mutation of octatonic chordal/regional space. Each "mysterium" region shown in boldface represents a macromodulatory area, and each pc designation stands for a micromodulatory area. The location of a micromodulatory area is named, with one exception, by the bass note that supports that point in the piece. The exception occurs at bars 19–20, whose bass note is E♭ but whose continuation by descending minor thirds in bars 21–27 requires the location by analogy to be A. Scriabin makes the adjustment in bar 21 by reverting to a transposition of the opening chord. The path in Figure 7.24b plots the transpositions in Figure 7.24a.

The salience rule helps determine whether a pitch at the scalar level also belongs to the chordal level. For example, is the melodic F♯ in bar 15 harmonic or nonharmonic? By the anchoring/reduction rule, it can be treated as ornamental to the following melodic F on the fourth eighth note. But by parallelism (salience condition [10]), if A♭ in bar 1 is harmonic, so is F♯ in bar 15. And A♭ in bar 1 is highly salient (conditions [2], [6], [8]). Salience seems to win over anchoring, so that A♭ in bar 1 and F♯ in bar 15 are chordal.

Even though these pitches (A♭ in bar 1, F♯ in bar 15) count as harmonic, they are not completely so. The whole-tone and mysterium verticalities in which they participate do not form the harmonic bedrock of the piece. The chords underneath the winding melody all fall within the octatonic collection. From this angle, the piece is essentially octatonic with whole-tone and mystic offshoots. There are just two chord-types: the [0 2 6 8] or French-sixth chord and the [0 1 6 7] chord. Both are self-symmetrical subsets of **oct0** and both meet the basic-space well-formedness halving criterion in relation to the scale level. Figure 7.25 illustrates their characteristic manifestations (the notes in parentheses signify lesser harmonic status). Bars 1–3 oscillate between the French sixth and a [0 1 6 7] chord. Then comes a second [0 1 6 7] in bar 4. In both [0 1 6 7] chords there are added "sevenths," but these are ornamental in the sense that sevenths in dominants are ornamental. Bar 15 merges the transposed [0 2 6 8] and [0 1 6 7] from bar 1 into a six-note sonority by transposing one of the tritones up a minor third and adding it to the chord. The same combined chord ends the piece, in the tonic region and freed of any mysterium-derived melodic note.

The cadential structure requires elucidation before we undertake a reductional analysis. The opening chord, a French sixth built over C, is the referential T-

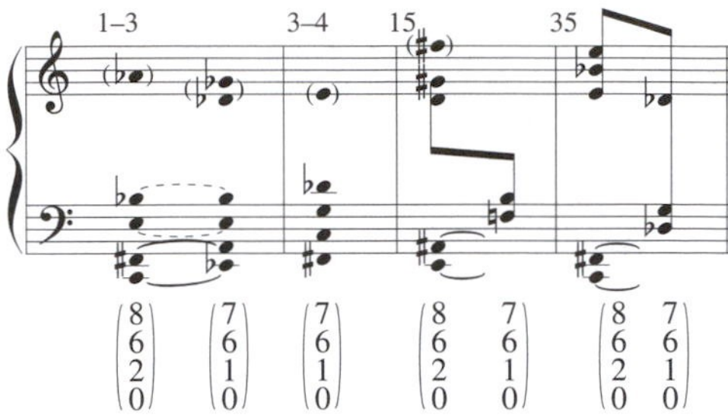

FIGURE 7.25 Some structural chords in Op. 67, no. 1.

functional sonority. The piece's D-functional sonority, the chord that ends the first phrase in bar 4 and its extension in bar 6, is [0 1 6 7] built over F♯, shown in Figure 7.26a. The two basic chord-types are thus associated with the two primary functions. It suits these chord-types and their octatonic basis for the tritone C-F♯ to replace the fifth C-G as the governing bass-interval progression. Since the F♯^{0167} ends the first phrase, its role there is half-cadential. At first its structural melodic pitch, after reduction by anchoring, is C, as in bar 4 (see Figure 7.18). In bar 6, however, the structural melodic pitch of the F♯^{0167} is D♭ because this time D♭ does not anchor on C. In this way an implication is set in motion that D♭ will rise to another stable pitch. This melodic tendency seeks realization at the end of the A section by rising in bars 12–13 through a passing D♯ to E, which is potentially stable because it belongs to the tonic chord. However, as shown in Figure 7.26b, this resolution is undercut by a deceptive motion in the other voices as **oct1** begins to penetrate the texture; in particular, the F in bars 13–14 belongs not to **oct0** but to **oct1**. The half-cadential F♯^{0167} returns at the end of the B section (bars 23–26) and in the course of the reprise. In bars 32–35, shown in Figure 7.26c, F♯^{0167} at last finds harmonic and melodic resolution, F♯^{0167}→ C$^{F6/0167}$, with the melodic line rising from D♭ through E♭ to E. The full cadence at the end of the A' section thereby answers the deceptive cadence at the end of the A section.

Figure 7.27 gives a reductional analysis of Op. 67, no. 1. The surface has already been reduced to the time-span quarter-note level by applying the anchoring/reduction rule as in Figure 7.18, and then by applying the salience rule (mostly

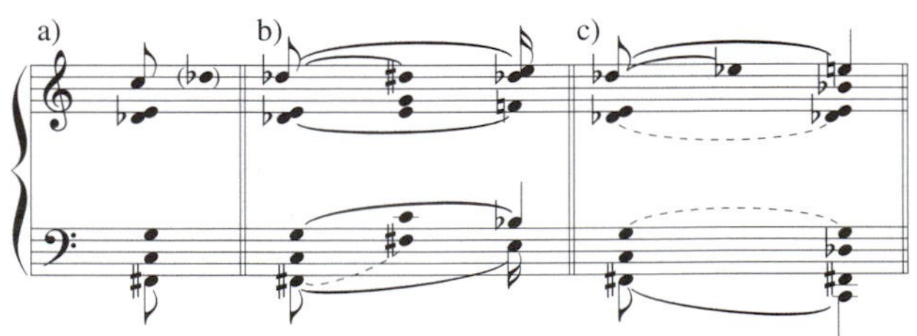

FIGURE 7.26 Cadential structure in Op. 67, no. 1: (a) half-cadence; (b) deceptive cadence; (c) full cadence.

conditions [2] and [6]) to eliminate inessential eighth notes. The meter is normalized from $\frac{5}{8}$ to $\frac{2}{4}$ by shortening the first dotted-quarter beat. Against the irregular phrase groupings appears a periodic four-bar hypermeter (assisted by the deletion of bars 5–6 at time-span level e). There are grouping overlaps at bars 13 and 17. In the time-span analysis the soprano and bass notes are compressed into one stave. As in time-span reduction in the Classical idiom, cadences are labeled and retained according to level. In the deceptive cadence, the departing second member of the cadence is not retained at larger levels. Level f reduces level g by salience criteria. For the rest of the time-span analysis, choices are made in the A and A' sections on the basis of T-functional stability and D-functional cadential retention in conjunction with the time-span structure. In the B section, salience (chiefly metrical position) and stability reinforce each other in the selection of events. "Stability" in this case refers to local T-functions—chords with a French sixth component—in correspondence with the path in Figure 7.24b. Level c shows the structural beginnings and cadences of each section, level a the structural beginning and cadence of the entire piece.

Refer now to the δ values calculated in Figure 7.28 to supplement the prolongational derivation. In all cases but one, the chord-type changes, so it is necessary to invoke δ_{is} instead of just δ_{oct}. The initial referential state of the basic space is that in Figure 7.28a, C^{F6}/$\mathbf{C}^{oct0}$ (or C^{F6}/**oct0**). The opening and closing T-functions, which are somewhat different structures, obtain the short distance in Figure 7.28b. Somewhat larger are the distances for the full cadence, $F\sharp^{0167}\rightarrow C^{F6/0167}$ in Figure 7.28c, and for the progression from the opening C^{F6} to the half-cadential $F\sharp^{0167}$ in Figure 7.28d.

These distances shape the global prolongational structure, which is reconstructed in Figure 7.29 with local distance values included in the tree. Prolongational level a derives from time-span level a in Figure 7.27. Prolongational level b in Figure 7.29b invokes the interaction principle to reach down to time-span level c for the C^{F6} at the reprise in bar 27 and for the $F\sharp^{0167}$ in bar 12. This brings two strong prolongations, the C^{F6} that connects the A section to the A' section and the $F\sharp^{0167}$ that connects the end of the A section to the end of the B section. The dramatic action in the B section takes place within this prolonged $F\sharp^{0167}$. Figure 7.29c adds prolongational levels c–d from the rest of time-span level c and all of time-span level d. δ($F\sharp^{0167}$/**oct0**→$E^{F6/0167}$/**oct1**) in Figure 7.28e is appropriately large. This right-branching departure is answered, on the basis of both the balance constraint and a smaller δ value, by a left-branching return, $E\flat^{F6/0167}$/**oct0**→$F\sharp^{F6}$/**oct0**; compare Figures 7.28f–g. The only place that requires explanation in prolongational level e is the branching between the $E\flat^{F6/0167}$ and $F\sharp^{F6}$, shown in Figure 7.29d. The short distance for $F\sharp^{F6}$/**oct0**→$F\sharp^{0167}$/**oct0** in Figure 7.28h, together with their common root, causes these chords to attach as a weak prolongation. Within this context there is a balancing tension and relaxation between F6 and [0 1 6 7] chords a minor third apart, for which $\delta_{is} = (0 + 4) + (0 + 1) + 5 = 10$. The remaining branchings can be consulted directly in Figure 7.27.

It may be felt that this analysis does not do justice to the descending harmonic sequence in bars 19–27. There are two responses. First, the sequence is reflected

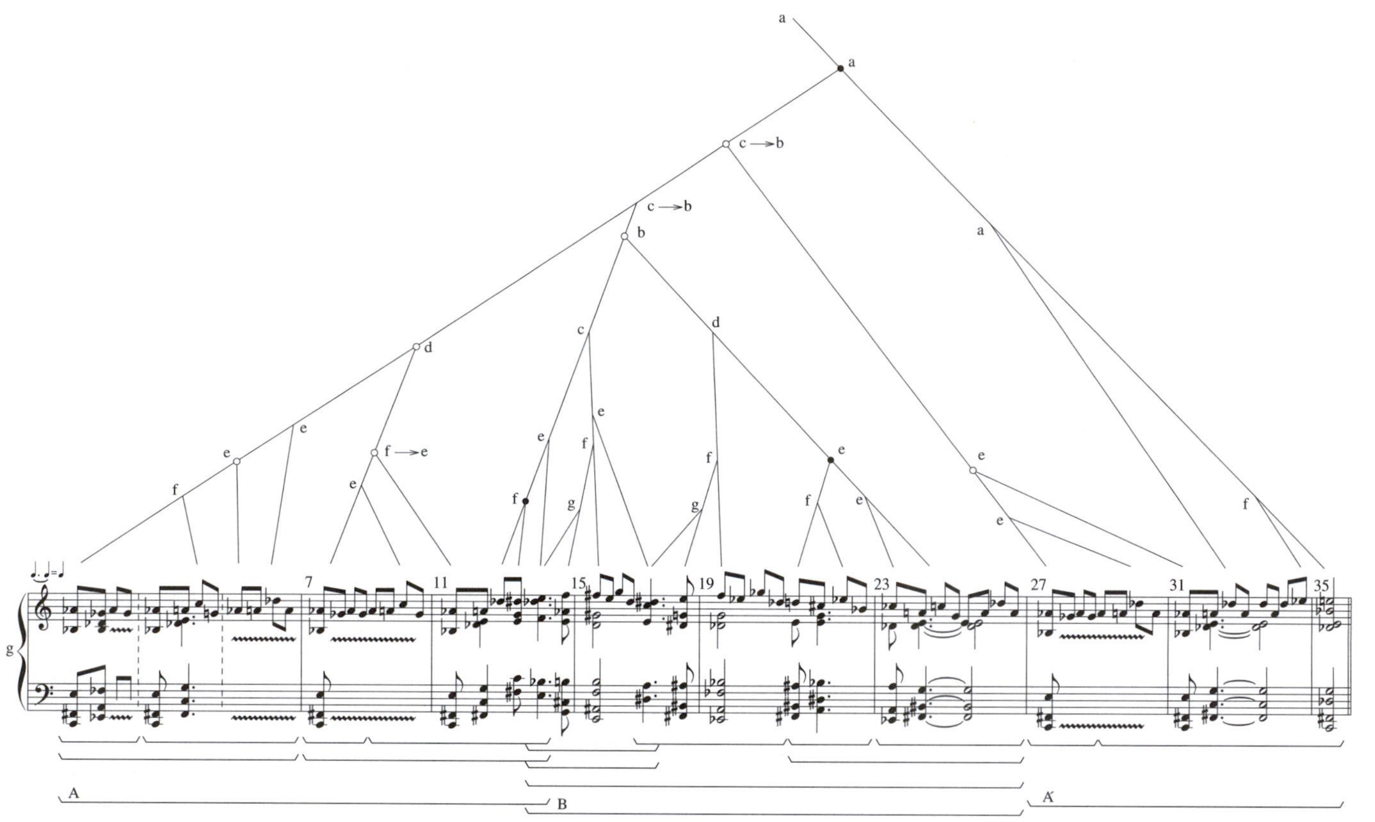
a
a
c → b
c → b
b
a
c
d
d
e
e
f → e
e
f
f
e
f
g
f
g
e
e
f
e
e
e
f
g
7
11
15
19
23
27
31
35
A
B
A′

FIGURE 7.27 Grouping, metrical, time-span, and prolongational analysis of Scriabin's Op. 67, no. 1.

a)

```
0
0                 6
0          4      6            10
0  1    3  4      6  7      9  10
0  1  2  3  4  5  6  7  8  9  10  11
```

C^{F6}/**C^{oct0}**

b)

```
0
0                 6
0  1       4      6  7         10
0  1    3  4      6  7      9  10
0  1  2  3  4  5  6  7  8  9  10  11
```

δ_{is}(C^{F6}/**oct0→**C$^{F6/0167}$/**oct0**)
= (0 + 3) + (0 + 0) + 2 = 5

c)

```
0
0                 6
0  1       4      6  7         10
0  1    3  4      6  7      9  10
0  1  2  3  4  5  6  7  8  9  10  11
```

δ_{is}(F♯^{0167}/**oct0→**C$^{F6/0167}$/**oct0**)
= (0 + 3) + (0 + 2) + 3 = 8

d)

```
                  6
   1              6
0  1      (4)     6  7
0  1    3  4      6  7      9  10
0  1  2  3  4  5  6  7  8  9  10  11
```

δ_{is}(C^{F6}/**oct0→**F♯^{0167}/**oct0**)
= (0 + 4) + (0 + 2) + 4 = 10

e)

```
           4
           4                   10
      2    4  5        8       10  11
   1  2    4  5     7  8       10  11
0  1  2  3  4  5  6  7  8  9  10  11
```

δ_{is}(F♯^{0167}/**oct0→**E$^{F6/0167}$/**oct1**)
= (0 + 3) + (1 + 1) + 12 = 17

f)

```
         3
         3                  9
   1     3  4        7      9  10
0  1     3  4     6  7      9  10
0  1  2  3  4  5  6  7  8  9  10  11
```

δ_{oct}(E$^{F6/0167}$/**oct1→**E♭$^{F6/0167}$/**oct0**)
= 1 + 1 + 11 = 13

g)

```
                  6
0                 6
0          4      6            10
0  1    3  4      6  7      9  10
0  1  2  3  4  5  6  7  8  9  10  11
```

δ_{is}(E♭$^{F6/0167}$/**oct0→**F♯^{F6}/**oct0**)
= (0 + 3) + (0 + 1) + 5 = 9

h)

```
                  6
0                 6
0  1              6  7
0  1    3  4      6  7      9  10
0  1  2  3  4  5  6  7  8  9  10  11
```

δ_{is}(F♯^{F6}/**oct0→**F♯^{0167}/**oct0**)
= (0 + 3) + (0 + 0) + 2 = 5

FIGURE 7.28 Some chordal/regional distances in Op. 67, no. 1.

in the regional path in Figure 7.24b (in terms of Figure 7.27, this path is taken at prolongational level e). Second, a point of the sequence—and this would also be true of many sequences in the Classical idiom—is that its prolongational structure changes. Bars 23–24 transpose bars 21–22 exactly, but in bars 21–22 the first chord is superordinate and in bars 23–24 the second chord is superordinate. This happens because in bars 23–24 the sequence comes around to the D-functional F♯^{0167} that plays such a major role in the piece. It would be possible, however, to bring out the sequence more clearly in the reduction if the cadences were not labeled. The F♯^{0167} chords would be eliminated at local time-span levels, and the analysis would emphasize transpositions of the opening sonority over anything else. But among other things, this step would treat the final four bars as an afterthought. To avoid such a counterintuitive outcome, it is necessary to label cadences as in Figure 7.27 and retain them at global levels (as discussed in "A Representative Analysis" in chapter 1).

Figure 7.30 performs a hierarchical tension analysis and a functional analysis for prolongational levels a–f of the Prelude. Consider first the tension analysis. For simplicity, repetitious events are removed, particularly from the A section. The local distance values included in the trees of Figure 7.29 represent T_{loc} values for the short version of the hierarchical tension rule. These are added down the tree structure to produce the T_{glob} values beneath the music in Figure 7.30. For example, T_{loc} for the climactic E$^{F6/0167}$ chord in bar 15 equals 17, and it inherits 5

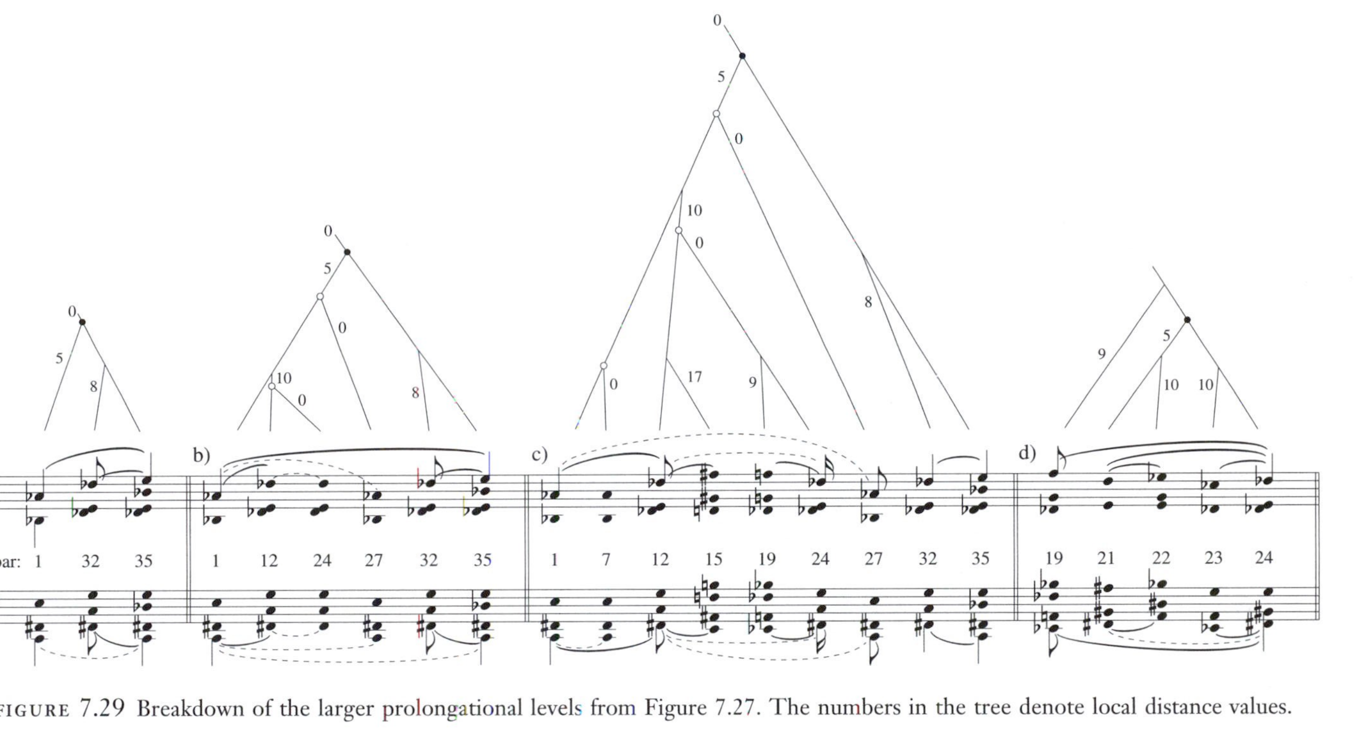

FIGURE 7.29 Breakdown of the larger prolongational levels from Figure 7.27. The numbers in the tree denote local distance values.

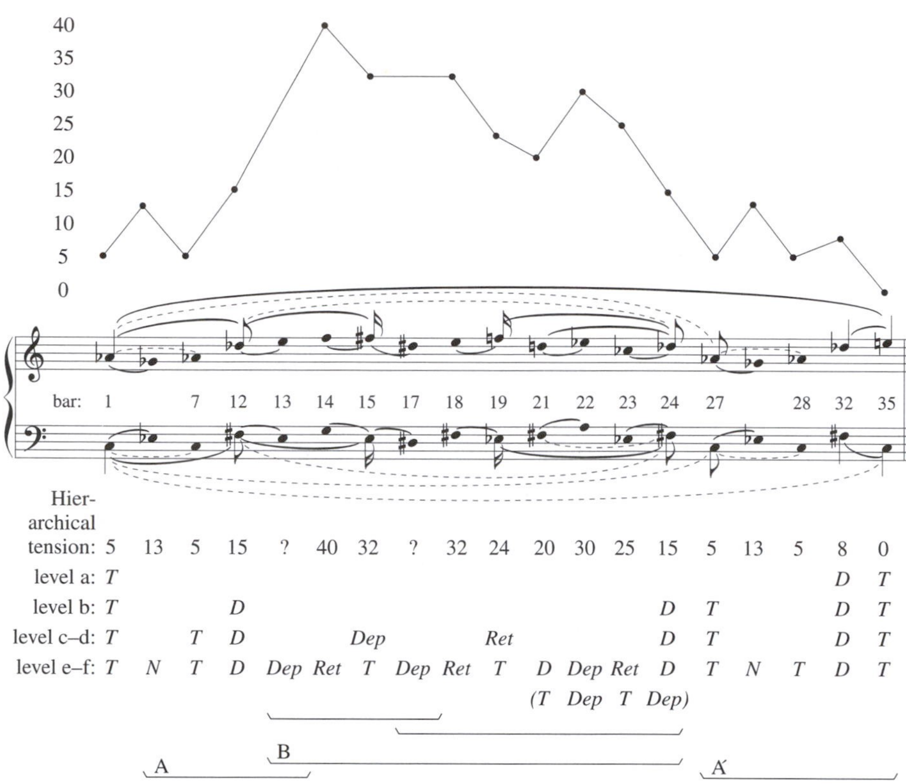

FIGURE 7.30 Hierarchical tension analysis and functional analysis of Op. 67, no. 1.

+ 10 down the tree, so its total tension is 32. In terms of the rule: $T_{glob}(E^{F6/0167}) = T_{loc}(E^{F6/0167}) + T_{inh}(F\sharp^{0167}{}_{dom}) = 17 + (5 + 10) = 32$. The curve above the music represents the T_{glob} values graphically. The overall pattern is of low tension sharply increasing to high tension into the climax at bar 15 and a gradual return to low tension into the reprise and close.

A different decision at the outset would change the curve somewhat. $\delta = 5$ between the opening and closing T-functions, so a choice must be made as to which T is set to 0. On the somewhat arbitrary assumption that this piece attains closure in the manner of a Classical piece, I have chosen final T = 0; hence the resulting highest branchings in Figures 7.27 and 7.29a–c. The alternative of initial T = 0 would decrease all values by 5 except for the two-membered final cadence, which would increase by 5.

No tension value is given for the deceptive resolutions in bars 13 and 17. Mysterium collections overlap in bars 13–14 and 17–18, and these chords do not conform to the standard types for the Prelude, [0 2 6 8] and [0 1 6 7]. In a sense they do not count as chords in this music; they are dissonant verticalities. Extra steps could be taken to assign them tension values, but I shall not do so here. These values would be high in relation to their immediate contexts.

This raises once again the issue of the role of sensory dissonance. The chords at bars 13 and 17 are tense not only because they are atypical sonorities deeply embedded in the tree but also because they are psychoacoustically rough even in comparison with the chords that surround them. To a lesser extent it might be argued that final T in bar 35 is rougher than initial T in bar 1 and therefore that initial T should be set to 0. However, the virtual-pitch root of initial T is less clear than that of final T, so these factors (conditions [1] and [2] of the sensory consonance rule) largely cancel each other out. Melodically, the opening A♭ feels less stable than the final E. The latter is comparatively stable partly because of the realized implication from bar 13 discussed earlier and also because it fits the harmonic template of the bass C. In short, the issue of sensory consonance is complex for this piece. Scriabin seems to have sought a fairly high and constant dissonance level against which the melody and harmony grope toward cognitive resolution.

The functional analysis at the bottom of Figure 7.30 reads off the prolongational tree in a mostly straightforward manner. The parenthesized interpretation for bars 21–24 at levels e–f follows from a local view of the path. In a larger view, this is the third instance of Dep→Ret in the B section, a pattern replicated on a larger scale at levels c–d. In two of these instances—the $E\flat^{F6/0167}$ in bar 19 at level d and the $E\flat^{F6}$ in bar 23 at level e—Ret strictly should be designated S. But it is not clear that S is an acting functional category in this music. The Prelude avoids any S-function in the A and A' sections. Except for a few neighboring chords, these sections alternate between T and D, and normative prolongational structure is not fulfilled. This is one reason that the ending is only partly closed. (It may also explain why Scriabin asks for an accelerando and ritardando in the final phrase; slowing down compensates for syntactic incompleteness in bringing about a degree of closure.) Rather than approach the final cadence through some form of S, Scriabin merges D-function into the final T through the combined chord $C^{F6/0167}$. The effect is less one of resolution than one of an encompassing resonance.

Leading tone formations in Bartók and Stravinsky

Charles Morrison (1991) proposes the construct in Figure 7.31 based on a statement by Bartók (1976), who completes the chromatic aggregate by a combination of Lydian and Phrygian modes over a single tonic. The Lydian/Phrygian poly-

FIGURE 7.31 Bartók's Lydian/Phrygian polymode, with double leading tones indicated by the arrows (from Morrison 1991).

FIGURE 7.32 Leading-tone progressions in Bartók's Fifth Quartet: (a) the ending of the first movement; (b) the ending of the fifth movement.

mode yields double leading tones around the tonic and dominant pitches, indicated by the arrows in Figure 7.31a. Figure 7.31b treats these tendencies as a voice-leading harmonic progression. The four leading tones together form a chord that can be arranged in fourths, and they resolve on an open fifth.

The closing gestures of the first and last movements of Bartók's Fifth Quartet in Figure 7.32 illustrate double leading tones taken from segments of the polymode in Figure 7.31a. In both passages there is an axis of symmetry, B♭–E. Starting from E in Figure 7.32a, the leading tones that circle around E♭ in the upper line provide the inversional complement of those around F in the lower line. In a combination of descending Phrygian and ascending Lydian tetrachords, the two lines then converge through leading-tones C♭ and A on tonic B♭. In Figure 7.32b, a Phrygian tetrachord ascends to E, from which it continues to ascend by a Lydian tetrachord to A→B♭ while the lower line enters and descends by a Phrygian tetrachord to C♭→B♭. Both movements exploit an ambiguity as to whether salient tritone E or stable fifth F is more structural in relation to tonic B♭. The prolongational sketches favor the fifth, but the tritone alternative is also viable.

In harmonic passages these modal constructs tend to be less relevant than their reductions to leading tones of tonic and dominant pitches in Figure 7.31b. As in Schoenberg's Opp. 9 and 10, Bartók sometimes adds leading tones to the third of the triad ($\hat{3}$ or ♭$\hat{3}$, as the case may be). The third movement of the Sixth Quartet begins with such a progression, shown in Figure 7.33a; the movement ends with a variant of the same progression. Of the double leading tones to the pitches of the F major triad, all are present except G♭ (which appears in that role in the next bar), and all resolve to their strongest virtual attractions (B→C by octave displacement).

The fourth movement of the Sixth Quartet closes with the structurally similar but more elaborated passage in Figure 7.33b. The graph shows the strongest virtual attractions, indicated by slurs to parenthetical notes, of the dissonant major seconds in the upper register in bars 79–81. The tendency of these seconds is to

FIGURE 7.33 Leading-tone progressions in Bartók's Sixth Quartet: (a) the beginning of the third movement; (b) the ending of the fourth movement.

resolve by semitone to pitches of the D minor triad. The triad answers, but with added pitches and in a lower register. These leading-tone attractions do not reach full fruition until—after a last recall of the *mesto* theme and a return to registrally shifting chords—the arrival on the tonic D-A fifth in bar 85 (with a momentary F♯) in multiple registers.

Morrison offers the constructs in Figure 7.31 to develop a prolongational analysis of the first section (bars 1–148) of the fifth movement of the Fourth Quartet. In order to provide a pitch-space foundation for his approach, Figure 7.34a ignores the modes in Figure 7.31a and casts Figure 7.31b as fifth/leading-tone space. The scalar level consists of the tonic and dominant pitches, the four leading tones, and an optional filling in of the space between pc1 and pc6 by pc3 or pc4. At the chordal level is the fifth to which the leading tones resolve. The scalar level can be interpreted as an altered diatonic scale with $\flat\hat{2}$, $\sharp\hat{4}$, $\flat\hat{6}$, and $\sharp\hat{7}$. Viewed as a scale per se, however, this level fails most of the preferential conditions for basic spaces. It depends for its validity instead on the powerful voice-leading attractions it elicits, demonstrated in Figure 7.34b. The weakness of the other stepwise attractions in Figure 7.34c only magnifies the strength of the leading tones.

Fifth/leading-tone space evokes interesting historical associations. It unites the voice leading in the fourteenth-century leading-tone cadence ($\sharp\hat{4}$ and $\sharp\hat{7}$ in Figure 7.19a) with the voice leading in the late-nineteenth-century dominant-substitute $\flat II^{+6}$ cadence ($\flat\hat{2}$, $\flat\hat{6}$, and $\sharp\hat{7}$ in Figure 7.15b). As intimated earlier, the space is central to Schoenberg's tonal period before he plunged into atonality. (In addition to Figure 7.20, see, for example, the final bars of his tone poem *Pelleas und Melisande*, Op. 5, in which all four leading tones resolve directly or indirectly to a D minor triad.) More generally, the symmetry of double leading tones around the tonic and dominant pitches is a special case of axis-of-symmetry formations based on interval cycles, proposed by George Perle (1977, 1990) for the music of Scriabin, Bartók, Berg, Varèse, and others and applied to Bartók's music in detail by

a)

0											
0							7				
0	1		(3)			6	7	8			11
0	1	2	3	4	5	6	7	8	9	10	11

or

0											
0							7				
0	1			(4)		6	7	8			11
0	1	2	3	4	5	6	7	8	9	10	11

b)

$\alpha(B \rightarrow C) = \frac{4}{2} \times \frac{1}{1^2} = 2$

$\alpha(Db \rightarrow C) = \frac{4}{2} \times \frac{1}{1^2} = 2$

$\alpha(F\sharp \rightarrow G) = \frac{3}{2} \times \frac{1}{1^2} = 1.5$

$\alpha(A\flat \rightarrow G) = \frac{3}{2} \times \frac{1}{1^2} = 1.5$

c)

$\alpha(E\flat \rightarrow D\flat) = \frac{2}{2} \times \frac{1}{2^2} = 0.25$

$\alpha(E \rightarrow F\sharp) = \frac{2}{2} \times \frac{1}{2^2} = 0.25$

$\alpha(Eb \rightarrow C) = \frac{4}{2} \times \frac{1}{3^2} = 0.22$

$\alpha(E \rightarrow G) = \frac{3}{2} \times \frac{1}{3^2} = 0.17$

FIGURE 7.34 The Lydian/Phrygian polymode treated as fifth/leading-tone space: (a) two slightly different versions of the space; (b) the leading-tone attractions; (c) the other stepwise attractions in the space.

Elliot Antokoletz (1984) (including the passages in Figure 7.32). Not included in their approach, however, is the hierarchy of a basic space and the resulting account of voice-leading attractions. The strength of double leading-tone attractions causes this symmetry to stand out perceptually more than other intervallic symmetries do.

The first section of the fifth movement of the Fourth Quartet symmetrically freezes leading tones into the tonic and dominant pitches to which they resolve, forming [0 1 6 7] chords. Figure 7.35a gives the opening: D♭ and F♯ occur within the C-G fifth, which is superordinate by virtue of registral placement (salience condition [5]). **C** is in turn tonic of the C-G fifth because it is the virtual root (sensory consonance condition [2]). In bar 3 the cello enters with symmetrical fifths around C, including an F that lies outside the fifth/leading-tone spatial framework. Starting in bar 12, the viola-cello ostinato accompaniment in Figure 7.35b adds another leading tone, the grace note A♭. The accompaniment eventually modulates to new frames of reference, **A** in bars 44–72 and **F♯** in bars 76–98. The excerpts in Figures 7.35c–d show that the leading tones on $\flat\hat{2}$, $\sharp\hat{4}$, and $\flat\hat{6}$ (to use the altered diatonic description) continue with the structural fifths A-E and F♯-C♯. After a transition, the texture from bars 1–11 returns transposed to **A♭** in bars 121–141, excerpted in Figure 7.35e. The leading tones, again on $\flat\hat{2}$, $\sharp\hat{4}$, and $\flat\hat{6}$, transfer to the offbeat cello attacks, creating a tritone polarity in which D

FIGURE 7.35 Excerpts from the first section of the fifth movement of Bartók's Fourth Quartet.

a)

0
0 7
0 1 6 7
0 1 3 4 6 7 9 10
0 1 2 3 4 5 6 7 8 9 10 11

C^{0167}/**oct0**

b)

$\underline{3}$
$\underline{3}$ $\underline{10}$
$\underline{3}$ $\underline{4}$ $\underline{9}$ $\underline{10}$
0 1 3 4 6 7 9 10
0 1 2 3 4 5 6 7 8 9 10 11

δ(C^{0167}/**oct0**→A^{0167}/**oct0**)
= 0 + 1 + 7 = 8

c)

$\underline{6}$
$\underline{1}$ $\underline{6}$
0 1 6 7
0 1 3 4 6 7 9 10
0 1 2 3 4 5 6 7 8 9 10 11

δ(C^{0167}/**oct0**→F♯^{0167}/**oct0**)
= 0 + 2 + 3 = 5

d)

$\underline{8}$
$\underline{3}$ $\underline{8}$
$\underline{2}$ $\underline{3}$ $\underline{8}$ $\underline{9}$
0 $\underline{2}$ 3 $\underline{5}$ 6 $\underline{8}$ 9 $\underline{11}$
0 1 2 3 4 5 6 7 8 9 10 11

δ(C^{0167}/**oct0**→A♭^{0167}/**oct2**)
= 1 + 1 + 11 = 13

FIGURE 7.36 [0167]/oct space and some pertinent distances within it.

momentarily triumphs in bars 145–47 before sliding down to **C** via leading-tones D♭ and A♭. Against this modulating ostinato the violin melody in bars 16–98 takes place almost entirely within **oct0**.

In keeping with the harmonic character of this movement, Figure 7.36a treats octatonic space so that [0 1 6 7] is the prevailing chord, yielding [0167]/oct space oriented to **C**^{oct0}. The superordinate fifths [0 7] appear at the next higher level, and the root of the fifth is at the top. Pcs 9 and 10 at the scalar level in **oct0** do not fit into the scalar level of fifth/leading-tone space in Figure 7.34a. The music thus employs two overlapping pitch organizations, one for the accompaniment and the other for the melody. The difference is small because the primary leading tones in the ostinati, ♭$\hat{2}$ and ♯$\hat{4}$, belong to both scales. Moreover, once the leading tones are reduced out, the fifths that remain in leading-tone space match up with the fifths level in octatonic space. The [0 1 6 7] chords stay within **oct0** when moved around the minor-third cycle C→A→F♯. (In this respect this passage resembles the Scriabin Prelude.) Fifth/leading-tone space plays a local role, and the passage as a whole is governed by [0167]/oct space.

Figures 7.36b–d give enough distances in [0167]/oct space to project the chordal/regional structure in Figure 7.37. Strictly speaking, the arrangement within a region should reflect the shorter distances between chords a tritone apart (δ = 5) compared to those a minor third apart (δ = 8), by curving the space along the lines suggested for the diagram of F6/oct space in Figure 6.22b; but a simple squarelike arrangement will suffice. The resulting geometry corresponds to that of triadic/oct space with collapsed parallel triads (compare Figure 6.11). The path taken in Figure 7.37 follows the course of the ostinati in Figure 7.35: starting at C, it moves to A and F♯, all within **oct0**, then to A♭ in **oct2**, and finally back to C in **oct0**.

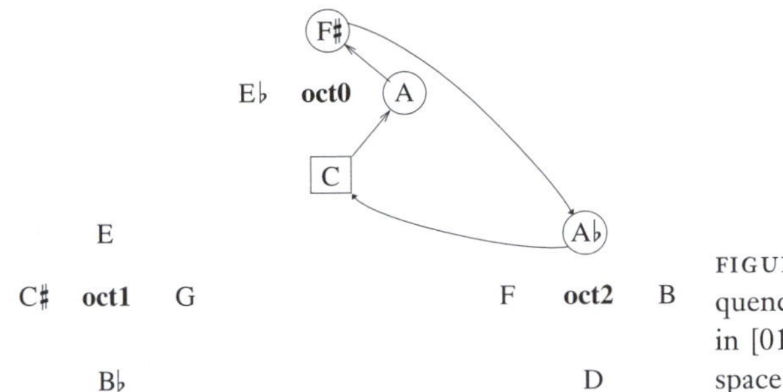

FIGURE 7.37 Path for the sequence in Figure 7.35 represented in [0167]/oct chordal/regional space.

Figure 7.38 is a prolongational sketch of the entire section based on the representative fragments in Figure 7.35. As in Classical tonal music, reduction in this dissonant idiom is both horizontal and vertical; that is, it both removes subordinate events and simplifies the contents of the events that remain. But there are differences as well. Dissonant nonharmonic tones in Classical music reduce out just

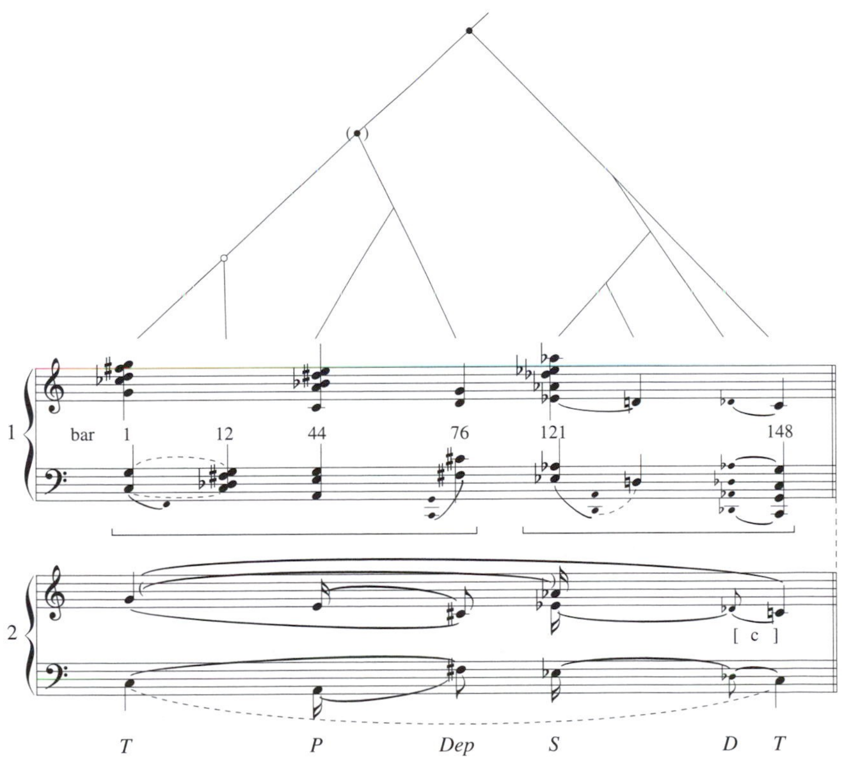

FIGURE 7.38 Prolongational analysis of the first section of the fifth movement of Bartók's Fourth Quartet, based on the excerpts in Figure 7.35.

below the musical surface. Further deletion of inner voices at underlying levels applies to pitches that belong to triads of which the structural outer voices are also members. Here, however, vertical reduction is more far-reaching. Nonharmonic tones are retained as far as level 1 in Figure 7.38, which is already a considerable abstraction from the surface. The basis for their further reduction at level 2 is both the salience of the fifths and the force of the leading-tone attractions. The latter factor can be viewed as assimilation by attractors. In effect, because of the deep level at which their reduction takes place, the leading tones are treated as both harmonic and nonharmonic. Through level 1, the characteristic chord is [0 1 6 7]; from level 2 on down, it becomes [0 7].

The large-level grouping boundary beneath level 1 in Figure 7.38 provides enough time-span information to make the specific prolongational connections in level 2. The analysis raises two questions. First, within the first large time span, does C^{0167} prolong directly to $F\sharp^{0167}$, within which A^{0167} nests, or does it prolong to A^{0167} and then the latter to $F\sharp^{0167}$, in embedded right branches? Morrison argues for the former reading, which this analysis also adopts. In its favor are the distances in Figure 7.36: $\delta(C^{0167}\rightarrow F\sharp^{0167})$ is less than $\delta(C^{0167}\rightarrow A^{0167})$. By the rule of prolongational connection, $F\sharp^{0167}$ attaches to C^{0167} directly. Then, by the recursion constraint, A^{0167} attaches to $F\sharp^{0167}$. Another way of arriving at this conclusion is to observe that the chords at bars 1 and 76 share the same pcs except for D in bar 76 and are thus virtually in a relationship of weak prolongation. That is, by analogy with weak prolongation in triadic/diatonic music, the pcs in the two chords are largely the same but in a different disposition. Hence the filled-in node in parentheses in the tree.

The second issue is what constitutes a cadence in this idiom. Despite its brevity, the grace-note D♭-A♭ fifth falling into bar 148 is labeled as the first member of the full cadence, giving it structural importance. This move enables the functional analysis at the bottom of the graph to be normative. In particular, the $A\flat^{0167}$ area (bars 121–141) receives S-function. But the real justification for labeling the D♭-A♭ as cadential is that this is the role that leading-tone formations play in this piece when they are not frozen into their governing fifths. Such is the implication of Morrison's abstracted progression in Figure 7.31b. In support of this interpretation is the final cadential gesture of the movement (identical to the ending of the first movement), given in Figure 7.39a with its prolongational analysis. The E♭ in the head motive suspends into the downbeat and immediately resolves to D♭ before the structural resolution to C. Meanwhile in the soprano, F♯ tends toward G but resolves to its secondary attractor E. The counterpoint frees leading tones D♭ and F♯ from the C^{0167} that begins the movement so that they can assume a separate D-function. The functional expression of the final cadence thus becomes D→T. Figure 7.39b brings out this interpretation by rhythmically normalizing the displacement caused by the quasi suspension.

The force of this cadence relies not only on leading-tone attractions but also on the resolution of sensory dissonance. From the perspective of salience, the dissonant [0 1 4] trichords on the upbeat and downbeat in Figure 7.39a move to an implied C major triad, obliquely resolving the roughness. The rhythmic nor-

FIGURE 7.39 The ending of Bartók's Fourth Quartet: (a) the music and its prolongational analysis; (b) rhythmic normalization of the cadence, with functions added.

FIGURE 7.40 The beginning of Stravinsky's *Les noces* and its prolongational analysis (including implied resolutions of leading tones).

FIGURE 7.41 The beginning of the "Danse sacrale" from Stravinsky's *Le sacre du printemps*, together with its prolongational analysis.

malization in Figure 7.39b yields the same picture: a dissonant [0 1 6], standing for the [0 1 6 7] chords, resolves to an underlying triad.

Stravinsky of the Russian period precedes Bartók of the later quartets in the dual employment of diatonic-modal and octatonic scales with leading-tone formations. The beginning of *Les noces* in Figure 7.40 provides an example. Against a modal vocal line centered on **E** by salience, the pianos strike leading-tone D♯. In bars 11–20 the accompaniment fills in the texture with leading-tones B♭ (= A♯) and F, creating the [0 1 6] sonority that prevails in subsequent phrases. In bars 21–23 the soprano embellishes leading-tone F with G♭ while the pianos state leading-tones E♭-B♭ (= D♯-A♯) before both parts return, an octave lower, to the sonority of bars 11–20. From bar 24 on, the pattern of bars 21–23 repeats with some of the pitches in lower octaves and with leading-tones D♯-A♯ in the pianos in turn embellished by D-A. The prolongational sketch in Figure 7.40 brings out these relationships. (As van den Toorn [1983] and Taruskin [1996] observe, bars 11–20 also combine incomplete diatonic and octatonic collections.)

The opening of the "Danse sacrale" from *Le sacre du printemps*, sketched in Figure 7.41, can be seen through the same lens. A distinctive surface sonority in *Le sacre* is the dominant seventh, usually in closed position, in an octatonic context, and with an added pitch a major seventh below its root acting as an octave-displaced leading tone. (Other displaced leading tones can appear as well; for example, in the famous thumping chord of the "Danses des adolescentes," an acoustically reinforcing third and fifth are added to F♭ a seventh below the E♭^{7} chord.) The dominant-seventh-including structure typically functions as T. Bar 1 of Figure 7.41 exhibits all these features in a D^7 chord with E♭ beneath. Leading-tone E♭ to **D**^{oct2} is reinforced by its fifth, leading-tone B♭, which unlike the other pitches does not belong to **oct2**. In bar 2 another leading tone, C♯, enters. The continuation in bar 3 sustains C♯ while the upper voices move in parallel neighboring motion. Bars 10–11 project a D minor triad in the bass and soprano over a sustained E♭ minor triad, which is an octave-shifted elaboration of leading-tones E♭-B♭ from bar 1. Meanwhile the inner voices descend in **oct2** by triads symmetrically arrayed around D. After a return to the opening material, the bass begins to move in bars 21–22, against the tonic-functioning dominant seventh with leading tones, by outlining D-F from the D minor triad, in motivic answer to F-A in the soprano in bars 10–11.

The prolongational graph beneath the music in Figure 7.41 highlights by means of stemmed note heads the structural role of the D minor triad, primarily on the basis of its registral salience (condition [5]). At an underlying level the pitches that complete the dominant sevenths and the appended leading tones reduce out vertically, leaving the D minor triad as a residue. This is what enables the dominant sevenths to function as T: the reduced-out pitches are inner-voice colorations. This reading is supported both by the Introduction to Part II of *Le sacre*, in which leading-tone e♭ and c♯ triads oscillate in eighth notes over sustained low D minor triads, and by the ending of the "Danse sacrale" which resolves a long quasi-dominant A pedal by a crunching D-A-(E) fifth with frozen leading-tone G♯. Its great surface dissonance notwithstanding, *Le sacre* still evokes levels of pitch space (diatonic and octatonic scales, leading tones, triads and their roots, prolongations of a tonic). In this critical sense the work remains marginally tonal.

8 *Atonal Structures*

PRELIMINARIES TO PROLONGATIONS IN FLAT SPACE

Remnants of the chord distance rule

The analyses of music by Bartók and Stravinsky in chapter 7 stretch the applicability of the concept of the basic space to its breaking point. This chapter explores the analytic potential of the theory for music in which there is no referable basic space. Whether or not such music has pitch centricity established by salience, it is atonal in the sense that its pitch space is flat. The only basic-space level is the chromatic. There is no stratified distinction between harmonic and nonharmonic tones or, more generally, between stable and unstable structures. Despite the flat space, however, there remain enough rules in force to assign meaningful prolongations and functions.

Although any version of δ would appear to be inapplicable in such a context, with small adjustments a few of its variables remain operational. Consider the most elaborated form of δ, the interspatial rule $\delta_{is}(x \rightarrow y) = ([sc + 1] + ch) + (i + j) + k$. Variables *sc*, *i*, and *j* do not apply because there is no scalar or chordal level. Variable *ch*, however, can be reinterpreted as measuring ic similarity not between two chords as represented at a chordal level but between any two event structures: the more differences in the presence or absence of ics between the two structures, the more dissimilar they are, hence the greater the distance between them. Variable *k* measures pc similarity not by comparing basic-space configurations but by directly comparing surface events: the more distinctive pcs between two event structures or pc sets, the more dissimilar they are, hence the greater the distance between them. The rule becomes a pared down version of δ_{is}:

FLAT-SPACE DISTANCE RULE $\delta_{flat}(x \rightarrow y) = ch + k$, where $\delta_{flat}(x \rightarrow y)$ = the distance between event-structure x and event-structure y; *ch* = the number of differences in the presence or absence of ics between x and y; and *k* = the number of distinctive pcs in y compared to those in x.

An event structure is defined not just as a pitch event in GTTM's sense but also as a set of pitches transformed into a verticality by a fusion rule introduced later.

An advantage of δ_{flat} is that it takes the parsimonious course of adjusting existing versions of δ to the new context rather than injecting foreign elements into δ. δ_{is} in particular is modified because only this version includes variable *ch*, which measures ic commonality between different pitch structures. One could imagine, however, a more complex measure of distance between two atonal pitch formations. Yet it is far from obvious what the best solution might be. (There is an inconclusive literature on pc-set similarity.) As suggested in "Related Issues" in chapter 6, the use of ic vectors is problematic because they make finer distinctions than appear to be warranted on perceptual grounds. One might go to the opposite end of the spectrum and ask whether the abstraction of pc and ic content is justified at all. Yet description at the level of pitches and intervals, though more precise in one sense, pays a price in loss of generality. A proper balance must be sought between concrete pitches and intervals, on the one hand, and abstract pcs and ics, on the other, in contributing to judgments of similarities between atonal events. I shall not explore this complex topic here (see Väisälä [1999] for some ideas in this regard).

Despite these qualifications, the flat-space rule succeeds in the modest role for which it is designed. Its function is to help decide right or left branchings by the principle of the shortest path. Refinements missed by δ_{flat} are largely neutralized in any case, by virtue of its interaction with the rules of prolongational good form and the three perceptual rules of salience, anchoring/reduction, and sensory dissonance.

Figure 8.1 gives a few illustrations of the flat-space rule in relation to {0 1 6 7}. (The curly brackets denote not general—transpositionally and inversionally equivalent—set-class types but sets with specific pcs.) The first two cases in Figure 8.1a simply transpose [0 1 6 7], so *ch* = 0 and *k* sums the new pcs. In the third case in Figure 8.1a, the set type changes to [0 1 5 6], introducing a single ic not present in [0 1 6 7], ic4, so that *ch* = 1. But the distance {0 1 6 7}→{0 1 5 6} remains small because only one new pc is introduced. In Figure 8.1b, {0 1 6 7} is compared to transpositions of [0 1 4], so that *ch* is constant and *k* varies. A similar pattern holds in Figure 8.1c, where {0 1 6 7} is compared to one of the two all-interval tetrachords, and in Figure 8.1d, where it is compared to dominant-seventh structures. (As with the interspatial distance rule, a comparison of sets of different cardinality results in an asymmetry between δ(x→y) and δ(y→x), because of the differing values for *k*. I shall not pursue an adjustment for this slightly awkward result.)

a)

$\delta_{flat}(\{0167\} \rightarrow \{1278\}) = 0 + 2 = 2$
$\delta_{flat}(\{0167\} \rightarrow \{4,5,10,11\}) = 0 + 4 = 4$
$\delta_{flat}(\{0167\} \rightarrow \{0156\}) = 1 + 1 = 2$

b)

$\delta_{flat}(\{0167\} \rightarrow \{014\}) = 2 + 1 = 3$
$\delta_{flat}(\{0167\} \rightarrow \{125\}) = 2 + 2 = 4$
$\delta_{flat}(\{0167\} \rightarrow \{458\}) = 2 + 3 = 5$

c)

$\delta_{flat}(\{0167\} \rightarrow \{0146\}) = 3 + 1 = 4$
$\delta_{flat}(\{0167\} \rightarrow \{3589\}) = 3 + 4 = 7$

d)

$\delta_{flat}(\{0167\} \rightarrow \{0269\}) = 3 + 2 = 5$
$\delta_{flat}(\{0167\} \rightarrow \{2,4,8,11\}) = 3 + 4 = 7$

FIGURE 8.1 Illustrations of the flat-space distance rule.

A geometric mapping of distances between all possible pc sets would require so many spatial dimensions as to be unintelligible. δ_{flat} does not yield a small number of regular patterns. In this respect flat space resembles what an associational space of motivic relationships would look like. Even supposing one could adequately measure the relative similarity and dissimilarity—hence their distances from one another—of all the motives in, say, a Brahms symphony, the tangle of motivic relationships would not be constrained or regular enough to yield an illuminating geometry. Just so with distances among pc sets in flat space.

"The Harmonic Tension Model" in chapter 4 offered a quantitative gloss on the three kinds of prolongational branching by the pattern of entries for $T_{loc}(\mathbf{y})$, which utilizes δ, in the associated tables for hierarchical tension. Now that we have δ_{flat}, can atonal prolongations fit into this scheme? The answer is no: the tonal gloss relies on distinctions between the root and the other pitches in a triad and also between harmonic and nonharmonic tones, and these conditions do not hold in flat space. True, one could erect a partial analogue by equating bass with root—or, better, by deriving the strongest virtual pitch as root in an updated Hindemithian approach. But any successes in this direction would be overwhelmed in practice by salience and other contextual factors. Let us instead adopt a simple treatment of the three branching categories:

ATONAL BRANCHING WELL-FORMEDNESS CONDITION An event e_i can be a direct elaboration of another event_j in any of the following ways:
(1) e_i is a strong prolongation of e_j if the two events share all the same pcs
(2) e_i is a weak prolongation of e_j if the two events share approximately half the same pcs
(3) e_i is a progression to or from e_j if the two events share less than half the same pcs.

This rule, which modifies GTTM's PRWFR 2, ignores the *ch* variable in δ_{flat} in favor of the *k* variable and does not attempt to build on what would frequently be a perceptually flimsy assignment of roots or nonharmonic tones. It also accepts indefiniteness in distinctions between branching categories. In particular, the distinction is fuzzy between weak prolongation and progression; in such cases, the filled-in node that represents weak prolongation is placed in parentheses. This fuzziness is, I believe, less a theoretical weakness than the recognition of a perceptual reality about music not constructed out of levels of basic spaces.

Atonal functions

Functions can be read off the prolongational tree in atonal music much as in tonal music. But there are differences. Without a stratified basic space, it seems unwarranted to refer to a global atonal tonic and to subsidiary atonal regions as local tonics. Rather, certain atonal sonorities are contextually referential by salience. Let us therefore replace tonal T-function by atonal RS-function (for "referential sonority"). Without T-functions it is pointless to refer to D-functions; moreover, in atonal music there are no fixed cadential formulae, hence no cadential labelings. Similarly, there are no S-functions because there are no D- or T-functions. Right-branching progressions act as Dep, left-branching progressions as Ret. N-functions and P-functions are analogous to the tonal case—albeit without the support of a stratified space—in that they express neighboring or passing motion between superordinate events. We arrive at a modification of the tonal function rule:

ATONAL FUNCTION RULE Assign the repertory of functions RS (referential sonority), Dep (departure), Ret (return), N (neighboring), and P (passing), by prolongational position from global to local levels, such that

(1) RS belongs to
  (a) the prolongational head or
  (b) an event that contains Dep and Ret within a strong prolongation of itself
(2) Dep belongs to any event assigned a right-branching progression
(3) Ret belongs to any event assigned a left-branching progression
(4) N belongs to any pitch or chord that is directly subordinate within a strong prolongation
(5) P belongs to any pitch or chord that is
  (a) directly subordinate within a weak prolongation
  (b) a left branch off Dep or
  (c) a right branch off Ret
(6) all functions transmit intact through strong or weak prolongations
(7) parallel passages preferably receive parallel functions.

Condition (1a) in effect replaces the action of the tonic-finding rule by the conditions of the salience rule (since, as will be discussed shortly, salience is the primary determinant of time-span head) and, secondarily, of the sensory consonance rule. Condition (1b) allows the possibility of subordinate RS-functions, by analogy with subordinate tonic regions. Its inclusion of the combination of Dep and Ret fills the place of the self-contained tonal regions on which the tonic-finding rule relies, the idea being that a departure and return within a repeated sonority sufficiently establishes the sonority as contextually referential. Conditions (5b) and (5c) complement each other and enable P-functions between events that do not form weak prolongations. Condition (5b) corresponds to condition (7b) in the tonal function rule. The latter does not include a corresponding case to atonal condition (5c) because in tonal music left branching usually involves S and D instead of Ret.

Derivational principles

Atonal prolongational analyses derive in the same general way as tonal prolongational analyses: via grouping and meter (although the latter may not be applicable in atonal textures that do not give rise to the inference of periodic beats), to time-span segmentation and time-span reduction, and then via the application of the interaction principle to prolongational reduction. The segmentation problem that besets pc-set theory finds a solution here, in a rather different form, in procedures that are already in place. That is, rather than search for a principled basis for circling horizontal, vertical, or diagonal adjacent pitches as perceptually viable pc-sets (as in Hasty 1981), this procedure achieves rhythmic units, hence pc groupings, by means of the time-span segmentation and derives atonal prolongations from them. The cognitive claim is that there is continuity in this regard between tonal and atonal music.

The role of prolongational good form does not change when moving from tonal to atonal analysis. Recursive branching remains a preferred branching pattern, and departure and return are preferably in balance.

The principal difference between tonal and atonal prolongational derivations lies in the relative roles of stability and salience (see "Psychoacoustic Factors in Prolongational Analysis" in chapter 7). In the atonal case, in the absence of a stratified hierarchy of stability, the salience rule usually holds sway. The rule of time-span stability and its associated rule of prolongational connection, both of which call up δ_{flat}, play a correspondingly smaller role. Because of this redistribution in weightings (which I shall not attempt to quantify) and because salience affords fewer and less regular hierarchical distinctions than does stability, atonal prolongational structures tend to be perceptually fragile and of limited hierarchical depth. (Some empirical evidence for the influence of salience in construing atonal surfaces appears in Cuddy [1997] and Dibben [1999]; much remains to be explored in this area.)

"The Harmonic Tension Model" in chapter 4 showed how intuitions of tension and relaxation are measured by distances traversed in tonal space as traced down the prolongational tree. Without an ordered space and with the concomitant perceptual dependency on salience for organizing prolongational structure, there is a relatively weak correlation in most atonal music between elaboration and tension. Hence it is preferable to refer not to atonal prolongational tension and relaxation but just to atonal departure and return. Strong prolongation yields no departure or return, weak prolongation some departure or return, and progression a comparatively large degree of departure or return.

This picture of the interaction of stability and salience, while cogent as far as it goes, ignores the potential role of sensory consonance in atonal music. Even without a stratified space, sensory consonance plays a structural role when an atonal surface projects significant and patterned differences in consonance. Daniel Pressnitzer, Stephen McAdams, Susan Winsberg, and Joshua Fineberg (2000) report experiments that use complex sonorities in which salience is neutralized and roughness is varied. They find that listeners reliably correlate roughness and tension. The implication for this theory is that low roughness might partly replace the role of high salience in atonal prolongation. That is, within each prolongational region, relatively rough events might be reduced out, leaving more consonant events for the next reductional stage. A problem for this hypothesis is that relatively rough events also tend to be relatively salient. As a result, salience may conflict with and even overwhelm sensory consonance as a reductional factor. Formally, the issue concerns the relative weight of the salience rule compared to that of the rule of sensory consonance. The hypothesis is attractive, however, in its appeal to intuitions of tension and relaxation, which are the starting point in GTTM's conception of tonal prolongation. The difference between tonal and atonal music in this regard is that for tonal music the chief measure of tension, once local dissonance is reduced out, is a cognitive one, based on distances from triad to triad in the elaborate mental schema that is tonal pitch space, whereas for atonal music the chief measure of tension is psychoacoustic at all levels.

The relative inattention in the theoretical literature given to the organizing potential of degrees of sensory consonance may partly be an effect of the influence of Schoenberg's (1941/1975) doctrine of the emancipation of dissonance. Nevertheless, composers have frequently exploited this potential in largely atonal contexts. We have seen fragments of this approach in the closing gesture of Bartók's Fourth Quartet (Figure 7.39), a work that moves between chromatic pitch spaces and flat space, and we shall see it later in analyses of Schoenberg's Op. 11, no. 1, and Webern's Op. 7, no. 1. Hindemith's (1937/1942) theory of harmony fits within this general framework, as do techniques of the spectral school of composition (Fineberg 2001).

To summarize the foregoing discussion of atonal prolongational derivation, the picture that emerges for both tonal and atonal musics, assuming similar rhythmic frameworks, is that there are three broad, interactive factors in the listener's inference of prolongational reduction. Pitch-space distance (representing cognitive distance) plays a major role in tonal music but a minor role in atonal music. Psychoacoustic roughness is a factor only at the surface of tonal music but has the potential for significance also at underlying levels of atonal music. Psychoacoustic salience is important in both idioms but is more so in atonal music, in compensation for its lack of accessible forms of cognitive distance.

A further derivational complication that arises from flat space is that with no scalar or chordal level, hence with no stratified distinction between harmonic and nonharmonic tones, it is often ambiguous whether nonsimultaneous, temporally adjacent pitches form a single prolongational event. If they do, the event is arpeggiated and can be fused in the reduction; if not, the pitches do not form one event and require further prolongational treatment. The essential variables, leaving aside factors as such as timbral contrast, are as follows:

FUSION TRANSFORMATION RULE Temporally contiguous events may be fused if

(1) they are not separated by a grouping boundary
(2) they are at least a minor third apart
(3) they are temporally proximate (the closer, the more fusible)
(4) the duration of one overlaps that of the other.

These factors are psychoacoustic in nature (Bregman 1990). Condition (2) complements the anchoring/reduction rule. The fusion transformation rule has its counterpart in GTTM's TSRWFR 3b and is useful in tonal reduction not only for accompanimental figures but also in the verticalization of underlying events whose components are temporally distributed at the surface. The rule is in operation, for example, for the opening V^7 and closing I in the analysis of Debussy's "La terrasse" in Figure 7.14a. Fusion is notated there by a bracket over the fused pitches at the leaf of a branch. The absence of basic-space distinctions in atonal music both gives fusion a greater role than in tonal music and renders uncertain when the rule should be triggered. This uncertainty is less a deficiency of the theory than an acknowledgment of the cognitive effects of a flat space. Listening to any piece of Boulez from *Pli selon pli* onward, for instance, involves the awareness that sometimes for vast stretches the individual lines are also arpeggiations of single proliferating vertical events. This is the chief reason that the music sounds static. Instead of assigning progressions to events, the ear delves inside the shifting events themselves. The interest resides in nuances of "subevents." While it is not in principle beyond the reach of this theory to assign prolongational structure to subevents, this volume does not attempt this task but stops at assigning prolongational structure to atonal pitch events at a perceptual level comparable to that for events in tonal music.

It should be eminently clear by this point that when I invoke "atonal prolongation" I am not attempting to revive the Schenkerian conception of prolongation in context for which it was not designed. Rather, I use the term "prolongation" in the same way that it has been employed throughout GTTM and this volume, as a commonplace word adapted to precise meanings within the theory. A prolongational analysis represents hierarchical connections across musical events and does so in terms of three categories: the same (strong prolongation); the same in altered form (weak prolongation); and different (progression). This categorization is deliberately broad and could even be applied to nonmusical phenomena such as narrative structure in literature and phonological patterns in poetry (Lerdahl and Halle 1991). Only an abstract categorization at the theoretical foundation can accommodate contrasting musical idioms and hence can support an inclusive theory of musical cognition. Particular settings of formalisms (such as the particular basic space and the version of δ) account for specific stylistic features within this general framework. In this respect the approach resembles that in linguistic theory between universal grammar and particular grammars (Chomsky 1965). The fruitfulness of the approach is demonstrated not only by its psychologically grounded application to music of the Classical period but also by its modification for chromatic tonal music from Schubert to Bartók. Except for the change to flat space, the situation does not fundamentally alter once the stylistic line into atonality is crossed. One does not hear *Elektra* and *Erwartung* in entirely different ways. The historical development from tonality to atonality (and back) is richly continuous. Theories of tonality and atonality should be comparably linked. (For related discussion, see Travis 1966, 1970; Straus 1987, 1997; Larson 1997; and Lerdahl 1989a, 1997a, 1999.)

ATONAL PROLONGATIONS AND FUNCTIONS

Three Schoenberg analyses

In discussing melodic fragments from his orchestral song "Seraphita," Op. 22, no. 1, Schoenberg (1965) emphasizes the pitches marked by an "x" in Figure 8.2a, connecting them as lines, apparently on the basis of streaming. In the second fragment of Figure 8.2a Schoenberg treats the second pitch, F, as a neighboring ornament between E and E♭. From my perspective, this is so because F and E♭ occur in the same time-span segment and within a minor third. By the anchoring/reduction rule, F is a quasi appoggiatura and reduces out. The first note, E, is structural in comparison to F on grounds of salience, because it abuts a grouping boundary (salience condition [8]). Schoenberg's interest is in bringing out motivic relationships, but the distinctions in question hold from a prolongational perspective as well. Continuing from Schoenberg's remarks, Jack Boss (1994) similarly

FIGURE 8.2 Analysis of melodic fragments from Schoenberg's Op. 22, no. 1: (a) from Schoenberg (1965); (b) from Boss (1994); (c) the prolongational analysis of (b).

treats the two parenthesized As in bars 1–2 of Figure 8.2b as embellishing neighbors. This theory can extend this approach. Again by anchoring, D♯ in bar 3 acts as a quasi appoggiatura to C♯. The A in bar 3 resolves to A♯ by the same factor, and similarly with C→B in bars 4–5 and E♭→D in bar 5. Although A♯→G♯ in bar 4 could be treated in parallel fashion, in this case the comparative salience of the A♯ seems to override the anchoring rule. That is, salience condition (7) and the anchoring/reduction rule vie for dominance. Under this view, the A♯ is selected because of its relative length and the G♯ functions as a quasi échappée. Similarly, B in bar 1 is sufficiently prominent by virtue of its beginning the phrase (condition [8]) that it dominates B♭ later in the same bar.

Figure 8.2c slots these choices for Figure 8.2b into a prolongational analysis of the entire line, divided into two streams. The structural notes of the two lines form intervallic successions that are inversionally equivalent: B–C♯–A♯ in the upper stream, C♯–B–D in the lower. In this approach, motivic relatedness is a consequence rather than a cause of reductional levels. (At the next reductional level, the two streams would coalesce into one, showing a motion from the opening B to the closing D.)

Schoenberg's little piano piece Op. 19, no. 6, given in Figure 8.3 along with its prolongational and functional analysis, builds off reiterations of the opening sonority. (Pc-set and transformational analyses of this piece appear in Forte [1973] and Lewin [1987].) No metrical grid is supplied because the distances between attack points at the musical surface do not facilitate the inference of a hierarchy of periodic beats. Beneath the music appears the grouping structure, which falls into four short quasi phrases at grouping level b (bars 1–4, 4–6, 7–8, 9) by virtue of the intervening silences. At grouping level a, symmetry causes both the first and second phrases and the third and fourth phrases to group together. Phrases 1 and 3 subdivide at grouping level c. The time-span analysis fuses the opening trichords into a single six-note chord because after the attacks both trichords sound together (fusion condition [4]). The hierarchy of the time-span analysis is presented in compressed form, with the parenthesized letters that appear beneath level d indicating the levels to which superordinate events rise. There is no cadential labeling, as there is no formulaic repertory of cadences in this idiom.

The prolongational analysis, derived as usual from global-to-local levels of the associated time-span reduction, displays the opening sonority as strongly prolonging first to bar 3, then to bar 5, and finally to bar 9. After each of these prolongations there is a right-branching departure to a melodic tag. Bars 7–8 develop this feature into the entire third phrase, which returns to the home sonority in bar 9 via the neighboring chord on the second beat of bar 8. Thus bar 7 is prolongationally as well as texturally the most remote passage in the piece. By the balance constraint, bars 7–8 are left-branching so as to stabilize the right-branching departure in bars 5–6.

The functional analysis in Figure 8.3 shows the opening referential sonority, labeled RS, prolonging at level a, with a major departure–return pattern at levels b–d in bars 5–8. Level d further decomposes into locally departing melodic tags.

Figure 8.4 isolates the melodic tags to reveal a prolongational rhyme between phrases 1 and 3 and phrases 2 and 4. The tag for the first phrase is the neighboring motion (D♯→E→D♯) in Figure 8.4a. This motive inverts and transforms at the beginning of the third phrase (D→C♯→D), after which further elaboration takes place. To project this relationship, the beginning of bar 7 in Figure 8.4c is treated as not fused, leading to a different prolongational analysis than that indicated by the prolongational slurs in Figure 8.3. Similarly, the descending whole step at the end of the second phrase (G♯→F♯) in Figure 8.4b turns into the descending major ninth at the end of the fourth phrase (B♭→A♭) in Figure 8.4d. In Figure 8.4b the second pitch dominates by the anchoring/reduction rule. Figure 8.4d follows by parallelism as well as registral extreme (salience conditions [10] and [5]). The arrows bring out this pair of correspondences.

In Figure 8.5 the application of δ_{flat} to the primary sonorities in Op. 19, no. 6, supports the branchings at levels a–b in Figure 8.3. The distance from the sonority in bar 1 to that in bars 5–6 is small, encouraging a right-branching elaboration. The sonority in bar 8 is slightly closer to the final sonority in bar 9 than to the one in bars 5–6 and preferably connects as a left branch. This result reinforces that of the balance constraint. But is δ_{flat} really doing what it is supposed to do? In every calculation, $ch = 0$, since all three chords include all ic types. This is a probable outcome of comparing atonal chords that contain six or more notes. Should variable *ch* be replaced by a more complex measure of ic distance that differentiates the ic content of these chords? Pending relevant empirical evidence, I surmise that *ch* is behaving correctly: chords with many pcs do tend to sound alike in terms of ic content.

Figure 8.6 gives the opening section of Schoenberg's piano piece Op. 11, no. 1. The analysis of the truncated antecedent–consequent period—bars 1–8 and 9–11—appears in Figure 8.7, minus the slightly varied repetitions of the close of the first phrase in bars 5–8. In bars 4–9 the meter effectively goes into $\frac{2}{4}$. At time-span reductional level d in Figure 8.7, E in bar 3 and B♭ in bar 11 are selected by the anchoring/reduction rule. At level c the melodic notes in bars 1 and 9 are reduced out because they are unaccompanied (salience condition [6]). The fused events on the downbeat of bar 2 and on the notated third beat of bar 4 are superordinate to the chord in bar 3 because they are next to a larger grouping boundary; the same holds at time-span level b for the fused event in bar 11.

The event on the third beat of bar 4 dominates at time-span level a not because of its grouping position but because it yields an optimal global prolongational connection (GTTM's TSRPR 6). To clarify, Figure 8.8 shows the recapitulatory phrase of the piece, the most important of a number of large-scale prolongational references to the opening. Bars 53–54 telescope the head motive from bars 1–2 against the closural harmony of bars 4–5, which itself verticalizes the head motive (B-G♯-G). This powerful prolongational connection between exposition and reprise can be achieved only if the event in bar 4 is treated as the referential sonority of the first phrase.

Once this choice at time-span level a is in place, the prolongational analysis in Figure 8.7 follows straightforwardly by the interaction principle. The chord in bar 4 dominates at prolongational level a. At prolongational level b, the chord in bar 11 attaches as a marginally weak prolongation to the chord in bar 4 (because they share pcs G and B). At prolongational level c, bar 2 attaches to bar 4 for the

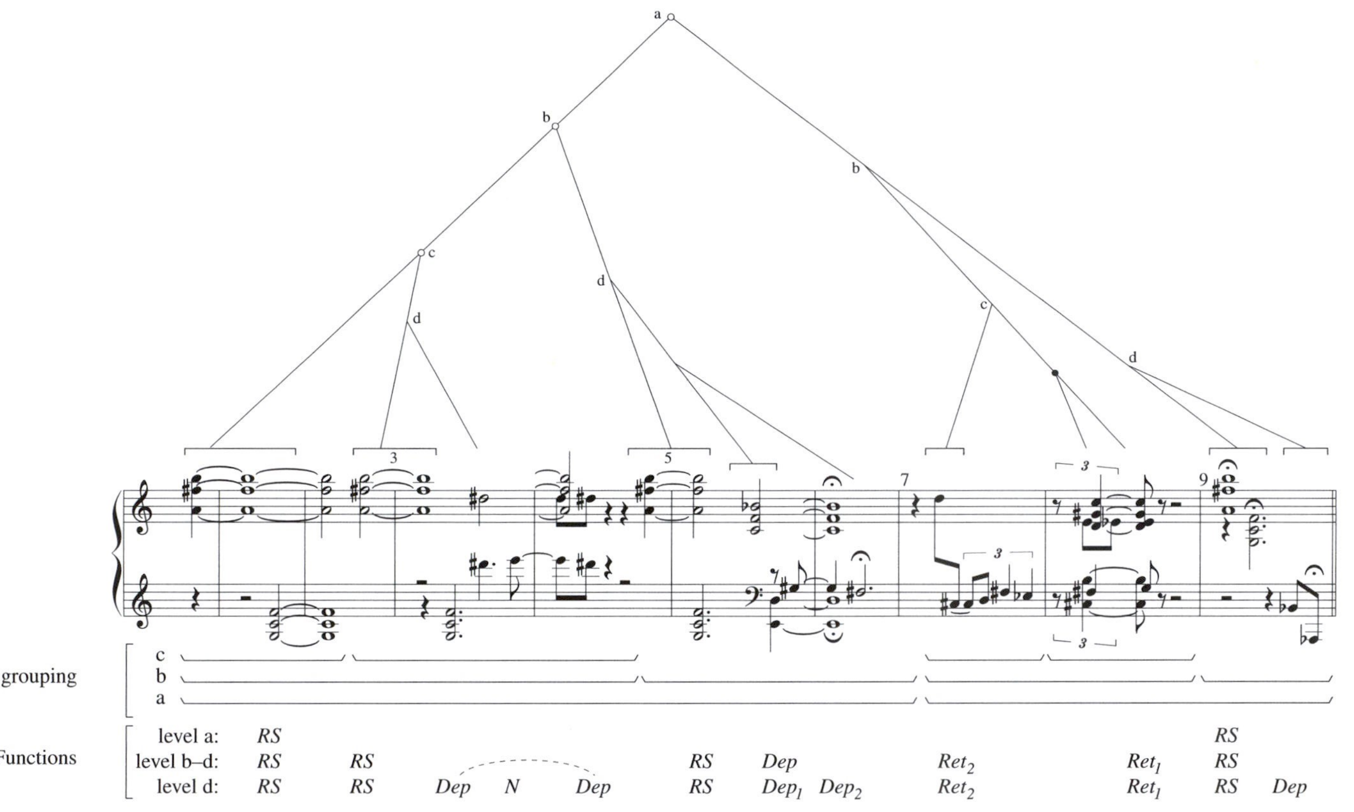
a
b
c
d
3
5
7
9
grouping
c
b
a
Functions
level a: RS RS
level b–d: RS RS RS Dep Ret_2 Ret_1 RS
level d: RS RS Dep N Dep RS Dep_1 Dep_2 Ret_2 Ret_1 RS Dep

FIGURE 8.3 Schoenberg's Op. 19, no. 6, together with its prolongational and functional analysis.

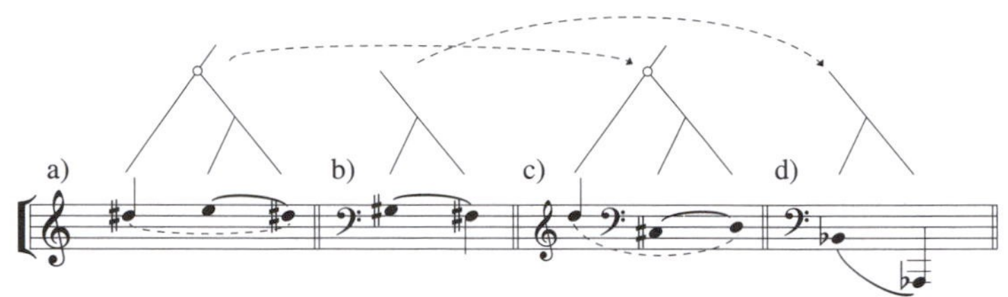

FIGURE 8.4 Connections between melodic tags in Op. 19, no. 6.

same reason. The connection between bars 2 and 4 is stronger, however, because here G and B repeat in the same register. Within this framework, bar 3 becomes a departure from bar 2, and the C-E anacrusis in bar 4 acts as a return to the referential sonority. The events in bars 9–10 in turn elaborate bar 11. The functional assignments in Figure 8.7 clarify these relationships.

Figure 8.9a highlights these same functions for the melody in bars 1–4. Figures 8.9b–c continue the melodic analysis by computing the melodic and metrical attractions, respectively, from one pitch to the next. The semitonal attractions G♯→G and F→E stand out in Figure 8.9b. For Figure 8.9c the quarter-note level is set at L(0) = 1, with the half-note level at L(2) = 2 and the eighth-note level at L(−1) = 0.5. As in Figure 8.7, the notated third beat of bar 4 is taken to be a downbeat (locally in $\frac{2}{4}$). A rescaling coefficient is required for combining the melodic and metrical values. Here—to try out a different procedure from that undertaken in Figure 6.49—the metrical values are divided in half. Figure 8.9d sums the resultant values to arrive at an overall tension curve for the melody. The effect of flat pitch space, because the first factor in the melodic equation must always be $\frac{1}{1}$ rather than some higher value caused by differences in basic-space levels, is proportionally to reduce the melodic values in comparison with the metrical values. In other words, the melodic and metrical attraction rules together predict that durational and metrical factors play a greater role in the perception of tension in atonal than in tonal music. The value for the quickly passing A→F seems high, however, suggesting that an additional temporal smoothing function is needed; I shall not pursue this. The main analytic result obtained from this exercise is that the melodic/metrical attractions to G in bars 2 and 4 are relatively strong, rein-

δ_{flat}({G,C,F,A,F♯,B}→{E,D,F♯,C,F,B♭}) = 0 + 3 = 3

δ_{flat}({E,D,F♯,C,F,B♭}→{C♯,G,B,D,Eb,G♯,C}) = 0 + 6 = 6

δ_{flat}({C♯,G,B,D,E♭,G♯,C}→{G,C,F,A,F♯,B}) = 0 + 5 = 5

FIGURE 8.5 Distances between the primary sonorities in Op. 19, no. 6.

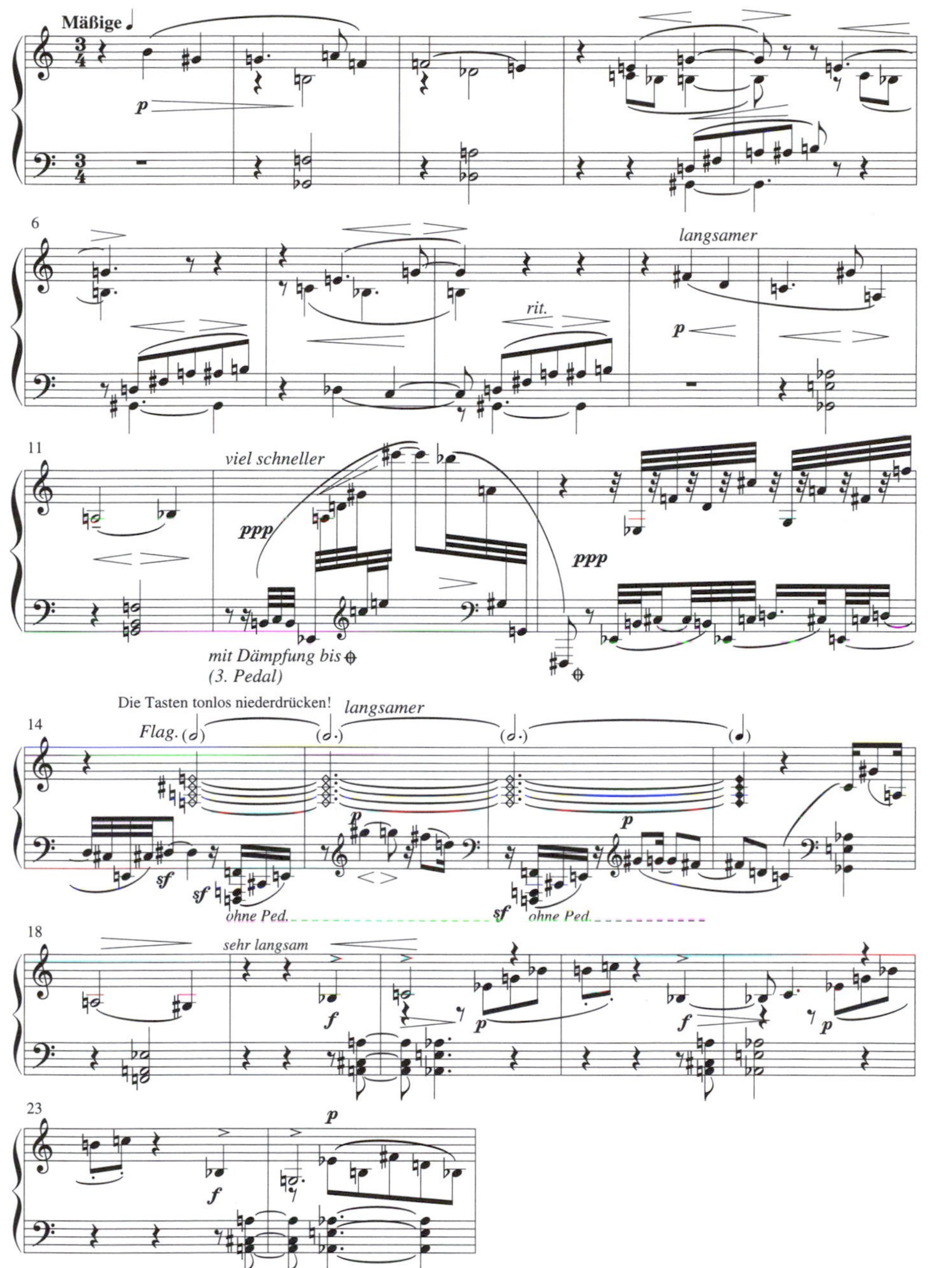

FIGURE 8.6 The first section (bars 1–24) of Schoenberg's Op. 11, no. 1.

a
b
c
d
e
e
d
e
3
5
9
11
(in 2)
grouping
d
c
b
Functions
level a–b:
level c–e:
(RS) (RS) Dep Ret RS (P) P Dep
(RS) P (RS) P Dep RS Dep
e

FIGURE 8.7 The first two phrases of Op. 11, no. 1, together with their prolongational and functional analysis.

FIGURE 8.8 The recapitulatory phrase (bars 53–58) of Op. 11, no. 1.

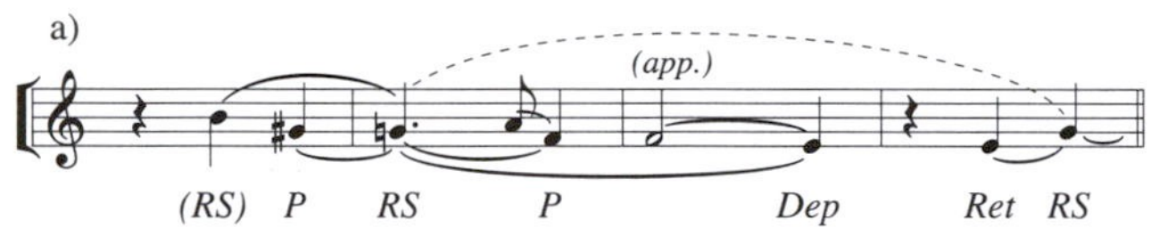

b)

$\alpha(\mathrm{B}\rightarrow\mathrm{G}\sharp) = {}^{1}/_{1} \times {}^{1}/_{3^2} = 0.11$

$\alpha(\mathrm{G}\sharp\rightarrow\mathrm{G}) = {}^{1}/_{1} \times {}^{1}/_{1^2} = 1.0$

$\alpha(\mathrm{G}\rightarrow\mathrm{A}) = {}^{1}/_{1} \times {}^{1}/_{2^2} = 0.25$

$\alpha(\mathrm{A}\rightarrow\mathrm{F}) = {}^{1}/_{1} \times {}^{1}/_{4^2} = 0.06$

$\alpha(\mathrm{F}\rightarrow\mathrm{E}) = {}^{1}/_{1} \times {}^{1}/_{1^2} = 1.0$

$\alpha(\mathrm{E}\rightarrow\mathrm{G}) = {}^{1}/_{1} \times {}^{1}/_{3^2} = 0.11$

c)

$\alpha(b_2\rightarrow b_3) = {}^{1}/_{1} \times {}^{1}/_{1} = 1.0$

$\alpha(b_3\rightarrow b_1) = {}^{2}/_{1} \times {}^{1}/_{1} = 2.0$

$\alpha(b_1\rightarrow b_{2\&}) = {}^{0.5}/_{2} \times {}^{1}/_{1.5} = 0.17$

$\alpha(b_{2\&}\rightarrow b_3) = {}^{1}/_{0.5} \times {}^{1}/_{0.5} = 4.0$

$\alpha(b_3\rightarrow b_1) = {}^{2}/_{1} \times {}^{1}/_{1} = 2.0$

$\alpha(b_1\rightarrow b_3) = {}^{1}/_{2} \times {}^{1}/_{2} = 0.25$

$\alpha(b_3\rightarrow b_2) = {}^{1}/_{1} \times {}^{1}/_{2} = 0.5$

$\alpha(b_2\rightarrow b_1) = {}^{2}/_{1} \times {}^{1}/_{1} = 2.0$

d)

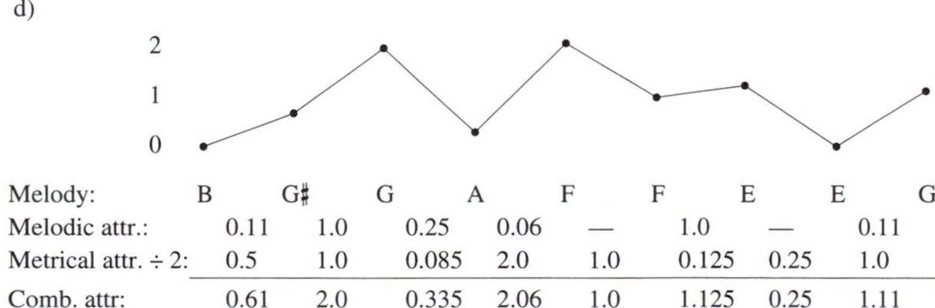

Melody:	B		G♯		G		A		F		F		E		E		G
Melodic attr.:		0.11		1.0		0.25		0.06		—		1.0		—		0.11	
Metrical attr. ÷ 2:		0.5		1.0		0.085		2.0		1.0		0.125		0.25		1.0	
Comb. attr:		0.61		2.0		0.335		2.06		1.0		1.125		0.25		1.11	

FIGURE 8.9 The melody in bars 1–4 of Op. 11, no. 1: (a) functional analysis: (b) computations for the melodic attractions; (c) computations for the metrical attractions; (d) combined melodic/metrical tensional analysis.

forcing the intuition that the two Gs connect and dominate the phrase prolongationally.

Subsequent events bear out the global referentiality of G. The consequent phrase in bars 9–11 is interrupted by the contrasting fast arpeggiations in bars 12–14 (see Figure 8.6). The consequent phrase resumes in bars 15–16 and reaches completion by a continuation in bars 19–24 that parallels bars 4–8. Figure 8.10 shows how deeply reductional this parallel is. As illustrated by the dashed circles and the arrow at (a), the closing melodic E→G in bar 4 derives from the melodic heads of bars 2–3; that is, the ending of the phrase compresses and reverses the motion of the first three bars. One might expect an analogous pattern after the second phrase—specifically B♭→C, since C and B♭ are the heads of bars 10–11. After the interruption and resumption of the phrase, the expected B♭→C indeed arrives in bars 19–20, as shown by the circles and arrow at (b). The material in bars 19–20, parallel to that in bars 4–5, repeats in rhythmic variation, just as in bars 5–6; but the third time, in bars 23–24, it changes to B♭→G, an inversion of the parallel place in the grouping structure, E→G in bar 7. Finally, G and B♭ happen to be the melodic heads of the entire passage shown in Figure 8.7. Thus the process of reversal and compression continues down one more reductional level, as shown by the circles and arrow at (c). With this arrival on G, supported as in bar 4 by A♭ (=G♯) in the bass, the first section achieves prolongational closure.

The recapitulatory phrase in Figure 8.8 accomplishes closure in a somewhat different way, by finally attaining G in place of G♯/A♭ in the bass in bar 56 and, via chromatic descent, a new stable pitch D in the soprano. The echoing alto implies D but stops short on E♭ in bar 58. The arrival in bars 56–58 nonetheless feels as resolved as is consistent with this dissonant idiom, largely by the outer voices that come to rest on a consonant fifth. Despite the resolution, however, this is not the ending: the E♭-G in the bass and the E♭ in the alto in bars 56–58 point toward the final E♭ in bar 64, which in turn recalls the departure in bar 12. But this final progression does not cancel the prior resolution on G. It is characteristic of Schoenberg in this period—for example, in a number of songs in *The Book of the Hanging Gardens*, Op. 15, or the second of the *Five Orchestra Pieces*, Op. 16 (respectively written immediately before and after the Op. 11 pieces)—to trail tonic resolution by a final move away in which the resulting tonal instability is compensated by a web of motivic recall.

Figure 8.11 lists in order the phrase-beginning and phrase-ending chords in Op. 11, no. 1, that both project the centrality of G and include some form of [0 1 4]. These chords bear a family resemblance. Just as a tonic chord can take many surface forms in jazz, so chords that share related pc and ic features can function as global referential sonorities in atonal music. The extent to which these structural chords pervade Op. 11, no. 1, suggests that an atonal prolongational analysis of the entire piece is feasible. Because of Schenker's influence, it is often assumed that complete reductions of extensive tonal pieces are less idealized than they in fact are. Conversely, perhaps because of the influence of pc-set theory, it is often

FIGURE 8.10 Motivic consequences in bars 16–24 of the prolongationally important melodic notes in Figure 8.7.

FIGURE 8.11 Structural chords in Op. 11, no. 1, that both center on G and include [0 1 4] trichords.

assumed that reductional analysis is irrelevant for atonal pieces. The reality of the cognition of both idioms lies somewhere in between, with tonal prolongations more robust and nested than atonal prolongations.

Figures 8.12a–e sketch prolongational analyses for the rest of the phrase groups in Op. 11, no. 1, without showing the time-span structure and the derivation of

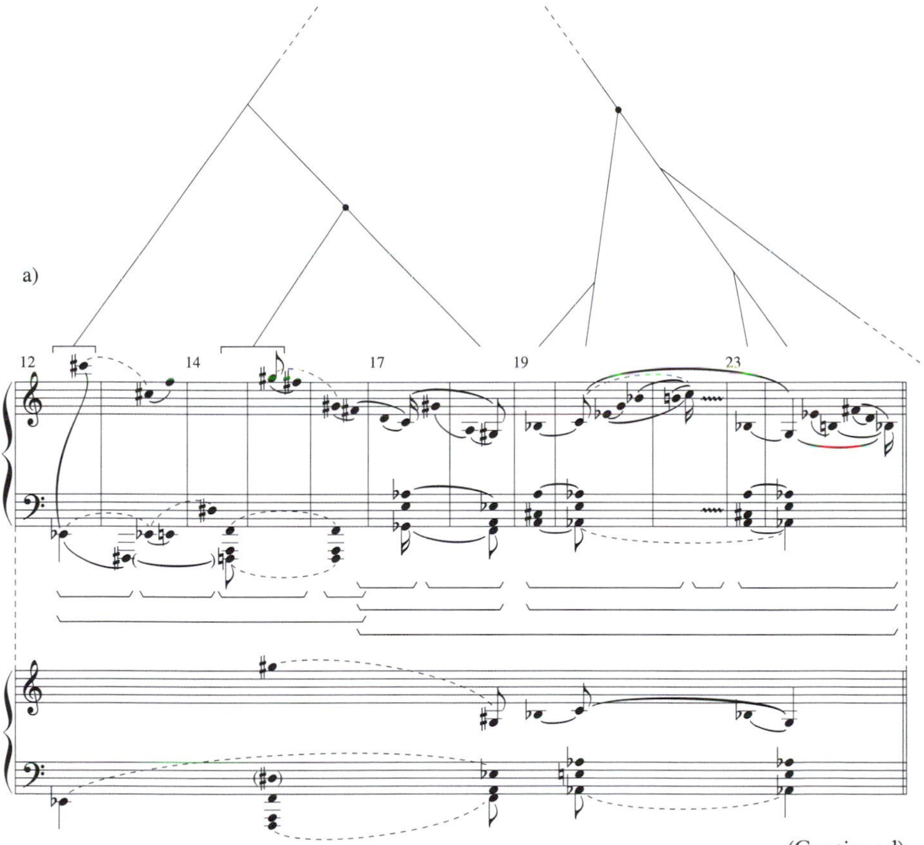

(Continued)

FIGURE 8.12 Prolongational analyses of the rest of the phrases in Op. 11, no. 1.

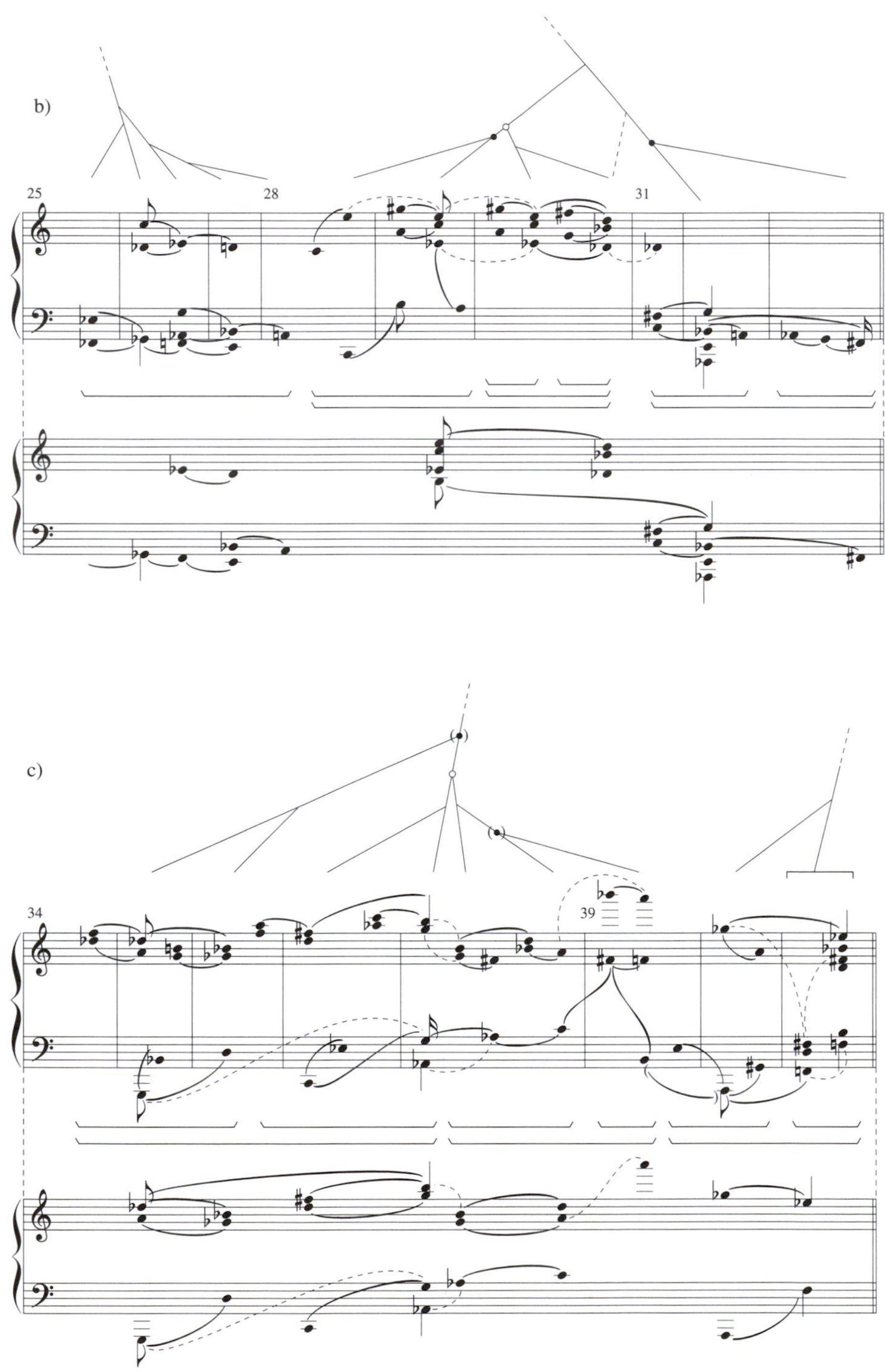

FIGURE 8.12 (Continued)

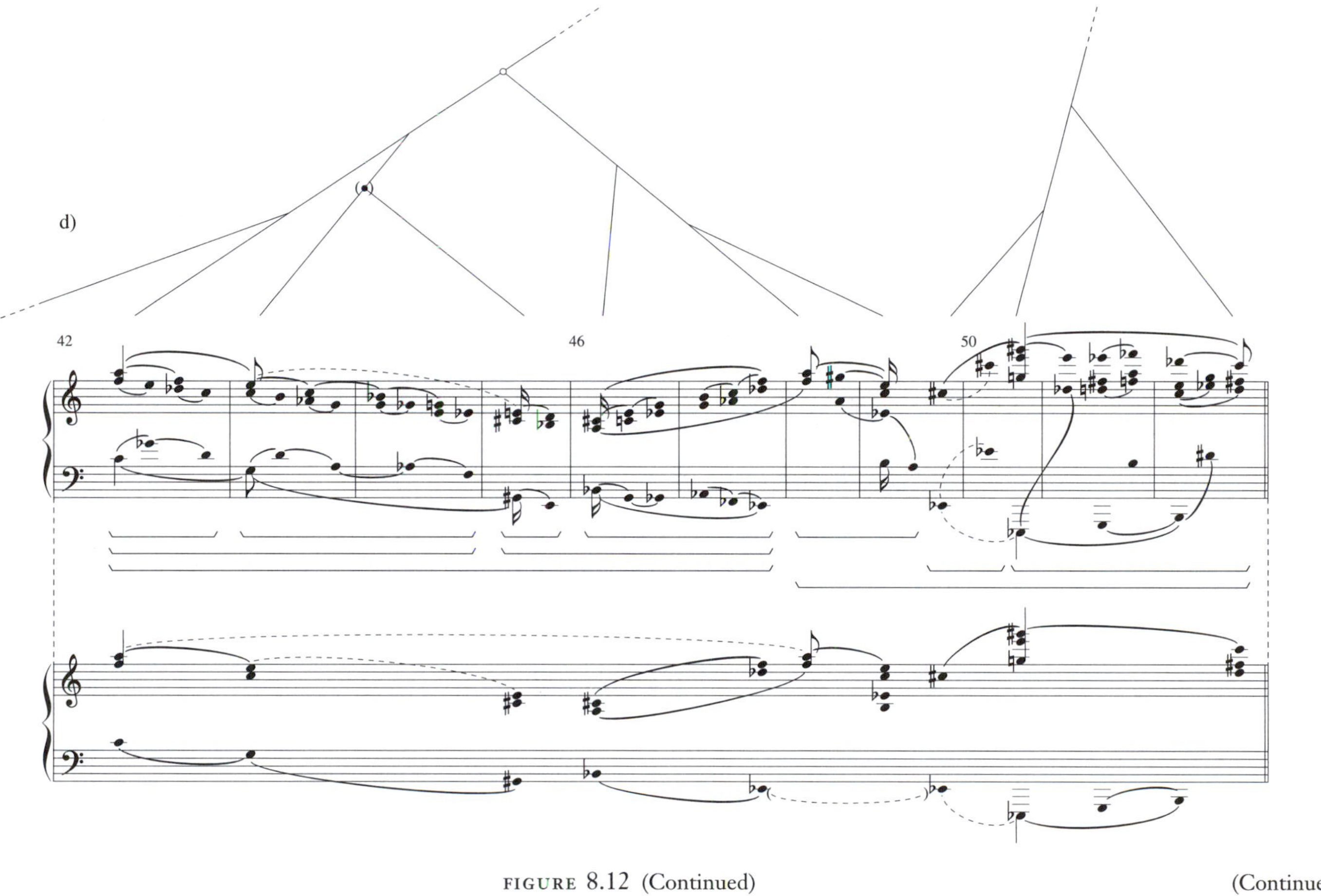

FIGURE 8.12 (Continued)

(Continued)

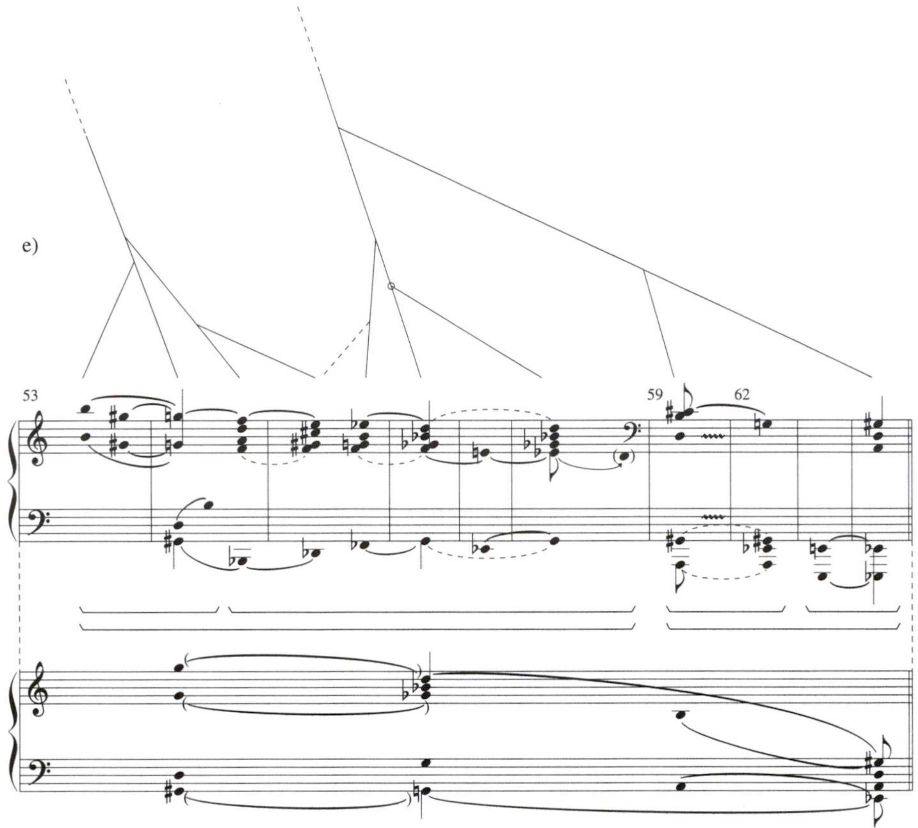

FIGURE 8.12 (Continued)

the prolongational connections from it. Figure 8.13a combines these fragments up to the level of the principal sections of the piece, designated for convenience as exposition, development, and recapitulation. Subordinate events are omitted. Branches in the development and recapitulation that do not connect to one another attach at a still larger level. Figure 8.13b assembles the remaining unattached branches into the global prolongational structure of Op. 11, no. 1. This graph projects the extent to which the similar chords in Figure 8.11 frame the piece as a whole. Much could be said about the details of this analysis, including options not taken. Given the relatively large scope of the piece, the aural and analytic grasp of the entire prolongational structure is bound to be more fragile and conflicted than is the case for previous analyses in this book. (For a contrasting quasi-tonal analysis of Op. 11, no. 1, see Ogdon [1981].)

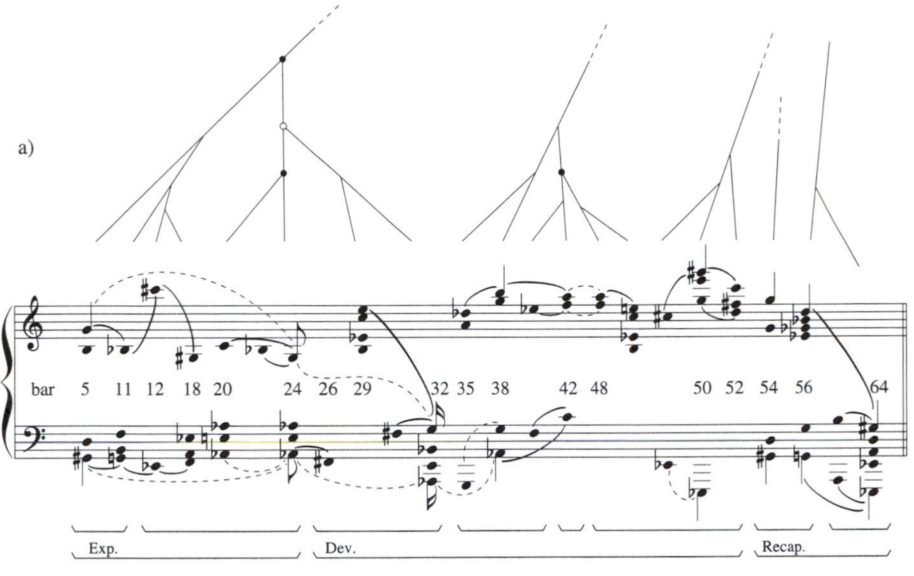

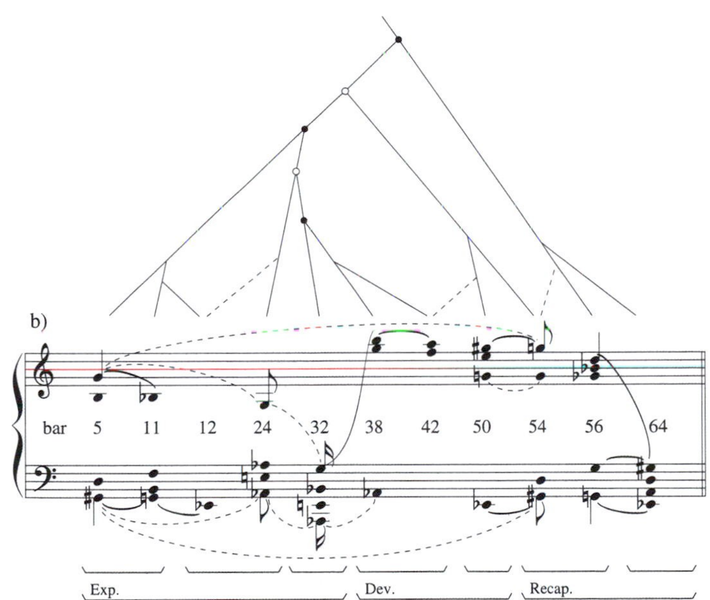

FIGURE 8.13 Global prolongational analysis of Op. 11, no. 1, assembled from the fragments in Figure 8.12: (a) at the level of the exposition, development, and recapitulation; (b) the entire piece.

FIGURE 8.14 Webern's Op. 7, no. 1.

A Webern analysis

The score of Webern's Op. 7, no. 1, for violin and piano appears in Figure 8.14, its analysis in Figure 8.15. The music has three polyphonic strands: the violin line, the trichords in the piano right hand, and the bass line. To achieve a unitary reductional analysis, the fusion rule must be applied liberally so that the grouping boundaries for each stream align vertically to permit one overall nested grouping structure. (The alternative would be to assign polyphonic groupings and to reduce each line until all three converge into a single homophonic grouping, along lines presented in "Issues in Prolongational Theory" in chapter 1. In the absence of a clear metrical structure and of the constraints of tonal harmony, however, this procedure would be rather tenuous.)

Time-span level f in Figure 8.15 normalizes the surface to the eighth-note level. The time-span reduction passes through levels f–d by a combination of the anchoring/reduction and salience criteria. Consider, for example, the five-note violin melody in bars 4–5. In bar 4 at level e, D dominates E by the anchoring/reduction rule and G dominates D by beginning the phrase and by being higher (salience conditions [8] and [5]). In bar 5, F dominates G♭ by being higher and longer (salience conditions [5] and [7]). Thus G in bar 4 and F in bar 5 continue to level d. At this level the introductory quality of bars 1–2 lends the G in the violin in bar 4 the role of a structural beginning; hence its dominance over F. Moreover, when combined with the other streams, the G is supported by a more salient sonority than is the F (condition [5]).

The rest of the time-span analysis proceeds in similar fashion. By level c there are four fused sonorities, one per group at grouping level c. The low E♭ in bar 3 is verticalized to bar 1. This transformation is plausible because of the vacuum created by the silence in the low register in bars 1–2. The choice at level b is decided by position at the largest grouping boundary. The choice of the triad in bar 9 for time-span level a comes from its comparative psychoacoustic consonance (sensory consonance condition [1]).

Prolongational levels 1 and 2 derive as usual from their time-span equivalents. The second sonority in time-span level c attaches to the first sonority as a weak prolongation (by $\delta_{\text{flat}} = 0 + 1 = 1$), and the third attaches to the fourth by the balance constraint. As prolongational level 1 projects, the piece prolongs E♭, first by a high E♭ pedal, then by rocking between E♭ and C♯, with C♯ embellishing E♭ within the attraction band, and finally by the E♭ triad. (Wallace Berry 1976 offers a related interpretation.) The connection between the high E♭ in bar 1 and the undulating E♭ in bars 6–8 is strengthened by the timbral similarity, compared to a normal violin sound, between the harmonic of the former and the *col legno* of the latter. Both pitches are highly salient (conditions [4], [5], [7], and [8]). The inner-voice pitch E♭ in the final E♭ triad, however, is structurally important for a different reason: E♭ is the unambiguous virtual pitch, or root, of the sonority (sensory consonance condition [2]). The euphony and root-clarity of the final sonority bring pc E♭ out of its previous dissonant haze. Although in other pieces Webern often seeks an open form, in this instance there is prolongational resolution. The E♭ triad fulfills this purpose. A triad with any other root would create an open form by not prolonging the E♭, and a dissonant chord that contained a salient E♭ would manifest weak prolongation but not closure.

Prolongational level 1 includes the verticality in bar 5 from level d, as well as the four sonorities of level c, in order to exhibit the normative functional progression RS→Dep→Ret→RS. The Ret-function, however, already contains seeds of the RS-function to which it resolves, by virtue of the prolonged pitches E♭ and B♭. In addition to representing a global level of horizontal reduction, prolongational level 1 expresses vertical reduction in two ways, by distinguishing between stemmed and unstemmed notes and by deleting less salient inner voices. The resulting linear motion is essentially stepwise in all voices: in the soprano, E♭ by octave transfer throughout, with an inner-voice G→F→E♭ descent in bars 3–6 in

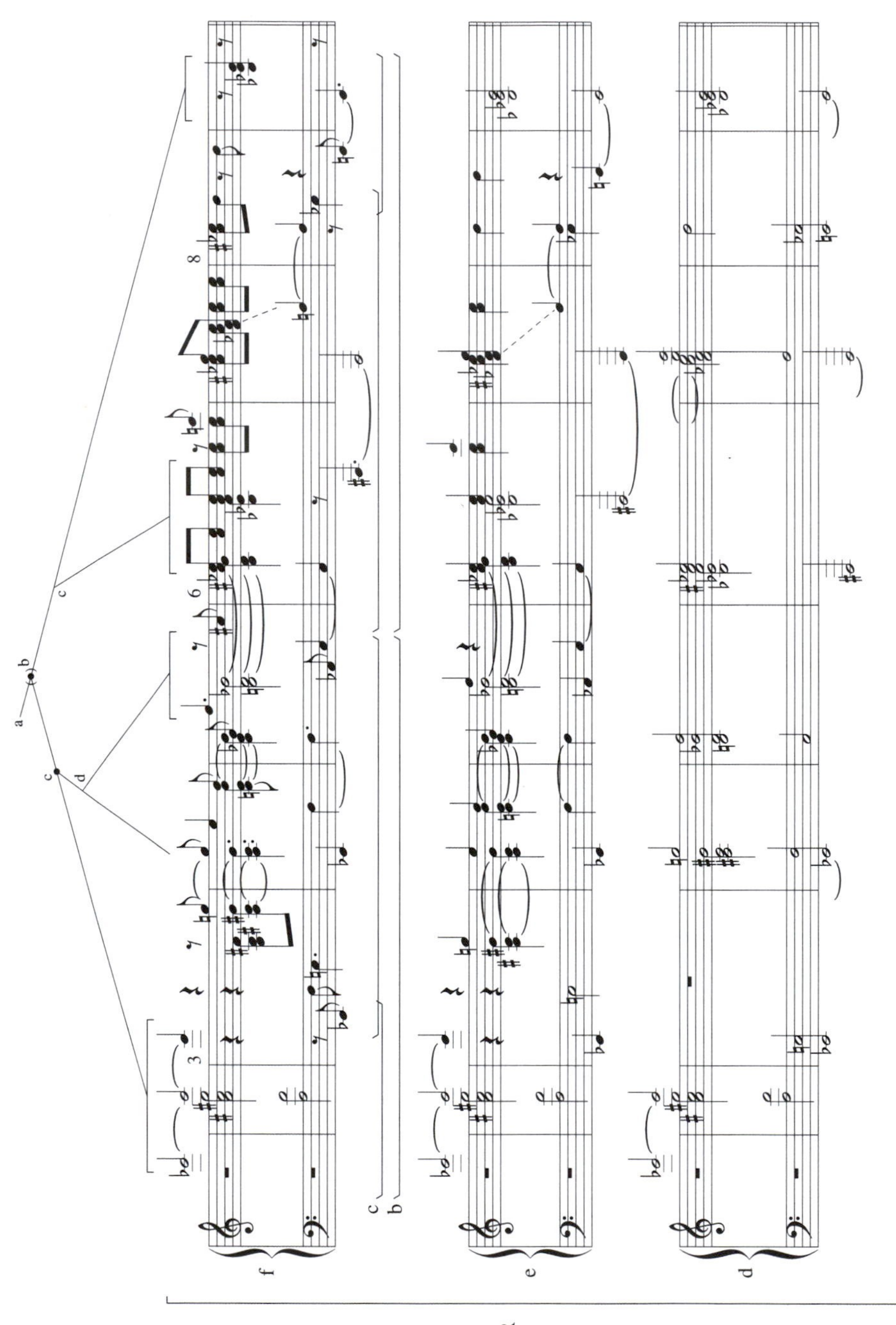
a
b
c
d
c
3
6
8
c
b
f
e
d
TSR

FIGURE 8.15 Analysis of Op. 7, no. 1.

the violin; in the alto, G♯→B♭→A→G; in the tenor, A→B→B♭; in the bass, E♭→E, internally elaborated by F♯. The attractions of these nearby pitches in each voice create and maintain the polyphonic strands.

At prolongational level 2 the analysis accommodates independent streams. The piano right hand in bars 3–6 moves in parallel trichords. Meanwhile a new violin gesture, the rocking C♯-E♭, has begun at the end of bar 5. Prolongational level 2 treats these two parts independently, causing overlapping slurs. This violation of strict branching is repaired by the fusion of sonorities at prolongational level 1; that is, the local streams are understood within this underlying homophonic framework (for a less extreme tonal counterpart, compare Figure 1.29).

Some interesting details in prolongational level 2 concern double leading tones. The undulating E♭ and C♯ anchor locally on D in the violin in bar 8 (Webern's spelling also implies this reading). In a more global perspective, however, this D embellishes the earlier E♭ of bars 6–7. The D in bar 8 is then left hanging, in symmetry around E♭ with low E in the piano; both express an unrealized attraction to E♭ in their own registers. The double leading tones to E♭ in bar 8 are in turn prefigured in the inner voice of the right-hand piano parallel trichords in bars 3–6. As shown in Figure 8.16, the last two trichords (B-D-B♭, B♭-E♭-A), are formed by swapping E♭ and D from what otherwise would be a pattern of continuing [0 1 5] trichords that begins in bar 3 (Morris 1994). The reversal creates a double-leading-tone attraction to middle-voice E♭ in bar 6.

In these Schoenberg and Webern analyses I have mostly ignored a pc-set approach to atonal music. I see analysis of that kind as supplementary to a prolongational approach. For example, the [0 1 4 7] tetrachord and closely related sets are prevalent throughout the Webern. It is the E in the bass, placing the E♭ triad in a [0 1 4 7] context, that allows the triad to conclude the piece without violating stylistic consistency. Similarly, family resemblances among the harmonies of Op. 11, no. 1, can be elucidated by pc-set analysis (Forte 1981; Perle 1962; Wittlich 1975) or, alternatively, by a constraint formalism that favors the prominently stated trichords [0 1 4], [0 1 5], [0 1 6], and [0 4 8] as well as selected tetrachordal concatenations of them and that disfavors such chords as major or minor triads and chromatic clusters. By itself, however, a pc-set analysis tends to leave a piece in a jumble of fragments. The same holds for the Schoenbergian motivic approach propounded by Ethan Haimo (1996) for Op. 11, no. 1. Assuming a viable set segmentation or motivic analysis, what makes this particular set or that particular motive appear where it does and at that particular pitch level? The answer lies in

FIGURE 8.16 Trichords in bars 3–6 of the Webern: (a) implied pattern of parallel [0 1 5] trichords; (b) reversal of E♭ and D in the last two trichords in (a) so as to form a double-leading-tone attraction to E♭ in bar 6.

a prolongational approach, one that places set succession or motivic variation in a larger context of departure and return, linear connection, and function.

Prolongations and tone rows

Whatever success the atonal prolongational approach enjoys in the preceding analyses is partly a consequence of its having been applied to pieces of the early atonal period, in which frequent harmonic return and semitonal voice leading remain as stylistic features carried over from chromatic tonal practice. How well does the method survive for later atonal music? The answer varies. I believe it will be useful for analyzing the pedals and proliferations of Boulez's mature style, for example, but not the stochastic textures of Xenakis (unless the "event" is redefined in terms of global texture rather than individual pitch events). Here I shall consider briefly the effect of the classical twelve-tone technique on atonal prolongations.

Figure 8.17 gives the music up to the beginning of the second theme group of Schoenberg's piano piece Op. 33a, a twelve-tone work in his quasi-neoclassic style. To simplify, let us accept the notated meter (the perceived meter is a complex issue outside our concerns here). Beneath level f of the time-span reduction for bars 1–9 in Figure 8.18 appears the grouping analysis, labeled according to schematic function as in "Functions and Schemas" in chapter 5. After a two-bar introductory head-motive there is a sentence, lengthened from four to five bars by a quasi-sequential repetition in bar 7, followed by two bars of characteristically Schoenbergian liquidation (extension with motivic dissolution), which replaces the articulative function of the tonal cadence. That the phrasal-formal structure of this music takes this form will be no surprise to anyone who has browsed Schoenberg (1967). However, this sentence reflects only the grouping-motivic aspects of the classical model and does not incorporate an analogy to its schematic pitch structures as discussed in chapter 5. Level f already vertically reduces out inner voices in favor of the more salient outer voices (condition [5]). Time-span levels e–a continue the horizontal reduction by selecting salient events according to loudness, registral extreme, duration, and presence at a (relatively large) grouping boundary (conditions [3], [5],[7], and [8]). These choices are often conflicted, and other options are viable.

The time-span analysis illuminates the role of contour in the delineation of motivic material. In the head motive (bars 1–2) parallel chords rise and descend. The rise in contour is imitated at the musical surface in the statement, counterstatement, and continuation of the sentence (bars 3–5 in Figure 8.17). Level d in Figure 8.18 demonstrates that the entire sentence (bars 3–7) manifests the rising–falling contour of the head motive, and level e likewise shows that the liquidation (bars 8–9) follows an abbreviated version of the same pattern.

The prolongational analysis in Figure 8.18 derives in customary fashion from the time-span reduction. The absence of inner voices seems to be a more significant omission even than in Op. 11, no. 1, probably because this music is so intervallically conceived. This shortcoming could be rectified by a more detailed analysis. Less remediable, however, is the absence of strong and weak prolonga-

FIGURE 8.17 Bars 1–14 of Schoenberg's Op. 33a. Used by permission of Belmont Music Publishers.

tions. Harmonic nonrepetition weakens the effect of hierarchy. Continuing the analysis to larger levels, however, demonstrates significant prolongational returns. Bar 1 returns in bar 10 for a combinatorially elaborated statement of the head motive, followed by a rhythmically compressed sentence in bars 12–13 (parallel to bars 3–7), after which follows the second theme, which also begins with the pcs of the head motive. As sketched in Figure 8.19, the prolongational analysis connects these events as weak prolongations at a global level.

The prolongational analysis at the more local level of Figure 8.18 is not particularly revealing. The continual cycling of the complete aggregate is one cause, leading to the dearth of strong or weak prolongations at local levels; another is the stylistic focus on surface intervallic patterns, which quickly disappear in a reduction. Because both result from the twelve-tone organization, let us briefly refer to Op. 33a from that point of view. The prime and semicombinatorial-inversion rows are given in Figure 8.20. Much of the pitch interest of the piece results from partitionings of only these two row forms and their retrogrades. Bars 1–13 project the tetrachordal partitionings isolated by the dashed vertical lines in Figure 8.20; the second theme that starts in bar 14 begins hexachordal partitionings, shown by the solid vertical line; the development begins with trichordal partitionings. The time-span and prolongational analyses in Figure 8.18 have little to do with these structures.

Analyzing this music would be much easier if listeners apprehended its twelve-tone structure. But twelve-tone technique is a compositional method. It is important to distinguish between compositional and analytic theory (see the preface to Morris 1987; also Lerdahl 1988a). There is no reason to suppose that listeners identify rows when hearing twelve-tone works. Schoenberg himself was emphatic on this point (see Schoenberg 1958/1965, letter to Rudolf Kolisch, 27 July 1931). This is not to say that the row structure for Op. 33a has no effect on how the piece is grasped aurally. Rather, its effect is indirect. On the one hand, the twelve-tone organization interferes with the establishment of prolongational relationships; on the other, it supplants them with an emphasis on surface intervallic patternings and with associations among subsets of the row.

Why are twelve-tone rows not heard as such? The difficulty listeners have in hearing tone rows and their transformations cannot be attributed to their intrinsic complexity, which does not exceed that of tonal basic spaces and their configurations. Nor can it be attributed to lack of exposure: even experienced twelve-tone composers rarely identify tone rows when listening to twelve-tone pieces (unless they have deciphered the rows in advance). Rather, the intrinsic organization of these structures makes them difficult to cognize. This cognitive opacity provides potent evidence that the musical mind inclines toward other ways of structuring musical materials.

Twelve-tone rows are cognitively opaque for a number of reasons. (I concentrate on serialism in its classical Schoenbergian variety.) The first and most significant reason is that tone rows are permutational rather than elaborational structures. Most pitch organizations—whether of species counterpoint, classical variation, jazz, Indian raga, or Japanese koto—are elaborational. This feature enables pitch relations to be described by a tree or comparable notation. Serialism

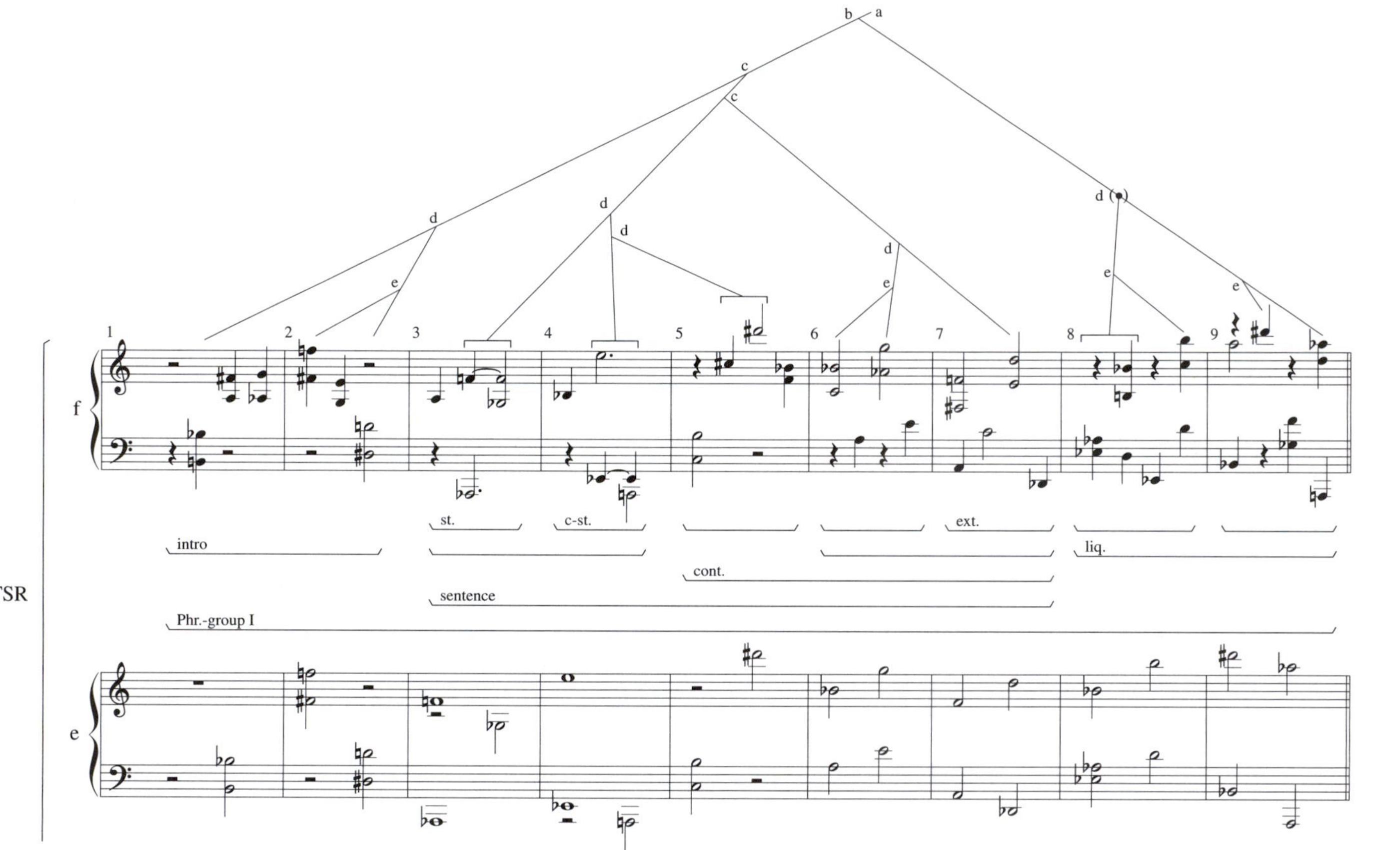

TSR
intro
st.
c-st.
cont.
ext.
liq.
sentence
Phr.-group I

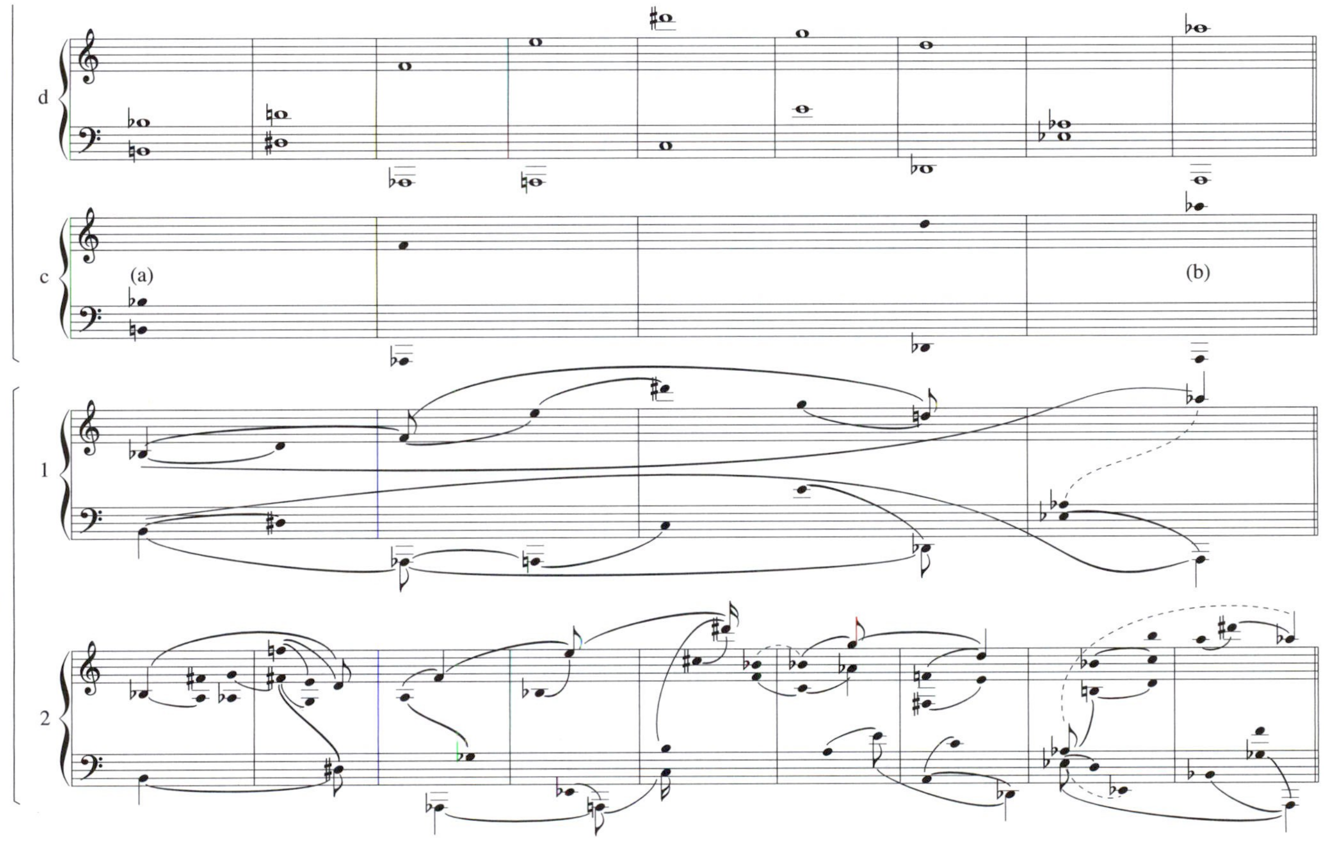

FIGURE 8.18 Reductional analysis of bars 1–9 of Op. 33a.

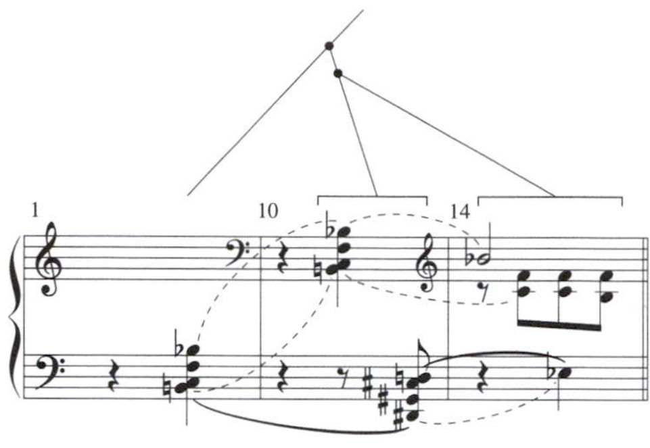

FIGURE 8.19 Prolongational sketch of global prolongations for bars 1–14 of Op. 33a.

instead depends on specific orderings of the pcs of a set, which are essential to the identity of individual set forms. Thus the internal elaboration of a pitch by other pitches would undermine the identity of a set form. Composers have found ways to overcome this condition, but this does not change the essentially non-elaborational nature of tone rows.

The little cognitive research that has been directed toward serialism (as in Francès 1988; Dowling 1972; and Deutsch 1982b) supports the contention that permutational structures are difficult to learn and remember. Since other human activities are not organized in such a fashion, it is hardly surprising that the issue has in general been ignored by psychologists. The situation is reminiscent, however, of Chomsky's (1965) observation that many logically possible syntactic constructions never occur in language, such as forming interrogatives from declaratives by word reversal or by exchange of odd and even words. The human mind gravitates toward treelike (elaborational) structures.

A second reason concerns row transformations rather than rows themselves. When intervallic direction is preserved, transposition is easily heard. When reverse intervallic direction is maintained, inversion is relatively easy to identify. But if, as is customary in the idiom, these operations are realized by preserving ic sequences rather than interval sequences—that is, by ignoring contour—they become difficult to identify (Dowling and Harwood 1986). Retrograde is troublesome to grasp by ear even if intervallic direction is preserved, retrograde inversion still more so. In short, the basic twelve-tone operations, and hence the various instantiations of a row, are difficult to detect.

A third reason for the cognitive opacity of twelve-tone rows is that twelve items well exceed the optimal number for comprehension (Miller 1956). People parse telephone numbers into two or three units so as to learn and remember them better. Pc sets with four members are easier to recognize than sets with eight

P_0:	10	5	0	11	9	6	1	3	7	8	2	4
I_5:	3	8	1	2	4	7	0	10	6	5	11	9

FIGURE 8.20 Basic set forms for Op. 33a.

members. Partly for this reason, Schoenberg and Webern divide their rows into subsets that are comparatively memorable. If all the other causes of opacity could be discounted, it would be advisable from the viewpoint of ease of processing for composers to employ three- or four-note rows.

A fourth reason is that tone rows do not project a space in which spatial distance correlates with cognitive distance. A step in tonal music is usually by half- or whole-tone motion. This is not reflected in the rows in Figure 8.20 or in tone rows generally. One might assert instead that a step occurs from a pc to an adjacent pc in the row. But then step distance varies greatly from one adjacency to the next, and there is no correlation with the log-frequency distance registered tonotopically in the auditory system (see "Empirical Issues" in chapter 2). Serialism does not incorporate a psychologically coherent notion of step and skip. The listener consequently has difficulty locating a pitch as close to or far from another pitch.

The dissociation of spatial and cognitive distance has the further effect of neutralizing the proximity factor in melodic and voice-leading attractions. The role of semitonal proximity is contradicted by intervallic patterns in the row and its subsets. The "will of the tones" is not a factor in Op. 33a.

At levels above the set it remains possible to conceive of combinations and sequences of rows in a spatial manner. As noted in "The Regional Level" in chapter 2, Schoenberg's row transpositions are broadly analogous to regional modulation in tonal music. In Op. 33a the row transpositions in the development section to P_2/I_7 and P_7/I_0 (bars 28–32) take a quasi-modulatory role characteristic of classical developments. As with many tonal modulations, these particular transpositions are motivated by motivic relationships (the intervallic fifths at the beginning of the row are highlighted at the onset of the development; see Perle [1962]). But these relationships are not easy to comprehend in terms of relative distance because no matter what the transposition is, the total aggregate is always completed. Variation in the content of subsets of the aggregate does not provide contrast comparable to tonal modulation. (Composers in search of pc variety have found ways to avoid continual completion of the aggregate, but this does not obviate the source of the problem, which is that a twelve-tone row typically goes through all twelve pcs before repeating.)

A fifth reason for tone-row opacity is that the convention of inventing a new row for each piece does not allow the listener consistent exposure to a limited number of pitch alphabets (Deutsch and Feroe 1981). The twelve-tone idiom relies instead on contextual associations within a particular piece. This may be a source of aesthetic richness, but it also creates obstacles to comprehension.

A sixth reason is that tone rows do not incorporate consonance and dissonance in any systematic way. As has been remarked concerning the development of highly chromatic spaces such as F6/oct space, and especially with the historical evolution into flat space, the decreasing correlation between sensory consonance and levels of a basic space weakens the cognition of hierarchy and leads to an increasing reliance on psychoacoustic principles, especially salience, in organizing musical surfaces. But as we have just seen, the hierarchical organization of Op.

33a as derived by salience conditions is not very convincing. In the absence of effective hierarchy, the listener's tendency is to resort instead to associations across partitionings of the row. These relationships may be fascinating, but they are relatively difficult to cognize if only because they are not heard in a hierarchical fashion.

Schoenberg (1941/1975) supports the elimination of the distinction between consonance and dissonance by arguing that consonance and dissonance fall on a continuum rather than in separate categories and that the higher dissonant partials have achieved greater "comprehensibility" through stylistic change. On that basis he claims the emancipation of dissonance. This view overlooks the fundamental distinction between sensory and musical dissonance and appears to confuse cultural with biological evolution. It is correct that sensory dissonance lies on a continuum. Musical consonance and dissonance, however, might or might not fall in different categories, depending on the musical idiom in question. Schoenberg can define musical consonance and dissonance out of existence for his own idiom (with the exception of the octave: pcs are needed), but this move does not neutralize sensory consonance/dissonance, which is a matter not of cultural practice or definition but of biology. The sensory dissonance of a seventh remains greater than that of a sixth, regardless of the musical purposes to which these intervals are put. By disregarding sensory distinctions, Schoenberg does not erase them but rather leaves them—at least at the level of compositional theory—in an uncontrolled state.

A seventh reason, which overlaps with a number of the other causes and which is shared with nonserial atonal music, is that tone rows and their combinations (as in Figure 8.20) do not take the form of basic spaces. This volume has demonstrated the multiple purposes of basic spaces. The specific point here is that musical idioms that employ preferred basic spaces are cognitively more transparent than those that do not. Tone rows manifest a different kind of organization.

These seven considerations go a considerable way toward explaining why twelve-tone rows are not apprehended and partly account for why twelve-tone pieces are often harder for listeners to assign structure to than even short pieces in the early atonal idiom, let alone pieces that utilize basic spaces. As for the analysis of Op. 33a, the comparative failure of the prolongational method when coupled with salience criteria, together with the perceptual inaccessibility of the row structure per se, suggests that a somewhat different approach, perhaps incorporating aspects of pc-set theory, is needed for representing and deriving how listeners understand this idiom. Such a development lies beyond the scope of this book.

PROSPECTS

The last three chapters have shown how the entire tonal theory—grouping and meter, time-span and prolongational reduction, pitch space with its versions of δ, prolongational paths, tension curves and attractions, functions and phrasal-formal schemas—can be applied, with appropriate modifications, to highly chromatic and atonal music. In the process, however, the theory has gradually become less systematic, with increasing reliance on the underspecified interaction of unquantified rules of salience and consonance. Changes in the basic spaces themselves cause this decrease in derivational clarity. If the musical signal does not facilitate the inference and transformation of stratified basic spaces, the listener turns to psychoacoustic factors to organize the stimulus. The precision afforded by basic spaces gives way to less structured, more continuous forms of mental processing. The ambiguities of derivation reflect the uncertainties in listening to atonal music.

At the same time, the atonal theory as it stands is incomplete in its interface with psychoacoustics. Tools such as spectograms or measures of sensory dissonance do not easily translate into music-theoretic concepts, whether of prolongations or of pc sets. Music theory has almost always assumed the transformation of the auditory signal into quantized pitches, intervals, and durations. This idealization of auditory experience is necessary for a clear account of cognitive musical structures, but much is lost in the process, including dynamic variation, expressive timing, textural density, and timbral modulation. This loss is critical when music does not employ stratified basic spaces. A full integration of the concepts and representations of psychoacoustics into those of music theory—for which computer modeling is essential—will facilitate the analysis of atonal music.

Although the analyses in this study end with music of the early twentieth century, there is no reason in principle that the theory could not be adapted to more recent music (or, for that matter, to Renaissance music or to music of different cultures). What interests me most is the potential of the theory for future music. Much twentieth-century music arose from compositional systems spawned not by knowledge of how the musical mind works (this knowledge is only now emerging) but by the ideology of historical progress. Schools of composition grew around various ideas of what the next historically significant step ought to be. These steps led to mutually incompatible and largely private compositional codes. Without guidance from study of music cognition, this result was in retrospect predictable, for the musical mind does not spontaneously learn arbitrary syntaxes. Cultural variation is infinite but constrained. (For related discussion, see Lerdahl 1988a and 1997a.)

Beyond its theoretical and psychological interest, the theory presented here holds promise, both in its specific ideas and in its general approach of formal modeling in dialogue with empirical research, for future compositional practice. Many of its proposals can be instantiated in computer programs that serve as compositional aids. The theory and its overall approach can help pave the way for a kind of compositional thought based less on aesthetic-historical dialectics than on the growing understanding of the musical mind.

Rule Index

RULES INTRODUCED IN THIS VOLUME

PROLONGATIONAL GOOD FORM

(1) *Normative prolongational structure* For cadenced groups, prefer to include
   (a) a structural beginning and a cadence
   (b) optionally, a right-branching prolongation that is the most important direct elaboration of the structural beginning
   (c) a right-branching progression that, except for (b), is the most important direct elaboration of the structural beginning
   (d) a left-branching progression that is the most important direct elaboration of the first element of the cadence.

(2) *Balance constraint:* At any level, for events e_2 and e_3 immediately subordinate within the strong or weak prolongation e_1–e_4, prefer the attachment of e_2 to e_1 and e_3 to e_4.

(3) *Recursion constraint:* At any level, for events e_j and e_k subordinate to e_i, prefer, if e_j directly attaches to e_i, the direct attachment of e_k to e_j; and if e_k directly attaches to e_i, prefer the direct attachment of e_j to e_k; both subject to the conditions that
   (a) e_j and e_k are both to the left or to the right of e_i
   (b) e_i, e_j, and e_k form all progressions or all prolongations
   (c) e_i, e_j, and e_k are all either harmonic events within a region or events located in different regions.

CHORDAL CIRCLE-OF-FIFTHS RULE Move the pcs at levels a–c of the basic space four steps to the right (mod 7) on level d or four steps to the left.

REGIONAL CIRCLE-OF-FIFTHS RULE Move the pcs at level d of the basic space seven steps to the right (mod 12) on level e or seven steps to the left.

CHORD DISTANCE RULE (full version) $\delta(x \rightarrow y) = i + j + k$, where $\delta(x \rightarrow y)$ = the distance between chord x and chord y; i = the number of applications of the regional circle-of-fifths rule needed to shift the diatonic collection that supports x into the diatonic collection that supports y; j = the number of applications of the chordal circle-of-fifths rule needed to shift x into y; and k = the number of distinctive pcs in the basic space of y compared to those in the basic space of x.

REGION DISTANCE RULE $\Delta(\mathbf{I} \rightarrow \mathbf{R}) = [\delta_1(\mathbf{P}_1 \rightarrow \mathbf{P}_2)] + [\delta_2(\mathbf{P}_2 \rightarrow \mathbf{P}_3)] \ldots + \delta_n(\mathbf{P}_n \rightarrow \mathbf{R})$, where $\Delta(\mathbf{I} \rightarrow \mathbf{R})$ = distance from the home pivot-region tonic **I** to the target region **R**; δ_1 = the pivot-region step from the first pivot-region tonic $\mathbf{P}_1$ to the second pivot-region tonic $\mathbf{P}_2$, and so on; and $\delta_n(\mathbf{P}_n \rightarrow \mathbf{R})$ = the distance from pivot-region tonic $\mathbf{P}_n$ to **R**, once **R** lies within the shifted pivot region. Steps within square brackets apply only if the condition for $\delta_n(\mathbf{P}_n \rightarrow \mathbf{R})$ is not met.

CHORD/REGION DISTANCE RULE $\Delta(C_1/\mathbf{R}_1 \rightarrow C_2/\mathbf{R}_2) = [\delta_1(C_1/\mathbf{R}_1 \rightarrow I/\mathbf{P}_1)] + [\delta_2(\mathbf{P}_1 \rightarrow \mathbf{P}_2)] + [\delta_3(\mathbf{P}_2 \rightarrow \mathbf{P}_3)] \ldots + \delta_n(I/\mathbf{P}_n \rightarrow C_2/\mathbf{R}_2)$, where $\delta_1(C_1/\mathbf{R}_1 \rightarrow I/\mathbf{P}_1)$ = the distance of C_1 in $\mathbf{R}_1$ to pivot-region tonic $\mathbf{P}_1$, which contains $C_1/\mathbf{R}_1$; $[\delta_2(\mathbf{P}_1 \rightarrow \mathbf{P}_2)] + [\delta_3(\mathbf{P}_2 \rightarrow \mathbf{P}_3)] \ldots$ = intermediate pivot-region shifts; and $\delta_n(I/\mathbf{P}_n \rightarrow C_2/\mathbf{R}_2)$ = the distance from pivot-region tonic $\mathbf{P}_n$, which contains $C_2/\mathbf{R}_2$, to C_2 in $\mathbf{R}_2$.

PRINCIPLE OF THE SHORTEST PATH The pitch-space distance between two events is preferably calculated to the smallest value.

TIME-SPAN STABILITY Of the possible choices for the head of a time-span T, prefer the event that yields the smallest value for δ (or Δ if necessary) in relation to the superordinate context for T.

PROLONGATIONAL CONNECTION Of the possible connections within a prolongational region R, prefer the attachment that yields the smallest value for δ (or Δ if necessary) in relation to the superordinate end points of R.

SEQUENTIAL TENSION RULE (short version) $T_{seq}(\mathbf{y}) = \delta(x_{prec} \rightarrow \mathbf{y})$, where **y** = the target chord, x_{prec} = the chord that immediately precedes **y** in the sequence, $T_{seq}(\mathbf{y})$ = the tension associated with **y**, and $\delta(x_{prec} \rightarrow \mathbf{y})$ = the distance from x_{prec} to **y**.

HIERARCHICAL TENSION RULE (short version) $T_{loc}(\mathbf{y}) = \delta(x_{dom} \rightarrow \mathbf{y})$; and $T_{glob}(\mathbf{y}) = T_{loc}(\mathbf{y}) + T_{inh}(x_{dom})$, where **y** = the target chord, x_{dom} = the chord that directly dominates **y** in the prolongational tree; $T_{loc}(\mathbf{y})$ = the local tension associated with **y**; $\delta(x_{dom} \rightarrow \mathbf{y})$ = the distance from x_{dom} to **y** (= $i + j + k$); $T_{glob}(\mathbf{y})$ = the global tension associated with **y**; and $T_{inh}(x_{dom})$ = the sum of distance values inherited by **y** from chords that dominate x_{dom}.

SURFACE TENSION RULE $T_{diss}(\mathbf{y})$ = scale degree (add 1) + inversion (add 2) + nonharmonic tone (add 1 for sevenths, 3 for diatonic nonharmonic tones, and 4 for chromatic nonharmonic tones), where $T_{diss}(\mathbf{y})$ = the surface tension associated with chord **y**; scale degree = chords with $\hat{3}$ or $\hat{5}$ in the melodic voice; inversion = chords with $\hat{3}$ or $\hat{5}$ in the bass; and nonharmonic tone = any pc in **y**'s span that does not belong to **y.**

SEQUENTIAL TENSION RULE (long version) $T_{seq}(\mathbf{y}) = T_{diss}(\mathbf{y}) + \delta(x_{prec} \rightarrow \mathbf{y})$.

HIERARCHICAL TENSION RULE (long version) $T_{loc}(\mathbf{y}) = T_{diss}(\mathbf{y}) + \delta(x_{dom} \rightarrow \mathbf{y})$; and $T_{glob}(\mathbf{y}) = T_{loc}(\mathbf{y}) + T_{inh}(x_{dom})$.

INTERACTION PRINCIPLE (revised from GTTM) To assign the prolongationally most important event e_k within prolongational region $(e_i–e_j)$,

(1) derive prolongational level ${}_{p}L_n$ from the most global available time-span level ${}_{ts}L_n$
(2) within $(e_i–e_j)$, choose from ${}_{ts}L_n$
   (a) the e_k that forms the smallest value between $T_{loc}(e_i \rightarrow \mathbf{e_k})$ and $T_{loc}(e_j \rightarrow \mathbf{e_k})$, and attach e_k to that e_i or e_j
   (b) except if there is a $T_{loc}(e_i \rightarrow \mathbf{e_k}) = 0$ at ${}_{ts}L_{n-1}$, in which case attach that e_k to e_i before returning to step (2a)
(3) repeat steps (2a–b) at ${}_{ts}L_{n-1}$ and ${}_{p}L_{n-1}$, and continue recursively until all events are assigned.

MELODIC ATTRACTION $\alpha(p_1 \rightarrow p_2) = \frac{s_2}{s_1} \times \frac{1}{n^2}$, where p_1 and p_2 are pitches, with $p_1 \neq p_2$; $\alpha(p_1 \rightarrow p_2)$ = the attraction of p_1 to p_2; s_1 = the anchoring strength of p_1 and s_2 = the anchoring strength of p_2 in the current configuration of the basic space; and n = the number of semitone intervals between p_1 and p_2.

VOICE-LEADING ATTRACTION $\alpha_{rvl}(C_1 \rightarrow C_2) = \alpha_{r1} + \ldots \alpha_{rn}$, where C_1 and C_2 are chords in which (at the very least) not all the pitches are identical;

$\alpha_{rvl}(C_1 \rightarrow C_2)$ = the realized voice-leading attraction of C_1 to C_2; and $\alpha_{r1} + \ldots \alpha_{rn}$ = the sum of the realized melodic attractions for all the voices in C_1 to C_2.

HARMONIC ATTRACTION $\alpha_{rh}(C_1 \rightarrow C_2) = K[\alpha_{rvl}(C_1 \rightarrow C_2)/\delta(C_1 \rightarrow C_2)]$, where $\alpha_{rh}(C_1 \rightarrow C_2)$ is the realized harmonic attraction of C_1 to C_2; constant $K = 10$; $\alpha_{rvl}(C_1 \rightarrow C_2)$ is as in the voice-leading attraction rule; and $\delta(C_1 \rightarrow C_2)$ is the distance from C_1 to C_2, with $C_1 \neq C_2$.

EVENT GOVERNANCE Assume any pitch p_x, chord C_x, and region $\mathbf{R}_x$. Then,
(1) p_x is governed by C_x if p_x takes place in the span over which C_x extends, from the onset of C_x to the onset of C_{x+1}; and
(2) C_x is immediately governed by $\mathbf{R}_x$ if C_x takes place in the span over which $\mathbf{R}_x$ extends, from the onset of $\mathbf{R}_x$ to the onset of $\mathbf{R}_{x+1}$; but
(3) if there is a pivot chord C_p, the span of $\mathbf{R}_x$ overlaps with that of $\mathbf{R}_{x+1}$, such that $\mathbf{R}_x$ ends and $\mathbf{R}_{x+1}$ begins with C_p.

ATTRACTIONAL CONTEXT Assume pitches p_1 and p_2, chords C_1 and C_2, and regions $\mathbf{R}_1$ and $\mathbf{R}_2$, such that
(1) $p_1 \neq p_2$, but possibly $C_1 = C_2$ and $\mathbf{R}_1 = \mathbf{R}_2$
(2) p_1 is governed by C_1 and C_1 is governed by $\mathbf{R}_1$; p_2 is governed by C_2 and C_2 is governed by $\mathbf{R}_2$;
(3) if a realized attraction is computed and if
 (a) p_1 and p_2 are in the same stream and
 (b) $p_2/C_2/\mathbf{R}_2$ directly succeeds $p_1/C_1/\mathbf{R}_1$ at any prolongational level,
then $\alpha(p_1/C_1/\mathbf{R}_1 \rightarrow p_2/C_2/\mathbf{R}_2)$, such that
(4) if p_1 is nonharmonic, it is evaluated within the basic-space configuration of $C_1/\mathbf{R}_1$
(5) if p_1 is harmonic, it is evaluated within the the basic-space configuration of $I/\mathbf{R}_2$.

TONIC-FINDING RULE To establish tonic orientation in any time span or prolongational region at any level,
(1) if single pitches are under consideration, prefer the interpretation that places the pitches at the highest locations in the current basic-space configuration
(2) if chords are under consideration, prefer the interpretation that connects the chords by the shortest chordal/regional paths, both
 (a) with respect to one another and
 (b) with respect to the putative tonic at that level (without violating characteristic diatonic inflections in minor)
(3) if two events within a region are equally close to a tonic under different interpretations or if the events do not fit in the same region, prefer the

interpretation that forms the shortest path to the governing tonic at the next larger reductional level.

FUNCTION RULE Given the repertory of functions T (tonic), D (dominant), S (subdominant), Dep (departure), Ret (return), N (neighboring), and P (passing), assign them by prolongational position from global to local levels, such that

(1) T belongs to any pitch chord that is a (local) tonic as established by the tonic-finding rule
(2) D belongs to any chord
  (a) that is part of a labeled cadence, such that
    (i) for a full cadence, it left-branches into T, or
    (ii) for a half- or deceptive cadence, it left-branches to an underlying implied T, or
  (b) that is an applied (secondary) dominant
(3) S belongs to any chord that left-branches to D
(4) Dep belongs to any chord that is assigned a right-branching progression
(5) Ret belongs to a noncadential chord that is assigned a left-branching progression to a chord that itself is a right prolongation
(6) N belongs to any pitch or chord that is
  (a) directly subordinate within a strong prolongation or
  (b) a diatonic or chromatic step away from one of its directly superordinate events but not from the other ("incomplete N")
(7) P belongs to any pitch or chord that is
  (a) directly subordinate within a weak prolongation or
  (b) a left branch off Dep
(8) all functions transmit intact through strong or weak prolongations
(9) parallel passages preferably receive parallel functions.

OCTATONIC INTRAREGIONAL CHORD-CYCLE RULE To move from one triad to another within an octatonic collection,

(1) move the pcs at levels a–c of the triadic/octatonic basic space two steps to the right (mod 8) on level d or two steps to the left; and/or
(2) move the single pc that is at level c but not at level b an ic1 to the only such option available at level d.

OCTATONIC REGION-CYCLE RULE Move the pcs at level d of the octatonic basic space one/four/seven/ten steps to the right (mod 12) on level e or the same to the left.

OCTATONIC CHORD DISTANCE RULE $\delta_{oct}(x \rightarrow y) = i + j + k$, where $\delta_{oct}(x \rightarrow y)$ = the distance between chord x and chord y; i = the number of applications of the octatonic region-cycle rule needed to shift the octatonic collection that supports x into the octatonic collection that supports y; j = the number of applications of condition (1) of the octatonic intraregional chord-cycle rule needed to shift x into y; and k = the number of distinctive pcs in the basic space of y compared to basic space of x.

Corollary: When calculating distances between chords across octatonic regions, let j always equal 1.

HEXATONIC INTRAREGIONAL CHORD-CYCLE RULE To move from one triad to another within a hexatonic collection,

(1) move the pcs at levels a–c of the hexatonic basic space two steps to the right (mod 6) on level d or two steps to the left, or
(2) move the single pc that is at level c but not at level b an ic1 to the only such option available at level d.

HEXATONIC REGION-CYCLE RULE Move the pcs at level d of the hexatonic basic space one/five/nine steps to the right (mod 12) on level e or the same to the left.

HEXATONIC CHORD DISTANCE RULE $\delta_{hex}(x \rightarrow y) = i + j + k$, where $\delta_{hex}(x \rightarrow y)$ = the distance between chord x and chord y; i = the number of applications of the hexatonic region-cycle rule needed to shift the hexatonic collection that supports x into the hexatonic collection that supports y; j = the number of applications of condition (1) of the hexatonic chord-cycle rule needed to shift x into y; and k = the number of distinctive pcs in the basic space of y compared to basic space of x.

Corollary: When calculating distances between chords across hexatonic regions, let j always equal 1.

CONSTRAINTS ON BASIC SPACES

Well-formedness conditions A basic space must

(1) consist of a closed group of pcs, with a single modulus operative at all levels (here the modulus is the octave)
(2) be hierarchically organized such that
    (a) at the lowest level, intervals between adjacent pcs are equal (here it is the twelve semitones)
    (b) every pc above the lowest level is also a pc at all lower levels
    (c) a pc that is relatively stable at level L is also a pc at L + 1
    (d) L + 1 has fewer pcs than L

Preferential conditions A basic space preferably

(1) correlates height of level in the space with the degree of sensory consonance of adjacent intervals within a level
(2) has almost half the pcs at L + 1 as at L

(3) expresses maximal evenness in its distribution of pcs at a given level (alternatively, has coherent steps at a given level)
(4) expresses a unique distribution of directed intervals
(5) has two step sizes at the scale level
(6) has two intervallic generators at the scale level, such that the starting point is reached again without intervening pc duplication
(7) has steps no larger than ic2 between adjacent pcs at the scale level.

INTERSPATIAL DISTANCE RULE (final version) $\delta_{is}(x^{chord}/x^{scale} \rightarrow y^{chord}/y^{scale}) = ([sc + 1] + ch) + (i + j) + k$, where $\delta_{is}(x^{chord}/x^{scale} \rightarrow y^{chord}/y^{scale})$ = the distance between x^{chord}/x^{scale} and y^{chord}/y^{scale}; *sc* = the number of differences in the presence or absence of adjacent intervals between x^{scale} and y^{scale}; *ch* = the number of differences in the presence or absence of ics between x^{chord} and y^{chord}; *i* = the number of applications of the y^{scale} region-cycle rule to move the tonic orientation of x^{scale} to the tonic orientation of y^{scale}; *j* = the number of applications of either the y^{chord} intraregional chord-cycle rule or the corollary to the y^{chord} chord distance rule (as the case may be) to move the root of x^{chord} to the root of y^{chord}; and *k* = the number of distinctive pcs in the basic space of y^{chord}/y^{scale} compared to the basic space of x^{chord}/x^{scale}.

METRICAL ATTRACTION RULE (full version) $\alpha(b_x \rightarrow b_{x+1}) = {}^{S_x + 1}/_{S_x} \times {}^{1}/_{r}$, where $\alpha(b_x \rightarrow b_{x+1})$ = the attraction of b_x to b_{x+1}; b_x and b_{x+1} are adjacent beats at the same metrical level; s_x = the anchoring strength of b_x and s_{x+1} = the anchoring strength of b_{x+1} in the metrical grid; and r = the ratio of a beat's span to its normal span.

SALIENCE CONDITIONS Of the possible choices for the head of a time-span T, choose an event that is
(1) attacked within the region
(2) in a relatively strong metrical position
(3) relatively loud
(4) relatively prominent timbrally
(5) in an outer-voice (high or low) registral position
(6) relatively dense (simultaneous attacks)
(7) relatively long in duration
(8) next to a (relatively large) grouping boundary
(9) relatively important motivically
(10) parallel to a choice made elsewhere in the analysis.

ANCHORING/REDUCTION RULE In a melodic sequence, if temporally adjacent pitches in a stream are less than a minor third apart and are comparably dissonant, choose the second pitch.

SENSORY CONSONANCE RULE In a harmonic sequence, choose the chord that is more consonant according to
(1) roughness
(2) clarity of harmonic root.

FLAT-SPACE DISTANCE RULE $\delta_{flat}(x \rightarrow y) = ch + k$, where $\delta_{flat}(x \rightarrow y)$ = the distance between event-structure x and event-structure y; *ch* = the number of differences in the presence or absence of ics between x and y; and *k* = the number of distinctive pcs in y compared to those in x.

ATONAL BRANCHING WELL-FORMEDNESS CONDITION An event e_i can be a direct elaboration of another event e_j in any of the following ways:
(1) e_i is a strong prolongation of e_j if the two events share all the same pcs
(2) e_i is a weak prolongation of e_j if the two events share approximately half the same pcs
(3) e_i is a progression to or from e_j if the two events share less than half the same pcs.

ATONAL FUNCTION RULE Assign the repertory of functions RS (referential sonority), Dep (departure), Ret (return), N (neighboring), and P (passing), by prolongational position from global to local levels, such that
(1) RS belongs to
 (a) the prolongational head or
 (b) an event that contains Dep and Ret within a strong prolongation of itself
(2) Dep belongs to any event assigned a right-branching progression
(3) Ret belongs to any event assigned a left-branching progression
(4) N belongs to any pitch or chord that is directly subordinate within a strong prolongation
(5) P belongs to any pitch or chord that is
 (a) directly subordinate within a weak prolongation
 (b) a left branch off Dep or
 (c) a right branch off Ret
(6) all functions transmit intact through strong or weak prolongations
(7) parallel passages preferably receive parallel functions.

FUSION TRANSFORMATION RULE Temporally contiguous events may be fused if
(1) they are not separated by a grouping boundary
(2) they are at least a minor third apart
(3) they are temporally proximate (the closer, the more fusible)
(4) the duration of one overlaps that of the other.

RULES FROM GTTM REFERRED TO IN THIS VOLUME

MWFR 2 Every beat at a given level must also be a beat at all smaller levels present at that point in the piece.

MWFR 3 At each metrical level, strong beats are spaced either two or three beats apart.

MWFR 4 The tactus and immediately larger metrical levels must consist of beats equally spaced throughout the piece. At subtactus metrical levels, weak beats must be equally spaced between the surrounding strong beats.

TSRWFR 3B If time-span T contains other time spans, let $T_1, \ldots, T_n$ be the (regular or augmented) time spans immediately contained in T and let $e_1, \ldots, e_n$ be their respective heads. Then if $e_1, \ldots, e_n$ are not separated by a group boundary, the head of T may be the superimposition of two or more of $e_1, \ldots, e_n$.

TSRPR 2 Of the possible choices for head of a time-span T, prefer a choice that is
(1) relatively intrinsically consonant
(2) relatively closely related to the local tonic.

TSRPR 6 In choosing the head of a time-span T, prefer a choice that results in a more stable choice of prolongational reduction.

PRWFR 2 An event e_i can be a direct elaboration of another event e_j in any of the following ways:
(1) e_i is a strong prolongation of e_j if the roots, bass notes, and melodic notes of the two events are identical
(2) e_i is a weak prolongation of e_j if the two events are identical, but the bass and/or melodic notes differ
(3) e_i is a progression to or from e_j if the harmonic roots of the two events are different.

PRPR 3 In choosing the prolongationally most important event e_k in a prolongational region (e_i–e_j), prefer an e_k that attaches so as to form a maximally stable prolongational connection with one of the end points of the region.

Bibliography

Abrams, R. M., and K. K. Gerhardt (1997). Some Aspects of the Foetal Sound Environment. In I. Deliège and J. Sloboda, eds., *Perception and Cognition of Music*. Hove, East Sussex: Psychology Press.

Agmon, E. (1996). Coherent Tone-Systems: A Study in the Theory of Diatonicism. *Journal of Music Theory*, 40, 39–59.

Aldwell, E., and C. Schachter (1979). *Harmony and Voice Leading*, Vol. 2. New York: Harcourt Brace Jovanovich.

Antokoletz, E. (1984). *The Music of Béla Bartók: A Study of Tonality and Progression in Twentieth-Century Music*. Berkeley: University of California Press.

Archangeli, D., and D. T. Langendoen (1997). *Optimality Theory: An Overview*. Oxford: Blackwell.

Babbitt, M. (1962). Twelve-tone Rhythm and the Electronic Medium. *Perspectives of New Music*, 1, 49–79.

Bailey, R. (1977). The Structure of the Ring and Its Evolution. *Nineteenth Century Music*, 1, 48–61.

Bailey, R. (1985). An Analytical Study of the Sketches and Drafts. In R. Bailey, ed., *Wagner: Prelude and Transfiguration from* Tristan and Isolde. New York: Norton Critical Scores.

Baker, J. (1986). *The Music of Alexander Scriabin*. New Haven: Yale University Press.

Balzano, G. J. (1980). The Group-theoretic Description of 12-fold and Microtonal Pitch Systems. *Computer Music Journal*, 4 (4), 66–84.

Balzano, G. J. (1982). The Pitch Set as a Level of Description for Studying Musical Pitch Perception. In M. Clynes, ed., *Music, Mind, and Brain*. New York: Plenum.

Bartók, B. (1976). The Relation between Folk Music and Art Music. In B. Sachoff, ed., *Béla Bartók Essays*. London: Faber & Faber.

Beach, D. (1967). The Functions of the Six-Four Chord in Tonal Music. *Journal of Music Theory*, 11, 2–31.

Beach, D. (1990). Apples and Oranges: Neumeyer's Reading of the Octave Line. *In Theory Only*, 11(5), 9–18.

Berger, A. (1963). Problems of Pitch Organization in Stravinsky. *Perspectives of New Music*, 2.1, 11–42. (Reprinted in B. Boretz and E. T. Cone, eds., *Perspectives on Schoenberg and Stravinsky*. New York: Norton, 1972.)

Berger, K. (2000). *A Theory of Art*. New York: Oxford University Press.

Bernstein, D. (1991). Arnold Schoenberg and the Austro-German Theoretical Legacy: Stufen, Regions, and the Theory of Tonal Function. New York: Paper delivered at the joint meeting of the Arnold Schoenberg Institute and the Music Theory Society of New York State.

Berry, W. (1976). *Structural Functions in Music*. Englewood Cliffs, NJ: Prentice-Hall. (Reprinted New York: Dover, 1987.)

Bharucha, J. J. (1984a). Anchoring Effects in Music: The Resolution of Dissonance. *Cognitive Psychology*, 16, 485–518.

Bharucha, J. J. (1984b). Event Hierarchies, Tonal Hierarchies, and Assimilation: A Reply to Deutsch and Dowling. *Journal of Experimental Psychology: General*, 113, 421–425.

Bharucha, J. J. (1987). Music Cognition and Perceptual Facilitation: A Connectionist Framework. *Music Perception*, 5, 1–30.

Bharucha, J. J. (1991). Pitch, Harmony and Neural Nets: A Psychological Perspective. In P. M. Todd and D. G. Loy, eds., *Music and Connectionism*. Cambridge, MA: MIT Press.

Bharucha, J. J. (1996). Melodic Anchoring. *Music Perception*, 13, 383–400.

Bigand, E., R. Parncutt, and F. Lerdahl (1996). Perception of Musical Tension in Short Chord Sequences: The Influence of Harmonic Function, Sensory Dissonance, Horizontal Motion, and Musical Training. *Perception and Psychophysics*, 58, 125–141.

Boretz, B. (1972). Meta-Variations, Part IV: Analytic Fallout (I). *Perspectives of New Music*, 11, 146–223.

Boss, J. (1994). Schoenberg on Ornamentation and Structural Levels. *Journal of Music Theory*, 38, 187–216.

Boulez, P. (1966). *Relevés d'apprenti*. Paris: Editions du Seuil. (Tr. S. Walsh, *Stocktakings from an Apprenticeship*, Oxford: Clarendon, 1991.)

Bregman, A. S. (1990). *Auditory Scene Analysis*. Cambridge, MA: MIT Press.

Brown, H., and D. Butler (1981). Diatonic Trichords as Minimal Tonal Cue-Cells. *In Theory Only*, 5, 39–55.

Brown, M. (1993). Tonality and Form in Debussy's *Prélude à l'après-midi d'un faune*. *Music Theory Spectrum*, 15, 127–143.

Browne, R. (1981). Tonal Implications of the Diatonic Set. *In Theory Only*, 5, 3–21.

Bruner, C. (1984). The Perception of Contemporary Pitch Structures. *Music Perception*, 2, 25–40.

Burns, E. M., and W. D. Ward (1982). Intervals, Scales, and Tuning. In D. Deutsch, ed., *The Psychology of Music*. New York: Academic.

Butler, D. (1989). Describing the Perception of Tonality in Music: A Critique of the Tonal Hierarchy Theory and a Proposal for a Theory of Intervallic Rivalry. *Music Perception*, 6, 219–241.

Callender, C. (1998). Voice-Leading Parsimony in the Music of Alexander Scriabin. *Journal of Music Theory*, 42, 219–233.

Caplin, W. (1998). *Classical Form*. New York: Oxford University Press.

Carpenter, P. (1983). *Grundgestalt* as Tonal Function. *Music Theory Spectrum*, 5, 15–38.

Chomsky, N. (1965). *Aspects of the Theory of Syntax*. Cambridge, MA: MIT Press.

Christensen, T. (1993). *Rameau and Musical Thought in the Enlightenment*. Cambridge: Cambridge University Press.

Churchland, P. (1986). *Neurophilosophy: Toward a Unified Science of the Mind-Brain*. Cambridge, MA: MIT Press.

Clough, J., and J. Douthett (1991). Maximally Even Sets. *Journal of Music Theory*, 35, 93–173.

Clough, J., N. Engebretsen, and J. Kochavi (1999). Scales, Sets, and Interval Cycles: A Taxonomy. *Music Theory Spectrum*, 21, 74–104.

Cohn, R. (1988). Inversional Symmetry and Transpositional Combination in Bartók. *Music Theory Spectrum*, 10, 19–42.

Cohn, R. (1996). Maximally Smooth Cycles, Hexatonic Systems, and the Analysis of Late-Romantic Triadic Progressions. *Music Analysis*, 15, 9–40.

Cohn, R. (1997). Neo-Riemannian Operations, Parsimonious Trichords, and Their *Tonnetz* Representations. *Journal of Music Theory*, 41, 1–66.

Cohn, R. (1998). Square Dances with Cubes. *Journal of Music Theory*, 42, 283–296.

Cohn, R. (1999). As Wonderful as Star Clusters: Instruments for Gazing at Tonality in Schubert. *Nineteenth Century Music*, 22, 213–232.

Cohn, R., and D. Dempster (1992). Hierarchical Unity, Plural Unities: Toward a Reconciliation. In K. Bergeron and P. V. Bohlman, eds., *Disciplining Music: Musicology and Its Canons*. Chicago: University of Chicago Press.

Cook, N. (1987). The Perception of Large-scale Tonal Closure. *Music Perception*, 5, 197–205.

Cook, N. (1994). Perception: A Perspective from Music Theory. In R. Aiello and J. Sloboda, eds., *Musical Perceptions*. New York: Oxford University Press.

Cooke, D. (1959). *The Language of Music*. Oxford: Oxford University Press.

Cooper, G., and L. B. Meyer (1960). *The Rhythmic Structure of Music*. Chicago: University of Chicago Press.

Cowell, H. (1930). *New Musical Resources*. New York: Alfred A. Knopf.

Cuddy, L. L. (1997). Tonal Relations. In I. Deliège and J. Sloboda, eds., *Perception and Cognition of Music*. Hove, UK: Psychology Press.

de la Motte, D. (1988). *Harmonielehre*. Munich: Bärenreiter.

Deliège, I. (1987). Grouping Conditions in Listening to Music: An Approach to Lerdahl and Jackendoff's Grouping Preference Rules. *Music Perception*, 4, 325–360.

Deutsch, D. (1969). Music Recognition. *Psychological Review*, 76, 300–307.

Deutsch, D. (1980). The Processing of Structured and Unstructured Tonal Sequences. *Perception & Psychophysics*, 28, 381–389.

Deutsch, D. (1982a). Grouping Mechanisms in Music. In D. Deutsch, ed., *The Psychology of Music*. New York: Academic. (Reprinted in D. Deutsch, ed., *The Psychology of Music*, second edition, New York: Academic, 1999.)

Deutsch, D. (1982b). The Processing of Pitch Combinations. In D. Deutsch, ed., *The Psychology of Music*. New York: Academic. (Reprinted with revisions in D. Deutsch, ed., *The Psychology of Music*, second edition, New York: Academic, 1999.)

Deutsch, D. (1984). Two Issues concerning Tonal Hierarchies: Comment on Castellano, Bharucha, and Krumhansl. *Journal of Experimental Psychology: General*, 113, 413–416.

Deutsch, D., and J. Feroe (1981). The Internal Representation of Pitch Sequences in Tonal Music. *Psychological Review*, 88, 503–522.

Dibben, N. (1999). The Perception of Structural Stability in Atonal Music: The Influence of Salience, Stability, Horizontal Motion, Pitch Commonality, and Dissonance. *Music Perception*, 16, 256–294.

Dogantan, M. (1997). *Mathis Lussy's Theory of Rhythm as a Basis for a Theory of Expressive Performance*. Columbia University: Ph.D. dissertation.

Douthett, J., and P. Steinbach (1998). Parsimonious Graphs: A Study in Parsimony, Contextual Transformations, and Modes of Limited Transposition. *Journal of Music Theory*, 42, 241–263.

Dowling, W. J. (1972). Recognition of Melodic Transformations: Inversion, Retrograde, and Retrograde-Inversion. *Perception and Psychophysics*, 12, 417–21.

Dowling, W. J., and D. L. Harwood (1986). *Music Cognition*. New York: Academic.

Drobisch, M. W. (1855). Über musikalische Tonbestimmung und Temperatur. *In Abhandlungen der Koniglich sachsischen Gesellschaft der Wissenschaften zu Leipzig*, 4, 3–121. Leipzig: Hirzel.

Dubiel, J. (1990). When You Are a Beethoven: Kinds of Rules in Schenker's *Counterpoint*. *Journal of Music Theory*, 34, 291–340.

Epstein, D. (1979). *Beyond Orpheus*. Cambridge, MA: MIT Press. (Reprinted New York: Oxford University Press, 1987.)

Erpf, H. (1927). *Studien zur Harmonie-und Klangtechnik der Neuen Musik*. Leipzig: Breitkopf & Härtel.

Euler, L. (1739). *Tentamen novae theoriae musicae*. St. Petersburg. New York: Broude, 1968.

Fétis, F.-J. (1844). *Traité complet de la théorie et de la pratique de l'harmonie*. Paris and Brussels.

Feynman, R. (1965). *The Character of Physical Law*. Cambridge, MA: MIT Press.

Fineberg, J. (2001). Spectral Music. *Contemporary Music Review*, 19 (2–3).

Fodor, J. A. (1983). *The Modularity of Mind*. Cambridge, MA: MIT Press.

Forte, A. (1959). Schenker's Conception of Musical Structure. *Journal of Music Theory*. 3, 1–30. (Reprinted in M. Yeston, ed., *Readings in Schenker Analysis*. New Haven: Yale University Press, 1977.)

Forte, A. (1973). *The Structure of Atonal Music*. New Haven: Yale University Press.

Forte, A. (1981). The Magical Kaleidoscope: Schoenberg's First Musical Masterwork, Opus 11, No. 1. *Journal of the Arnold Schoenberg Institute*. 5, 127–168.

Forte, A. (1988). New Approaches to the Linear Analysis of Music. *Journal of the American Musicological Society*. 41, 314–347.

Forte, A., and S. Gilbert (1982). *Introduction to Schenkerian Analysis*. New York: Norton.

Francés, R. (1988). *The Perception of Music*. Tr. W. J. Dowling. Hillsdale, NJ: Erlbaum. (Originally published Paris: Vrin, 1958.)

Fyk, J. (1995). *Melodic Intonation, Psychoacoustics, and the Violin*. Zielona Góra, Poland: Organon.

Gjerdingen, R. O. (1988). *A Classic Turn of Phrase*. Philadelphia: University of Pennsylvania Press.

Gjerdingen, R. O. (1994). Apparent Motion in Music? *Music Perception*, 11, 335–370.

Gjerdingen, R. O. (1996). Courtly Behaviors. *Music Perception*, 13, 365–382.

Graybill, R. (1994). Prolongation, Gesture, and Tonal Motion. In R. Atlas and M. Cherlin, eds., *Musical Transformation and Musical Intuition: Eleven Essays in Honor of David Lewin*. Roxbury, MA: Ovenbird Press.

Haimo, E. (1996). Atonality, Analysis, and the Intentional Fallacy. *Music Theory Spectrum*, 18, 167–199.

Halle, J., and F. Lerdahl (1994). A Generative Textsetting Model. *Current Musicology*, 55, 3–23.

Handel, S. (1989). *Listening*. Cambridge, MA: MIT Press.

Harrison, D. (1994). *Harmonic Function in Chromatic Music: A Renewed Dualist Theory and an Account of Its Precedents*. Chicago: University of Chicago Press.

Hasty, C. (1981). Segmentation and Process in Post-tonal Music. *Music Theory Spectrum* 3, 54–73.

Hasty, C. (1997). *Meter as Rhythm*. New York: Oxford University Press.

Hayes, B. (1989). The Prosodic Hierarchy in Poetry. In P. Kiparsky and G. Youmans, eds., *Phonetics and Phonology: Rhythm and Meter*. New York: Academic.

Heider, F., and M. Simmel (1944). An Experimental Study of Apparent Behavior. *American Journal of Psychology*, 57, 243–259.

Heinichen, J. D. (1728). *General-Bass in der Composition*. Dresden: Facs. Hildesheim: Olms, 1969.

Helmholtz, H. von (1863/1885). *On the Sensations of Tone*. Tr. A. Ellis. London: Longmans, Green, 1885. (Reprinted New York: Dover, 1954.)

Hindemith, P. (1937/1942). *The Craft of Musical Composition*. Vol. 1. New York: Belwin-Mills.

Hoffman, M. (1980). Gottfried Weber. *The New Grove Dictionary of Music and Musicians*. London: Macmillan.

Hubel, D. H., and T. N. Wiesel (1962). Receptive Fields, Binocular Interaction and Functional Architecture in the Cat's Visual Cortex. *Journal of Physiology*, 160, 106–154.

Huron, D. (2000). A Derivation of the Rules of Voice-Leading from Perceptual Principles. Unpublished manuscript.

Hutchinson, W., and L. Knopoff (1978). The Acoustical Component of Western Consonance. *Interface*, 7, 1–29.

Hyer, B. (1989). *Tonal Intuitions in* Tristan und Isolde. Yale University: Ph.D. dissertation.

Hyer, B. (1995). Reimag(in)ing Riemann. *Journal of Music Theory*, 39, 101–138.

Imig, R. (1970). *Systeme der Funktionsbezeichnung in den Harmonielehren seit Hugo Riemann*. Düsseldorf: Gesellschaft zur Förderung der systematischen Musikwissenschaft.

Ito, J. (1998). Swing Rhythm: Toward an Empirical Study. Columbia University: Seminar paper.

Jackendoff, R. (1982). *Semantics and Cognition*. Cambridge, MA: MIT Press.

Jackendoff, R. (1987). *Consciousness and the Computational Mind*. Cambridge, MA: MIT Press.

Jackendoff, R. (1991). Musical Parsing and Musical Affect. *Music Perception*, 9, 199–230.

Johnson, M. (1987). *The Body in the Mind: The Bodily Basis of Meaning, Imagination, and Reason*. Chicago: University of Chicago Press.

Jones, M. R., and M. Boltz (1989). Dynamic Attending and Responses to Time. *Psychological Review*, 96, 459–491.

Keiler, A. (1977). The Syntax of Prolongation I. *In Theory Only*, 3 (5), 3–27.

Kellner, D. (1737). *Treulicher Unterricht im General-Bass*. Hamburg: Christian Herold.

Kerman, J. (1980). How We Got into Analysis, and How to Get Out. *Critical Inquiry*, 7, 311–331. (Reprinted in J. Kerman, *Write All These Down*. Berkeley: University of California Press, 1994.)

Koffka, K. (1935). *Principles of Gestalt Psychology*. New York: Harcourt, Brace & World.

Komar, A. (1971). Schumann *Dichterliebe*. New York: Norton Critical Scores.

Kopp, D. (1995). *A Comprehensive Theory of Chromatic Mediant Relations in Mid-Nineteenth-Century Music*. Brandeis University: Ph.D. dissertation.

Kramer, J. (1988). *The Time of Music*. New York: Schirmer.

Krumhansl, C. L. (1979). The Psychological Representation of Musical Pitch in a Tonal Context. *Cognitive Psychology*, 11, 346–374.

Krumhansl, C. L. (1983). Perceptual Structures for Tonal Music. *Music Perception*, 1, 28–62.

Krumhansl, C. L. (1990). *Cognitive Foundations of Musical Pitch*. New York: Oxford University Press.

Krumhansl, C. L. (1996). A Perceptual Analysis of Mozart's Piano Sonata K. 282: Segmentation, Tension, and Musical Ideas. *Music Perception*, 13, 401–432.

Krumhansl, C. L. (1998). Evidence Supporting the Psychological Reality of Neo-Riemannian Transformations. *Journal of Music Theory*, 42, 265–281.

Krumhansl, C. L., J. J. Bharucha, and E. Kessler (1982). Perceived Harmonic Structure of Chords in Three Related Musical Keys. *Journal of Experimental Psychology: Human Perception and Performance*, 8, 24–36.

Krumhansl, C. L., and E. Kessler (1982). Tracing the Dynamic Changes in Perceived Tonal Organization in a Spatial Representation of Musical Keys. *Psychological Review*, 89, 334–368.

Krumhansl, C. L., and M. A. Schmuckler (1986). The *Petroushka* Chord. *Music Perception*, 4, 153–184.

Kurth, E. (1920). *Romantische Harmonik und ihre Krise in Wagners "Tristan"* Bern: Haupt. (Reprinted Hildesheim: Olms, 1975.)

Lake, W. (1987). *Melodic Perception and Cognition: The Influence of Tonality*. University of Michigan: Ph.D. dissertation.

Lakoff, G., and M. Johnson (1980). *Metaphors We Live By*. Chicago: University of Chicago Press.

Larson, S. (1994). Musical Forces, Step Collections, Tonal Pitch Space, and Melodic Expectation. *Proceedings of the Third International Conference on Music Perception and Cognition*, 227–229.

Larson, S. (1995). Musical Forces and Melodic Expectations: Comparing Computer Models with Human Subjects. Unpublished manuscript.

Larson, S. (1997). The Problem of Prolongation in Tonal Music: Terminology, Perception, and Expressive Meaning. *Journal of Music Theory*, 41, 101–136.

Lecanuet, J. P. (1996). Prenatal Auditory Experience. In I. Deliège and J. Sloboda, eds., *Musical Beginnings*. Oxford University Press.

Leman, M. (1995). *Music and Schema Theory: Cognitive Foundations of Systematic Musicology*. Berlin: Springer.

Lendvai, E. (1971). *Béla Bartók: An Analysis of His Music*. London: Kahn & Averill.

Lerdahl, F. (1987). Timbral Hierarchies. *Contemporary Music Review*, 1, 135–160.

Lerdahl, F. (1988a). Cognitive Constraints on Compositional Systems. In J. Sloboda, ed., *Generative Processes in Music*. Oxford: Oxford University Press. (Reprinted in *Contemporary Music Review*, 6, 97–121.)

Lerdahl, F. (1988b). Tonal Pitch Space. *Music Perception*, 5, 315–350.

Lerdahl, F. (1989a). Atonal Prolongational Structure. *Contemporary Music Review*, 4, 65–87.

Lerdahl, F. (1989b). Les relations chromatiques come moyen d'extension d'une théorie générative de la musique tonale. *Analyse musicale*, 16, 54–60.

Lerdahl, F. (1991). Underlying Musical Schemata. In I. Cross and P. Howell, eds., *Representing Musical Structure*. New York: Academic.

Lerdahl, F. (1992). Pitch-Space Journeys in Two Chopin Preludes. In M. R. Jones and S. Holleran, eds., *Cognitive Bases of Musical Communication*. Washington, DC: American Psychological Association.

Lerdahl, F. (1994a). Octatonic and Hexatonic Pitch Spaces. *Proceedings of the Second International Conference for Music Perception and Cognition*.

Lerdahl, F. (1994b). Tonal and Narrative Paths in *Parsifal*. In R. Atlas and M. Cherlin, eds., *Musical Transformation and Musical Intuition: Eleven Essays in Honor of David Lewin*. Roxbury, MA: Ovenbird Press.

Lerdahl, F. (1996). Calculating Tonal Tension. *Music Perception*, 13, 319–363.

Lerdahl, F. (1997a). Composing and Listening: A Reply to Nattiez. In I. Deliège and J. Sloboda, eds., *Perception and Cognition of Music*. Hove, UK: Psychology Press.

Lerdahl, F. (1997b). Issues in Prolongational Theory: A Response to Larson. *Journal of Music Theory*, 41, 141–155.

Lerdahl, F. (1999). Spatial and Psychoacoustic Factors in Atonal Prolongation. *Current Musicology*, 63, 7–26.

Lerdahl, F., and J. Halle (1991). Some Lines of Poetry Viewed as Music. In J. Sundberg, L. Nord, and R. Carlson, eds., *Music, Language, Speech, and Brain*. Wenner-Gren International Symposium Series. London: Macmillan.

Lerdahl, F., and R. Jackendoff (1977). Toward a Formal Theory of Tonal Music. *Journal of Music Theory*, 21, 111–171.

Lerdahl, F., and R. Jackendoff (1983). *A Generative Theory of Tonal Music*. Cambridge, MA: MIT Press,.

Lester, J. (1992). *Compositional Theory in the Eighteenth Century*. Cambridge, MA: Harvard University Press.

Lewin, D. (1968). A Study of Hexachordal Levels in Schoenberg's Violin Fantasy. *Perspectives of New Music*, 6, 18–32. (Reprinted in B. Boretz and E. T. Cone, eds., *Perspectives on Schoenberg and Stravinsky*. New York: Norton, 1972.)

Lewin, D. (1982). A Formal Theory of Generalized Tonal Functions. *Journal of Music Theory*, 26, 23–60.

Lewin, D. (1984). Amfortas's Prayer to Titurel and the Role of D in Parsifal: The Tonal Spaces of the Drama and the Enharmonic C♭/B. *Nineteenth Century Music*, 7, 336–349.

Lewin, D. (1987). *Generalized Musical Intervals and Transformations*. New Haven: Yale University Press.

Lewin, D. (1992). Some Notes on Analyzing Wagner: The *Ring* and *Parsifal. Nineteenth Century Music*, 16, 49–58.

Liberman, M., and A. Prince (1977). On Stress and Linguistic Rhythm. *Linguistic Inquiry*, 8, 249–336.

Litterick, L. (1996). Recycling Schubert: A Review of Richard Kramer's *Distant Cycles. Nineteenth Century Music*, 20, 77–95.

Lobe, J. C. (1851). *Katechismus der Musik*. Leipzig: J. J. Weber.

Locke, D. (1982). Principles of Offbeat Timing and Cross-Rhythm in Southern Ewe Dance Drumming. *Ethomusicology*, 26, 217–246.

London, J., and R. Rodman (1998). Musical Genre and Schenkerian Analysis. *Journal of Music Theory*, 42, 101–124.

Longuet-Higgins, H. C. (1962). Two Letters to a Musical Friend. *Music Review*, 23, 244–248 and 271–280. (Reprinted in H. C. Longuet-Higgins, *Mental Processes: Studies in Cognitive Science*. Cambridge, MA: MIT Press, 1987.)

Longuet-Higgins, H. C., and M. Steedman (1971). On interpreting Bach. (Reprinted in H. C. Longuet-Higgins, *Mental Processes: Studies in Cognitive Science*, Cambridge, MA: MIT Press, 1987.)

Lubin, S. (1974). *Techniques for the Analysis of Development in Middle Beethoven*. New York University: Ph.D. dissertation.

Lussy, M. (1874). *Traité de l'expression musicale: Accents, nuances et mouvements dans la musique vocale et instrumentale*. Paris: Berger-Levrault & Heugel.

Marr, D. (1982). *Vision*. San Francisco: Freeman.

Martino, D. (1961). The Source Set and Its Aggregate Formations. *Journal of Music Theory*, 5, 224–273.

Marvin, E. W., and A. R. Brinkman (1999). The Effect of Modulation and Formal Disruption on Perceived Tonic Closure. *Music Perception*, 16, 389–407.

Marx, A. B. (1837–1847). *Die Lehre von der musikalischen Komposition*. Leipzig: Breitkopf & Härtel.

Mattheson, J. (1735). *Der kleine generalbass Schule*. Hamburg: Johann Christoph Kißner.

McAdams, S., and A. Bregman. (1979). Hearing Musical Streams. *Computer Music Journal*, 3 (4), 26–43. (Reprinted in C. Roads and J. Strawn, eds., *Foundations of Computer Music*. Cambridge: MIT Press, 1985.)

McCreless, P. (1982). *Wagner's* Siegfried: *Its Drama, History, and Music*. Ann Arbor: UMI Research Press.

Mehra, J. (1994). *The Beat of a Different Drum: The Life and Science of Richard Feynman*. Oxford: Oxford University Press.

Messiaen, O. (1944). *Technique de mon langage musical*. Paris: Alphonse Leduc.

Meyer, L. B. (1956). *Emotion and Meaning in Music*. Chicago: University of Chicago Press.

Meyer, L. B. (1961). On Rehearing Music. *Journal of the American Musicological Society*, 14. (Reprinted in L. B. Meyer, *Music, the Arts, and Ideas*, second edition. Chicago: University of Chicago Press, 1994.)

Meyer, L. B. (1973). *Explaining Music*. Berkeley: University of California Press.

Mickelsen, W. C. (1977). *Riemann's History of Harmonic Theory with a Translation of Harmonielehre*. Lincoln: University of Nebraska Press.

Miller, G. A. (1956). The Magical Number Seven, plus or minus Two: Some Limits on Our Capacity for Processing Information. *Psychological Review*, 63, 81–96.

Miller, G. A., E. Galanter, and K. Pribram (1960). *Plans and the Structure of Behavior*. New York: Holt.

Mitchell, W. J. (1967). The Tristan Prelude: Techniques and Structure. In W. J. Mitchell and F. Salzer, eds., *The Music Forum*, Vol. 1. New York: Columbia University Press.

Momigny, J.-J. de (1806). *Cours complet d'harmonie et de composition*. Paris.

Mooney, M. K. (1996). *The Table of Relations and Music Psychology in Hugo Riemann's Harmonic Theory*. Columbia University: Ph.D. dissertation.

Morris, R. D. (1980). A Similarity Index for Pitch Class Sets. *Perspectives of New Music*, 18, 445–460.

Morris, R. D. (1987). *Composition with Pitch Classes*. New Haven: Yale University Press.

Morris, R. D. (1994). Conflict and Anomaly in Bartók and Webern. In R. Atlas and M. Cherlin, eds., *Musical Transformation and Musical Intuition: Eleven Essays in Honor of David Lewin*. Roxbury, MA: Ovenbird Press.

Morrison, C. D. (1991). Prolongation in the Final Movement of Bartók's String Quartet No. 4. *Music Theory Spectrum*, 13, 179–196.

Narmour, E. (1977). *Beyond Schenkerism*. Chicago: University of Chicago Press.

Narmour, E. (1990). *The Analysis and Cognition of Basic Melodic Structures*. Chicago: University of Chicago Press.

Narmour, E. (1996). Analyzing Form and Measuring Perceptual Content in Mozart's Sonata K. 282: A New Theory of Parametric Analogues. *Music Perception*, 13, 265–318.

Nattiez, J.-J. (1990). *Music and Discourse: Toward a Semiology of Music*. Tr. C. Abbate. Princeton: Princeton University Press.

Neisser, U. (1967). *Cognitive Psychology*. Englewood Cliffs, NJ: Prentice-Hall.

Neumeyer, D. (1987). The Urlinie from $\hat{8}$ as a Middleground Phenomenon. *In Theory Only*, 9 (5–6), 3–26.

Oettingen, A. von (1866). *Harmoniesystem in dualer Entwicklung*. Dorpat and Leipzig: Gläser.

Ogdon, W. (1981). How Tonality Functions in Schoenberg's Op. 11, No. 1. *Journal of the Arnold Schoenberg Institute*, 5, 169–181.

Palmer, C. (1996). Anatomy of a Performance: Sources of Musical Expression. *Music Perception*, 13, 433–453.

Parncutt, R. (1989). *Harmony: A Psychoacoustical Approach*. Berlin: Springer-Verlag.

Parncutt, R. (1994). Template-Matching Models of Musical Pitch and Rhythm Perception. *Journal of New Musical Research*, 23, 145–167.

Perle, G. (1962). *Serial Composition and Atonality*. Berkeley: University of California Press.

Perle, G. (1977). *Twelve-Tone Tonality*. Berkeley: University of California Press.

Perle, G. (1984). Scriabin's Self-Analyses. *Music Analysis*, 3, 101–122.

Perle, G. (1990). *The Listening Composer*. Berkeley: University of California Press.

Pinker, S. (1997). *How the Mind Works*. New York: Norton.

Piston, W. (1941/1978). *Harmony*, fourth edition, revised and expanded by M. DeVoto. New York: Norton.

Plomp, R., and W. J. M. Levelt (1965). Tonal Consonance and Critical Bandwidth. *Journal of the Acoustical Society of America*, 38, 548–560.

Pople, A. (1983). Skryabin's Prelude, Op. 67, No. 1: Sets and Structure. *Music Analysis*, 2, 151–173.

Povel, D.-J. (1996). Exploring the Elementary Harmonic Forces in the Tonal System. *Psychological Research*, 58, 274–283.

Pressing, J. (1983). Cognitive Isomorphisms between Pitch and Rhythm in World Musics: West Africa, the Balkans and Western Tonality. *Studies in Music*, 17, 38–61.

Pressnitzer, D., S. McAdams, S. Winsberg, and J. Fineberg (2000). Perception of Musical Tension for Nontonal Orchestral Timbres and Its Relation to Psychoacoustic Roughness. *Perception and Psychophysics*, 62, 66–80.

Proctor, G. (1978). *Technical Bases of Nineteenth-Century Chromatic Tonality*. Princeton University: Ph.D. dissertation.

Rahn, J. (1983). *A Theory for All Music: Problems and Solutions in the Analysis of Non-Western Forms*. Toronto: University of Toronto Press.

Rameau, J.-P. (1722). *Traité de l'harmonie réduite à ses principes naturels*. Paris: Ballard. (Tr. P. Gosset, New York: Dover, 1971.)

Rameau, J.-P. (1737). *Génération harmonique*. Paris: Prault fils.

Reise, J. (1983). Late Skriabin: Some Principles behind the Style. *Nineteenth Century Music*, 6, 220–231.

Restle, F. (1970). Theory of Serial Pattern Learning: Structural Trees. *Psychological Review*, 77, 481–495.

Riemann, H. (1880). *Skizze einer neuen Methode der Harmonielehre*. Leipzig: Breitkopf & Härtel.

Riemann, H. (1893). *Vereinfachte Harmonielehre, oder die Lehre von den tonalen Funktionen der Akkorde*. (Tr. H. Bewerunge, London: Augener, 1896.)

Riemann, H. (1902). *Grosse Kompositionslehre*, Vol. 1. Berlin: W. Spemann.

Riemann, H. (1903). *System der musikalischen Rhythmik und Metrik*. Leipzig: Breitkopf & Härtel.

Riemann, H. (1915). Ideen zu einer "Lehre von den Tonvorstellung." *Jahrbuch der Musikbibliothek Peters*, 21–22, 1–26. (Tr. R. Wason and E. W. Marvin, *Journal of Music Theory*, 36, 69–117.)

Riepel, J. (1755). *Grundregeln zur Tonordnung insgemein*. Frankfurt and Leipzig.

Roederer, J. G. (1973). *Introduction to the Physics and Psychophysics of Music*. New York and Berlin: Springer Verlag. (Second edition 1979.)

Rosch, E. (1975). Cognitive Reference Points. *Cognitive Psychology*, 7, 532–547.

Rosch, E., and C. B. Mervis (1975). Family Resemblances: Studies in the Internal Structure of Categories. *Cognitive Psychology*, 7, 573–605.

Rothfarb, L. A. (1988). *Ernst Kurth as Theorist and Analyst*. Philadelphia: University of Pennsylvania Press.

Rothstein, W. (1989). *Phrase Rhythm in Tonal Music*. New York: Schirmer.

Rothstein, W. (1990). Rhythmic Displacement and Rhythmic Normalization. In A. Cadwallader, ed., *Trends in Schenkerian Research*. New York: Schirmer.

Rumelhart, D. E., and J. L. McClelland (1986). *Parallel Distributed Processing: Explorations in the Microstructure of Cognition*. Cambridge, MA: MIT Press.

Sadai, Y. (1986). L'application du modèle syntagmatique-paradigmatique à l'analyse des fonctions harmoniques. *Analyse musicale*, 2, 35–42.

Salzer, F. (1952). *Structural Hearing: Tonal Coherence in Music*. New York: Charles Boni. (Reprinted New York: Dover, 1962.)

Schachter, C. (1980). Rhythm and Linear Analysis: Durational Reduction. In F. Salzer, ed., *The Musical Forum*, Vol. 4. New York: Columbia University Press. (Reprinted in C. Schachter [ed. J. Straus], *Unfoldings*. New York: Oxford University Press, 1998.)

Schachter, C. (1995). The Triad as Place and Action. *Music Theory Spectrum*, 17, 149–169. (Reprinted in C. Schachter [ed. J. Straus], *Unfoldings*. New York: Oxford University Press, 1998.)

Scharf, B., S. Quigley, C. Aoki, N. Peachey, and A. Reeves (1987). Focused Auditory Attention and Frequency Selectivity. *Perception & Psychophysics*, 42, 215–223.

Schellenberg, E. G. (1997). Simplifying the Implication-Realization Model of Musical Expectancy. *Music Perception*, 14, 295–318.

Schenker, H. (1906). *Harmony*. Tr. E. M. Borghese. Chicago: University of Chicago Press, 1980.

Schenker, H. (1910–1922). *Counterpoint*. Tr. J. Rothgeb and J. Thym. New York: Schirmer, 1987.

Schenker, H. (1921–1924). *Der Tonwille*. Vienna: A. Gutmann Verlag.

Schenker, H. (1932). *Funf Urlinie-Tafeln*. Vienna: Universal. (Republished as *Five Graphic Music Analyses*, New York: Dover, 1969.)

Schenker, H. (1935/1979). *Free Composition*. Tr. E. Oster. New York: Longman.

Schoenberg, A. (1911/1978). *Theory of Harmony*. Tr. R. Carter. Berkeley: University of California Press.

Schoenberg, A. (1941/1975). Composition with Twelve Tones. In A. Schoenberg, *Style and Idea*. New York: St. Martin's Press.

Schoenberg, A. (1954/1969). *Structural Functions of Harmony*, rev. ed. New York: Norton.

Schoenberg, A. (1958/1965). *Letters*. (Selected and ed. by E. Stein.) New York: St. Martin's Press.

Schoenberg, A. (1965). Analysis of the Four Orchestral Songs, Op. 22. *Perspectives of New Music*, 3, 1–21.

Schoenberg, A. (1967). *Fundamentals of Musical Composition*. (Eds. G. Strang and L. Stein.) New York: St. Martin's Press.

Schumann, R. (1971). *Tagebücher* i (1827–1838). Leipzig: Deutsche Verlag für Musik.

Sechter, S. (1853). *Die Grundsätze der Musikalischen Komposition*. Leipzig: Breitkopf & Härtel.

Shepard, R. N. (1982). Structural Representations of Music Pitch. In D. Deutsch, ed., *The Psychology of Music*. New York: Academic.

Shepard, R. N., and L. A. Cooper (1982). *Mental Images and Their Transformations*. Cambridge, MA: MIT Press.

Simon, H. A. (1962). The Architecture of Complexity. *Proceedings of the American Philosophical Society*, 106, 467–482. (Reprinted in H. A. Simon, *The Sciences of the Artificial*. Cambridge, MA: MIT Press, 1981.)

Simon, H. A., and R. K. Sumner (1968). Pattern in Music. In B. Kleinmuntz, ed., *Formal Representation of Human Judgment*. New York: Wiley.

Sloboda, J. A. (1985). *The Musical Mind*. Oxford: Oxford University Press.

Spotts, F. (1994). *Bayreuth: A History of the Wagner Festival*. New Haven: Yale University Press.

Stockhausen, K. (1957). Wie die Zeit vergeht. . . . *Die Reihe*, 2, 64–75. (English version London: Universal, 1975.)

Straus, J. N. (1987). The Problem of Prolongation in Post-tonal Music. *Journal of Music Theory*, 31, 1–21.

Straus, J. N. (1997). Voice Leading in Atonal Music. In J. M. Baker, D. W. Beach, and J. W. Bernard, eds., *Music Theory in Concept and Practice*. Rochester: University of Rochester Press.

Stumpf, C. (1890). *Tonpsychologie*, 2 vols. Leipzig: Hirzel.

Swain, J. P. (1997). *Musical Languages*. New York: Norton.

Taruskin, R. (1988). Review of James M. Baker, *The Music of Alexander Scriabin* and Boris de Schloezer, *Scriabin: Man and Artist. Music Theory Spectrum*, 10, 143–169.

Taruskin, R. (1996). *Stravinsky and the Russian Traditions*. Berkeley: University of California Press.

Taruskin, R. (1997). Scriabin and the Superhuman. In R. Taruskin, *Defining Russia Musically*. Princeton: Princeton University Press.

Temperley, D. (1996). *The Perception of Harmony and Tonality: An Algorithmic Approach*. Columbia University: Ph.D. dissertation.

Temperley, D. (1997). An Algorithm for Harmonic Analysis. *Music Perception*, 15, 31–68.

Temperley, D., and D. Sleator (1999). Modeling Meter and Harmony: A Preference Rule Approach. *Computer Music Journal*, 23, 10–27.

Terhardt, E. (1974). Pitch, Consonance, and Harmony. *Journal of the Acoustical Society of America*, 55, 1061–1069.

Terhardt, E., G. Stoll, and M. Seewann (1982). Pitch of Complex Tonal Signals according to Virtual Pitch Theory: Tests, Examples and Predictions. *Journal of the Acoustical Society of America*, 71, 671–678.

Thompson, W. F., and R. Parncutt (1997). Perceptual Judgments of Triads and Dyads: Assessment of a Psychoacoustic Model. *Music Perception*, 14, 263–280.

Travis, R. (1966). Directed Motion in Schoenberg and Webern. *Perspectives of New Music*, 4, 85–89.

Travis, R. (1970). Tonal Coherence in the First Movement of Bartok's Fourth String Quartet. In W. Mitchell and F. Salzer, eds., *The Music Forum*, Vol. 2. New York: Columbia University Press.

Tversky, A., and J. W. Hutchinson (1986). Nearest Neighbor Analysis of Psychological Spaces. *Psychological Review*, 93, 3–22.

Väisälä, O. (1999). Concepts of Harmony and Prolongation in Schoenberg's Op. 19/2. *Music Theory Spectrum*, 21, 230–259.

van den Toorn, P. (1983). *The Music of Igor Stravinsky*. New Haven: Yale University Press.

Vial, F.-G. (1767). *Arbre généalogique de l'harmonie*. Paris.

Wagner, R. (1992). *My Life*. Tr. M. Whittall. New York: Da Capo Press. (Originally published Munich: Paul List Verlag, 1963.)

Wason, R. (1985). *Viennese Harmonic Theory from Albrechtsberger to Schenker and Schoenberg*. Ann Arbor: UMI Research Press.

Weber, G. (1821–1824). *Versuch einer geordeneten Theorie der Tonsetzkunst*. Mainz: B. Schotts Söhne.

Weinberger, N. M. (1999). Music and the Auditory System. In D. Deutsch, ed., *The Psychology of Music*, second edition. New York: Academic.

Werts, D. (1983). *A Theory of Scale References*. Princeton University: Ph.D. dissertation.

Wittlich, G. (1975). Sets and Ordering Procedures in Twentieth-Century Music. In G. Wittlich, ed., *Aspects of Twentieth-Century Music*. Englewood Cliffs, NJ: Prentice-Hall.

Youmans, G. (1994). The Vocabulary-Management Profile: Two Stories by William Faulkner. *Empirical Studies of the Arts*, 12, 113–130.

Zuckerkandl, V. (1956). *Sound and Symbol*. Tr. W. R. Trask. Bollingen Series 44. Princeton: Princeton University Press.

Index